THE DOW JONES

INVESTOR'S HANDBOOK

1987

THE DOW JONES

INVESTOR'S HANDBOOK

1987

Edited by PHYLLIS S. PIERCE

DOW JONES-IRWIN
Homewood, Illinois   60430

ISBN 0-87094-995-0
Library of Congress Catalog Card No. 82-71541

Printed in the United States of America

1 2 3 4 5 6 7 8 9 0 K 4 3 2 1 0 9 8 7

Contents

How Long Can the Expansion
Keep Rolling Along?

IT'S most remarkable, but the latest upturn in the business cycle simply won't quit.

To be sure, it staggers and stumbles, huffs and puffs, teeters and totters and, in general, teases everyone time and again into fearing that at last a new recession is at hand.

But the next recession never seems quite to develop. The economy somehow manages to keep expanding, albeit woefully weakly at some times. And, as this most unusual behavior continues month after month after month, some most unusual records are beginning to be approached.

The latest expansion, which began near the close of 1982, recently entered its fifth year, and in the long history of the U.S. business cycle, dating back before the Civil War, only four of 30 previous up-phases of the cycle endured beyond the four-year mark.

Indeed, if this expansion lasts only through this summer, it will become the longest cyclical upswing ever in peace-time, assuming peace persists in 1987 for America. It would surpass the economy's 58-month advance of 1975-80, but still remain well short of the extraordinary advance of the so-called Soaring Sixties, which lasted 106 months, a period encompassing the Vietnam War.

What explains this extraordinary staying power? And how likely is the economy to keep rolling along, recession-free, through expansionary year number five and on into expansionary year number six?

The considerations that underlie the upturn's durability are easier to fathom than the chances that the long cyclical advance will continue through 1987 and beyond.

To a notable extent, the latest expansion has been long not because it has been strong, but for quite the opposite reason—because its growth has been unusually sluggish. But this sluggishness, whose accompaniments range from painfuly high jobless levels to painfully low plant-utilization rates, has served to forestall a buildup in constraints to further economic growth, constraints that normally develop after long periods of expansion.

Typically, as an expansion ages, shortages develop of production facilities, materials and labor-power. The resulting bottlenecks, delays in deliveries, excessive labor-cost increases and the like all act to complicate smooth, continuing gains in overall business activity.

And, besides such tightening physical constraints, pressures of a financial sort typically build as well. Interest rates tend to climb. Inflation tends to accelerate, often to painful levels. And the money supply, as reflected in the various monetary aggregates monitored by the Federal Reserve Board, tends to tighten. Again, further economic advance is made more difficult.

Indeed, this is how recessions normally develop—because a briskly growing economy is running out of elbowroom for additional expansion. It is a myth, albeit a popular one, that recessions develop on account of some mysterious economic inertia or lethargy.

The encouraging fact about the latest expansion is that, despite its longevity, it remains remarkably free so far of the sorts of constraints, physical as well as financial, that normally reach cumbersome, constrictive levels after so long a time of economic upswing. There are not the usual scarcities or bottlenecks or cost increases. Nor do the various interest-rate, price or monetary indicators signal any serious buildup of restrictive pressure.

The upshot, in the view of most business forecasters, is that the economy will indeed manage to make it through yet another year of growth. The consensus, to be sure, anticipates a continuing sluggish pace of advance. But no recession is foreseen any time soon. For example, not a single member of the nonprofit Conference Board's Economic Forum, comprising 14 eminent forecasters, expects a recession to set in during 1987 and, daring to peer still farther down the road, the Forum consensus anticipates a recession-free 1988 as well.

Edgar R. Fiedler, a member of the Conference Board group, reports that its best guess is for the economy, as gauged by the inflation-adjusted gross national product, to "advance by 3%" this year, which would slightly exceed the modest 1986 gain. Such rates of growth in an up-phase of the business cycle, it should be noted, are decidedly subpar. Over many decades, the economy has expanded at an average annual of roughly 3%, the projected 1987 pace, but that long-term average encompasses many intervals of sharp economic contraction as well as the expansionary times.

Other features of the Forum's forecast for the new year reasonably resemble the 1987 estimates of most economists around the nation.

Prices, as measured by the broad-ranging gauge which economists call the GNP deflator, are expected to climb 3.8%, an appreciably faster rate of increase than the 1986 price gain of about 3%. Still,

4

the projected rise would be moderate by recent post-World War II standards.

Unemployment is expected by the Forum economists to average about 6.7% of the labor force, which would represent a very slight improvement over jobless rates prevailing in much of 1986.

Interest rates, generally, are seen remaining moderately close to where they were late last year. The average prime rate charged by commercial banks, for instance, is expected to average 7.6%, which would come in within a whisker of the late-1986 readings.

And, most importantly, corporate profits, which generally rose in 1986 despite deep trouble in some businesses, are expected to rise once more in 1987. The Forum's estimates regarding the profits outlook vary more widely, it should be added, than its forecasts for other economic sectors. The high-end forecast is for a gain of nearly 14% and the low-end for only a 5% rise. The group's median works out to 6.7%, which would be reasonably close to the actual profits increase in 1986.

Profits, of course, are a vital consideration for investors. What a company earns, after all, constitutes a fundamental factor in shareownership dicisions. For all its sluggishness, 1986 with its generally rising profits was a fruitful year for shareowners, with the Dow Jones Industrial Average, for instance, achieving new high territory late in the year.

Economists, while they will happily attempt to pinpoint the future course of the economy as a whole, tend to eschew the guessing game of where the stock market is likely to be heading. However, the general share-price level is in fact considered a highly reliable leading indicator of the economy in general. For all its sudden day-to-day fluctuations, the stock market has tended over the many decades of business-cycle history to move in rough tandem with the economy, only slightly ahead of it, up or down as the case may be.

Accordingly, the prevailing view that the economy is likely to keep expanding in 1987 and beyond, albeit slowly, surely augers well for most share prices. If the economy keeps rising moderately, so will the stock market, experience teaches—at least until a new recession begins to form on the horizon.

One brave forecaster who does occasionally dare to look ahead in the market is Morris Cohen, an economic consultant based in Hackensack, N.J., well enough away from Wall Street perhaps for him to be able to distinguish the stock-market forest from the trees daily share-price volatility. He anticipates a higher market, generally, as 1987 goes along—precisely because he foresees a "continuing moderate gain in the economy and improvement in profits."

It must be added, of course, whether the focus is on the stock market or the broader economic scene, that forecasting is a perennially hazardous endeavor. And the riskiness is especially great at a time such as now, when as we have seen an expansion's longevity begins to defy the law of averages.

Extraordinary developments, in addition, surround the present economic situation. The federal budget deficit, which typically dwindles or disappears entirely as an economic upswing proceeds, in this long expansion remains Brobdingnagian. Unprecedented as well is the shortfall in foreign trade. And, unlike the federal budget balance, the trade balance usually tends to worsen as an upturn in the cycle goes along. This is a worrisome consideration when the trade deficit already provokes strong protectionist calls, and casts such deep doubt on America's ability to compete in world markets, even now that the dollar's international value has eroded sharply.

The importance of the trade balance to the overall economic outlook is underscored by David D. Hale, chief economist of Kemper Financial Services in Chicago. "If the expansion is to continue through a fifth year," he warns, "the U.S. must revive employment and income growth in the manufacturing sector by reducing the trade deficit." While he stresses that such a reduction is far from guaranteed, he hopes that, with a cheaper dollar and leaner production facilities in many U.S. industries, "by late 1987 there should be a sufficiently large improvement occurring in trade" to ensure continued growth in the economy as a whole.

On top of all of these concerns is the hard-to-weigh impact of America's increased dependency on foreign capital. As the foreign-made goods have flowed into the U.S., the dollars used to buy them have flowed out, eventually to reenter as investment from abroad in U.S. brick and mortar as well as in all manner of governmental and private securities.

This inflow serves, of course, to stimulate business within America, providing among other benefits financial support for U.S. money-raisers, from Uncle Sam on down the list. By the same token, however, the investment inflow has rendered America increasingly dependent on funds from abroad. If for any reason the inflow should dry up, serious problems could ensue, such as sharply rising interest rates in credit markets deserted by a major source of funds.

Perhaps the most difficult imponderable in the year ahead, however, is the impact of latest tax overhaul. For all the studies of its likely repercussions, no forecaster can ascertain with reasonable assurance just how things really will work out. The best guess seems to be that in the shorter term, mainly in early 1987, its overriding effect will be to slow general business activity. Partly, this should reflect tax-law changes that presumably prompted many consumers to buy goods and services in 1986 rather than now. Last year, of course, state and local sales taxes still were deductible from federal levies, as was the interest on most consumer borrowing.

In addition, tax incentives to invest in new capital projects are less alluring now than before the overhaul, whose provisions also include removal of the investment tax credit and generally less liberal depreciation rules. Here again, the assumption must be that some potential 1987 activity was transacted earlier, thus serving to slow the current business tempo.

In the longer term, the impact of the tax overhaul may well prove more benign. For one thing, hopefully, it will channel investment away from relatively unproductive avenues that no longer are tax-sheltered into ones that are more conducive to fresh economic growth-for example, into a new factory whose products will compete in world markets instead of into still another sparsely-occupied office building that nonetheless affords its developers enormous write-offs. For another thing, at least for many consumers, the overhaul, with its sharply lower rates, presumably will lighten the tax load, and this in turn should provide a spur to economic activity.

Whatever does develop, however beneficial or disruptive the new tax regulations prove to be, however long- or short-lived the economic upswing turns out to be, one fact of business-cycle history stands out. The record leaves no doubt that, sooner or later, expansions end, and when they do and recessions take hold, varying degrees of economic distress inevitably follow.

Precisely how much distress is difficult to foresee and rarely has hinged on the length of a preceding expansion. Much will depend, however, on the general financial health of individuals, private businesses and the government itself. And, in this regard, today's scene is troubling, for even though the economy has been in an expansionary mode for more than four years, huge amounts of debt, much of it of highly questionable quality, permeate the environment. The catalogue of borrowing ranges from so-called junk bonds used in the corporate takeover game to uncollectable bank loans unwisely extended to impoverished Third World countries. And, to worsen matters, the debt burden has kept rising while savings have kept eroding.

No wonder that various indicators of how readily the debt load is being serviced—for instance, the delinquency rate on consumer-installment loans—depict a worsening situation. This is not the sort of trend that usually occurs in the midst of a sustained business upturn. Normally, at such a point in the business cycle, the debt burden is easing.

A consequence of this shakiness now is that, if a recession were to develop any time soon, it could be severe indeed, with many borrowers simply unable to keep servicing their debt.

In such a climate, the matter of whether a new recession is imminent assumes, quite obviously, even more than the usual degree of urgency. And, by the same token, the consensus view that the expansion will keep rolling along as year number five unfolds seems especially welcome news.

—ALFRED L. MALABRE JR.

Mr. Malabre is an editor of The Wall Street Journal and author of the paper's Monday morning "Outlook" column. His latest book, published this spring by Random House, is titled "Beyond Our Means." It traces America's economic growth since World War II and weighs the problems that now confront us. His earlier books include "Investing for Profit in the Eighties," published by Doubleday, and "Understanding the Economy: For People Who Can't Stand Economics," published by Dodd Mead.

The Dow Jones Averages

THE first stock index in history was compiled by Charles Henry
Dow, first editor of *The Wall Street Journal* and co-founder (in
1882) of Dow Jones & Co. He made a list of 11 stocks, including nine
railroads and only two industrials. He added up the closing prices of
these 11 stocks, divided the total by 11 and produced a stock market
average, which was first published on July 3, 1884, in the *Customer's
Afternoon Letter*, a two-page financial news bulletin.

On May 26, 1896, Dow published the first industrial stock
average made up of 12 components. Like his earlier average, this too
was computed simply by adding the closing prices of the individual
issues and dividing the total by 12. At this time he also devised a
20-stock railroad average and publication of the two averages was
begun October 7, 1896 on a continuous basis. The list of 12 industrial
issues was expanded to 20 in 1916 and to 30 in 1928. Publication of a
utility average was begun in January 1929.

The additions to the industrial average together with substitutions and stock splits that occurred through the years made it
necessary to change the original simple method of computing the
average. If continuity were to be maintained it no longer was possible
to just add up the closing prices of the various components and divide
the total number of stocks in the index. For instance, if the index
consisted of three component stocks with closing prices of 36, 15 and
24 it would be calculated under the original method by adding the
total of the three (75) and dividing by the denominator three; this
would produce an average of 25. But if the stock selling at 36 were
split 2-for-1 its closing price would be 18; this would produce a
three-stock total of 57 which divided by three would be 19. Thus, the
average would drop by more than 20% although the total value of the
stocks was unchanged.

The problem of compensating for such occurrences so that the
average could remain consistent was solved by adjusting the divisor,
or denominator. In this case, instead of dividing by three the divisor
was adjusted to 2.28 with the result that the average showed the same
figure it did before the split of the component stock. Therefore,
whenever one of the average's stocks split, a substitution was
made or a stock dividend was declared, the divisor was adjusted to
compensate the change.

The divisor is changed from time to time to maintain the
historical continuity of the average, one of its most popular features.

This is true also of the railroad average, which on January 2, 1970, was revised to become the transportation average with the substitution of some airline and trucking companies for nine of the 20 railroad issues.

The 30 Dow Industrials are chosen as representative of the broad market and of American industry. The companies are major factors in their industries and their stocks are widely held by individuals and institutional investors.

Changes in the components are made entirely by the editors of *The Wall Street Journal* without consultation with the companies, the stock exchange or any official agency. For the sake of continuity, such changes are made rarely. Most substitutions have been the result of mergers, but from time to time changes may be made to achieve a better representation.

No change was made in 1986. The last such change occurred in October 1985 when Philip Morris replaced General Foods and McDonald's was substituted for American Brands. General Foods was dropped from the list because of its acquisition by Philip Morris. Standing alone, this change would overweight the indicator, which is designed to reflect price trends in the broader stock market, in the tobacco products and processed foods sectors. For this reason, American Brands, formerly known as American Tobacco and a component of the 30 industrials since their inception, was dropped from the list. McDonald's, a major food service company, was among the largest companies in market value, was widely owned and would cover a previously unrepresented sector.

Charles Henry Dow could hardly have imagined that the occasional stock average he computed with paper and pencil would one day become part of the language of American finance.

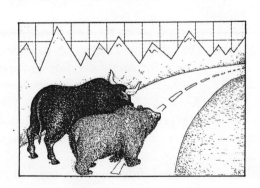

The Dow Jones Averages

The Dow Jones Stock Averages are compiled daily by using the New York Stock Exchange only closing prices and adjusting by the then current appropriate average divisor. The divisor for the Industrial Average is 0.889; Transportation, 1.032; Utilities, 2.171; 65 Stocks, 4.025. A list of the stocks on which these averages are based follows:

30 Industrial Stocks

Allied-Signal
Alcoa
American Can
Amer Express
AT&T
Bethlehem Steel
Chevron
Du Pont
Eastman Kodak
Exxon

General Electric
General Motors
Goodyear
Inco
IBM
Inter Paper
McDonald's
Merck
Minnesota M&M
Navistar Inter

Owens-Illinois
Philip Morris
Procter & Gamble
Sears Roebuck
Texaco
Union Carbide
United Technologies
USX Corp.
Westinghouse Electric
Woolworth

20 Transportation Stocks

AMR Corp.
Amer President
Burlington North
CSX Corp.
Canadian Pacific
Carolina Freight
Consolidated Freight

Delta Air Lines
Federal Express
Leaseway Tran
NWA Inc.
Norfolk Southern
Pan Am Corp.
Piedmont Aviation

Ryder System
Santa Fe So Pacific
TWA
UAL Inc.
Union Pac Corp.
USAir Group

15 Utility Stocks

Amer. Elec. Power
Centerior Energy
Columbia Gas Sys.
Com'wealth Edison
Consol. Edison

Consol. Nat. Gas
Detroit Edison
Houston Indus.
Niagara Mohawk Pr.
Pacific Gas & El.

Panhandle Eastern
Peoples Energy
Philadelphia Elec.
Pub. Ser. Enterp.
Sou. Cal. Edison

The Dow Jones Averages

20 Bonds

The Dow Jones Bond Averages are a simple arithmetic average compiled daily by using the New York Exchange closing bond prices. A list of the bonds on which these averages are based follows:

10 PUBLIC UTILITIES

Alabama Power	9¾s	'04	Detroit Edison	9s	'99
Am T&T deb.	8.8s	'05	Mich Bell	7s	'12
Commonwealth Edison	8¾s	'05	Pacific G&E	7¾s	'05zz
Consolidated Edison	7.9s	'01	Philadelphia Elec.	7⅜s	'01
Consumers Power	9¾s	'06	Public Service (Ind.)	9.6s	'05

10 INDUSTRIALS

BankAmerica	7⅞s	'03	General Elec	8½s	'04
Beth Steel	6⅞s	'99	GM Acceptance	12s	'05
Eastman	8⅝s	'16	Pfizer	9⅛s	'00
Exxon	6s	'97	Socony Mobil	4⅛s	'93
Ford Motor	8⅛s	'90	Weyerhaeuser	5.20s	'91

A list of Bonds on which the Confidence Index is based follows:

Barron's Best Grade Bonds

Amer. Tel. & Tel.	8¾s	2000	IBM	9⅜s	2004
Balt G&E	8⅜s	2006	Ill Bell Tel	7⅝s	2006
Exxon Pipeline	9s	2004	Pfizer	9¼s	2000
Gen Elec	8½s	2004	Proc. & G	8¼s	2005
GMAC	8¼s	2006	Sears Roe	7⅞s	2007

Barron's Intermediate Grade Bonds

Alabama Power	9¾s	2004	Firestone	9¼s	2004
Beneficial Corp	9s	2005	GTE	9⅜s	1999
Cater Trac	8s	2001	Union Carbide	8½s	2005
Comwlth Edison	9⅛s	2008	US Steel	7¾s	2001
Crown Zeller	9¼s	2005	Woolworth	9s	1999

Commodity Futures

The Dow Jones Commodity Futures index is compiled daily by using the following commodities:

Cattle	Cotton	Silver
Coffee	Gold	Soybeans
Copper	Hogs	Sugar
Corn	Lumber	Wheat

Stock and Bond Yields

Monthly averages, in percent. ▪▪▪▪▪ Bonds ▬DJIA

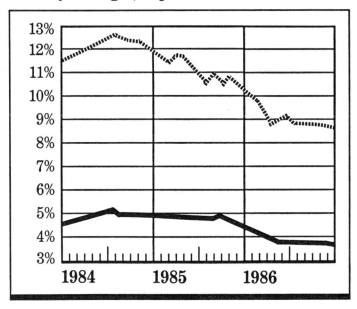

Changes in Dow Jones Industrials

The present Dow Jones industrial average of 30 stocks began October 1, 1928, when the list was expanded to 30 from 20 and several substitutions were made. On October 1, 1928, the stocks making up the industrial average were:

Allied Chemical	General Railway Signal	Sears, Roebuck
American Can	Goodrich	Standard Oil (N.J.)
American Smelting	International Harvester	Texas Corp.
American Sugar	International Nickel	Texas Gulf Sulphur
American Tobacco B	Mack Truck	Union Carbide
Atlantic Refining	Nash Motors	U.S. Steel
Bethlehem Steel	North American	Victor Talking Machine
Chrysler	Paramount Publix	Westinghouse Electric
General Electric	Postum Inc.	Woolworth
General Motors	Radio Corp.	Wright Aeronautical

The divisor on October 1, 1928, was 16.67.

Subsequent changes in stocks making up the industrial average and changes in the divisor, together with the dates, were:

Date		Divisor	Explanation
1928 November	5	16.02	Atlantic Refining Split 4 for 1
December	13	14.65	General Motors split 2½ for 1
			International Harvester split 4 for 1
December	26	13.92	International Nickel reorganization
1929 January	8	12.11	American Smelting split 3 for 1
			Radio Corp. split 5 for 1
			National Cash Register replaced Victor Talking Machine
May	1	11.7	Wright-Aeronautical split 2 for 1
May	20	11.18	Union Carbide split 3 for 1
June	25	10.77	Woolworth split 2½ for 1
July	25	10.77	Postum name changed to General Foods
September	14	10.47	Curtiss-Wright replaced Wright Aeronautical
1930 January	29	9.85	General Electric split 4 for 1
			Johns-Manville replaced North American
July	18	10.38	Borden replaced American Sugar
			Eastman Kodak replaced American Tobacco B
			Goodyear replaced Atlantic Refining
			Liggett & Myers replaced General Railway Signal
			Standard Oil of California replaced Goodrich
			United Air Transport replaced Nash Motors
			Hudson Motor replaced Curtiss-Wright
1932 May	26	15.46	American Tobacco B replaced Liggett & Myers
			Drug Inc. replaced Mack Trucks
			Procter & Gamble replaced United Air Transport
			Loew's replaced Paramount Publix
			Nash Motors replaced Radio Corp.
			International Shoe replaced Texas Gulf Sulphur

Changes in Dow Jones Industrials

Date			Divisor	Explanation
1932 May	26		15.46	International Business Machines replaced National Cash Register
				Coca Cola replaced Hudson Motor
1933 August	15		15.71	Corn Products Refining replaced Drug Inc.
				United Aircraft replaced International Shoe
1934 August	13		15.74	National Distillers replaced United Aircraft
1935 November	20		15.1	DuPont replaced Borden
				National Steel replaced Coca Cola
1937 January	8		15.1	Nash Motors name changed to Nash Kelvinator
1939 March	14		15.1	United Aircraft replaced Nash Kelvinator
				American Tel. & Tel. replaced I.B.M.
1945 May	10		14.8	Loew's Inc. split 3 for 1
May	11		14.2	Westinghouse Mfg. split 4 for 1
October	23		13.6	Sears Roebuck split 4 for 1
1946 August	1		13.3	National Distillers split 3 for 1
1947 May	16		12.2	Eastman Kodak split 5 for 1
June	2		11.76	Johns-Manville split 3 for 1
July	14		11.44	Chrysler Corp. split 2 for 1
December	3		11.36	American Smelting 20% stock dividend
1948 January	19		10.98	Bethlehem Steel split 3 for 1
May	17		10.55	Union Carbide split 3 for 1
June	7		10.20	International Harvester split 3 for 1
November	26		10.14	National Steel 10% stock dividend
1949 June	3		9.88	U.S. Steel split 3 for 1
June	16		9.06	DuPont split 4 for 1
1950 March	22		8.92	Procter & Gamble split 1½ for 1
March	31		8.57	National Steel split 3 for 1
September	5		7.76	Allied Chemical split 4 for 1
October	3		7.54	General Motors split 2 for 1
1951 March	12		7.36	Standard Oil of California split 2 for 1
May	2		7.33	United Aircraft 20% stock dividend
June	12		7.14	Texas Corp. split 2 for 1
June	13		6.90	Standard Oil (N.J.) split 2 for 1
September	11		6.72	Goodyear split 2 for 1
December	3		6.53	American Smelting split 2 for 1
1952 May	2		6.16	American Can split 2 for 1; 100% stock dividend
1954 June	14		5.92	General Electric split 3 for 1
July	1		5.89	United Aircraft distributed 1 share of Chance-Vought for every 3 United Aircraft held
1955 January	24		5.76	Goodyear split 2 for 1
May	23		5.62	Corn Products Refining split 3 for 1
June	3		5.52	U.S. Steel split 2 for 1
September	26		5.46	United Aircraft 50% stock dividend (3 for 2)
November	10		5.26	General Motors split 3 for 1
December	19		5.11	Sears Roebuck split 3 for 1
1956 March	19		4.89	Standard Oil (N.J.) split 3 for 1
March	26		4.79	Johns-Manville split 2 for 1
June	8		4.69	General Foods split 2 for 1
June	11		4.56	Texas Co. split 2 for 1
June	18		4.452	Standard Oil (Calif.) split 2 for 1

Changes in Dow Jones Industrials

Date		Divisor	Explanation
1956 June	25	4.351	Procter & Gamble split 2 for 1
July	3	4.581	International Paper replaced Loew's Inc.
September	11	4.566	American Tel & Tel rights offering (1 share for each 10 held)
1957 February	7	4.283	Bethlehem Steel split 4 for 1
November	18	4.257	United Aircraft 20% stock dividend (6 for 5)
1959 April	14	4.13	Eastman Kodak split 2 for 1
June	1	3.964	American Tel & Tel split 3 for 1
			Anaconda replaced American Smelting
			Swift & Co. replaced Corn Products
			Aluminum Co. of America replaced National Steel
			Owens-Illinois Glass replaced National Distillers
December	29	3.824	Goodyear split 3 for 1
1960 January	25	3.739	Allied Chemical split 2 for 1
February	2	3.659	Westinghouse Electric split 2 for 1
May	3	3.569	American Tobacco split 2 for 1
May	31	3.48	International Nickel split 2 for 1
August	24	3.38	General Foods split 2 for 1
December	30	3.28	International Paper Co. split 3 for 1
1961 April	10	3.165	Procter & Gamble split 2 for 1
August	11	3.09	Texaco split 2 for 1
1962 May	1	3.03	American Tobacco split 2 for 1
June	5	2.988	DuPont distributed ½ share of General Motors
1963 May	13	2.914	Chrysler Corp. split 2 for 1
November	21	2.876	DuPont distributed 36-100 share General Motors stock for each share of DuPont common held
1964 January	13	2.822	Chrysler Corp. split 2 for 1
June	18	2.754	F. W. Woolworth split 3 for 1
June	23	2.670	American Tel & Tel split 2 for 1
November	19	2.615	DuPont distributed ½ share of General Motors
1965 March	23	2.543	Sears Roebuck split 2 for 1
April	12	2.499	International Harvester split 2 for 1
May	24	2.410	Eastman Kodak split 2 for 1
June	1	2.348	Owens-Illinois Glass split 2 for 1
June	16	2.278	Union Carbide split 2 for 1
November	1	2.245	United Aircraft split 3 for 2
1967 June	6	2.217	Swift split 2 for 1
June	12	2.163	Anaconda split 2 for 1
1968 May	27	2.078	Eastman Kodak split 2 for 1
August	19	2.011	International Nickel split 2½ for 1
1969 April	1	1.967	Johns-Manville split 2 for 1
May	7	1.934	Goodyear split 2 for 1
August	11	1.894	Texaco split 2 for 1
1970 May	19	1.826	Procter & Gamble split 2 for 1
1971 March	30	1.779	General Foods split 2 for 1
June	8	1.712	General Electric split 2 for 1
December	16	1.661	Westinghouse Electric split 2 for 1
1972 November	1	1.661	Standard Oil (N.J.) name changed to Exxon
1973 May	30	1.661	Swift name changed to Esmark
December	11	1.626	Standard Oil (Calif.) split 2 for 1
1974 February	4	1.598	Aluminum Co. of America split 3 for 2

Changes in Dow Jones Industrials

Date		Divisor	Explanation
1975 May	1	1.598	United Aircraft name changed to United Technologies
October	1	1.588	Esmark split 5 for 4
1976 April	21	1.588	International Nickel name changed to Inco
May	19	1.554	United Technologies split 2 for 1
June	2	1.527	U.S. Steel split 3 for 2
July	26	1.473	Exxon split 2 for 1
August	9	1.504	Minnesota Mining & Manufacturing replaced Anaconda
1977 April	11	1.474	Owens-Illinois split 2 for 1
July	18	1.443	Sears, Roebuck split 2 for 1
1979 June	29	1.465	International Business Machines replaced Chrysler
			Merck replaced Esmark
			DuPont split 3 for 1
1981 February	23	1.431	Aluminum Co. of America split 2 for 1
March	11	1.388	Standard Oil (Calif.) split 2 for 1
May	26	1.348	American Brands split 2 for 1
June	12	1.314	Exxon Corp. split 2 for 1
1982 August	30	1.359	American Express Co. replaced Manville Corp.
1983 February	11	1.344	American Express Co. split 4 for 3
February	22	1.292	Procter & Gamble split 2 for 1
June	2	1.248	General Electric split 2 for 1
August	11	1.230	American Express Co. split 3 for 2
1984 January	4	1.194	"New" AT&T replaced "Old" AT&T
May	30	1.160	Allied Corp. split 3 for 2
			Westinghouse Electric split 2 for 1
June	11	1.132	United Technologies split 2 for 1
July	2	1.132	Standard Oil (Calif.) name changed to Chevron
1985 May	20	1.116	Eastman Kodak split 3 for 2
September	19	1.116	Allied Corp. name changed to Allied-Signal Inc.
October	30	1.090	Philip Morris Cos. replaced General Foods Corp.
			McDonald's Corp. was substituted for American Brands Inc.
1986 February	20	1.090	International Harvester name changed to Navister International Corp.
March	4	1.044	Union Carbide split 3 for 1
April	11	1.008	Philip Morris split 2 for 1
May	27	0.956	Merck split 2 for 1
May	28	0.953	Distribution of one share of Henley Group Inc. common for each four shares of Allied-Signal common held.
May	30	0.929	F.W. Woolworth split 2 for 1
June	17	0.908	Owen-Illinois split 2 for 1
June	26	0.889	McDonald's split 3 for 2

The Dow Jones Industrials—1985

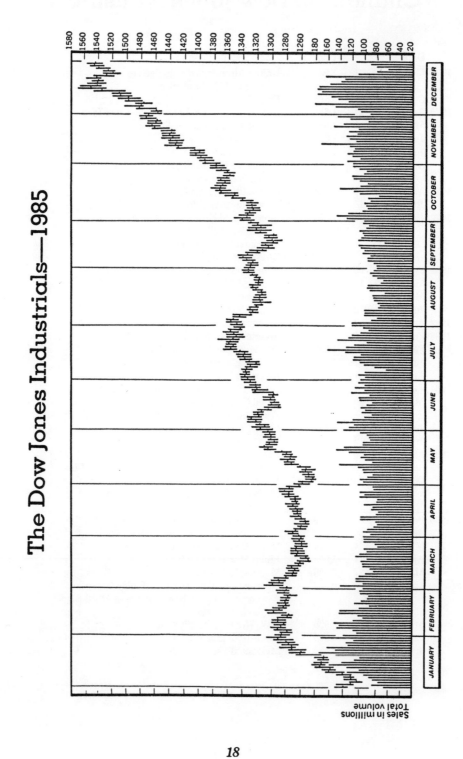

Sales in millions
Total volume

The Dow Jones Industrials—1986

1960 1940 1900 1860 1820 1780 1740 1700 1660 1620 1580 1540 1500 240 220 200 180 160 140 120 100 80 60 40

| JANUARY | FEBRUARY | MARCH | APRIL | MAY | JUNE | JULY | AUGUST | SEPTEMBER | OCTOBER | NOVEMBER | DECEMBER |

Sales in millions
Total volume

Dow Jones Industrial Average
Earnings, Dividends and Price-Earnings Ratio

	Price	Earnings (by qtrs)	Preceding 12 mos. earnings	Price Earnings Ratio (col. 1 ÷ col. 3)	Dividends
1986 December 31	1895.95	. . . .	. . . .	. . . .	17.09
September 30	1767.58	33.01	118.80	14.9	16.79
June 30	1892.72	36.37	103.39	18.3	16.94
March 31	1818.61	24.73	96.43	18.9	16.22
					67.04
1985 December 31	1546.67	24.69	96.11	16.1	17.19
September 30	1328.63	17.60	90.78	14.6	15.02
June 28	1335.46	29.41	102.26	13.1	14.95
March 29	1266.78	24.41	107.87	11.7	14.87
					62.03
1984 December 31	1211.57	19.36	113.58	10.7	16.99
September 28	1206.71	29.08	108.11	11.2	14.72
June 29	1132.40	35.02	102.07	11.1	14.98
March 30	1164.89	30.12	87.38	13.3	13.94
		113.58			60.63
1983 December 30	1258.94	13.89	72.45	17.4	14.77
September 30	1233.13	23.04	56.12	30.0	13.98
June 30	1221.96	20.33	11.59	105.4	13.70
March 31	1130.03	15.19	9.52	118.7	13.88
		72.45			56.33
1982 December 31	1046.54	d2.44	9.15	114.4	13.03
September 30	896.25	d21.49	35.15	25.5	13.44
June 30	811.93	18.26	79.90	10.2	13.75
March 31	822.77	14.82	97.13	8.5	13.92
		9.15			54.14
1981 December 31	875.00	23.56	113.71	7.7	14.44
September 30	849.98	23.26	123.32	6.9	13.73
June 30	976.88	35.49	128.91	7.6	14.19
March 31	1003.87	31.40	123.60	8.1	13.86
		113.71			56.22

Earnings and Price-Earnings Ratio

Earnings on the Dow Jones industrial average are computed by adding the per share results of the latest quarter of each of the 30 components. This total is then divided by the then-current divisor. Having obtained the figure for the quarter, the four most recent quarterly figures are totaled to give the 12-month figure.

The industrial average stood at 1767.58 on September 30, 1986, for instance (see above). The 12-month earnings for that date were 118.80, being the sum of the four previous quarters ended September.

To obtain the price-earnings ratio on the industrials, the industrial average on a given date is divided by the 12-month earnings of the same date.

Dow Jones Industrial Average
Earnings, Dividends and Price-Earnings Ratio

	Price	Earnings (by qtrs)	Preceding 12 mos. earnings	Price Earnings Ratio (col. 1 ÷ col. 3)	Dividends
1980 December 31	963.99	33.17	121.86	7.9	14.40
September 30	932.42	28.85	111.58	8.4	13.53
June 30	867.92	30.18	116.40	7.5	13.20
March 31	785.75	29.66	120.77	6.5	13.23
		121.86			54.36
1979 December 31	838.74	22.89	124.46	6.7	13.87
September 28	878.67	33.67	136.26	6.4	12.51
June 29	841.98	34.55	128.99	6.5	12.49
March 30	862.18	33.35	124.10	6.9	12.11
		124.46			50.98
1978 December 29	805.01	34.69	112.79	7.1	14.34
September 29	865.82	26.40	101.59	8.5	11.41
June 30	818.95	29.66	91.37	9.0	11.62
March 31	757.36	22.04	89.23	8.5	11.15
		112.79			48.52
1977 December 30	831.17	23.49	89.10	9.3	13.24
September 30	847.11	16.18	89.86	9.4	10.73
June 30	916.30	27.52	97.18	9.4	11.41
March 31	919.13	21.91	95.51	9.6	10.46
		89.10			45.84
1976 December 31	1004.65	24.25	96.72	10.4	12.13
September 30	990.19	23.50	95.81	10.3	9.85
June 30	1002.78	25.85	90.68	11.1	10.19
March 31	999.45	23.12	81.87	12.2	9.23
		96.72			41.40
1975 December 31	852.41	23.34	75.66	11.3	9.63
September 30	793.88	18.37	75.47	10.5	9.05
June 30	878.99	17.04	83.83	10.5	8.97
March 31	768.15	16.91	93.47	8.2	9.81
		75.66			37.46
1974 December 31	616.24	23.15	99.04	6.2	10.45
September 30	607.87	26.73	99.73	6.1	9.43
June 28	802.41	26.68	93.26	8.6	8.87
March 29	846.68	22.48	89.46	9.5	8.97
		99.04			37.72
1973 December 31	850.86	23.84	86.17	9.9	10.62
September 28	947.10	20.26	82.09	11.5	8.36
June 29	891.71	22.88	77.56	11.5	8.27
March 30	951.01	19.19	71.98	13.2	8.08
		86.17			35.33

Dow Jones Industrial Average
Earnings, Dividends and Price-Earnings Ratio

		Price	Earnings (by qtrs)	Preceding 12 mos. earnings	Price Earnings Ratio (col. 1 + col. 3)	Dividends
1972	December 29	1020.02	19.76	67.11	15.2	8.99
	September 29	953.27	15.73	62.15	15.3	7.76
	June 30	929.03	17.30	58.87	15.8	7.87
	March 30	940.70	14.32	56.76	16.6	7.65
			67.11			32.27
1971	December 31	890.20	14.80	55.09	16.2	7.85
	September 30	887.19	12.45	53.43	16.6	7.51
	June 30	891.14	15.19	53.45	16.7	7.80
	March 31	904.37	12.65	52.36	17.3	7.70
			55.09			30.86
1970	December 31	838.92	13.14	51.02	16.4	8.25
	September 30	760.68	12.47	51.83	14.7	7.80
	June 30	683.53	14.10	53.18	12.8	7.80
	March 31	785.57	11.31	54.07	14.5	7.68
			51.02			31.53
1969	December 31	800.36	13.95	57.02	14.0	8.63
	September 30	813.09	13.82	59.60	13.6	7.82
	June 30	873.19	14.99	59.47	14.7	8.08
	March 28	935.48	14.26	59.34	15.8	9.37
			57.02			33.90
1968	December 31	943.75	16.53	57.89	16.3	8.59
	September 30	935.79	13.69	57.05	16.4	7.73
	June 28	897.80	14.86	55.71	16.1	7.73
	March 29	840.67	12.81	53.98	15.6	7.29
			57.89			31.34
1967	December 29	905.11	15.69	53.87	16.8	8.03
	September 29	926.66	12.35	52.73	17.6	7.25
	June 30	860.26	13.13	54.27	15.8	7.36
	March 31	865.98	12.70	56.67	15.3	7.55
			53.87			30.19
1966	December 30	785.69	14.55	57.68	13.6	10.01
	September 30	774.22	13.89	57.36	13.5	7.18
	June 30	870.10	15.53	56.23	15.5	7.26
	March 31	924.77	13.71	55.05	16.8	7.44
			57.68			31.89
1965	December 31	969.26	14.23	53.67	18.1	8.54
	September 30	930.58	12.76	52.74	17.6	6.58
	June 30	868.03	14.35	50.84	17.1	6.79
	March 31	889.05	12.33	48.55	18.3	6.70
			53.67			28.61

Dow Jones Industrial Average
Earnings, Dividends and Price-Earnings Ratio

	Price	Earnings (by qtrs)	Preceding 12 mos. earnings	Price Earnings Ratio (col. 1 + col. 3)	Dividends
1964 December 31	874.13	13.30	46.43	18.8	10.46
September 30	875.37	10.86	45.88	19.1	5.79
June 30	831.50	12.06	44.46	18.7	7.16
March 31	813.29	10.21	42.60	19.1	7.83
		46.43			31.24
1963 December 31	762.95	12.75	41.21	18.5	7.39
September 30	732.79	9.44	40.18	18.2	5.35
June 28	706.68	10.20	38.71	18.3	5.52
March 29	682.52	8.82	37.35	18.3	5.15
		41.21			23.41
1962 December 31	652.10	11.72	36.43	17.9	7.66
September 28	578.98	7.97	35.52	16.3	5.26
June 29	561.28	8.84	34.74	16.2	5.23
March 30	706.95	7.90	34.11	20.7	5.15
		36.43			23.30
1961 December 29	731.13	10.81	31.91	22.9	7.57
September 29	701.21	7.19	29.03	24.2	5.09
June 30	683.96	8.21	29.29	23.4	5.05
March 30	676.63	5.70	29.53	22.9	5.00
		31.91			22.71
1960 December 31	615.89	7.93	32.21	19.1	6.55
September 30	580.14	7.45	31.64	18.3	4.86
June 30	640.62	8.45	31.26	20.5	4.83
March 31	610.59	8.38	33.82	18.2	5.12
		32.21			21.36
1959 December 31	679.36	7.36	34.31	19.8	6.73
September 30	631.68	7.07	35.70	17.7	4.53
June 30	643.60	11.01	35.71	18.0	4.59
March 31	601.71	8.87	31.04	19.4	4.89
		34.31			20.74
1958 December 31	583.65	8.75	27.95	20.9	5.83
September 30	532.09	7.08	27.97	19.0	4.59
June 30	478.18	6.34	29.41	16.3	4.62
March 31	446.76	5.78	32.56	13.7	4.96
		27.95			20.00
1957 December 31	435.69	8.78	36.08	12.1	6.91
September 30	456.30	8.51	36.70	12.4	4.91
June 28	503.29	9.49	34.82	14.4	4.79
March 29	474.81	9.30	34.30	13.8	5.00
		36.08			21.61

Dow Jones Industrial Average
Earnings, Dividends and Price-Earnings Ratio

		Price	Earnings (by qtrs)	Preceding 12 mos. earnings	Price Earnings Ratio (col. 1 ÷ col. 3)	Dividends
1956	December 31	499.47	9.40	33.34	15.0	8.17
	September 28	475.25	6.63	33.65	14.1	4.83
	June 29	492.78	8.97	35.51	13.9	4.98
	March 29	511.79	8.34	36.02	14.2	5.01
			33.34			22.99
1955	December 30	488.40	9.71	35.78	13.7	8.13
	September 30	466.62	8.49	34.41	13.6	4.25
	June 30	451.38	9.48	32.11	14.1	4.24
	March 31	409.70	8.10	29.65	13.8	4.96
			35.78			21.58
1954	December 31	404.39	8.34	28.18	14.4	5.76
	September 30	360.46	6.19	26.99	13.4	3.75
	June 30	333.53	7.02	27.52	12.1	3.92
	March 31	303.51	6.63	27.20	11.2	4.04
			28.18			17.47
1953	December 31	280.90	7.15	27.23	10.3	4.86
	September 30	264.04	6.72	27.63	9.6	3.53
	June 30	268.26	6.70	26.93	10.0	3.95
	March 31	279.87	6.66	25.78	10.9	3.77
			27.23			16.11
1952	December 31	291.90	7.55	24.78	11.8	4.62
	September 30	270.61	6.02	24.37	11.1	3.55
	June 30	274.35	5.55	24.06	11.4	3.55
	March 31	269.46	5.66	25.11	10.7	3.71
			24.78			15.43
1951	December 31	269.23	7.14	26.59	10.1	5.25
	September 28	271.16	5.71	29.02	9.3	3.72
	June 29	242.64	6.60	31.83	7.6	3.48
	March 31	247.94	7.14	32.40	7.7	3.89
			26.59			16.34
1950	December 30	235.41	9.57	30.70	7.7	6.26
	September 29	226.36	8.52	27.15	8.3	3.87
	June 30	209.11	7.17	24.99	8.4	2.98
	March 31	206.05	5.44	23.20	8.9	3.02
			30.70			16.13
1949	December 31	200.13	6.02	23.54	8.5	5.02
	September 30	182.51	6.36	24.66	7.4	2.32
	June 30	167.42	5.38	23.95	7.0	2.85
	March 31	177.10	5.78	23.79	7.4	2.60
			23.54			12.79

d-Deficit.

Dow Jones Transportation Average
Earnings, Dividends and Price-Earnings Ratio

		Price	Earnings (by qtrs)	Preceding 12 mos. earnings	Price Earnings Ratio (col. 1 ÷ col. 3)	Dividends
1986	December 31	807.17	. . . .	. . . .	. . . .	4.14
	September 30	800.38	19.92	14.09	56.8	4.05
	June 30	782.75	(d9.81)	9.99	78.3	4.15
	March 31	830.84	(d4.51)	35.65	23.3	4.02
			. . .			16.36
1985	December 31	708.21	8.49	47.27	15.0	3.93
	September 30	640.57	15.82	51.35	12.5	3.93
	June 28	664.09	15.85	55.31	12.0	3.88
	March 29	603.08	7.11	58.39	10.3	3.70
			47.27			15.44
1984	December 30	558.13	12.57	62.37	8.9	3.51
	September 28	517.61	19.78	62.22	8.3	3.71
	June 29	474.18	18.93	58.17	8.1	3.56
	March 30	510.19	11.09	52.93	9.6	3.51
			62.37			14.29
1983	December 30	598.59	12.42	38.84	15.4	3.06
	September 30	561.58	15.73	36.32	15.4	3.68
	June 30	585.92	13.69	31.12	18.8	3.85
	March 31	507.39	(d3.00)	28.91	17.5	3.54
			38.84			14.13
1982	December 31	448.38	9.90	29.46	15.2	3.53
	September 30	360.46	10.53	28.06	12.8	3.88
	June 30	320.59	11.48	35.69	9.0	3.54
	March 31	333.08	(d2.45)	35.34	9.4	3.93
			29.46			14.88
1981	December 31	380.30	8.50	46.17	8.2	4.27
	September 30	350.03	18.16	51.40	6.8	3.56
	June 30	415.18	11.14	45.35	9.1	4.26
	March 31	437.62	8.37	44.14	9.9	3.95
			46.17			16.04
1980	December 31	398.10	13.73	43.14	9.2	3.42
	September 30	333.86	12.11	39.99	8.3	3.55
	June 30	273.50	9.93	37.95	7.2	3.54
	March 31	246.30	7.37	42.99	5.7	3.11
			43.14			13.62
1979	December 31	252.39	10.58	42.77	5.9	3.37
	September 28	260.47	10.07	42.17	6.2	2.95
	June 29	242.26	14.97	45.87	5.3	3.22
	March 30	225.17	7.15	45.31	5.0	2.83
			42.77			12.37

Dow Jones Transportation Average
Earnings, Dividends and Price-Earnings Ratio

		Price	Earnings (by qtrs)	Preceding 12 mos. earnings	Price Earnings Ratio (col. 1 + col. 3)	Dividends
1978	December 29	206.56	9.98	41.42	5.0	3.01
	September 29	244.11	13.77	39.98	6.1	2.73
	June 30	219.86	14.41	36.48	6.0	2.87
	March 31	207.15	3.26	32.59	6.4	2.59
			41.42			11.20
1977	December 30	217.18	8.54	34.44	6.3	2.71
	September 30	215.48	10.27	33.36	6.5	2.46
	June 30	238.80	10.52	31.76	7.5	2.59
	March 31	222.97	5.11	29.31	7.6	2.34
			34.44			10.10
1976	December 31	237.03	7.46	27.47	8.6	2.45
	September 30	217.34	8.67	25.10	8.7	2.21
	June 30	224.77	8.07	22.83	9.8	2.26
	March 31	207.97	3.27	17.63	11.8	2.09
			27.47			9.01
1975	December 31	172.65	5.09	13.68	12.6	2.10
	September 30	155.97	6.40	12.46	12.5	1.96
	June 30	171.13	2.87	14.03	12.2	2.23
	March 31	165.48	(d0.68)	19.06	8.7	2.16
			13.68			8.45
1974	December 31	143.44	3.87	23.45	6.1	2.38
	September 30	128.48	7.97	25.06	5.1	2.15
	June 28	162.18	7.90	22.64	7.2	2.12
	March 29	185.08	3.71	19.87	9.3	1.99
			23.45			8.64
1973	December 31	196.19	5.48	19.22	10.2	1.97
	September 28	176.96	5.55	18.67	9.5	2.13
	June 29	156.18	5.13	18.64	8.4	2.03
	March 30	200.13	3.06	18.83	10.6	2.03
			19.22			8.16
1972	December 29	227.17	4.93	18.75	12.1	2.03
	September 29	217.70	5.52	18.36	11.8	1.89
	June 30	233.30	5.32	18.28	12.8	2.00
	March 30	258.93	2.98	17.23	15.0	1.88
			18.75			7.80
1971	December 31	243.72	4.54	15.25	16.0	1.77
	September 30	237.18	5.44	12.80	18.5	1.83
	June 30	215.60	4.27	10.56	20.4	2.31
	March 31	200.00	1.00	8.17	24.5	1.72
			15.25			7.63

Dow Jones Transportation Average
Earnings, Dividends and Price-Earnings Ratio

		Price	Earnings (by qtrs)	Preceding 12 mos. earnings	Price Earnings Ratio (col. 1 ÷ col. 3)	Dividends
1970	December 31	171.52	2.09	8.52	20.5	2.42
	September 30	153.45	3.20	10.74	14.3	1.86
	June 30	120.57	1.88	11.98	10.1	2.32
	March 31	173.06	1.35	13.89	12.5	1.92
			8.52			8.52
1969	December 31	176.34	4.31	15.39	11.5	3.14
	September 30	196.60	4.44	16.34	12.0	2.50
	June 30	211.99	3.79	15.60	13.6	2.85
	March 28	243.69	2.85	16.56	14.7	2.54
			15.39			11.03
1968	December 31	271.60	5.26	17.59	15.4	3.32
	September 30	267.69	3.70	16.61	16.1	2.53
	June 28	261.77	4.75	15.16	17.3	2.96
	March 29	218.99	3.88	13.86	15.8	2.66
			17.59			11.47
1967	December 29	233.24	4.29	12.79	18.2	3.28
	September 29	261.83	2.25	15.07	17.4	2.60
	June 30	254.84	3.45	17.84	14.3	2.86
	March 31	230.59	2.81	20.06	11.5	2.53
			12.80			11.27
1966	December 30	202.97	6.56	20.90	9.7	3.71
	September 30	193.49	5.02	20.75	9.3	2.53
	June 30	226.06	5.67	21.20	10.7	2.75
	March 31	249.17	3.65	20.68	12.0	2.39
			20.90			11.38
1965	December 31	247.48	6.41	19.35	12.8	3.73
	September 30	222.91	5.47	16.89	13.2	1.93
	June 30	193.69	5.15	15.17	12.8	2.16
	March 31	210.77	2.32	14.16	14.9	2.26
			19.35			10.08
1964	December 31	205.34	3.95	14.49	14.2	2.92
	September 30	218.17	3.75	13.61	14.0	1.82
	June 30	213.56	4.14	14.82	14.4	1.86
	March 31	191.83	2.65	14.54	13.2	1.80
			14.49			8.40
1963	December 31	178.54	5.07	12.69	14.1	2.37
	September 30	170.53	2.96	12.33	13.8	1.60
	June 28	173.66	3.86	11.90	14.6	1.73
	March 29	152.92	0.80	9.86	15.5	1.72
			12.69			7.42

Dow Jones Transportation Average
Earnings, Dividends and Price-Earnings Ratio

		Price	Earnings (by qtrs)	Preceding 12 mos. earnings	Price Earnings Ratio (col. 1 ÷ col. 3)	Dividends
1962	December 31	141.04	4.71	9.38	15.0	2.12
	September 28	115.68	2.53	8.11	14.2	1.53
	June 29	118.63	1.83	8.67	13.7	1.69
	March 30	144.28	0.32	6.75	21.4	1.69
			9.38			7.03
1961	December 29	143.84	3.44	4.89	29.4	1.97
	September 29	143.96	3.09	4.28	33.6	1.60
	June 30	139.47	d.09	1.16	119.3	1.77
	March 30	146.20	(d1.54)	3.43	42.6	1.77
			4.89			7.11
1960	December 31	130.85	2.82	6.71	19.5	2.38
	September 30	125.42	(d.03)	7.31	17.2	1.79
	June 30	143.19	2.18	8.54	16.8	1.98
	March 31	143.74	1.73	10.71	13.4	1.93
			6.70			8.08
1959	December 31	154.05	3.42	11.11	13.9	2.26
	September 30	157.40	1.20	12.99	12.2	1.75
	June 30	167.62	4.36	16.36	10.2	1.87
	March 31	158.65	2.13	13.89	8.8	1.87
			11.11			7.75
1958	December 31	157.65	5.30	12.34	12.8	2.04
	September 30	144.61	4.58	10.91	13.2	1.71
	June 30	118.75	1.89	10.06	11.8	1.85
	March 31	103.88	0.58	12.25	8.5	1.89
			12.35			7.49
1957	December 31	96.96	3.87	15.55	6.2	2.19
	September 30	123.70	3.72	17.66	7.0	2.23
	June 28	146.46	4.08	18.55	7.9	2.25
	March 29	144.05	3.88	19.65	7.3	2.29
			15.55			8.96
1956	December 31	153.23	5.98	19.52	7.9	2.79
	September 28	154.01	4.61	16.76	8.2	1.86
	June 29	166.69	5.18	19.49	8.5	1.90
	March 29	171.82	3.75	19.32	8.9	2.23
			19.52			8.78
1955	December 30	163.29	5.22	19.79	8.2	2.82
	September 30	155.05	5.34	20.66	7.5	1.62
	June 30	160.95	5.01	18.88	8.5	1.69
	March 31	150.32	4.22	16.69	9.0	1.91
			19.79			8.04

Dow Jones Transportation Average
Earnings, Dividends and Price-Earnings Ratio

		Price	Earnings (by qtrs)	Preceding 12 mos. earnings	Price Earnings Ratio (col. 1 ÷ col. 3)	Dividends
1954	December 31	145.86	6.09	14.98	9.7	2.42
	September 30	115.18	3.57	14.19	8.1	1.44
	June 30	112.70	2.81	15.66	7.2	1.51
	March 31	101.42	2.51	17.65	5.7	1.55
			14.98			6.92
1953	December 31	94.03	5.30	19.65	4.8	2.38
	September 30	93.90	5.04	21.39	4.4	1.86
	June 30	104.77	4.80	20.81	5.0	1.46
	March 31	107.02	4.51	19.76	5.4	1.40
			19.65			7.10
1952	December 31	111.27	7.04	19.20	5.8	2.03
	September 30	100.35	4.45	18.44	5.4	1.31
	June 30	102.73	3.76	16.65	6.2	1.41
	March 31	94.36	3.95	16.13	5.8	1.30
			19.20			6.05
1951	December 31	81.70	6.28	14.87	5.5	1.62
	September 28	84.76	2.66	15.48	5.5	1.22
	June 29	72.39	3.24	17.53	4.1	1.07
	March 31	80.58	2.69	17.82	4.5	1.01
			14.87			4.92
1950	December 30	77.64	6.89	17.11	4.5	1.38
	September 29	67.64	4.71	13.60	5.0	.78
	June 30	52.24	3.52	10.76	4.9	.84
	March 31	54.83	1.99	9.26	5.9	.85
			17.11			3.85
1949	December 31	52.76	3.37	8.79	6.0	1.12
	September 30	47.87	1.88	9.54	5.0	.76
	June 30	42.57	2.02	11.84	3.6	.99
	March 31	49.02	1.51	13.39	3.7	.93
			8.78			3.80
1948	December 31	52.86	4.13	13.89	3.8	1.19
	September 30	58.33	4.18	12.96	4.5	.69
	June 30	62.76	3.57	10.30	6.1	.79
	March 31	53.73	2.01	8.66	6.2	.82
			13.89			3.49
1947	December 31	52.48	3.20	8.52	6.2	1.05
	September 30	48.43	1.52	8.18	5.9	.79
	June 30	45.88	1.93	8.74	5.2	.67
	March 31	48.64	1.88	6.43	7.6	.83
			8.53			3.34

d-Deficit.

Dow Jones Utility Average
Earnings, Dividends and Price-Earnings Ratio

		Price	Preceding 12 mos. earnings	Price Earnings Ratio (col. 1 ÷ col. 2)	Dividends
1986	December 31	206.01	....	....	3.94
	September 30	199.71	14.91	13.4	3.79
	June 30	200.10	13.95	14.3	3.92
	March 31	193.73	19.40	10.0	3.64
					15.29
1985	December 31	174.81	18.27	9.6	3.56
	September 30	150.29	17.60	8.5	3.55
	June 28	164.85	18.74	8.8	3.54
	March 29	153.01	19.15	8.0	3.49
					14.14
1984	December 31	149.52	21.02	7.1	3.46
	September 28	139.16	21.49	6.5	3.63
	June 29	124.28	21.18	5.9	3.38
	March 30	126.83	20.75	6.1	3.34
					13.81
1983	December 30	131.84	19.79	6.7	3.27
	September 30	134.68	18.90	7.4	3.26
	June 30	127.63	16.78	7.6	3.24
	March 31	124.54	17.77	7.0	3.19
					12.96
1982	December 31	119.46	18.34	6.5	3.15
	September 30	115.36	18.86	6.1	3.12
	June 30	107.70	19.31	5.6	3.21
	March 31	108.25	18.09	6.0	2.96
					12.44
1981	December 31	109.02	18.31	5.9	3.02
	September 30	102.21	17.65	5.8	2.78
	June 30	107.98	16.33	6.6	2.72
	March 31	109.02	15.96	6.8	2.71
					11.23
1980	December 31	114.42	15.58	7.3	2.60
	September 30	107.82	15.21	7.1	2.57
	June 30	113.33	15.20	7.5	2.57
	March 31	99.70	15.47	6.4	2.49
					10.23
1979	December 31	106.60	15.49	6.9	2.40
	September 28	106.90	15.76	6.8	2.36
	June 29	105.45	15.10	7.0	2.35
	March 30	104.19	14.91	7.0	2.33
					9.44

Dow Jones Utility Average
Earnings, Dividends and Price-Earnings Ratio

	Price	Preceding 12 mos. earnings	Price Earnings Ratio (col. 1 ÷ col. 2)	Dividends
1978 December 29	98.24	14.29	6.9	2.23
September 29	106.12	13.85	7.7	2.19
June 30	104.94	14.03	7.5	2.19
March 31	105.68	13.92	7.6	2.18
				8.79
1977 December 30	111.28	14.27	7.8	2.09
September 30	113.25	14.99	7.6	2.08
June 30	114.68	14.91	7.7	2.07
March 31	106.02	14.48	7.3	1.99
				8.23
1976 December 31	108.38	13.59	8.0	1.93
September 30	97.78	12.50	7.8	1.88
June 30	87.55	12.01	7.3	1.87
March 31	87.55	11.99	7.3	1.87
				7.55
1975 December 31	83.65	11.58	7.2	1.82
September 30	76.97	11.59	6.6	1.80
June 30	85.99	11.63	7.4	1.79
March 31	77.20	11.77	6.6	1.79
				7.20
1974 December 31	68.76	11.57	5.9	1.75
September 30	61.16	11.38	5.4	1.72
June 28	68.22	11.11	6.1	1.67
March 29	90.75	10.69	8.5	1.77
				6.91
1973 December 31	89.37	10.79	8.3	1.75
September 28	103.40	10.83	9.5	1.73
June 29	102.12	10.79	9.5	1.72
March 30	108.00	10.99	9.8	1.72
				6.92
1972 December 29	119.50	10.94	10.9	1.70
September 29	110.56	10.65	10.4	1.68
June 30	106.63	10.42	10.2	1.68
March 30	112.47	10.17	11.1	1.67
				6.73
1971 December 31	117.75	10.12	11.6	1.65
September 30	109.31	10.09	10.8	1.64
June 30	118.45	9.92	11.9	1.64
March 31	122.83	9.79	12.5	1.63
				6.56

Dow Jones Utility Average
Earnings, Dividends and Price-Earnings Ratio

		Price	Preceding 12 mos. earnings	Price Earnings Ratio (col. 1 ÷ col. 2)	Dividends
1970	December 31	121.84	9.69	12.6	1.61
	September 30	108.19	9.64	11.2	1.60
	June 30	95.86	9.70	9.9	1.58
	March 31	117.75	9.68	12.2	1.58
					6.37
1969	December 31	110.08	9.54	11.5	1.56
	September 30	111.16	9.44	11.8	1.55
	June 30	122.09	9.39	13.0	1.55
	March 28	129.67	9.32	13.9	1.55
					6.21
1968	December 31	137.17	9.23	14.9	1.54
	September 30	130.37	9.32	14.0	1.53
	June 28	132.60	9.15	14.5	1.53
	March 29	121.58	9.46	12.8	1.51
					6.11
1967	December 29	127.91	9.24	13.8	1.50
	September 29	130.34	9.03	14.4	1.49
	June 30	131.39	8.96	14.7	1.46
	March 31	138.55	8.95	15.5	1.44
					5.89
1966	December 30	136.18	8.75	15.6	1.69
	September 30	124.72	8.80	14.2	1.41
	June 30	131.60	8.76	15.0	1.38
	March 31	141.24	8.66	16.3	1.36
					5.84
1965	December 31	152.63	8.53	17.9	1.34
	September 30	157.60	8.38	18.8	1.31
	June 30	154.15	8.12	19.0	1.28
	March 31	162.36	7.88	20.6	1.26
					5.19
1964	December 31	155.17	7.88	20.3	1.24
	September 30	153.16	7.31	21.0	1.32
	June 30	143.40	7.25	19.8	1.19
	March 31	137.30	7.11	19.3	1.19
					4.94
1963	December 31	138.99	7.04	19.7	1.72
	September 30	139.95	7.06	19.8	1.31
	June 28	139.08	6.95	20.0	1.07
	March 29	136.19	6.68	20.4	1.04
					5.14

Dow Jones Utility Average
Earnings, Dividends and Price-Earnings Ratio

	Price	Preceding 12 mos. earnings	Price Earnings Ratio (col. 1 ÷ col. 2)	Dividends
1962 December 31	129.23	6.48	19.9	1.04
September 28	117.62	6.07	19.4	1.13
June 29	108.28	6.05	17.9	.99
March 30	130.01	6.02	21.6	.98
				4.14
1961 December 29	129.16	5.86	22.0	97
September 29	122.44	5.78	21.2	1.17
June 30	111.74	5.78	19.5	.93
March 30	111.91	5.67	19.7	1.24
				4.31
1960 December 31	100.02	5.61	17.8	1.09
September 30	91.29	5.54	16.5	1.09
June 30	93.39	5.51	16.9	.90
March 31	88.20	5.36	16.5	.90
				3.98
1959 December 31	87.83	5.31	16.5	.94
September 30	87.91	5.27	16.7	.98
June 30	87.30	5.23	16.7	.87
March 31	99.43	5.16	18.1	.87
				3.66
1958 December 31	91.00	4.96	13.3	.85
September 30	80.71	4.87	16.6	.97
June 30	78.92	4.84	16.3	.84
March 31	74.00	4.83	15.3	.83
				3.49
1957 December 31	68.58	4.70	14.6	.94
September 30	66.67	4.63	14.4	.82
June 28	69.84	4.66	15.0	.82
March 29	71.47	4.28	16.7	.81
				3.39
1956 December 31	63.54	4.71	14.6	1.04
September 28	65.57	4.68	14.0	.76
June 29	67.38	4.73	14.2	.77
March 29	67.39	4.58	14.7	.76
				3.33
1955 December 30	64.16	4.34	14.8	.82
September 30	63.14	4.19	15.1	.70
June 30	64.34	4.08	15.8	.73
March 31	63.57	4.09	15.5	1.32
				3.57

Daily Closing 1986 Dow Jones Averages

January

	—30 Industrials—			—20 Transport Cos.—			—15 Utilities—			Daily Sales —000—	20 Bonds	Commodity Futures
	High	Low	Close	High	Low	Close	High	Low	Close			
1						HOLIDAY						
2	1551.95	1523.74	1537.73	714.03	698.24	706.55	175.63	172.80	174.45	98,960	84.10	133.23
3	1557.11	1534.98	1549.20	711.30	695.75	702.99	176.29	173.78	175.88	105,030	84.31	132.36
6	1577.00	1537.04	1547.59	705.84	691.95	697.06	177.06	174.65	176.14	99,610	84.47	134.87
7	1573.74	1544.50	1565.71	711.66	694.33	706.79	179.83	175.78	179.06	152,950	84.67	136.51
8	1578.10	1516.63	1526.61	717.24	691.48	693.49	179.83	174.04	174.75	180,330	84.65	136.85
9	1530.85	1495.64	1518.23	696.11	674.74	686.97	174.09	172.04	172.04	176,460	84.39	137.13
10	1530.96	1500.57	1513.53	701.09	679.13	686.97	174.09	171.16	172.75	122,780	84.12	138.19
13	1526.83	1502.29	1520.53	698.12	681.39	692.31	173.73	170.60	172.39	108,680	83.95	136.39
14	1530.62	1508.03	1519.04	698.84	687.20	692.78	173.98	171.52	172.55	113,920	83.73	135.90
15	1535.32	1512.96	1527.29	701.80	691.00	698.84	173.68	171.62	173.01	122,420	84.11	136.28
16	1547.71	1517.09	1541.63	714.27	693.97	712.49	174.96	171.42	173.63	130,460	84.15	135.65
17	1552.52	1519.72	1536.70	723.29	707.03	716.64	175.01	171.88	172.75	132,130	84.28	134.49
20	1536.01	1516.86	1529.13	719.25	706.08	715.81	173.11	171.11	172.34	85,340	84.15	133.87
21	1535.89	1502.87	1514.45	725.07	709.64	715.93	172.91	169.52	170.80	128,310	83.84	132.69
22	1525.57	1494.84	1502.29	723.77	708.81	712.13	171.06	168.39	169.47	131,180	83.80	132.07
23	1519.38	1491.74	1511.24	724.00	706.67	719.37	170.60	167.98	170.09	130,310	84.14	132.66
24	1537.39	1507.68	1529.93	742.40	715.93	739.91	171.57	168.80	171.21	128,930	83.88	133.84
27	1548.17	1524.43	1537.61	757.95	735.64	746.44	173.73	170.55	172.55	122,930	83.96	133.49
28	1561.35	1530.50	1556.42	757.48	739.43	753.68	175.01	171.68	174.39	145,660	84.15	132.17
29	1578.10	1548.05	1558.94	768.87	749.41	755.58	176.75	173.68	174.65	193,800	84.17	131.44
30	1572.59	1545.76	1552.18	758.67	740.27	745.01	175.73	172.80	173.88	125,340	84.33	130.03
31	1582.91	1548.17	1570.99	754.99	739.20	748.46	177.52	172.91	176.91	143,519	84.25	128.93
High			1570.99			755.58			179.06		84.67	138.19
Low			1502.29			686.97			169.47		83.73	128.93

Daily Closing 1986 Dow Jones Averages

February

	—30 Industrials—			—20 Transport Cos.—			—15 Utilities—			Daily Sales —000—	20 Bonds	Commodity Futures
	High	Low	Close	High	Low	Close	High	Low	Close			
3	1600.11	1564.33	1594.27	759.85	743.71	756.29	179.06	175.52	178.14	145,280	84.74	127.21
4	1611.47	1575.46	1593.23	765.55	744.66	755.22	178.96	174.50	176.45	175,730	85.11	125.08
5	1601.83	1576.26	1593.12	758.19	744.78	753.44	177.06	174.39	175.83	134,310	85.19	126.40
6	1616.51	1587.50	1600.69	762.11	748.69	756.65	176.96	174.34	176.04	146,100	85.19	127.04
7	1622.82	1576.83	1613.42	766.38	745.61	762.35	177.37	173.73	176.75	144,400	85.08	128.22
10	1633.14	1605.16	1626.38	773.15	756.29	767.92	178.65	175.63	178.29	129,910	85.06	128.85
11	1637.50	1613.30	1622.82	773.27	759.26	764.84	179.73	177.16	178.65	141,250	85.18	129.15
12	1640.48	1611.70	1629.93	770.89	760.21	766.98	179.22	176.75	178.19	136,370	85.44	128.72
13	1649.31	1616.86	1645.07	777.90	760.92	768.16	179.63	177.22	179.11	136,490	86.06	127.00
14	1668.81	1636.12	1664.45	777.78	761.51	772.91	181.01	177.99	180.70	155,590	86.29	125.94
17						HOLIDAY						
18	1685.55	1649.43	1678.78	787.27	769.35	784.78	183.78	179.52	183.27	160,200	86.33	130.41
19	1689.22	1651.03	1658.26	791.90	776.83	784.43	184.40	181.11	182.60	152,030	86.45	131.42
20	1675.46	1641.97	1672.82	794.28	778.37	792.14	184.29	181.01	183.99	139,740	86.43	131.67
21	1702.75	1668.69	1697.71	803.54	789.41	797.72	186.24	183.06	185.53	177,590	87.07	132.74
24	1709.75	1678.67	1698.28	801.99	785.73	792.97	186.14	182.65	184.65	144,670	87.85	134.12
25	1709.52	1674.08	1692.66	792.50	773.62	780.39	185.88	182.65	184.65	147,960	87.86	133.98
26	1714.79	1679.59	1696.90	787.04	772.55	781.46	185.22	182.76	183.73	158,020	88.45	132.33
27	1728.90	1683.37	1713.99	795.94	778.25	791.43	186.24	182.70	185.32	181,740	89.11	132.67
28	1732.57	1687.50	1709.06	804.37	784.78	792.26	187.17	183.68	185.83	191,660	89.28	132.04
High			1713.99			797.72			185.83		89.28	134.12
Low			1593.12			753.44			175.83		84.74	125.08

35

Daily Closing 1986 Dow Jones Averages

March

	-30 Industrials-			-20 Transport Cos.-			-15 Utilities-			Daily Sales -000-	20 Bonds	Commodity Futures
	High	Low	Close	High	Low	Close	High	Low	Close			
3	1714.33	1684.63	1696.67	800.54	777.48	789.62	185.83	183.06	184.29	142,670	89.45	131.57
4	1718.63	1679.72	1686.42	802.99	779.44	786.92	186.19	183.01	184.24	174,510	90.08	132.93
5	1695.40	1663.07	1686.66	792.20	776.13	785.57	184.45	180.55	182.45	154,560	89.38	132.68
6	1711.21	1681.75	1696.60	797.11	780.05	789.01	184.09	181.11	182.19	158,990	89.28	133.58
7	1713.48	1682.83	1699.83	797.23	782.26	791.34	183.94	179.68	181.83	163,230	89.21	133.14
10	1715.16	1688.70	1702.95	799.80	784.59	793.06	184.19	180.50	182.81	129,930	89.88	133.71
11	1752.17	1704.26	1746.05	806.55	786.43	801.52	187.73	182.60	186.81	187,270	89.53	134.18
12	1773.35	1733.48	1745.45	815.75	796.49	806.18	190.45	186.14	188.40	210,250	90.03	134.92
13	1768.80	1729.53	1753.71	817.22	800.54	810.48	189.99	186.04	188.04	171,480	89.83	134.67
14	1799.93	1745.21	1792.74	822.37	801.40	816.24	190.14	186.45	189.47	181,870	90.00	134.40
17	1790.59	1758.38	1776.82	814.77	797.72	804.10	188.55	185.53	186.65	137,460	89.91	133.93
18	1806.75	1763.65	1789.87	810.72	791.71	802.75	187.94	185.01	186.50	148,010	89.89	133.11
19	1806.99	1773.47	1787.95	812.44	798.21	805.57	187.06	184.04	185.01	149,990	89.79	133.56
20	1820.76	1784.36	1804.24	820.17	799.31	812.07	185.68	183.11	184.65	147,950	90.06	133.85
21	1821.24	1764.85	1768.56	823.60	799.68	804.71	187.01	183.22	184.60	199,220	90.04	133.07
24	1796.22	1763.29	1782.93	817.47	798.09	809.74	187.68	183.73	186.76	143,810	90.19	132.01
25	1794.30	1762.09	1778.50	811.46	796.00	803.61	188.24	185.17	187.73	139,250	90.19	131.23
26	1817.41	1775.98	1810.70	819.19	800.42	816.24	190.30	187.06	189.37	161,460	90.39	131.55
27	1849.74	1806.51	1821.72	835.99	817.35	828.39	192.40	189.37	191.53	178,100	90.68	132.12
28						HOLIDAY						
31	1841.83	1803.16	1818.61	842.98	821.64	830.84	194.60	190.40	193.73	134,440	90.72	130.75
		High	1821.72			830.84			193.73		90.72	134.92
		Low	1686.42			785.57			181.83		89.21	130.75

36

Daily Closing 1986 Dow Jones Averages

April

	–30 Industrials–			–20 Transport Cos.–			–15 Utilities–			Daily Sales –000–	20 Bonds	Commodity Futures
	High	Low	Close	High	Low	Close	High	Low	Close			
1	1829.02	1777.54	1790.11	834.15	808.27	813.05	195.27	190.40	191.32	167,390	90.81	129.00
2	1803.64	1769.76	1795.26	816.85	797.60	813.67	192.50	188.81	191.27	145,300	91.12	128.62
3	1809.27	1753.71	1766.40	819.80	796.74	800.66	192.50	188.24	189.68	148,230	91.09	126.67
4	1772.87	1728.45	1739.22	803.73	774.78	779.32	190.55	185.73	186.55	147,270	91.03	125.43
7	1749.04	1712.52	1735.51	785.33	765.46	778.83	186.35	182.55	185.27	129,760	90.89	126.43
8	1779.57	1737.07	1769.76	794.90	775.39	788.40	188.40	184.19	187.63	146,290	90.96	126.75
9	1807.71	1754.19	1778.62	800.05	780.42	786.80	190.14	186.29	188.60	156,250	91.14	126.15
10	1807.83	1768.20	1794.30	794.90	781.77	787.41	190.09	187.42	189.17	184,760	91.26	126.27
11	1812.50	1779.14	1790.18	796.00	775.76	786.06	190.24	186.76	188.19	139,440	91.49	127.05
14	1811.38	1781.00	1805.31	793.67	779.32	788.27	189.94	187.68	189.17	106,730	91.64	126.31
15	1822.05	1789.68	1809.65	795.39	777.97	789.13	190.71	188.30	189.73	123,650	91.55	125.09
16	1859.62	1814.73	1847.97	816.98	790.97	813.30	193.07	189.01	191.22	173,830	91.67	124.18
17	1870.16	1831.72	1855.03	826.18	805.81	817.96	193.17	189.47	192.50	161,400	91.86	124.80
18	1870.16	1830.98	1840.40	822.74	804.96	812.56	192.60	190.04	191.78	153,640	91.75	124.99
21	1864.21	1829.86	1855.90	826.67	806.67	822.13	193.42	189.83	192.24	136,090	91.94	123.49
22	1866.44	1815.97	1830.98	830.35	808.88	815.63	192.86	187.37	190.04	161,510	91.92	124.29
23	1841.27	1803.94	1829.61	824.34	804.47	813.79	189.83	186.24	187.63	149,690	91.37	124.37
24	1848.46	1818.95	1831.72	821.03	807.41	811.46	189.12	185.94	186.86	146,560	91.26	124.98
25	1848.46	1813.74	1835.57	818.03	801.69	810.97	187.83	184.86	186.70	142,310	90.91	123.96
28	1852.68	1817.71	1843.75	820.78	802.38	815.26	187.63	187.09	185.58	123,860	90.95	124.08
29	1856.15	1813.12	1825.89	821.76	799.68	807.41	186.09	178.96	182.65	148,770	91.17	125.30
30	1831.23	1777.90	1783.98	809.13	787.78	792.20	182.40	178.34	179.63	147,460	91.59	126.44
High			1855.90			822.13			192.50		91.94	129.00
Low			1735.51			778.83			179.63		90.81	123.49

37

Daily Closing 1986 Dow Jones Averages

May

	— 30 Industrials —			— 20 Transport Cos. —			— 15 Utilities —			Daily Sales —000—	20 Bonds	Commodity Futures
	High	Low	Close	High	Low	Close	High	Low	Close			
1	1796.88	1761.04	1777.78	799.80	783.61	791.95	180.95	177.69	179.71	146,480	91.64	124.65
2	1795.88	1763.14	1774.68	797.72	780.42	786.56	182.75	179.09	181.41	126,270	91.11	124.24
5	1800.35	1770.96	1793.77	796.74	783.49	792.44	184.45	180.95	183.58	102,440	91.48	124.53
6	1803.32	1775.92	1787.95	797.47	783.00	789.62	185.28	182.08	183.73	121,180	91.60	124.29
7	1790.05	1755.21	1775.30	791.71	775.64	783.37	183.73	179.55	181.77	129,890	91.68	123.59
8	1797.87	1768.48	1786.21	789.99	777.23	783.00	184.82	181.31	183.73	136,030	91.65	124.76
9	1797.12	1767.73	1789.43	793.92	773.31	788.03	184.15	181.15	182.91	137,400	91.74	124.72
12	1804.32	1774.80	1787.33	794.28	778.70	784.96	183.58	180.58	181.98	125,360	91.66	122.85
13	1804.07	1772.32	1785.34	793.55	774.90	782.88	183.47	180.07	181.46	119,160	91.39	122.37
14	1815.23	1775.55	1808.28	791.83	775.64	786.43	183.32	180.33	182.70	132,140	91.71	122.26
15	1808.78	1766.99	1774.68	788.76	772.20	776.50	183.78	180.38	182.34	131,570	91.70	121.81
16	1775.67	1749.88	1759.80	778.21	765.58	771.71	182.96	180.12	181.05	113,540	91.18	120.84
19	1769.84	1746.53	1758.18	777.48	765.95	771.10	182.70	179.76	181.72	85,840	90.98	119.07
20	1788.44	1752.48	1783.98	788.03	768.89	785.45	182.60	179.86	182.08	112,990	90.43	118.47
21	1798.61	1766.62	1775.17	788.27	777.11	780.30	183.11	179.71	181.15	117,090	90.56	117.98
22	1813.74	1774.18	1806.30	797.72	778.21	795.02	184.45	180.58	183.68	144,920	90.59	117.95
23	1842.14	1804.69	1823.29	803.97	790.73	797.96	185.54	182.65	184.35	130,160	91.25	118.21
26						HOLIDAY						
27	1856.56	1823.48	1853.03	812.19	795.88	809.25	187.04	183.37	186.47	121,160	90.59	117.47
28	1891.79	1851.92	1878.28	819.80	804.96	810.84	189.51	185.69	187.91	159,590	90.66	117.43
29	1892.97	1857.42	1882.35	814.89	802.13	809.74	190.29	186.31	189.82	135,670	90.54	116.16
30	1898.22	1857.95	1876.71	814.77	798.09	803.36	190.96	187.29	189.62	151,200	90.19	115.36
	High		1882.35			810.84			189.82		91.74	124.76
	Low		1758.18			771.10			179.71		90.19	115.36

Daily Closing 1986 Dow Jones Averages

June

	−30 Industrials−			−20 Transport Cos.−			−15 Utilities−			Daily Sales −000−	20 Bonds	Commodity Futures
	High	Low	Close	High	Low	Close	High	Low	Close			
2	1886.17	1845.53	1861.95	809.13	793.06	798.58	190.13	186.93	188.33	120,590	90.14	114.53
3	1875.54	1854.67	1870.43	803.75	791.63	797.88	189.25	185.85	188.02	114,710	90.09	114.50
4	1882.00	1846.34	1863.29	805.25	790.00	798.00	188.74	183.58	186.57	116,960	89.84	114.57
5	1880.79	1851.18	1879.44	809.25	791.88	804.50	189.46	185.28	188.69	110,920	89.33	115.60
6	1894.38	1866.12	1885.90	805.50	791.50	795.38	189.20	186.26	187.76	110,910	89.50	115.55
9	1880.25	1833.83	1840.15	793.63	774.63	778.38	187.65	182.49	183.89	123,330	89.64	115.00
10	1852.80	1816.07	1837.19	781.88	767.38	774.13	184.40	181.41	183.47	125,020	89.42	114.53
11	1854.68	1825.75	1846.07	782.13	764.88	774.63	185.13	182.39	183.78	127,350	89.43	113.98
12	1851.86	1826.29	1838.13	785.63	770.25	779.38	185.88	182.75	185.06	109,060	89.52	114.03
13	1883.21	1843.92	1874.19	792.38	777.63	786.50	189.17	185.11	187.69	141,200	89.86	114.15
16	1890.61	1863.29	1871.77	793.50	779.00	786.63	189.78	186.54	188.90	112,120	90.04	112.92
17	1886.98	1853.94	1865.78	794.00	775.25	785.13	190.00	187.64	188.52	123,090	90.06	113.31
18	1881.33	1843.75	1868.94	787.75	774.88	781.63	190.05	187.14	189.17	117,040	89.98	114.69
19	1883.12	1851.46	1855.86	784.63	770.38	772.75	189.72	187.31	188.02	128,980	89.81	115.26
20	1882.85	1847.60	1879.54	781.00	767.75	778.13	190.99	187.31	190.49	149,140	89.86	115.19
23	1883.40	1853.39	1864.26	794.00	761.63	782.63	190.82	187.69	189.17	123,750	89.91	114.09
24	1891.80	1853.94	1875.55	793.25	775.25	781.13	192.25	187.86	191.04	140,620	90.00	113.67
25	1903.36	1870.32	1885.05	790.50	777.88	782.13	194.66	190.77	193.02	161,790	90.20	113.11
26	1897.22	1867.41	1880.20	784.63	768.63	776.13	196.59	192.52	195.49	134,070	90.30	113.21
27	1898.90	1871.34	1885.26	784.63	772.13	777.50	199.99	196.09	198.78	123,810	90.47	112.39
30	1908.62	1876.12	1892.72	787.75	774.25	782.75	201.75	197.90	200.10	135,130	90.50	112.33
High			1892.72			804.50			200.10		90.50	115.60
Low			1837.19			772.75			183.47		89.33	112.33

Daily Closing 1986 Dow Jones Averages

July

	–30 Industrials–			–20 Transport Cos.–			–15 Utilities–			Daily Sales –000–	20 Bonds	Commodity Futures
	High	Low	Close	High	Low	Close	High	Low	Close			
1	1911.28	1878.52	1903.54	788.00	775.50	781.88	200.87	197.68	199.55	147,670	90.81	112.62
2	1922.67	1891.31	1909.03	786.63	775.50	780.63	201.20	198.07	200.32	150,000	90.84	112.23
3	1918.59	1887.23	1900.87	784.88	772.50	777.75	201.91	198.84	200.76	108,260	90.97	112.57
4						HOLIDAY						
7	1895.53	1834.08	1839.00	777.63	760.00	765.25	200.87	196.97	198.95	138,230	91.47	111.72
8	1834.36	1794.99	1820.73	763.88	742.38	752.50	198.95	194.61	198.23	174,060	91.09	111.26
9	1838.58	1807.65	1826.07	759.63	741.75	750.00	200.81	196.48	199.00	142,880	91.24	111.70
10	1842.94	1799.07	1831.83	759.50	740.13	753.38	201.14	197.13	200.54	146,160	91.06	111.59
11	1840.97	1810.88	1821.43	757.88	744.63	751.38	204.60	199.99	204.05	124,470	91.05	112.03
14	1816.65	1785.29	1793.45	750.38	736.88	740.00	206.19	200.98	204.16	123,170	91.06	112.54
15	1805.54	1760.12	1768.70	741.38	716.88	721.75	206.30	199.17	200.81	183,980	91.17	114.12
16	1794.29	1759.70	1774.18	735.38	718.00	723.63	204.49	197.68	200.92	160,810	91.24	115.31
17	1802.73	1762.09	1781.78	731.63	719.00	725.13	203.17	198.89	200.98	132,390	91.20	114.76
18	1807.37	1754.64	1777.98	734.13	713.38	727.25	202.68	196.81	200.48	149,680	91.21	115.07
21	1792.60	1763.92	1779.11	728.00	715.25	720.38	204.55	200.15	203.61	106,280	91.41	115.76
22	1810.46	1769.12	1795.13	734.75	714.38	729.75	207.02	202.24	205.31	138,470	91.45	115.25
23	1813.70	1780.09	1798.37	736.63	721.25	726.38	207.40	203.28	205.42	133,270	91.06	115.68
24	1806.81	1778.68	1791.62	729.75	707.88	715.38	206.96	202.62	205.42	134,710	90.34	115.64
25	1821.57	1791.06	1810.04	725.38	710.00	720.50	208.39	204.55	207.45	131,960	90.41	116.04
28	1815.24	1760.26	1773.90	725.25	708.88	713.63	207.78	201.64	203.01	127,990	90.22	116.29
29	1788.95	1752.95	1766.87	724.38	704.63	711.00	204.44	200.65	203.28	115,690	90.08	115.61
30	1794.15	1741.56	1779.39	727.00	704.38	718.88	205.26	201.14	203.94	146,690	89.94	114.99
31	1794.29	1764.20	1775.31	725.13	709.88	716.13	205.31	202.13	204.05	112,660	89.93	114.17
High			1909.03			781.88			207.45		91.47	116.29
Low			1766.87			711.00			198.23		89.93	111.26

Daily Closing 1986 Dow Jones Averages

August

	–30 Industrials–			–20 Transport Cos.–			–15 Utilities–			Daily Sales –000–	20 Bonds	Commodity Futures
	High	Low	Close	High	Low	Close	High	Low	Close			
1	1788.81	1753.09	1763.64	726.75	706.13	713.00	205.09	202.29	203.28	114,920	89.78	113.99
4	1785.15	1730.60	1769.97	717.50	697.13	709.13	204.44	200.59	203.01	129,990	89.53	113.37
5	1800.20	1766.87	1777.00	720.63	701.50	710.88	204.38	201.20	202.95	153,090	89.67	111.93
6	1788.67	1759.84	1779.53	715.13	702.25	709.38	204.66	201.53	202.39	127,510	89.57	112.54
7	1802.02	1766.17	1786.28	723.75	706.88	716.75	205.26	202.24	204.38	122,440	89.69	113.33
8	1799.78	1769.69	1782.62	720.00	708.50	712.88	206.25	202.92	204.00	106,300	89.82	114.84
11	1824.66	1779.25	1811.16	726.00	711.00	721.75	207.02	203.61	205.64	125,600	90.13	116.44
12	1840.55	1804.92	1835.49	734.38	717.75	732.50	207.73	204.77	207.13	131,710	90.09	114.76
13	1860.66	1822.98	1844.49	753.63	731.00	748.13	209.60	205.70	209.16	156,400	90.05	115.27
14	1859.81	1832.54	1844.91	759.50	745.13	754.00	210.77	208.00	210.04	123,770	90.07	115.13
15	1863.61	1829.02	1855.60	761.00	750.00	756.00	211.79	209.10	211.24	123,490	90.27	115.50
18	1875.14	1842.66	1869.52	757.75	745.38	753.38	212.23	208.94	211.13	112,840	90.53	116.13
19	1880.20	1846.88	1862.91	754.75	738.63	744.00	214.15	210.09	213.38	109,310	90.59	116.11
20	1889.34	1849.97	1881.33	755.50	741.25	752.13	220.41	213.33	219.15	156,600	91.09	116.58
21	1899.47	1864.31	1881.19	762.38	750.13	757.13	220.85	216.29	218.21	135,180	91.60	117.65
22	1899.04	1868.11	1887.80	765.50	754.25	761.75	217.15	215.96	217.39	118,130	91.79	117.82
25	1893.42	1860.52	1871.77	772.13	752.63	761.75	217.45	215.38	214.37	104,350	91.85	118.89
26	1911.28	1870.50	1904.25	780.13	759.88	774.00	218.65	214.48	217.72	156,640	91.80	119.04
27	1918.59	1887.80	1904.53	781.50	787.75	781.50	218.82	216.13	217.78	143,270	91.65	120.65
28	1912.26	1882.73	1900.17	785.25	771.88	777.75	219.20	215.85	217.50	125,080	91.74	120.57
29	1913.53	1883.44	1898.34	781.38	768.63	772.00	220.25	216.57	219.15	125,270	91.72	121.15
High			1904.53			781.50			219.15		91.85	121.15
Low			1763.64			709.13			202.95		89.53	111.93

41

Daily Closing 1986 Dow Jones Averages

September

	— 30 Industrials —			— 20 Transport Cos. —			— 15 Utilities —			Daily Sales –000–	20 Bonds	Commodity Futures
	High	Low	Close	High	Low	Close	High	Low	Close			
1						HOLIDAY						
2	1913.39	1857.42	1870.36	775.75	756.75	759.88	219.92	213.99	215.42	135,530	91.85	122.84
3	1888.22	1852.78	1881.33	771.75	754.13	769.50	217.45	212.89	216.68	154,310	91.56	123.22
4	1927.87	1877.25	1919.71	792.88	768.75	790.13	219.97	215.58	218.82	189,420	91.59	124.01
5	1933.35	1890.19	1899.75	792.50	772.75	777.50	218.54	212.12	213.71	180,620	91.49	124.94
8	1907.06	1866.84	1888.64	787.38	767.88	777.75	214.15	208.06	210.69	153,300	91.45	124.40
9	1909.45	1874.02	1884.14	790.75	773.50	782.50	213.55	208.61	210.47	137,520	91.65	123.24
10	1897.50	1863.05	1879.50	789.88	776.00	782.63	213.33	209.38	211.35	140,300	91.60	122.70
11	1868.67	1780.79	1792.89	779.38	741.88	749.00	209.98	197.24	202.24	237,570	91.30	123.27
12	1805.40	1733.55	1758.72	753.00	723.00	737.38	202.95	194.22	198.78	240,490	91.34	123.87
15	1786.98	1746.20	1767.58	748.50	729.25	740.75	201.20	197.19	200.21	155,620	91.34	124.30
16	1785.01	1739.60	1778.54	742.50	727.13	739.25	200.65	201.20	199.93	131,180	91.08	124.84
17	1799.35	1757.87	1769.40	756.25	737.00	747.25	203.01	198.67	200.65	141,040	90.98	125.29
18	1789.93	1748.03	1774.18	775.63	754.13	766.25	202.51	198.23	200.10	132,240	91.10	125.62
19	1783.04	1747.61	1762.65	783.38	758.25	780.13	201.47	197.30	201.09	153,860	90.73	127.98
22	1797.81	1761.67	1793.45	788.38	773.38	784.63	203.56	199.44	202.84	126,060	90.71	127.73
23	1809.76	1778.54	1797.81	799.88	780.38	794.38	204.87	201.20	203.23	132,570	90.59	127.15
24	1820.02	1786.28	1803.29	803.25	784.38	792.13	205.42	202.08	204.16	134,570	90.62	125.90
25	1803.15	1753.80	1768.56	797.75	773.75	784.50	205.04	202.00	201.75	134,290	90.96	125.43
26	1788.10	1750.14	1769.69	793.50	775.13	784.25	203.06	200.10	201.75	115,270	91.00	123.75
29	1768.98	1732.99	1755.20	794.38	777.63	789.63	201.09	199.60	198.84	115,610	90.66	124.20
30	1790.35	1750.14	1767.58	809.63	788.63	800.38	201.14	197.79	199.71	124,880	90.75	124.14
High			1919.71			800.38			218.82		91.85	127.98
Low			1755.20			737.38			198.78		90.59	122.70

42

Daily Closing 1986 Dow Jones Averages

October

	—30 Industrials—			—20 Transport Cos.—			—15 Utilities—			Daily Sales –000–	20 Bonds	Commodity Futures
	High	Low	Close	High	Low	Close	High	Low	Close			
1	1805.82	1762.65	1782.90	824.63	803.63	815.13	201.80	198.29	119.93	143,550	90.87	122.65
2	1796.54	1767.72	1781.21	821.63	805.13	813.88	200.54	197.43	199.33	128,050	91.12	123.51
3	1806.38	1761.25	1774.18	823.50	806.75	811.88	201.58	198.47	199.62	128,090	91.19	122.58
6	1794.85	1763.36	1784.45	827.25	808.13	822.25	201.12	198.24	200.20	88,250	91.31	123.01
7	1799.35	1765.19	1784.45	828.50	814.13	818.13	200.77	197.72	199.27	125,100	91.45	124.20
8	1812.43	1772.22	1803.85	834.38	815.38	828.13	199.97	197.43	198.81	141,700	91.31	123.70
9	1824.24	1785.85	1796.82	839.13	821.50	826.38	200.37	197.37	199.22	153,390	91.37	122.75
10	1806.38	1780.93	1793.17	830.63	817.75	824.13	199.50	196.86	198.18	105,050	91.21	121.93
13	1806.95	1781.50	1798.37	831.63	817.75	829.38	199.50	196.74	198.76	54,990	91.45	123.65
14	1816.51	1783.32	1800.20	841.25	822.13	827.63	199.74	196.80	198.30	116,820	91.40	122.74
15	1835.77	1792.18	1831.69	839.75	826.13	836.13	201.52	197.49	201.06	144,310	91.35	122.95
16	1852.64	1819.18	1836.19	843.38	826.00	828.88	203.25	199.85	201.81	156,920	91.25	122.48
17	1844.91	1817.07	1837.04	831.38	817.13	823.88	201.92	199.16	201.06	124,110	91.40	121.35
20	1826.63	1793.87	1811.02	823.00	806.50	815.25	200.94	197.32	199.33	109,010	91.32	121.39
21	1822.98	1792.04	1805.68	823.63	807.38	817.63	200.60	197.84	199.68	110,000	91.47	121.67
22	1821.29	1793.59	1808.35	824.50	812.63	818.75	200.77	198.12	199.56	113,990	91.54	121.75
23	1845.05	1806.95	1834.93	834.25	816.88	829.38	202.84	199.04	202.15	150,940	91.75	120.88
24	1851.66	1821.71	1832.26	834.88	819.75	825.00	203.59	200.77	202.27	137,480	91.58	120.58
27	1850.11	1817.49	1841.82	832.38	818.50	827.63	204.34	201.29	203.65	133,240	91.43	121.37
28	1863.47	1830.99	1845.47	840.00	825.75	834.25	206.30	203.25	205.09	145,870	91.45	121.22
29	1863.33	1834.51	1851.80	847.38	829.63	839.88	207.28	203.82	206.99	164,430	91.38	119.56
30	1894.69	1862.77	1878.37	851.63	829.75	835.88	210.56	207.45	208.72	194,220	91.83	120.97
31	1891.73	1858.13	1877.81	842.63	826.50	835.38	210.04	207.05	209.41	147,210	91.80	120.25
High			1878.37			839.88			209.41		91.83	124.20
Low			1774.18			811.88			198.18		90.87	119.56

Daily Closing 1986 Dow Jones Averages

November

	– 30 Industrials –			– 20 Transport Cos. –			– 15 Utilities –			Daily Sales –000–	20 Bonds	Commodity Futures
	High	Low	Close	High	Low	Close	High	Low	Close			
3	1902.28	1870.78	1894.26	844.38	830.75	841.38	211.48	208.60	210.67	138,220	92.03	121.42
4	1902.00	1873.88	1892.44	849.00	834.75	844.50	211.14	208.60	210.39	163,240	92.00	120.50
5	1911.14	1876.55	1899.04	856.63	839.13	849.63	211.25	208.14	210.44	183,170	92.02	120.25
6	1907.48	1868.95	1891.59	857.50	839.25	849.25	211.77	208.26	210.56	165,290	92.23	120.96
7	1899.47	1870.78	1886.53	853.25	838.25	845.00	211.14	208.08	209.81	142,300	91.64	121.07
10	1901.01	1871.20	1892.29	847.75	837.88	844.63	211.02	208.08	210.27	120,220	91.24	120.99
11	1904.95	1882.45	1895.95	842.13	831.00	836.63	211.60	209.24	210.44	118,520	91.22	119.90
12	1909.31	1876.97	1893.70	845.00	829.63	840.13	211.88	209.35	211.54	162,190	91.87	120.43
13	1901.01	1857.28	1862.20	849.38	828.75	834.25	212.11	209.18	209.87	163,950	91.89	119.95
14	1883.58	1848.28	1873.59	842.63	827.75	838.25	211.54	208.31	210.16	172,060	92.23	118.47
17	1879.92	1846.74	1860.52	838.13	824.25	829.25	210.73	207.62	209.24	133,250	92.10	117.38
18	1864.31	1806.52	1817.21	832.13	808.88	813.88	210.33	203.07	204.17	185,260	92.41	118.25
19	1838.02	1797.10	1826.63	821.63	805.38	816.50	206.13	202.56	205.03	183,290	92.59	117.83
20	1866.28	1823.12	1860.66	831.00	814.00	826.75	208.03	203.71	207.22	158,120	92.57	117.20
21	1901.86	1853.07	1893.56	844.25	823.13	838.88	212.40	206.59	211.48	200,650	92.61	116.55
24	1921.40	1879.08	1906.07	849.25	832.75	844.50	214.19	209.58	213.27	150,820	92.48	117.39
25	1922.81	1890.04	1912.12	850.38	837.25	846.13	213.96	210.44	212.81	154,570	92.71	117.60
26	1926.46	1895.11	1916.76	849.75	836.88	844.75	213.73	210.79	212.29	151,990	92.69	117.94
27						HOLIDAY						
28	1923.51	1903.82	1914.23	848.30	839.80	845.91	213.44	210.44	213.09	95,530	92.81	119.41
	High		1916.76			849.63			213.27		92.81	121.42
	Low		1817.21			813.88			204.17		91.22	116.55

44

Daily Closing 1986 Dow Jones Averages

December

	— 30 Industrials —			— 20 Transport Cos. —			— 15 Utilities —			Daily Sales —000—	20 Bonds	Commodity Futures
	High	Low	Close	High	Low	Close	High	Low	Close			
1	1915.92	1880.48	1912.68	848.18	832.02	844.83	212.34	208.37	211.48	133,750	92.92	119.76
2	1958.80	1914.93	1955.57	863.39	844.35	858.84	214.94	210.85	214.47	230,350	93.01	119.22
3	1971.74	1933.91	1947.27	870.09	855.24	863.75	214.88	211.48	213.84	200,140	93.15	119.04
4	1963.30	1930.26	1939.68	876.32	858.72	866.74	215.05	212.29	213.90	156,910	93.41	119.58
5	1950.22	1911.70	1925.06	871.29	856.08	860.87	214.71	210.44	211.94	139,820	92.96	118.53
8	1946.71	1906.92	1930.26	863.86	846.86	853.69	213.50	209.93	212.17	158,980	93.10	117.66
9	1939.82	1909.87	1916.90	855.60	837.76	841.48	213.38	210.44	211.31	128,690	93.27	116.75
10	1943.05	1908.32	1932.93	850.69	833.69	845.31	213.09	209.93	212.23	139,670	93.21	116.38
11	1947.41	1904.81	1923.65	850.22	831.54	841.12	212.98	208.89	210.04	135,990	93.20	116.46
12	1932.09	1904.39	1912.26	845.07	831.54	834.77	211.02	208.43	209.64	126,610	93.01	116.17
15	1925.34	1887.09	1922.81	833.81	820.16	830.10	210.50	206.70	209.98	148,220	93.06	116.09
16	1942.91	1912.40	1936.16	838.84	821.72	833.33	213.15	208.95	212.40	157,040	93.17	115.63
17	1937.57	1909.45	1918.31	838.30	824.37	829.58	212.29	209.64	210.67	148,840	93.29	115.84
18	1927.02	1900.17	1912.82	835.88	821.83	825.34	212.11	209.01	211.02	155,430	93.27	115.31
19	1935.18	1899.89	1928.85	837.21	819.65	835.88	212.75	208.83	212.06	244,680	93.65	114.88
22	1938.84	1907.76	1926.18	836.24	823.64	830.91	212.46	209.24	211.83	157,610	93.50	114.72
23	1933.77	1902.28	1914.37	835.15	816.25	824.13	212.00	208.60	209.70	188,700	93.62	114.53
24	1937.57	1910.01	1926.88	828.85	815.53	820.37	210.73	208.37	209.98	95,410	93.43	114.76
25						HOLIDAY						
26	1939.12	1919.71	1930.40	823.52	816.38	819.65	210.27	208.54	209.47	48,860	93.36	115.01
29	1931.38	1904.53	1912.12	820.86	809.96	813.23	209.52	206.70	208.03	99,800	93.37	114.84
30	1920.70	1894.69	1908.61	816.62	805.47	810.20	208.43	204.51	205.78	126,180	93.21	114.52
31	1920.42	1885.40	1895.95	813.71	800.99	807.17	207.34	204.28	206.01	139,170	93.43	115.84
High		1955.57				866.74			214.47		93.65	119.76
Low		1895.95				807.17			205.78		92.92	114.52

DOW JONES INDUSTRIAL MONTHLY CLOSING AVERAGES

1986 Month ended		D-J Ind.	1985 Month ended		D-J Ind.	1984 Month ended		D-J Ind.
December	31	1895.95	December	31	1546.67	December	31	1211.57
November	28	1914.23	November	29	1472.13	November	30	1188.94
October	31	1877.81	October	31	1374.31	October	31	1207.38
September	30	1767.58	September	30	1328.63	September	28	1206.71
August	29	1898.34	August	30	1334.01	August	31	1224.38
July	31	1775.31	July	31	1347.45	July	31	1115.28
June	30	1892.72	June	28	1335.46	June	29	1132.40
May	30	1876.71	May	31	1315.41	May	31	1104.85
April	30	1783.98	April	30	1258.06	April	30	1170.75
March	31	1818.61	March	29	1266.78	March	30	1164.89
February	28	1709.06	February	28	1284.01	February	29	1154.63
January	31	1570.99	January	31	1286.77	January	31	1220.58

1983 Month ended		D-J Ind.	1982 Month ended		D-J Ind.	1981 Month ended		D-J Ind.
December	30	1258.64	December	31	1046.54	December	31	875.00
November	30	1276.02	November	30	1039.28	November	3 0	888.98
October	31	1225.20	October	29	991.72	October	30	852.55
September	30	1233.13	September	30	896.25	September	3 0	849.98
August	31	1216.16	August	31	901.31	August	31	881.47
July	29	1199.22	July	30	808.60	July	31	952.34
June	30	1221.96	June	30	811.93	June	30	976.88
May	31	1199.98	May	28	819.54	May	29	991.75
April	29	1226.20	April	30	848.36	April	30	997.75
March	31	1130.33	March	31	822.77	March	31	1003.87
February	28	1112.62	February	26	824.39	February	27	974.58
January	31	1075.70	January	29	871.10	January	30	947.27

1980 Month ended		D-J Ind.	1979 Month ended		D-J Ind.	1978 Month ended		D-J Ind.
December	31	963.99	December	31	838.74	December	29	801.05
November	28	993.34	November	30	822.35	November	30	799.03
October	31	924.49	October	31	815.70	October	31	729.45
September	30	932.42	September	28	878.58	September	29	865.82
August	29	932.59	August	31	887.63	August	31	876.82
July	31	935.32	July	31	846.42	July	31	862.27
June	30	867.92	June	29	841.98	June	30	818.95
May	30	850.85	May	31	822.33	May	31	840.61
April	30	817.06	April	30	854.90	April	28	837.32
March	31	785.75	March	30	862.18	March	31	757.36
February	29	863.14	February	28	808.82	February	28	742.12
January	31	875.85	January	31	839.22	January	31	769.92

Month ended		D-J Ind.	1977 Month ended		D-J Ind.	Month ended		D-J Ind.
December	30	831.17	August	31	861.49	April	29	926.90
November	30	829.70	July	29	890.07	March	31	919.13
October	31	818.35	June	30	916.30	February	28	936.42
September	30	847.11	May	31	898.66	January	31	954.37

46

DOW JONES INDUSTRIAL MONTHLY CLOSING AVERAGES

1976 Month ended		D-J Ind.	1975 Month ended		D-J Ind.	1974 Month ended		D-J Ind.
December	31	1004.65	December	31	852.41	December	31	616.24
November	30	947.22	November	28	860.67	November	29	618.66
October	29	964.93	October	31	836.04	October	31	665.52
September	30	990.19	September	30	793.88	September	30	607.87
August	31	973.74	August	29	835.34	August	30	678.58
July	30	984.64	July	31	831.51	July	31	757.43
June	30	1002.78	June	30	878.99	June	28	802.41
May	28	975.23	May	30	832.29	May	31	802.17
April	30	996.85	April	30	821.34	April	30	836.75
March	31	999.45	March	31	768.15	March	29	846.68
February	27	972.61	February	28	739.05	February	28	860.53
January	30	975.28	January	31	703.69	January	31	855.55

1973 Month ended		D-J Ind.	1972 Month ended		D-J Ind.	1971 Month ended		D-J Ind.
December	31	850.86	December	29	1020.02	December	31	890.20
November	30	822.25	November	30	1018.21	November	30	831.34
October	31	956.58	October	31	955.52	October	29	839.00
September	28	947.10	September	29	953.27	September	30	887.19
August	31	887.57	August	31	963.73	August	31	898.07
July	31	926.40	July	31	924.74	July	30	858.43
June	29	891.71	June	30	929.03	June	30	891.14
May	31	901.41	May	31	960.72	May	28	907.81
April	30	921.43	April	28	954.17	April	30	941.75
March	30	951.01	March	30	940.70	March	31	904.37
February	28	955.07	February	29	928.13	February	26	878.83
January	31	999.02	January	31	902.17	January	29	868.50

1970 Month ended		D-J Ind.	1969 Month ended		D-J Ind.	1968 Month ended		D-J Ind.
December	31	838.92	December	31	800.36	December	31	943.75
November	30	794.09	November	28	812.30	November	29	985.08
October	30	755.61	October	31	855.99	October	31	952.39
September	30	760.88	September	30	813.09	September	30	935.79
August	31	764.58	August	29	836.72	August	30	896.01
July	31	734.12	July	31	815.47	July	30	883.00
June	30	683.53	June	30	873.19	June	28	897.80
May	29	700.44	May	29	937.56	May	31	899.00
April	30	736.07	April	30	950.18	April	30	912.22
March	31	785.57	March	28	935.48	March	29	840.67
February	27	777.59	February	28	905.21	February	29	840.50
January	30	744.06	January	31	946.05	January	31	855.47

1967 Month ended		D-J Ind.	Month ended		D-J Ind.	Month ended		D-J Ind.
December	29	905.11	August	31	901.29	April	28	897.05
November	30	875.81	July	31	904.24	March	31	865.98
October	31	879.74	June	30	860.26	February	28	839.37
September	29	926.66	May	31	852.56	January	31	849.89

YEARLY HIGHS AND LOWS OF DOW JONES AVERAGES

		—Industrials—		—Transportation—		—Utilities—	
		High	Low	High	Low	High	Low
1986	. . . .	1955.57	1502.29	866.74	686.97	219.15	169.47
1985	. . . .	1553.10	1184.96	723.31	553.03	174.96	146.54
1984	. . . .	1286.64	1086.57	612.63	444.03	149.93	122.25
1983	. . . .	1287.20	1027.04	612.57	434.24	140.70	119.51
1982	. . . .	1070.55	776.92	464.55	292.12	122.83	103.22
1981	. . . .	1024.05	824.01	447.38	335.48	117.81	101.28
1980	. . . .	1000.17	759.13	425.68	233.69	117.34	96.04
1979	. . . .	897.61	796.67	271.77	205.78	109.74	98.24
1978	. . . .	907.74	742.12	261.49	199.31	110.98	96.35
1977	. . . .	999.75	800.85	246.64	199.60	118.67	104.97
1976	. . . .	1014.79	858.71	237.03	175.69	108.38	84.52
1975	. . . .	881.81	632.04	174.57	146.47	87.07	72.02
1974	. . . .	891.66	577.60	202.45	125.93	95.09	57.93
1973	. . . .	1051.70	788.31	228.10	151.97	120.72	84.42
1972	. . . .	1036.27	889.15	275.71	212.24	124.14	105.06
1971	. . . .	950.82	797.97	248.33	169.70	128.39	108.03
1970	. . . .	842.00	631.16	183.31	116.69	121.84	95.86
1969	. . . .	968.85	769.93	279.88	169.03	139.95	106.31
1968	. . . .	985.21	825.13	279.48	214.58	141.30	119.79
1967	. . . .	943.08	786.41	274.49	205.16	140.43	120.97
1966	. . . .	995.15	744.32	271.72	184.34	152.39	118.96
1965	. . . .	969.26	840.59	249.55	187.29	163.32	149.84
1964	. . . .	891.71	766.08	224.91	178.81	155.71	137.30
1963	. . . .	767.21	646.69	179.46	142.03	144.37	129.19
1962	. . . .	726.01	535.76	149.83	114.86	130.85	103.11
1961	. . . .	734.91	610.25	152.92	131.06	135.90	99.75
1960	. . . .	685.47	566.05	160.43	123.37	100.07	85.02
1959	. . . .	679.36	574.46	173.56	146.65	94.70	85.05
1958	. . . .	583.65	436.89	157.91	99.89	91.00	68.94
1957	. . . .	520.77	419.79	157.67	95.67	74.61	62.10
1956	. . . .	521.05	462.35	181.23	150.44	71.77	63.03
1955	. . . .	488.40	388.20	167.83	137.84	66.68	61.39
1954	. . . .	404.39	279.87	146.23	94.84	62.47	52.22
1953	. . . .	293.79	255.49	112.21	90.56	53.88	47.87
1952	. . . .	292.00	256.35	112.53	82.03	52.64	47.53
1951	. . . .	276.37	238.99	90.08	72.39	47.22	41.47
1950	. . . .	235.47	196.81	77.89	51.24	44.26	37.40
1949	. . . .	200.52	161.60	54.29	41.03	41.31	33.36
1948	. . . .	193.16	165.39	64.95	48.13	36.04	31.65
1947	. . . .	186.85	163.21	53.42	41.16	37.55	32.28
1946	. . . .	212.50	163.12	63.31	44.69	43.74	33.20
1945	. . . .	195.82	151.35	64.89	47.03	39.15	26.15
1944	. . . .	152.53	134.22	48.40	33.45	26.37	21.74

YEARLY HIGHS AND LOWS OF DOW JONES AVERAGES

	—Industrials—		—Transportation—		—Utilities—	
	High	Low	High	Low	High	Low
1943	145.82	119.26	38.30	27.59	22.30	14.69
1942	119.71	92.92	29.28	23.31	14.94	10.58
1941	133.59	106.34	30.88	24.25	20.65	13.51
1940	152.80	111.84	32.67	22.14	26.45	18.03
1939	155.92	121.44	35.90	24.14	27.10	20.71
1938	158.41	98.95	33.98	19.00	c25.19	c15.14
1937	194.40	113.64	64.46	28.91	37.54	19.65
1936	184.90	143.11	59.89	40.66	36.08	28.63
1935	148.44	96.71	41.84	27.31	29.78	14.46
1934	110.74	85.51	52.97	33.19	31.03	16.83
1933	108.67	50.16	56.53	23.42	37.73	19.33
1932	88.78	41.22	41.20	13.23	36.11	16.53
1931	194.36	73.79	111.58	31.42	73.40	30.55
1930	294.07	157.51	157.94	91.65	108.62	55.14
1929	381.17	198.69	189.11	128.07	144.61	64.72
1928	300.00	191.33	b152.70	b132.60	....	....
1927	202.40	152.73	144.82	119.92	....	....
1926	166.64	135.20	123.23	102.41	....	....
1925	159.39	115.00	112.93	92.82	....	....
1924	120.51	88.33	99.50	80.23	....	....
1923	105.38	85.76	90.63	76.78	....	....
1922	103.43	78.59	93.99	74.43	....	....
1921	81.50	63.90	77.56	65.52	....	....
1920	109.88	66.75	85.37	67.83	....	....
1919	119.62	79.15	91.13	73.63	....	....
1918	89.07	73.38	92.91	77.21	....	....
1917	99.18	65.95	105.76	70.75	....	....
1916	110.15	84.96	112.28	99.11	....	....
1915	99.21	54.22	108.28	87.85	....	....
1914	a83.43	a71.42	a109.43	a89.41	....	....
1913	88.57	72.11	118.10	100.50	....	....
1912	94.15	80.15	124.35	114.92	....	....
1911	87.06	72.94	123.86	109.80	....	....

a—The high and low figures for the industrials and transportation are for the period ended July 31, 1914. The industrial average was composed of 12 stocks when the New York Stock Exchange closed in July 1914 because of World War I. In September 1916, a new list of 20 stocks was adopted and computed back to the opening of the Exchange on December 12, 1914. On October 1, 1928, the stocks comprising the industrial average was increased to 30. The high and low for the industrial average for December 1914 was 56.76 and 53.17, respectively. The high and low for transportation for December 1914 was 92.29 and 86.40.

b—On March 7, 1928, transportation components were increased to 20 from 12.

c—Since June 2, 1938, the utility average has been based on 15 stocks instead of 20.

DOW JONES COMPOSITE AVERAGE—65 STOCKS

Year	High	Date		Low	Date	
1986	767.89	December	2	602.83	January	10
1985	619.41	December	16	480.93	January	4
1984	514.02	January	6	421.36	July	24
1983	515.11	November	29	401.03	January	3
1982	416.33	December	27	299.44	August	12
1981	394.56	April	20	320.59	September	25
1980	388.87	November	28	271.73	March	27
1979	315.05	August	15	274.27	February	28
1978	315.26	September	8	260.66	March	6
1977	324.86	January	3	274.31	October	25
1976	325.49	December	31	264.50	January	22
1975	268.20	July	15	205.32	January	2
1974	282.51	March	13	184.24	October	3
1973	334.08	January	3	247.67	December	5
1972	338.54	December	11	302.13	October	16
1971	318.44	April	28	270.18	January	4
1970	273.21	December	30	208.66	May	26
1969	346.23	February	7	252.99	December	17
1968	353.09	November	29	290.09	March	25
1967	337.32	August	4	282.69	January	3
1966	352.40	February	11	261.27	October	7
1965	340.88	December	31	290.37	June	28
1964	314.15	November	20	269.09	January	2
1963	269.08	December	18	228.67	January	2
1962	245.80	January	3	187.41	June	26
1961	251.43	November	15	204.77	January	3

YEARLY HIGHS AND LOWS OF DOW JONES BOND AVERAGES

20 Bonds	1986	1985	1984	1983	1982	1981
High	93.65	83.73	72.92	77.84	71.52	65.78
Low	83.73	72.27	64.81	69.35	55.67	54.99
10 Public Utilities						
High	95.79	82.88	70.31	78.88	72.71	66.18
Low	81.85	68.62	59.43	65.76	53.80	53.61
10 Industrials						
High	91.64	84.58	76.22	77.13	71.23	66.15
Low	84.82	75.61	69.61	71.51	57.36	56.32

NET ASSETS PER SHARE ON DOW JONES INDUSTRIAL STOCKS

As of 12/31	1985	1984	1983	1982	1981	1980	1979
Allied-Signal	25.09	23.93	31.52	52.14	50.85	47.48	40.47
Alum. Co. Am.	39.52	40.23	38.89	38.51	41.19	78.50	70.42
Amer. Brands	....	27.54	25.95	26.13	24.05	45.65	30.28
Amer. Can	44.19	40.70	40.28	40.19	53.79	50.89	49.08
Amer Express	22.82	20.21	18.95	23.87	....	....	....
Amer. Tel.	13.68	13.26	62.41	68.55	67.52	65.51	63.43
Anaconda	....	....	....	....	....	....	....
Bethlehem Steel	15.13	20.02	23.53	28.32	63.13	59.89	58.72
Chevron	45.47	43.15	41.23	38.72	37.13	64.76	54.31
Chrysler	....	....	....	....	....	....	....
duPont	51.62	48.88	45.76	44.87	40.40	39.26	36.87
Eastman Kodak	28.28	45.84	45.41	45.51	41.27	37.27	33.40
Esmark	....	....	....	....	....	....	....
Exxon	39.80	36.85	34.80	32.84	32.84	58.81	51.39
General Electric	30.01	27.09	24.04	43.12	35.51	35.67	32.08
General Foods	....	40.92	39.15	36.06	32.88	32.58	29.15
General Motors	51.57	66.00	68.59	60.99	60.48	61.49	66.86
Goodyear	32.44	29.78	28.61	33.14	32.96	32.09	30.18
Inco	9.68	9.32	10.54	12.99	16.80	23.57	21.67
IBM	49.99	43.23	38.02	33.66	31.09	28.49	25.87
Int. Paper	66.60	66.04	65.30	63.36	64.40	56.66	52.95
Manville	....	....	....	....	38.36	40.29	40.18
Merck	36.15	35.29	32.59	29.49	26.73	24.64	22.10
Minnesota Mining	34.98	32.79	31.54	30.10	29.36	28.09	25.15
Navistar	d22.02	d19.15	d28.96	nil	39.76	53.30	69.85
Owens-Illinois	51.03	47.07	46.86	50.22	47.07	43.56	39.72
Philip Morris	39.69	....	....	....	....	....	....
Proc. & Gamble	31.49	30.42	27.76	50.35	46.69	43.52	39.07
Sears Roebuck	30.61	28.39	26.51	25.08	22.74	24.38	23.06
Texaco	57.04	55.15	56.86	55.11	53.11	46.64	39.22
Union Carbide	59.46	69.89	69.95	73.54	76.74	70.89	62.95
USX	38.18	38.41	36.94	58.09	69.01	59.98	57.07
United Technologies	29.11	25.72	45.47	41.32	36.29	31.29	26.68
Westinghouse	17.22	18.06	32.08	30.12	25.92	29.81	25.63
Woolworth	37.60	32.67	31.92	31.58	43.85	45.29	41.23
Total	1,030.02	1,037.70	1,092.50	1,197.97	1,281.92	1,360.25	1,259.04
Divided	1.090	1.132	1.230	1.359	1.314	1.465	1.465
(D-J Indus. Divisor)							
Average	944.97	916.70	888.21	881.51	975.59	928.50	859.41
Next year mkt low	1,502.29	1,184.96	1,104.57	1,027.04	776.92	824.01	759.13
Ratio mkt to book value	164	129	124	116	80	89	88

d-Deficit.

This compilation has not been adjusted for stock splits. For most recent splits, see page 17.

Barron's Confidence Index

Barron's Confidence Index is the ratio of Barron's average of the yield on 10 best grade corporate bonds to the yield on 10 intermediate grade corporate bonds. The ratio is high when investors are confidently buying bonds below top grade. It is low when they take refuge in top grade issues.

(For bonds used in this tablulation, see page 12—the Dow Jones Averages.)

		Index col. 3 ÷ col. 2	10 Intermediate Grade Bond Yield	10 Best Grade Bond Yield			Index col. 3 ÷ col. 2	10 Intermediate Grade Bond Yield	10 Best Grade Bond Yield
1986					April	25	92.1	9.62	8.86
December	26	92.1	9.26	8.53		18	91.1	9.52	8.67
	19	91.1	9.33	8.50		11	90.4	9.75	8.81
	12	90.8	9.36	8.50		4	90.6	9.69	8.78
	5	90.5	9.41	8.52	March	27	90.6	9.77	8.85
November	28	89.9	9.55	8.59		21	92.5	9.71	8.98
	21	91.9	9.42	8.66		14	92.1	9.74	8.97
	14	92.6	9.46	8.76		7	91.6	9.88	9.05
	7	91.8	9.51	8.73	February	28	90.4	10.08	9.11
October	31	92.0	9.61	8.84		21	90.7	10.50	9.52
	24	92.0	9.64	8.87		14	91.8	10.59	9.72
	17	91.9	9.68	8.90		7	91.3	10.66	9.73
	10	92.2	9.65	8.90	January	31	91.5	10.72	9.81
	3	92.5	9.63	8.91		24	91.9	10.80	9.93
September	26	93.0	9.59	8.92		17	92.3	10.81	9.98
	19	93.4	9.55	8.92		10	90.9	10.84	9.85
	12	92.0	9.56	8.80		3	90.6	10.77	9.76
	5	92.1	9.51	8.76	**1985**				
August	29	92.2	9.50	8.76	December	27	91.3	10.86	9.92
	22	90.0	9.70	8.73		20	92.1	10.79	9.94
	15	91.6	9.74	8.92		13	92.9	10.92	10.13
	8	92.3	9.64	8.90		6	93.7	11.01	10.32
	1	92.7	9.65	8.95	November	29	93.3	11.09	10.35
July	25	92.4	9.60	8.87		22	93.7	11.10	10.40
	18	92.6	9.56	8.85		15	92.5	11.30	10.45
	11	92.2	9.58	8.83		8	93.4	11.30	10.55
	3	93.2	9.57	8.92		1	94.1	11.39	10.72
June	27	92.4	9.71	8.97	October	25	95.4	11.39	10.87
	20	93.5	9.71	9.08		18	94.4	11.55	10.90
	13	93.7	9.76	9.15		11	94.9	11.56	10.97
	6	93.3	9.74	9.09		4	94.3	11.57	10.91
May	30	93.4	9.70	8.98	September	26	93.4	11.62	10.85
	23	92.7	9.65	8.95		20	93.9	11.62	10.91
	16	92.1	9.60	8.84		13	93.2	11.71	10.92
	9	91.9	9.53	8.76		6	92.9	11.56	10.74
	2	93.0	9.52	8.85					

BARRON'S CONFIDENCE INDEX

Month		Index col. 3 + col. 2	10 Intermediate Grade Bond Yield	10 Best Grade Bond Yield	Month		Index col. 3 + col. 2	10 Intermediate Grade Bond Yield	10 Best Grade Bond Yield
August	30	92.1	11.60	10.68	October	26	93.7	12.97	12.16
	23	92.6	11.63	10.77		19	94.8	13.18	12.49
	16	92.3	11.87	10.96		12	95.4	13.29	12.68
	9	94.0	11.82	11.11		5	92.6	13.73	12.71
	2	94.5	11.70	11.07	September	28	92.1	13.74	12.65
July	26	94.6	11.60	10.97		21	91.6	13.72	13.56
	19	93.5	11.53	10.78		14	91.6	13.90	12.72
	12	92.6	11.58	10.72		7	92.1	14.03	12.93
	5	93.2	11.57	10.78	August	31	92.1	14.00	12.90
June	28	94.4	11.58	10.93		24	92.1	13.97	12.87
	21	93.9	11.38	10.69		17	91.8	14.00	12.86
	14	93.8	11.45	10.74		10	92.3	13.91	12.85
	7	93.9	11.42	10.72		3	91.3	14.23	12.99
May	31	92.4	11.85	10.95	July	27	90.8	14.50	13.17
	24	93.7	11.90	11.15		20	91.2	14.51	13.22
	17	92.8	12.17	11.30		13	92.8	14.60	13.55
	10	93.2	12.42	11.58		6	93.5	14.65	13.70
	3	92.6	12.54	11.61	June	29	93.7	14.66	13.73
April	26	92.4	12.59	11.63		22	93.6	14.52	13.59
	19	92.7	12.40	11.49		15	92.9	14.55	13.51
	12	93.3	12.63	11.78		8	93.2	14.57	13.58
	5	94.4	12.68	11.97		1	95.0	14.58	13.85
March	29	93.8	12.83	12.04	May	25	93.2	14.58	13.59
	22	93.9	12.89	12.11		18	93.6	14.54	13.61
	15	94.0	12.90	12.13		11	94.6	14.19	13.43
	8	95.7	12.80	12.25		4	94.4	13.94	13.16
	1	95.7	12.74	12.20	April	27	94.9	13.72	13.02
February	22	95.6	12.50	11.95		19	95.6	13.67	13.07
	15	94.2	12.45	12.72		13	94.0	13.63	12.81
	8	94.7	12.41	11.75		6	95.2	13.62	12.97
	1	93.3	12.41	11.57	March	30	94.5	13.55	12.80
January	25	93.6	12.50	11.70		23	95.4	13.52	12.90
	18	93.8	12.69	11.90		16	95.3	13.47	12.83
	11	93.4	12.70	11.86		9	95.8	13.23	12.68
	4	93.0	12.77	11.87		2	96.3	12.99	12.51
1984					February	24	95.5	12.92	12.33
December	28	92.7	12.76	11.83		17	95.0	12.80	12.15
	21	92.5	12.76	11.80		10	94.9	12.72	12.07
	14	93.7	12.96	11.96		3	95.8	12.71	12.18
	7	93.6	12.72	11.90	January	27	95.6	12.78	12.22
November	30	94.2	12.53	11.81		20	95.3	12.85	12.24
	23	94.1	12.78	12.02		13	94.2	12.98	12.23
	16	94.3	12.87	12.13		6	94.3	13.08	12.34
	9	94.6	12.80	12.11					
	2	93.9	12.73	12.16					

BARRON'S CONFIDENCE INDEX

		Index col. 3 + col. 2	10 Intermediate Grade Bond Yield	10 Best Grade Bond Yield
1983				
December	30	91.0	12.92	11.76
	23	91.6	12.94	11.85
	16	90.3	13.17	11.89
	9	89.3	12.82	11.45
	2	91.3	12.60	11.50
November	25	90.7	12.61	11.44
	18	91.1	12.55	11.43
	11	91.8	12.50	11.47
	4	91.2	12.51	11.41
October	28	93.7	12.42	11.64
	21	93.3	12.37	11.54
	14	92.9	12.43	11.55
	7	91.6	12.36	11.32
September	30	89.4	12.58	11.25
	23	89.2	12.62	11.26
	16	90.4	12.67	11.46
	9	90.5	12.71	11.50
	2	89.9	12.72	11.44
August	26	89.6	12.64	11.32
	19	90.0	12.68	11.41
	12	90.3	12.85	11.60
	5	91.3	12.75	11.64
July	29	91.5	12.55	11.48
	22	91.2	12.50	11.40
	15	89.9	12.48	11.22
	8	91.3	12.36	11.28
	1	91.1	12.17	11.09
June	24	91.1	12.10	11.02
	17	90.1	12.17	10.97
	10	91.5	12.08	11.05
	3	89.9	11.99	10.78
May	27	90.2	11.89	10.72
	20	91.2	11.71	10.68
	13	90.7	11.53	10.46
	6	91.2	11.48	10.48
April	29	91.1	11.67	10.63
	22	91.6	11.73	10.74
	15	89.9	11.93	10.72
	8	89.6	12.12	10.86
March	31	89.5	12.03	10.77
	25	90.1	12.08	10.89
	18	88.7	12.26	10.87
	11	89.1	12.29	10.95
	4	87.0	12.35	10.75

		Index col. 3 + col. 2	10 Intermediate Grade Bond Yield	10 Best Grade Bond Yield
February	25	88.3	12.55	11.08
	18	88.5	12.67	11.22
	11	88.7	12.81	11.36
	4	89.5	12.76	11.42
January	28	88.6	12.81	11.35
	21	89.3	12.63	11.28
	14	88.6	12.68	11.24
	7	87.4	12.80	11.19
1982				
December	31	86.4	12.94	11.18
	24	87.9	12.77	11.22
	17	88.0	12.74	11.21
	10	87.3	12.89	11.25
	3	86.7	12.98	11.26
November	26	87.1	12.82	11.17
	19	86.5	12.89	11.15
	12	87.0	12.91	11.23
	5	85.9	13.02	11.19
October	29	85.2	13.35	11.38
	22	87.4	13.13	11.47
	15	88.2	13.18	11.62
	8	88.9	13.67	12.16
	1	88.6	13.77	12.20
September	24	88.9	13.82	12.29
	17	87.4	14.14	12.36
	10	88.8	14.00	12.43
	3	89.5	14.14	12.66
August	27	88.3	14.16	12.50
	20	87.9	14.28	12.56
	13	90.5	14.70	13.31
	6	89.2	14.81	13.21
July	30	89.3	15.00	13.39
	23	90.9	14.77	13.42
	16	90.5	14.92	13.51
	9	91.7	14.93	13.69
	2	90.2	15.06	13.59
June	25	89.4	14.95	13.37
	18	90.5	14.71	13.31
	11	88.2	14.88	13.13
	4	87.5	14.82	12.97
May	28	88.6	14.60	12.94
	21	88.5	14.59	12.92
	14	88.8	14.59	12.96
	7	89.5	14.64	13.10

BARRON'S CONFIDENCE INDEX

Month		Index col. 3 + col. 2	10 Intermediate Grade Bond Yield	10 Best Grade Bond Yield	Month		Index col. 3 + col. 2	10 Intermediate Grade Bond Yield	10 Best Grade Bond Yield
April	30	89.2	14.70	13.11	June	29	90.0	13.89	12.50
	23	88.4	14.91	13.18		22	88.2	13.86	12.37
	16	89.4	14.93	13.35		15	88.5	14.21	12.58
	9	89.3	15.07	13.45		8	89.0	14.18	12.62
	2	88.1	15.10	13.30		1	89.4	14.30	12.79
March	26	87.8	15.05	13.21	May	25	90.5	14.39	13.02
	19	88.0	15.12	13.30		18	91.6	14.51	13.29
	12	87.7	15.00	13.15		11	90.2	14.59	13.16
	5	88.5	14.94	13.23		4	90.4	14.34	12.97
February	26	89.3	15.02	13.42	April	27	90.3	14.05	12.69
	19	89.0	15.39	13.70		20	90.1	14.02	12.63
	12	90.6	15.19	13.77		13	88.3	13.97	12.33
	5	91.4	15.03	13.74		6	87.0	13.89	12.08
January	29	90.5	15.27	13.82	March	30	87.0	13.66	11.88
	22	91.4	15.28	13.96		23	86.3	13.61	11.74
	15	91.7	15.31	14.04		16	86.4	13.78	11.91
	8	89.5	15.25	13.65		9	88.3	13.77	12.16
1981						2	86.7	13.81	11.98
December	28	88.8	14.99	13.31	February	23	87.4	13.71	11.99
	21	88.9	14.83	13.18		16	87.4	13.63	11.91
	14	88.1	14.58	12.84		9	86.7	13.58	11.78
	7	87.7	14.43	12.65		2	86.0	13.50	11.69
November	30	88.7	14.40	12.78	January	26	88.7	13.31	11.81
	23	88.8	14.38	12.77		19	87.7	13.17	11.55
	16	90.0	14.52	13.07		12	87.3	13.65	11.92
	9	90.6	14.86	13.46		5	86.1	13.82	11.90
	2	90.1	15.23	13.72	**1980**				
October	26	90.1	15.23	13.72	December	29	84.0	13.69	11.50
	19	93.1	14.77	13.75		22	87.4	14.05	12.28
	12	91.6	15.09	13.82		15	89.3	13.78	12.31
	5	91.5	15.19	13.90		8	86.0	13.68	11.77
September	28	93.1	14.69	13.67		1	86.9	13.60	11.82
	21	93.1	14.56	13.56	November	24	87.8	13.51	11.86
	14	93.9	14.66	13.76		17	90.9	13.09	11.90
	7	90.8	14.67	13.32		10	91.3	13.02	11.89
August	31	89.7	14.72	13.21		3	92.4	12.98	11.99
	24	90.8	14.54	13.20	October	27	91.8	12.75	11.71
	17	91.9	14.26	13.11		20	89.9	12.73	11.45
	10	92.9	14.27	13.26		13	89.4	12.87	11.50
	3	92.2	14.32	13.20		6	89.5	12.93	11.57
July	27	91.7	14.21	13.03	September	29	88.5	12.77	11.30
	20	90.3	14.10	12.73		22	90.7	12.63	11.46
	13	90.5	14.13	12.79		15	90.8	12.51	11.36
	6	89.5	14.11	12.63		8	90.0	12.37	11.13
						1	88.0	12.61	11.10

BARRON'S CONFIDENCE INDEX

Month		Index col. 3 + col. 2	10 Intermediate Grade Bond Yield	10 Best Grade Bond Yield	Month		Index col. 3 + col. 2	10 Intermediate Grade Bond Yield	10 Best Grade Bond Yield
August	25	88.1	12.48	10.99	October	29	89.4	11.25	10.06
	18	87.2	12.32	10.74		22	89.3	10.82	9.66
	11	87.1	12.28	10.69		15	90.0	10.67	9.60
	4	88.7	11.96	10.61		8	90.8	10.26	9.32
July	28	88.6	11.86	10.51		1	91.0	10.06	9.16
	21	89.4	11.70	10.46	September	24	92.1	9.94	9.15
	14	89.6	11.58	10.38		17	91.2	9.93	9.06
	7	89.3	11.57	10.33		10	92.4	9.79	9.05
June	30	89.3	11.24	10.04		3	93.0	9.74	9.06
	23	88.4	11.30	9.99	August	27	92.7	9.68	8.97
	16	86.9	11.77	10.23		20	93.0	9.64	8.97
	9	87.4	11.87	10.38		13	92.4	9.65	8.92
	2	88.5	11.94	10.57		6	93.3	9.67	9.02
May	26	88.8	11.94	10.60	July	30	93.3	9.68	9.03
	19	86.8	12.12	10.52		23	93.3	9.67	9.02
	12	85.7	12.10	10.37		16	92.7	9.68	8.97
	5	86.5	12.41	10.73		9	92.7	9.65	8.95
April	28	87.3	12.64	11.03		2	91.8	9.67	8.88
	21	85.5	13.02	11.13	June	25	91.5	9.70	8.88
	14	89.5	13.31	11.91		18	91.4	9.76	8.92
	7	90.5	13.50	12.22		11	91.4	9.84	8.99
March	31	90.0	13.42	12.08		4	91.7	9.91	9.09
	24	91.9	13.25	12.18	May	28	91.4	9.96	9.10
	17	93.6	13.28	12.43		21	92.1	9.96	9.17
	10	92.3	13.27	12.25		14	91.8	10.03	9.21
	3	89.8	13.28	11.93		7	90.8	9.99	9.07
February	25	92.3	12.99	11.99	April	30	90.7	9.94	9.02
	18	90.2	12.61	11.38		23	90.0	9.94	8.95
	11	90.7	12.32	11.18		16	90.7	9.91	8.99
	4	90.1	12.17	10.97		9	90.7	9.88	8.96
January	28	91.7	11.91	10.92		2	91.1	9.83	8.96
	21	90.6	11.74	10.63	March	26	91.4	9.83	8.99
	14	90.9	11.67	10.61		19	91.7	9.84	9.02
	7	90.0	11.81	10.63		12	92.1	9.78	9.01
1979						5	91.4	9.81	8.97
December	31	89.2	11.77	10.50	February	26	91.4	9.77	8.93
	24	89.2	11.64	10.38		19	92.4	9.68	8.95
	17	91.3	11.38	10.39		12	92.7	9.65	8.95
	10	90.9	11.27	10.24		5	92.7	9.65	8.95
	3	91.5	11.26	10.30	January	29	91.5	9.75	8.92
November	26	92.3	11.31	10.44		22	91.1	9.80	8.93
	19	90.9	11.28	10.25		15	91.3	9.86	9.00
	12	92.6	11.22	10.39		8	91.4	9.84	8.99
	5	92.0	11.22	10.33		1	90.8	9.81	8.91

Barron's Group Stock Averages

Barron's group stock averages are a simple arithmetic average based on closing prices as of Thursday each week. In cases where there have been stock splits, stock dividends or substitutions of the individual group components, adjustments have been made to the individual stock multiplier and/or to the group divisor to keep the averages comparable throughout the period for which they have been computed. A list of the stocks on which these averages are based together with their respective multipliers and group divisors follows:

AIRCRAFT (Mfg.)÷5
 Boeing x 81
 Curtiss-Wright x 1.173
 Lockheed x 18.8448
 McDonnell Douglas x 2.83575
 United Technologies x 12.96

AIR TRANSPORT÷4
 AMR x 20
 PanAm World Airways x 8
 TWA x 3.3021
 UAL Inc. x 2

AUTOMOBILES÷6
 American Motors x 5.1936
 Chrysler x 12
 Ford Motor x .8184375
 General Motors x 6

AUTOMOBILE EQUIP.÷4
 Borg-Warner x 24
 Champion Spark Plug x 7.609
 Eaton x 6
 Timken x 4

BANKS÷25
 BankAmerica x 96
 Chase Manhattan x 38.178
 Citicorp x 72
 Continental Illinois x 73.895
 Morgan (J.P.) x 48

BUILDING MAT. & EQUIP.÷4.4458
 American Standard x 2
 Crane x 12
 Lone Star Indus. x 7.5
 USG Corp x 40

CHEMICALS÷5
 Allied-Signal x 12
 Am. Cyanamid x 8
 Monsanto x 18
 Olin Corp. x 6
 Union Carbide x 30.667

CLOSED END INVEST. COS.÷3.2629
 Gen'l American Investors x 2.25
 Lehman x 2
 Tri-Continental x 2

DRUGS÷4
 Abbott Laboratories x 192
 Bristol-Myers x 96
 Merck x 4
 Sterling Drug x 27

ELECTRICAL EQUIPMENT÷3.188
 General Electric x 12
 Square D x 33.75
 Westinghouse Elec. x 32

FARM EQUIPMENT÷3.862
 Allis-Chalmers x 7
 Deere x 48
 Varity x 10.76

FOODS & BEVERAGES÷5.2459
 Borden x 12
 Coca-Cola x 6
 General Mills x 36
 Kraft x 12
 PepsiCo x 62.22

GOLD MINING÷4
 ASA Ltd. x 39.912
 Dome Mines x 36
 Homestake Mining x 10
 LAC Minerals Ltd. x 3.1319

GROCERY CHAINS÷.82066
 Great A&P Tea x 3.418
 Kroger x 24

INSTALMENT FINANCING÷1.7725
 Beneficial x 4.125
 Household Int'l. x 18

Barron's Group Stock Averages

INSURANCE÷33
  Aetna Life & Cas. x 426
  CIGNA x 88.172
  Continental x 44.53
  Travelers x 400
  USLIFE x 271.336

LIQUOR÷1.949
  Brown-Forman "A" x 6.809
  National Distillers x 6
  Seagram x 60

MACHINE TOOLS÷1.4502
  Acme-Cleveland x 3.7117
  Cinn. Milacron x 12

MACHINERY (Heavy)÷3.3071
  Foster Wheeler x 48
  Harnischfeger x 3.5
  Wean United x 3.86

MOTION PICTURE÷2.50425
  Walt Disney x 83.744
  MCA x 24.652

NON-FERROUS METAL÷4.339
  Asarco x 12.7998
  INCO x 2.242
  Newmont Mining x 9.44
  Reynolds Metals x 2

OFFICE EQUIPMENT÷6.84675
  IBM x 234.856
  NCR x 24
  Unisys Corp. x 4

OIL÷5.633
  Amoco x 18.86
  Chevron x 16
  Exxon x 24
  Mobil x 9.6
  Phillips x 48
  Texaco x 16

PACKING÷3.3984
  Hormel x 64.65424
  Wilson Foods x 71.359

PAPER÷4.6376
  Internat'l Paper x 3.046
  Kimberly-Clark x 16
  Mead Corp. x 7.5
  Union Camp x 18

RAILROAD EQUIPMENT+.85267
  General Signal x 4
  Portec x 3.792

RETAIL STORES÷7
  K mart x 4.339
  May Dept. Stores x 14.9268
  J.C. Penney x 18
  Sears, Roebuck x 48
  Stop & Shop x 111.825
  Walgreen x 32
  Woolworth (F.W.) x 6

RUBBER÷3.3632
  Firestone x 24
  Goodrich x 9
  Goodyear x 24

STEEL & IRON÷4.688
  Armco x 6
  Bethlehem Steel x 12
  National Intergroup x 6.60
  USX x 9

TELEVISION÷10.3705
  CBS x 6
  Capital Cities/ABC x 2
  General Instrument x 3
  GTE Corp. x 3

  Oak Indus x 329.94
  Sony x 6.25
  Texas Instruments
  Zenith Electronics x 36

TEXTILES÷4
  Burlington Ind. x 10
  Celanese x 2.5
  Stevens (J.P.) x 18.40
  West Point-Pepperell x 8.7466

TOBACCO÷5
  Am. Brands x 16
  Culbro x 14.33
  Philip Morris x 8
  RJR Nabisco x 20
  U.S. Tobacco x 11.517

Barron's Group Stock Averages

	1981		1982		1983		1984		1985		1986	
	High	Low	High	Low	High	Low	High	Low	High	Low	High	Low
Aircraft manufacturing	607.11	371.86	581.88	310.08	815.05	583.99	961.62	631.98	1,176.20	893.12	1,443.47	1,099.97
Air transport	137.50	67.44	156.16	65.50	233.34	127.09	247.91	163.05	305.97	216.87	364.00	252.56
Automobiles	71.33	42.88	94.89	44.18	132.13	87.03	134.24	98.61	143.68	118.97	191.66	133.91
Automobile equipment	235.19	179.74	240.16	160.02	321.43	235.60	324.19	239.58	302.57	264.15	424.77	297.31
Banks	350.73	290.03	352.30	225.91	383.58	287.44	342.01	229.57	381.86	290.67	491.81	360.57
Bldg mat and equipment	271.66	200.07	231.96	140.32	254.14	211.70	262.90	209.60	267.00	250.67	559.36	343.02
Chemicals	391.55	303.85	373.85	271.55	510.40	354.77	475.85	384.10	507.80	389.50	717.88	493.60
Closed-End Invest	48.12	37.76	48.11	32.69	48.69	41.33	49.18	35.53	41.02	35.85	45.39	37.88
Drugs	1,614.22	1,333.69	2,005.41	1,440.62	2,601.34	1,867.78	2,534.34	2,210.00	3,530.81	2,396.81	5,106.37	3,349.94
Electrical equip	673.33	497.56	748.17	482.22	925.44	729.30	929.75	738.20	1,171.99	880.50	1,439.56	1,147.35
Farm equipment	660.27	430.57	460.89	286.92	555.56	408.28	542.21	330.95	426.55	326.97	446.49	279.66
Foods and beverages	386.30	308.75	508.32	344.39	581.83	454.24	663.16	520.41	923.54	593.73	1,315.45	863.11
Gold Mining	888.75	624.01	894.61	344.46	1,050.78	698.17	933.24	581.86	713.22	494.24	594.44	416.14
Grocery chains	335.05	234.31	488.72	265.95	519.96	419.00	516.23	395.45	659.64	501.02	1,083.27	620.29
Installment financing	224.48	178.40	309.04	210.45	415.83	252.56	424.61	303.49	532.67	408.22	698.43	521.93
Insurance	1,296.11	969.59	1,287.29	884.84	1,343.56	1,050.19	1,356.98	985.12	1,809.29	1,361.24	2,208.32	1,778.22
Liquor	798.20	653.33	958.12	635.41	1,415.73	982.90	1,372.99	1,160.51	1,753.38	1,340.26	2,304.18	1,629.57
Machine tools	271.85	167.94	219.82	132.39	284.11	213.29	262.19	169.08	218.26	143.54	234.07	157.95
Machinery (heavy)	260.86	155.39	172.12	116.40	203.80	156.98	194.75	132.00	184.87	148.55	209.74	162.04
Motion pictures	571.46	417.72	733.02	454.12	1,051.12	660.13	896.06	726.90	1,479.94	752.97	2,316.70	1,444.23
Non-Ferrous metals	347.22	187.73	223.15	133.75	276.39	204.96	238.37	142.50	200.36	153.67	213.61	151.99

Barron's Group Stock Averages

	1986		1985		1984		1983		1982		1981	
	High	Low	High	Low	High	Low	High	Low	High	Low	High	Low
Office equipment	5,640.94	4,316.55	5,435.15	4,195.54	4,432.93	3,558.33	4,709.59	3,374.31	3,385.44	2,007.77	2,432.67	1,742.12
Oil	942.40	698.44	846.06	710.69	769.64	621.26	648.44	523.50	569.74	418.94	769.44	568.64
Packing	871.09	556.90	619.65	470.69	594.39	425.31	630.05	473.78	506.08	280.96	318.96	238.84
Paper	670.42	478.99	496.23	393.00	428.72	347.19	443.10	311.31	332.51	227.36	341.65	258.92
Railroad equipment	341.12	261.73	306.42	255.37	272.40	216.42	248.67	180.82	204.05	139.55	266.87	194.20
Retail merchandise	1,795.11	1,256.48	1,462.79	1,094.54	1,379.52	1,004.56	1,578.07	851.39	888.04	409.05	491.08	355.92
Rubber	675.14	461.61	466.07	354.38	442.22	333.94	472.12	396.94	432.19	238.97	287.53	228.37
Steel and iron	152.16	79.00	167.85	132.72	215.75	136.30	192.46	136.44	178.16	109.76	237.06	170.27
Television	332.05	269.37	284.08	236.81	389.47	231.28	537.86	340.88	852.10	410.84	1,074.56	679.95
Textiles	556.88	383.03	413.78	270.85	351.64	250.55	357.90	283.89	285.85	187.91	236.73	197.77
Tobacco	709.65	465.19	470.84	385.66	410.84	349.78	388.97	286.17	304.16	216.15	244.18	204.40

New York Stock Exchange

Composite Stock Index

Year	Open	High	Low	Close	Chg.
1986	120.74	*145.75	117.75	138.58	— .54
1985	96.38	121.90	94.60	121.58	+25.20
1984	95.18	98.12	85.13	96.38	+ 1.3
1983	79.79	99.63	79.79	95.18	+14.15
1982	81.33	82.35	58.80	81.03	+ 9.92
1981	78.26	79.14	64.96	71.11	— 6.75
1980	60.69	81.02	55.30	77.86	+15.91
1979	53.93	63.39	53.88	61.95	+ 8.33
1978	51.82	60.38	48.37	53.62	+ 1.12
1977	57.69	57.69	49.78	52.50	— 5.38
1976	48.04	57.88	48.04	57.88	+10.24
1975	37.06	51.24	37.06	47.64	+11.51
1974	51.98	53.37	32.89	36.13	—15.69
1973	65.06	65.48	49.05	51.82	—12.66
1972	56.23	65.14	56.23	64.48	+ 8.05
1971	49.73	57.76	49.60	56.43	+ 6.20
1970	52.10	52.36	37.69	50.23	— 1.30
1969	58.94	59.32	49.31	51.53	— 7.37
1968	53.68	61.27	48.70	58.90	+ 5.07
1967	43.74	54.16	43.74	53.83	+10.11
1966	49.86	51.06	39.37	43.72	— 6.28
1965	45.37	50.00	43.64	50.00	+ 4.35
1964	40.47	46.49	40.47	45.65	+ 5.73
1963	34.41	39.92	34.41	39.92	+ 6.11
1962	37.34	38.02	28.20	33.81	— 4.58
1961	31.17	38.60	31.17	38.39	+ 7.45
1960	31.99	31.99	28.38	30.94	— 1.21
1959	29.54	32.39	28.94	32.15	+ 3.30
1958	21.71	28.85	21.45	28.85	+ 7.74
1957	24.43	26.30	20.92	21.11	— 3.24
1956	23.56	25.90	22.55	24.35	+ 0.64
1955	19.05	23.71	19.05	23.71	+ 4.31
1954	13.70	19.40	13.70	19.40	+ 5.80
1953	14.65	14.65	12.62	13.60	— 0.89
1952	13.70	14.49	13.31	14.49	+ 0.89
1951	12.28	13.89	12.28	13.60	+ 1.59

*Record high, September 4, 1986.

The New York Stock Exchange composite stock index has been computed on a daily basis since June 1, 1964. Prior to that date it was on a weekly basis. December 31, 1965, equals 50.

New York Stock Exchange

Volume, Shares and Turnover Rate

(Millions of Shares)

Year	Reported Stock Volume	Average of Shares Listed	Per Cent Turnover	Year	Reported Stock Volume	Average of Shares Listed	Per Cent Turnover
1986	35,680.0	56,023.8	64	1950	524.8	2,259.4	23
1985	27,510.7	N.A.	54	1949	272.2	2,091.6	13
1984	23,071.0	47,104.8	49	1948	302.2	1,962.0	15
1983	21,589.6	42,316.9	51	1947	253.6	1,839.0	14
1982	16,458.0	38,907.0	42	1946	363.7	1,681.8	22
1981	11,853.7	36,003.5	33	1945	377.6	1,542.2	24
1980	11,352.3	31,871.0	36	1944	263.1	1,490.8	18
1979	8,155.9	28,803.0	28	1943	278.7	1,479.9	19
1978	7,205.1	26,833.2	27	1942	125.7	1,466.9	9
1977	5,273.8	25,296.5	21	1941	170.6	1,459.0	12
1976	5,360.1	23,489.0	23	1940	207.6	1,445.1	14
1975	4,693.4	22,108.0	21	1939	262.0	1,429.8	18
1974	3,517.7	21,351.8	16	1938	297.5	1,418.1	21
1973	4,053.2	20,062.6	20	1937	409.5	1,386.2	30
1972	4,138.2	18,329.4	23	1936	496.0	1,339.1	37
1971	3,891.3	16,782.1	23	1935	381.6	1,311.6	29
1970	2,937.4	15,573.6	19	1934	323.8	1,299.4	25
1969	2,850.8	14,139.1	20	1933	654.8	1,302.6	50
1968	2,931.5	12,410.0	24	1932	425.2	1,315.3	32
1967	2,529.9	10,079.5	22	1931	576.8	1,307.8	44
1966	1,899.5	10,495.0	18	1930	810.6	1,212.2	67
1965	1,556.3	9,641.0	16	1929	1,124.8	942.5	119
1964	1,236.6	8,668.8	14	1928	930.9	706.2	132
1963	1,146.3	7,883.7	15	1927	581.7	620.3	94
1962	962.2	7,373.6	13	1926	451.9	538.6	84
1961	1,021.3	6,773.2	15	1925	459.7	462.5	99
1960	766.7	6,152.8	12	1924	284.0	424.8	67
1959	820.3	5,432.0	15	1923	236.5	393.2	60
1958	747.1	4,910.2	15	1922	260.9	337.2	77
1957	559.9	4,632.9	12	1921	172.8	292.7	59
1956	556.3	4,149.2	13	1920	227.6	251.1	91
1955	649.6	3,505.3	19	1919	318.3	208.0	153
1954	573.4	3,050.4	19	1918	143.3	193.9	74
1953	354.9	2,857.4	12	1917	184.6	179.7	103
1952	337.8	2,702.0	13	1916	232.6	160.2	145
1951	443.5	2,484.6	18	1915	172.5	155.8	111

N.A.-Not available.
Source: NYSE Fact Book.

New York Stock Exchange

All Listed Stocks

End of Year	Number of Companies	Number of issues	Shares Listed (millions) Number	Market Value	a-Inst. Holdings
1986	1,575	2,257	59,620	$2,199,258.0	....
1985	N.A.	2,290	N.A.	N.A.	....
1984	1,543	2,319	49,092.0	1,586,098.0	....
1983	1,550	2,307	45,118.0	1,584,155.0	....
1982	1,526	2,225	39,516.0	1,305,355.0	....
1981	1,565	2,220	38,298.0	1,143,794.0	....
1980	1,570	2,228	33,709.0	1,242,803.0	....
1979	1,565	2,192	30,032.8	960,606.1	....
1978	1,581	2,194	27,573.1	822,735.9	....
1977	1,575	2,177	26,093.2	796,639.0	....
1976	1,576	2,158	24,499.8	858,299.2	....
1975	1,557	2,111	22,478.0	685,110.0	32.9%
1974	1,567	2,080	21,737.0	511,055.0	32.8
1973	1,560	2,058	20,967.0	721,012.0	31.8
1972	1,505	2,003	19,159.0	871,540.0	31.7
1971	1,426	1,927	17,500.0	741,827.0	30.1
1970	1,351	1,840	16,065.0	636,380.0	27.6
1969	1,311	1,789	15,082.0	629,453.0	26.0
1968	1,273	1,767	13,196.0	692,337.0	24.8
1967	1,274	1,700	11,622.5	605,816.8	24.0
1966	1,286	1,665	10,938.6	482,540.9	23.7
1965	1,273	1,627	10,057.7	537,480.6	22.7
1964	1,247	1,606	9,229.4	474,322.3	22.2
1963	1,214	1,572	8,108.2	411,318.0	21.3
1962	1,186	1,559	7,659.2	345,846.1	20.4
1961	1,163	1,541	7,088.0	387,841.2	19.4
1960	1,143	1,528	6,458.4	306,967.1	18.7
1959	1,116	1,507	5,847.3	307,707.7	18.1
1958	1,100	1,507	5,016.7	276,665.2	17.9
1957	1,107	1,522	4,803.8	195,570.2	17.8
1956	1,087	1,502	4,462.1	219,175.9	17.1
1955	1,087	1,508	3,836.3	207,699.2	16.2
1954	1,089	1,532	3,174.3	169,148.5	....
1953	1,084	1,530	2,926.6	117,257.2	....
1952	1,084	1,522	2,788.2	120,536.2	....
1951	1,075	1,495	2,615.1	109,483.6	....
1950	1,057	1,472	2,353.2	93,807.3	....
1949	1,043	1,457	2,165.7	76,292.0	14.5
1948	1,017	1,419	2,017.5	67,048.3	....
1947	996	1,379	1,906.5	68,312.5	....
1946	962	1,334	1,771.4	68,594.9	....
1945	912	1,269	1,592.1	73,765.3	....

a-Estimated holdings of New York Stock Exchange-listed stocks include insurance companies, investment companies, non-insured pension funds, non-profit institutions, common trust funds and mutual savings banks. The holdings do not include foreign institutions, mutual funds that aren't registered with the Securities and Exchange Commission, private hedge funds, non-bank trusts and bank-administered personal trusts. N.A.-Not available.

Source: NYSE Fact Book.

New York Stock Exchange

Daily Reported Stock Volume: Average, High and Low Record Days

(Thousands of Shares)

Year	a-Average Daily Volume	High Day Volume	Date	b-Low Day Volume	Date	Year	a-Average Daily Volume	High Day Volume	Date	b-Low Day Volume	Date
1986	141,028	244,293	12-19	48,864	12-26	1951	1,674	3,877	1-17	973	7-11
1985	109,170	181,026	12- 5	62,054	12-26	1950	1,980	4,859	6-27	1,061	3-13
1984	91,190	236,565	8- 3	46,364	10- 8	1949	1,023	2,212	12-14	541	6-17
1983	85,334	129,411	1- 6	53,033	8-29	1948	1,132	3,837	5-14	465	8-16
1982	65,051	149,385	11- 4	36,760	1- 4	1947	952	2,197	4-14	476	8-27
1981	46,853	92,881	1- 7	23,945	12-24	1946	1,370	3,624	9- 4	487	7- 5
1980	44,871	84,297	11- 5	16,132	12-26	1945	1,422	2,936	6-28	492	8- 6
1979	32,237	81,619	10-10	18,346	1- 2	1944	958	2,517	6-16	337	5-15
1978	28,591	66,370	8- 3	c7,580	1-20	1943	1,012	2,805	5- 4	335	8-30
1977	20,928	35,261	11-11	10,582	10-10	1942	455	1,441	12-29	207	7- 1
1976	21,186	44,513	2-20	10,301	1- 2	1941	619	2,925	12-29	224	5-19
1975	18,551	35,158	2-13	8,670	9-15	1940	751	3,940	5-21	130	8-19
1974	13,904	26,365	10-10	7,402	7- 5	1939	955	5,934	9- 5	235	7- 3
1973	16,084	25,962	9-20	8,970	8-20	1938	1,080	3,100	11- 9	278	6- 8
1972	16,487	27,555	12-29	7,945	10- 9	1937	1,492	7,288	10-19	424	6-21
1971	15,381	31,731	8-16	7,349	10-25	1936	1,791	4,718	2-17	586	5-13
1970	11,564	21,345	9-24	6,660	5-11	1935	1,385	3,948	11-14	345	2- 4
1969	11,403	19,950	10-14	6,758	12-26	1934	1,178	4,940	2- 5	275	8-20
1968	12,971	21,351	6-13	6,707	3-25	1933	2,519	9,572	7-21	477	1-30
1967	10,080	14,954	12-29	5,998	7- 3	1932	1,541	5,461	8- 8	385	10-31
1966	7,538	13,121	5- 6	4,268	6- 6	1931	2,090	5,346	2-24	536	9- 1
1965	6,176	11,434	12- 6	3,028	7- 7	1930	2,959	8,279	5- 5	1,090	8- 1
1964	4,888	6,851	4- 2	3,051	8-10	1929	4,277	16,410	10-29	1,996	12-24
1963	4,567	9,324	11-26	2,513	7-26	1928	3,416	6,943	11-23	1,090	6-25
1962	3,818	14,746	5-29	1,946	10- 8	1927	2,111	3,214	10- 4	1,219	1-28
1961	4,085	7,077	4- 4	2,184	7- 3	1926	1,643	3,860	3- 3	607	5- 6
1960	3,042	5,303	12-30	1,894	10-12	1925	1,663	3,391	11-10	790	4-13
1959	3,242	4,884	3-13	1,745	10-12	1924	1,029	2,584	11-20	316	6- 2
1958	2,965	5,368	10-17	1,566	2-24	1923	863	1,559	11-22	283	7-16
1957	2,222	5,093	10-22	1,256	9- 4	1922	950	2,008	4-17	236	7- 3
1956	2,216	3,921	2-29	1,233	10- 9	1921	632	1,290	3-23	280	8- 8
1955	2,578	7,717	9-26	1,230	8-15	1920	828	2,008	4-21	227	6-29
1954	2,275	4,433	12-29	1,215	1-11	1919	1,179	2,697	11-12	299	2- 7
1953	1,414	3,119	3-31	738	9- 8	1918	529	1,692	5-16	136	8- 2
1952	1,297	2,352	11-19	780	5-19	1917	678	2,048	2- 1	236	10-24

a-A trading session of three hours or less is counted as one-half day.
b-Full days only.
c-Opened at noon due to snow storm.
Source: NYSE Fact Book.

New York Stock Exchange

Cash Dividends and Yields on Common Stocks

Calendar Year	Number of Issues Listed at Year End	Number Paying Cash Dividends During Year	Estimated Aggregate Cash Payments (Millions)	a-Median Yield (%)	Calendar Year	Number of Issues Listed at Year End	Number Paying Cash Dividends During Year	Estimated Aggregate Cash Payments (Millions)	a-Median Yield (%)
1986	2,257	1,180	$76,161	N.A.	1962	1,168	994	$11,203	3.8
1985	N.A.	1,206	N.A.	N.A.	1961	1,145	981	10,430	3.3
1984	1,511	1,243	68,215	3.8	1960	1,126	981	9,872	4.2
1983	1,518	1,259	67,102	3.5	1959	1,092	953	9,337	3.8
1982	1,499	1,287	62,224	4.1	1958	1,086	961	8,711	4.1
1981	1,534	1,337	60,628	5.0	1957	1,098	991	8,807	6.1
1980	1,540	1,361	53,072	4.6	1956	1,077	975	8,341	5.2
1979	1,536	1,359	46,937	5.0	1955	1,076	982	7,488	4.6
1978	1,552	1,373	41,151	4.8	1954	1,076	968	6,439	4.7
1977	1,549	1,360	36,270	4.5	1953	1,069	964	5,874	6.3
1976	1,550	1,340	30,608	4.0	1952	1,067	975	5,595	6.0
1975	1,531	1,273	26,901	5.0	1951	1,054	961	5,467	6.5
1974	1,543	1,308	25,662	7.4	1950	1,039	930	5,404	6.7
1973	1,536	1,276	23,627	5.0	1949	1,017	887	4,235	7.0
1972	1,478	1,195	21,490	3.0	1948	986	883	3,806	7.8
1971	1,399	1,132	20,256	3.2	1947	964	851	3,255	6.3
1970	1,330	1,120	19,781	3.7	1946	933	798	2,669	4.8
1969	1,290	1,121	19,404	3.6	1945	881	746	2,275	3.6
1968	1,253	1,104	18,124	2.6	1944	864	717	2,223	5.0
1967	1,255	1,116	16,866	3.2	1943	845	687	2,063	6.1
1966	1,267	1,127	16,151	4.1	1942	834	648	1,997	7.8
1965	1,254	1,111	15,300	3.2	1941	834	627	2,281	9.3
1964	1,227	1,066	13,555	3.3	1940	829	577	2,099	6.1
1963	1,194	1,032	12,096	3.6					

a-Based on cash payments during the year and price at end of year for dividend-paying stocks only. N.A.-Not available.

Source: NYSE Fact Book.

Stock and Bond Trading for 1986

NEW YORK STOCK EXCHANGE COMPOSITE

The following tabulation gives the 1986 sales, high, low, last price and net change from the previous year in stocks listed on the New York Stock Exchange.

Stock	Div.	P-E Ratio	Sales 100s	High	Low	Last	Net Chg.
—A—							
AAR s	.44	17	70342	26½	17	23⅜	+ 6⅛
ADT	.92	...	95573	30	21¾	27	+ 1¾
AFG s	.12i	14	150565	33	16¾	28⅞	+ 12⅛
AGS		18	50428	29	16¾	28	+ 4⅞
AMCA		...	5619	15	6¾	7	− 4
AMR		12	f13230	62⅛	39¼	53⅝	+ 12¼
ANR pf	2.67	...	8281	27½	23⅞	26	+ 1⅝
ANR pf	2.12	...	6859	24¾	20⅛	24	+ 3¾
ARX	.71t	11	32643	16½	10	11¾	− 3¾
ASA	2.00a	...	168589	41½	28¾	37½	+ 2⅝
AVX		...	96943	18⅜	9¾	10⅝	− 3⅞
AZP	2.72	8	564699	32	26	28⅜	+ 1⅛
AbtLb s	.84	20	837050	55	31⅝	45⅝	+ 11½
AccoWd	.56	17	67319	32	25	25¾	− ½
AcmeC	.40	...	58483	14⅞	9	10⅜	− 2⅛
AcmeE	.32b	16	7930	9¼	6⅛	6¼	− 2⅛
AdaEx	4.45e	...	32379	23⅞	17½	19⅛	− ¼
AdmM s		...	14568	16⅝	9¾	13½	+ 2¼
AdvSys	1.45t	15	43788	20⅜	12⅛	18½	+ ¾
AMD		...	965800	32⅞	12⅞	13¾	− 15¼
Adobe		...	37379	12⅝	5¼	6⅝	− 5⅝
Adob pf	1.84	...	17913	18⅜	13¾	16¼	− 1¼
Adob pf	2.40	...	16749	20¼	16⅜	18	+ ⅛
Advest	.12a	9	94463	18⅜	11⅛	11¾	− 1
AetnLf	2.64	8	f11692	66¼	52¼	56⅜	+ 2⅞
AetL pf	3.94e	...	53425	54⅝	51⅛	51¾	− 1⅜
AetL pfC	5.95e	...	5401	101½	87¼	89¾	...
AfilPb s	.44	34	55045	73⅜	34⅞	70⅛	+ 34⅜
Ahmns s	.46	7	964616	28¾	15¾	21⅝	+ 5⅜
Aileen		63	47886	5¾	2⅞	4⅜	+ 1
AirPrd s	.80	439	397015	41⅝	29⅛	35⅛	+ 3⅛
AirbFrt	.60	21	90482	32	16	29⅞	+ 10⅝
Airgas n		...	2337	8⅞	8⅛	8⅜	...
Airlse n	.49e	...	12286	20⅜	17⅛	17¼	...
AlMoan	1.60c	...	72094	2	¼	13/32	− 1 19/32
AlaP pf	1.94e	...	20292	29	25⅜	25⅜	− 1⅝
AlaP dpf	.87	...	46156	10¾	8⅜	9⅞	+ 1½
AlaP pf	9.00	...	2550	106½	87	102¼	+ 14¼
AlaP pf	11.00	...	z41660	109½	86	107½	+ 2
AlaP pf	9.44	...	1899	107½	90	106	+ 15⅝
AlaP pf	8.16	...	3734	103½	77½	98¾	+ 19¼
AlaP pf	8.28	...	1420	95	74¾	91¼	+ 16¼
AlskAir	.16	15	246955	22¾	14¼	20	+ 3⅞
Albrto s	.21	29	36065	25	13½	19½	+ 4⅞
AlbCulA	.21	25	34974	23¼	13½	16¾	...
Albtsns	.84	15	129739	49½	30½	43	+ 10½
Alcan	.80	...	796074	34⅝	27⅝	28¼	− ¾
AlcoStd	1.28	16	73535	46¾	35½	41⅞	+ 3¾
AlexAlx	1.00	126	322921	42⅜	25⅛	26½	− 6¾
Alexdr		116	30639	49	34½	39½	+ ⅝
AllgCp	1.54t	11	22334	116½	83¼	105	+ 16⅝
AlgCp wi		...	219	67½	65½	67½	...
AlgCp pf	2.86	...	5967	29¼	26⅝	28⅛	+ ⅞
AlgInt	.35j	...	153007	25¼	11⅜	12½	− 6⅞
AlgIn pr	1.64j	...	14417	19¾	9½	13¼	− 3½
AlgI pfC	8.44j	...	14202	93½	39	45¾	− 39⅝
AllgPw	2.92	11	412671	53⅞	31⅝	44¼	+ 11⅛
AllenG s	.56	15	71753	27¼	14¾	15¾	− 5½
Allen pf	1.75	...	13195	28⅞	20⅞	22¼	...
AlldPd		11	52995	45½	22½	33⅛	+ 9½
AldSgnl	1.80b	...	f12670	49½	36¾	40⅛	− 2⅜
AldStr s	1.16	69	f14057	68⅞	33	68¾	+ 35⅜
AlldSup		13	96429	10⅛	5⅜	7⅛	+ 1½
AllisCh		...	118802	6¾	2⅛	2⅝	− 1½
AlisC pf		...	4163	40¾	25¼	28	− 2½
ALLTL	2.04	11	41912	45	29	39⅜	+ 9⅞
ALLT pf	2.06	...	237	57¼	38¼	52½	+ 14
Alcoa	1.20	...	771214	46⅜	32⅝	33⅞	− 4⅝
Amax		...	339996	16⅜	10½	12⅛	− 1½
Amax pf	3.00	...	849	36¾	29¾	35½	+ 5¼
AmHes	.27j	...	f10296	29	16½	23¾	− 3½
AHes pf	3.50	...	591	121⅝	82¼	105½	− 13½
AmAgr		...	149428	1⅞	½	¾	− ⅝
ABakr		19	40134	45¾	24	43¾	+ 17½
ABrnd s	2.08	14	582313	52½	31¼	42½	+ 9⅝
ABrd pf	2.75	...	37865	34⅞	30⅜	32¾	+ 1⅞
ABrd pf	2.67	...	1198	101	64	84¼	+ 17
ABldM	.90	14	13592	29	20⅞	21⅜	− 3⅝
ABusPr	.76	13	12547	36⅞	23¼	25¾	− 8¼
AmCan	2.90	12	292316	91⅞	59⅝	84⅛	+ 24⅛
ACan pf	3.00	...	7714	79	51¾	73	+ 21½
ACan pf	13.75	...	7578	119½	113	113½	− 2
ACapBd	2.20	...	22647	25⅜	20⅞	24⅛	+ 2½
ACapCv	5.82e	...	6793	35	28⅞	31	+ 2⅜
ACMR n	.60	14	96575	24¼	14⅝	21⅛	...
ACentC		...	18777	7⅞	3⅜	3¾	− 1⅜
ACyan	1.90	22	471185	89⅞	54¼	77⅞	+ 20⅜
AEIPw	2.26	11	f11773	31½	22¾	27½	+ 3⅞
AmExp	1.44	10	f20150	70⅛	50½	56⅝	+ 3⅝
AFaml s	.44	14	193378	37⅜	20⅝	26	+ 5⅜
AGnCp	1.12	10	736534	46¾	33⅜	36⅞	+ 2
AGnl wt		...	95536	24	14	15¾	+ 1½
AGnl pfA	4.28e	...	72504	55⅜	51⅞	52	− 1⅞
AHerit	1.32	8	2924	44⅛	38	38½	− 4
AHoist		...	45098	10⅞	6⅛	7½	− 1⅝
AHoist pf	1.95	...	13637	25¼	18¾	19¾	...
AHome	3.10	15	760198	94⅞	61¼	76⅞	+ 14
AHme pf	2.00	...	27	405¾	284	344	+ 52¼
Amrtch	7.50	12	383395	152¼	98	132½	+ 26
AInGr s	.25	18	411631	71¾	52	61⅛	+ 8⅛
AMI	.72	...	974815	23⅛	13⅜	14¾	− 4¾
AmMot		...	963627	5	2½	2⅞	+ ⅛
AMotr pf	2.37	...	48056	31½	22	24⅞	...
APresd	.50	145	180352	29	16⅞	26⅛	+ 7¼
APrsd pf	3.50	...	11742	59	48½	57½	...
ASLFla		2	78534	19⅜	8	16	+ 7¼
ASLFl pf	2.19	...	21358	24⅜	16½	22⅞	+ 5¾
AShip	.80	16	29799	12½	8¾	9⅛	− 3⅛
AmStd	1.60	16	303072	46⅞	36	42⅞	+ 4⅛
AmStor	.84	14	159420	71¼	51⅝	54⅜	− 10⅜
AStr pfA	4.38	...	29588	81	63¼	64⅝	− 9⅜
AStr pfB	6.80	...	6702	61½	56¼	58½	+ ¼
AT&T	1.20	15	f52868	27⅞	20⅞	25	...
AT&T pf	3.64	...	135949	52½	41	49⅝	+ 8
AT&T pf	3.74	...	239879	52½	42	50¼	+ 7½
AmWtr	1.12	12	53040	44½	27¾	40⅜	+ 8¼
AWat pr	1.43	...	z11070	108½	76	104	+ 23¼
AWat pr	1.25	...	z65680	17½	12¾	15½	+ 2¾
AWa 5pr	1.25	...	z15100	17½	12½	16½	+ 3½
AmHotl		...	54205	13	9¼	10½	...
ATr pr	5.92	...	14615	81¼	69⅝	76	+ 3⅛
ATr sc		...	13033	44⅝	19⅛	36¾	+ 14¾
ATr un	5.92	...	2782	123½	88	113¾	+ 20¾
Amern s	.96	12	13804	33	22	30⅛	+ 6⅛
AmesDp	.10	21	447545	34⅝	19¼	23⅝	− 1¾
Ametek	1.00	17	73109	31	23⅜	26⅛	− 2⅛
AmevSc	1.08	...	16579	12¼	10¼	12	+ 1⅜
Amfac		...	77620	31¾	21½	22	− 4½
Amfac pf	1.87	...	1250	26⅝	25⅜	25¾	...
vjAmfsc		...	80755	6⅞	1¼	2	+ ⅝
Amoco	3.30	17	f11260	72⅛	53⅛	65¼	+ 3⅜
AMP	.72	24	626991	45	32⅞	36⅛	+ ⅛
Ampco	.30	...	45920	16½	12¾	13	− 1⅜
Amrep s		10	34595	23⅜	11¼	12¾	− 2¾
AmSth	1.16	10	37711	38½	26¼	31½	+ 4½
Anacmp		75	373159	6⅝	2¾	3¾	+ ⅜
Anadrk	.30	61	254877	23	18⅜	20⅛	...
Anlog s		31	197162	24¾	14¼	15⅝	− 4⅛
Anchor	1.48	...	133221	35	23¼	29	+ 2¾
Angelic	.64	14	50894	29¾	22	24	− 3
AnglCr n	.26e	...	7272	16	13½	14⅛	...
Anheu s	.48	17	f11920	29¼	19¾	26⅛	+ 5
Anheu pr	3.60	...	35899	113¼	63½	101⅞	+ 18⅜
Anixtr s	.16	23	184455	14	8½	14	+ 4⅛
Anthem	.02j	26	51662	19⅛	8⅜	11¾	− 4⅛
Anthny s	.44	...	10896	14⅜	8¼	10⅞	− ⅞
Apache	.28	...	99172	12	7⅝	9	− 1⅞
ApcP un	.70	...	217444	18⅛	6	6⅜	− 10⅜
ApPw pf	8.12	...	1313	101¼	75⅝	98⅛	+ 20⅜
ApPw pf	7.40	...	1627	94⅜	67½	93	+ 20
ApPw pf	2.65	...	1933	29¼	25½	29	+ 2½
ApPw pf	4.18	...	4382	34¼	30	32	− 2
ApPw pf	3.80	...	2209	32	28⅝	30½	− 1¼
ApplMg		18	28572	20¼	12¾	14⅞	...
ArchD s	.10b	11	f12201	23⅜	16¼	18⅜	+ 1⅛
Aristc n		...	95882	18⅝	17¾	18¼	...
AriP pf	6.91e	...	6622	100	80	89	− 8¼

NEW YORK STOCK EXCHANGE COMPOSITE

Stock	Div.	P-E Ratio	Sales 100s	High	Low	Last	Net Chg.
AriP pf	3.58	...	8377	33⅛	29½	30	− ½
ArkBst s	.36	13	66286	27⅞	14¾	26¾	+ 12¼
Arkla	1.08	17	439492	21⅛	16	19	+ 1⅜
Armada		66	4410	15⅛	8¼	13¼	− 1⅞
Armco		...	565790	12	4⅛	5⅛	− 4¼
Armc pf	2.10	...	9417	26½	13	15⅝	− 3⅜
ArmsRb	.48	...	57230	17⅛	13½	13⅞	− 2
ArmWI s	.84	13	200212	35	19¾	29⅞	+ 7⅝
ArmW pf	3.75	...	z50800	56	38¼	54	+ 14
ArowE	.20j	...	74524	17⅛	3⅛	6⅛	− 9⅝
ArowE pf	1.94	...	23176	24¾	9¼	13⅝	...
Artra	.16j	35	14495	31⅞	19¾	25¼	+ 2⅜
Arvin	.68	11	78981	35	19	28	+ 6⅛
Arvin pf	2.00	...	183	110⅛	61	89⅞	+ 21⅜
Asarco		...	204687	22⅞	10	14⅞	− 3½
Asarc pf	2.25	...	30207	35	24¼	31¼	...
AshlOil	1.80	9	424947	64¼	35½	56	+ 18⅝
AtalSo n		10	8222	14½	9¼	10⅜	...
Athlone	1.60	...	9245	22	15½	16	− 5¼
AtCyEl	2.62	11	104147	46⅝	28¼	37⅜	+ 8⅞
AtlCE pf	5.87	...	10	133	122	131¾	+ 43¼
AtlRich	4.00	16	f14486	64⅜	45¼	60	− 3¾
AtlRc pr	3.00	...	103	434¼	336½	412¾	− 9½
AtlRc pr	2.80	...	987	153	109	144	− 7½
AtlasCp		...	14744	17	11⅞	16	+ 3¾
AudVd		13	225383	17⅜	6⅝	7¾	− 5¾
Augat	.40	34	160292	27½	15	15¾	− 10¼
Ausimt	.20e	14	97162	31	12¼	18⅞	+ 5⅛
AutoDt s	.38	24	307069	38¾	28	35¼	+ 5¾
Avalon		23	13151	5	3⅛	4½	+ ¼
AVMC s	.50	11	12434	32	19½	26¼	+ 1⅝
Avery	.76	19	102092	47½	34½	41¼	+ 4⅜
Avnet	.50	40	362440	40⅜	25¼	25¾	− 8½
Avon	2.00	...	631848	36⅜	25¾	27	− ⅝
Aydin		15	30370	27⅝	17½	23⅝	+ 2¾

—B—

Stock	Div.	P-E Ratio	Sales 100s	High	Low	Last	Net Chg.
BMC		...	48335	7¾	3¼	7½	+ 2⅜
Bairnco	.70	15	51493	31⅛	23½	29¾	+ 2½
BkrIntl	.34	10	444640	17⅞	8⅞	11⅞	− 6
Baldor	.44	17	18574	24	17⅛	19⅝	− ½
Ball	.82	14	60971	45½	26¼	35¼	+ 4⅜
BallyMf	.20	20	497306	24⅛	14⅝	19¾	+ 3¼
BaltGE	1.80	11	441860	39⅞	23	33⅞	+ 8⅞
Balt pfB	4.50	...	z61870	62	47	60	+ 12½
BncOne	.84	10	212617	33⅛	22⅝	22⅞	− ½
BncCtr	.71e	...	5577	35⅛	10¾	34¼	+ 23¾
BanTex		...	171973	2	¼	⅜	− 1⅝
Bandag	1.40	16	39495	91½	57	87⅛	+ 27½
BkBos s	1.50	8	230922	44⅞	28⅞	39⅞	+ 8⅝
BkB pfA	3.38e	...	5102	53	47⅜	50⅝	− 2¼
BkB pfB	3.32e	...	9420	53⅞	46⅛	51	+ ¾
BkB pfC	6.10e	...	4579	100½	82	93	− 2½
BkNE dpf	3.96e	...	1422	54½	51¼	52¼	− 2¾
BkNY s	1.68	8	142241	46¾	32¾	38⅞	+ 4⅝
BnkAm		...	f19790	18½	9½	14⅝	− 1
BkA pf	3.58e	...	43656	43	26	31	− 6
BkA pf	6.07e	...	18607	73½	44¾	58¾	+ ½
BkA pf	2.88	...	58365	15⅞	7¼	9⅛	− 5⅝
BkARty	2.40	7	18997	34¼	26	29⅞	+ 3⅞
BnkTr s	1.66	8	597975	52½	33⅜	45¼	+ 8½
Banner	.06	10	43061	24	15½	21	+ 4¼
Barcly n	.64e	...	3877	31	26½	30¾	...
Bard s	.36	22	239286	40⅜	18¾	36¼	+ 14¼
BarnGp	1.00	12	18103	34½	26⅞	30½	+ 3
Barnet s	.80	11	157915	40⅞	31⅛	31¼	+ 1½
BaryWr	.60	14	52573	24½	14⅜	15⅛	− 4⅞
BASIX	.14t	...	56024	12⅛	6⅞	7¼	− 3⅛
Bausch	.78	16	321691	44	31¾	39⅛	+ 7
BaxtTr	.40	11	f16547	21¼	15⅛	19¼	+ 3½
BxtT pfA	3.25e	...	79919	50¼	44½	45⅞	− 2⅜
BxtT pfB	3.50	...	104246	72½	56¼	69	+ 11⅞
BayFin	.20	44	21336	33¼	22	24½	− 4
BaySG s	1.44	10	12390	27½	16¼	22½	+ 4¾
BearSt	.44	8	357249	26⅝	14⅞	16½	+ 1⅛
Bearing	1.00	67	16212	45¾	31	33⅜	− 4⅛
Becor	.20	63	90064	15¼	9¾	11¼	− 3¾
BectD s	.74	18	395431	61¼	30⅞	50	+ 19
vjBeker		...	71915	1⅞	9/32	5/16	− 15/16
vjBekr pf		...	4726	4⅛	7/16	⅝	− 2½
BeldnH	.40	12	12694	22⅜	17	19¼	− ¾
BelHwl	.62	12	110144	47⅝	30⅛	37	+ 6
BelHw pf	.74	...	4499	46⅝	29½	36½	+ 6
BellAtl s	3.60	12	546057	77	50	67½	+ 14¼
BCE g	2.40	7	124712	30	24⅞	27	− 3⅛
BellInd	.32	37	19587	27⅜	16⅜	20½	− 6
BellSou	3.04	11	f15310	69	45	57¾	+ 8¾
BeloAH	.80	26	55856	62¼	48⅜	51	− 1¼
Bemis s	.60	16	28932	30⅞	19⅝	28¼	+ 6
BenfCp	2.00	...	405260	78⅝	44¼	55½	+ 7
Benef pf	4.30	...	5579	62	40¼	51	+ 10¼
Benef pf	4.50	...	z33720	62	41	48	+ 7
Benef pf	5.50	...	z10360	351	204	236	+ 23½
Benef pf	2.50	...	1084	38	22⅞	26¼	+ 3¼
Beneqt n	1.20	...	16880	26⅝	19¼	24⅜	+ 5
BengtB		...	127169	6½	3⅛	4⅞	+ ⅞
Berkey		...	65810	8⅜	2⅞	5⅛	− 2
BestPd	.24	...	308887	16⅜	8½	9⅜	− 5¾
BethStl		...	831258	22	4⅝	6¼	− 9⅜
BethSt pf	2.50j	...	48667	54¼	12¾	17⅜	− 22
BethS pfB	1.25j	...	85475	27⅝	6⅝	8⅞	− 10⅝
Bevrly s	.20	14	965890	22½	14⅛	16⅜	− 1¾
BevIP n	1.38e	...	56083	29	19⅛	25¼	+ 6¼
Biocft		36	80051	24⅛	11⅞	15½	+ 1⅞
BlackD	.40	33	771380	25¼	14½	16¼	− 5¼
BlkHC s	1.14	13	28022	29	18½	21¾	+ 1⅜
BlairJn	1.50r	...	347322	15½	10⅛	12⅞	+ 1½
BlkHR	1.48	21	137037	52½	35¾	45	+ 6½
Boeing	1.20	12	f13289	64⅞	45¾	51⅛	− 1⅛
BoiseC	1.90	21	271257	64⅞	44½	59¾	+ 12¾
Boise pfC	3.50	...	19791	57	48¼	54	...
BoltBer	.10	28	42161	47⅞	33⅝	39⅜	+ 4
Borden s	1.12	17	393404	52½	31¾	46⅞	+ 12½
BorgWa	1.00	16	f10569	44⅝	21⅞	38⅛	+ 13½
Bormns	.20e	8	34406	25¾	10	17⅝	+ 5⅝
BCelts n		...	18414	18⅜	15¼	15¾	...
BosEd s	1.78	10	181184	28	21⅛	25¾	+ 2⅞
BosE pf	8.88	...	z84750	102	83½	101	+ 15
BosE pr	1.17	...	10379	13¼	10⅝	11⅞	+ ½
BosE pr	1.46	...	6014	16⅝	14¼	15¾	+ 1¼
Bowatr	.72	19	246258	33⅛	23⅜	30⅜	+ 5¾
BrigSt	1.60	16	76665	40¼	28¾	35¼	+ 5
BrGas pp		...	256471	9⅞	8⅝	9¾	...
BristM	2.80	20	f10378	88½	60¼	82⅝	+ 16⅜
BrstM pf	2.00	...	147	185¼	127½	174	+ 33¾
BritLnd		...	4634	4⅜	2⅞	3¼	− ⅞
BritPt	2.44e	15	336393	43¾	30⅛	43½	+ 11⅛
BritTel	1.33e	14	64354	44	26	32⅝	...
Brock n		...	22044	12⅛	7½	8⅜	...
Brckw s	.88	...	48555	24⅝	22	22	+ 3⅜
BkyUG s	1.66	12	49198	28⅞	21	23	+ ¾
BkUG pf	2.47	...	2678	29½	25¾	27⅞	+ 1¾
BwnSh	.40	18	16314	30½	17½	19⅛	− 3
BrwnGp	1.50	16	102506	43⅜	31	34½	+ ¾
BrwnF	.80	24	401971	47⅜	30¼	44¾	+ 12¾
Brnsw s	.60	14	367910	39⅜	21⅝	33⅞	+ 12⅛
BrshWl	.56	22	100055	39⅞	25⅛	26¾	− 7¼
Buckeye n		...	24166	20⅞	19¾	20⅝	...
Bundy	.80	10	11151	28⅞	17½	22⅞	+ 3⅜
BunkrH	2.16	...	5770	23⅜	18¾	22½	+ 2¾
BKInv n	1.10e	...	44440	24⅜	17¾	20½	...
BurlnCt		16	42685	26½	15⅞	24	+ 5¼
BurlInd	1.64	21	199611	45	29½	41½	+ 9⅝
BrlNth	2.00	9	759622	82⅜	46½	53¼	− 15
BrlNo pf	.55	...	11783	9⅛	7⅜	8⅜	+ ⅞
Burndy		...	55495	15⅛	10⅝	12¾	+ 1½
Butlrln	.52	36	71437	20¼	14¾	18⅜	+ 1¼

—C—

Stock	Div.	P-E Ratio	Sales 100s	High	Low	Last	Net Chg.
CBI In	.60	16	201996	31⅞	19¼	28⅞	+ 9
CBI pf		...	3597	51¾	50	50⅝	...
CBS	3.00	14	299529	151½	110	127	+ 11⅛
CBS pf	1.00	...	53	99½	85	87	+ 7
CCX		...	21371	5½	3⅞	4½	− ¼
CCX pf	1.25	...	z18100	12¾	10½	11¾	+ 1¼
CIGNA	2.60	...	724067	77¼	51⅛	55	− 9¼
CIG pf	2.75	...	48642	37⅞	29½	30¾	− 3¾
CIG pf	4.10	...	77086	64	53½	55	− ⅝
vjCLC		...	28793	3⅜	11/16	1	− ⅝
CNA Fn		13	136306	75	47¼	53¾	− 10¾
CNAI	1.24	...	24543	13⅜	11⅝	12⅞	+ 1¼
CNW		038	146045	30½	16½	20¾	− 1½
CNW pf	2.12	...	42061	32¼	23	28⅜	...
CPC Int	2.48	20	670317	88½	46½	79¼	+ 28¼
CP Ntl	1.60	11	55403	39½	26	32⅝	+ 5⅜
CRIIM	3.35e	12	38828	24⅝	21⅛	23¼	+ 1⅞
CRI II n	1.70	...	18550	21	18¾	20½	...
CRSS	.34	13	10344	17⅞	13	14⅜	+ ¼
CSX	1.16	...	963894	37½	25⅝	29⅛	− 1⅛
CSX pf	7.00	...	107	220	168	177	− 11
CTS	1.00	...	49376	44¾	27½	32¼	+ ⅝
C 3 Inc		...	61854	14¼	6⅞	12⅜	+ 3½
Cabot	.92	12	156210	35⅜	23⅜	30	+ 4½

NEW YORK STOCK EXCHANGE COMPOSITE

		P-E Ratio	Sales 100s	High	Low	Last	Net Chg.
Caesar		13	351111	22⅞	14¾	19	+ 3
CalFIP n		...	20549	10⅞	9⅞	10⅝	...
CalFed	.60	5	554681	42	26¾	33½	+ 6⅛
CalRE	1.28	14	16404	13¼	10	11⅜	− ⅜
Callhn	.25b	...	28961	24⅝	13½	16⅞	− 1¾
Calmat	.68	15	45268	43	26½	40⅝	+ 12⅜
Calton n		...	81130	8¼	4⅝	5⅝	...
Camrnl	.04	...	42365	13⅜	8⅜	10⅛	− 2¾
CRLk g	.40	...	219728	24½	14⅛	19⅝	− 2⅛
CmpR g	.16t	...	103984	2⅝	¾	1⅛	− 1⅛
CamSp	1.44	16	266141	68½	44	57	+ 7⅝
CdPac s	.48	...	f10243	14⅝	10	12⅞	− ⅝
CanonG		17	267835	45½	9½	11⅜	− 18⅛
CapCits	.20	29	95871	279¾	208¼	268⅛	+ 43⅝
CapHld	.88	12	204377	38¾	25¾	30⅝	+ 1¼
CapH pf	6.99e	...	22127	107½	102	103¾	− ¾
Carlng g	.48	...	12833	11¾	8⅜	9½	− ¼
Carlisle	1.10	16	33123	39⅜	28½	29⅞	− 4⅜
CarolP n		...	21183	9⅜	7⅛	9⅜	...
CaroFt	.44	13	76574	42½	26¼	35	+ 6¼
CarPw	2.76	10	560465	42¾	28⅝	38⅝	+ 8½
CarP pr	2.67	...	3925	30⅞	25¾	28½	+ 2½
CarTec	2.10	21	66148	37¾	28½	31	− 3¼
Carrol	.10	...	69604	11¼	6½	11⅛	+ 3⅝
CarPir s	.70	22	161663	40¼	23½	36	+ 9⅝
CartHw	1.22	31	404157	57½	26½	48	+ 19⅜
CartWl	.80	19	41303	86⅛	48	75	+ 26⅞
CartSv n	.07r	6	13423	22⅝	13⅝	13⅞	− 4¼
CascNG	1.28	19	15627	20	14⅞	15⅞	− 2¼
CastlCk		14	274366	20¼	13	19¼	+ 6¼
CstlC pf	.90	...	43505	21⅛	15⅛	20	+ 4⅞
Caterp	.50	13	914166	55⅜	36⅝	40⅛	− 1⅞
Celans	5.20	14	157087	247½	140¼	240⅛	+ 89⅞
Celan pf	4.50	...	3446	97½	45¾	93½	+ 47½
Cengy	.01e	...	44302	9⅛	4⅜	5⅛	− 2⅝
Centel	2.50	12	99836	65⅛	45	56	+ 8¾
CentE n	2.56	8	594721	27¾	22⅛	22¾	...
Centex	.25	11	202316	40½	24	31¼	+ 5⅞
CenSoW	2.14	9	545500	37½	26½	34¼	+ 6¾
CenHud	2.96	6	113570	39⅞	26⅝	30⅛	+ ⅛
CHud pf	1.86e	...	3195	27	21½	26	...
CnILt pf	4.50	...	z23780	55½	44¼	54½	+ 10¼
CnIIPS	1.68	13	241861	30¾	19¾	28	+ 8⅛
CnLaEl	2.08	11	52789	38	28½	34¼	+ 4¼
CLaEl pf	4.18	...	4185	38¼	32¾	35¼	...
CeMPw	1.40	233	109765	20	13⅜	18⅝	+ 4⅜
CVtPS	1.90	8	22999	29¼	21	27⅛	+ 5¼
CentrDt		36	497513	8¼	4⅛	4⅜	− ⅝
CntryTl	.84	11	40426	18¾	13	16⅛	+ 2⅝
Cenvill	2.00	9	15480	20	15⅝	18⅞	+ 1⅞
Crt-teed	.90	9	88282	38½	22⅝	31¼	+ 4⅞
Chmpln	.52	17	f10573	34	22½	30¾	+ 5⅞
ChamSp	.20j	...	273550	11⅞	8⅝	10⅞	+ 1¼
vjChrtC		...	107176	4¼	2⅛	3⅞	+ 1½
vjCht wt		...	17339	1	¼	9/32	− 7/32
vjChrt pf		...	19811	3¾	1⅞	3⅝	+ 1⅛
Chase s	2.05	5	f10200	49½	34	35⅝	− ⅝
Chase pf	6.75	...	4929	94½	67	91	+ 23
Chase pf	7.60	...	5496	97¾	73	95¾	+ 23¼
Chase pf	5.25	...	13403	57¼	49¼	54¼	+ 5
Chse pf	4.46e	...	61732	55¼	51¼	51⅝	− 1½
Chse pf	4.14e	...	62773	54½	49½	50¼	− 1½
Chaus n		15	114386	25⅛	15⅝	18½	...
Chelsea	.72	11	15149	32⅜	24½	30⅞	+ 4⅞
Chemed	1.56	15	35297	40	29½	33¼	+ ¼
ChmNY	2.60	6	514557	56¼	40¾	42¼	− 3⅛
ChNY pf	1.87	...	2877	55	41	43⅛	− 2⅞
ChNY pf	4.46e	...	41951	55	50¾	51¾	− 1½
ChNY pf	3.98e	...	21161	54¼	51	51½	− 1½
ChWst n		40	164024	25¾	18	23	...
Chspk s	.88	37	18857	36⅞	25¼	33⅝	...
ChesPn	2.08	20	976296	72¼	38	71⅞	+ 29½
Chevrn	2.40	11	f16983	48⅛	34	45⅜	+ 7¼
ChiMlw		12	9872	154	128	132⅝	− 3⅜
ChiMl pf		...	1884	88½	57	57½	− 4¼
ChiPnT		...	51880	39⅞	19¾	37¾	+ 17½
ChkFull	.35t	14	76766	14⅜	8⅛	9¼	...
ChrisC s		34	32163	25⅞	17¼	18⅞	+ 1⅝
ChCft pf	1.00	...	73	12½	10¼	11½	− ¾
ChCft pf	1.40	...	49	550	425	475	+ 50
Christn		...	12495	9¼	4½	5⅛	− 3⅜
Chroma		10	192387	25⅛	15¼	21⅞	+ 6⅛
Chrys s	1.40	4	f17442	47⅛	27⅛	37	+ 6
Chubb	1.68	20	308094	78⅛	54	59¼	+ 4⅜
Churchs	.46	41	594496	18½	10⅞	11⅛	− 6⅞
Chyron	.12	26	72847	7¾	4	5⅞	− 1⅜
Cilcorp	2.28	12	54850	42½	26½	38⅝	+ 11⅝
CinBel s	1.76	11	28016	47¾	27⅜	41	+ 13⅜
CinGE	2.16	7	537175	31⅛	20⅜	26⅝	+ 4½
CinG pf	4.00	...	z53650	47	33	43½	+ 9½
CinG pf	4.75	...	z37090	54	41	53	+ 12½
CinG pf	9.30	...	2258	102½	80⅞	98½	+ 17½
CinG pf	7.44	...	2934	85⅝	65	81⅛	+ 15⅛
CinG pf	9.28	...	3900	103⅜	81	101	+ 19⅜
CinG pf	9.52	...	2761	103	83⅞	100	+ 16¼
CinG pf	10.20	...	3911	109	99½	106	+ 5⅞
CinMil	.72	26	113958	26	17⅝	19⅞	+ 2⅛
CirclK s	.28	18	307722	18⅝	9⅝	16⅛	+ 5⅞
CirCty s	.06	23	285951	34¼	11¾	30⅝	+ 18¼
Circus s		23	155011	21⅛	13⅜	17⅞	+ 3¼
Citicrp	2.46	8	f11658	63¾	46⅞	53	+ 3⅝
Citcp pf	6.00e	...	78597	90½	78¾	83⅝	+ 4⅞
Citcp pfA	7.00e	...	24410	103½	94⅛	98½	+ 1½
Citcp pfB	6.01e	...	3169	102¼	98½	99½	− ⅜
Clabir	.72	...	33860	8¼	6¾	7½	...
ClairSt	.10	42	220500	11⅝	6¼	8¾	− 2¼
ClarkE		...	136215	28⅝	15¾	19¾	− 5½
ClayHm		15	53775	21	10½	12⅛	− ⅞
ClvClf	.60j	...	106164	19⅜	6	9½	− 8⅜
ClvCl pf	2.00	...	33940	23	10¾	14⅜	− 6⅛
ClvEl pf	7.40	...	2290	81	62	74½	+ 11½
ClvEl pf	7.56	...	3201	81½	63½	77	+ 12¼
ClvEl pf	7.94e	...	1213	102½	80	82½	− 17¾
Clorox	1.52	14	204012	60⅜	44	50⅝	+ 3
ClubMd	.20	15	35243	32¼	21¼	25¼	+ 1½
Coachm	.40	65	126734	22½	9⅞	12⅜	− 1
CoastSL		...	426669	19½	11¼	12¾	− 1¼
Coastal	.40	45	209236	40	23½	35	− 4⅛
Cstl pf	1.19	...	176	64¼	50½	58⅛	+ ⅛
Cstl pf	1.83	...	383	64	41	56	− 3½
Cstl pf	2.11	...	21618	30	24⅝	29	...
CocaCl s	1.04	18	f15017	44⅞	25½	37¾	+ 9⅝
CocCE n		...	487613	16⅝	13⅞	14¼	...
Coleco		44	315626	20½	8¼	8⅜	− 7⅝
Colemn	1.20	14	36995	46¾	29¾	30¾	− ½
ColgPal	1.36	24	652570	47	30⅜	40⅞	+ 8⅛
ColgP pf	4.25	...	z15570	67	50½	64⅜	+ 14⅛
ColAik	.88	17	254143	53	31	52½	+ 21
ColFds	.12	40	181492	19⅜	11½	16⅜	+ 2⅝
Colt n		...	79598	11⅞	9¼	10	...
ColGas	3.18	27	263114	46	34¾	45¼	+ 5¾
ColGs pf	5.48	...	504	58	49½	55⅞	+ 5⅜
ColGs pf	5.12	...	8077	57	50	57	+ 7¼
ColGs pf	4.06e	...	5142	53	48	51½	− ½
ColumS s	.24	3	256118	17⅜	8⅞	10½	+ ½
ColSv pf		...	35639	16½	9¾	10⅝	...
CSO pf	3.45	...	7260	29¾	26½	27¾	− ⅛
CSO pf	2.42	...	357	27¼	21¼	26½	+ 4½
CSO pf o	15.25	...	z25950	118½	111	115¾	+ 3¼
CSO pr n	15.25	...	z77020	118½	109½	117	+ 4
Combln	2.24	10	113824	65½	51	52¾	+ 1
CmbEn	1.00	20	211923	36¾	27	30¾	− ⅛
Comdta	.20	16	373937	14⅞	9½	10	− 2¾
Comds s	.16	8	405437	25	12	15¾	− 3¼
CCred n	.06e	...	274310	22¾	19¾	20½	...
CmMtl s	.32	11	31770	22½	14½	15¾	− ¾
Comdre		...	353813	11⅜	4¾	8⅞	− 1¾
CmwE	3.00	7	f19800	35¾	28⅝	33⅞	+ 4½
CwE wtA		...	16	11⅜	9⅝	10¾	+ 1⅝
CwE wtB		...	9	11⅜	9⅝	10¾	+ ½
CwE pf	1.42	...	646	35¾	29	34⅜	+ 5⅛
CwE pr	1.90	...	20050	22¾	17⅜	21½	+ 4⅛
CwE pr	2.00	...	15482	23¾	18¼	22½	+ 4¼
CwE pf	12.75	...	z24500	115	103¾	115	+ 6¼
CwE pf	11.70	...	1639	115¾	106½	108	...
CwE pfB	8.40	...	8870	103½	89	101½	+ 13
CwE pf	8.38	...	12869	96¾	77½	90¼	+ 11¼
CwE pr	2.37	...	7751	26⅜	24⅜	25½	+ 1⅛
CwE pf	2.87	...	7116	29⅝	26⅛	27½	+ 1⅜
CwE pf	8.40	...	17441	96¾	77¾	90¼	+ 12¼
CwE pr	7.24	...	5974	84	66½	79½	+ 11
ComES	2.72	9	26024	45¾	29¼	38	+ 7¼
ComES pf	9.80	...	z13480	108½	93	104	+ 16
CmwM n	1.00	...	21811	10⅛	9⅝	9¾	...
Comsat	1.20	...	200230	40½	28⅛	28⅛	− 7⅜
CPsyc	.48	18	429684	39⅞	22	30¼	+ 2
Compaq		15	789497	21⅝	11⅝	19¼	+ 6
Compgr	.60	33	14783	28	15½	19	− 8⅜
CmpAs s		28	225536	30⅞	16¼	27½	+ 10
CompSc		22	156052	44⅞	29½	42¼	+ 8¾
Cptvsn		...	305911	18⅝	10⅛	13⅜	+ ¾
ConAg s	.58	17	175195	32⅛	19⅜	28⅝	+ 7⅜
ConnE	1.68	14	7563	27	18⅛	24	+ 5⅝
CnnNG s	1.30	13	10740	24½	17	19½	+ 1½
Conrac	.40b	11	43707	17⅞	12¼	12¾	− 1¾

NEW YORK STOCK EXCHANGE COMPOSITE

		P-E Ratio	Sales 100s	High	Low	Last	Net Chg.
Consec n		13	10988	13¾	10⅝	11¼	...
ConsEd	2.68	11	626332	52⅞	37⅝	47⅛	+ 7⅝
ConE pr	6.00	...	77	335	250	304	+ 67½
ConE pf	4.65	...	5946	65⅝	46½	62¼	+ 15¼
ConE pf	5.00	...	4451	63⅜	48⅝	60⅞	+ 11⅞
CnsFrt s	.82	13	239117	36½	23⅝	30	+ 3½
CnsNG s	1.50	14	198834	35⅛	21¾	32⅝	+ 7¼
CnStor s		33	213117	23⅝	7⅜	13½	+ 5¾
ConsPw		...	806658	17⅜	7½	15⅝	+ 8⅛
CnP pfA	4.16	...	z58370	46	30½	43	+ 11½
CnP pfB	4.50	...	1266	49½	35	47	+ 12
CnP pfC	4.52	...	z94490	63½	41¾	63	+ 22
CnP pfD	7.45	...	3477	78¼	54	74½	+ 20
CnP pfE	7.72	...	5182	80¾	55	77⅛	+ 21⅝
CnP pfG	7.76	...	4711	81¾	55⅝	77¾	+ 21¾
CnP prV	4.40	...	35214	35	28¼	32½	+ 3⅛
CnP prU	3.60	...	16763	32	24⅛	30	+ 5⅜
CnP prT	3.78	...	11450	32¼	25⅞	29⅝	+ 3⅜
CnP pfH	7.68	...	5598	80¾	55	77¼	+ 22¼
CnP prP	3.98	...	7707	31⅛	26½	29¼	+ 2⅝
CnP prN	3.85	...	7742	31	26	30	+ 4
CnP prM	2.50	...	5817	26	17¼	24⅜	+ 6⅝
CnP prL	2.23	...	7511	24¼	16	23	+ 6¾
CnP prS	4.02	...	8978	32½	26½	30⅛	+ 3
CnP prK	2.43	...	7884	25½	16⅞	24	+ 7⅛
Contel	1.88	9	471200	35⅜	25⅜	28⅜	+ 2¾
CntlCp	2.60	30	379128	55	42	44¾	− 2¼
Contlll	.02e	9	262989	10¼	5	5⅜	− 4½
Cntlll pf	3.93e	...	14300	46½	40⅞	44¾	+ ⅞
CtllHld		...	178071	1¼	¼	9/32	− 19/32
Cntlnf s		8	94628	12⅜	5⅞	8½	+ 1⅛
CtData		...	558306	28¾	18¾	26⅜	+ 5⅝
CnDt pf	4.50	...	z36250	56½	35¼	50	+ 14
CookU n		...	13527	7¼	1¾	2⅜	...
Cooper	1.60	14	349210	51½	35⅝	41⅜	− ⅝
CoprTr	.44	12	36303	28¾	17¼	26¼	+ 6⅞
Coopvis	.40	43	383935	28½	14⅜	17½	− 9¾
Copwld		...	12306	10⅞	6¼	7⅜	− 1¾
Cpwld pf	2.48	...	3796	19⅞	16	17⅞	+ 1¾
Coreln	.60	20	28860	15½	11⅜	12½	− ⅞
CornGl	1.40	16	407299	81½	46⅝	54⅞	− 6⅞
CorBlk s	.65	15	128996	43½	27⅞	32⅜	+ 2¼
CTSF n		...	7109	10½	9¾	10⅛	...
CTSF pf		...	4040	50¼	49⅛	49¾	...
CntCrd s	.13i	15	104087	14½	5⅜	12⅜	+ 6⅝
CntrMt	2.01e	8	84720	19⅛	10	18	+ 7⅝
Craig		18	9991	21¾	9⅛	14¼	+ 4⅞
Crane s	1.20	19	59227	37⅜	24⅝	34¼	+ 7¼
CrayRs		22	525198	99⅝	57¼	80⅞	+ 15⅜
CrmpK	1.28	14	14345	39⅛	24½	36¼	+ 9⅞
CrwnCk		14	49951	114¼	77¼	103⅛	+ 13½
CrysBd		30	146765	24⅜	17¼	17¾	− 5
Culbro	.80a	14	9485	46¾	32	38½	+ 5¾
Culinet		...	495915	19¼	6¼	6⅞	− 12⅛
CumEn	2.20	...	127011	78¾	51¼	67⅛	− 4⅞
Cumn pr	3.50	...	1236	56½	54½	55½	...
Curlnc	1.10a	...	8419	13¼	10¾	12¾	+ 1¾
CurtW	1.60	...	15787	57⅛	43½	52⅝	+ 8
Cyclops	1.10	12	42235	78	51⅜	64⅜	+ 8¾

—D—

		P-E Ratio	Sales 100s	High	Low	Last	Net Chg.
DCNY	2.15e	8	15968	59⅞	38	54½	+ 9
DPL	2.00	16	401378	29⅛	19½	25½	+ 5
Dallas	.66	126	21252	19½	12½	13⅞	− 4⅜
DamonC	.20	...	38671	23⅛	11½	13¼	− 3⅞
DanaCp	1.28	16	381770	36½	25½	34⅞	+ 7⅝
Danahr		10	56281	13⅜	7	12⅜	+ 4½
Daniel	.18	...	35383	8¼	6	8	+ ⅛
DataGn		141	477599	48½	25	29⅝	− 15¾
Datapt		...	222442	9¼	4¾	6⅜	+ 1⅛
Datpt pf	4.94	...	1287	33	31½	31⅞	...
DtaDsg	.24	5	28720	8¾	5⅛	5¼	− 2½
Dayco	.40	12	131443	30½	18	28	+ 9¾
Dayc pf	4.25	...	z5020	160	96½	150	+ 55
DaytHd	.84	15	797322	58½	40	42½	− 3⅜
DPL pf	7.48	...	z75500	88	67	86⅝	+ 18⅞
DPL pf	7.70	...	1164	89	69⅝	86	+ 14½
DPL pf	7.37	...	1165	87½	65½	83½	+ 16½
DeanF s	.46	19	64721	33⅝	25⅛	27¾	− ⅜
DecCa n	.13e	...	8674	19⅝	15	15½	...
DIC		38	206322	14¾	7½	8¾	− 4½
Deere	.25	...	473308	35⅛	21½	22⅞	− 5⅞
DelmP	2.12	11	163715	38⅛	25⅜	33	+ 5⅛
DeltaAr	1.00	27	707988	51⅞	37¾	48⅛	+ 9⅛
Deltona		...	27979	10¼	4⅞	5⅛	− 2
DlxCh s	.64	26	216649	38	21½	35¼	+ 11⅞
DensMf	1.20	35	59191	30⅜	23½	27¾	+ ½
DeSoto	1.40	17	14695	41⅜	34¼	38⅛	+ 2⅞
DetEd	1.68	6	f13284	19⅜	15⅜	16½	+ ⅝
DetE pf	5.50	...	230	107	88	95½	+ 8
DetE pf	9.32	...	2674	97½	79½	93½	+ 14½
DetE pf	7.68	...	6760	88¼	68½	81¾	+ 13¼
DetE pf	7.45	...	6984	86⅝	68¼	78⅝	+ 11⅛
DetE pf	7.36	...	7716	85⅛	66¾	76¾	+ 8⅞
DE pfF	2.75	...	3135	27	25⅛	26	+ ⅛
DE prR	3.24	...	7462	29⅞	26¾	28⅝	+ 1⅛
DE pfQ	3.13	...	16453	29¼	26	27¾	+ 1
DE pfP	3.12	...	4868	30	25¾	28	+ 1¼
DE pfB	2.75	...	5600	26⅞	25	26¼	+ ¼
DE prO	3.40	...	9263	29⅞	27½	28⅜	+ ½
DE pfM	3.42	...	13294	33	27¼	28⅛	+ ¼
DE prL	4.00	...	7244	33¾	27⅝	28⅛	− 3½
DE prK	4.12	...	12246	34¾	26⅛	27¾	− 4⅞
DetE pf	9.72	...	4117	108	99	101	+ 1½
DetE pr	2.28	...	11095	25¼	19⅞	23⅜	+ 3¼
Dexter s	.60	17	60162	23¼	16⅞	22¼	+ 5
DiGior	.64	10	96836	27	17⅞	21½	+ 2¼
DiaBth	.20	35	61232	35⅛	10½	12¼	− 14⅜
DiamS	.70r	...	890024	15⅜	9½	12¼	− 1⅝
DiaSh pf	4.00	...	15569	42	31⅝	38¾	+ 3⅜
DiaSO	2.80e	...	95399	20⅜	13¾	16¼	− 2¼
DianaCp	.30	17	7470	13	10⅞	11	− ½
Diebold	1.20	17	118088	47	35	45¾	+ 4⅜
Digital s		19	f16185	109	65¾	104¾	+ 38½
Disney s	.32	24	f12451	54⅞	28	43⅛	+ 15
DEI	1.44	...	73960	29	19½	23¼	+ 2⅞
Divrsln		11	29806	7¾	5⅜	6	− ⅜
Dome g	.06	...	504121	12¼	4⅞	7¾	− 1⅜
DomRs	2.96	12	617210	52⅛	33¾	44¼	+ 8¾
Donald	.66	11	29073	39¾	24⅛	33⅞	+ 6½
Donley	1.28	16	160196	80	58⅞	61½	− 2⅛
Dorsey s	.64	13	37759	28½	18	21¾	+ 2⅛
Dover	.92	18	178720	48½	37	44½	+ 4⅛
DowCh	2.00	43	f15336	61¾	39⅞	58½	+ 17½
DowJn s	.56	21	192800	42⅛	28	39	+ 7½
Downey	.12i	4	59882	27	16¾	19⅝	+ 1⅛
Dravo	.50	41	144718	20	13¼	18⅜	+ 1⅝
Dresr	.40	161	559676	20⅜	14	19⅜	+ 1¼
DrexB	2.00	...	6969	24	20⅛	23⅝	+ 1¾
Dreyfs s	.28a	16	253877	39½	23⅞	29	+ ⅛
duPont	3.20	13	f10781	92½	59½	84	+ 16⅛
duPnt pf	3.50	...	4653	51	37½	50	+ 11¼
duPnt pf	4.50	...	8287	64½	48	63⅜	+ 12⅞
DukeP	2.68	11	494990	52	34⅞	45¼	+ 9⅞
Duke pf	6.75	...	80	203	148	202	+ 48
Duke pf	8.70	...	3123	105	87½	101¾	+ 13¾
Duke pf	8.20	...	7093	102¾	81	99	+ 16
Duke pf	7.80	...	11310	102	19⅛	98½	+ 18¾
Duke pf	2.69	...	3733	28½	25½	25¾	− ⅞
Duke pr	3.85	...	13392	36¾	29¼	30¾	− 5¼
Duke pf	11.00	...	z34350	107⅝	103	106	+ ¼
Duk pfN	8.84	...	3976	107¼	99	105¾	+ 6
Duk pfM	8.84	...	3204	108¼	89⅜	104¾	+ 16¾
Duke pf	8.28	...	7650	104½	81½	101	+ 17
DukeRln	.52e	...	15356	8¾	6¾	8½	...
DukeRCa		...	15701	1⅞	1	1⅛	...
DunBrd	2.56	24	284850	120⅜	80¾	105¼	+ 21½
DuqLt	1.20	6	717186	19⅜	12⅛	12¼	− 4
Duq pfA	2.10	...	1754	24½	18	21¼	+ 2½
Duq pf	1.87	...	z81430	21	15¼	18¼	+ 2⅛
Duq pf	2.00	...	1419	21⅝	16⅝	19½	+ 3
Duq pf	2.05	...	z37150	22¼	17½	20¼	+ 3¼
Duq pf	2.07	...	1207	22½	17¼	22½	+ 5¾
Duq pfG	2.10	...	z23820	24	17⅞	21½	+ 4½
Duq prK	2.10	...	7536	23½	18	21¼	+ 3¼
Duq pr	2.31	...	8767	25¾	19	23	+ 3¼
Duq pr	2.75	...	z47700	28½	24	26½	+ 1½
Duq pf	7.20	...	1852	78¾	61⅞	74	+ 11½
Dynlct	.27e	28	103599	18⅞	12¾	14¾	− ¼
DynAm	.20	8	24790	33¼	23¾	24¾	− 3¾

—E—

		P-E Ratio	Sales 100s	High	Low	Last	Net Chg.
EGG	.56	15	178714	43	27⅝	28¼	− 10⅛
EQK G n	1.00	...	30537	11¼	9¾	10½	...
EQK Rt	1.66	23	45970	18¼	14½	15	-- 2⅜
ERC		14	36876	15⅞	8⅛	10¾	+ 2⅝
E Syst	.50	20	267224	39⅝	23½	29⅞	+ ¼
EagleP	1.04	...	55280	41¾	28¼	36	+ 6⅛
EastGF	1.30	13	208976	30⅞	22¼	28	+ 3¾
EastUtl	2.18	14	93989	39½	25¾	38½	+ 12⅝
EKodk	2.52	47	f24041	70	45⅞	68⅝	+ 18
Eaton	1.60	17	225783	79⅞	63	73¾	+ 9⅝
Eaton pf	10.00	...	78	314	255	302	+ 46
Echlin	.50	17	447491	20⅝	14¼	19½	+ 5⅛

NEW YORK STOCK EXCHANGE COMPOSITE

Stock	Div	P-E Ratio	Sales 100s	High	Low	Last	Net Chg.
Ecolab s	.58	...	11197	29¼	20½	23	+ 2⅜
EdisBr	1.60	12	20783	43¾	32½	33⅞	− ¾
EDO	.28	18	56543	19⅞	14¼	15¾	− ⅛
EdCmp	.16	19	28377	13¾	8⅞	11½	+ ¼
Edwrd s	.60	11	147571	31	21⅝	25¾	+ 2¾
ElToro	.08	22	71123	20½	10⅝	20¼	+ 7⅝
Elcor	.36	12	11892	17⅞	10	16½	+ 6¼
Eldon	.20	15	18488	17½	14⅝	16⅛	− 2⅛
ElecAs		...	17444	7	3⅝	4¾	+ ½
Elctspce	.08	21	57701	28	13⅝	16¾	− 7⅜
Elgin	.40j	...	16908	18	12½	14⅛	+ ⅞
Elscint		...	54702	4⅛	1⅜	1⅞	− 1
EmrsEl	2.88	15	359548	92⅝	78⅛	83¾	+ 2½
ERad s		16	273327	11¾	3¾	9½	+ 5¼
EmryA	.50j	...	222812	22⅛	11	11⅜	− 5⅝
Emhart	1.40	...	157074	42⅝	30¼	32¼	− ¼
Emht pf	2.10	...	42	139	113½	120	+ 21½
EmpDs	2.00	11	22611	36	23¼	32¼	+ 7⅞
Emp pf	.47	...	3012	6⅜	4¾	5⅞	+ ¾
Emp pf	.50	...	z72250	6⅞	5	6½	+ 1½
Energen	1.08	42	11552	21⅝	13⅝	20⅜	+ 4⅞
EnglCp	.76	15	104401	33¾	22⅞	28	+ 3¾
EnisBu	.68	14	31198	28	21⅛	26½	+ 3½
Enron	2.48	29	335747	50⅝	33¾	39½	− 5½
Enrn pfD	6.40	...	z1600	86	81½	85	+ 3
Enrn pfE	6.84	...	z840	88	82	88	+ 6
Enrn pfG	8.48	...	z19190	101	91¾	92	...
Enrn pfJ	10.50	...	1517	175	130¼	139⅛	− 15⅞
Enrn pfH	10.50	...	13318	111¼	97⅞	99	− 3¼
Ensrch	.80b	...	473762	25⅛	13⅛	16¼	− 6
Ensch pf	10.32	...	z37810	106	100⅜	105¾	+ 3¾
Ensch pr	4.00e	...	8076	53⅝	39	47	− 6
Ensch pf	7.36e	...	4580	103⅝	72½	86⅝	− 16
EnsExp	1.20	15	103518	18⅞	10⅛	13½	− 3⅝
Ensrce s		...	43695	22½	5⅜	6⅛	− 13⅞
Entera		...	43117	12¼	4½	5½	− 6½
EntexE	.60	...	46695	11¾	3⅛	3⅜	− 7¾
EntexIn	1.40	...	135280	24¼	13½	14⅞	− 3¼
EnvSys		30	147201	24½	11¾	18½	+ 5⅞
Equifx s	.68	19	51322	28½	19	21⅞	+ 2⅛
Equimk		9	169596	7⅛	4⅛	4⅜	− ⅞
Eqmk pf	2.31	...	2979	25¼	21½	23⅝	+ ⅞
EqtRE n		...	3590	10¾	10	10⅛	...
EqtRes	1.80	12	66677	55⅝	33⅛	54¾	+ 16
Equitec	.16	14	28909	11¾	6	6⅝	− 3
Erbmnt	.40	14	144191	34⅜	14⅝	22⅛	+ 6½
EssBus	.56	16	21317	37¼	24	30¾	+ 6⅛
EsxCh s	.60	13	21330	29½	15⅝	20⅝	+ 4¾
Estrlne	.54j	138	36752	24¼	10¼	15⅛	− 2⅝
Ethyl s	.38	15	363950	22½	13½	18¾	+ 5⅛
Ethyl pf	2.40	...	60	421	322	385	+ 79¾
Excelsr	1.78e	...	5826	20¾	17⅞	18½	+ ¼
Exxon	3.60	9	f24134	74⅛	48⅜	70⅛	+ 15
—F—							
FGIC n	.02e	13	64172	36	23⅛	23⅝	...
FMC		16	189439	26⅜	15½	25¾	...
FPL Gp	2.04	11	850509	38	26⅜	31⅝	+ 3⅜
FabCtr	.28	34	14102	12¾	8⅞	11¾	+ 1
Facet		16	14280	13⅛	8¾	12¾	+ 2
Fairchd	.20	10	83452	14	7⅞	10⅛	− ⅝
Fairc pf	3.60	...	8434	38	29½	35⅛	+ 3⅞
Fairfd	.20	17	65432	14	7	8⅛	− 5¼
FamDlr	.24	16	191445	28⅛	15⅜	16¾	− 3⅝
Fanstel	.60	19	20829	17	11⅝	12¾	− 3¾
FrWst s	.40	4	40902	20⅛	11⅛	13⅞	− 2⅝
Farah	.88j	9	70243	26⅝	13	13⅝	− 7½
FayDrg	.20	58	59158	11¾	8½	8⅝	− ⅛
Feders	.20b	12	133607	12⅞	5⅛	9½	+ 4⅜
FedlCo s	1.18	11	90739	44	26½	40¼	+ 11¾
FedExp		...	752174	73¾	51	63⅛	+ 2½
FdHm pf	4.53e	...	84372	66¾	36¾	63	+ 26¼
FdMog	1.60	10	49901	46¼	36½	40	+ 1⅝
FedNM	.32	25	f14907	42	22¾	40¾	+ 14⅞
FedlPB	.70	19	113412	32½	18¾	27⅞	+ 7⅞
FPap pf	1.20	...	187	79⅜	47½	69	+ 21½
FPap pf	2.31	...	24509	39½	29	36⅛	+ 6⅜
FedRlt s	1.08	14	29274	23¼	16⅛	19⅞	+ 3
FdSgnl	.80	17	49970	24⅝	17	18	− 1⅞
FedDSt	2.68	14	425443	100⅜	63½	83¼	+ 16⅝
Ferro	1.20	16	52249	41⅜	30¼	39	+ 6⅞
Fldcst s	.68	19	55128	43	17¼	33½	+ 16⅛
Filtrk s	.44	16	28219	20½	9½	15⅛	+ 5⅜
FinCpA		2	825127	17¼	6⅞	7½	− 2½
FinCp pf	.60	...	1736	10¾	5½	6½	+ ⅝
FinC pf	4.50e	...	13714	44¼	30	31½	− 5⅞
FnSBar		4	73145	17⅝	7¾	10¾	+ 1⅞
FireFd	.30	...	448641	44½	30⅝	35⅛	+ 4¼
Firestn	.80	13	433779	29½	21⅝	27⅞	+ 4
FtAtl pf	4.37e	...	6769	56¼	51¾	52⅛	− 2⅜
FtBkSy	2.00	8	259524	59¾	40⅞	52⅜	+ 10⅝
FtBkS s		...	264279	29⅞	20⅜	25	+ 4⅛
FBostn	1.00	9	294079	62¾	40	42⅛	− 1⅝
FCapHd		24	200440	17⅜	5½	14⅞	+ 8⅞
FstChic	1.32	6	460719	34⅞	18⅞	28⅝	− ⅞
FCh a pf	3.78e	...	30840	53	46	51	+ 3
FCh pfB	6.82e	...	15574	95	71¼	89¾	+ 20¾
FCh pfC	7.27e	...	5980	103	87⅛	100	+ 11⅜
FtBTex	.07j	...	164890	14	3	3⅜	− 9½
FBTx pf	4.09e	...	14140	38¼	15¼	17¾	− 18⅛
FBTx pf	3.71e	...	6403	35¼	14½	14½	− 18½
FtCity		6	17662	9½	4¼	6	− 1⅝
FFB s	1.68	9	68069	42½	28⅜	35	+ 4¼
FFid pf	7.70e	...	z79090	111½	103½	104⅝	− 6⅞
FFnFd n	.16	...	57866	9¾	6½	7	...
FIntste	2.66	7	243315	67⅜	50¾	52	− ⅞
FIntst pf	2.37	...	12525	38½	27	30	− 1⅞
FtMiss	.24	10	114755	8⅛	5¼	6⅜	− ⅞
FstPa		13	244835	9¾	6⅞	9	+ ⅜
FstPa pf	2.62	...	70792	34¼	27¾	29¼	− 3¼
FUnRl s	1.50	19	47972	26⅛	16¾	25	+ 7½
FtVaBk	1.00	10	47057	37½	25⅜	28⅜	+ 1⅝
FtWach	1.08	11	145282	46⅛	32⅜	36⅜	+ 2⅜
FtWisc s	.84	10	36546	33	20¼	24	+ 2⅛
FWisc pf	6.25	...	1862	60	54½	58	+ 1¾
FWisc pf	3.05e	...	685	106	99⅞	103¾	...
Fischb		...	12155	37	25	26⅛	− 1⅜
FishFd	.05e	...	14623	16⅝	10¼	14	+ ½
FltFnG	1.60	9	87860	56⅛	37¼	46½	+ 5⅞
FltF pf	3.15e	...	11209	52⅝	46	49⅛	− 1⅝
FleetEn	.52	17	309693	33½	20¾	25⅜	+ 1
Flemng	1.00	14	187689	44⅞	31	34⅝	− 4¼
Flexi pf	1.61	...	14847	15⅞	12⅝	15½	+ 2⅜
FlghtSf	.20	16	99695	30¼	19¾	22½	− 2½
FloatPt		...	221433	46	10½	11¼	− 24¼
FlaEC	.20a	17	10158	51¼	38½	46¼	+ 4⅞
FlaPrg	2.40	11	473268	47	30¼	39⅝	+ 8⅞
FlaStl	.80	9	50022	34⅛	17⅞	24⅛	+ 5½
FlwGen		...	51950	7¾	4½	4⅞	− 2¾
Flower	.54	20	74864	29	20	24⅛	+ ⅞
Fluor	.40	...	403395	19¼	11⅛	11½	− 4
FooteC	2.20	13	29069	67½	44	48¾	+ ¼
FordM s	2.60	5	f18403	63½	35¾	56¼	+ 17⅝
FtDear	1.36	...	13416	16⅛	13¼	15¼	+ 1¾
FtHowd	1.00	19	286307	60½	42⅞	46	− 3
FostWh	.44	19	155389	15	10⅝	13⅛	+ ⅜
FoxPhot	.68	32	40520	30⅛	12	30⅛	+ 16¼
Foxbro	.25e	...	66713	31⅞	22½	23¾	− 2¼
Franc n		...	75448	12⅛	8¾	11⅜	...
FrnkR s	.24	22	131328	35¾	31⅜	33⅛	+ 12⅜
FMEP	2.20	...	87090	18⅛	14	15⅛	− 1⅜
FMGC	.05e	47	82347	13⅝	6¾	10¾	− ¾
FMOG	.92e	2	69015	7⅞	4	4⅞	− 2½
FrptMc	2.00e	63	419122	21	14¼	18¼	+ ¼
FMRP n	2.40	...	54212	21½	17⅝	20⅛	...
Fruehf	.52j	24	530847	49⅞	24¼	40⅞	+ 15⅝
FruhfB		...	1216	4	3½	4	...
Frhf pfA	3.68	...	2150	21¾	21	21½	...
Fuqua s	.24	10	83411	25½	16⅞	22¾	+ 4⅛
—G—							
GAF s	.10	15	426782	44	23⅞	36¾	+ 7¼
GATX	1.50	17	173833	42	30	33⅝	− ⅜
GATX pf	2.50	...	404	52	42	44¾	+ 2¾
GATX pf	3.17e	...	841	50½	49	49½	− ⅞
GCA		...	208801	7⅝	2	2	− 5½
GEICO	1.08	12	31250	105½	77¾	98½	+ 11½
GEO		...	66608	4	1½	2⅛	− 1¼
GF Cp		...	8211	6½	3⅜	5¼	− ½
GTE	3.66	...	f13116	63⅞	45¼	58⅜	+ 12⅜
GTE pf	2.50	...	559	56¼	40¼	51⅝	+ 10½
GTE pf	2.00	...	6799	34½	26⅜	31	+ 4¼
GTE pf	2.48	...	10749	31½	24⅛	28⅞	+ 4
Gabeli n		...	66820	10⅛	8½	8⅝	...
GalHou		...	26832	4⅛	1	2¾	− ⅞
Gannett	1.84	22	361383	87⅛	59¼	72⅛	+ 10⅞
Ganet wi		...	28	37⅞	36	36½	+ 5⅞
Gap s	.50	23	215424	45⅞	15½	35¾	+ 20¼
Gearht	.20j	...	209460	8⅜	⅞	1⅞	− 5¾
Gelco	.42j	...	250166	25½	12¾	19	− ¾
Gelco pf		...	12932	16	15½	16	...
GemII C		...	64663	13	10⅜	12⅛	+ 1⅛
GemII I	1.33e	...	43072	14⅜	11¾	13⅝	+ 2

NEW YORK STOCK EXCHANGE COMPOSITE

		P-E Ratio	Sales 100s	High	Low	Last	Net Chg.
GnCorp	1.50b	16	202049	84½	64¾	74	+ 4⅞
GAInv	3.31e	...	31375	21	16⅝	18	- 1¼
GCinm	.60	13	195799	59	36⅝	44¼	+ 5⅝
GCin pf	.66	...	3246	57	36½	43⅜	+ 5
GnData		31	88981	14½	7½	8	− 3¾
GenDev		7	96341	25¼	14⅛	17½	+ 2
GnDev wt		...	19176	11¼	5⅛	8¼	+ 2⅝
GnDyn	1.00	8	309874	89¼	64¼	67¾	− 1
GenEl	2.52	16	f18962	88¾	66½	86	+ 13¼
GnHme		6	59678	15¼	5⅞	7¼	+ 1⅜
GHost s	.24	11	207069	25⅝	11¾	13¼	− 1¼
GnHous	.24	36	12256	13⅝	9⅝	10⅞	− ½
GnInst	.25	38	372119	24⅝	15¾	18¾	+ 1⅛
GnMill s	1.28	18	420757	47¼	28¼	43⅛	+ 12⅝
GMot	5.00e	6	f22135	88⅝	65⅞	66	− 4⅜
GMot pf	3.75	...	6517	54½	41½	53¾	+ 12
GMot pf	5.00	...	9049	72	54⅜	66½	+ 12
GM E	.40	12	385502	49⅝	24¾	24⅞	− 16
GM H	.45e	...	128705	49¼	32⅝	38⅝	+ ⅜
GNC	.16	...	38384	6¾	4¾	5¼	− ¼
GPU		9	527719	25	16½	22⅝	+ 5½
GenRe s	.88	21	461086	69½	49¼	55½	+ 5½
GnRefr		6	18815	17⅜	9¾	15	+ 3⅝
GnSignl	1.80	37	175972	54¼	39¼	44¼	− 2⅛
GTFI pf	1.25	...	3640	17¾	12⅝	16⅞	+ 4¼
GTFI pf	1.30	...	1925	18½	13	17½	+ 4½
GTFI pf	8.16	...	2474	104¼	81	103	+ 23¼
Gensco		...	87187	4¼	2⅜	3⅜	− ⅛
GnRad		...	145607	14¼	5⅛	7¼	− 5⅞
GenuPt	1.28a	19	170271	48⅜	35⅜	43⅛	+ 5
GaPac	1.00	17	960285	41¼	24¾	37	+ 10½
GaPc pf	2.24	...	17537	45¼	37	43½	+ 6½
GaP prB	2.24	...	2685	45¼	35¾	43⅞	+ 8⅛
GaPc prC	2.24	...	4310	45	35	43	+ 8½
GaPwr pf	2.30	...	4558	27⅜	24½	24⅞	...
GaPwr pf	2.47	...	3854	28¼	25¼	26¼	...
GaPw pf	1.91e	...	2506	24	20	21½	...
GaPw pf		...	13275	23¼	19½	21	...
GaPw pf	3.00	...	11106	30¼	23⅞	28¾	+ 2⅞
GaPw pf	2.05e	...	12907	26¼	22	23	− 2
GaPw pf	3.44	...	10071	30⅞	27¼	29¼	+ 1
GaPw pf	3.76	...	15548	33¼	27⅞	31⅛	+ 2
GaPw pr	2.56	...	10936	27¾	22¼	26¾	+ 4
GaPw pf	2.52	...	4400	27½	22	25⅝	+ 3½
GaPw pf	2.75	...	8904	28	25	26½	+ ¾
GaPw pr	7.80	...	5818	91	68	86½	+ 17¼
GaPw pr	7.72	...	z73740	86¾	66¼	83½	+ 16½
GerbPd	1.32	20	268523	57⅝	35¾	41⅜	− 1
GerbSc	.12	16	123585	24⅝	13⅛	17¼	− 3¼
GerFd n		...	42823	11⅛	8⅞	10⅛	...
Getty s	.16b	12	38919	33½	18¼	20⅞	− ¼
GIANT		10	46832	27	12⅜	23⅞	+ 10
GibrFn	.15e	4	465642	13⅝	9⅜	10¾	+ ⅛
Gillet s	1.36	17	f10379	68⅞	34⅜	49¼	+ 14½
GleasC		5	35601	27	15	18	+ 1⅛
Glenfed	.40	5	280960	27⅜	17¼	24¼	+ 6¾
GGCap n		...	2964	10⅜	9⅜	9¾	...
GGInc n	.25e	...	13754	12	10⅛	11⅜	...
vjGlbM	.12j	...	165617	1⅝	¾	1	− ⅜
vjGlM pf	1.75j	...	14231	5	2¼	2⅝	− 1½
GlbYld n	.41e	...	156375	10	8¼	8¾	...
GldNug		77	394063	16	9⅛	9¼	− 2⅜
GldN wt		...	110720	4	1⅛	1⅜	− ⅝
GldWF	.20	6	323558	46¾	30⅜	34⅞	+ 3⅞
Gdrich	1.56	...	203056	47⅞	32⅛	42⅝	+ 9¾
Gdrch pf	7.85	...	z85590	100	88	100	+ 13½
Gdrch pf	.97	...	z23960	12	9½	11	+ 1
Goodyr	1.60	11	f22541	50	29	41⅞	+ 10⅝
GordnJ	.52	16	17248	22½	16⅜	20	+ 2⅛
Gotchk n		123	29366	21⅝	13¾	19¾	...
Gould	.34j	...	659823	32¾	14¾	16¼	− 14⅜
Grace	2.80	16	731501	60¾	45¼	48⅜	+ ½
Graco	.60	10	49960	32	19¼	24⅞	+ 5⅛
Graingr	.72	15	97450	46½	37¼	43½	+ 5⅛
GtAFt s	.40	5	202224	24¾	13¾	17½	+ 2⅝
GtAtPc	.40	10	154472	27¾	19¼	23½	+ 1⅝
GNIrn	2.72e	7	9794	27	16	25⅝	+ 9⅜
GtNNk	1.72	29	263566	68¾	40¼	64½	+ 22⅝
GtWFin	1.20	7	757369	48¼	33⅛	46½	+ 11⅞
GMP	1.80	10	12303	30⅞	19⅜	27½	+ 7⅝
GrenT s		11	170205	29¼	16⅝	24	+ 6¾
Greyh	1.32	12	458691	38	27⅛	31	− 1⅜
Greyh pf	4.75	...	1094	57½	46½	57½	+ 10⅝
Grolier		11	382119	14	6	9⅝	+ 3⅛
GrowGp	.30b	18	44336	12¾	10	11⅝	+ ⅞
GthStk n		...	57871	10¾	8¾	9	...
GrubEl	.08a	...	107156	10¾	4⅞	5⅛	− 4⅝
Grumn	1.00	10	212839	33⅛	23	24½	− 7⅛
Grum pf	2.80	...	3752	28¾	26⅜	27⅝	+ ⅞
Gruntal	.16	8	49445	10¼	6⅜	6¾	...
Gulfrd s	.60	13	36385	29	21	24⅞	+ 3⅝
GlfWst	.90	16	495909	72½	47¾	63⅜	+ 13⅝
GlfW pf	5.75	...	201	77	68¾	75¾	+ 7
GulfRs		...	38607	15⅜	10¼	12	− 1⅞
GulfR pf	1.30	...	1143	21⅛	16½	17⅝	− ⅝
GlfStUt	.67j	4	f11289	15	7	7⅜	− 5⅝
GlfSU pf	4.40	...	z49410	44	34	36¼	− 5¾
GlfSU pf	4.52	...	z2580	43	34½	37	− 3
GlfSU pf	5.08	...	z19740	50½	38¼	40	− 7
GlfSU pf	5.59e	...	7954	53¼	27⅛	27½	− 23¾
GlfSU pr	3.85	...	16621	32½	22½	25⅛	− 6
GlfSU pr	4.40	...	17705	34⅞	25	26⅝	− 7¼
GlfSU pf	8.80	...	1984	93	67	72	− 19½
—H—							
HRE	2.28	14	21605	27½	23⅛	26¾	+ 2¼
HallFB	1.00j	...	188473	29¼	14¼	14¼	− 13
Halbtn	1.00	...	936741	28	17⅜	24⅜	− 3⅛
Halwd n	1.12	11	88066	22½	16¾	18¾	+ 1¼
HanJS	1.47a	...	19757	17⅝	15⅛	16⅞	+ 1⅛
HanJI	1.84a	...	14751	25⅜	21¼	23¾	+ 1⅜
Handlm	.56	16	128915	38	23	28½	− ⅜
HandH	.66	...	44566	24	16¾	19¾	+ 1⅜
Hanna	.40	24	48343	26⅜	15¾	19⅛	− 1⅛
Hanna pf	2.12	...	7346	26½	23½	26	...
Hanfrd	.50	16	20545	40½	24½	33¾	+ 7⅛
Hansn n		...	194926	15¾	13⅜	14½	...
HarBJ s	.40	14	216922	38¾	22⅛	27⅛	+ 2⅜
Harlnd	.68	24	47888	50⅞	34⅛	49¼	+ 14⅜
Harnish		...	304961	19¾	11½	14⅞	+ 2
Harn pfB	3.40	...	28575	29¾	26¼	28	+ 1¼
HrpRwe	.60	14	14129	26½	19⅛	20⅞	− 1½
Harris	.88	19	443261	36⅞	25½	29¾	+ 2½
HarGrp		...	116377	22½	12	21⅞	+ 6½
Harsco s	1.00	16	90587	28⅞	20⅞	25⅝	+ 2⅝
Hartfd pf	2.83e	...	8688	48	45	47⅛	...
Hrtmx s	.92	19	120129	32	23½	27	+ ¾
HattSe	1.80	14	4586	21	17⅛	20⅜	+ 2¾
HawEl	1.80	12	48492	35½	24½	31½	+ 6⅜
HayesA	.40	...	39234	14½	8⅛	12½	+ 2⅜
HazLab	.40	21	33349	23¾	13⅛	22½	+ 9
HltRhb n		...	2823	19⅞	18⅝	19⅜	...
HlthCP	2.30e	...	57175	31¼	20¼	29⅛	+ 8¼
HltUSA		...	79211	13½	5	13⅜	+ 3¾
Hecks	.09j	...	116371	17¼	10	10¾	− 3
HeclaM	.05j	...	159093	16¼	8¼	10⅞	− 2⅞
Heilmn	.52a	13	187548	30	19⅞	23¼	+ 3⅜
Heilig s	.28	80	55776	39¼	21⅜	29½	+ 6½
Heinz	1.00	18	532729	48¼	29¼	40½	+ 8⅛
Heinz pf	1.70	...	1963	206	144	182	+ 39½
HelneC	.15e	13	28486	38¼	20	28⅞	+ 5¾
HelmP	.36	74	123868	24½	16⅞	20¾	+ ½
Herculs	1.76	14	489937	60	37	50⅝	+ 11¼
HeritC	.04i	...	136016	28¼	19	25⅛	+ 4⅛
Hrshy s	.54	18	228006	30	15½	24⅝	+ 7½
Hesston		...	16312	6⅞	2⅝	3⅝	− 2⅜
Hestn pf		...	1414	10¼	6¾	8¾	− ⅝
HewlPk	.22	21	f15687	49⅝	35¾	41⅞	+ 5⅛
Hexcel	.60	18	30043	45⅞	28⅛	36½	+ 8¾
HiSher s	.44	9	26560	22⅞	16	17⅞	− ⅞
HiVolt	.17	15	32286	14⅝	11⅜	12¾	− ⅞
Hilnbrd	.56	20	45495	49⅝	25¼	46⅝	+ 19⅞
Hilton	1.80	17	125768	80¼	60½	67¼	+ 2⅜
Hitachi	.52e	32	181152	74	35½	69	+ 30¼
Holiday	1.12j	15	550513	81	54¼	70½	+ 11
HlidyA	1.70t	...	691	114¾	83½	104½	+ 16⅞
HollyS	1.00	36	15390	131¼	96¾	97½	− 33¼
HomeD		24	282967	21¾	10¾	17⅞	+ 5⅜
HmFSD	.20	5	216423	38⅝	24¾	26⅜	− ⅛
Hmstke	.20	52	309732	29⅝	20⅛	25⅜	+ 2¼
HmstF s	.40b	3	23869	23⅜	14¼	17¾	+ 3⅜
Honda	.61e	15	189869	88⅞	55	85¾	+ 26½
Honwell	2.00	12	663000	84¼	58¼	59⅛	− 15
HrznBn	1.36	14	33957	56½	36	51½	+ 13⅝
HrzBn pf	1.98e	...	2183	27	24½	25⅜	− 1⅛
Horizon		...	14200	6⅜	4⅜	4⅞	− 1⅛
HCA	.66	11	768918	43⅛	30	30⅜	− 5⅜
Hotlln s	2.00	...	41441	23¾	19⅞	22¼	+ 1¼
HougM s	.58	18	23261	33½	21	32¼	+ 9
HouFab	.48	17	47103	21⅛	13¼	13½	− 1¼
HousInt	1.86	11	402410	52½	39⅛	47¾	+ 5½
HoInt pf	2.37	...	231	114⅞	91	108½	+ 15½
HoInt pf	2.50	...	315	77¼	60¼	72	+ 10¼
HoInt pf	6.25	...	7526	110	82	103½	+ 19½

NEW YORK STOCK EXCHANGE COMPOSITE

Stock	Div.	P-E Ratio	Sales 100s	High	Low	Last	Net Chg.
HouInd	2.80	9	824852	37	27¼	34¾	+ 6¾
HouOR	.90e	...	12991	9	4	4⅛	− 3⅜
HowlCp	.28a	...	5566	16⅜	7⅞	8	− 6⅜
Huffy	.40	15	36860	15⅞	10⅝	11¾	+ ¼
HughTl	.08	...	332267	13⅜	6¾	8¾	− 4½
HughSp	.40	11	25077	30⅜	20⅝	22¼	− 1⅜
Human	.76	48	917073	33⅞	19⅛	19⅛	− 12⅛
HuntMf	.44	22	28238	36⅜	20½	22	− 1¾
HuttEF	.88	26	950011	54¼	32	38⅛	+ 3¼
Hydral	2.08	12	10767	44⅝	30⅜	37¾	+ 3⅜
—I—							
IC Ind s	.80	...	516605	30⅜	17¾	23	+ 3⅞
ICM	1.36e	13	23856	16¼	13¼	14⅝	− ⅛
ICN		...	799662	34	10¼	17¾	+ 4¼
IE Ind	1.98	13	121981	27¾	20	23⅜	+ 2⅝
INAIn	1.80	...	8617	20¾	18⅛	19	+ ¾
IPTim n	2.72e	11	57079	28⅜	22⅛	26¾	+ 4½
IRT s	1.28a	16	21631	19	15¾	16⅜	+ 3⅜
ITT Cp	1.00	22	f16434	59½	35⅜	53⅜	+ 15⅜
ITT pfH	4.00	...	349	109	70	101½	+ 29¾
ITT pfJ	4.00	...	612	101	68	92½	+ 22½
ITT pfK	4.00	...	16442	97½	70	92	+ 22
ITT pfO	5.00	...	7274	95	69⅝	90	+ 20
ITT pfN	2.25	...	2890	76⅞	49½	69	+ 17¼
ITT pfI	4.50	...	4226	100	71¼	94	+ 22⅛
IU Int	.60	...	213217	17⅞	12	14¾	+ ¼
IdahoP	1.80	13	134491	30⅞	22¾	26¼	+ 3¼
IdealB		...	131645	5¼	1⅛	2⅜	− 1¾
IllPowr	2.64	7	989317	32	23⅛	29⅜	+ 5½
IlPow pf	2.04	...	2012	25	18¼	22½	+ 4
IlPow pf	2.10	...	1086	26½	19	24½	+ 4½
IlPow pf	2.13	...	1420	26¾	18⅝	24⅛	+ 4⅜
IlPow pf	2.21	...	1075	27⅛	19	26¼	+ 6¼
IlPow pf	2.35	...	2069	28⅝	20½	26	+ 4
IlPow pf	4.12	...	4227	49½	4	46	+ 8
IlPow pf	3.78	...	5246	45½	33	43	+ 8½
IlPow pf		...	841	52	50	52	...
IlPow pf	3.64e	...	17631	52¼	46	48	− 2¼
IlPow pf	5.75	...	1336	59½	55	58¼	+ 2½
IlPow pf	3.04e	...	16084	46⅛	37	39	− 2
IlPow pf	5.83	...	919	58½	52¼	55	+ 2
IlPow pf	4.47	...	5786	51½	39	49⅛	+ 8⅛
IlPow pf	4.00	...	10684	48	35½	45⅝	+ 9
ITW	.72	32	100304	53½	31	51⅞	+ 16⅞
ImoDv n		...	496	16⅛	13⅜	13⅝	...
ImpCh	2.81e	12	447511	65⅝	42⅛	63	+ 19
ImplCp		11	191785	19⅜	7⅝	13¾	+ 3½
INCO	.20	...	667517	16⅞	10½	11¾	− 1½
IndiM pf	7.08	...	1451	88½	65	78	+ 12
IndiM pf	7.76	...	2354	94½	69¼	85⅛	+ 16⅝
IndiM pf	8.68	...	1520	102½	78½	97⅜	+ 20⅜
IndiM pf	12.00	...	z13540	107	99½	103	+ 1¾
IndiM pf	2.15	...	12342	25½	19½	23¾	+ 4⅜
IndiM pf	2.25	...	9154	26⅝	20⅜	24½	+ 4⅛
IndiM pf	3.63	...	2971	31⅝	27	28¾	− ⅜
IndiM pf	2.75	...	1322	29	25	27⅜	+ ⅜
IndiEn	2.12	11	11047	37½	26⅞	31⅜	+ 1⅞
IngerR	2.60	14	118062	68⅞	50⅞	55¾	+ 2¼
IngR pr	2.35	...	4003	45¾	34½	37	...
IngrTec	.54	18	10027	24	15½	23½	+ 5½
InldStl	.38j	...	198887	28⅜	14½	18⅞	− 3¾
InldSt pf	4.75	...	11417	55½	42½	49	+ 1⅞
Insilco	1.00b	14	129665	24¾	17½	19⅞	− ½
InspRs		...	139165	6⅝	4⅛	4¾	− ¼
IntgRsc		11	143705	40¼	16¼	21¾	− 3
IntgR pf	4.72e	...	1034	50	37¾	37¾	− 8½
IntgR pf	4.25	...	17685	51	34¼	38½	+ 2½
IntgR pf		...	8836	20¾	16¼	18	...
Intlog	1.62t	3	215415	18	5½	6⅝	− 3⅛
Intlog pf	1.50	...	6312	11½	9¾	9⅞	− ½
IntRFn		...	33667	16½	10⅞	12¾	+ ⅛
ItcpSe	2.10a	...	15839	24½	20	23⅛	+ 2⅞
Interco s	1.60	12	120742	47¾	33½	36⅞	+ 1½
Inter pf	7.75	...	2153	203	149¼	165⅛	+ 13⅝
Intrfst	.18j	...	480261	10⅝	4⅜	4⅝	− 5¾
Intlk s	1.30	15	38039	41¾	21½	38⅝	+ 15⅝
Intmed		28	110607	16½	6⅜	15⅜	+ 5⅞
IntAlu	.72	15	16827	24¾	17¼	19¼	− 1¾
IBM	4.40	12	f40760	161⅞	119¼	120	− 35½
IntCtrl	.50	51	26530	36¾	22⅞	23½	− 7¾
IntFlav	1.24	17	192763	48⅞	34½	37¼	− 2¾
IntMin	1.00	...	237806	36¼	25	26½	− 8¼
IntMn pf	4.00	...	367	46	36½	45	+ 7¾
IntM pfA	3.75	...	22258	50⅞	45½	46¾	...
InMult s	1.18	16	62259	31⅝	22½	24¼	− 2¼
IntPapr	2.40	16	848504	80⅛	48⅜	75⅛	+ 24⅜
IntRc s		...	82517	11½	5¼	5⅞	− 2¾
IT Crp s		24	180233	27⅜	13¼	16	+ 1⅝
IntpbG s	.60	16	71273	30½	21	27⅜	+ 6
IntBkr s		11	26522	25⅝	16⅛	23⅞	+ 7¼
IntstPw	1.96	12	32527	31⅝	21⅛	26⅜	+ 4¼
InPw pf	2.28	...	1043	27½	21½	26½	+ 4⅞
IntSec	.40	9	27594	15¾	11	11¾	+ ½
IowIIG	2.90	12	58905	46¾	34½	44⅜	+ 8½
IowIll pf	2.31	...	6541	27½	22⅜	25½	+ 2
IowaR s	1.64	13	59476	27½	17¼	24¾	+ 6¾
Ipalco s	1.52	12	155800	29½	18½	24⅛	− 5⅜
IpcoCp	.36	150	52066	16	10	12	− 1⅞
IrvBnk	2.08	7	171900	59¼	41	45⅞	+ 1¾
IrvBk pf	3.40e	...	15470	54	49	51½	− ⅛
Italy n		...	98623	17⅞	9	9⅞	...
—J—							
JP Ind s		15	74320	20¼	13½	15¾	+ 1⅜
JWP s		18	121468	27½	10⅛	17⅜	+ 5¼
JWT	1.12	14	76553	41½	24⅝	29¾	− ¾
JRiver s	.40	20	558413	35	22	33⅞	+ 7½
JRvr pf	3.37	...	5602	56¾	51	56	...
Jamswy	.12	15	92503	31	19	22⅝	+ 1½
JapnF	4.69e	...	120970	15⅞	10¼	14¾	+ 3⅛
JeffP s	1.12	13	148329	40½	30¾	33⅞	+ ¾
JerC pf	4.00	...	z41220	45½	35	44	+ 7
JerC pf	9.36	...	1327	104¾	82½	103	+ 18¼
JerC pf	8.12	...	1186	97	72	90½	+ 16¾
JerC pf	8.00	...	2075	95½	71½	92	+ 19
JerC pf	7.88	...	1562	95	70¼	92	+ 20
JerC pf	2.18	...	25271	26⅛	19½	25⅝	+ 5⅜
Jewlcr s		4	14490	20¼	9½	10¼	− 2
JohnJn	1.40	33	f15912	74¼	45¾	65⅝	+ 13
JohnCn	2.12	12	118572	72	47¾	57¼	+ 8¼
JhnC pf	4.25	...	13798	73	59	66	+ 6¼
JhnCR n	1.70	...	7421	15½	9¾	12¼	...
JhCR wt		...	561	15/16	⅜	9/16	...
Jorgen	1.00	25	11206	27½	21½	22¾	− 3⅝
Jostn s		19	69539	20¼	12¾	18	+ 3⅝
JoyMfg	1.40	...	238602	34⅞	19⅝	34¾	+ 11
—K—							
KDI	.30	13	79934	19⅛	10¼	13⅝	+ 2¾
KLM	.69e	12	260711	23⅞	17½	18⅛	− ⅝
K mart	1.48	19	f17059	57⅜	33⅝	43⅞	+ 8½
KN En n	1.48	94	106840	24¼	15⅝	20¾	+ 4⅝
KaisrAl	.15j	...	399898	23¼	12½	13⅞	− 3⅛
KaiAl pf	4.12	...	58	81	55	64	− 1
Kai 57pf	4.75	...	52	91	65	72½	+ 8
Kai 59pf	4.75	...	87	91	53½	53½	− 9
Kai 66pf	4.75	...	26	77	65	71¾	+ 7¾
KaisCe	.20	53	64018	27⅜	13¼	26½	+ 11¼
KaiC pr	1.37	...	7197	25⅞	14½	25½	+ 8½
KanbE n	2.40	...	19547	13	5⅜	6½	...
Kaneb	.14j	...	235115	7⅜	2⅛	2¼	− 4⅞
Kaneb pf	6.40j	...	z80650	102	30	30	− 70½
KCtyPL	2.00	8	228584	32¼	22⅛	28	+ 5⅜
KCPL pf	3.80	...	z28380	43	32½	42	+ 9½
KCPL pf	4.35	...	z82260	50½	38	49¾	+ 11¼
KCPL pf	4.50	...	z45449	52½	40	50⅛	+ 8⅝
KCPL pf	2.20	...	2740	26¼	19⅝	25	+ 5⅜
KCPL pf	2.33	...	2822	27⅞	20⅝	26¼	+ 5⅞
KCSou	1.08	394	82620	64⅞	46½	47¼	− 1
KCSo pf	1.00	...	z71700	17	11¼	15½	+ 3½
KanGE	1.36	17	377485	23½	14	22⅞	+ 8¾
KanPLt	3.16	11	98089	65	39⅝	54⅜	+ 14⅝
KaPL pf	2.32	...	4920	29⅞	24	28½	+ 4⅛
KaPL pf	2.23	...	5160	29	22	27½	+ 5
KatyIn		...	40627	20½	12⅞	13⅜	− 2½
Katy pf	1.46	...	544	51⅞	34	35¼	− 6⅝
KauBH n	.05e	...	15872	13⅝	9	10⅞	...
KaufB s	.33	12	223250	25⅞	10½	18	+ 6¾
Kauf pf	1.50	...	5159	29⅛	16¼	22¾	+ 6
Kauf pf	8.75	...	10476	139	84	105½	+ 21¼
Kellog s	1.08	21	439664	58¾	32⅜	51¾	+ 17
Kelwd s		12	71323	24⅜	22¾	23⅝	+ 7⅜
Kenmt	1.00	45	49565	26¾	20	24	+ 1¾
KPToy		...	154290	24	15⅛	18⅜	+ 2⅝
KyUtil	2.52	14	119797	48⅛	30	41⅜	+ 10¾
KerrGl	.44	...	16353	17½	11	12⅞	+ ⅞
KerG pf	1.70	...	2670	25½	19⅞	21⅛	+ ½
KerrMc	1.10	...	320931	33⅞	23½	28⅛	− 5⅞
Keycp s	1.00	8	52157	30⅝	21	22⅛	− 3⅜
KeysCo		...	3871	9¾	3⅛	7⅛	+ 3½
KeyInt	.48b	20	100573	19⅝	11⅜	14¾	− 1
Kidde	1.20	27	109058	38½	28⅜	31¼	− 3½

NEW YORK STOCK EXCHANGE COMPOSITE

		P-E Ratio	Sales 100s	High	Low	Last	Net Chg.
Kid prB	4.00	...	159	88	70	73¾	− 2⅜
Kid pfC	4.00	...	192	87	69	70¼	− 8⅛
Kidde pf	1.64	...	158	58	45	47	− 4⅝
KimbCl	2.48	14	224520	92⅝	63⅜	79⅞	+ 12⅞
KngWd s		22	157618	19¼	10⅛	14	+ 3¾
Klnwrt n		...	7592	10¼	9¾	10⅛	...
KnghtRd	1.00	20	251960	57⅞	37½	46⅞	+ 7
Knogo		17	73016	29⅝	19	22½	+ 1¾
Koger	2.60	55	47619	34	25¼	31⅞	+ 5⅞
Kolmor	.32	...	56668	19¼	12¼	12⅞	− 1½
Kopers	.80	...	279659	30½	20	29⅜	+ 8⅜
Kopr pf	4.00	...	z39930	51	36½	51	+ 15¾
Korea	.44e	...	110189	39¾	16½	34	+ 16⅜
Kraft		...	f11379	65⅞	38⅞	47⅜	+ 7½
Kroger s	1.05	15	439863	35	21⅜	29⅞	+ 6
Kubota	.52e	84	806	55	32½	44½	+ 8
Kuhlm	.40	177	21074	21⅞	12	12⅜	− 7⅝
Kyocer	.53e	...	15191	58¼	39⅝	50½	+ 4½
Kysor	.88	10	22487	27	19½	24¾	+ 2⅝
—L—							
LAC n	.30	...	166563	29⅞	12½	19¾	− 6¼
LN Ho	2.26e	12	16531	34⅜	17	26½	− 5
LLE Ry	1.44e	...	125487	11¾	7⅜	8¾	− 1½
LLCCp		3	186883	4⅞	1⅝	3⅝	+ 1⅜
vjLTV		...	f13208	9⅞	1⅜	1⅝	− 5⅛
vjLTVA		...	1139	14½	2⅛	2½	− 7
vjLTV pf		...	666	46	10¼	10¼	− 25¾
vjLTV pfB		...	41893	18¼	2⅞	3	− 9¾
LTV pfC		...	13118	53¾	7⅞	8¾	− 30¼
LTV pfD		...	32998	14	1⅞	2⅜	− 7⅞
LVI Gp		...	138429	5⅜	2⅛	3½	+ 1
LQuint		144	148830	16¾	11¼	11½	− ⅞
LQuMt n		...	12024	19⅞	17⅝	17¾	...
LaclGs	2.10	10	14396	39¾	28	36	+ 6⅛
Lafarge	.20	16	42062	12⅛	8	9⅜	+ 1
Lafrg pf	2.44	...	10091	30½	25¼	26¾	+ 1¼
Lamaur	.24	18	26876	16½	9⅝	11⅜	+ 1½
LamSes		...	24945	5	2⅝	4½	+ ⅝
Lawtlnt	.56	29	73947	17⅜	11½	16⅛	+ 3½
LearPt	.05j	...	155441	10¾	4⅛	4¾	− 5⅝
LearP pf	.72j	...	20610	22	8¼	9¼	− 10½
LearSg	2.00	28	383893	92	47¾	91⅛	+ 42⅝
LearS pf	2.25	...	751	230	121¼	226⅝	+ 104
LeaRnl s	.40	16	15944	16½	12⅝	14½	+ ⅞
LswyTr	1.50	18	79886	50⅛	33¼	48¼	+ 14½
LeeEnt	.60	19	42220	27⅝	20½	23⅞	+ 1½
LegMa s		14	42042	25⅜	16	21¼	+ 4¾
LegPlt s	.40	13	61502	36⅜	20⅝	25¾	+ 3⅝
Lehmn	3.60e	...	91270	17½	14¼	15	− 1
Lennar	.20	15	52152	21⅝	12½	18½	+ 5⅞
LeslFy n		...	51451	17⅞	10⅝	11¾	...
LeucNt		7	28403	39¼	22	34	+ 10¾
Leucd pf	4.67e	...	29	52	50	51	− 1
LibAS n		...	34365	10¼	8⅞	9⅝	...
LibtyCp	.72	11	16400	45⅜	32⅞	36¾	+ 2⅝
Lilly s	2.00	19	747454	83½	50⅝	74¼	+ 18½
Lilly wt		...	465143	29¼	8	19⅞	...
Limitd s	.16	30	787224	34½	20½	31¾	+ 11
LncNtC n		...	12321	17¼	14⅞	15¾	...
LincNtl	2.16	9	235811	62¾	45⅝	46⅜	− 3¾
LincN pf	3.00	...	147	249¼	187¼	188	− 12
LincPl	2.28	...	4176	27½	23¾	25¾	+ 1½
Litton		33	271022	92¼	71¾	74	− 9¾
Litton pf	2.00	...	584	32	23⅝	25¾	+ 1⅞
Lockhd	1.00	8	919882	60¼	43	50⅛	+ 1
Loctite	.88	18	54171	49¾	33¼	47½	+ 13½
Loews	1.00	9	514800	72⅜	53¾	58¼	+ 3¾
Logicon	.28	12	44065	41⅜	21⅞	24⅛	− 16⅞
LomFn s		13	312416	35¼	23¼	29¼	+ 4¾
LomMt	2.68e	12	67781	34	26	30¼	+ 4
LomM wt		...	57512	7	2⅝	3½	+ ⅞
LomasM	2.32	25	51861	27¾	20	26⅜	+ 6⅛
LnStar	1.90	18	118916	36¾	27⅜	32¾	+ 2¼
LoneS pf	5.37	...	10471	62	53¼	55⅞	− 2½
LILCo		3	913063	14⅝	8	10⅛	+ 2⅛
LIL pfB		...	z23190	45	30½	41	+ 11¼
LIL pfE		...	1021	43	27	36	+ 10½
LIL pfI		...	111	97½	64	73	+ 9½
LIL pfJ		...	1528	72¼	47½	63	+ 15¾
LIL pfK		...	1882	75	47½	67	+ 17½
LIL pfX		...	32218	29¾	21½	26¼	+ 4¼
LIL pfW		...	16025	30	22	27⅜	+ 5⅜
LIL pfV		...	23342	30⅛	21⅜	26½	+ 4⅝
LIL pfU		...	16211	33⅝	25⅛	29¼	+ 4¼
LIL pfT		...	21880	28⅛	20⅛	25	+ 4¾
LIL pfS		...	2144	87½	64½	84	+ 18¾
LIL pfP		...	7901	23⅜	14⅞	21¼	+ 6¼
LIL pfO		...	6628	23⅞	18	23½	+ 5¼
LongDr	.76	18	110335	38¾	26⅝	29½	− 1⅛
Loral	.60	17	210794	48¾	33⅞	38⅜	+ 1⅞
LaGenl	.62	20	12125	15	10½	14	+ ⅜
LaLand	1.00	72	285398	32¾	23	27¼	− 3
LaPac	.80b	22	269072	33⅜	21	30⅝	+ 8⅜
LaP pfA	4.80	...	6420	36⅜	31⅜	34¼	+ 2¾
LaPL pf	3.16	...	18339	29¾	24¼	29	+ 4⅝
LouvGs	2.60	12	118562	44⅜	29	37⅜	+ 7⅜
Lowes	.40	18	375129	41½	22½	26	+ ⅛
Lubrzl	1.20	16	290134	35⅛	25⅝	31½	+ 3½
Lubys s	.44	22	51950	29	22½	26¼	− 1
LuckyS	1.16j	21	912661	37⅞	23¼	26⅝	+ 1⅝
LckSt wd		...	7826	28	25¾	26⅝	...
Lukens	.48	32	18095	16½	11⅝	14¾	+ 1¼
—M—							
MACOM	.24	...	500354	18⅝	11⅝	12⅝	− 2⅜
MAIBF		9	20877	14⅞	10⅛	11	...
MCA	.68	16	730076	56½	37⅞	38⅜	− 10⅞
MCorp	1.05j	...	264481	22⅝	9⅛	10⅛	− 10⅛
MCor pf	3.50	...	2121	43	35	36½	− 2
MDC n		...	10212	14⅞	14	14⅛	...
MDC	.40	6	248870	22½	11⅜	13¼	+ 1½
MDU s	1.42	11	40698	27⅞	19¼	23¼	+ 3⅞
MEI		...	119526	10	5	8⅝	...
MFM n		...	33326	10½	10	10⅜	...
MGMUA		31	46219	18¼	8	9½	...
ML CvC n		...	102006	9¾	6½	6⅞	− ¾
ML CvI n	1.35e	...	76050	14⅛	11	13⅜	+ 1½
Macmil	.60	17	167570	54¼	34	43	+ 5
Manhln	.20b	9	26271	19½	11½	12¼	− 3⅝
ManhNt	.16j	...	31171	14⅝	8	8⅛	− 3
ManrCr	.12	18	257519	25½	15¾	16⅝	− 1¼
Manpwr	.52t	23	169824	45	23¼	41⅜	+ 16½
MfrHan	3.28	5	447123	57¾	41⅛	45⅛	− 2
MfrH pf	4.46e	...	35492	55	50	51½	...
MfrH pf	4.24e	...	56641	52⅝	46	50⅞	+ 2⅛
vjManvl		1	455174	8⅞	1⅝	1⅞	− 4⅛
vjMnvl pf		...	37194	21¼	13½	19¼	+ 2⅜
MAPCO	1.00	14	156629	62⅛	36	59¼	+ 21¼
Marntz		...	56873	14⅞	3½	5¾	+ 2¼
Marcde		37	73284	2¼	⅜	1½	+ 15/16
MarMid	2.04	7	66101	56½	37½	45¼	+ 7⅝
MarM pf	3.28e	...	12367	52¾	47⅜	50½	− ½
Marion s	.28	48	356894	50	22⅜	37¾	+ 14⅞
MarkC	.32	26	17035	13½	9⅞	11½	− ½
Mark pf	1.20	...	3238	19¾	15½	17	− 1¼
Mariot s	.16	21	468858	39	20⅝	29	+ 7⅛
MrshM s	1.90	19	255905	76¾	40⅝	60¾	+ 20
Msrhln s		11	21517	13⅜	8¼	10	− ¾
MartM	1.00	10	422057	48½	32¼	38⅝	+ 3⅛
Masco s	.36	20	520796	34½	19½	29	+ 8⅞
MasCp	3.60	...	10605	45	30½	41¾	+ 11⅛
Maslnc	1.24e	...	20311	14¼	11¾	12	− ½
MatsuE	.54e	235	217346	135½	60	126¾	+ 62⅜
Mattel		25	506587	15½	7¾	8¼	− 4
MauLo n	.55e	...	22002	10⅞	9¾	10½	...
Maxam		...	79466	20¼	8⅜	8¾	− 2¼
MayDS s	1.04	15	834763	44⅛	30	35½	+ 4¼
Maytag	1.60a	17	339886	54⅞	36	47¼	+ 8⅜
McDr pf	2.20	...	11510	28½	20⅛	25⅞	+ 3⅝
McDr pf	2.60	...	32674	28	19⅞	26⅜	+ 3⅛
McDerl	1.80	4	667414	23⅜	13⅝	21¾	+ 3½
McDrl wt		...	77158	3⅞	1½	3⅛	+ ¼
McDld	.20	11	14342	14¾	9½	10	− 2½
McDnl s	.66	17	906594	76¾	48⅝	60⅞	+ 7
McDnD	2.08	10	227429	91⅛	71	71¼	− 3
McGrH	1.52	18	298860	64	46½	54⅝	+ 6⅝
McInt g		8	3024	33⅜	25⅛	27¼	− 1⅜
McKes s	1.28	15	135024	35¼	24¾	31¾	+ 5⅝
McK pf	1.80	...	233	108¾	80½	104	+ 19
vjMcLe		...	63809	9¾	45/64	1⅜	− 8¼
McLea wt		...	70178	3⅛	3/32	5/32	− 2 3/32
Mead	1.20	19	204160	60⅞	42½	54⅝	+ 10¼
Mesrux	.36	19	108405	42¾	25⅞	42½	+ 14¼
Medtrn	.88	18	150256	92½	42⅞	76⅞	+ 33⅜
Mellon	2.76	8	219463	72½	51⅞	55⅜	+ 3¼
Mellon pf	2.80	...	8384	32¾	28⅛	29¼	+ ¼
Mellon pf	1.69	...	9065	28½	23⅜	24½	...
Melvill	1.56	13	248897	73¾	49¼	54	+ 3½
MercSt	1.50	13	34930	117	72¾	95¾	+ 17⅝
Merck s	2.20	27	811403	129½	67⅛	123⅞	+ 55⅜
MercSL	.40b	4	34057	17	10¼	10⅝	− ⅛
Merdth s		12	35865	41⅜	29¼	32¾	− 1
MerLyn	.80	11	f18728	43¾	32⅜	36½	+ 2⅛

NEW YORK STOCK EXCHANGE COMPOSITE

		P-E Ratio	Sales 100s	High	Low	Last	Net Chg.
MesaLP	2.00	...	742624	18¼	12¼	16⅞	+ 4¼
MesLP pf	1.50	...	458223	15⅞	11⅝	15⅝	...
MesaOf		...	371868	2¼	1	1⅛	− 1
MesaPt		2	600810	3⅞	2¼	3¾	+ 1
MesaR	1.17e	...	7045	38	28¼	37⅝	+ 6⅜
Mesab	.10e	...	63719	6¾	1	1¼	− 4⅝
Mestek		...	9219	7½	4¼	7½	+ 3⅝
MtE pfC	3.90	...	z14800	45	34	42½	+ 8¼
MtE pfF	8.12	...	1150	98½	73¼	92	+ 19
MtE pfG	7.68	...	2484	93	67	87½	+ 20½
MtE pfJ	8.32	...	1177	100½	72⅜	95¼	+ 21¼
MtE pfI	8.12	...	2573	98	72¼	89½	+ 17¼
MtE pfH	8.32	...	1890	99⅝	72½	92	+ 19
MetrF s	.44	3	33878	20⅜	11¼	12⅜	+ ⅝
MexFd	.26e	...	112672	3⅝	2	3⅝	+ 1½
MhCn pf	2.05	...	9923	26½	22⅞	25¾	+ 2¾
MchER	1.44	58	10536	27⅞	18⅛	25	+ 5⅜
Micklby	.06	...	9761	6¼	3⅜	3⅞	− ⅝
MidSUt		7	f15045	15	10½	13⅛	+ 2½
MWE s	1.48	14	53343	26	19½	22⅜	+ 6⅜
MiltnR	.44	59	13583	15⅜	9½	10⅝	− 2½
MMM	3.60	17	761834	118⅞	86	116⅝	+ 26⅞
MinPL s	1.52	11	92984	34⅞	19⅛	29⅝	+ 9⅞
Mitel		1	156954	6¾	4⅛	4⅜	− 1⅞
Mobil	2.20	10	f26265	40⅞	26¼	40⅛	+ 9⅞
MoblHo		...	57753	3⅜	½	1¼	+ ¾
Mohsc s	.36	18	59119	31¾	20¼	25⅝	+ 5¼
MohkDt		...	131123	3½	1⅞	2⅞	+ ⅜
MonCa	1.05j	9	51148	79½	53½	66¼	+ 11
MonCa pf	3.00	...	4862	64	52⅜	55½	+ 3
Monrch	.80	33	13357	19⅞	12⅞	15	− 1⅞
Monsan	2.60	174	681657	81½	44¾	76½	+ 28¾
MonPw	2.68	7	289312	43⅜	31⅜	38½	+ 6⅛
MonSt	1.80a	...	16819	23½	19	21⅞	+ 1⅛
MONY	.88	16	34859	11½	8¾	10⅝	+ 1¾
Moore	.72	14	52337	27⅝	18⅝	20⅝	+ ⅜
MoorM	.52	...	64554	28¼	14½	20½	− 5⅛
MorM pf	2.50	...	9908	32½	24¼	25½	− 2½
Morgan	2.72	9	871268	96	59	82½	+ 18⅜
Morgn wi		...	517	48	29½	41⅞	+ 9⅞
Morgn pf	5.02e	...	21067	91¾	83	87½	+ 2½
MorKeg s	.20	11	16817	16⅝	10⅛	12⅝	+ 2⅜
MorgS n	.35e	8	123024	82	61⅜	64⅞	...
MorKnd	1.48	11	78137	52¼	39¼	42¼	− 5
MorseS	.80	19	33609	33½	23	31	+ 5⅞
MtgRty	2.13e	11	64094	23⅜	17¾	22½	+ 4⅝
Morton	.76	13	517922	42½	30	37⅛	+ ⅜
Motel6 n		...	27359	13⅝	12¾	13⅛	...
Motorla	.64	25	f13036	50	33⅝	35⅝	− 3¼
Munfrd	.54	19	19207	24⅝	16⅝	18⅛	− ⅞
Munsg s		11	42532	18⅞	11	11⅜	− ¼
MurpO	1.00	28	164079	31⅞	20⅜	25	− 4½
MurryO	.60	16	13805	26¼	19⅛	20⅛	− 2⅝
MutOm	1.44	...	14236	17½	14⅛	16⅝	+ 1¼
MyerL		...	43458	8¼	2⅛	5⅜	+ 3
Mylan s		17	474184	18	10	11⅛	− 1⅛

—N—

		P-E Ratio	Sales 100s	High	Low	Last	Net Chg.
NAFCO	1.00b	25	23059	28¼	15½	17⅞	+ 1
NBD s	1.20	8	114571	37½	27⅛	29⅛	+ 2½
NBI		...	106061	14¼	7½	8⅞	− 4
NCH	.72	15	19778	33½	24½	29⅝	+ 3⅝
NCNB s	.84	9	284849	27¾	20	21½	− 1⅛
NCR	.92	13	958731	57	38⅝	44⅛	+ 3⅞
NL Ind n	.07i	...	150210	6⅝	3⅜	5	...
NL Ind pf		...	209253	13	10¼	11⅝	...
NUI	2.32	...	4712	36	28⅞	30¾	− 5
NWA	.90	25	458830	62⅞	41½	61	+ 15
Nacco s	.50	7	21692	29¾	20½	26⅜	+ 3⅛
Nalco	1.20	12	233873	31¼	23½	27⅜	+ ⅝
Nashu s	.05i	10	86688	28⅛	15	23⅜	+ 7¾
NtlCnv	.36	54	231407	13½	7¾	9⅛	− 1¼
NatDist	2.20	29	196249	47¾	30	42⅝	+ 7⅜
NDist pf	4.25	...	z940	89½	83	89½	+ 4
NDist pf	2.25	...	125	41	35½	39½	+ 3⅝
NDist pr	1.85	...	29039	22¾	20	22¼	+ 2¼
NatEdu s		20	96800	23⅜	12⅜	17¾	+ 3½
NtEnt		61	61574	9	3⅝	4¼	− ¼
NatFGs	2.28	11	19397	41½	28⅝	38⅞	+ 10⅛
NII	.25	...	153239	28½	13	14	− 13⅜
NII pf	5.00	...	10772	59½	47	50	− 7¼
NMedE	.60	21	823579	26¾	19¼	22½	+ ⅛
NMineS		...	7121	8¼	2⅞	3⅜	− 3½
NtPrest	1.14	15	20580	37⅛	27¼	35⅛	+ 5⅜
NtSemi		...	f11879	15⅝	8½	10⅝	− 2
NtSem pf	4.00	...	23379	65¼	45	52½	− 2¼
NtSvl s	.96	15	94043	39⅞	28⅞	33⅜	+ 4½
NStand	.40	24	12869	15	11½	12	− 1⅝
NtWst n		...	43198	24⅜	20⅞	24¼	...
Navistr		...	f21718	11⅝	4¾	4¾	− 3¾
Nav wtA		...	148027	7¾	2⅛	2½	− 2⅝
Nav wtB		...	115336	5⅝	1	1⅛	− 1½
Nav wtC		...	15465	3¾	1¼	1⅜	...
Nav pfC		...	15790	77	47⅞	76¾	+ 25
Nav pfD		...	22260	36¾	15	15	− 10⅞
Nerco	.64	11	20027	13¾	9⅛	11⅞	+ ⅛
NevPw s	1.44	13	71721	25⅜	16	20¼	+ 3½
NevP pf	1.60	...	2929	20½	15⅛	19⅛	+ 3⅛
NevP pf	1.74	...	z49570	23	17¾	20	+ 1¼
NevP pf	1.95	...	2361	22⅞	18¼	21⅝	+ 2⅞
NevSvL	.60	7	44302	25½	12¾	24⅞	+ 11⅞
NEngE s	2.00	9	331308	35¼	24⅜	28	+ 3
NJRsc	2.32	21	8839	33⅞	25⅝	29½	+ 3⅞
NPlnR s	.80	18	40178	15¼	11	14	+ 3
NYSEG	2.64	8	463193	38½	27⅛	31⅜	+ 2¾
NYS pf	3.75	...	z87130	44	33¼	41	+ 6¾
NYS pf	8.80	...	z64590	97½	75½	93	+ 16
NYS pfA	2.02e	...	18359	28½	25⅛	25½	− 1⅛
NYS pf	2.12	...	3235	26	19⅜	23⅝	+ 3⅝
NYS pfD	3.75	...	3908	32⅛	26½	26⅞	− 3⅝
Newell	.84	13	68810	36¾	21	27	+ 4⅞
Nwhall s	.48a	16	50946	43¾	30⅞	31½	− ⅛
Newhll	8.00e	1	16869	20¼	8¾	9¼	− 7⅛
NwhlRs	.75e	10	5147	8⅞	5⅞	6¼	− 2
NwmtG n	.05e	59	67899	17⅝	8⅝	16⅝	...
NwmtM	1.00	34	213279	63⅜	41	61½	+ 14⅜
Nwpark		...	56931	1½	11/32	⅜	− ½
NewsL n	.11e	32	20279	48⅜	22¾	47	...
NiaMP	2.08	6	f11516	25½	15½	16¾	− 3¾
NiaMpf	3.40	...	z91840	38¼	30¾	34½	+ 3½
NiaMpf	3.60	...	1284	39½	31½	35⅛	+ 3⅝
NiaMpf	3.90	...	z98680	42½	33½	39	+ 3½
NiaMpf	4.10	...	z99720	47	36¾	41⅛	+ 4⅛
NiaMpf	4.85	...	2337	56⅛	43⅛	49½	+ 6⅜
NiaMpf	5.25	...	1632	61	46½	53⅛	+ 8⅛
NiaMpf	6.10	...	3291	72	55½	62	+ 4¾
NiaM pf	2.42e	...	22644	28⅜	23½	23½	− 3¾
NiaM pf	1.92e	...	12777	26½	19	19	− 6
NiMpf	10.60	...	z31180	107¼	98	101¼	− 2¾
NiaMpf	7.72	...	2509	89	71	78⅛	+ 8⅝
NiagSh	3.21e	...	22566	16⅞	14⅛	14¾	− 1⅝
Nicolet	.12	10	63064	22⅛	12¼	19½	+ 4
NICOR	1.80	...	196570	31½	21⅝	27⅜	+ 5¾
NICO pf	1.90	...	173	30¾	25¾	27½	+ 2
NoblAf	.12	...	229268	14	7⅞	11⅛	− 2⅜
NordR s		16	92000	25¼	8½	21¼	+ 12¾
NorfkSo	3.40	10	313217	99¼	73⅞	84½	+ 3¼
Norsk n	.65e	...	89827	23⅛	16⅞	19⅜	...
Norstr	1.40	10	92432	33	25	26½	− 2¼
Norstr pf	3.44e	...	15029	53½	44¼	49	− 1½
Nortek s	.10	7	133234	19⅛	10⅝	13	+ 1¾
NAPhil	1.00	25	68173	48	35⅛	41⅜	+ 4⅛
NEurO	2.42e	8	23965	21⅜	15⅛	20¼	+ 3¾
NoestUt	1.68	9	740733	28¼	17⅜	24¼	+ 6½
NIndPS		...	573946	13½	9⅜	11¾	+ 1⅞
NIPS pf	3.10e	...	12813	44½	33½	39	+ 4
NoStP s	1.90	11	302418	40⅛	25	34½	+ 8
NSPw pf	3.60	...	1219	49	35	45	+ 10
NSPw pf	4.08	...	z66220	57¼	39	54½	+ 15½
NSPw pf	4.10	...	z76980	58	40	55¾	+ 15½
NSPw pf	4.11	...	z70680	58¼	41½	55½	+ 14
NSP pf	4.16	...	z73060	60	43	59	+ 16
NSPw pf	4.56	...	5045	64⅝	45½	61¼	+ 16¼
NSPw pf	6.80	...	2140	95	68	90½	+ 23½
NSPw pf	7.84	...	7430	103¼	79	98¼	+ 20¼
NSPw pf	8.80	...	1119	105⅛	87½	103	+ 16
NSPw pf	7.00	...	4311	98¼	69	93¼	+ 21⅞
NorTel	.40	...	379660	38⅜	25¼	31⅝	− 3⅜
Nthgat g		...	46694	5⅛	3	4⅝	+ 1¼
Nortrp	1.20	32	376089	51⅝	36⅞	39¼	− 4⅞
NwCP pf	3.42e	...	2039	51	40	41¼	− 10
NwtP pf	2.50	...	1610	26¾	24	25⅝	+ 1⅜
NwtP pf	2.36	...	3738	26	22⅜	26	+ 3¾
NwStW		38	29122	21	13¼	18⅛	+ 4¾
Norton	2.00	...	161754	43	35	37	− 1⅝
Norwst	1.80	11	215382	41⅜	28	36⅜	+ 5⅛
Nwst pf	4.09e	...	13752	53½	50¼	51½	+ ⅝
Nwst pf	3.93e	...	5584	53⅛	51⅛	51⅞	+ ⅜
Novo	.34e	15	173885	35½	25⅞	32⅞	+ 3½
Nucor s	.32	11	145554	46⅛	29⅛	30½	− 5⅜
Nynex s	3.48	11	695961	73¼	46⅜	64⅛	+ 15¼

—O—

		P-E Ratio	Sales 100s	High	Low	Last	Net Chg.
OakInd		...	706663	2½	¾	⅞	− 1

NEW YORK STOCK EXCHANGE COMPOSITE

		P-E Ratio	Sales 100s	High	Low	Last	Net Chg.
OakiteP	1.52	15	4447	34	26⅞	27⅛	– 7⅛
Oakwd s		14	27323	19	11	14⅛	– 1⅞
OcciPet	2.50	28	f18696	31¼	22⅝	27½	– 3½
OcciP wt		...	17041	12¾	9	11⅝	– 1¼
OcciP pf	6.25	...	61076	58⅜	52⅝	56⅜	+ ⅞
Occi pf	14.00	...	z15330	124¼	115	120½	– ½
ODECO	.35j	...	170554	20¼	10⅝	12⅜	– 7½
Ogden	1.80	...	176310	48	27½	40	+ 6⅞
Ogdn pf	1.87	...	76	132¾	86	129	+ 34½
OhioEd	1.92	8	f15334	22½	15⅞	19½	+ 3⅛
OhEd pf	3.90	...	z35600	44	32¼	41	+ 8½
OhEd pf	4.40	...	z32640	46½	36	44	+ 7½
OhEd pf	4.44	...	z80120	48⅛	36	46¼	+ 10¾
OhEd pf	4.56	...	z49740	48½	36⅞	46⅛	+ 8⅝
OhEd pf	7.24	...	2272	77½	31	73	+ 14½
OhEd pf	7.36	...	2726	79	60	74½	+ 11⅝
OhEd pf	2.01e	...	10593	27½	21¼	23⅜	– 2⅞
OhEd pf	8.20	...	1923	85⅝	66	82	+ 15⅛
OhEd pf	2.16e	...	4450	44	35	42½	+ 6½
OhEd pf	3.50	...	7499	32¼	27⅝	31	+ 1⅝
OhEd pr	3.92	...	7544	34¾	30¾	33⅜	+ 1¾
OhEd pr	1.80	...	2592	22¼	16¼	19⅞	+ 3⅜
OhEd pf	9.12	...	4870	96¾	75¼	93½	+ 19½
OhEd pf	8.64	...	1627	89	69	86	+ 17
OhE pf	10.48	...	1444	105½	92½	101	+ 8½
OhE pf	10.76	...	z73900	106⅞	93½	105	+ 9
OhMatr	.40	25	74956	17⅜	11¼	16⅝	+ 4
OhP pf	8.04	...	z46810	91	71	89¼	+ 19¼
OhP pfB	7.60	...	4138	95	71	92¾	+ 19¾
OhP pfC	7.60	...	3857	94⅝	72¾	93¾	+ 21¼
OhP prH	3.75	...	2403	33¾	29⅜	30¼	– ¾
OhP pfG	2.27	...	34322	27⅜	21⅝	25¾	+ 3⅞
OhP pfA	14.00	...	z43580	118½	108	110½	+ 2
OhP pfF	14.00	...	z17740	118	107½	112	+ 3½
OhP pfE	8.48	...	2254	102	80	98¾	+ 17⅝
OhP pfD	7.76	...	4225	96¾	73	94	+ 20
OklaGE	2.18	13	276158	38¾	26⅛	34½	+ 7⅛
OklaG pf	.80	...	1069	12	8½	10	+ 1½
Olin	1.60	13	188809	53¼	34⅝	41	+ 3⅞
Omncre		40	64111	9	6⅝	7¼	– ⅛
Oneida	.40	37	33242	18⅝	9⅞	13⅝	– 2¼
ONEOK	2.56	14	93951	35¾	27¼	33½	+ 1⅝
OranRk	2.18	12	54856	40	26¼	34⅞	+ 6¾
Orange		...	41644	9½	6¼	8⅝	– ⅛
Orient		...	47544	4⅛	1½	1⅝	– 2½
OrionC	.76	...	61312	40¼	26⅜	27⅛	– 4⅝
OrionC pf	1.12	...	11666	34¼	25¾	25¾	– 4¼
OriC adj	3.95e	...	692	51	44¾	44¾	...
OrionP		...	283832	18⅛	10	12⅛	+ 1⅞
Orion pr	.50	...	10984	11½	7¾	9	+ 1
OutbdM	.64	32	175065	38½	23⅞	27	– 1
OvShip	.50	14	111212	30¼	17⅞	20⅛	+ ⅜
OwenC n		...	219402	13⅞	8⅞	13¾	...
OwnIll s	.95	17	578873	53	25¾	53	+ 26⅝
OwnIl pf	4.00	...	109	89	75	79¼	+ 4¼
OwnIl pr	4.75	...	117	315	155	313	+ 157
Oxford	.46	14	38532	18¾	13⅛	14	– 1¾

—P—

		P-E Ratio	Sales 100s	High	Low	Last	Net Chg.
PHH	1.04	15	140110	41	29⅛	31⅝	– 6¾
PPG	1.92	14	315620	77⅝	45	72⅞	+ 21⅞
PS Grp	.60	...	97729	38¼	25	35½	+ 9⅞
PacAS	1.54	...	11034	17½	14¼	16⅜	+ 1¾
PacGE	1.92	9	f16105	27½	18¾	24¼	+ 4¼
PacLtg	3.48	32	240893	57½	45	49	+ ½
PacRes		8	81458	17⅜	10⅜	14¾	+ 3⅝
PacRs pf	2.00	...	18003	26⅜	20¼	26	+ 5⅜
PacSci	.40	19	17581	17⅞	13	14	– ⅜
PacTel s	3.04	11	702104	62¼	38¾	53¼	+ 11
Pacifcp	2.40	11	428945	38	30⅛	35⅞	+ 4⅝
PainW s	.52	13	483680	39⅛	26	31½	+ 3½
PanAm		...	f15090	9½	4	4¼	– 3½
PanA wt		...	68569	3⅝	1⅛	1⅜	– 1⅛
Pandck n	.20	27	239348	26¾	13	25⅛	+ 6¼
PanEC n	2.00	...	259179	28⅛	24¼	27¾	...
Panill n		13	111810	28⅛	14⅜	16	...
Pansph	.24	15	81017	36	23⅝	25⅞	+ 1⅜
Pardyn		...	227203	11	3⅝	5	– 2
ParkEl	.12	16	15403	18⅞	13⅝	16	...
ParkDrl	.04	...	107637	5⅛	2⅞	3¼	– 1⅜
ParkH s	.80	13	184305	30½	20¼	25¾	+ ⅛
PatPtr		...	32477	4	2⅝	3	– ¼
Patten s	.98t	17	87013	20⅝	5⅛	16	+ 11
PayNP	.40	12	102295	19⅜	9½	11⅛	– 1¾
PayCsh	.16	16	383475	27½	14½	19⅛	+ 3⅜
PenCen	.05	24	266484	62½	50½	53¾	+ 3
Penney	2.48	12	623197	88⅜	52⅝	72¼	+ 16¾
PaPL	2.60	13	393141	43⅜	27⅝	36½	+ 7¾
PaPL pf	4.40	...	z64840	54½	39¾	53⅛	+ 13⅛
PaPL pf	4.50	...	z78190	53⅜	39½	50½	+ 10½
PaPL pf	8.60	...	z88970	100	77⅛	96½	+ 18¼
PaPL dpr	2.90	...	4347	30¼	26⅞	28½	+ 1½
PaPL pr	8.40	...	1339	98⅞	72½	93	+ 17½
PaPL pf	9.24	...	2690	107	99	105	+ 6½
PaPL pr	11.00	...	z99320	110½	99¼	104	+ 2
PaPL pr	8.00	...	2195	95	69	88½	+ 19½
PaPL pr	8.70	...	1659	99¾	75½	97¾	+ 22¼
Penwlt	2.20	19	52858	59	40¾	49¾	+ 7
Penw pr	2.50	...	155	87½	62½	75¾	+ 12¼
Penw pr	1.60	...	6380	34¾	24½	29¾	+ 4
Pennzol	2.20	65	457225	91	48⅛	67	+ 3
PeopEn	1.32	9	144562	23¾	18⅝	20¾	+ 1
PepBoy	.22	28	107532	48¼	25⅛	41⅞	+ 14⅞
PepsiC s	.64	16	f14956	35⅝	22	26	+ 1¾
PerkF n	.25e	...	16904	13⅛	10⅝	10¾	...
PerkEl	.60	17	426420	36⅞	23⅛	25½	– 5⅜
Prmian	.60e	6	204173	7⅞	5½	6⅛	– ¾
PeryDr	.22	21	69142	20⅞	12	12¼	– 4⅞
Petrie s	.70	16	225374	35¾	22⅛	26½	+ 2½
PetRs	4.34e	...	19126	31⅛	22¾	29	+ 2¼
PetRs pf	1.57	...	8518	20	16	18⅞	+ 2¼
PtrInv	.30j	...	24076	3	1	1⅜	– 1¼
Pfizer	1.64	15	f11760	72⅞	46¼	61	+ 10⅜
PhelpD		22	324197	32½	16	20¾	– 2¼
Phelp pr	5.00	...	27373	63	48¾	56¾	+ ½
PhilaEl	2.20	8	f17127	24⅛	16⅞	22⅝	+ 5¼
PhE pfA	3.80	...	z93400	43	30	39½	+ 8½
PhE pfB	4.30	...	z74830	49⅜	33¾	43⅛	+ 8⅛
PhE pfC	4.40	...	z45040	48	35½	44	+ 7½
PhE pfD	4.68	...	1011	51⅜	37	49	+ 12½
PhE pfE	7.00	...	1318	78	58	75¼	+ 16¼
PhE pfG	8.75	...	4222	95	68	88½	+ 20½
PhE pfS	9.50	...	1973	105	100½	104¾	...
PhE pfR	1.41	...	17484	13⅞	11¼	13	+ 1⅜
PhE pfQ	14.62	...	491	125	106¾	122¼	+ 12¼
PhE pfP	1.33	...	28615	13¼	10⅜	12¼	+ 1⅝
PhE pfH	7.85	...	4910	87⅛	32	80¾	+ 19¼
PhE pfO	1.28	...	31120	12⅞	10⅛	11¾	+ 1⅝
PhE pfN	17.12	...	2084	134¼	122½	127	+ 3
PhE pfM	15.25	...	1246	124	105⅛	115½	+ 2½
PhE pfL	9.52	...	z61200	103	84	98¼	+ 14¼
PhE pfK	9.50	...	3095	99	74	92½	+ 16½
PhE pfJ	7.80	...	3632	85¼	60½	81½	+ 19
PhE pfI	7.75	...	z37300	82	59	76	+ 15½
PhilSb s	.94	14	21698	19¼	12⅝	17⅜	+ 3¼
PhilMr s	3.00	12	f17418	78	43⅞	71⅞	+ 27¾
Philpl s	.36	13	100746	19	12⅜	14⅝	+ ¾
PhilIn pf	1.00	...	255	89¼	64¼	74¼	+ 8¼
PhilPet	.60	9	f22763	12¾	8¼	11¾	– ⅜
PhlPt pf	2.02e	...	94130	24¼	19¼	24	+ 1⅜
PhilVH	.40	14	49832	44¼	31½	40½	+ 9
Phlcrp n		...	3746	13½	9	9½	...
PiedAv	.32	12	217727	50⅝	31½	45½	+ 11¾
PiedA pf		...	24588	62½	49½	58½	...
PieNG s	1.20	15	25612	23¼	17	22⅝	+ 4⅜
Pier 1 s		22	79705	22⅜	12	16⅜	+ 3½
PierI wi		...	3	16¾	8¼	13⅜	+ 3¾
PilgRg n	.17e	...	85160	11½	7½	7⅞	...
PilgPr n		...	17853	12¼	9¼	10⅛	...
Pilsby s		14	362287	41⅛	29⅛	33⅞	+ 3⅛
PionrEl	.13e	...	12917	33½	16	32	+ 14¼
PitnyB s	.66	18	215882	38¼	22¾	36⅝	+ 12⅜
PitnB pf	2.12	...	5671	150	93	145½	+ 51
Pittstn		53	268835	15⅞	10½	11¾	– ⅝
Plains n		60	54126	26⅞	15	23⅞	+ 7⅝
Plantrn	.16	14	32666	19½	14	15¾	+ 1½
Playboy		...	26835	10	5⅞	8¾	– ½
Plesey	.91e	14	5314	37¾	21¾	27	+ ¼
PogoPd	.20	...	133845	11¾	4¼	5¾	– 5⅛
Polarid	1.00	23	621877	74¾	42¼	66½	+ 23¼
Pondrs	.40b	23	241423	29	12¼	28¾	+ 15¾
PopTal	.80b	17	34095	25⅜	17¼	23	+ 3⅞
Portec	.60	13	10682	21½	14¼	14¼	– 4
Portr pr	5.50	...	z10220	88	80	88	+ 5½
PortGC	1.96	10	384506	36¾	21⅞	29	+ 7
PorG pf	2.60	...	3057	29⅝	24¾	28¾	+ 3⅜
PorG pf	4.40	...	13086	35⅞	32⅛	32¾	– ⅜
PorG pf	4.32	...	7167	35	31⅜	32	– 2
Potltch	1.68	15	60668	61	35½	57½	+ 19¾
Potlth pf	6.19e	...	z10600	108⅞	107½	108	+ 3
Potlt pf	3.75	...	7362	66¼	54	64	...
PotmEl	2.36	12	220452	59¼	33¾	48⅝	+ 14
PotEl pf	2.44	...	73	173½	99¼	149	+ 51
PotEl pf	4.04	...	4902	54	42	52½	+ 9½

NEW YORK STOCK EXCHANGE COMPOSITE

		P-E Ratio	Sales 100s	High	Low	Last	Net Chg.
PotEl pf	4.23	...	5818	59	48¾	58¼	+ 10⅛
Premk n	.05e	...	100231	21½	17½	19⅝	...
Premln	.44	20	28195	35½	25¼	29	...
Primrk	1.30	9	77521	29	22½	24¾	+ ¾
PrimeC		16	795937	28	15⅝	16⅜	− 5¼
PrimM s	.08	26	252920	45⅜	24½	37¼	+ 6⅛
PrmMLt n		...	6981	20⅞	20	20⅞	...
ProctG	2.70	18	770305	82½	63¾	76⅜	+ 6⅝
PrdRs	.28	21	60183	19⅛	13⅞	16¼	− ⅜
Proler	1.40	...	6032	43	27	33⅞	− 8¾
PruRtC		...	24401	2	1⅛	1⅛	− ⅝
PruRl	.68e	...	24908	8⅜	7⅜	7¾	+ ⅛
PSvCol	2.00	13	541411	22⅜	16	18¾	− 2⅜
PSCol pf	7.15	...	2129	90⅞	66¼	78⅞	+ 10⅞
PSCol pf	2.10	...	11333	26	21	23⅜	+ 2⅜
PSInd		7	923048	18⅝	7¼	14¾	+ 7½
PSIn pfA		...	z98650	42	20¾	37¾	+ 13½
PSIn pfB		...	5025	13¼	6⅞	12¼	+ 4⅜
PSIn pfC		...	7356	14	6⅝	12¼	+ 4¾
PSIn pfD		...	4183	85	43⅛	81	+ 35⅛
PSIn pfE		...	3310	104½	54	101¾	+ 41
PSIn pfF		...	4247	97	50	95½	+ 41
PSIn pfG		...	4677	96	50	94¼	+ 40¾
PSIn pfI		...	3017	102½	60¾	101½	+ 39¼
PSIn pfH		...	2343	98⅝	53	97½	+ 39½
PSvNH		4	277255	11⅜	7⅜	8⅜	...
PSNH pf		...	2320	25⅛	17	17½	− 2¾
PNH pfB		...	6489	25½	17	18⅜	− 3¼
PNH pfC		...	3722	33¼	24	25¼	− 2¼
PNH pfD		...	6003	31¼	21¾	22¾	− 1½
PNH pfE		...	8679	31¾	22	22¾	− 1⅞
PNH pfF		...	8365	27¾	18⅞	19⅝	− 2⅜
PNH pfG		...	11528	28⅞	19⅛	20⅝	− 2⅝
PSvNM	2.92	10	384219	37⅞	28	33	+ 3½
PSvEG	2.96	10	747486	48¼	30¾	40¼	+ 8⅝
PSEG pf	4.08	...	z89510	54⅜	39½	52⅛	+ 12¾
PSEG pf	4.18	...	1581	56	40⅜	52	+ 11⅝
PSEG pf	4.30	...	2982	58½	41½	54⅝	+ 13
PSEG pf	5.05	...	1927	69½	48½	64¼	+ 15¾
PSEG pf	5.28	...	1709	71	51	65	+ 14¾
PSEG pf	11.62	...	524	121	108½	120	+ 15¾
PSEG pf	12.80	...	938	124	110	112¾	+ 2¾
PSEG pf	8.16	...	2977	103	79	99½	+ 20½
PSEG pf	2.17	...	17810	26⅜	20¼	25⅛	+ 3¾
PSEG pf	6.80	...	3596	91¼	65¼	83	+ 17¼
PSEG pf	2.43	...	7881	27⅝	23½	26	+ 2⅛
PSEG pf	7.70	...	5615	101	74	94⅝	+ 21
PSEG pf	7.80	...	11627	101¼	75	96	+ 19
PSEG pf	8.08	...	z65790	93	73	90	+ 16
PSEG pf	7.52	...	4403	99	72	91	+ 18¾
PSEG pf	7.40	...	3503	98½	71⅝	90	+ 18½
PSEG pf	9.62	...	1417	105	92⅛	102⅜	+ 10¼
Publick		65	55847	3⅞	2⅜	3¼	+ ⅜
Pueblo	.20	12	30169	24⅜	15¾	19⅝	+ 1½
PR Cem	.10e	7	12942	20⅞	7½	17⅜	+ 9¼
PugetP	1.76	11	303237	25¼	17⅝	20⅞	+ 2½
PulmPe	.12	19	293715	10⅝	6⅞	7½	− ⅝
PulteHm	.12	16	207613	24	10½	12⅛	− 1⅝
Purolat	.64j	...	133947	28⅞	15	28⅝	+ 4⅞
Pyro		10	82567	8	4⅞	5⅛	− 1

—Q—

QMS		18	2702	16⅜	8⅛	14½	+ 5⅜
QuakO s		18	281003	44⅞	27⅜	40	+ 11⅜
QuakSO	.80a	12	133205	30	23	25	+ ¾
Quanex		...	57695	8	3	3¼	− 2⅞
Questar	1.80	15	67975	39⅛	25⅜	37¼	+ 5½
QkReil	.32a	12	60295	40¾	22½	26¾	− 5¾

—R—

RBInd	.04j	...	15846	10	5⅞	7¾	+ 1⅞
RJ Fin	.16	9	16271	20	11¼	12⅛	+ ⅞
RJR Nb	1.60	13	f17764	55⅛	31	49¼	+ 17⅞
RJR pf	11.50	...	18195	126¾	110⅜	121¼	+ 10⅝
RLC	.20	14	90826	11⅞	8¼	10⅛	+ 1⅛
RPC		...	27989	3⅝	1¾	2⅜	− 1⅛
RTE	.60	20	54919	29⅝	20⅛	29	+ 7¾
Radice		12	59443	17⅝	7¾	9¼	− 5⅜
RalsPur	1.10	21	465278	77	45½	70¾	+ 23¾
Ramad		24	519958	11	6	6⅝	− ⅞
Ranco	.84	21	26416	38⅞	18⅜	38¾	+ 17¾
RangrO		66	412605	5⅛	2⅝	4⅝	+ 1⅛
Raycm	.44	19	159290	140	66¼	88⅝	− 9⅜
Rayonr	2.60	...	43701	27¼	19	20¾	...
Raytch		...	17299	13⅞	4½	7	− 4½
Raythn	1.80	13	505784	71¾	52⅜	67¼	+ 13⅝

		P-E Ratio	Sales 100s	High	Low	Last	Net Chg.
ReadBt	.02j	...	200342	5½	1¼	1⅜	− 3¼
RdBat pf	1.06j	...	16637	14	4¾	5⅜	− 6⅞
RdBat pf	1.38j	...	7634	18	3	3¾	− 14¾
RltRef	1.40	9	2581	18¼	13¾	16	+ 2¼
RecnEq		17	136506	16½	10¼	15½	+ 2
Redmn	.32	15	76266	12⅝	6⅞	8¾	− ¾
Rebok s		10	f12802	35¼	8⅜	23⅜	+ 14⅛
Reece		49	6220	15⅛	9⅛	10¾	− 4
Regal		...	28689	1	5/16	13/32	− 11/32
ReglFn n		...	42101	9⅞	6⅞	7⅛	...
ReichC	.80	...	39525	38¼	28⅜	32½	− ⅝
RelGp n	.04e	...	159921	10⅝	7½	7⅞	...
RepGyp	.36	10	75523	14¼	7⅝	8¾	− 1⅞
RpNY s	1.12	14	66719	57¾	34½	57½	+ 23⅝
RNY pfA	3.89e	...	17604	55¼	51	51⅞	− 2⅛
RNY pfB	3.01e	...	6385	54⅝	51½	52	...
RepBk	1.64	8	194371	35	17⅞	19	− 14⅛
RepBk pf	2.12	...	10473	30⅜	24¾	25⅜	− 3⅛
RepBk adj	4.46e	...	2891	101½	65	65	− 35
RshCot	.32	13	43619	32⅝	24⅝	27⅞	+ 2⅜
Revco	.80	21	746521	39⅞	25½	38¼	+ 12¾
Revere		...	63660	22½	11¼	22⅜	+ 10¾
Revlon		...	511057	19¼	9	11⅜	+ 1⅝
Rexhm	.80	13	19208	33¼	24½	31⅝	+ 4⅞
Rexnrd	.44	...	317629	22⅝	14⅛	22	+ 5⅛
ReyMtl	1.00	16	209030	52¾	36⅜	40	+ 2¼
ReyM pf	4.50	...	1413	111	78	88	+ 6½
ReyM pf	2.30	...	66156	36¼	28⅝	30½	+ ⅝
Rhodes	.36	12	95652	32	16¾	18⅞	− ⅜
RiteAid	.58	17	247046	35½	24¼	29½	+ 3⅝
RvrOak		...	73812	4⅜	¼	15/32	− 2 29/32
Robtsn	1.20j	...	31581	24¼	10⅞	12⅜	− 11¼
vjRobins		3	121656	15⅝	7½	7⅞	− 3⅝
RochG	2.20	7	175422	29⅞	21¼	22½	− 1
RochTl	2.64	12	46816	52	36	44¾	+ 6
RckCtr	1.76	17	285575	22⅛	17⅞	21½	+ 2⅞
Rockwl	1.20	11	634333	48⅞	31⅜	45⅜	+ 9⅝
RkInt pf	4.75	...	28	475	360	447	+ 107
RkInt pf	1.35	...	148	170	124	162	+ 40
RodRn n		8	13918	13	9	10⅛	...
RHaas s	.80	18	183581	38¾	23⅞	34⅞	+ 9⅜
Rohr		12	178073	36⅜	25½	29	...
RolnCm	.42	44	45801	41¼	25¼	41¼	+ 12⅜
RolinE s	.08	43	233362	29⅞	11½	25⅞	+ 14
Rollins	.48	20	54964	18¼	12⅝	16¾	+ 3⅛
Roper s		...	60928	21¼	7⅞	18⅜	+ 10½
Rorer	1.16	6	406356	47½	32½	37⅜	+ 1⅝
Rothch n		9	190022	28⅞	12⅛	13	...
Rowan	.06j	...	388484	8¼	3⅜	4	− 3⅞
Rown pf	2.12	...	8230	24¾	22	23⅜	...
RoylD	5.29e	10	f10135	96	59¾	95½	+ 32½
RoyInt		102	41890	17⅝	5¾	6⅛	− 11
Royce n		...	15162	10⅛	9⅝	9⅞	...
Rubmd	.28	26	169170	28½	16⅝	24¼	+ 7
RussBr	.40e	16	61894	35½	22½	31¾	+ 8⅜
RusTog	.76	11	18040	33⅛	21¾	29⅛	+ 6⅞
Rusel s		12	80760	19⅝	9¼	17⅛	+ 7¾
RyanH	1.20	13	223649	50¾	26	45⅝	+ 18⅝
RyanH wd		...	5839	46	45½	45⅝	...
Ryder s	.44	17	359210	35½	21½	33⅜	+ 11⅛
Rykoff	.60	27	43408	32⅜	22½	26⅜	+ 2⅝
Rylnd s	.40	11	162663	27⅝	11¼	19⅞	+ 5⅛
Rymer		93	18826	23	15⅛	19⅝	+ 1½
Rymer pf	1.17	...	14802	14⅜	11½	12⅞	+ ⅛

—S—

SL Ind s	.17b	11	12523	13	8½	8¾	− 1
SPSTec	.96	13	19459	45¾	31¼	37¾	+ 2⅞
SSMC n		...	41981	17½	11½	14½	...
Sabine	.04	...	61321	17⅜	10⅝	12⅝	− 4¼
SabnR	1.48e	8	46252	15½	10⅞	12½	− 1⅜
SfgdBs	.30	32	160167	22⅜	13¾	20¼	+ ¼
SfgdSc		15	43473	16½	10	13¾	+ ¾
SfgdS wt		...	17593	5¾	2¾	3¼	+ ¼
SaftKln	.32	28	84657	38¾	25¾	33⅜	+ 7⅝
StJoLP	1.88	10	12168	39	22¼	37	+ 13⅝
vjSalant		10	36081	17½	8	10½	+ ⅞
SallieM	.36	22	246276	68⅝	35¼	66⅛	+ 29⅛
SallM pf	2.56e	...	30576	52¼	49⅛	50⅛	− ⅜
Salomn	.64	10	f14298	59⅜	37⅜	38⅜	− 5⅛
SDieGs	2.38	10	410496	42½	26¾	33⅞	+ 6⅞
SJuanB	.45e	...	182164	8⅞	6⅞	7⅞	− ⅜
SJuanR	2.00c	...	5416	12⅝	8¼	8¾	− 1⅞
SAnitRt	2.04	17	23021	32¾	23⅜	29½	+ 6
SFeEP n	2.88	...	72361	26⅜	16¼	17	...
SFeSoP	1.00	19	f11110	39⅝	26¼	29⅝	− 5¼
SaraLe	2.00	17	301771	73⅝	47⅛	69¼	+ 18⅝

NEW YORK STOCK EXCHANGE COMPOSITE

		P-E Ratio	Sales 100s	High	Low	Last	Net Chg.
SaraLe s		...	313811	36¾	23½	33⅞	+ 8½
SaraL pf	2.77e	...	12933	51½	49¼	50	...
SaulRE	.20	42	3949	19	16	16½	+ ⅜
SavEP s	.88	10	47936	23⅛	10¾	19⅝	+ 8¼
SavE A	1.34	...	504	47¼	23	43½	+ 19¼
SavE pf	1.28	...	3811	14½	11¼	13	+ 1¼
Savin		...	72698	4½	1⅝	2¼	− 1¾
Savin pf		...	3265	6½	3⅛	3⅝	− 1¾
SCANA	2.24	13	221512	42⅞	27⅛	36⅝	+ 8¾
Schfr n		...	13688	10	8⅛	8¾	...
SchrPlo	1.80	20	641340	88	56	79	+ 20⅞
Schlmb	1.20	...	f19652	37¾	27¼	31¾	− 4¾
SciAtl	.12	...	227094	14¾	8½	11⅛	− ½
ScottP	1.36	13	277680	66⅝	48	62¾	+ 12⅛
Scottys	.52	15	55712	18⅛	12	12¼	− 2⅝
SeaCnt	.42	...	60398	34¼	12¾	13⅝	− 16⅞
SeaCt pf	1.46	...	8736	14⅛	7¾	10½	− 2
SeaC pfB	2.10	...	10002	16⅞	10½	13¼	− 3
SeaC pfC	2.10	...	17903	17	9¾	12⅞	− 3
SeaC pfD	4.12	...	14000	51¼	34½	35½	...
Seagrm	1.00	13	462649	65⅛	37⅜	60¾	+ 12¾
Seagul		...	34230	17⅛	12⅛	16	...
SealAir	.48	19	43716	43¾	33⅛	40½	+ 5
SealPw	1.10	12	58944	31¼	23⅛	26⅛	− 1⅝
Sears	1.76	11	f21006	50⅜	35⅞	39¾	+ ¾
Sear pf	7.13e	...	49408	106½	102¼	103¾	− 1¼
SecPac	1.48	7	464357	40¼	27⅛	34⅝	+ 2¾
SvceCp	.48	21	166742	37½	27⅝	37⅛	+ 5⅞
SvcRes		...	40825	17⅜	4¼	15½	+ 10⅞
Svcmst n		...	4120	21⅞	21	21⅝	...
Shaklee	.72	4	159223	28	14⅝	17¾	+ 1¾
Shawln s	.40	14	78238	23⅜	15¼	20½	+ 7⅜
ShellT	2.97e	10	385846	58⅞	36	58½	+ 19¾
Shrwin s	.50	16	260393	32¼	21¼	27⅝	+ 5½
Shoetwn		10	201071	12	6⅛	6½	− 1½
Showbt	.58e	17	29190	22¾	15¼	19⅝	+ 3⅜
SierPac	1.72	14	93523	29	19⅛	25⅛	+ 5
Signet	1.24	9	110210	38½	28	32	+ 1⅞
Singer	.40b	9	466013	55⅞	35¼	37⅜	− 2
Singr pf	3.50	...	3584	41⅜	31⅞	39	+ 6¾
Skyline	.48	15	100659	21	12⅜	14⅝	− 2¾
Slattery		...	2152	29¾	20⅜	27⅛	− 2⅜
vjSmith	.08j	...	289134	7½	1¼	4½	− 2¼
SmkB	3.00	15	565444	105⅜	73⅝	95⅛	+ 19½
Smuckr	.60	20	19993	50	37¼	45	− 2½
SnpOn s	.64	16	146536	32⅛	20⅜	25⅝	+ 3¾
Snyder	1.50	...	64667	12	9½	10¾	− 1⅛
Snydr pf	2.09	...	1297	19½	18⅝	19½	...
Sonat	2.00	...	281133	35¾	21⅜	26	− 8
SonyCp	.23e	18	572727	23½	18⅛	20½	+ ⅛
SooLin	.60j	...	38992	36⅞	18¾	19¼	− 6½
SourcC	3.40	...	12306	45⅞	39½	41	− ¾
SrcCp pf	2.40	...	3616	27½	22⅞	26¼	+ 2⅞
SCrE pf	2.50	...	393	34½	23⅝	30½	+ 6⅞
SoJerIn	2.52	14	11664	42¾	28⅜	36¾	+ 7¾
Soudwn	1.00b	...	46500	44⅜	26¾	27⅝	− 15⅛
SoetBk	1.32	9	116537	46½	35⅛	37⅝	+ 1⅜
SoetBk pf		...	509	85	72½	83	...
SCalEd	2.28	10	f13322	38¾	25¼	33⅞	+ 7¼
SouthCo	2.14	8	f17531	27¼	20⅜	25⅜	+ 3⅛
SolndGs	1.96	12	32827	41¼	25½	39	+ 11¾
SNETI	2.88	13	103897	61½	43	53⅞	+ 8⅞
SoRy pf	2.60	...	3397	36¼	26¼	33½	+ 6⅝
SoUnCo	.80	...	121509	25⅜	10¼	10¾	− 14¼
Soutlnd	1.12	11	558584	60½	40⅜	47	+ 3
Soutld pf	4.00	...	27328	76	57½	68	+ 7¾
Soumrk	.24b	7	439711	14	8	8⅜	− 1⅜
Somk pf	5.19e	...	18829	51¾	39	39⅜	− 9⅞
Somk pf		...	89	25½	25	25½	...
SwAirl	.13	14	509861	27½	18¼	20⅝	− 6¼
SwtFor		...	153384	19¾	11⅞	17⅞	+ 5⅛
SwtGas	1.28	11	63641	21⅜	16⅝	17⅞	− ⅛
SwGas wi		...	15	17¾	17¾	17¾	...
SwBell	6.40	12	464185	116⅜	79	112¼	+ 26¾
SwEnr	.52	10	38955	22⅝	16¼	17⅝	− 3½
SwtPS	2.12	12	234694	37⅞	25¼	31	+ 4⅞
Sparton	.52	13	27389	20¼	14	17⅞	+ 1½
SpectP		209	46336	29⅞	18⅛	23	− 1¾
Springs	1.52	19	30010	56⅞	41	49⅞	+ 5⅞
SquarD	1.84	13	166721	50	39¼	46⅜	+ 3⅝
Squibb	2.00	23	458289	124⅛	76¼	114	+ 34
Staley	.80	29	413685	34⅝	22⅞	25¼	− 1¼
Staley pf	3.50	...	1602	50¾	48¾	50¼	...
StBPnt	.58	17	112886	27	19⅜	21⅛	+ 1
StMotr	.32	15	53047	20⅛	11⅞	19⅞	+ 7⅝
StdOil	2.80	...	773761	51¾	40¼	49⅜	− ½
StOil pf	3.75	...	z3710	73¾	70¼	72¾	+ 1

		P-E Ratio	Sales 100s	High	Low	Last	Net Chg.
StPac s	.10c	13	141387	33¾	13½	26½	+ 10⅝
StPc wi		...	1235	27¼	25¾	27¼	...
StdPrd s	.64	12	35375	37¾	18¾	37	+ 17⅜
Standex	.52	13	37195	17	14½	15⅞	+ 1⅛
Stanh s	.84	11	38513	26¾	13	22¾	+ 9
StanW s	.76	13	143249	30¾	20½	25½	+ 4¼
Starrett	1.08	11	3587	44⅞	35⅜	40¾	+ 1⅝
StaMSe	1.20	...	13011	13⅜	10⅞	12¾	+ 1¾
Steego	.11t	69	24085	4⅜	2½	4⅛	+ 1½
StrlBcp	.80	10	39677	16⅞	12⅝	14	− ½
SterlDg	1.32	22	750455	52	36⅜	46⅜	+ 8¾
StevnJ	1.20	13	247145	39⅝	26⅞	37⅞	+ 6⅞
StwWrn	1.68	27	18662	31½	26⅜	27½	− 2
StkVC pr	1.00	...	1848	14¼	12	13½	+ ¼
Stifel		11	2631	11	9⅜	9⅞	+ 2½
StoneW	1.60	13	17398	58¼	44	49⅛	− 5⅝
StoneC	.60	132	119212	60	33⅞	58	+ 20⅛
StneC pf	3.50	...	26204	62	48	59¾	...
StopShp	1.10	16	210182	61¾	39⅛	51	+ 11¾
StorEq	1.40	14	58410	21⅛	13⅞	15⅛	− 3⅛
vjStorT		4	543343	7⅜	1¾	3½	+ 1¾
StratMt	2.27e	10	33868	23½	17½	22¾	+ 4⅛
StridRt	.80	13	79943	36	20⅛	28½	+ 7⅞
SuavSh		9	27625	10⅝	5	8¾	+ 2⅞
SunCh	.48	23	103507	84¾	34¾	70⅛	+ 33
SunC A n		...	680	69	65	66¾	...
SunChB n		...	721	71¾	68¼	70⅝	...
SunCh pf	5.00	...	2	93	92	93	...
SunEl		56	82823	14¼	8½	11¼	+ 1⅜
SunEng	1.20	...	65664	24	13⅜	16⅞	− 5⅛
SunCo	3.00	8	261075	59½	42¼	54¼	+ 2½
SunC pf	2.25	...	600	122¼	90½	113	+ 9
Sundstr	1.80	12	91644	64⅜	49¼	53¼	− 1¼
SunMn		...	364581	7⅛	2	3⅛	− 2⅜
SunM pf	1.19	...	56460	8¾	4⅞	6½	− 1
SunTr s	.64	11	163292	28	17¼	20	+ ⅞
SupVal s	.42	21	345991	27⅞	19¾	24½	+ 2⅛
SupMk s	.28	14	152871	32¼	22½	23¼	− 2
Swank	.24j	29	12355	16⅜	11¾	12	− 3
SymsCp		16	28353	14¾	10¼	10¾	− 1⅜
Syntex	1.60	17	749104	74¾	40½	57⅝	+ 10⅞
Sysco s	.28	22	160941	33⅞	22⅜	30	+ 7⅝
—T—							
TDK	.41e	17	12772	53¾	38¾	48	+ 4⅛
TECO	2.52	13	144897	54⅞	34	46	+ 11⅜
TGIF		28	41927	10	6½	6⅝	− 1½
TNP	1.32	11	21158	24	19⅜	22⅛	+ 2
TRE	1.20	17	84414	46½	26½	45⅞	+ 14½
TRW	3.20	18	148850	110	82¼	84½	− 3½
TRW pf	4.40	...	51	221	180	189	− 3
TRW pr	4.50	...	472	201	155	157¾	− 6¼
TW Svc n		...	2307	14½	14⅛	14⅜	...
vjTacBt		...	33354	1⅞	¾	1⅜	+ 9/16
TaftBrd	1.16	643	73252	121	82	115	+ 28¾
Talley	.30	11	78043	24¼	17	18	− 1
Talley pf	1.00	...	7324	25½	19½	20⅛	− ⅞
Tambd	3.60	21	60783	121¾	87	118¾	+ 28⅝
Tambd s		...	63206	60⅞	43½	55¼	+ 10¼
Tandy	.12i	19	984073	45	30½	42½	+ 1¾
Tndycft		17	10797	20⅞	14⅞	16½	− 1⅜
Tektrnx	1.20	24	150844	70¼	54½	68	+ 11¾
Telcom		...	8406	3⅜	1⅜	1½	− 1¼
Teldyn	17.50t	12	75393	367¾	291	301½	− 28⅞
Telrate	.48	33	213165	29⅞	16¾	29	+ 12
Telex		14	269149	70⅛	52¼	67	+ 7⅜
Templn	.72	19	141661	59⅛	42	57¼	+ 13⅝
Tennco	3.04	18	929785	43⅛	34½	38¼	− 1½
Tenc pr	11.00	...	8885	107	101	102	− ⅞
Tenc pr	7.40	...	10818	96	86	93⅛	+ 6⅞
Terdyn		409	253705	29⅝	15⅝	16⅜	− 6¾
Tesoro	.30j	...	111754	15	7½	10¾	+ 1¼
Tesor pf	2.16	...	5731	27	19⅝	22½	+ 1⅛
Texaco	3.00	9	f20647	37⅛	26	35⅞	+ 5⅞
TxABc	.40	...	57334	30⅜	13¾	14¼	− 15⅝
TexCm	1.56	72	508784	31	16½	26½	− 1½
TexEst	1.00	...	444979	41¼	24	27⅛	− 7⅞
TxET pf	4.48e	...	11609	55¾	45¾	51¼	− 2¾
Texlnd	.80b	20	35810	35	23½	23⅝	− 6¾
Texlnst	2.00	...	333835	148¼	102¾	118⅛	+ 12⅝
TxPac	.40	17	9270	30½	23¾	24¼	− 6⅜
TexUtil	2.68	7	f13575	37½	29½	31½	+ 1⅝
Texfi In		...	39407	5⅝	3	5¼	+ 1⅝
Textron	1.80	11	355626	70	48⅝	63	+ 14
Textr pf	2.08	...	1294	76	53	69	+ 15⅜
Textr pf	1.40	...	577	60¾	43⅜	56¼	+ 12½
Thack		53	9295	12¼	8	9½	− 2¼

NEW YORK STOCK EXCHANGE COMPOSITE

		P-E Ratio	Sales 100s	High	Low	Last	Net Chg.
ThrmE s		22	71659	23	13¼	17	+ 3⅝
ThmBet	1.52	17	58777	49¾	37	43⅛	+ 2⅜
Thomln	.68b	10	27205	24¼	15½	16⅛	− 4⅝
ThmMed	.40	14	30069	21	11⅜	13½	− ¾
Thorln s		12	25500	18½	9⅛	15⅛	+ 5⅝
Tidwtr	.27j	...	145550	13⅜	3	4¼	− 8¼
Tidwt pf	5.32j	...	260	99¼	87½	87½	− 11¾
Tigerln		...	383270	9¾	3⅝	8⅝	+ ¾
Time	1.00	11	579800	91⅜	57½	70	+ 7⅞
Timplx		14	104906	25⅛	13¾	23⅜	+ ¼
TimeM	1.64	11	200147	73⅞	50⅛	63½	+ 5⅞
Timken	1.00	...	39230	53⅜	39½	43¼	− 1¾
Titan		14	66993	11⅞	6⅜	6⅝	− 2⅜
Titan pf	1.00	...	2941	13	11¼	11¾	+ ¼
TodShp	1.32	025	32830	30⅞	18¼	20½	− 7¼
TodSh pf	3.08	...	8211	30	25	29½	...
Tokhm s	.48	47	39404	23¾	16¾	20	+ ¾
TolEd pf	1.61e	...	12738	25⅛	21⅝	22	...
TolEd pf	3.72	...	5089	32¾	28⅞	30¾	+ 1¾
TolEd pf	3.75	...	5531	33⅛	29⅛	29⅞	+ ½
TolEd pf	3.47	...	4997	32¼	28	31¼	+ 2¾
TolEd pf	4.28	...	3280	37⅝	33½	34⅜	+ ⅝
TolEd pf	2.36	...	4722	26	19⅝	23⅞	+ 4¼
TolEd pf	2.21	...	4736	24½	18½	22⅜	+ 3⅞
TolE adjpf	2.51e	...	8081	27⅜	19¾	20	− 4⅞
TollBr n		19	36584	17¾	9	17⅛	...
Tonka s	.07	7	145035	32¼	15⅞	19⅞	+ 1⅝
TootRl s	.40	18	9049	54	33½	53	+ 13⅝
Trchmk	1.00	9	358961	38½	21¼	26	+ 4
Trch pf	7.35e	...	6607	110	103½	105⅜	− 5⅛
ToroCo	.50	10	37413	29¼	17¼	21¾	+ 2⅛
Tosco		...	238062	4⅝	1⅝	2	− 1⅞
vjTowle		...	47356	7	2	2⅜	− 4¼
vjTwle pf		...	2828	3¾	1⅜	1½	− 1⅝
ToyRU s		32	872281	34½	26⅝	28¾	...
Tracor	.36	91	141834	24⅛	16½	17¼	− 2½
Tramel	1.40	...	35308	15⅜	12½	14⅞	+ 1½
TWA		...	507849	28	12⅞	23¼	+ 7
TWA pf	2.25	...	63426	18	9	16¾	+ 2⅛
Transm	1.76	11	378704	40⅛	31¾	32⅝	− 1⅛
Trnsam wi		...	2	33¾	33¾	33¾	...
Tranlnc	2.28	...	8628	26⅝	21¼	24⅜	+ 2½
TrnCda g	1.12	10	22701	15½	11¼	12¼	− 3⅛
Trnscap		4	19539	19⅛	12	12⅜	− 1
Trncp rt		...	91	1/32	1/32	1/32	...
Transco	2.72	...	383943	63½	35	41⅜	− 13¼
Trnsc pf	3.87	...	13038	75	45¼	54	− 13
Trnsc pf	4.75	...	34392	59	48¾	53⅜	− 2⅞
TranEx	2.36	...	126383	18⅞	11¾	14⅜	− 4
Transcn		20	34487	11⅝	7⅜	8⅛	+ ¼
TrGP pf	6.65	...	z28890	95¼	85¼	95¼	+ 7¼
TrG pf	10.32	...	z71040	104	99	101½	+ 1½
TrGP pf	8.64	...	z96810	103½	94½	101¼	+ 5¼
TrGP pf	2.50	...	3875	27	25	27	+ ½
Trnwld s	.40b	10	f10647	42⅝	22¼	32⅜	+ 6
Twld pf	2.00	...	13173	49½	30	49½	+ 18¼
TrwdLq n		...	3395	32½	32¼	32½	...
Travler	2.16	9	f10507	59½	42½	44⅝	− 3⅜
Trav pf	4.16	...	42518	68¾	53⅞	56⅞	− ⅝
TriCon	7.93e	...	71877	30¼	23	28⅝	+ 5
TriCn pf	2.50	...	1975	35¾	26⅛	33⅜	+ 6¾
Trialn s	.12	7	222735	31¾	16¼	25¼	+ 8⅝
Trilnd pf	.12	...	21812	29¾	16	24½	...
Tribune	1.20	7	191846	78	49½	57	+ 1¼
Tricntr	.04e	3	51110	4⅝	1⅜	2⅛	− 2⅛
Trico	.20	18	32519	7⅞	4⅞	7⅝	+ ⅞
Trinty	.50	45	122231	20	13¼	16⅝	+ 1⅜
Trinov s	1.00	...	102555	54⅛	31	47⅛	+ 14⅜
Trinv pf	4.75	...	4555	121½	76½	107	+ 27¾
TritEng	.10b	11	63677	26⅜	13⅜	14½	− 11
TritE pf	2.00	...	18982	28⅛	20¾	24¼	...
TucsEP	3.30	13	132248	65	41	58¼	+ 15½
Tultex s	.32	15	73425	22¾	9⅛	18⅛	+ 8⅝
TwinDs	.70	...	4686	18¾	14¼	14¾	− 3⅝
TycoL s	.40	18	150490	42½	23⅜	40¾	+ 17⅛
Tyler	.40	17	70235	17¾	11¼	12	− 2¾

—U—

		P-E Ratio	Sales 100s	High	Low	Last	Net Chg.
UAL	1.00	...	897388	64¾	46¼	52¼	+ 2½
UCCEL		24	62924	27⅜	15¼	24⅝	+ 7¼
UDC s	2.00	6	78105	26¾	15	20⅜	+ 4
UGI	2.04	...	72724	28¼	21⅛	25⅝	+ 4½
UNCInc		16	96850	13¾	8¼	8¾	− ¾
UNUM n		...	156807	28⅝	25¾	26⅞	...
URS	.25r	...	49363	18⅜	11¾	15½	+ 2⅜
USFG	2.32	16	924334	46¾	36¼	39¾	+ ¾
USFG pf	4.10	...	19042	58½	52¾	57⅛	...
USG s	1.12	11	525783	46½	22¼	37¾	+ 12½
USG pf	1.80	...	166	160	82	136	+ 47½
USPCI s		...	73882	32¾	17⅝	24¾	+ 5⅛
USX	1.20	...	f43505	28¾	14½	21½	− 5⅛
USX pf	4.40e	...	46267	54¾	23⅝	33¾	− 19⅞
USX pf	2.25	...	95607	28⅞	22⅞	25	− 3
USX pf	10.75	...	22427	106	86¾	88	...
USX wt		...	87540	1⅜	¼	⅜	...
UniFrst	.20	16	13599	32⅜	16¾	26⅝	+ 10⅛
Unilvr	2.98e	17	4556	132	76	132	+ 51½
UniNV	6.14e	17	71068	238	137¾	237⅞	+ 90⅝
UCamp	1.64	23	319683	58¼	38⅜	51	+ 11¼
UCarb s	1.50	10	f18754	25½	18¾	22½	...
UnionC		10	56230	13¼	7¾	8⅝	+ ⅞
UnElec	1.92	10	580977	31¾	20⅞	28¾	+ 7⅜
UnEl pf	3.50	...	z33360	41	31½	38¾	+ 4⅞
UnEl pf	4.00	...	z89302	52	36	50½	+ 13¼
UnEl pf	4.50	...	z31590	51½	39¼	50	+ 10
UnEl pf	4.56	...	6233	58⅛	41½	57	+ 15½
UnEl pf	6.40	...	1711	81	59	79	+ 16⅝
UnEl pfM	4.00	...	16237	34¼	27½	28⅜	− 4⅞
UEl pfL	8.00	...	2111	97½	73¼	90⅝	+ 15⅜
UnEl pf	2.98	...	11911	29¾	26¾	28⅞	+ 1¼
UnEl pf	2.13	...	17917	26½	20	25½	+ 3⅞
UnEl pf	2.72	...	2468	28¼	26	27½	+ ⅜
UnEl pf	7.44	...	5465	93⅝	67⅝	90¼	+ 20¼
UEl pfH	8.00	...	1736	94	70	85	+ 13
UnEx n	1.88e	...	77415	19¾	13	16⅛	− 2⅜
UnPac	2.00	...	699184	67⅜	46½	62¼	+ 8⅜
UnPc pr	7.25	...	22990	139½	104½	130¼	+ 14
Unisys	2.60	14	891744	86½	57½	80	+ 16⅝
Unisy pf	3.75	...	332764	60⅜	48¾	56½	...
Unit		...	17965	2¾	1	1½	− 1⅛
UAM n	.06e	34	25081	18¾	15½	17½	...
UnBrnd		9	25357	37	22⅛	33¼	+ 5½
UCbTV s	.08	80	77752	32⅞	23½	25¾	+ 3⅛
UIllum	2.32	5	99588	36¼	26⅞	29¼	+ 2¼
UIllu pr	2.20	...	1503	24½	18½	23	+ 4⅞
UIllu pf	1.90	...	3366	17	14¾	15¾	+ ¾
Unitlnd	.64b	13	57134	27⅜	14	14¾	− 7¾
Unitlnn	.22j	...	7918	51¾	36	37¼	− 5¾
UJerB s	.86	10	90829	31½	22¼	23¾	...
UJBk wi		...	25	11¼	11¼	11¼	...
UtdMM		...	76829	21½	9⅜	13⅝	− 5⅜
UPkMn		1	6378	3½	2¼	2⅝	− ½
UsairG	.12	9	467090	41	30⅛	36¼	+ 1⅞
USHom		...	548673	9¼	4⅛	5⅝	− ⅛
USLeas	.88	11	35267	46¾	37½	42⅛	+ 1⅜
USSho s	.46	24	275574	27¼	19½	20¾	− ⅝
USTob	1.96	12	264683	45½	30	44⅜	+ 9½
USWst s	3.04	11	603922	62	41⅝	54	+ 9½
UnStck		8	17476	11⅛	7½	8¼	− 1¾
UStck pf	1.30	...	967	11½	8½	9¼	...
UnTech	1.40	13	f10193	56¼	39¼	46	+ 2¼
UniTel	1.92	...	710389	31¼	23¼	25½	+ 1¾
UniTl pf	1.50	...	163	45	35	38¼	+ 3
UniT 2pf	1.50	...	392	37½	29½	31⅜	+ 2⅛
UWR s	.92	15	27807	22⅝	14½	17⅞	+ 2⅞
Unitrde	.20	...	73332	27⅛	10½	12¼	− 9¼
Univar	.20	6	22072	15½	9⅜	10⅝	− 4⅝
UnvFd s	.80	18	56561	28	19	23½	+ 3¾
UnvHR n		...	1163	10¾	10⅛	10½	...
UnLeaf	1.08	10	69368	31	23¼	26⅞	+ 2⅝
UMtch n		...	49538	22⅜	13¾	15⅜	...
Unocal	1.00	...	f11011	28¼	15⅝	26⅝	− ¼
Upjohn s	1.52	24	448644	106¼	61¾	93¼	...
USLIFE	1.20	10	128323	49½	35¾	43½	+ 5¾
USLF pr	3.33	...	830	37	33⅝	36⅛	+ 2⅛
UslfeF	1.08a	...	8692	12¾	10⅝	11⅜	+ ¾
UtaPL	2.32	13	285004	37¼	24⅞	27¾	+ 2¼
UtPL pf	2.36	...	8545	29¼	23⅝	27¼	+ 3⅝
UtPL pf	2.04	...	17514	26⅞	20⅜	25⅛	+ 4⅛
UtiliCo	1.48b	11	42192	34¾	22½	31⅞	+ 9⅜
UtilCo pf	2.44	...	1306	27	21¾	25⅛	+ 3⅛
UtilCo pr	2.61	...	4555	29⅝	24	28¼	+ 4¼
UtilCo pf	4.12	...	2101	37⅝	32½	33⅞	− 1⅝

—V—

		P-E Ratio	Sales 100s	High	Low	Last	Net Chg.
VF Cp s	.72	14	281739	36	24	30⅞	+ 5
Valero		...	180400	14¼	6⅝	6⅞	− 6⅞
Valer pf	3.44	...	9462	25⅝	18⅞	20¾	− 4⅝
Valeyln		38	15126	2⅞	1	1½	− ⅞
VanDrn	1.10	11	17063	37⅛	27⅛	29⅞	+ ¼
Varco		...	34219	5	1⅞	2⅜	− 1⅝
Varco pf		...	3105	15½	7¼	8	− 6⅛
Varian	.26	...	261798	30½	22⅜	22⅞	− 5¾
Varity		...	694079	3½	1¾	1⅞	− ¼
Varo	.40	24	35859	17¾	12	12¼	− 2¼

NEW YORK STOCK EXCHANGE COMPOSITE

		P-E Ratio	Sales 100s	High	Low	Last	Net Chg.
Veeco	.40	363	59857	19¾	12	14½	– 3½
Vendo		...	21580	11⅛	5¾	9½	– 1¼
VestSe	1.20a	...	13721	14¾	11⅝	13⅞	+ 2⅛
Vestrn		9	182090	15¼	4½	4¾	– 8⅜
Viacm s	.28	...	934793	44⅞	25¼	39½	+ 12¼
VaEP pf	5.00	...	z30610	66	48	62	+ 14
VaEP pf	7.72	...	2646	101⅝	74⅞	95½	+ 18
VaEP pf	8.84	...	1285	103	87	99	+ 11
VaEP pf	8.60	...	139	99¾	86	97½	+ 13½
VaEl pf	8.60	...	1088	107½	93½	105	+ 11½
VaE pfJ	7.72	...	3994	101⅝	75	95⅛	+ 19¾
VaEP pf	7.20	...	3513	96½	71	89	+ 17
VaEP pf	7.45	...	2601	99½	73	91⅝	+ 17⅜
Vishay		13	16582	24⅞	17	19¾	– 2¼
VistaC n		...	23230	18¾	17	18¾	...
Vornad		18	9353	80¾	64	69¾	– ⅝
VulcM	2.96	16	22547	125½	88¼	124½	+ 33½
–W–							
WICOR	2.60	12	17367	46	29⅜	42¼	+ 11¼
WabR pf	4.50	...	z39850	56½	43¾	56½	+ 13½
Wackht	.60	17	25462	40	17½	21⅛	– 5⅛
Wainoc		...	41426	8	4	5	– 3
WalMrt	.17	33	f10554	53⅞	29⅛	46½	+ 14⅝
Walgrn	.54	19	317590	39½	24¼	32⅜	+ 4¼
WalCSv	.60	18	35564	50⅛	37	43½	+ 3⅞
WaltJ s	1.40	9	277587	54⅝	32⅝	47¼	+ 12¼
WaltJ pf	1.00	...	z59200	12¾	9¼	12½	+ 2¼
WaltJ pf	1.60	...	456	90¾	56	81	+ 24
WrnC s	.30	13	940957	28⅜	17⅞	22½	+ 3⅞
WrnC pf	3.62	...	48998	53⅝	46¼	52⅞	...
WarnrL	1.68	...	687895	63⅛	45	58⅝	+ 11⅛
WashGs	1.76	11	44261	30⅜	20⅛	25¾	+ 3⅜
WshNat	1.08	10	50410	35⅜	24⅝	32	+ 5¾
WasN pf	2.50	...	421	65	50	60	+ 11¾
WshWt	2.48	11	118282	31⅝	24¼	25¼	+ ¼
Waste	.56	28	758506	59¾	34½	55⅝	+ 20⅛
WatkJn	.40	15	85374	42½	24¼	32¾	+ 5½
WayGos	.20	20	15818	28½	9¼	24	+ 12⅛
WayG pf	1.60	...	1728	56½	21¼	48¼	+ 25
WeanU		...	9406	4⅞	1⅞	2⅛	– 2¾
Wean pf	.63k	...	262	10⅜	8¾	9	– ⅝
WebbD	.20	10	93629	28¼	19⅛	22¼	+ 1⅛
vjWedtc			183899	11¾	¼ 13/32	-- 10 19/32	– 96.3
WeingR	1.56	17	43846	25	19½	21⅜	+ 1½
WeisMk	.54	18	22206	41¾	33⅛	37	– 3¾
WellsF	3.12	11	162672	115	61	101½	+ 38⅛
WllsF wi		...	15	57½	30½	50⅞	+ 19¼
WelF pf	3.15e	...	43723	52⅛	46	49⅛	+ 1⅜
WelF pf	2.45e	...	20632	50½	44	48½	...
WelFM	2.80	12	40417	29½	23⅝	28¼	+ 4⅝
Wendy s	.24	79	968669	17¾	10	10¼	– 3⅛
WestCo	.52	14	16110	34¼	24½	28¼	+ 2⅜
WPenP pf	4.50	...	z36040	58½	43	57	+ 14
WstPtP	2.20a	13	95873	60⅜	41½	52⅛	+ 8¾
WstctT g	.80	...	21766	12⅞	8⅞	9½	– 3¼
WnAirL		26	f16808	13	6⅜	12¾	+ 5⅞
WCNA		...	253694	2¼	¼	¾	– 1½
WCNA pf	1.81j	...	9820	19	3⅜	4⅛	– 14⅞
WPacl	2.25e	19	12386	174	131¾	161¾	+ 22¼
WstnSL	.24	6	86805	28	12⅛	18¼	+ 5¾
WUnion		...	416160	13⅛	3¼	4	– 8⅜

		P-E Ratio	Sales 100s	High	Low	Last	Net Chg.
WnUn pf		...	1114	40	18	19½	– 20
WnU pfC		...	276	42	19½	19⅝	– 23⅜
WnU pfS		...	29318	7⅜	1¾	2	– 4¼
WnU pfE		...	31587	13½	2⅜	2⅝	– 10¼
WUTI pf		...	755	43⅜	19	26¾	– 12¾
WUTI pfA		...	9790	17½	6¾	7¾	– 5⅞
WstgE	1.40	13	f11457	62½	42	55¾	+ 11¼
Wstvc s	1.00	16	148376	43½	27¼	40¾	+ 12½
Weyerh	1.30	23	801551	41¼	29⅝	37¾	+ 7
Weyr pf	2.80	...	27788	55⅞	42⅝	52⅞	+ 10
WheILE	5.75	...	5212	98	75	95	+ 17½
vjWhPit		...	18821	13⅜	6⅞	7¾	– ½
vjWPit pfB		...	z53830	29	18	19	+ ¾
vjWhPit pf		...	z65930	23	13	13¼	– 1
Whirlpl	2.20	12	262650	83	48½	67¾	+ 18⅜
Whirlp wi		...	6	41½	24¼	33¾	+ 9⅛
WhitC pfA	1.50e	...	32	49⅝	48	49⅝	+ ⅞
Whitehl		22	38876	34⅞	21	21¾	– 9¾
Whittak	.60	...	194897	35	18⅝	29½	+ 9½
Wilfred	.12	9	18624	17¼	8¾	8¾	– 3¾
WillcxG	.15	9	38808	18½	11⅞	15⅞	+ 2⅜
William	1.40	...	323460	29½	17⅝	23¼	– 6½
WilmEl		...	77837	12¼	4⅝	5⅝	– ⅝
WilshrO		21	15487	7⅛	4	5⅛	– ⅜
Winchl n		...	9973	17¾	17⅜	17½	...
WinDix	1.80	17	91334	59	34⅞	45⅞	+ 7½
Winnbg	.20	14	311824	20¾	9	11½	– 1
Winner		...	24688	8	3⅜	3⅝	– 3
WinterJ	.16e	20	11910	10⅝	5¾	6¾	– 2½
WiscEP	2.68	11	142442	64½	38⅜	52⅝	+ 12⅞
WisE pf	8.90	...	1950	105	91	102	+ 11
WisE pf	7.75	...	2558	102¼	81	101	+ 20
WisG pf	2.55	...	1120	31	26	28⅛	+ 1⅜
WiscPL	2.96	12	37849	60¼	39	50	+ 9⅝
WiscPS	3.00	12	43145	63	38⅜	49⅜	+ 10¼
Witco s	1.12	13	74715	40	26⅜	38⅝	+ 11½
WolvrW	.12j	...	66855	13½	8⅛	9	– 4½
Wlwth s	1.12	12	445768	49	29	38⅝	+ 8⅝
Wolw pf	2.20	...	715	137	83	110	+ 26
WrldAr		2	19305	5¼	2	4⅛	+ ¼
WrldVl n		...	8317	19¾	14⅜	15¼	...
Wrigly s	.96	19	42848	52	27½	45¾	+ 14¾
Wurltzr		...	14323	4⅛	1⅜	2⅞	– ¼
WyleLb	.32	29	52435	17½	11	13⅝	– 1⅛
Wynns	.60	...	22095	25¾	15	19⅞	+ 3⅜
–X-Z–							
Xerox	3.00	13	f10558	72¼	48⅝	60	+ ¼
Xerox pf	5.45	...	80132	58¼	54	55⅛	+ ⅞
XTRA	.64	...	75213	28¾	21⅛	26⅞	+ 4⅜
Yorkln n		...	69702	18¾	13½	16¼	...
ZaleCp	1.40	...	83683	50⅛	28½	48¼	+ 18⅞
Zale pfA	.80	...	147	39½	22⅞	39½	+ 16⅝
Zapata	.03j	...	178502	8⅞	2¼	3	– 4⅝
Zayre s	.32	17	626222	43⅞	20¾	24	– 6¾
Zemex	.40	20	3658	17	9¾	12½	...
ZenithE		...	332200	29⅞	17⅞	21⅞	+ 1⅜
ZenLb s		53	441430	18¼	8	8½	– 3⅞
Zero s	.29	15	42424	22⅜	12⅜	14¾	– 3⅝
Zurnln	1.32	15	40504	45¾	32¾	38½	– ⅛
Zweig n	.10e	...	67098	10⅜	8¾	9⅛	...

Footnotes on Following Page

NEW YORK STOCK EXCHANGE COMPOSITE

Sales figures are unofficial.

g-Dividend or earnings in Canadian money. Stock trades in U.S. dollars. No yield or PE shown unless stated in U.S. money. n-New issue in the past year. The range begins with the start of trading in the new issue and does not cover the entire year. s-Split or stock dividend of 25 per cent or more in the past year. The high-low range is adjusted from the old stock. Dividend begins with the date of split or stock dividend. The net change is from an adjusted previous year's closing price. v-Trading halted on primary market.

Unless otherwise noted, rates of dividends in the foregoing table are annual disbursements based on the last quarterly or semi-annual declaration. Special or extra dividends or payments not designated as regular are identified in the following footnotes.

a-Also extra or extras. b-Annual rate plus stock dividend. c-Liquidating dividend. e-Declared or paid in preceding 12 months. i-Declared or paid after stock dividend or split-up. j-Paid this year, dividend omitted, deferred or no action taken at last dividend meeting. k-Declared or paid this year, an accumulative issue with dividends in arrears. r-Declared or paid in preceding 12 months plus stock dividend. t-Paid in stock in preceding 12 months, estimated cash value on ex-dividend or ex-distribution date. z-Sales in full.

pf-Preferred. pp-Holder owes 2 instalments of purchase price. rt-Rights. un-Units. wd-When distributed. wi-When issued. ww-With warrants. wt-Warrants. xw-Without warrants.

vj-In bankruptcy or receivership or being reorganized under the Bankruptcy Act, or securities assumed by such companies.

NEW YORK BONDS

The following tabulation gives the 1986 sales, high, low, last price and net change from the previous year in bonds listed on the New York Stock Exchange.

		Sales $1,000	High	Low	Last	Net Chg.
		—A—				
AGS 7½11	cv	1480	121½	94½	121½	...
AMR 10¼06	10.1	7013	102⅜	87¼	101½	+ 12
ANR 8⅝93	8.8	438	100	93⅜	98⅛	+ 7¼
ANR 9⅝94	9.6	198	100	97⅝	100	+ 5⅜
ANR 10⅝95	10.6	340	103½	99⅛	100½	+ 3¾
ANR 13¼97	12.4	77	107½	100¼	107¼	+ 3¼
ANR 11¾97	11.4	115	103½	100	103	+ 5
ARX 9⅜05	cv	2950	131	107	111	– 16
AVX 13½00	13.0	513	105¼	96	104	+ 9
AbbtL 6¼93	6.5	95	96	85	96	+ 7⅞
AbbtL 7⅝96	7.6	253	100	86	99¾	+ 14⅝
AbbtL 9.2s99	9.0	288	103	93⅛	102⅝	+ 8¼
AbbtL 11s93	10.1	275	112	104½	109	+ 6
Advst 9s08	cv	11452	121½	98½	103	+ 1¾
AetnLf 8⅛07	8.5	3776	98¼	81	95¾	+ 11⅜
AirPr 11⅝10	10.6	100	110	104½	110	+ 8
AirPr 14⅝87	14.0	752	109½	104⅝	104⅝	– 4⅜
AirPr 11½95	9.7	198	121	113⅝	119	+ 14
AirbF 7½11	cv	1590	117	90	114	...
AlaBn 6.8s99t	6.8	925	101	99¾	100⅛	+ ¼
AlaP 9s2000	8.9	3262	102	87⅜	100¾	+ 11¼
AlaP 8½s01	8.6	2907	98⅝	84⅜	98⅜	+ 12¾
AlaP 7⅞s02	8.4	1471	95	80	93⅜	+ 13⅛
AlaP 7¾s02	8.4	2263	92½	78⅜	91¾	+ 12
AlaP 8⅞s03	8.8	4859	100½	86⅛	100½	+ 12½
AlaP 8¼s03	8.7	2418	96¾	81	95⅜	+ 13¼
AlaP 9¾s04	9.5	4425	103¾	92¾	102½	+ 8¼
AlaP 10⅞05	10.3	1524	108⅝	100	106	+ 4
AlaP 10½05	9.9	3399	107¾	98⅝	105¾	+ 5¾
AlaP 8⅞06	9.0	2354	99¾	85½	98¾	+ 11⅛
AlaP 8¾07	9.0	4013	98½	84⅛	96⅞	+ 10⅞
AlaP 8⅝87	8.6	2916	101⅝	99¼	100½	+ 1⅛
AlaP 9¼07	9.2	3637	101	89⅜	100½	+ 11⅝
AlaP 9½08	9.3	3405	102⅜	90¼	101¾	+ 10¼
AlaP 9⅝08	9.5	3852	102⅞	91	101¾	+ 8⅛
AlaP 12⅝10	11.6	6273	111⅞	105	108⅜	+ ⅜
AlaP 9⅜16	9.4	60	99½	98½	99½	...
AlskA 9s03	cv	7016	126	103	116	+ 7
AlskH 16¼94	14.5	3568	115⅞	101	111¾	+ 3½
AlskH 16¼99	13.4	3223	121	110¼	121	+ 8
AlskH 17¾91	14.4	2051	124¼	116	123⅜	+ 3⅜
AlskH 15¼92	14.1	1570	110⅞	103½	108⅜	+ 2⅜
AlskH 11¾92	11.2	465	105½	98¼	105	+ 3
AlskH 11½93	11.3	320	107	100⅞	101⅝	+ ⅝
AlskH 11⅜93	11.2	205	104⅝	100⅝	101¾	+ ¼
AlskH 10¾93	10.3	1119	105½	100⅝	104	+ 2
AlskH 11½93I	11.1	326	109¾	99⅝	104	+ 4
AlskH 12⅞93	11.9	1052	108⅛	102	108	+ 2½
Alco 8½10	cv	6154	119	104¼	114	+ 9½
AllgWt 4s98	6.4	222	63	52	62½	+ 8¾
Allgl 10¾99	14.5	2766	90	53	74	– 3
Allgl 10.4s02	14.3	9667	87½	30	72¾	– 3¼
Allgl 9s89	10.1	1961	93¼	63	89	...
AlldC 5.2s91	5.9	249	89	79⅛	88	+ 9⅝
AlldC 6.6s93	6.8	388	100⅞	81	97	+ 19
AlldC 7⅞96	8.0	828	99¾	87	99	+ 15⅝
AlldC 9s2000	9.0	854	100	90	100	+ 15
AlldC zr87	...	5195	98⅞	86½	96 9/32	+ 9 25/32
AlldC zr92	...	7924	64⅝	50⅛	64¼	+ 12⅝
AlldC zr96	...	2844	47½	35	45½	+ 10⅛
AlldC zr98	...	6614	37	26⅝	36⅞	+ 9⅜
AlldC zr2000	...	13366	30½	21	30¼	+ 7½
AldC dc6s88	6.2	4917	99⅜	91⅛	97½	+ 5½
AldC dc6s90	6.3	2523	96½	84⅝	94½	+ 7¾
AlldC zr87	...	464	96½	87	96 1/32	+ 8 1/32
AlldC zr89	...	116	83	74⅛	82⅛	+ 10⅛
AlldC zr91	...	301	70½	60½	70½	+ 11½
AlldC zr9	...	340	60	48	58½	+ 12¾
AlldC zr95	...	485	49½	36⅝	49½	+ 15
AlldC zr97	...	797	42	30	41½	+ 11½
AlldC zr99	...	2002	33½	24¼	32⅛	+ 7⅜
AlldC zr01	...	2231	28	19	28	+ 8
AlldC zr03	...	2128	25	16¼	22¼	+ 5¾
AlldC zr05	...	3155	19½	13	19⅛	+ 6⅛
AlldC zr07	...	860	15½	9⅜	15½	+ 8½
AlldC zr09	...	13724	14½	8⅛	13⅜	+ 4⅝
AldSig 9.4s88	9.1	23	103½	101½	103¼	...
AldSig 9⅞97	9.4	60	105½	100¼	104½	...
AlldSt 10⅜90	10.3	1735	104	100	100¼	– 1⅞
AlsCha 10.35s99	10.5	378	102	87½	98⅛	+ 9
AlsCha 12s90	11.9	704	103¼	97	100½	+ ⅛
AlsCha 16s91	14.5	2501	113½	107	110⅛	+ 1
AllstF 8⅛87	8.1	415	101	99⅜	100 1/16	+ 15/16
AllstF 7⅞87	7.8	1245	101	99⅜	100⅜	+ ½
Alcoa 6s92	6.5	891	92¾	80⅜	92⅝	+ 14
Alcoa 9s95	9.0	3015	103	92⅛	100½	+ 8
Alcoa 7.45s96	7.8	1067	95¾	81¾	95	+ 13¼
Alcoa 9.45s00	9.3	1273	102	91	102	+ 11
AluCa 14¼92	12.8	342	116	105¼	111¾	+ ¾
AluCa 9⅞98	9.5	35	104	104	104	...
AMAX 8½96	10.0	1000	88	70¼	85⅛	+ 15⅛
AMAX 9⅜00	10.5	1720	89½	72	89⅜	+ 18¼
AMAX 8⅝01	10.3	411	86	71⅛	83⅜	+ 16⅜
AMAX 14¼90	13.0	6859	110½	101¼	109½	+ 6
AMAX 14½94	12.8	13536	114	100¾	113¼	+ 9¾
AHes 7⅛96	7.8	121	94	87	91	+ 2¼
AFoP 4.8s87	4.8	2639	100	95	99 13/16	+ 5 3/16
AFoP 4.8s87r	4.8	608	99⅞	5 15/16	99	...
AForP 5s30	9.1	2751	59⅞	44	55	+ 8⅝
AFor 5s30r	9.0	358	57	42½	55½	...
AAirl 4¼92	5.2	2678	83⅜	69⅝	82⅛	+ 13⅛
AAirl 5¼98	7.4	217	71⅛	61	71⅛	+ 10⅛
ABrnd 4⅝90	5.1	135	92	85	91½	+ 6½
ABrnd 5⅞92	6.4	1041	94	81⅛	92¼	+ 12¾
ABrnd 11⅛89	10.7	1612	107	102⅝	103¾	+ ⅜
ABrnd 9¾87	9.6	955	102⅝	101	101 1/16	– 7/16
ABrnd 9⅛16	9.1	100	103	98¾	100	...
ACan 4¾s90	5.2	136	91⅝	80¾	91¼	+ 10¼
ACan 4¾90r	5.5	30	88	85⅛	87	...
ACan 6s97	7.4	744	81⅝	70⅝	81¼	+ 11¼
ACan 7¾s01	8.5	1057	91⅜	80	91⅜	+ 14⅝
ACan 13¼93	11.4	3414	118	107	116½	+ 8¼
ACeM 6¾91	cv	1365	70⅜	46½	54	– 8
ACyan 7⅜01	8.2	317	90	76¾	90	+ 12⅜
ACyan 8⅜06	8.6	262	97¼	82⅞	97¼	+ 16¼
AExC 7.8s92	7.9	440	101⅝	90	98½	+ 6
AExC 10.1s90	10.0	2989	104	100⅛	100½	– 2¼
AExC 11¼00	10.0	406	112	103⅝	112	+ 6¾
AExC 12⅞91	12.0	986	111	105½	107	...
AExC 14¾92	12.7	890	119⅝	114	116½	– ⅜
AExC 11⅝92	10.9	589	113½	105⅜	106⅞	+ ⅝
AExC 11¾12	10.6	100	112	103	111	+ 9½
AmGn 9⅜08	9.1	227	103½	91	103½	+ 13½
AmGn 11s07	cv	5605	246	190	194½	– ½
AmGn 11s08	cv	2151	237	188	201	+ 6
AHoist 5½93	cv	950	77	66	66	– 4
AHosp 7⅞07	8.7	542	91	79	90½	+ 18½
AInvt 8¾s89	8.8	343	100	95⅛	99	+ 5⅛
AmMed 9½01	cv	24744	111¾	96	101	– 2
AmMed 8¼08	cv	8659	98	85	89	+ 4½
AmMed 11s98	11.0	685	103½	98	100¼	+ ¼
AmMed 11¾99	11.4	199	107	100¼	103½	+ ⅝
ASmel 4⅝88	4.9	293	93⅝	83	93⅝	+ 9⅛
AmStr 12s90	11.8	115	104	101½	102⅛	– 1
ATT 2⅝s86	2.6	6184	99 31/32	98	99⅞	+ 1⅞
ATT 2⅞s87	2.9	13441	98¾	93¾	98 23/32	+ 4 23/32
ATT 3⅞s90	4.2	14400	93	85	91⅝	+ 5⅞
ATT 3⅞90r	4.2	2078	92⅞	84⅞	91½	...
ATT 8¾00	8.6	1098	102¾	25	101⅜	+ 10
ATT 7s01	8.0	35191	90	74¼	87⅞	+ 10¾
ATT 7⅛s03	8.1	30519	90⅞	73⅝	88½	+ 12⅛
ATT 8.80s05	8.8	77482	101⅛	87	100	+ 10
ATT 8⅝s07	8.7	42091	100⅜	84⅝	99⅝	+ 10¾
ATT 8⅝26	8.7	2604	99⅝	90¼	99⅜	...
Ames 10s95	9.9	518	101	91½	101	+ 10½
Amfac 5¼94	cv	1338	91¼	80⅜	87	+ 6¼
Amoco 6s91	6.2	3758	99	84¼	96¼	+ 9⅝
Amoco 6s98	6.8	3143	88	74	88	+ 12⅛
Amoco 9.2s04	8.8	6411	105½	92¾	104	+ 9
Amoco 8⅜05	8.5	2296	99⅞	85¼	98	+ 10¾
Amoco 7⅞07	8.5	2108	94¼	80¼	92¼	+ 10¼
Amoco 14s91	12.6	4597	113⅞	109⅛	111½	+ ⅛
Amoco 7⅞96	7.8	598	101½	97½	101½	...
Ancp 13⅞02f	cv	6599	102½	82½	100	+ 11
Andarko 14¾91	13.0	99	113½	105⅛	113½	+ 4¼
Andarko 14.70s94	13.0	34	113¼	106¼	113¼	+ 5¾
Anchr 8⅝06	9.5	66	90⅝	83⅝	90⅝	+ 5⅝
Anhr 11⅞12	10.6	630	112¾	106½	111¾	+ 5
Anhr 8s96	7.8	1445	102½	99¼	102½	...
Anhr 8⅝16	8.7	5	99½	99½	99½	...
Anhr 5.45s91	5.9	192	93	86⅜	92⅛	+ 6⅞
Anhr 6s92	6.5	362	95	82¼	92¼	+ 10
Anhr 7.95s99	8.4	149	97½	83⅛	95	+ 11⅞

NEW YORK BONDS

		Sales $1,000	High	Low	Last	Net Chg.
Anhr 9.20s05	8.9	1316	103	89	103	+ 16
Anhr 8.55s08	9.2	36	95	86½	93⅜	+ 18⅜
Anxtr 8¼03	cv	7844	115	99¾	100⅞	– 1¼
Apch 8.5s06	8.0	3612	109	97¾	106½	...
Arco 7¾86	7.8	1190	100⅛	99⅛	99 29/32	+ 19/32
Aristr 9½89	9.5	194	101	94⅝	100¼	+ 5⅝
Aristr 8½90	8.6	173	100⅝	97¼	99	+ 7
Aristr 14½99	13.4	80	115½	108½	108½	– 3¼
Aristr 14¼94	12.8	10	111	111	111	– ¼
ArizP 7.45s02	8.7	1957	88	73⅝	86	+ 11¾
ArizP 10⅝00	10.1	1913	106½	97½	105	+ 5
ArkBst 7s11	5.9	2924	122	103	119	...
ArmS 5.9s92	7.4	183	88⅛	80	80	+ ⅜
ArmS 8.7s95	12.7	2985	89	60	68¼	– 8¾
ArmS 9.2s00	14.4	7134	85⅝	54½	63¾	– 8¾
Arms 8½01	15.6	9182	80⅝	52	54½	– 10¾
ArCk 8s96	8.0	568	101	86½	99½	+ 13
ArRub 8⅝96	9.1	143	97	90¼	95	+ 10
ArRub 11½95	10.8	25	106	106	106	...
ArRub 7¾11	cv	2098	103	94	98	...
Asar 9¾2000	10.8	1675	91½	77⅞	89⅞	+ 11
AshO 6.15s92	6.8	223	91	81¼	91	+ 10¾
AshO 4¾93	cv	109	179	111	171	+ 59
AshO 8.8s00	9.1	888	98	84½	97	+ 15½
AshO 8.2s02	9.0	545	92¼	77⅛	91¼	+ 13⅛
AshO 11.1s04	10.6	952	108	97⅜	105	+ 4
AsCp 12⅛00	11.4	85	106	102¾	106	+ 6
AsCp 13⅛00	11.6	180	116	109½	112¾	+ 7⅛
AsCp 13⅞90	13.0	154	109⅛	106⅛	106⅝	– 2⅜
AsCp 14½90	13.2	167	109½	107½	109½	+ 1⅞
AsCp 12⅜89	11.7	237	106¾	103	105½	+ 1¾
AsCp 11.85s89	10.9	62	110	108½	109	+ 2⅝
AsCp 11¾88	10.9	326	109	103⅞	108	+ 3⅞
AsCp 12.55s88	11.6	47	108½	105⅜	107⅞	+ ⅞
AsCp 11½89	10.5	15	109½	109½	109½	+ 4⅞
AsCp 11s90	10.2	105	108	105⅛	108	+ 4½
AsCp 11⅝89	10.7	135	111½	109⅛	109⅛	...
AsCp 9¾90	9.2	260	106	101½	106	+ 4¼
AsCp 10½91	9.5	100	110⅞	110⅞	110⅞	+ 10½
AtalSos 7⅛01	cv	87	101	91	94	...
Atchn 4s95st	5.1	183	80	62	78	+ 15
Atchn 4s95st r	5.5	15	72⅜	63⅛	72⅜	...
Atchsn 4s95	5.3	1138	76½	60⅞	75	+ 9¾
Atchn 4s95r	5.4	338	76	65	74½	...
Athlne 11s93	12.1	306	96½	90¾	91	– ⅞
Athlne 15⅝91	13.7	4	114	113	114	+ 7
AtlCL 4.95s88	5.1	195	96⅞	91⅞	96⅞	+ 6⅞
AtlCL 4.95s88r	5.1	25	96⅞	92½	96⅞	...
AtlCSt 4¾88	5.0	131	97⅝	90½	94¾	+ 7⅛
AtlCst 4¾88r	4.6	26	96	92½	96	...
ARich 5⅝97	6.4	467	88	72¾	88	+ 14½
ARich 8⅝00	8.7	2674	100¾	88¼	99½	+ 9½
ARich 7.7s00	8.3	1595	94½	81½	93	+ 10¾
ARich 7¾03	8.4	1664	93	79¾	92	+ 10½
ARich 11⅜10	10.5	1522	111½	100½	108½	+ 1½
ARich 13⅝11	11.9	1144	120	111	114⅝	+ ⅛
ARch dc7s91	7.1	3596	98⅝	88	98⅝	+ 8⅞
ARch 12½12	11.4	698	116⅝	109⅝	110⅛	+ 1⅝
ARch 11s13	10.0	581	109½	100	109½	+ 9
ARch 11⅛15	10.1	837	110½	102	110	+ 5
ARch 10⅜95	9.2	3278	113⅞	102¼	112⅞	+ 7⅜
ARch 10⅞05	9.3	1525	117¼	102	117¼	+ 16
ARch 9¾89	9.2	2250	107⅛	101⅜	106½	+ 3¾
ARch 10½95	9.4	463	112½	103¾	112	+ 7½
ARch 9½96	9.0	9887	106	97½	105½	...
ARch 9¼93	8.6	1592	107⅛	101¾	107	...
ARch 9⅛11	9.0	127	102	98	101	...
AutDt 6½11	cv	14547	115	99	113	...
Avaln 7s92f	cv	820	82	71½	82	+ 10½
AvcoC 5½93	cv	1001	93	88⅛	91	+ 1⅜
AvcoC 7½93	8.0	3865	95	81	93¾	+ 10¾
AvcoC 12s90	12.0	399	105	100⅛	100⅛	– 1⅞
AvcoF 6⅛87	6.1	231	100½	97⅝	100	+ 2
AvcoF 7⅞89	7.9	237	103	95	100¼	+ 4¼
AvcoF 7⅞92	8.0	240	100½	91½	98	+ 7
AvcoF 7⅝97	8.0	249	95¼	80	95¼	+ 20⅜
AvcoF 8.35s	8.5	234	98½	84½	98½	+ 19½
AvcoF 8⅞91	8.8	282	101½	93⅞	100⅜	+ 6⅜
AvcoF 9⅜93	9.5	67	100	94⅛	99	+ 9⅜
AvcoF 9⅛98	9.1	267	100	92⅛	100	+ 9⅞
AvcoF 9⅜98	9.3	184	102	85	101	+ 9
AvcoF 9¾99	9.6	813	103	100	102	+ 2
Avnet 8s13	cv	9351	109½	95	98	– 1½
Avon 11¾90	10.9	291	109½	103	108	+ 6
—B—						
BPNA 10s00	9.8	619	104	97¼	102	+ 2
BPNA 9¼01	9.3	803	100½	91¾	99⅞	+ 10¾
Bally 6s98	cv	15209	97½	75⅛	90¼	+ 14¼
Bally 10s06	cv	23453	107½	91¾	102	+ 10
BalPP 13⅞03	12.4	30	112⅛	112⅛	112⅛	+ 12⅛
B O 4¼95	4.7	468	90⅞	70¾	90⅝	+ 20⅝
B O 4¼95r	4.7	89	90⅝	70	90⅝	...
B O 4½10A	cv	1246	226	117	124¼	– 29⅞
BalGE 3s89	3.2	754	92¾	83½	92½	+ 7⅝
BalGE 3s89r	3.3	92	92	90	92	...
BalGE 3¼90	3.7	754	90	78	88¼	+ 8⅝
BalGE 3¼90r	3.7	71	88⅜	81	88⅜	...
BalGE 4s93	4.8	338	83	70¼	83	+ 11
BalGE 4s93r	5.3	5	75⅝	75⅝	75⅝	...
BalGE 9⅞05	9.3	1587	109	95	105⅞	+ 9⅞
BalGE 8⅜06	8.5	2427	98½	82⅜	98⅜	+ 14⅞
BalGE 8¼07	8.6	1515	97	82	96⅛	+ 12⅞
BalGE 9⅜08	9.1	2930	104⅛	90⅝	102½	+ 9½
BalGE 14¾92	13.4	905	115⅝	107	110	– ⅛
BkBos 10.65s87	10.4	1174	105⅞	101⅛	102¼	– ¾
BkNE 8.85s99	8.9	616	101	85⅜	99	+ 14
BkNY 8¼10	cv	11822	136¾	108¼	126	+ 16
Banka 7⅞03	9.4	4708	87⅜	72⅞	83⅞	+ 9⅛
Banka 8⅞05	9.8	11164	95	75⅜	90⅞	+ 7⅝
Banka 8¾01	9.7	6909	94½	78⅛	89¾	+ 7
Bkam 8.35s07	9.7	6326	89⅞	72⅝	86⅜	+ 8½
Bkam zr87A	...	20151	95	83	94⅜	+ 9¼
Bkam zr90s	...	11852	72¼	59	71	+ 6
Bkam zr92s	...	53321	58⅝	20	56¼	+ 5⅜
Bkam zr87D	...	18538	92½	78⅛	91 21/32	+ 7 13/32
Bkam zr91s	...	9077	69½	55⅞	68⅝	+ 6⅝
Bkam zr93s	...	34120	55	41⅛	53	+ 5⅛
Bkam 13¼88	12.3	1811	110¼	102	107⅞	– ⅛
BkAm 11½95	11.5	677	102½	99½	100	– 2¼
BkAm 11⅜96	11.4	579	103	97	100⅛	– 2⅛
BkAm 7.65s94	7.9	1877	103	94½	96⅝	– 5
Bkamrt 9½00	cv	10	178⅛	178⅛	178⅛	+ 4⅛
BkamRt 9½08	cv	4074	112	100	109	+ 10
BnkTr 8⅛99	8.4	1820	99	82¾	97	+ 12¼
BnkTr 8⅝02	8.7	1224	99¼	84⅛	99¼	+ 10⅞
Baner 13⅛06	12.4	10	106	106	106	...
BarcA 7.95s92	7.9	171	100½	94	100½	+ 13¼
BarcA 8¾97	8.7	450	101	91	100½	+ 9½
BarcA zr90s	...	6742	76	63⅛	74⅛	+ 10⅛
BarcNA 14⅝91	13.3	95	112¼	109¾	109¾	– 1⅞
BarcNA 11⅝03	9.9	114	117¾	105	117¾	+ 15¾
BASX dc11⅝03	12.4	151	97½	87	94	+ 9
BASIX 8¾05	cv	6770	119½	87¾	90	– 20
BaxL 4⅜s91	cv	43	197½	156	197	+ 41
BaxL 4¾s01	cv	825	179½	132	170	+ 38
Bearng 8½09	cv	2470	119	104½	106	– ½
BecD 4⅛s88	cv	374	248	128	200	+ 65¾
vjBeker 15⅞03f	...	16183	76⅞	16⅛	19⅝	– 47
BellCn 8¾06	9.0	1699	101	86½	96¾	+ 7¼
BellCn 9s08	9.0	1075	101½	87½	99½	+ 11⅞
BellCn 13⅜10	10.2	43	130½	111¼	130½	+ 20½
BellCn 14½91	13.1	615	112¾	110½	110½	+ ⅞
BellPa 8⅝06	8.7	7055	99¾	84¼	99¼	+ 12¼
BellPa 7⅛12	8.2	3037	88	70⅜	87⅜	+ 14⅜
BellPa 7½13	8.2	4230	91	73¼	91	+ 15½
BellPa 9⅝14	9.3	9522	106½	92½	103⅝	+ 8⅛
BellPa 8¾15	8.8	3032	100¾	84⅝	99½	+ 10½
BellPa 8⅛17	8.6	2628	96	79½	94½	+ 12½
BellPa 9¼19	9.1	4462	104¼	87⅞	102	+ 10¾
Bemi 6⅜92	7.3	18	87¼	80	87¼	+ 11¼
Bendx 6⅝92	6.9	518	96¼	82¼	96¼	+ 10¾
Bendx 11.20s05	10.4	261	107⅞	100⅛	107⅞	+ 7⅞
BenCp 7½96	8.2	518	95⅛	82¼	91	+ 9
BenCp 7.45s00	8.5	698	88⅜	71½	87½	+ 13⅜
BenCp 7½02	9.0	340	85½	74	83	+ 12
BenCp 7½98	8.2	135	92	81	92	+ 12
BenCp 8s01	8.0	53	100⅛	99⅝	100	+ 1¼
BenCp 8.3s03	8.7	265	95	80	95	+ 12¾
BenCp 8.4s07	9.2	906	94	79⅛	91⅛	+ 12⅛
BenCp 8.4s08	8.4	2261	102½	99¼	100⅜	+ ½
BenCp 6½87t	6.5	569	99 19/32	94¼	99 5/16	+ 1 5/16
BenCp 9s05	9.2	345	97⅞	88½	97⅞	+ 13⅞
BenCp 13⅜91	12.7	769	109¼	102½	105⅛	– 2⅞
BenCp 12¾13	11.8	100	114	107⅞	107⅞	+ 1⅞
BenCp 12½93	10.4	70	119⅞	108	119⅞	+ 24⅞
BenCp 12.45s94	10.9	285	121	114¼	114½	+ 13
BenCp 12.60s94	10.7	74	121¾	112	118	+ 10½
BenCp 12⅜88	12.0	50	103	103	103	– 1½
BenCp 9⅜90	8.9	69	105¼	105¼	105¼	...
BestPrd 9s94	10.1	47	89⅜	76⅜	89⅜	+ 13¾
BestPr 12⅝96	12.6	113	100½	99½	100	...
BethSt 4½90	8.3	11956	82⅞	50	54	– 20¼
BethSt 5.4s92	9.3	2761	78⅝	50⅜	58	– 10½

NEW YORK BONDS

		Sales $1,000	High	Low	Last	Net Chg.
BethSt 6⅞99	15.3	5020	71¾	39	44⅞	−13⅛
BethSt 9s00	16.8	16759	84⅝	41⅜	53½	−18
BethSt 8.45s05	18.2	64494	78	38⅝	46½	−18½
BethSt 8⅜01	17.4	14540	79	38	48	−16¼
Bevrly 7⅝03	cv	18883	114	95	99½	−7
Beverly zr03	...	36764	32½	25⅜	27¾	+1¾
Boeing 8⅜96	8.1	835	104	98⅛	103¼	...
BoisC 13⅛94	12.3	35	107⅛	107	107	−2½
BoisC 11⅞93	10.1	12	117	100	117	...
Bordn 4⅜91	5.2	24	84	77⅛	84	+8¾
Bordn 5¾97	6.7	459	86	73	86	+15⅝
Bordn 8½04	8.6	1160	99	85¼	99	+15
Bordn 9⅜09	9.0	561	104¼	97	104¼	+15⅜
Bordn 10¼95	9.8	10	105	105	105	...
BorW 7⅞s91	8.1	288	100	95	97⅝	+5⅛
BorW 7½s93	7.7	66	97	89¾	97	+10⅜
BorgW dc6s01	8.8	227	74	58⅝	68	+9¾
BorW 5½s92	6.1	289	91	82¼	90	+12¼
BosE 9¼07	9.3	1222	101¾	88	99¾	+9¾
Bowatr 9s09	cv	4041	133½	112	118½	+5½
Bowatr 12⅜15	10.9	109	113½	104	113½	+14⅜
BrkUn 4⅜88	4.5	277	97⅜	92½	97⅛	+7⅝
BrkUn 4⅝90	5.0	122	93	84½	93	+9
BrkUn 6¼92	6.7	241	95	88⅞	93	+12⅞
BrkUn 9⅛95	8.8	1350	103½	94	103¼	+8½
BrkUn 7⅞97	7.9	79	100	86	100	+21⅜
BrkUn 8¾99	8.8	756	100½	93½	100	+15⅝
BrkUn 9⅝96	9.4	375	105	97¼	102	+8⅛
BwnSh 9¼05	cv	4030	108	91½	100	+6¼
BrnGp 7⅜98	8.1	178	94⅛	90	90½	+9⅜
BrnGp 9⅞00	10.1	34	100	95⅛	98¼	+8¼
BucyE 9s99	9.2	95	98	89¼	98	+18¾
Bulova 6s90	cv	337	90	78⅝	88	+10
BurlInd 5s91	cv	1193	105½	90	104⅛	+13⅛
BurlInd 9s95	9.0	548	101	90⅝	100½	+9⅞
BurlInd 11¼90	11.1	1003	103⅞	99½	101	+¾
BurlInd 8¾08	cv	8985	110	93	105½	+12
BurNo 8½96	8.3	998	102¾	88½	102¾	+14¾
BurNo 8.6s99	8.5	710	102	86⅝	101½	+14⅛
BurNo 12⅞05	11.2	564	114¾	108¼	114½	+1½
BurNo 9⅝96	9.2	543	105¾	103⅝	104¾	...
BurNo 9s16	9.5	42	100	94½	95	...

—C—

		Sales $1,000	High	Low	Last	Net Chg.
CBS 10⅞95	10.0	12749	112¾	102	109	+4⅜
CBS 7.85s01	8.4	27	94½	87	93½	+16
CIGNA 8s07	cv	9934	117½	102	107	+4
CIT 9½95	9.3	1769	103½	97½	102⅝	+3⅝
CIT 8⅜s01	8.5	429	98⅝	83⅛	98⅝	+14¼
CIT 9s91	9.0	971	103	97⅛	100¼	+3¼
CIT 8.8s93	8.6	2097	102½	92⅞	102½	+8
CIT 8¾08	9.0	400	99⅜	83¼	97⅛	+12⅛
CIT 9.85s04	9.9	118	101	91⅛	100	+11¾
CIT 9⅝09	9.6	270	100½	91	100	+15⅞
CIT 11½05	10.2	852	112½	100⅝	112½	+8
CIT 15½87	14.6	1804	111½	105	106¼	−4¾
CNA 8½95	8.5	1036	100¼	87⅜	100	+12⅞
CNA Inc 94s	...	1	113	113	113	...
CSX 9½16	9.5	258	101	98	100½	...
CTI 18¼89	17.2	148	113	105	106	−5⅞
Caesr 12½90	12.0	1657	110	101½	104	+2
Caesr 11¼97	11.0	897	104½	92	102½	+7
Caesr 12s94	11.6	290	107	96¼	103½	+9½
Caesr 12½00	12.5	376	104½	97	100	...
Caesr cv6⅞06	...	4980	114	96¼	104	...
CampTag 15⅜91	13.7	128	114½	110¾	112	−1
CPc4s perp	9.2	4584	50	39½	43½	+3⅝
CPC 4sr	8.9	310	46¾	39⅝	45	...
CapHd 12¾06	10.4	1435	124	105	123	+16¾
CCOh 4½90	5.2	8	87	85	87	+10¾
CaroFrt 6¼11	cv	2031	109	98¼	105	...
CarPL 7¾02	8.4	1577	92¼	78⅛	92¼	+14⅛
CaroT 5¾88	cv	105	131	97¼	125	+27¾
CaroT 9⅛00	9.1	825	104½	89⅝	100⅜	+10⅞
CaroT 7¾01	8.2	616	95⅜	79⅞	95	+18
CaroT 8.1s03	8.7	490	96¾	81	93	+12¾
CaroT 9s08	8.9	613	101¼	88¾	101¼	+11⅜
Carr 8⅛s96	8.2	201	100	90	98½	+11½
Carr 7¾s98	8.4	50	92⅝	92⅝	92⅝	+11⅝
Carsn 7½11	6.8	8597	111	98	110	...
CartH 9¼96	9.3	523	100	91	100	+11
CarH 9.45s00	9.5	45	99	86	99	+20½
CartH 9⅛08	10.1	1300	96⅝	84⅛	90	+10½
CartH 11⅞10	11.4	300	107¾	100	104½	+7½
CasNG 10½92	10.1	293	104¼	98⅛	104¼	+6⅛
Case 5½s90	6.0	262	93¼	83⅛	91¾	+5¾
CastlC 8½97	9.3	103	91⅞	73⅞	91⅞	+21⅞
CatTr 5.3s92	5.9	30	91¼	88	89⅝	...
Caterp 6⅞92	7.3	62	95	93½	94⅛	−¾
Caterp 8.6s99	8.8	545	99½	91⅝	98⅛	+8⅛
Caterp 8¾99	8.9	170	99	89	98½	+13
Caterp 5½00	cv	13282	121	95	99	+¾
Caterp 8s01	8.6	700	93	83¼	93	+10⅜
Caterp 12½90	11.6	617	109¾	106¼	108	+2
Cave 11½00O	12.0	1740	100	85⅛	96	+10¼
Cave 11½00N	12.0	1582	99⅝	83⅞	96	+11
Celanse 11⅞05	11.0	134	111	103	108⅛	+4⅛
Celanse 9¾06	cv	515	336½	205	335	+124
Cenco 5s96	cv	366	73½	65½	65⅝	−6⅞
Cenco 4¾97	cv	161	62½	50	55½	+3
Centel 8.1s96	8.2	545	100	83⅛	98¼	+15⅛
CtrlTel 8s96	8.2	1324	100¼	84⅜	98⅛	+11¼
CATS zr11-88	...	1429	88⅞	77½	88	+8⅜
CATS zr11-91	...	2334	72	56⅜	72	+16⅝
CATS zr05-92	...	672	69	54⅛	66¼	+12½
CATS zr11-94	...	598	57⅝	43¼	56¼	+10½
CATS zr05-95	...	296	53⅞	41	53	+10
CATS zr11-96	...	2295	47⅞	34⅜	47¾	+10⅞
CATS zr05-97	...	1780	44½	33⅜	44½	+9¾
CATS zr05-98	...	2088	42⅞	29	39	+8⅜
CATS zr11-99	...	907	36	27¼	34¼	+6¾
CATS zr11-01	...	1636	33½	23	29½	+6¾
CATS zr11-02	...	717	29	20¾	29	+9
CATS zr11-03	...	2365	25	18	24½	+5⅝
CATS zr2006-11	...	13095	20½	12¾	18¾	+5½
ChSp 5⅞s92	6.0	74	98	90	97⅝	+18⅛
Champ 6½11	cv	3016	116½	96	116	...
vjChtCo 10⅝98f	...	7656	65¾	46¼	64⅞	+12¾
vjChtC dc14¾02f	...	13022	62	46⅛	62	+4⅛
ChsCp 6½96	cv	3085	167	119	129¼	+3¾
ChsCp 6.35s99t	6.5	1004	101	97¼	98⅜	+1⅛
ChsCp 6½09t	6.7	4763	98¼	85⅞	97	+4½
ChsCp flt96t	...	5	99½	99½	99½	...
Chelse 5¼93	cv	335	143	115	138	+22
Chmtrn 9s94	11.1	2035	87⅞	74¼	81	+1
ChNY 5s93	cv	73	174	134½	139	−2½
ChNY 5½96	cv	213	172	132	137½	−5½
ChNY 8.4s99	8.7	1312	97	85	96⅛	+13⅞
ChNY 8¼02	8.7	1190	96	79⅝	95¼	+18¼
ChNY 7.40s04t	7.3	864	102	98	102	+2
ChORA 4s89	4.3	91	92⅞	87	92⅞	+7⅛
C&O 4½92	5.3	295	86¼	77	84¾	+7¾
CPoM 7¼12	8.5	1839	87⅞	70⅛	85⅝	+14⅝
CPoM 8⅞09	8.9	2755	100	85¼	99½	+13¼
CPoM 9s18	9.0	2699	101	84½	100¼	+11¾
CPom 11¼25	9.5	28	119	104	119	+21
CPoV 7¼12	8.4	1750	90½	71⅜	86½	+14⅞
CPoV 8⅝09	8.8	3879	99⅛	83½	97⅝	+12⅛
CPoV 9¼15	9.1	3078	102¾	88⅝	101⅜	+10⅜
CPoV 9½19	9.2	1347	105⅛	89⅝	103½	+11½
CPoWas 7¾	8.8	912	89	74¼	88½	+14⅞
CPWV 7¼13	8.5	683	86⅞	69¾	85⅝	+15⅝
CPoWV 9s15	9.2	1377	101¾	85½	97¾	+11⅞
CPWV 9¼19	9.1	1986	101⅝	89½	101⅝	+11⅝
ChvrnC 12¾87	12.3	8065	107 23/32	103¼	103¼	−2⅝
ChvrnC 11¾88	10.9	2285	109¾	105¼	108	+1
ChvrnC 12s94	10.4	4489	117⅞	108½	115½	+5
ChvrnC 11s90	10.2	6851	109⅛	104	107½	+2⅝
ChvrnC 10¾95	9.6	4010	113	104	112½	+6⅜
Chvrn 5¾92	6.2	2299	92⅞	81⅜	92⅜	+9
Chvrn 7s96	7.3	3754	95¾	83¼	95¼	+9⅝
Chvrn 8¾05	8.7	4701	101½	86⅞	100⅝	+10¾
Chvrn 8½95	8.5	4616	102	92⅜	100¼	+6½
Chvrn 8¾96	8.4	899	103¾	101	103¾	...
Chvrn 9⅜16	9.4	157	102¼	98¾	99¾	...
ChNWn 3s89	3.4	69	87⅝	79⅝	87⅝	+10¾
ChNwn 3s89r	3.4	2	87⅝	87⅝	87⅝	...
ChNWT 14¼04	12.8	16	111½	102⅛	111½	+7½
ChNwt 15¾04	13.7	138	116½	113	115	+10⅞
ChiBQ 3s90	3.5	19	85	83	85	+20
CGtW 4s88	4.2	274	96	91	95	+5¾
CGtW 4½38f	...	80	47	39⅛	46	+7⅜
ChCft 13s99	12.7	681	105⅞	99	102¾	+1¾
ChCft 15s99	14.2	1447	109⅞	101⅛	106	...
Chrysl 8⅞95	8.9	7038	101	91⅛	100⅛	+8⅛
Chryslr 8s98	8.5	10729	95	79⅛	94½	+13⅜
Chryslr 12¾92	10.8	2124	118⅛	109⅛	118⅛	+8½
Chryslr 13s97	10.8	1890	123⅜	109⅜	120	+7⅞
Chryslr 12s15	10.7	2504	112¾	103	112¼	+6¼
ChryF 8.35s91	8.3	3200	102	90⅝	100¼	+10¼
ChryF 7.7s92	7.8	1429	100	88½	99	+11¼
ChryF 9⅜87	9.4	3272	103¾	99⅞	100	...
ChryF 13¼88	12.1	2496	111¾	107⅛	109⅞	+1⅞
ChryF zr89	...	181	80	72⅞	80	...

NEW YORK BONDS

		Sales $1,000	High	Low	Last	Net Chg.
ChryF zr90	...	1029	78	61⅛	73⅛	...
ChryF 13½91	12.3	1394	114½	105½	110	+ 5⅜
ChryF 94t	...	5	99⅛	99⅛	99⅛	...
ChryF 13¼99	10.7	35	123¾	122	123¾	+ 15⅞
ChryF 12¾99	10.3	239	124	109¼	124	+ 16⅝
ChryF 11¾90	10.7	755	111⅞	104⅞	109⅞	+ 6⅛
ChryF 12s92	10.5	760	116	105¼	114½	+ 7⅜
ChryF 12⅛90	10.9	1486	112½	105½	111½	+ 6
ChryF 10.6s90	9.9	2137	109	101½	106⅝	+ 4⅝
ChryF 9.8s88	9.4	1314	105⅛	102	104	...
ChryF 9⅜89	8.9	1268	106	99⅝	105	...
ChryF 9¾90D	9.2	2684	107	99½	106½	...
ChryF 9¾90F	9.2	1334	107	101	106	...
ChryF 9⅜91	9.0	1262	105⅞	100⅜	104⅜	...
ChryF 9¼91	8.9	986	105¼	99⅝	104½	...
ChryF 7¼89	7.3	29	100	99½	100	...
ChryOv 5s88	cv	12	87	80	87	+ 11
CinGE 4⅛87	4.2	337	98⅞	93	98 23/32	+ 4 23/32
CinGE 4⅛87r	4.2	6	99	97	99	...
CirclK 8¼05	cv	6394	140½	99	130½	+ 30¼
CirclK 7¼06	cv	1440	107¼	101	102¼	...
Citicp 7.2s89t	7.2	4471	102⅞	98	99½	+ ⅝
Citicp 5¾00	cv	405	151⅜	119½	127½	+ 7½
Citicp 8.45s07	8.9	12791	97	81	94½	+ 10¾
Citicp 8⅛07	8.8	6061	93½	79¼	92	+ 11
Citicp 8.4s98t	8.4	4217	102	94	99⅞	+ 2⅞
Citicp 7s04t	7.0	4807	100⅞	95½	99¾	+ 2¼
Citicp 89t	...	71	101½	98	98	– 1¾
Citicp 6.09s95t	6.1	5	99⅞	99⅞	99⅞	+ 3¾
Citicp 7s98t	7.0	45	100	98	100	+ ⅜
Citicp flt98t A	...	14	99½	97	97	+ ¼
Citicp 12¼93	11.3	3392	110	105¾	108	+ 1¼
Citicp 12s90	11.5	5090	107	103⅜	104	– 1⅛
Citicp 12½93	11.3	2131	111	106	110¼	+ 4
Citicp 8s99	7.9	3617	106	98	101⅛	– 1⅜
Citicp 12⅞89	12.3	1195	108	104	104⅞	– 1⅛
Citicp 11.60s89	11.2	951	106½	103½	103⅞	– ⅛
Citicp 11⅞95	10.7	997	112	107⅜	111	+ 6¼
CitiPP 12½96	cv	347	118	105½	118	+ 12½
CitSv 6⅛97	8.0	984	76¼	66½	76¼	+ 8¼
CitSv 6⅝99	8.3	1385	80	68	79½	+ 10
CitSv 7.65s01	9.0	727	87	72⅞	85⅛	+ 8⅝
CitSv 9¾00	9.9	1107	100¼	86⅝	98	+ 11⅜
CitSv 13⅞11	12.4	1797	115	110	111¾	– 1¼
CitSvc zr87	...	7788	94¾	83¾	93 15/32	+ 9 23/32
CitSvc zr88	...	11370	86⅛	76	86	+ 9½
CitSvc zr89	...	20081	79½	68	79	+ 10
CitSvG 13s05	12.4	430	110	102	105⅛	+ 1⅝
Clmt zrD88	...	9	84	84	84	...
Clmt zrD96	...	20	12	12	12	...
Clmt zrD04	...	1	16	16	16	...
Clmt zrD05	...	28	7	7	7	...
ClkEq 9⅝99	10.3	108	99	91	93	+ 5
ClkEq 7.85s91	8.0	890	98	86	98	+ 9⅝
ClkEq 8s87	8.2	1454	100¼	98	98 1/32	– 7/32
Claytn 7¾01	cv	5794	130	95¼	102½	...
ClevEl 7⅛90	7.3	2604	98	89⅝	97½	+ 7
ClevEl 3s89	3.4	669	89¾	80⅛	89¼	+ 9
ClevEl 3⅞93	5.0	265	77⅞	68	77⅞	+ 10
ClevEl 3⅞93r	5.1	21	75½	75½	75½	...
ClevEl 4⅜94	5.7	389	79½	65⅝	76⅜	+ 11⅜
ClevEl 8⅜91	8.4	2458	101	90¾	100¼	+ 9½
ClevEl 8¾05	9.3	3733	94½	79¾	94	+ 12
ClevEl 9¼09	9.5	3561	99	83½	97¼	+ 11¼
ClevEl 9.85s10	9.8	3364	102	88	100½	+ 10¼
ClevEl 8⅜11	9.4	2978	90¾	77⅛	89¼	+ 9½
ClevEl 8⅜12	9.4	1986	89⅜	77	88⅞	+ 9¾
Coastl 11¼96	11.7	2267	103	96	96⅛	...
Coastl 11¾06	11.8	2962	104	98	99¼	...
Coastl 11.48s91	9.3	149	91	88	91	...
Coleco 14⅜02	14.2	7489	105⅛	97	101	– 1⅜
Coleco 11s89	cv	5282	147½	98½	100	– 25
Coleco 11⅛01	13.7	2658	88⅞	79⅝	81½	...
ColnFd 12s08	11.9	1080	103⅞	97	100½	+ 5⅛
ColonSt 8s96	11.0	38	73	60¼	73	+ 16⅜
ColInt 8½91	9.3	68	93	90½	91⅛	– 8⅞
ColUte 13s02	10.8	10	120	120	120	+ 10
ColtIn 10⅛95	10.5	7440	100¼	91	96¾	...
ColtIn 11¼15	11.3	2341	103	95	99⅛	...
ColtIn 12½01	11.9	2784	108	102	104⅞	...
ColuG 9s94	9.0	2148	103⅛	91¾	100½	+ 6⅝
ColuG 8¾95	8.8	1301	101½	90⅝	99¾	+ 8¾
ColuG 9⅛95	8.9	1735	102½	92⅝	102	+ 8⅝
ColuG 8⅜96	8.6	1068	98⅝	87⅞	97	+ 8⅜
ColuG 8¼96	8.6	1218	98	86⅞	96⅛	+ 8⅝
ColuG 7½97M	8.2	487	94	82	91⅞	+ 11¼
ColuG 7½97J	8.3	545	93	80⅜	90¼	+ 10
ColuG 7½97O	8.0	465	94	80⅛	94	+ 14
ColuG 7½98	8.1	325	92⅜	77¾	92⅜	+ 12⅜
ColuG 9⅞99	9.8	278	103	98	100⅝	+ 10½
ColuG 9⅝89	9.4	944	104½	98	102⅛	+ 4⅛
ColuG 10⅛95	9.9	381	105	100	102	+ 1⅞
ColuG 9⅛96	9.1	732	102	93¼	100½	+ 7⅞
ColuG 10¼99	9.9	380	103½	100	103⅜	+ 7⅝
ColuG 11¾99	11.1	697	108	101½	105⅝	+ 1⅝
ColuG 12¾00	11.8	658	110	103⅜	107⅝	+ 1⅞
ColuG 15⅜97	13.2	268	116½	112	116½	+ 3¾
ColuG 10¼11	10.0	65	102½	101¾	102½	...
ColSO 4½87	4.5	515	99½	94¼	99 15/32	+ 4 11/32
ColSo 13¾93	12.6	100	110¼	109	109	– 1
CEn 7.45s96	7.8	195	95	83	95	+ 16½
Cmdis 8s03	cv	21353	112½	85½	99	– 2
Cmdis 9.65s02	10.9	6041	92½	71	88¾	+ 9¼
Cmdis 10s94	10.0	435	100⅞	98	100¼	...
CmlCr 8¾91	8.7	3718	101⅛	84⅞	100⅝	+ 14⅞
CmlCr 7¾92	8.0	1474	96¾	78⅝	96⅝	+ 17⅜
CmlCr 7¾93	8.1	1919	99	77½	95¾	+ 19
CmlSo 4½91	cv	250	83	73⅛	80¾	+ 7⅝
CmwE 2¾99	4.3	26	64	58	64	+ 9⅞
CmwE 3s99	5.9	18	51¾	50⅛	50⅝	+ ⅝
CmwE 2⅞01	5.7	36	51⅛	46	50½	– 13½
CmwE 7⅝03F	8.8	1801	91	75¾	86⅞	+ 9½
CmwE 7⅝03J	8.5	1597	90½	76⅛	89¼	+ 11
CmwE 8s03	8.8	4356	92¼	77⅜	90¾	+ 10⅛
CmwE 8¾05	9.1	4267	98	84	96	+ 9
CmwE 9⅜04	9.3	4514	102½	89¾	100½	+ 9⅛
CmwE 8⅛07J	8.8	3462	94⅛	79	92⅜	+ 11⅝
CmwE 8⅛07D	9.1	2474	93	78¾	89¾	+ 8¾
CmwE 8¼07	9.0	4362	94⅞	78¾	91¾	+ 10⅛
CmwE 9⅛08	9.1	7467	100⅞	84⅛	100	+ 10⅞
CmwE 14⅞87	14.7	4421	107½	101¼	101¼	– 5⅝
CmwE 15⅜00	12.7	1373	126	116⅜	121¼	+ 1¼
CmwE 11⅛10	10.3	1870	109⅞	101	108⅜	+ 7¼
CmwE 14s91	13.0	10196	111¾	106⅛	107¾	+ 1⅝
CmwE 17½88	15.0	2813	122½	115¼	117	– 2
CmwE 16s90	15.2	7110	112¾	105	105½	– 7
CmwE 14s89	12.0	269	118	113¾	117	+ 3
CmwE 14⅜94	12.4	85	116	115	116	+ 1
CmwE 16¾11	14.8	11833	118	113	113½	– 2½
CmwE 14¼92	13.0	2113	115	108	110	+ ½
CmwE 15⅜12	13.2	723	120¼	114	116¾	...
CmwE 13s12	11.5	1262	116¼	109	112¾	+ 1¼
CmwE 12⅛13	10.8	695	113½	103	112⅝	+ 8
CmwE 12¼91	10.7	269	115	105½	115	+ 5
CmwE 13⅜13	11.5	393	118	109⅜	115⅞	+ 4¼
CmwE 10⅝95	9.8	198	110	106¾	108¾	+ 4⅛
CmwE 11¾15	10.5	528	113¾	103	111½	+ 5
Compq 9½05	cv	9336	185⅞	119	167½	+ 39
Cmpvsn 8s09	cv	12283	85¾	63½	83	+ 18½
ConnM 11½90	11.4	52	101½	100	101¼	– 1½
Conoco 9⅜09	9.2	638	102½	92⅜	102	+ 6¼
Conoco 13¼11	11.7	147	116⅞	110¼	113	...
ConEd 5s87	5.1	3209	99½	93⅛	99	+ 5
ConEd 5s87r	5.1	577	99	94	98¾	...
ConEd 4s88	4.1	2113	96⅞	89⅜	96⅝	+ 5⅝
ConEd 4s88r	4.2	688	97	89⅜	96⅜	...
ConEd 4¾90	5.1	774	93⅛	82	92⅞	+ 7⅜
ConEd 4¾90r	5.1	84	93	83	92½	...
ConEd 5s90	5.4	2056	93	84	91⅞	+ 7⅞
ConEd 5s90r	5.5	288	93	90½	91¼	...
ConEd 4¾91	5.3	688	90¾	80	89⅞	+ 8⅛
ConEd 4¾91r	5.2	54	91	86¼	91	...
ConEd 4⅝91	5.2	1051	90	78⅝	89	+ 10⅜
ConEd 4⅝91r	5.2	5	89	89	89	...
ConEd 4⅜92V	5.1	954	87⅛	75⅛	86⅝	+ 12⅛
ConEd 4⅜92v r	5.1	91	87	85⅝	86½	...
ConEd 4⅜92W	5.1	628	86⅝	75¾	86⅛	+ 13⅛
ConEd 4⅜92w r	5.2	37	85	81¾	84¼	...
ConEd 4⅝93	5.5	2328	84¾	72¼	84¼	+ 12⅞
ConEd 9⅜00	9.1	10012	103½	92¾	103⅛	+ 8¼
ConEd 7.9s01	8.3	6931	97	81¾	95½	+ 11½
ConEd 7.9s02	8.4	5622	95½	80⅝	94½	+ 11¾
ConEd 7¾03	8.3	4243	94	79	93⅛	+ 12⅞
ConEd 8.4s03	8.5	5971	99½	84	98⅜	+ 12
ConEd 9⅛04	8.9	9317	103	89	102	+ 10½
CFrt 7.95s96	8.6	32	95	77¾	92½	+ 15⅝
CnNG 4½87	4.5	168	99 21/32	94⅝	99⅜	+ 4¾
CnNG 4⅜88	4.5	216	98½	91	97¼	+ 6¼
CnNG 4¾90	5.1	150	94¼	86⅞	94	+ 15
CnNG 6⅛92	6.6	424	96	84⅜	92¼	+ 7¼
CnNG 7¾94	7.8	434	99¼	86⅜	99	+ 13⅞
CnNG 8¼94	8.3	864	101¾	92⅛	100	+ 8⅜
CnNG 9s95	8.9	1454	103	94⅛	101¼	+ 5¼
CnNG 7⅞95	8.2	403	101	88⅛	96	+ 6⅜
CnNG M 8⅜96	8.3	917	102	88⅝	100½	+ 10⅝
CnNG 7¾96	8.4	126	95½	84¾	92¼	+ 4¼

NEW YORK BONDS

		Sales $1,000	High	Low	Last	Net Chg.
CnNG 7⅝97	7.6	237	99¾	86½	99¾	+ 19⅝
CnNG 7¾98	8.1	246	96	85½	95⅝	+ 18⅝
CnNG 8⅝99	8.7	331	100	87⅞	99½	+ 11¾
CnNG 9¼95	9.1	1388	104	95½	102	+ 5⅞
CnNGS 8⅜96	8.4	291	100	92⅛	99½	+ 8
CnNG 8⅛97	8.3	409	99⅜	90⅞	98⅜	+ 9¼
CnNG 7⅝96	8.0	17	96¾	94⅜	95⅜	...
CnPw 4½88	4.8	1436	95⅛	83⅝	94⅜	+ 10⅞
CnPw 4⅝89	5.0	1174	93	79¼	92	+ 13⅞
CnPw 4⅝89r	5.1	79	91⅜	87½	91⅜	...
CnPw 4⅝90	5.4	890	87	73	86⅜	+ 12⅛
CnPw 4⅝90r	5.3	52	87¼	82¾	87¼	...
CnPw 4⅝91	5.5	1270	86	71	84½	+ 13
CnPw 5⅞96	7.4	3642	80½	62	79¾	+ 17½
CnPw 6⅞98	8.2	2549	84⅜	64⅝	83¾	+ 16¾
CnPw 6⅝98	8.2	2268	82¼	63⅛	81	+ 17½
CnPw 7⅝99	8.8	4360	89	68½	86¾	+ 17¾
CnPw 8⅝00	9.2	3628	93⅝	72¾	93⅝	+ 19
CnPw 8⅛01	9.2	3703	89	70¾	88¼	+ 17¼
CnPw 7½01	8.9	2345	85	65¾	84¼	+ 17¼
CnPw 7½02J	9.0	2746	84	65½	83⅝	+ 17⅝
CnPw 7½02O	9.0	4487	84⅞	65	83⅛	+ 17⅛
CnPw 8⅝03	9.5	3455	92	73	90¾	+ 16¾
CnPw 11⅜94	10.8	1729	108	97⅜	105	+ 5⅜
CnPw 11½00	10.8	3602	108⅜	94	106⅜	+ 6⅜
CnPw 9¾06	9.9	6909	100	80¾	98	+ 16⅜
CnPw 9s06	9.8	4929	94	74¾	92¼	+ 16⅜
CnPw 8⅞07	9.6	2812	92½	74	92¼	+ 17¼
CnPw 8⅝07	9.5	3952	91⅜	71⅞	90⅞	+ 18
CnPw 9s08	9.7	2592	94¼	74	93	+ 17½
Contel 13s07	11.9	39	109	102½	109	+ 3½
Contel 9⅛96	8.9	78	102	48¼	102	...
Ct IllCp 6.9s89t	7.0	319	100	94¾	98⅞	+ 6¼
CT IC 6s87t	6.2	315	971¾	97⅛	97 5/16	+ 5/16
Ct IC zr89	...	4693	79⅜	67⅞	78½	+ 10⅞
CtlInf 9s06	cv	3879	129¾	101¼	111½	...
CtlOil 4½91	5.0	322	89½	80⅛	89⅜	+ 7⅜
CtlOil 7½99	8.1	265	94¾	82½	93⅛	+ 11
CtlOil 9⅛s99	9.0	806	103	91½	101½	+ 8½
CtlOil 8⅞01	8.8	821	101⅝	93	101	+ 14½
CtlDat 5½87	5.6	1566	98	86½	98	+ 9⅝
CtlDat 12¾91	11.9	11383	110⅞	99½	107	...
CtlDat 8½11	cv	6783	122	99½	122	...
Coopvsn 8⅝05	cv	26421	118½	87	91½	− 25½
Copwld 7⅞01	10.5	130	75¼	70½	75⅛	+ 7⅞
CrnPd 5¾92	6.3	1100	93	80½	91⅜	+ 10½
CornG 7¾98	8.2	408	95	81	95	+ 14
CntryCr 7s11	cv	3337	122	99	119	...
Crane 6½92	6.9	392	94⅝	80¼	94⅜	+ 15⅛
Crane 7s93	8.0	629	92½	76¼	87¼	+ 9¼
Crane 7s94	8.1	4914	87¾	74¼	86	+ 11
Crane 10½94	10.4	838	103	94	100½	+ 4¼
Crane 8¾05	cv	3943	133¾	104¼	127	+ 20¾
CrayRs 6⅛11	cv	9803	132	103⅛	120	...
CrdF 8s92	8.0	318	100⅝	90½	99½	+ 10⅞
CrdF 8.2s87	8.2	438	100¼	98½	100¼	+ 1¾
CrdF 9⅜92	9.1	95	103	90⅛	103	+ 14⅞
CrdF 10½94	9.5	49	110½	101½	110½	+ 10
CrdF 15½91	13.7	164	118	112⅛	113⅛	+ 1⅝
CrdF zr90s	...	3505	74¾	62⅛	72⅞	+ 10⅝
CrdF 13⅞92	12.3	74	116	111⅜	113	+ 3
CrdF 12⅜94	...	20	108⅝	108⅝	108⅝	+ 1⅝
CrdF 12¼95	10.4	350	118⅞	117	117½	+ 15¾
CrdF 11½87	11.2	100	102⅞	102⅞	102⅞	...
CrdF 12¾94	10.6	18	120	120	120	+ 10
Crstwd 6¾90	cv	93	107½	88⅝	95	+ 6
Crstwd 6¼91	cv	459	91	80	91	+ 11
Crstwd 7s00	cv	44	95	93	95	− ½
CritAc 12.3s13	12.0	531	105½	101	102¼	+ ¾
CritAc 12s13	11.7	761	106	101	103	+ 1⅞
CritAc 12.15s13	11.9	622	104¾	101⅜	102½	+ ⅝
CritAc 11⅞14	...	523	104⅜	101	103¼	+ ½
CritAc 12¼14	12.0	800	106	101	102½	+ ½
CritAc 12.35s14	12.0	1029	106⅛	101	103	+ 1
CritAc 13.30s14	12.5	1668	109	103	106½	+ 1½
CritAc 13.10s14	12.3	1171	107¼	102	106½	+ ¾
CritAc 13⅛14	12.4	1623	108⅛	102¼	106	...
CritAc 11½15	11.2	897	107	100½	103	+ 3½
CritAc 11¼15	11.0	1150	105	100	102½	+ 3⅜
CritAc 11.85s15	11.4	965	104¼	102	103⅞	+ 2⅜
CrocN 8.6s02	9.0	1184	97⅛	79⅛	96	+ 15
CrwnC 4⅜88	4.6	50	97	89	95¾	+ 6
CrwnZ 9¼09	cv	5885	128	103¾	125	+ 19¾
Crucbl 6⅞92	6.9	37	99⅛	97½	99⅛	+ ⅛
Culb 11½05	11.2	417	103	94⅝	102½	+ 8⅞
CumE 8⅞95	8.9	348	100	92	99⅜	+ 11⅜

—D—

		Sales $1,000	High	Low	Last	Net Chg.
DCS 12.20s94	11.1	724	109½	99½	109½	+ 8½
Dana 6s91	6.5	46	96¼	78	92⅛	+ 16
Dana 7.3s96	7.8	238	93	82½	93	+ 10
Dana 9s2000	9.0	547	100	84¼	99½	+ 16⅝
Dana 8⅞08	9.1	89	97½	94	97½	+ 16⅜
Dana dc5⅞06	cv	14226	88½	71½	88	+ 16
DatGen 8⅜02	8.6	536	97½	79	97½	+ 17½
Datpnt 8⅞06	cv	26964	75¼	44	69	+ 23¾
DaytH 7¾94	7.8	684	99¾	87⅝	99	+ 12½
DaytH 9¾95	9.4	312	109	100⅛	104	+ 3½
DaytH 10⅞05	9.7	420	112	103	112	+ 13⅜
DaytH 14¾12	12.7	15	116	116	116	+ 12
DaytH 11⅞12	10.8	65	110	104	110	+ 7
DaytP 8⅛01	8.9	666	91⅛	78⅛	91⅛	+ 13
DaytP 8s03	8.8	770	91½	76	90⅞	+ 13½
DaytP 10.7s05	10.3	195	106	96¾	103¾	+ 6¾
DaytP 8¾06	9.1	279	96½	82	96½	+ 18
DaytP 8½07	9.0	726	94	79⅛	94	+ 14½
DaytP 16¾12	14.8	1774	120	112	113⅜	− 6⅝
Deere 8.45s	9.1	507	95¾	85⅛	93¼	+ 8¼
Deere 5½01	cv	1311	104	90	91½	+ ⅜
Deere 8s02	9.1	414	90¾	79¼	88	+ 12½
Deere 11½89	11.1	1915	104¾	100⅛	103½	− ½
Deere 9s08	cv	20831	110¾	93½	100¼	+ ¾
DeereCr 9.35s03	9.6	570	98⅛	89¼	97	+ 9½
DelPw 3⅞88	4.0	118	96⅝	89¾	96⅛	+ 6½
DelPw 3⅞88r	4.0	5	96⅛	96⅛	96⅛	...
DelPw 6⅜97	7.6	606	86¾	73½	84⅜	+ 8½
DlmP 4⅝94	5.7	189	82	72	81	+ 12½
Denn 8¼96	8.8	118	94	80½	94	+ 12
DetEd 6s96	7.3	2544	85¼	70	82½	+ 11⅜
DetEd 6.4s98	7.8	2776	84	70⅛	82¼	+ 10¼
DetEd 9s99	9.0	4179	101⅞	86	100	+ 12⅞
DetEd 9.15s00	9.3	5286	101½	86	98¼	+ 11¼
DetEd 8.15s00	8.9	3389	93½	79	91⅞	+ 10⅞
DetEd 8⅛01	8.7	2852	93⅝	79⅜	93⅛	+ 13
DetEd 7⅜01	8.6	2570	87⅛	72⅝	85¾	+ 10⅞
DetEd 7½03	8.7	2640	87½	73	85¾	+ 11⅝
DetEd 9⅞04	9.7	5107	103	89⅛	101⅝	+ 9⅛
DetEd 11⅞00	11.1	2048	108	102	106¾	+ 4½
DetEd 10⅝06	10.1	1610	105	96⅝	105	+ 9¼
DiaSh 9⅛00	9.6	197	96¾	84	94⅞	+ 7¼
DiaSh 8½08	10.1	413	89½	76	84	+ 6½
DiaSh 7.7s01	9.2	101	84½	75¼	84	+ 13
DiaSTel 7s08	8.4	159	84¼	73⅛	83	+ 12½
Digit 9⅜2000	9.1	159	104	90	103½	+ 12
Divers 10½91	10.8	300	101	90⅛	97	+ 7
DmBk 7¾96	7.9	348	98	82	98	+ 18
Dow 4.35s88	4.4	526	98	89⅛	98	+ 8⅞
Dow 6.70s98	7.8	1212	90	74	86⅛	+ 12⅞
Dow 7.75s99	8.2	1506	96	80½	94½	+ 13⅜
Dow 8⅞2000	8.7	2156	103¾	88	101⅞	+ 13⅝
Dow 8.92000	8.7	2598	103	89	102	+ 13
Dow 7.4s02	8.2	759	91¾	76½	90	+ 14¾
Dow 7⅝s03	8.4	778	91	77⅜	91	+ 12¼
Dow 8½s05	8.9	2484	97⅞	82	96	+ 11⅞
Dow 8½s06	8.7	2485	97⅝	81⅞	97⅝	+ 13⅝
Dow 7⅞07	8.7	1266	91	75¾	91	+ 12½
Dow 8⅝08	8.9	1679	99	83	97⅛	+ 16⅛
Dow 11¼10	10.3	2515	111	102	109	+ 4⅞
DwCrn 9⅝05	9.4	149	103⅝	88⅜	102	+ 13¼
Dresr 9⅜95	9.2	816	102⅞	94⅛	101⅝	+ 7½
Dresr 9⅜00	9.3	247	102	94¼	101	+ 9⅞
Dresr 11¾07	11.5	30	102½	102½	102½	− 4½
duPnt 8.45s04	8.6	6024	100	85⅝	98⅛	+ 10⅛
duPnt 8½06	8.6	4983	101	85⅝	98¾	+ 8¾
duPnt 14s91	12.4	5070	116¾	111½	112¾	+ ⅝
duPnt dc6s01	7.5	41449	82⅜	67	79½	+ 9⅞
duPnt 12⅞92	11.3	2527	115¾	110⅛	113¾	+ 1⅝
duPnt 8½16	8.6	86	99	97	98¾	...
duPnt 7½93	7.4	1848	101½	97½	101	...
DukeP 7⅜01	8.1	1705	92¾	77¼	91	+ 13½
DukeP 7¾02	8.2	2159	94½	79	94½	+ 13¾
DukeP 7⅜02	8.1	1892	91¼	76	91	+ 13¾
DukeP 7¾03	8.3	1998	93½	78⅛	93⅜	+ 13⅝
DukeP 8⅛03	8.4	3907	97	82	97	+ 13⅞
DukeP 9¾04	9.4	5287	105	95	104⅛	+ 9⅛
DukeP 9½05	9.1	3787	105½	91½	104⅝	+ 9⅞
DukeP 8⅜06	8.6	2346	99	83½	97½	+ 12¾
DukeP 8⅛07	8.8	2370	95⅜	81	92¼	+ 9⅛
DukeP 9⅜08	9.0	3898	104⅜	89½	103¾	+ 11
DukeP 10⅛09	9.6	2520	106⅞	97⅜	105¼	+ 6¼
DukeP 10⅞09	10.1	1850	110	100	107¾	+ 6¾
DuqL 3¾88	3.9	345	95¾	89⅝	95¾	+ 8¾
DuqL 4¼89	4.6	232	92⅛	83⅝	91⅞	+ 6⅜

NEW YORK BONDS

		Sales $1,000	High	Low	Last	Net Chg.
DuqL 5s2010	9.3	151	60	48	54	+6¾
DuqL 8¾00	9.1	2871	97⅜	82½	96⅜	+13⅝
DuqL 10¾95	10.4	42	108	100¼	103⅛	...
DuqL 9s06	9.4	2829	97	82¾	95¾	+13⅛
DuqL 8⅜07	9.3	1258	91	77⅝	90⅛	+10¼
DuqL 10⅛09	9.7	2457	104½	91	104½	+11½
DuqL 12¼10	11.3	1035	111	101¾	108	+5
DuqL 12⅛13	11.1	280	110	103⅛	109¼	+5¼
DuqL 13s13	12.0	161	110	105¼	108½	+3
Dyco 13s88	12.6	151	104⅛	102	103	+½

—E—

		Sales $1,000	High	Low	Last	Net Chg.
ECL 9s89f	...	2191	90	45	84	+37
EGG 3½s87	cv	12	340	253	262	−56
EKod 8⅝16	8.5	1551	101	95	101	...
EKod 4½88	cv	204	116	92	116	+14
Eaton 7.6s96	7.9	123	96	80	96	+14
Eaton 6s92	6.5	68	92¾	85¼	92¾	+7⅞
Eaton 7⅞03	8.8	233	92¾	74¼	90	+14
Eaton 8¾01	8.9	189	98	79⅝	98	+29
Eatn dc7s11	8.9	56	79	63½	79	+16
Eaton 8½08	cv	5879	130	111	124	+8¼
EdisEll 5s95	6.7	17	74¼	68	74¼	+15½
Ekco 4.60s87	4.7	92	96⅞	95½	96⅞	+4⅝
ElPas 12.45s97	11.6	406	108¼	103½	107⅛	+2⅝
ElPaso 15s00	13.2	1568	115	108	113⅝	+2¾
ElPaso 15¾92	14.0	855	118	108¼	112¼	−1¾
ElPaso 16.702	14.1	313	122½	112	118½	+2½
Emhrt 11.70s90	11.1	215	108⅜	103	105¼	+2¼
Ens 9¾s95	9.6	793	105	94⅜	102	+5⅝
Ens 7.65s98	8.4	371	91	80	91	+12
Ens 8.95s99	9.1	433	99	87⅜	98⅜	+13⅛
Ens 10⅝s00	10.2	449	104	94⅝	104	+6¼
Ens 8¾01	9.8	88	90¾	80½	89⅜	+8⅞
Ens 8½02	9.4	37	90⅞	80	90⅞	+15⅞
Ens 10⅞05	10.7	239	103	95⅞	102	+6⅛
Ens 10s01	cv	16360	108	97½	103½	+2
Ens 16⅜07	14.4	6	114	113	114	−3
Ens 11⅜95	10.3	26	110	100	110	+7
Entex 8⅞01	9.8	42	91½	90½	90½	+10½
Entex 12¾08	12.6	57	107½	101	101	...
EnvSys 6¾11	cv	1724	110	91	101	...
EqutR 9s96	9.0	221	102½	92	99¾	+11¾
EqutR 9½06	cv	209	215½	140	213	+45
Equitc 10s04	cv	6188	103	88	90	−2
EssxC 11⅜98	11.2	713	104⅜	93	102	+7
Estrl 12½95	12.1	224	103	95⅞	103	+2
Exxon 6s97	6.8	15893	89½	74	88¼	+12½
Exxon 6½98	7.1	13036	92¼	76⅛	91¾	+12¼
ExonFn 10½89	10.2	4104	107	102½	103⅛	+⅜
ExxP 9s04	8.6	4164	105	91½	105	+11⅞
ExxP 8⅞00	8.5	3241	104⅛	90½	103 29/32	+10 25/32
ExxP 8¼01	8.4	1608	101¼	86¼	98½	+10½
ExxP 5⅝97	6.8	235	82½	72	82½	+10¾
ExxP 6⅝98	7.4	227	90½	76	89½	+14⅝
ExxSh 7½11	7.5	5	99⅝	99⅝	99⅝	...

—F—

		Sales $1,000	High	Low	Last	Net Chg.
FMC 7½01	9.4	495	85	76	80	...
FMC 9½2000	9.7	528	101	90	98	+16½
Frch 9¾98	10.8	293	92	80	90	+10⅞
Fal 8.85s96	9.2	469	96	60	96	+17
Famly 4¾90	5.6	95	85	82⅛	85	+7½
Farah 5s94	cv	1120	85½	72½	76⅝	+4⅛
Feddr 5s96	cv	2298	69½	51	66	+13¼
Feddr 8⅞94	10.3	311	89½	73	86	+14½
FdHL zr92	...	451	64	53	64	+12½
FdHL zr19	...	20	6½	6½	6½	...
FdMog 7½98	8.6	115	91½	73½	87	+14⅞
FdMog 13s05	11.5	30	113	109¾	113	+13
FedN 4⅜s96	cv	1287	215	127¾	212	+75¼
FedN zr14s	...	1220	9	6	9	+4⅛
FedN zr19s	...	65	6¼	5¾	5¾	...
FdPapr 7.85s97	9.4	25	83½	83½	83½	...
FdRty 8¾10	cv	3714	142	105¼	127½	+21½
FedSt 8⅜95	8.4	264	102	93	100	+8½
FedSt 7⅛02	7.8	51	92	89	91	+6½
FedSt 10¼10	9.8	288	107¾	91	105	+8½
FedSt 10⅝13	9.8	42	108	94	107⅞	+8⅞
Ferro 5⅞92	6.5	23	89¾	88½	89¾	−¼
FinCpA 6s88	6.5	817	92	83	92	+8⅛
FinCpA 11⅞98	12.5	17243	98	85	95¼	+8⅜
FinCpA 6s10	10.9	664	61½	47	55	+8
FinCp dc11½02	cv	23052	125	95½	96⅛	−1⅞
FireO 5s88	5.0	60	100	99	100	+5
Firest 9¼04	9.4	993	98¾	85⅞	98	+10½
FtAtl 11¾93	11.4	22	103½	103	103½	−1⅝
FBkSy 6s89t	6.1	434	99¾	97¾	98⅛	−⅜
FtFid 8⅞88	8.9	536	100¼	99⅛	100	+1⅛
FtFid 11½93	10.6	66	109¼	104¾	108	+4
FMerBc 13¾92	12.6	119	113	108	109⅜	−1⅛
FtPenn 5½93	cv	1415	81¼	73	78⅝	+4⅝
FtSec 7s99t	7.1	869	100½	98⅛	98¾	−1¼
FUnRE 10¼09	cv	3437	130¾	105	127½	+21
FUnRE 10½90	10.0	315	107⅛	100¼	105½	+5½
FtWis 8½96	8.5	2173	100⅛	86	100	+13
FisbM 4¾97	cv	1076	75	59	67	+9½
FisbCp 8½05	cv	476	106	90	99⅞	+7⅞
FishF 6½94	cv	1167	87	77½	80	+2
FleetFn 9¼96	9.2	1142	104¼	92	100⅝	+6⅛
FleetFn 12½90	12.2	86	104	101	102¼	−2⅝
FleetF 11¼93	10.1	345	112¾	105	111⅝	+8⅝
FleetFn 8½10	cv	4086	145	115	140½	+21½
FlexiV 8.75s	9.0	45	97¾	95⅛	97¾	+40¾
FlexiV 12s00	11.5	44	106	94¼	104⅛	+10¼
FlaECs 5s01	7.3	71	68¼	56	68¼	+13¼
FlowGn 14.30s04	14.1	2309	104	96	101½	+3⅝
Flwr 8¼05	cv	7419	128	110½	116	+2⅞
FlyTigr 9s91	9.6	385	95	85⅜	93½	+3½
Ford 8⅛90	8.1	1346	105½	99	100⅝	+1⅝
Ford 7.85s94	7.9	743	107	88⅛	99½	+13⅜
Ford 14¼90	13.7	11208	108	103	103⅞	−3⅞
FrdC 7½91	7.5	3528	101⅞	91⅛	100	+9
FrdC 4½96	cv	784	227	135¾	203½	+66
FrdC 4⅞98	cv	235	244	155	233	+75
FrdC 7½92	7.5	999	102	88¾	100	+11
FrdC 8.7s99	8.6	2936	102	87¼	101	+10
FrdC 7½93	7.4	1176	103½	88⅛	100⅞	+13¾
FrdC 7⅞93	7.9	2897	101	90⅛	100¼	+10¼
FrdC 9.7s00	9.4	3010	105	93⅝	102⅞	+9
FrdC 9⅛01	8.9	2067	104	91	102½	+10
FrdC 8⅜01	8.6	3044	98⅝	82½	97¼	+12
FrdC 7⅞89	7.7	8341	101⅝	96	101⅝	+5
FrdC 8⅜02	8.6	2312	98¼	84½	97	+13
FrdC 8½02	8.8	1555	98	85¼	97⅛	+12⅛
FreptM 10½14	cv	15489	106½	95½	103½	+3½
FreptM 10⅞01	10.7	1	102	102	102	...
Frmnt 12⅞90	12.7	585	103⅞	98	101¾	−¼
Fruf 6s87	6.1	1236	99⅝	95¾	98½	+2¾
Fruf 5½94	cv	3790	160	91	139	+45
Fruf 9.7s96	9.7	208	101	88⅛	100	+11
FrufF 8s87	8.1	3192	100⅛	97 21/32	99⅜	+¾
Fruf 8½11	cv	3262	108½	101	107	...
FrufF 12½93	11.9	251	108¾	101⅛	105	+½
Fuqua 7s88	7.2	857	99	92	97½	+3¾
Fuqua 9½98	10.0	8256	98⅜	81⅝	94¾	+11
Fuqua 9⅞97	10.2	2558	99½	85	97	+12⅛

—G—

		Sales $1,000	High	Low	Last	Net Chg.
GAF 11⅜95	10.9	1972	105⅜	102	104	...
GATX 16⅜92	15.0	140	117½	106	109	−6
GATX 11½96	11.2	18904	105½	97½	102⅜	...
GTE 12¼94	10.6	294	118¾	104	113⅝	+11⅝
GTE 10⅝95	9.5	305	112½	104⅛	112	+9⅜
GTE 10s2000	9.7	362	105	97	102⅝	+7⅛
GardD 9¼05	9.8	160	96½	88	94¾	+14¾
Gelco 14⅝99	14.0	7393	108⅞	103¼	104½	−2¼
Gelco 14s01	cv	4520	109½	104	105½	−1
Gelco 14¼87	14.1	586	107	100¼	101¼	−3¼
GnCorp 11⅞93	11.5	131	105	94	103½	+11¼
GnCorp 12⅜03	12.0	22	103	96	103	+9
GnATr 5¾99	cv	6215	83	71	83	+8½
GCig 5½87	5.7	14	99	92½	96	+4½
GCinem 10s08	cv	5720	221	131½	209	+76
GCinem 10s09	cv	5549	191	116	172½	+55½
GnDev 12⅝05	12.3	3709	105	90	102¼	+11¼
GdDyn 5¾11	...	330	120	107	116	...
GnDyn 9s16	9.3	1	97	97	97	...
GnEl 5.3s92	5.8	2221	92½	80¼	91⅛	+9½
GnEl 7½96	7.5	5780	101	84½	99⅝	+11¼
GnEl 8½04	8.5	10076	100⅞	88	100	+8½
GElCr 7⅝88	7.6	6384	102½	98	100⅜	+1⅞
GElCr 8¼97	8.2	1866	103	89	101	+9⅝
GElCr 11½90	11.5	11306	104⅞	100 1/32	100¼	−3½
GElCr 11¾05	10.2	868	116½	106⅛	115	+10
GElCr 14s90	13.7	6918	107¾	101¼	102	−5⅝
GElCr 13⅝91	12.6	2440	111⅝	107⅛	108	−2¼
GElCr 8s11	7.9	495	102	100⅝	101	...
GElCr 8¼11	8.2	578	102¾	100⅜	101	...
GFood 14⅜89	14.1	4537	108¼	101¾	102	−4
GnHme 15½95	14.3	1161	115	105	108½	+3½
GHost 6s90f	6.8	283	92¼	77¾	88½	+13½
GHost 7s94	8.2	1021	86	74⅛	84⅞	+10⅞

NEW YORK BONDS

		Sales $1,000	High	Low	Last	Net Chg.
GnInst 5s92	cv	1356	118	96⅞	102½	+ 4½
GMills 8⅞95	8.6	1155	107	92⅛	103¼	+ 7⅜
GMills 8s99	8.0	559	100	83¼	100	+ 17
GMills 9⅜09	9.1	707	103	92⅞	102½	+ 16⅜
GMills zr88s	...	8516	93⅝	83⅛	93⅝	+ 9⅛
GMA 4⅞87	5.0	10625	99	93⅝	98 1/16	+ 4 3/16
GMA 6¼88	6.3	15022	99¾	93¼	98⅞	+ 4
GMA 7⅛90	7.1	16951	101¼	91⅜	100⅜	+ 8
GMA 8s93m	7.9	22495	101⅝	91¼	101⅛	+ 8⅛
GMA 7¾94	7.7	13951	101	86⅝	100⅜	+ 10⅞
GMA 7¼95	7.6	5635	98	84¼	95½	+ 9
GMA 7⅛92	7.2	10787	100	87½	99⅛	+ 9¾
GMA 7.85s98	8.1	4861	97¾	84⅛	96¾	+ 11¾
GMA 8⅞99	8.7	11879	102½	90½	102	+ 9
GMA 8¾s00	8.7	7923	101¾	90⅛	100⅜	+ 9⅜
GMA 8¾s01	8.7	3109	101⅝	88⅞	100½	+ 10
GMA 8⅛96	8.1	19824	101¼	88¼	100⅞	+ 9½
GMA 7.35s87	7.4	9632	100¾	98⅞	100	+ 1
GMA 8s02	8.4	2572	96½	83	95	+ 10¼
GMA 8s07	8.4	2922	95½	79⅛	95	+ 13
GMA 8¼06	8.6	3087	96¼	82	96¼	+ 10½
GMA 8.65s08	8.9	1670	99½	85⅜	97½	+ 8½
GMA 9¾03	9.4	2195	105⅜	96½	104⅛	+ 7
GMA 9.4s04	9.1	3753	103½	91⅛	103½	+ 10
GMA 12s05fb	10.3	2207	117½	107¾	116½	+ 8½
GMA 11⅝90	11.6	16885	104	100¼	100½	− 2⅝
GMA 12s05	10.5	4160	117¼	106	114	+ 6
GMA 11¾00	10.3	2073	114¾	106⅛	114½	+ 7½
GMA 14⅜91	13.2	6501	112⅞	109	109¼	− 2¼
GMA dc6s11	8.0	36862	79¼	61	75	+ 11
GMA 14⅝89	14.2	12948	108⅝	103⅛	103¼	− 4⅝
GMA 11¾89	11.3	2615	106¼	103¼	103⅝	− 1½
GMA zr12	...	1165	106⅝	60½	101¾	+ 41¾
GMA zr15	...	2401	100	63½	95	+ 35
GMA 13⅛87	13.1	1752	106	100⅛	100⅛	− 5⅞
GMA 12⅝88	12.2	1018	107½	103¼	103¼	− 3⅝
GMA 11⅞86	11.9	2034	103⅛	100	100	− 3 1/16
GMA 11s88	10.5	1631	107¼	103	105	+ ¼
GMA 10⅜88	9.9	2586	106	102⅝	104¾	+ 1⅝
GMA 10½89	9.7	2613	109⅞	103⅞	107¾	+ 2¾
GMA 9¾88	9.4	868	105¼	101⅜	103¾	+ 1¾
GMA 10¼90	9.8	1992	107¾	102½	104⅞	+ 1¾
GMA 10⅜95	9.3	4207	113⅛	102⅜	111¾	+ 5⅞
GMA 10s90	9.5	1633	107⅜	102	105⅜	+ 2⅜
GMA 8⅝89	8.4	1458	104⅞	101¼	102⅞	...
GMA 9¼93	8.8	992	105½	101⅝	105½	...
GMA 8½91	8.2	1649	105½	101⅛	104	...
GMA 8⅞96	8.5	1440	104½	100⅜	104⅛	...
GMA 8s96	8.0	5599	101¼	95⅜	100⅛	...
GMA 8¼16	8.7	263	97½	93	95	...
GMA 8.35s93	8.5	3	98	96¼	98	...
GMA 8s90	7.9	535	103½	100⅞	101¾	...
GMA 8⅛92	7.9	812	102¾	100	102¾	...
GMA 8s93J	7.9	9176	103	98⅞	101	...
GMA 7.80s93	7.8	515	100¼	99	100¼	...
GMA 7⅛89	7.1	60	100⅝	99¼	100⅝	...
GMA 8so	7.9	14	101	101	101	...
GM 8⅝s05	8.7	3937	100	86	99	+ 8¾
GM 8⅛91	7.9	876	103⅞	101	103⅜	...
GSignl 8⅞99	9.1	55	99½	91	98	+ 4¾
GTE 6⅝91	6.8	1778	97⅛	83⅛	96¾	+ 13¾
GTE 10⅛95	9.6	1751	110	100	105	+ 2
GTE 9⅜99	9.0	2654	105½	92	103⅞	+ 10⅞
GTCal 8⅞96	8.8	880	101⅞	90⅛	100⅝	+ 10⅝
GWat 8¾s96	8.8	342	102¼	88⅞	100	+ 14⅞
Gene 14¼94	14.1	793	105	88	101⅛	+ 11
Gene 15¼94	14.4	1251	106	93	106	+ 12
Gene dc9¾93	12.5	547	80	71	78	+ 1⅛
Genrad 7¼11	cv	2161	100	71	80	...
GaPac 6s87†	6.0	360	100	97⅛	100	+ ⅜
GaPw 8⅞00	9.2	7457	99½	84⅛	96⅛	+ 10⅜
GaPw 7⅜01	8.5	3052	87½	74	86½	+ 11½
GaPw 8⅛01	8.7	3818	94¼	78⅝	93⅛	+ 12½
GaPw 7⅝01	8.6	1685	89¾	74⅝	88½	+ 12½
GaPw 7½02J	8.6	2727	88¼	72¾	86⅞	+ 12¼
GaPw 7½02D	8.6	2065	88⅛	74	86¾	+ 11¾
GaPw 7⅞03	8.9	1901	90⅛	75⅝	88½	+ 11¼
GaPw 8⅝04	9.1	7052	97	80⅞	95¼	+ 14⅛
GaPw 11⅝00	11.0	4359	109	99¾	106	+ 3
GaPw 11¾05	10.9	5118	108⅞	100½	107½	+ 4⅛
GaPw 9⅞06	9.8	5055	103	91⅞	101⅛	+ 9
GaPw 9⅝08	9.6	3858	102	89	100⅝	+ 9⅝
GaPw 9¾08	9.6	3873	103	90	101⅜	+ 8⅜
GaPw 10½09	10.1	5347	105	95⅛	104	+ 7⅜
GaPw 11s09	10.6	5169	106	97⅜	104¼	+ 4½
GaPw 14½10	13.4	5377	113½	106¼	108	− 3
GaPw 16⅛11	16.1	11876	115	100	100 1/32	− 8 31/32
GaPw 16¼11	14.5	11310	114	107	112⅜	+ ⅛

		Sales $1,000	High	Low	Last	Net Chg.
GaPw 16¼12	14.3	12011	116	105	114	+ 1⅛
GaPw 13⅛12	11.7	2021	114	107	112⅛	+ 3½
GaPw 13¼13	11.8	805	114	104¾	112	+ 5¼
GaPw 16s14	13.9	8270	126⅞	106	115	− 5
GaPw 10s16J	9.8	1126	103⅛	98⅛	102½	...
GaPw 10s16A	9.6	450	104¾	99⅜	103⅞	...
Getty 14s00	12.4	2905	115	105	112½	+ 5½
GibFn 9¼08	cv	12948	117¼	101	105	+ 1
vjGloMr 12⅜98f	...	7263	28	17	20	− 6½
vjGloM dc16s01f	...	37401	30½	16	21	− 7¼
vjGloMr 16⅛02f	...	49973	31¼	15¼	20	− 8½
vjGloM dc13s03f	cv	25903	28	15	20¼	− 3
GloU 8s97	8.9	13	90	81⅛	90	+ 14⅝
GNgF dc8⅜93	9.4	2421	91⅝	77⅛	89	+ 10⅞
GdNgF 13¼95	12.5	2856	109⅜	98	106	+ 4
Gdrch 8¼94	8.6	1669	96⅞	85⅛	96¼	+ 10¼
Gdrch 7s97	8.8	649	80	70	80	+ 8
Gdyr 8.6s95	8.6	2531	101⅜	92	100½	+ 7¼
Gdyr 7.35s97	8.5	653	92⅞	79	86⅜	+ 6¼
Gould 9¼95	9.2	626	102	92	100⅝	+ 9⅜
Grace 4¼90	cv	2523	106¾	90¼	99¼	+ 9¼
Grace 6½96	cv	88	192½	156	190¼	+ 33¼
Grace 12¾90	11.8	326	110	106	108¼	+ ¾
Grace 11¾08	11.2	513	109	104	105⅛	...
Grace 10⅜97	10.2	273	105½	100	102	+ 3
GranC 4⅝94	cv	612	72⅞	64	66	...
GtNoN 7⅞98	8.6	48	93	87	92	+ 13⅞
GtNoN 8.7s08	9.6	56	93	87½	90⅜	+ 8⅜
GtNoR 3⅛00	5.6	712	58½	49	56¼	+ 10¼
GtNoR 2⅝10	6.5	1131	43½	35½	40½	+ 6¾
GtNor 2⅝10r	6.7	165	41	37	39	...
GtNoR 3⅛90	3.6	288	89¼	79	88	+ 9⅞
GWstFn 8½10	cv	8333	146	114½	140½	+ 25½
GGian 4¼92	cv	6	302	243	302	+ 59
GrnTr dc8¼95	9.4	756	88¼	76	87½	+ 10⅞
Greyh 6½90	cv	674	203⅜	170	178	− 5
Greyh 9⅜01	9.5	1931	101	87	99	+ 10⅞
Greyh 9⅞00	9.6	1172	102⅞	92	102¾	+ 8¾
GreyF 9¼92	9.2	666	101⅝	94⅝	100¼	+ 8¼
GreyF 12½00	11.6	976	111	103¼	108	+ 4
GreyF 14⅞91	13.6	1035	111⅛	106	109	+ ¼
GreyF 16⅛92	14.1	1807	119	111	114⅜	+ 4⅜
GreyF zr94	...	12378	50⅜	38	48	+ 8⅞
GreyF 13⅝94	11.8	58	117	109½	115¼	+ 7¼
GroIr 13⅝03	13.3	3849	105¼	95⅞	102¾	+ 4¾
GroIr 9½05	cv	3085	170½	103	135	+ 32¾
GrowGp 12½94	11.7	785	107	104	107	...
GrowGp 8½06	cv	6000	110	99	109½	...
Grumn 9¼09	cv	11442	111⅛	99¾	106¾	− 2¼
Gruntl 7½11	cv	4972	99	90	91	...
GlfWn 6s87	6.1	73	100	94¼	98⅜	+ 5¼
GlfWn 6s88	6.1	1646	98½	92	98⅛	+ 5⅜
GlfWn 7s03A	8.5	14903	83½	66½	81⅞	+ 13¼
GlfWn 7s03B	8.6	8839	82⅞	67⅛	81⅛	+ 13
GulfMo 5s56f	8.3	541	60⅞	56⅛	60	+ 1
GlfMo 5s56f rg	8.6	43	59¾	58	58	...
GlfRes 10⅞97	12.2	1352	95⅞	81	89½	+ 4½
GlfRes 12½04	12.7	3016	103¼	89	98⅜	+ 8¾
GlfStU 7¼92	cv	129	96	82	96	+ 14¼

—H—

		Sales $1,000	High	Low	Last	Net Chg.
Hallb 7.95s95	8.1	346	98⅞	89	98	+ 10
Hallb 9¼00	9.1	748	102	91	101⅝	+ 10⅜
HallB 10.20s05	9.8	377	105	95¼	103¾	+ 8
Harns 15s94	13.2	674	115⅜	104½	113½	+ 9⅞
Harns dc12s04	12.0	9797	103½	92	100⅛	+ 6⅛
Harra 9½96	9.5	1084	101⅞	92	100	+ 9⅞
Harris 7¾01	8.7	10	89½	89½	89½	+ 12½
Harris 11½10	10.6	60	108⅝	108	108	+ 10
Harsc 5½92	6.6	20	83½	83½	83½	+ 8½
Harsc 9⅞00	9.6	61	103	96	103	+ 17¼
Harsc 12¼10	11.1	64	110	104	110	+ 6¾
Hartfd 8½96	8.6	780	100½	85⅛	98½	+ 13
Hartmx 8½96	8.8	260	97½	85	97⅛	+ 12¼
Hawn 9s2000	9.0	894	101⅛	88	100⅛	+ 11¾
Hawn 8.2s01	8.5	445	97	82	97	+ 18¾
Hawn 7⅝02	8.8	160	91	76	87	+ 17¾
Hawn 8.35s03	8.7	213	95⅞	82½	95⅞	+ 13¾
Hazltn 6½06	cv	1379	107½	95	104	...
Heilm 11⅝05	11.0	227	111	99⅝	106	+ 8⅞
Heilm zr03	...	19305	34½	24¾	28¼	+ 3
Heinz 7¼97	7.6	161	96	77⅛	95⅞	+ 18¾
Hellr 9½89	9.3	1161	103½	99	101¾	+ 1¼
Hellr 9⅛91	9.1	1130	102½	94⅞	100⅛	+ 5¼
Hellr 7¾92	7.8	279	100	87	100	+ 12
Hellr 8s93	8.3	107	98	87⅛	96	+ 13⅞
Hellr 7¾93	7.8	435	99¾	84¾	99	+ 12⅝

NEW YORK BONDS

		Sales $1,000	High	Low	Last	Net Chg.
Hellr 8½93	8.7	72	98	97½	97½	+ 16¼
Hellr 10⅛91	9.7	282	106	98¼	104⅜	+ 5⅜
Hellr 8.1s87	8.1	1348	100¼	98	99⅞	+ 1⅛
Hellr 8¾02	8.9	185	98	84⅛	98	+ 18
Hercul 6½99	cv	4527	173	109	151	+ 36
Hercul 10½89	9.8	23	107¼	103⅝	107¼	+ 6⅝
Hercul na08	cv	1	135⅝	135⅝	135⅝	+ 35⅞
Hercul 8s10	cv	8836	145½	106½	138	+ 28
HerCm 7s11	cv	2249	122½	105	115	...
Hersh 9½09	9.2	430	104	93½	103½	+ 15¼
Hertz 8⅞s01	8.9	267	99¾	88	99¾	+ 12½
HltNJ 11⅜92	10.8	20	105¼	103	105¼	+ 3¾
HltNJ 10⅝94	10.5	25	101	101	101	− 4
HockV 4½99	6.8	78	66⅝	57⅜	66⅝	+ 8½
HockV 4½99r	6.7	42	67½	64	67½	...
Holidy 9½95	9.5	312	102	95⅛	100	+ 4⅞
Holidy 14⅛92	12.8	462	114⅛	107⅛	110⅛	+ ¾
Holidy 13¼99	13.0	35	103¼	102	102	...
Holidy 8⅜96	8.7	217	101	94	95¾	...
HmeDp 8½09	cv	19020	108¼	80½	103½	+ 23
HomFSD 6¾11	cv	3934	107¾	87	92¾	...
HonyF 8.2s98	8.3	373	98⅜	83	98⅜	+ 16⅝
Honey 6.1s92	6.6	352	98¾	81¼	92¾	+ 9¾
Honey 9⅜09	9.3	292	101	88½	101	+ 19
Honey 14⅛11	12.6	1322	118¾	110½	112	− ½
HookC 4⅞91	5.5	365	88½	76	88½	+ 10½
HoovU 8⅜96	9.1	40	94	87¾	92	+ 14¼
HosAff 10s99	10.0	713	103	86¼	100	+ 14¼
HosAff 10s91	9.8	896	103½	95	102	+ 6½
HoCp 10¾90	10.0	602	107	100¾	107	+ 6¼
HoCp 16½07	14.2	545	124½	114	116	− 2⅜
HoCp 8½08	cv	25277	108¾	95¾	104¼	+ 4¼
HoCp 9s98	cv	10189	108	95¾	103	+ 3½
HoCp 13s99	12.6	77	107	103	103	− ½
HousF 4⅜87	4.4	1318	99 3/32	94¼	98 13/16	+ 4 9/16
HousF 7½95	7.7	784	97½	85¼	97½	+ 10⅛
HousF 7¾99	8.2	442	95½	81¼	95	+ 21⅞
HousF 8½01	8.9	391	97¾	84½	96	+ 10
HouF 10½94.	10.1	429	105	101⅜	103½	+ 2⅝
HousF 9s00	9.0	717	100	88	100	+ 13
HousF 8⅜03	9.2	33	93	90⅝	90⅝	+ 8⅛
HouF 8.45s97	8.4	780	100¼	86	100¼	+ 15½
HousF 8.2s07	9.2	461	91	79¾	89½	+ 10½
HNG 10¼95	10.0	161	102	96⅞	102	+ 7
HNG 8.7s01	9.3	199	98¼	90	93⅞	+ 15⅜
HugheT 9s00	11.0	239	93½	75⅜	82	+ ¾
HugheT 9s08	10.8	10843	92	68⅜	83	+ 6½
HugheT 14¼88	13.8	6286	105½	99	103	− 1½
HugheT 9½06	cv	17747	96	76	92	+ 2¾
Humn 5s97	cv	4	99⅝	98⅛	98⅛	− 1⅞
Humn 9½98	9.5	337	101½	94⅛	99½	+ 4½
Humn dc13½02	13.2	1874	106	101	102	− 3¾
Humn 14½02	12.8	43	113¾	113	113	+ 4
Humn 13¾13	12.2	154	116	111¼	113	+ 12⅜
Humn 8½09	cv	29327	112½	99	100¼	− 5¾
Humn 10⅛91	9.4	91	108	98½	108	+ 7
vjHuntIR 9⅞04f	...	3746	12¼	2⅛	3½	− 8½
Hutton 12s05	11.3	4027	107¼	101	106½	+ 6⅜
Hutn 8½91	8.4	611	101¼	99½	100¾	...
Hutn 8⅞96	8.8	318	100⅞	98⅞	100⅜	...

—I—

		Sales $1,000	High	Low	Last	Net Chg.
IBM Cr 10¾96	10.6	1750	105½	101	101	− 4
IBM Cr 9⅞88	9.6	1770	105½	102	102½	+ ¾
IBM Cr 9s88	8.6	5511	105	100⅛	104¼	+ 3
IBM Cr 9⅝90	9.2	3854	106½	101¼	104½	+ 2⅛
IBM Cr 7⅛89	7.0	152	102	100½	102	...
ICN 12⅞98	12.9	855	104½	99½	100	...
ICPd 10¼95	10.2	201	103	97½	100½	+ ¾
ICI 9.05s95	8.9	75	102	92½	102	+ 10½
ICI 8⅞03	9.0	212	99	86½	98½	+ 12½
ITTF 8.1s92	8.1	395	100½	94	100¼	+ 13⅛
ITTF 10½95	10.2	658	104½	100	102¾	− ¾
ITTF 9⅝96	9.4	950	102½	95⅞	102½	+ 6½
ITTF 8½02	9.0	366	96⅝	82	94⅜	+ 12⅜
ITTF 8⅞03	8.7	725	101⅞	99½	101¾	+ 1¾
ITTF 11.85s99	11.1	210	111	101¼	106¾	+ ¾
ITTF 14¾91	13.5	1179	114	107½	109	− 2⅞
ITTF 11¼90	10.3	209	111	106	109½	+ 2½
ITTF 11⅜87	10.9	310	105¼	102½	104¼	+ 2¼
ITTF 10.80s92	10.0	73	107⅞	105	107⅞	+ 5⅜
ITTR 8s96	8.3	26	96	87⅜	96	+ 9⅝
ITTW 8½96	8.9	216	97⅛	88¾	96	+ 10⅞
IdelB 9¼00f	...	9034	83½	49	81⅛	+ 30⅝
IllBel 7⅝06	8.3	5398	93	76	91⅝	+ 12⅝
IllBel 8s04	8.4	5394	97⅞	81⅛	95¼	+ 13⅝
IllBel 8¼16	8.5	3263	99¾	80⅜	96½	+ 13
IlCnt 11¼99	11.0	879	103	95	102	+ 6
IlCnt 15½94	13.8	153	114	107½	112	+ 4½
IlCnt 3⅜89H	3.9	151	87	76½	87	+ 14⅞
IllPw 7.6s01	8.4	603	91	76⅛	90⅞	+ 13⅜
IllPw 7⅝03	8.6	677	88¾	74⅝	88¾	+ 17
IllPw 10½04	10.0	1198	107	96⅝	105⅛	+ 8⅝
IllPw 8⅝06	9.0	1589	96⅝	83½	95½	+ 12¾
IllPw 8¼07	9.0	727	93¼	77½	91¾	+ 12⅜
IllPw 8⅞08	9.1	1417	98¼	84	97	+ 12¾
IllPw 14½90	13.2	180	110	104¾	110	+ 4
IllPw 12s12	11.0	451	115½	102¾	109	+ 7
IllPw 10⅛16	9.7	197	104	100⅛	104	...
IllPw 9⅜16	9.3	191	103⅛	96¾	101	...
Inco 6.85s93	8.1	832	89	74	85	+ 5
Inco 12⅜10	12.0	570	106	93½	102⅞	+ 7⅛
InMic 11⅜90	10.8	820	105	101½	105	+ 2½
InMic 15⅝91	14.1	670	113	104¾	110¾	− ¼
IndBel 8⅛11	8.6	3159	95¾	79⅜	95	+ 13½
IndBel 10s14	9.3	2006	107⅝	95¾	107	+ 9
IndBel 8⅛17	8.6	2896	96	78	94	+ 12⅝
IndBel 8s14	8.6	1690	94¾	77⅝	93	+ 14
Inexc 8½00	cv	31155	81	32	77	+ 14½
IngR 8.05s04	8.5	584	95	78½	95	+ 17½
IngR 12⅜90	12.2	2331	103½	100⅛	101¼	− 1¾
IngR 12⅞10	11.8	28	109½	103¼	109½	+ 6½
InldStl 4⅜87	4.5	476	97 7/32	92⅛	97	+ 5⅞
InldStl 4½89	4.9	379	91	83	91	+ 7½
InldStl 6½92	7.8	282	84	76⅞	83	+ 6⅛
InldStl 8¾95	9.7	1106	96	82	90½	+ 6
InldStl 8⅞99	10.7	766	89½	80	83¼	+ 4¼
InldStl 9½00	10.6	851	91½	78	89¾	+ 9⅝
InldStl 7.9s07	11.2	2122	78½	63½	70¾	+ 2⅞
InldStl 11¼90	11.1	4730	102¾	95½	101	+ ½
Insilco 9s10	cv	5805	127	109	125	+ 12
IntgRs dc8⅝97	10.0	476	87	72½	86⅝	+ 15⅜
ItgRs 10¾96	11.2	708	102	95¼	96	...
Intlgc 11.99s96	12.6	375	104⅞	95	95	...
Intrco 14¼91	13.4	86	110⅝	105¾	106	+ ½
Intrfst 9¾99	10.8	1389	93	80	90⅛	+ 3¾
Intrfst 6.55s87t	7.4	540	96	88	89	− 5⅝
Intrfst 7¾05	cv	29068	77	60	70½	+ ¼
Intrlk 8.8s96	8.9	100	99	90⅛	99	+ 11
IBM 9⅜04	9.0	45876	106⅛	94¼	104¼	+ 6⅜
IBM 7⅞04	cv	1571	131	112	113⅛	− 9⅜
IBM 10¼95	8.9	1440	115⅝	103⅝	115⅝	+ 8¾
InMin 4s91	cv	24	137	124	129	− 25¼
InMin 9.35s00	9.4	727	100	92½	100	+ 14
InMin 11⅞05	11.2	55	106½	105⅛	105⅝	+ 5⅝
InMult 9⅛96	9.1	59	99¾	94	99¾	+ 16½
IPap 8.85s95	8.7	2097	102½	93¾	101½	+ 6¾
IPap 4¼96	cv	122	311¾	163½	284	+ 116
IPap 8.85s00	8.7	1648	103	88¾	101¼	+ 15¼
IPap dc5⅛12	...	3181	64	53	61	+ 7½
IPap 10⅞95	10.1	322	112	104½	108⅛	+ 8⅜
IntRec 9s10	cv	7638	96	70	72	− 12
IntSilvr 5s93	cv	314	112⅛	90⅛	102	+ 5½
IntTT 4.9s87	4.9	445	99 13/32	96	99¼	+ 3⅝
IntT 4.9s87r	11.0	90	99 13/16	12⅛	99 13/32	...
IntTT 8⅝00	cv	501	229	144	207	+ 62
IntTT 10s00	9.7	235	104⅞	96½	103½	+ 7½
InTT 14¾91	13.0	604	115¼	109¼	113¾	+ 1¾
Intnr 10¾90	10.7	1327	103¼	99⅛	100⅝	− ½
Intnr 10½08	cv	25715	120¼	102	120	+ 12¼
Intnr 11s93	10.6	260	110	101	104	...
Intnr 11½94	10.6	206	109¼	100	108⅞	...
Intnr 11s95	10.6	1195	109⅝	100	104	...
Intnr 12½02	12.1	26	103½	96¼	103½	...
IntrBk 5½87	cv	1383	102½	96	100½	+ 4½
IntSc 7¾11	cv	790	104	91	92	...
Ipco 5¼89	5.6	86	95¼	89	94½	+ 5½
IrvBk 8½02	8.7	172	97½	84⅞	97½	+ 16½
IrvBk 6¾04t	6.8	168	100	95	99⅝	+ ⅝

—J—

		Sales $1,000	High	Low	Last	Net Chg.
Jamswy 8s05	cv	4591	122	97½	106½	+ 4¾
JCP 9⅝06	9.6	1022	100½	87	100¼	+ 12⅞
JCP 9¾06	9.8	842	101	88	100	+ 13
JCP 8¾07	9.4	286	93¼	83½	93¼	+ 14½
JCP 9s08	9.4	164	95⅝	86	95⅝	+ 15⅛
vjJnM 7.85s04f	...	12912	109½	80	107	+ 23
vjJnM 9.7s85mf	...	25292	112	82 1/32	108	+ 17
vjJonsLI 6¾94f	...	11942	62½	14⅛	15⅛	− 39⅞
vjJonsLI 6½88f	...	1171	86½	15	15¼	− 64⅜
vjJoneL 6¾94f	...	3463	62¼	12¾	14	− 41¾
vjJoneL 9⅞95f	...	6231	79¾	37½	38⅛	− 30⅝
vjJoneL 8s98f	...	3383	67	38	38	− 16½
vjJoneL 9¾96f	...	2411	79	38	38⅛	− 26½

—K—

		Sales $1,000	High	Low	Last	Net Chg.
K Mart 12¾15	11.2	20	114	114	114	...
K mart 12⅛95	...	59	122½	113	120¾	+ 12¾
K mart 8⅛97	8.2	512	100	97½	99½	...
Kaisr 9s05	cv	6367	105	81	103	+ 22
KaufB 12¼99	12.3	1539	105⅞	98¼	100	+ 2¾
Kellwd 9s99	cv	504	265	158½	241¼	+ 80¼
Kenn 7⅞01	8.5	1052	94	82⅛	92⅞	+ 9⅞
KyCent 4s87	4.1	70	98 11/16	95	98 11/16	+ 8 1/16
KerrMc 8½06	9.0	184	94	82¼	94	+ 12¾
Keycrp 7¾02	8.9	955	90	79⅞	86¾	+ 15⅜
Kystn 8½05	cv	2423	122	102¾	111	+ 5
Kidde 8¾02	9.3	159	94	85½	94	+ 14
Kidde 9¾03	9.8	195	102¾	87	100	+ 15
KimCl 5⅞91	6.3	340	94¼	81½	94	+ 10½
KimCl 5⅞92	6.3	446	93⅜	83	93⅜	+ 10⅜
KimCl 11⅛90	10.7	180	108	104	104⅜	+ 1⅜
KimCl 11½13	11.1	19	109	102½	104	+ 7
KingCt 6s97	7.5	181	80	65	80	+ 17¼
Koger 2000s	...	530	137½	129½	136¾	+ 3¾
KogerP 9¼03	cv	4229	109¾	91	109¼	+ 15¾
Kolmrg 8¾09	cv	4669	99¼	85	90½	+ 4
Kraft 6⅞96	7.5	293	92⅛	81	92⅛	+ 11½
Kraft 8⅜04	8.5	1160	100	85	98½	+ 11½
Kraft 7.6s07	8.5	109	92⅛	77⅜	89	+ 13
Krogr 9s95	9.0	414	102	92	100½	+ 8⅜
Krogr 8.7s98	8.7	702	101	86¼	100	+ 11⅝
Krogr 8½01	8.7	144	97½	80¼	97⅜	+ 20⅝
Krogr 12⅜05	11.4	36	113⅞	105⅝	108⅝	+ 15⅝
Krogr 14⅜91	13.2	467	111¾	105¼	108½	+ ½
Krogr 11s95	11.0	13	100¼	99	100	+ 1
Krogr 8s93	8.0	155	102	98¼	100½	...

—L—

		Sales $1,000	High	Low	Last	Net Chg.
vjLTV 5s88f	...	60234	88	16	17½	− 63½
vjLTV 9¼97f	...	23517	79¾	24¼	25¾	− 41
vjLTV 11s07f	...	47890	82½	15	16½	− 54½
vjLTV 13⅞02f	...	42796	100	24¼	28	− 61⅝
vjLTV 14s04f	...	69664	98½	24	26	− 64½
vjLTV 10¼95f	cv	146	40	22	26	...
vjLTV 11½97f	...	4885	86⅛	15	15⅞	...
vjLTV 7⅞98f	...	3233	65	14	15½	...
vjLTV 8¾98f	...	6687	73⅞	14	15½	− 49¼
vjLTV Int 5s88f	cv	226	89	26⅛	26⅛	− 53⅞
LVI 14⅞95	14.0	37	106	103	106	...
LaQuin 10s02	cv	4861	109½	93⅛	103	+ 10
LearS 10s04	10.3	2555	102	87½	97½	+ 8½
LearS 11½98	11.4	4032	108	96⅝	100½	+ ½
LearS 11¼98	11.3	2771	105	95½	99½	− 1½
Lswy 12½89	12.4	25	100½	100½	100½	...
Leget 6½06	cv	4549	111½	99	100¼	...
Leucd 14s93	13.1	5	107	107	107	...
Leucd 7¾01	cv	515	131	103½	127½	...
LigGp 6s92	6.4	753	94	82⅝	94	+ 12⅜
LigGp 7.6s97	8.2	132	93	83	93	+ 15⅝
LigGp 8⅝01	9.2	484	95½	84½	93⅜	+ 6⅞
LincFt 8½96	8.5	322	99⅞	89	99⅞	+ 16
LincNtl 13⅞92	12.3	276	117	108¼	112⅞	+ 1⅜
Litton 3½87	cv	82	199½	166½	166½	− 16½
Litton 11½95	10.6	2536	112	102⅜	108⅛	+ 5½
Litton flt00	...	2007	101	98½	99¾	− 1¼
Litton 12⅝05	10.9	1569	118	106⅛	115¾	+ 9
LomN zr01	...	18239	33	25	29	+ 3½
LomN 9s10	cv	2411	145½	114	129	+ 13½
LomN 7s11	cv	5772	108½	91	99	...
LonSl 4⅞90	5.8	264	84	77	84	+ 6
LonSl 5⅛93	cv	53	128¼	116⅛	128	+ 11⅞
LonSl 11¾90	11.8	146	102⅜	100	100	...
LglsLt 12⅝92	12.0	1869	108	99½	104⅞	+ 4⅞
LglsLt 13½13	12.5	4186	109	100½	108	+ 5½
LglsLt 17½89	15.6	1816	116½	111½	112⅛	+ 1⅝
LglsLt 13¼95	12.4	4107	108⅛	101	106½	+ 3
LglsLt 11¼96	11.4	8217	101¼	94	98¾	...
LglsLt 11⅞15	11.9	8253	102½	96¾	99¾	...
LglsLt 11.7s93	11.7	393	100½	98⅞	100	...
LglsLt 11¾94	11.8	237	100⅛	98⅞	99⅞	...
LglsLt 11½14	12.3	177	94½	93⅜	93¾	...
Loral 10¾97	10.4	868	105	98¼	103	+ 4
Loral 7¼10	cv	8980	127	101	113¾	+ 9¾
Lorilld 6⅝93	7.0	506	97	80¼	94⅝	+ 12½
Lorilld 6⅞93	7.4	17385	94	81	93½	+ 10⅜
LouN 4⅞87	5.0	190	98¼	92⅞	98	+ 5
LouN 2⅞03	5.8	235	51	41½	50	+ 10½
LouN 3⅜03F	6.4	332	57	42⅞	52½	+ 12
LouN 3⅜03I	4.2	4	80	80	80	+ 2
LouN 3¾03	4.6	7	81½	81½	81½	+ 9½
LouN 7⅜93	7.8	189	95⅜	86⅛	94¼	+ 8¾
LouGs 4⅞87	5.0	313	98⅞	93⅞	98	+ 4¾
LouGs 4⅞90	5.2	210	93	86⅜	93	+ 12⅞
LouGs 4⅞90r	5.4	10	89¾	89¾	89¾	...
LouGs 9¼00	9.0	864	102⅝	90⅛	102½	+ 12
LouGs 8¼01	8.7	412	100	83¾	95¼	+ 12¼
LouGs 7½02	8.3	359	90	76⅞	90	+ 13⅝
LuckSt 5s93	cv	1	163¼	163¼	163¼	+ ¼
LuckSt 8½96	8.8	153	99½	88¼	97	+ 15¾
LuckSt 6¾00	cv	40	244¼	191	210	+ 81½
LuckSt 11¾05	11.1	290	105⅞	102	105⅞	+ 6⅞
vjLykes 7½94N f	...	3812	64	14	14⅜	− 43⅝
vjLykes 7½94f	...	27683	63½	14½	15¼	− 42
vjLykes 11s00f	...	11410	81¼	15	15⅞	− 57⅛

—M—

		Sales $1,000	High	Low	Last	Net Chg.
MACOM 9¼06	cv	11693	107½	89½	89½	− 6½
MCorp 9⅜01	10.2	1032	96	79	92	+ 13⅜
MGM 10s94	10.0	962	100½	93⅛	99¾	+ 8¾
MckF 9⅝90	9.6	540	101	95⅛	100	+ 4⅞
MckF 9¾91	9.8	221	101	93⅛	100	+ 5⅞
MckTr 7⅞97	9.2	580	90	80¼	85½	+ 7⅜
Macml 10¼01	10.3	39	99½	94½	99¼	+ 8¼
MacMl 7½10	...	4905	133½	106½	123¼	+ 15¾
McyCr 13⅞91	13.2	4892	108	104	105	− 2
McyCr 13¾88	13.8	2452	105	100	100	− 4
MeYk 9.1s02	9.2	1182	100	91¾	98⅞	+ 5⅜
MeYk 8½02	8.6	732	99⅛	88⅜	99	+ 10⅜
MeYk 7⅝02	8.3	273	92	82	92	+ 10⅜
MfrH 8⅛04	8.8	2105	94½	78	92	+ 13½
MfrH 8⅛07	8.9	2867	94½	77¼	91¼	+ 12⅛
MfrH 6s87t	6.1	1786	100	97 1/32	99	...
Mapco 10¾99	10.5	626	102	89	102	+ 9½
Mapco 11¾03	11.2	73	106½	100½	105	+ 9
MarO 4⅜87	4.4	328	99	93⅝	99	+ 5¼
MarO 8½00	9.7	1593	92	81	88	+ 6⅛
MarO 8.5s06	10.0	4802	89⅛	79	85	+ 4
MarO 10¼87	10.2	8618	102⅜	99½	100½	+ ⅛
MarO 12½94	12.4	1293	103¼	99⅛	100½	− 2⅜
Marcor 5s96	cv	12	110	104	110	+ 21
MarM 7⅝03	8.5	508	91	73	90	+ 15
MrtM d7s11	10.6	17	66	66	66	+ 2
Mattel 11⅝03	12.5	4071	101½	89⅞	93	+ ⅜
Mattel 14¾00	13.1	141	115½	107	113	+ 2
MayD 7.95s02	8.8	33	90½	80½	90½	+ 13½
MayDC 9s89	8.9	537	105½	98⅜	101⅛	+ 3⅛
Myr 7.85s96	7.9	573	99⅞	83½	99⅞	+ 18⅞
McCro 6½92	cv	137	72¾	66½	71¾	+ 5¾
McCro 7½94	10.9	782	76	66⅝	69	+ 2½
McCro 7½94N	10.6	267	79½	66⅛	71	+ 4⅝
McCro 7⅝97	10.9	465	72	63⅛	70¼	+ 8¼
McCro 7¾95	11.5	712	77½	65⅛	67⅛	+ 2
McDe 10.20s99	9.9	128	102¾	92⅛	102¾	+ 11⅝
McDe 9⅝04	10.1	144	95½	84¼	95½	+ 13
McDe 10s03	10.3	7792	100	84⅝	96¾	+ 10⅞
McDInv 8s11	cv	3040	110⅝	95	96¼	...
McDnl zr88	...	3177	90⅞	79½	90½	+ 10⅞
McDnl zr94	...	9298	58⅞	44½	57¾	+ 10¼
McDnl 11⅝95	10.5	30	114	106⅞	111	+ 6
McDnl 10⅞15	9.9	50	111⅝	103	110¼	+ 7⅜
McDD 4¾91	cv	129	289½	240	258½	+ 32
McGE 7½96	8.1	347	94½	82	92½	+ 10½
McGH 3⅞92	cv	3	190	190	190	+ 44
McKes 6s94	cv	45	215	162	215	+ 51
McKes 9¾06	cv	4360	159	119½	142	+ 19
vjMcLn 12s03f	...	47589	87	12⅜	12¾	− 67¼
vjMcLn 14¼94f	...	42074	98	12½	12⅞	− 80⅝
Mead 8½95	8.8	464	99¾	90½	97⅛	+ 8½
Mead 9⅞00	9.8	133	103	94	100½	+ 7¼
Mead 15⅞92	12.2	162	131	122	130	+ 11½
Melln 6.35s89t	6.4	858	101½	99⅛	100	...
Melln 6.05s89t n	cv	1824	99⅞	95	97	+ 1⅞
Melvl 4⅞s96	cv	20	426	348	379	+ 129
Memx 5¼90	cv	2562	93	83	92	+ 6⅛
MerSt 8.7s95	8.8	95	99⅛	94	99⅛	+ 12⅛
MLCPS 15¾06	13.2	1079	120	112⅝	119	+ 4
MerL 11⅝87	11.1	1009	109	103½	104⅝	+ ⅜
MerLy zr06	...	1919	25¼	20½	23½	+ 1½
MesaCap 12s96	11.7	1573	105½	102¾	103	...
MichB 3⅛88	3.3	1395	95⅜	87½	94⅜	+ 7⅞
MichB 3⅛88r	3.3	92	95⅛	92½	93½	...
MichB 4⅜91	4.9	584	89⅜	77⅞	88½	+ 10½
MichB 7¾11	8.5	3780	92¾	74⅞	90¾	+ 13¼
MichB 7s12	8.2	1955	85⅝	68⅞	85½	+ 16½
MichB 9.6s08	9.2	12148	105¼	90¾	104¼	+ 8⅞
MichB 8⅛15	8.6	4169	95¼	79⅛	94⅛	+ 13⅛

NEW YORK BONDS

		Sales $1,000	High	Low	Last	Net Chg.
MichB 9⅛18	9.1	5873	102	88	100½	+10½
MicG 8⅛98	8.8	733	94⅛	83	92⅝	+9⅝
MicG 10⅞95	10.5	80	105	99½	103½	+3⅜
MicG 13½03	11.6	6	116¾	106	116¾	+9⅞
Mickl dc11½98	12.2	494	94	84¼	94	+13⅞
Midcon 10¼09	cv	1099	192	157½	192	+27⅛
MidlBk 11.35s93	10.3	118	112	104¼	110⅜	+13
MileL 6½92	7.2	113	90½	83	90	+5
MileL 8.7s96	9.0	178	97½	89	96½	+18
MSPSS 4s91f	...	373	83	73½	80⅝	+5⅛
MMM 8.85s	8.8	1666	101½	91⅜	100¾	+8¾
MRvT 9¾90	9.6	385	103	98⅞	101⅛	+3½
MKT 4s90	4.8	979	86	74⅛	83⅛	+8¼
MKT 5½33f	...	3756	56	35⅝	50	+6⅝
MKT 5½33fr	...	478	55	36¼	48⅝	...
MPac 4¼90	4.6	3254	92¾	85⅛	92¾	+7¼
MPac 4¼90r	4.7	266	91½	84½	91¼	...
MPac 4¼05	7.4	2879	62½	50⅝	57½	+6
MPac 4¼05r	7.3	430	59⅞	49⅜	57⅞	...
MPac 4¾20f	...	2757	54	43⅝	52⅝	+8⅝
MPac 4¾30f	...	2862	54	43¾	52½	+8½
MPac 5s45f	...	10072	54¾	44	54¾	+10½
MoAl 8.4505	9.1	1553	97½	87	93	+4½
Mobil 8½01	8.6	33967	100½	86	99⅛	+10½
Mobil 14.4s04	12.4	37212	118¾	111	116	+1½
MobO 7⅜01	8.3	1574	93	78	89¼	+8¼
Mobil 10⅞92	10.5	8916	106⅞	102¾	103⅞	+¼
Mobil 13.76s04	12.0	29183	117½	110⅜	115	+2½
Mobil 8¾88	...	345	104½	100	103	+2
Mobil 7¼91	7.2	50	101	101	101	...
MohD 5½94	cv	347	50¼	41⅝	50	+9⅞
Monog 10s99	11.3	693	91¾	73⅛	88½	+11½
Monog 11s04	11.0	686	100	80	100	+16
Monon 6s07f	...	97	68½	61	66½	+7½
Mons 9⅛00	9.1	1410	101	90	100¼	+7¼
Mons 8½00	8.7	932	99¼	85¼	98⅛	+15⅛
Mons 8¾08	9.0	836	98¼	82	97¾	+15¾
MonW 4⅞90	5.4	1224	91⅞	79⅝	90⅝	+11⅝
MonW 9⅜00	9.7	1629	99⅜	84	97	+17
MntWC 6½87	6.6	1705	99⅝	94¼	99	+5⅛
MntWC 7⅜88	7.4	2544	100	93	99⅛	+5⅛
MntWC 9s89	9.0	3157	102½	94¼	100⅛	+3¼
MntWC 9¼90	9.2	3374	102	92⅝	101	+6
MntWC 9.6s95	9.6	445	102½	89⅛	100	+13
MntWC 8¼02	9.5	472	87	71	87	+18
MntWC 8⅜02	9.6	963	87	69⅝	87	+11
MntWC 8⅞03	9.9	618	92¼	76	90	+13½
MntWC 13½89	12.3	5	110	110	110	+8¾
MntWC 13¼94	11.3	131	117	108	117	+11½
MonyM 7s90	cv	422	101½	89	100	+12
Moran 8¾08f	cv	5431	76½	34	40	−35¾
Morgn 4¾98	cv	609	237	150	216	+54½
MortN 8⅞95	8.9	115	100⅞	95	100	+13⅝
MortN 9⅝00	9.5	61	103⅝	92	101	+21
Motrla 8s07	8.9	210	90	73⅞	90	+17
MtSTI 7⅜11	8.5	3065	89	71⅝	87	+12⅝
MtSTI 7¾13	8.5	3360	92¾	74⅝	91	+13
MtSTI 9¾12	9.3	4585	105¾	92¼	105	+10
MtSTI 9⅝15	9.3	4228	105½	92½	104	+11
MtSTI 7⅞16	8.5	1989	93½	75¾	92⅞	+14⅞
MtSTI 8s17	8.7	3960	94	77¼	92⅜	+14⅞
MtSTI 8⅝18	8.9	9015	98	82⅛	97¼	+11⅝
MtStTI 9¼14	9.1	5106	103¾	87⅝	102	+11⅝
MtStTI 12¼25	10.5	268	120	109⅛	117⅛	+8⅛
—N—						
NAFCO 9s03	cv	3234	114	91¼	97	+6
NBD 8¼10	cv	3123	138	107¾	120	+12½
NBI 8¼07	cv	6945	82½	67½	76⅝	+2⅝
NCNB 14½92	12.3	60	119¾	114	117¾	+5¾
NCNB 9.4s95	8.2	805	104⅞	94	102¾	+8¾
NCNB 8⅝97	8.6	617	100⅛	85	100⅛	+11⅛
NCNB 8⅜99	8.5	1441	100	83½	99	+16
NCNB 12.65s96	10.9	98	116	105½	115¾	+10¾
NLInd 7½95	9.5	539	92	71¾	79	−6¼
NLInd 9⅜00	10.8	1825	98	78½	87	−5⅝
NWA 7½10	cv	9039	123	98	118¼	+17¾
Nabis 7¾s01	8.2	842	95	77¼	95	+17
Nabis 7¾s03	8.1	431	95½	79	95½	+17
NBisc 4¾87	4.9	954	99¾	96	97¾	+1¾
NBsc 4¾87r	4.8	59	99⅜	12⅜	99⅜	...
NCash 4⅜87	4.4	459	101⅛	94⅞	99⅛	+4⅝
NCash 5.6s91	6.1	336	93	82¼	91⅞	+9⅞
NCash 7.7s94	7.8	661	99	86⅛	98⅜	+12¾
NConv 9s08	cv	6831	103	83½	93	+8
NDair 4⅜92	5.0	148	87	81⅛	87	+10½
NDist 4½92	cv	120	185	132½	173⅞	+29⅜
NtEdu 6½11	cv	5683	112	92	96½	...
NEnt 4¾96	cv	390	66¾	53	60	+7½
NtGyp zr04	...	77725	457⅛	40¼	47¼	...
NInd 10s99	10.7	608	97	79¼	93½	+14¼
NLead 4⅜88	4.7	558	96½	88	93	+6
NLead 4⅜88r	4.7	39	94	91	93¼	...
NtMed 12¾00	12.1	559	108	102⅝	105⅛	+1½
NtMed 9s06	cv	20456	117¾	103	109	−6¼
NMed 8s08	cv	26901	104	89	99¼	+4¾
NMed 12¾99A	12.0	1059	107⅜	103¼	106	+1
NMed 12⅛99B	11.5	499	107	101	105	+3⅜
NMEd 12s00	11.4	681	107⅞	100⅜	105	+4
NMed 12½00	11.8	1034	107¼	103	106	+3
NMed 12⅛95	9.9	50	123½	120	122	+14
NMed zr04	...	51008	31½	24¾	29	...
NRUt 7.40s07	9.3	30	80	75	80	+12
NRUt A9¾09	9.5	533	103	92½	103	+12
NRUt 13½10	12.4	110	108⅞	108½	108⅞	...
NRUt S9¾09	9.7	115	102½	98⅛	101	+6¼
NRUt 14¾11	12.9	280	118⅝	111	114	+1
NRUt 14⅞91	13.6	380	114	108	109½	−2½
NRUt 15¾91	13.8	334	117	111½	114½	+2⅝
NRUt 10½95	9.5	536	111¾	103½	110¾	+9½
NStl 4⅝89	5.3	550	91⅛	82⅞	86½	+4
NStl 8s95	9.6	1193	92½	76⅛	83	+4½
NStl 8⅜06	12.1	2335	78¾	62¼	69½	+1½
NtrlG 9¼95	9.3	107	100⅝	95	99¾	+9½
Navstr 4⅝88	5.0	416	100	92¼	92¼	−4¼
Navstr 4⅝88r	5.0	39	98½	93	93	+25
Navstr 4.8s91	4.9	663	99	89½	97¾	+1¾
Navstr 6¼98	9.6	2641	70½	57⅛	65⅛	+6⅝
Navstr 8⅝95	10.1	4388	87	74½	85½	+8⅜
Navstr 9s04	10.9	17304	85	65⅝	82½	+10½
Navstr 18s02	15.8	13459	122⅞	108⅛	114	−3½
Navst dc13¼95	12.6	17305	106⅜	95⅝	105	+5
Navstr 14½01	12.6	2012	116	105⅝	115	...
Navstr 13¼06	11.8	6097	112½	97	112¼	...
NavFin 8⅝91	9.2	2137	95	83	94	+11
NavFin 7⅝93	9.1	531	86⅞	73½	84¼	+12¼
NavFin ⅞½94	9.0	1799	83½	71⅝	83½	+12⅜
NavFin 13½88	12.7	5610	108	102⅝	106½	+3¼
NavFin 11.95s95	11.7	9030	102⅜	93	102	...
NEMtl 7⅜97	7.8	383	94⅞	80	94	+16⅛
NJBTI 3⅛88	3.3	605	96	89	95⅜	+5⅜
NJBTI 7¼11	8.3	2501	89	72¼	87½	+13¼
NJBTI 7⅜12	8.4	1784	89¾	73¾	88	+13
NJBTI 7¾13	8.5	2147	93⅛	75⅞	91⅜	+13¾
NJBTI 8¼16	8.6	1800	97⅜	80⅛	96¼	+12⅝
NJBTI 8s16	8.5	2056	96⅞	78⅛	94⅛	+14⅛
NJBTI 8¾18	8.7	3610	101¾	85⅛	101	+13
NwPlRt 8⅜00	cv	1776	128	96	125	+22½
NYEG 7⅝01	8.8	898	89½	74¼	87⅛	+13⅝
NYEG 9⅜05	9.3	2426	101	87½	100⅝	+10⅞
NYEG 9⅜06	9.5	744	101	89⅛	98¾	+9⅛
NYEG 8⅝07	9.1	442	95⅜	79¾	94½	+16
Newhal 6¾11	6.9	326	101½	98½	98½	...
NiMP 4⅞87	5.0	2357	99	93¾	98 11/32	+4 19/32
NiMP 4⅞87r	4.9	267	98⅝	6 1/16	98⅝	...
NiMP 10.2s05	9.9	1197	104	94½	103½	+7½
NiMP 8.35s07	9.1	1133	92⅝	79	92	+12¾
NblAfl 11½90	11.2	225	104½	100	102¼	−1¼
NorfW 4s96	5.6	307	73	62½	71⅜	+10⅝
NorfW 4s96r	5.7	99	73	70	70⅛	...
NorfW 4.85s15	8.2	521	62½	45½	59⅛	+11⅛
vjNACa 8.1s92f	7.9	250	102½	59½	102½	+42½
NoAPh 4s92	cv	60	76	69	75½	+6½
NoAPh 9¾00	9.7	262	103½	94	100½	+8½
NoIllG 8¾01	8.8	22	99½	95	99½	+14⅞
NoNG 8s91	8.2	515	99½	90⅞	97½	+6⅛
NoNG 7⅜92	7.8	303	95	87	95	+12⅞
NoNG 9s95	9.0	305	109	91	100	+9⅞
NoPac 4s97	5.1	1082	86	76½	78⅝	−⅜
NoPac 4s97r	4.9	373	86	76⅛	82⅛	...
NoPac 3s47	4.5	3168	85	65⅛	66⅞	−5⅛
NoPac 3s47r	4.8	1841	81	62	63	...
NoSP 4¼86r	4.1	25	99¾	99⅛	99¾	...
NoSP 4s88	4.1	312	96½	90½	96½	+6½
NoSP 4s88r	4.1	123	96½	88½	96½	...
NoSP 5s90	5.4	435	93	81⅝	92¼	+9⅛
NoSP 5s90r	5.4	36	92	87	92	...
NoSP 4⅞s91	5.4	207	91⅜	79⅜	91	+13
NoSP 4⅜s92	5.0	318	87	76¼	87	+13¼
NoSP 4⅜s93	5.4	106	81⅝	70⅝	81⅝	+12
NSPW 4⅝87	4.7	204	99¼	94¾	99	+5¼
NSPW 4⅝87r	4.7	39	99⅜	25	99⅜	...
NSPW 4½94	5.6	370	83¾	70	80	+13½
NoTel 12¼90	11.7	258	105½	103	105	+¾

NEW YORK BONDS

		Sales $1,000	High	Low	Last	Net Chg.
Norwst 7⅞86	7.9	300	100	98 17/32	99¾	+ 9/16
Norwst 6¾03	cv	478	131½	97	126½	+ 25½
Norwst 6s89t	6.2	642	99	96	97	− 1
NwPipl 10¼91	10.0	277	102¾	93⅛	102	+ 7
NwPipl 9½98	9.6	141	99	93⅜	98⅞	+ 8⅜
NwnBl 3¼96	4.5	240	72	58	72	+ 16⅜
NwnBl 7⅞11	8.5	4131	94½	76⅜	92⅛	+ 12⅞
NwnBl 7½05	8.3	2008	91½	75⅛	90⅝	+ 12⅜
NwnBl 10s14	9.4	3918	108	95½	106⅜	+ 8⅝
NwnBl 8⅝12	8.8	4093	98¾	83½	98½	+ 12⅞
NwnBl 8⅛17	8.6	1800	95¼	79⅝	94¼	+ 11¾
NwnBl 9½16	9.3	7021	104½	91¾	102¼	+ 10¼
Norton 9s95	9.1	82	102	93	99	+ 6
Norton 9⅞s00	10.3	14	96¼	95⅝	96¼	+ 9¼
Norton 9½05	cv	6724	109¾	97¾	107⅞	+ 10⅛
NortS 6s98	8.1	1322	83	63⅜	73⅝	+ 9⅛
NortS 7.7s96	8.7	268	89	80⅞	89	+ 7⅛
NortS 9½s99	9.9	715	96½	89	96	+ 12

—O—

		Sales $1,000	High	Low	Last	Net Chg.
OakIn d13.65s01	15.5	367	93	85	88	+ 3¾
OakIn 10½02	cv	2184	78½	61	76	+ 13
OcciP 16s89	15.6	8243	109¾	102½	102⅞	− 5⅝
OccP dc9.65s94	10.3	74339	98⅛	85	93⅝	− ⅜
OcciP d8.95s94	10.0	16840	95⅝	83	89¾	+ 1¾
OcciP 10s91	10.0	83179	102½	98⅜	100½	...
OcciP 10½93	10.4	45811	102	98	100½	...
OcciP 10⅞96	10.8	27713	103	97½	100⅞	...
OcciP 11¾11	11.6	64923	105	98⅝	101⅝	...
Ogden 5s93	cv	1282	144¼	90	135	+ 31
OhBIT 7½11	8.4	2600	91¼	74⅞	89⅝	+ 15⅜
OhBIT 7⅞13	8.5	3668	93½	75⅞	93	+ 14
OhBIT 9s18	8.9	4178	102	87	101¼	+ 14¼
OhBIT 8¾26	9.1	5	96	96	96	...
OhEd 9½06	9.6	4664	100½	86½	99	+ 11⅞
OhEd 8½06	9.3	1897	92½	78⅜	91½	+ 11⅞
OhEd 8⅜07	9.3	4677	90⅞	77½	90¼	+ 12¾
OhEd 9½08	9.6	7604	100	85¼	99	+ 12⅞
OhEd 15½10	12.8	1127	123½	113	121	+ 6
OhEd 11⅞10	11.1	3703	109	99¼	107	+ 4
OkIGE 4½87	4.5	648	99 29/32	96 1/32	99¾	+ 3⅞
OkIGE 4½87r	4.5	176	99¾	95½	99¾	...
OkIGE 3⅞88	4.0	320	97	90	96¾	+ 7⅝
OkIGE 3⅞88r	4.3	5	90	90	90	...
OkIGE 4¼93	5.1	233	83⅛	71	83⅛	+ 13⅛
OkIGE 4½95	5.9	110	77¾	67	75¾	+ 6¼
OkIGE 4½95r	6.0	7	75	66⅝	75	...
Olin 8¾08	cv	4803	140	109	111	− 2½
Orient 10¼98	13.1	2078	94¾	75½	78½	− 5½
OriCap 12½97	12.0	1480	106	98½	103¾	+ 2¾
Orion 11s98	12.2	6003	96¾	77½	90	+ 10¼
Orion 10s99	11.9	2175	92	72	84¼	+ 12¼
Orion dc10s94	11.6	1833	95¾	77½	86	+ 5¾
OutbM 7¾96	8.2	393	94	82⅝	94	+ 9
OwCor 9½00	9.4	616	101	94	101	+ 8⅜
OwCor 12s10	11.2	4095	107½	101⅝	106⅞	+ 2⅞
OwnIll 3¾88	3.9	43	96¼	89¾	96¼	+ 14⅜
OwnIll 6s92	cv	82	340	189	339	+ 157
OwnIll 7⅝01	9.0	878	92½	79⅜	85⅛	+ 5⅝
OwIll 9.35s99	9.4	483	101	93	100	+ 7¼

—P-Q—

		Sales $1,000	High	Low	Last	Net Chg.
PPG 9s95	8.9	975	105	93¾	101½	+ 5⅞
PPG 8½2000	8.5	260	100	88½	100	+ 13
PPG 9½91	8.9	303	106¾	103¼	106¾	...
PPG 10⅛95	9.5	470	109⅞	103	107⅛	...
PS Grp 14s93	12.8	4407	111	101⅜	109⅛	...
PS Grp 12½96	11.4	8596	110	99	109⅜	...
PGE 3⅜s87	3.5	606	97½	90⅝	97⅜	+ 5⅜
PGE 3⅜s88	3.6	338	93⅝	87	93½	+ 9⅝
PGE 5s89	5.1	1758	98	87¼	97¼	+ 8¼
PGE 5s89r	5.2	342	97	87	96⅛	...
PGE 4½s90	4.9	842	93¾	82	91½	+ 8¾
PGE 5s91	5.6	1974	91¾	79½	89½	+ 9⅜
PGE 5s91r	5.5	452	90¾	82	90⅛	...
PGE 4⅝s92	5.4	541	87⅛	75¼	86	+ 10½
PGE 4⅝92r	5.4	156	87	81	85½	...
PGE 4½s93	5.6	363	83⅞	70¾	81	+ 10¼
PGE 4⅜s94	5.6	303	79	66⅛	78⅝	+ 12⅝
PGE 4⅜94r	5.5	124	79⅜	70	79⅜	...
PGE 4¼s95	5.7	163	75	65⅜	74⅞	+ 8⅞
PGE 4¼95r	6.2	11	69	62	69	...
PGE 4½96JJ	6.1	472	76⅛	64⅞	73¾	+ 9⅛
PGE 4½96JJr	6.1	39	74	67	74	...
PGE 4½96KK	6.0	487	74⅞	62⅛	74¾	+ 10¾
PGE 8⅞s02	8.8	7504	101	86⅛	100½	+ 12⅜
PGE 8s2003	8.6	7137	94¾	79¼	93⅛	+ 12

		Sales $1,000	High	Low	Last	Net Chg.
PGE 7½s03	8.3	6269	90¼	75¼	90	+ 13
PGE 7½s04	8.4	5048	90⅜	75¼	89½	+ 13
PGE 7¾05ZZ	8.5	2469	92	76⅝	91⅝	+ 13⅝
PGE 7¾05A	8.4	1654	92⅛	77⅜	92	+ 13¾
PGE 9⅛s06	9.1	12994	101¼	87⅜	100½	+ 11
PGE 9⅝s06	9.4	14727	104⅝	90½	102⅞	+ 8⅛
PGE 8¼08	8.8	7765	94½	79⅞	93¾	+ 12¼
PGE 8½09	8.9	7480	96¾	81½	95¼	+ 11⅞
PGE 9⅜11	9.1	9330	103½	89¼	102¾	+ 11¾
PGE 10⅛12	9.6	11228	106½	94⅝	105½	+ 6½
PGE 15⅜92	14.0	2823	115½	108¾	110	− 4¼
PGE 12¼18	10.6	956	121¾	108	116	+ 6⅞
PNwT 8⅝10	8.9	6438	98¾	83¼	97	+ 11
PNwT 8¾08	8.8	5505	100¼	84⅛	99¼	+ 12⅜
PNwT 9s12	9.0	4920	101⅝	86½	99¾	+ 10⅜
PNwt 8¾18	8.8	2395	100	84⅜	99	+ 11
PNwT 10⅛19	9.7	4527	105⅝	96⅝	104 7/16	+ 6 5/16
PacSci 7¾03	cv	5539	91	74	85	+ 10½
PSwAir 6s87	6.2	669	100	93	97	+ 4
PacTT 3⅛87	3.2	2580	98	92⅛	97⅞	+ 5⅞
PacTT 3⅛87r	3.2	636	98⅛	92	97	+ 5⅜
PacTT 4⅜88	4.5	2439	97	90¼	96⅜	+ 5⅞
PacTT 4⅜88r	4.6	951	97	90½	96⅛	...
PacTT 3⅝91	4.3	787	87	75⅛	85	+ 9¼
PacTT 3⅝91r	4.2	222	87	77⅝	85½	...
PacTT 8.65s05	8.8	14469	99½	83¾	98¼	+ 11⅞
PacTT 8¾06	8.9	15306	99¾	83¾	98¾	+ 12
PacTT 7.8s07	8.5	6417	93	75⅞	91⅝	+ 13¼
PacTT 7¼08	8.4	8540	87¾	71⅝	86⅜	+ 12½
PacTT 7⅝09	8.5	5445	91	74¼	89¼	+ 12¼
PacTT 9½11	9.3	30483	104	89⅝	102⅜	+ 9⅝
PacTT 8⅞15	9.0	11050	99⅞	85¼	98⅞	+ 11⅛
PacTT 8⅜17	8.9	10182	96¼	79½	94¼	+ 10½
PacTT 9⅝14	9.3	9154	104⅞	90⅞	104	+ 11
PacTT 9s18	9.0	16874	101	85	100	+ 11¾
PacTT 9⅝18	9.3	9125	104¾	90¾	103⅞	+ 10¼
PacTT 9⅞16	9.4	8754	106¾	93¼	105⅜	+ 9¼
PacTT 9¾19	9.3	10004	106	92¼	104⅞	+ 10
PacTT 11.35s90	11.0	3694	104¼	101⅜	103⅜	+ ⅛
Paine 8¼08	cv	10467	108¾	91	103	+ 12
Paine 13⅜94	12.6	60	109	103	106½	+ ½
PAA 4½s86	cv	2918	99¾	95¾	99	+ 3
PAA 5¼s89	cv	6555	86	78½	78½	− 5½
PAA 11½94A	11.7	2805	103	94⅜	98	+ 1¾
PAA 11½94B	11.8	2569	107	94⅝	97⅝	+ 1⅜
PAA dc13½03	17.6	19924	101	75½	76½	− 18½
PAA 15s04	17.6	36128	107⅞	82¼	85	− 20⅛
PAA 9s10	cv	14433	123	76	77	− 32
PanEP 12s10	cv	8136	145	115¾	138	+ 20
PanEP 15¼97	13.7	482	115	110	111	− 2¼
ParkrH 4s92	cv	8	182	178	182	+ 25
Pembr 14s91	13.2	2195	107¼	104	106⅛	+ 1⅝
PenyF 5⅜87	5.4	763	99¾	97¼	99¾	+ 2¾
PenyF 7⅞91	7.9	2063	103½	91⅞	100	+ 6
PenyF 10.2s94	10.0	372	105	101⅛	102⅛	+ 2⅛
Penny 8⅞95	8.7	2213	102½	94⅜	102	+ 7¼
Penny 9s99	8.7	1986	104	91	103	+ 11½
Penny 10¾90	10.5	2722	105⅜	101½	102¾	...
Penny 11½10	10.8	298	111	101½	106	+ 4¾
Penny 12s10	10.9	437	112⅞	104¾	110	+ 2½
Penwl 9⅛95	9.1	762	100½	92⅛	100½	+ 6½
Pennzl 7½88	7.5	2048	101⅞	94⅞	100	+ 3⅛
Pennzl 7⅜88	7.4	1386	100½	95½	99½	+ 3⅞
Pennzl 8⅜96	8.8	1168	98½	89¾	95⅛	+ 4½
Pennzl 8¾01	9.0	395	97	83⅜	97	+ 13
Pennzl 14s91	12.8	1253	109½	104⅜	109	− ⅞
Pennzl 15s92	12.9	767	116½	112	116½	+ ½
Pennzl 12⅛07	11.2	357	111⅛	103	108¼	+ 13¾
Pennzl 8s88	8.0	136	103½	98	100	...
Pennzl 7⅞88	7.7	40	102	95	102	...
Pennzl 14⅝91	13.7	93	108	104¾	106⅝	...
Pennzl 15½92	13.2	34	117	112	117	...
Pennzl 8⅝96	8.5	16	101⅜	96¾	101⅜	...
Pennzl 9s01	9.4	2	96	96	96	...
PepBoy 6s11	5.8	2317	104¾	99¾	103¾	...
Pepsic 4¾96	cv	3	357	357	357	+ 67
PeryDr 8½10	cv	8797	129	101	101	− 11
Petrie 8s10	6.6	7371	144	109¼	121¼	+ 9¾
Petrie 7½10	6.0	2943	146	111½	125	+ 9½
Petrie 8s10d	cv	3535	164⅝	116	130	+ 10
Pfizer 4s97	cv	153	292	202½	258	+ 53½
Pfizer 8½99	8.4	1219	101½	86⅛	101½	+ 13½
Pfizer 9¼00	9.0	812	105⅞	92⅜	103	+ 12¾
Pfizer 8¾06	cv	2610	252½	164½	219	+ 40½
Phelp 8.1s96	9.3	1438	91	74¾	87½	+ 12⅝
PhilEl 4⅝87	4.7	1569	98½	91½	98 1/16	+ 5 1/16
PhilEl 4⅝87r	4.7	111	98⅛	96¼	98	...

NEW YORK BONDS

		Sales $1,000	High	Low	Last	Net Chg.
PhilEl 3¾88	3.9	1064	95⅞	87½	95⅞	+ 8½
PhilEl 3¾88r	3.9	83	95⅝	92⅞	95	...
PhilEl 5s89	5.4	1375	94⅜	81	92	+ 8
PhilaEl 5s89r	5.5	91	92⅝	84	90¼	...
PhilEl 6½93	7.2	1337	92	77⅛	90	+ 11
PhilEl 4½94	5.8	726	78	66⅛	78	+ 9
PhilEl 6⅛97	7.6	3492	81¼	67⅛	80⅛	+ 11
PhilEl 9s95	9.0	5121	102	88	100	+ 8⅜
PhilEl 7¾00	8.6	1909	90½	74¼	89⅝	+ 12⅝
PhilEl 8¼96	8.6	3642	96¼	82⅛	96¼	+ 11¾
PhilEl 7⅜01	8.6	2508	86½	71½	86	+ 14
PhilEl 7½98	8.5	1983	88¾	74	88½	+ 11⅛
PhilEl 7½99	8.5	2298	91⅛	74¼	87¾	+ 9
PhilEl 8½04	9.2	4601	93½	78⅛	92⅝	+ 12⅞
PhilEl 11⅝00	10.8	2819	109	100½	107½	+ 4½
PhilEl 11s00	10.5	2166	107½	99	104⅝	+ 4⅜
PhilEl 9⅛06	9.6	5480	98	82¼	95	+ 11¼
PhilEl 9⅝02	9.6	2894	101½	88	100¼	+ 11¼
PhilEl 8⅝07	9.4	1397	95	78⅛	91½	+ 11¾
PhilEl 8⅝03	9.4	1652	94	80	91⅝	+ 11⅛
PhilEl 9⅛08	9.6	4277	97⅛	81⅛	95⅛	+ 11½
PhilEl 12½05	11.4	4966	111	106	110	+ 3⅞
PhilEl 14⅛90	13.1	2545	109¾	104	107½	− 2½
PhilEl 14¾05	12.5	5361	120	110	118⅛	+ 3⅝
PhilEl 13¾92	13.0	978	110	105	106⅛	− ⅛
PhilEl 18s12	15.8	4701	121	113½	114	− 5
PhilEl 15⅜10	13.1	2989	121	114	117	+ ¾
PhilEl 13⅜13	11.8	1927	115½	105	113⅜	+ 4⅜
PhilEl 14½09	12.4	807	118⅞	112	116½	+ 5⅜
PhilEl 10⅞95	10.2	45	107	103	106⅝	+ 4⅝
PhilEl 11¾14	10.8	729	110¾	99⅝	109	...
PhilEl 11s11	10.6	21516	105⅝	95½	104¼	...
PhilEl 10⅜96	10.1	200	106	101¾	103	...
PhilEl 8¾94	8.5	1	103	103	103	...
PhilEl 10¼16	9.9	43	103¾	102	103¾	...
PhilM 6⅝93	7.1	591	95	81½	93	+ 12
PhilM 8⅞04	8.5	347	104½	90	104½	+ 12
PhilM 9⅛03	9.0	500	101½	91	101	+ 11¼
PhilM 14s91	13.0	772	113	107⅝	107⅝	+ ⅛
PhilM 15¼91	13.6	672	115¾	111⅛	112	− 3⅞
PhillP 7⅝01	9.4	5402	81½	68⅛	81½	+ 7½
PhillP 8⅞00	9.8	9319	91½	77	90⅞	+ 7¼
PhillP 12⅞92	11.8	33015	109⅝	99⅜	109	+ 1½
PhillP 12¼12	11.4	5252	108½	96	107½	+ 4
PhillP 11¼13	11.0	12316	103	89½	102½	+ 3½
PhillP 9.94s95t	11.0	35763	97¾	79⅛	90	− 7⅜
PhillP 13⅞97	11.6	48561	114	100	112	+ 2½
PhilP 14¾00	13.1	70259	117⅞	101½	114⅝	+ 3⅜
PiedNG 8⅝97	9.2	71	96	87¾	93¼	+ 8
PierOn dc11½03	11.4	1893	101	87¼	100⅞	+ 10⅝
Pillsb 14s91	12.7	240	111½	106⅝	110⅝	− ¼
Pillsb 12s99	11.0	15	109	106	109	+ 4
Pionr 12¼90	11.9	803	104	101¼	102⅝	− 2⅜
Pittstn 4s97	cv	1108	63½	49⅛	62⅛	+ 9⅝
Pittstn 9.2s04	cv	5166	100	80⅛	97	+ 16¾
Pneum 9⅝98	9.9	286	99⅝	86	97½	+ 10½
Pneum 11⅝94	11.4	22	102	101	102	+ 1¼
PogoP 8s05	cv	13164	66	52	58½	− 3½
PorG 9½s06	9.4	1367	115½	88¾	101½	+ 10¾
PorG 8¾07	8.9	1489	98¾	84	98⅜	+ 14⅜
PorG 13½12	12.1	726	115	108⅞	112	+ 3
PotEl 9½s05	9.2	5142	105	91⅝	102⅞	+ 7⅞
PotEl 7¾s07	8.4	1356	93¾	77⅜	92	+ 12⅝
PotEl 8⅜09	8.5	2794	98½	82⅜	98	+ 13
PotEl 10¾04	10.0	485	108	100⅛	107¼	+ 6¼
PotEl 14¼92	12.9	1604	115¼	108	110¼	− 1¾
PotEl 11⅞89	11.2	2095	107⅜	103⅝	105⅝	− ⅜
PotEl 11¼15	10.7	11	105½	104½	105½	...
PotEl 8¾16	8.7	30	100½	100½	100½	...
PrmeM 6⅝11	cv	9470	118½	95	107	...
ProcG 7s02	7.7	1591	92	75⅛	91	+ 13⅞
ProcG 8¼05	8.3	6039	100	85¼	99¾	+ 10
PrudRt zr87s	...	32	97 5/16	92	96	+ 9½
PrudRt zr88s	...	696	91⅞	80⅝	91⅞	+ 9⅞
PrudRt zr89s	...	470	84	72	82¼	+ 10½
PrudRt zr90s	...	229	77¼	65	76⅞	+ 13⅞
PrudRt zr91s	...	776	72	56⅛	69½	+ 12½
PrudRt zr92s	...	157	66	54	66	+ 15
PrudRt zr93s	...	627	59⅝	45¼	59⅝	+ 16⅝
PrudRt zr94s	...	357	57¼	48⅝	57⅛	+ 22¼
PrudRt zr95s	...	539	51⅞	37	50⅛	+ 12⅛
PrudRt zr96s	...	263	50	32⅛	50	+ 18
PrudRt zr97s	...	50	44	30¼	44	+ 17⅞
PSCol 8¾00	8.9	2348	100	86	98⅝	+ 12
PSCol 7¼01	8.5	971	88¾	76	85⅛	+ 8⅛
PSCol 7½02	8.7	1439	89	76⅜	85⅞	+ 9¾
PSInd 7⅝01	9.0	1235	87	65	85	+ 17⅜

		Sales $1,000	High	Low	Last	Net Chg.
PSInd 7s02	8.7	1036	80⅞	60½	80⅝	+ 17⅝
PSInd 8s04	9.3	792	87⅝	66¼	86	+ 20¼
PSInd 9.6s05	9.5	3594	101	76¾	101	+ 23½
PSInd 7⅝07	9.1	1293	85⅞	61½	83¾	+ 20¾
PSInd 8⅛07	9.2	2256	88⅞	67	88	+ 20⅛
PSInd 8⅞08	9.3	2235	96	71½	95⅞	+ 23½
PSInd 12⅛90	12.1	3450	104½	99⅝	100¼	− 1¾
PSInd 15¾11	14.4	750	115	109¼	109¼	− 1⅛
PSInd 12⅞12	11.8	1210	112	99¼	109¼	+ 10⅛
PSNH 12s99	12.2	11448	102	86⅛	98½	+ 5½
PSNH 14½00	13.7	5714	109	99¾	106	+ 3
PSNH 18s89	15.9	8731	115½	103⅛	113¼	+ 1¼
PSNH 15¾88	15.0	13518	109	98¼	104¾	...
PSNH 14⅜91	13.6	16473	109	94⅜	105½	+ 3½
PSNH 15s03	14.1	20576	111½	98⅛	106½	+ 2½
PSNH 17½04	15.0	49426	122	105	117	+ 3⅜
PSNH 13¾96	13.8	21449	100⅝	88½	100	...
PSEG 8s37	9.2	156	90	73¼	86½	+ 11½
PSEG 5s37	8.3	374	60	46	60	+ 13
PSEG 5s37r	8.5	107	59	47	59	...
PSEG 9s95	8.9	3903	103½	92¼	101½	+ 7
PSEG 8½04	8.7	2299	97½	83⅛	97½	+ 13⅜
PSEG 12s04	10.9	989	118	103	110	+ 5¾
PSEG 8¾06	8.8	2617	101⅜	85	99¼	+ 13¾
PSEG 8.45s06	8.8	1741	97⅛	82	96⅛	+ 12⅞
PSEG 8¼07	8.8	3152	95¼	80¾	94¼	+ 11¾
PSEG 9⅜08	9.2	2419	104	90⅝	102	+ 12¼
PSEG 9¾09J	9.4	792	104½	93⅛	103¾	+ 7¾
PSEG 14⅜12	12.2	322	117⅜	112⅝	117⅜	+ 2⅜
PSEG 12⅛12	10.9	395	114	105⅝	111⅝	+ 4⅛
PSEG 12⅝93	11.5	172	114¾	107½	110	+ 1
PSEG 9½15	9.3	20	102	100¼	102	+ 2¼
PSEG 9⅛16	9.1	101	100½	97½	100½	...
PSEG 7½96	7.7	462	98½	91⅜	97⅛	...
PSEG 8¾16	9.2	27	95½	92	95½	...
Pueblo 8½01	cv	1038	128	108½	119	...
PullL 7¾s92	7.9	90	97⅝	96⅛	97⅝	+ 17⅝
Quak 7.7s01	8.7	450	91⅜	82	88⅞	+ 6⅞
QuaStO 9s95	8.9	418	102	92	101⅜	+ 7⅜
Quanx 15¼99	16.9	4886	108	84	90	− 11⅞

—R—

		Sales $1,000	High	Low	Last	Net Chg.
RCA 11½90	11.2	1221	108½	101½	103	− 1½
RCA 12¾92	11.2	347	117	109⅜	113½	+ 2
RJR 7⅜01	8.4	1223	94	74⅜	87⅞	+ 14⅜
RJR 8s07	8.9	127	90½	74½	90⅛	+ 15
RJR 11.2s97	10.4	38463	109¾	102½	108⅛	+ 2¾
RalsP 7.7s96	8.0	433	98	81	96	+ 12¾
RalsP 5¾00	cv	19	460	349	460	+ 160
RalsP 9½16	9.5	83	102½	94	100½	...
RalsP 9s96	8.8	20	104	102½	102½	...
RalsP 9⅜16	8.9	564	105⅞	96	105⅜	...
RamIn 5s96	cv	1998	84½	69½	75	+ 4¾
RamIn 10s93	10.6	12805	99¼	84½	94¼	+ 9
RapA72 7s94	10.1	2885	76⅛	65⅛	69½	+ 4⅜
RapA69 7s94	10.0	2524	75½	64½	70	+ 4
RapA 6s88	6.6	4950	92¼	84⅝	90⅜	+ 4⅞
RapA 10¾03	13.1	5624	90	77⅝	82	+ 3¾
RapA 12s99	12.8	1227	100	87½	93¾	+ 4¼
RapA 10¾04	13.1	680	88½	75⅛	82	+ 3¾
RapA 11s05	12.9	952	90⅞	78⅛	85	+ 5½
RtyRef 12s98	12.1	1806	105	91½	99	+ 4⅜
RtyRef 11⅜98	11.4	646	102¾	92	100	+ 9⅛
Reichld 8s10	cv	1370	108¼	93	99½	+ 3½
RelEl 7¼s96	7.8	25	93½	88¾	93½	+ 14⅞
RelEl 9⅝s94	9.6	19	100	100	100	+ 16
RepNY 9s01	9.0	933	101½	87	100¼	+ 10¾
RepNY 8¾02	8.9	459	99½	85⅝	98½	+ 11½
RepNY 13¾05	11.6	169	120½	109¾	119	+ 7¼
RepNY 15¾91	12.1	139	130	121½	130	+ 8
RepNY 16s07	12.5	92	128½	123½	128½	+ 7
RepNY 8⅜96	8.2	83	102	97	102	...
vjRepStl 8.9s95f	...	7220	72	14	16½	− 49
vjRepStl 12⅛03f	...	87219	84⅞	11⅛	11½	− 62¼
RepBnc 9⅜01	9.7	760	97¾	85	97	+ 8⅛
RepBn 6¾04t	7.4	1235	97	91½	91½	− 5½
Revl 10⅞10	11.2	13514	100	82	97½	+ 12⅛
Revln 11¾95	11.7	55478	102	97	100¼	+ 3⅜
Revln 8¾98	cv	295	300	153	232	+ 72
Rexn 8.9s95	9.0	307	100	91½	99⅛	+ 9
Rexn 9¼05	cv	8509	112	104	106½	+ 1
ReyM 4½91	cv	5656	101½	81	93¼	+ 12¾
ReyTb 7s89	7.0	495	102⅛	92	100	+ 7¼
ReyTb 7⅞94	8.0	706	99⅝	90¼	99	+ 9⅜
Rics 7.35s97	8.0	73	92	83⅝	91⅝	+ 26
Riegel 5s93	cv	115	80½	78	78⅝	+ ⅛
RochG 9¼06	9.3	1379	100¼	85	100	+ 12⅞

NEW YORK BONDS

		Sales $1,000	High	Low	Last	Net Chg.
RochG 8⅜07	9.1	817	94	79	92½	+ 12
RochT 4¾94	cv	20	203	168¼	203	+ 47
RocIn 4¼91	cv	58	413	314	402	+ 51½
RocIn 5¾91	6.1	114	93½	80	93½	+ 11
RocIn 8.3s96	8.6	260	100	90¾	96	+ 7
RocIn 8½95	8.6	169	100⅜	90⅞	99	+ 7
RocIn 4⅞87	cv	1684	99 31/32	96	99⅞	+ 3⅞
RocIn 9⅜96	9.2	434	103½	96	101½	+ 5⅞
RohmH 9⅞00	9.4	294	104¾	95½	104¾	+ 7⅜
Rothch 7s11	cv	8978	105	75	76½	...
Rydr 11½90	11.2	290	105	101¾	103	+ 1½
Ryder 8⅛92	8.2	100	99	93¼	99	+ 9⅞
Ryder 10s94	10.0	136	102½	98¾	100¼	+ ½
Ryder 9¼98	9.3	47	100	84½	100	+ 12
Ryder 11⅝93	10.7	82	110¼	102¼	108⅝	+ 4⅝
Ryder 14s94	12.4	5	113	113	113	+ 8
Ryder 13⅜94	12.0	19	111½	111	111	− ½
Ryder 10⅞95	10.0	56	110	104	108½	...
Rykoff 9.2s05	cv	5123	133	111	116½	+ 3½
—S—						
SCM 5½s88	cv	113	164⅞	156¼	161¼	+ 4¼
SCM 9¼s90	9.2	135	100⅛	95	100⅛	+ 6⅛
SCM 10s09	cv	1	164	164	164	...
StLSaF 4s97	5.7	606	71	58½	70½	+ 12
StLSaF 4s97r	5.7	218	70½	61⅛	70½	...
StLSaF 5s06f	8.2	1952	66	51	61	+ 10
StLS1st 4s89	4.4	62	90	83⅛	90	+ 7
StL2nd 4s89	4.6	30	87⅜	76	87¼	+ 11⅞
StRegis 4⅞97	cv	1	245	245	245	+ 27
StReg 10⅝10	10.1	1070	105	92	105	+ 10⅞
SallM zr14	...	20	9	9	9	...
SallM 7¾09	cv	8017	194	117	186⅜	+ 67⅞
SalmnIn 90	...	1989	100¾	95	96	...
SalmnIn 10.7s92	9.8	50	109	109	109	+ 8
SalmnIn 11¾05	10.8	539	110	104	109⅛	+ 3⅛
SalmnIn 8s96	8.0	70	100	98⅝	100	...
SanD 10s06	9.4	1954	106½	95⅞	106 1/16	+ 9 11/16
SanD 8¾07	8.9	1389	100	84⅛	98¼	+ 12⅝
SanD 9¾08	9.4	1796	104½	93½	104	+ 9¼
SFeR 8.35s02	8.9	7	93½	93½	93½	+ 8¾
SaraL 7⅜96	7.7	93	96	83⅝	96	+ 15
Savin 11⅜98f	...	5402	74⅞	43½	69	+ 2½
Savin 14s00f	...	7033	90	46⅛	84	+ 5
Scher 9⅞88	9.5	5	104¼	104¼	104¼	+ 4¼
SciotoV 4s89	4.4	7	90	82	90	+ 10
Scot 8⅞2000	8.8	901	100½	88	100½	+ 10½
Scot 8¾2000	8.8	536	99	87⅛	99	+ 14¼
SeaCst 8.35s96	8.5	456	100½	85⅝	98⅝	+ 13⅜
SeaCst 7¾98	8.0	184	96½	80¾	96½	+ 19
Seafst 9¼01	9.8	2262	95	81⅞	94¼	+ 12¼
Seafst 10½90	10.4	2478	103	97⅝	100½	+ ¼
Seagrm zr06	...	29190	30	22¾	28¾	+ 4¼
SealPw 9s10	cv	1708	114¼	105¼	109	+ 4¾
Searl 8.7s95	8.8	221	100	92⅝	98⅞	+ 6⅝
Sears 6⅜93	6.6	1362	96½	83	96	+ 12⅜
Sears 8⅝95	8.4	3828	104	94	102¼	+ 6½
Sears 8s06	8.4	3226	96½	81	95½	+ 12
Sears 7⅞07	8.5	2880	94¾	80	93	+ 10
Sears 14⅛89	11.9	3385	121	114¾	118⅝	+ 4⅛
Sears 13¼92	10.6	2104	127	115	125¼	+ 8⅝
Sears 10¼88	9.9	7917	107	102⅝	103⅛	− 1⅛
Sears 10¾13	10.0	467	111½	100½	107	+ 3⅜
Sears 12s94	9.9	2615	123¼	111	120¾	+ 7½
Sears 12s87	11.8	137	104	102	102	− 3
Sears 11⅞14	10.6	198	115	109	111⅝	+ 1⅛
SearA 8⅜86	8.4	2277	100¼	99 17/32	100	+ ⅜
SecP 11¾93	10.5	513	113¼	106	111¾	+ 6
SvceCp 6½11	cv	2306	115	106½	113½	...
SLR 10¾03	10.3	1549	105¾	97⅛	103⅞	+ 4⅛
SLR 15¼90	14.5	1318	111	105¼	105¼	− 4¾
ShellO 5.3s92	5.8	1067	91⅜	81⅜	90⅝	+ 8⅝
ShellO 8½00	8.5	2935	100¼	86¾	100¼	+ 11⅛
ShellO 7¼02	7.8	1099	94½	77¼	93	+ 15⅝
ShellO 8¾05	8.7	1378	102½	87⅞	100½	+ 9
ShellO 8s07	8.4	1323	95	80¾	95	+ 11
ShellO 13⅞91	12.6	2325	114	108⅛	110½	+ 1¼
ShellO 14¼11	12.3	8677	121½	113½	116	...
ShllPL 7½99	7.7	537	99½	78½	97⅞	+ 18⅜
ShWi 5.45s92	6.1	384	89⅜	79	89⅜	+ 18⅛
ShWi 6¼95	cv	13	473	407	473	+ 157
ShWi 9.45s99	9.5	134	100	86	100	+ 17⅛
Showbt dc13s04	12.5	1996	105⅜	94½	103⅞	+ 8⅞
Signl 8.85s94	8.8	2173	103⅞	92½	100¾	+ 7½
Signl 5½94	cv	641	145	125	127	− 1½
Signl 5⅞97	7.2	213	82	68	82	+ 15
Signl 11¾05	10.9	839	114	102	107½	+ 5¾
Signl 8s09	cv	7172	101½	86¼	90½	+ 2¾
Sinclr 4.6s88	4.9	385	95⅞	90	94⅝	+ 5¾
Singer 8s99	8.7	2886	92½	80	92	+ 12
SkilCp 5s92	cv	22	195	178¼	195	+ 32
viSmith 9.85s04	...	2430	71	37½	70	...
Socny 4¼93	5.0	735	84¾	73	84¼	+ 9¾
SohioB 9¾99	9.5	908	104	95⅜	102½	+ 8
SohioP 8¾01	8.8	759	103	87⅝	99⅛	+ 10
SoestB 4¾97	cv	981	111½	95⅛	100¾	+ 6
SoCG 8.85s95	8.8	1200	102⅛	93⅛	100⅛	+ 4⅞
SoCG 7⅝97	8.4	82	93⅛	83⅜	90½	+ 9¼
SoCG 8¾s96	8.6	335	102½	98⅜	102	+ 10½
SoCG 8½97	8.4	146	101	92	101	+ 11¼
SoCG 12¾99	11.5	1115	111	106	111	+ 4⅝
SoCG 15s01	14.0	304	113¾	105	107½	− 2½
SoCG 17⅜01	15.1	5558	119	105	115	− 1¼
SoCG 15¾92	14.4	922	114⅛	107	109	− 4¾
SoCG 12¼93	11.2	90	113	107⅛	109½	+ 4½
SoCG 9⅜16	9.3	113	100½	99½	100½	...
SCouG 9½95	9.3	1007	104	96⅝	101⅝	+ 4
SoNG 7.7s91	7.9	577	100	94⅜	97⅝	+ 3⅞
SoNG 15s91	14.2	215	110¾	104	105½	− 3⅞
SoNG 11⅜94	10.9	346	107½	104	104	+ 1
SNET 8⅛08	8.5	4335	96	79⅝	95½	+ 13¾
SNET 9⅝10	9.2	2816	106⅛	93	104¼	+ 9¾
SPac 10.35s94	10.1	2344	107	99⅜	102½	+ 2⅜
SPac 2¾s96	4.3	157	64	56	63½	+ 13⅛
SPac 2¾96r	4.5	46	63	61¼	61¼	...
SPacTr 8.2s01	9.1	228	94	78	90¼	+ 13⅛
SouRy 4⅝88	4.8	417	98⅛	89¼	96¾	+ 6¾
SouRy 4½88	4.9	2	91	91	91	+ 6
SouRy 5s94	5.9	620	85	74¼	84¼	+ 9¼
SouRy 5s94r	6.3	136	81	74	79⅛	...
SouRy 8½01	8.6	144	99	84⅛	99	+ 21
SRyM 5s96	6.9	26	75	65⅛	72⅛	+ 9⅛
SthInd 8⅜02	9.1	257	94	79	91⅝	+ 16½
SthInd 9⅜03	9.2	150	102	87½	102	+ 21½
SthInd 9½04	9.9	75	98	88	95⅞	+ 7⅞
Soumrk 15¼91	14.3	30	109½	106½	106½	+ 6½
Soumrk 13¼94	12.9	2544	106	101⅛	102½	...
Soumrk 8½98	cv	5759	113⅛	94½	97	...
Soumrk 10⅞89	10.9	36	100	99	100	...
Soumrk 11⅞93	11.9	26	100	99½	99½	...
SwstFrst 12⅛01	12.1	682	103	98	100	...
SwEng 8½10	cv	6504	106	90	102	+ 5
Spiegl 5s87	5.1	402	99	94	98⅞	+ 6⅛
Spiegl 4½90	cv	16	80⅛	73¾	80⅛	+ 10¼
Staly 8⅞01	9.3	307	95⅜	84	95⅜	+ 12⅞
Staly zr01s	...	27088	41½	29	34¼	+ 3½
StBrn 6¾93	7.4	160	92	84⅞	91⅜	+ 8⅝
StBrn 7¾01	8.4	338	92	73¾	92	+ 17⅜
StBrn 9½04	9.5	191	100	91½	100	+ 14
StdOil 7.6s99	8.2	1029	94	79	92¾	+ 12¼
StdOil 8½00	8.7	3097	99⅞	86¼	97½	+ 9⅜
StdOil 8⅜07	8.6	1380	98	84⅝	97	+ 11⅝
StdOh 13⅜92	11.6	577	117	110	115⅛	+ 5½
StdOh 10⅞13	10.0	207	110	95	109	+ 13
StdOh 7⅝91	7.5	75	101¼	100¾	101¼	...
StdOh zr90	...	1016	102	99	99	...
StdOh zr92	...	31	105¾	104	104	...
StdOil 8s93	7.9	170	102	100	101¾	...
StdPac 12¾99	12.4	433	105½	98⅞	102¾	+ 4¾
StanW 9¼00	9.5	21	100	96	97	+ 8¼
Stauf 8⅛96	8.4	284	99½	87	96½	+ 8
Stauf 8.85s01	9.0	557	98⅛	84⅝	98⅛	+ 14⅛
SterlBn 6½90	cv	3160	112⅛	97½	99	− 1½
StrlBn na92	cv	8	178	165	165	+ 45¾
StrlBn na94s	...	79	145	131	142	+ 35
StrlBn na96s	...	108	134	109	134	+ 14
Stokly 8s98	8.2	119	98	82⅛	98	+ 18½
Stokly 10¼00	10.0	25	106	92½	102½	+ 18
StoneCn 13⅝95	12.4	4387	117⅝	102	110	+ 5⅛
StoneCn 6¾11	cv	1751	125	98	123	...
StopSh 10¾95	10.3	58	104	104	104	...
StrEq dc9⅞90	10.0	596	100	93¼	98½	+ 3½
StrTch 9s01f	cv	60915	101½	25	99	+ 73½
StrTch 11⅝93f	...	19045	92¼	49½	86	+ 36⅛
Suave 5s97	cv	161	75	55	75	+ 20
SunCh 11½96	11.3	132	103	91½	101½	+ 8
SunCh 11¼96	10.8	97	104	92	104	+ 10
SunCo 7⅛02	7.8	111	91	81⅛	91	+ 14
SunOil 4⅝90	4.9	60	94⅝	85½	94⅝	+ 8¼
SunOil 8½00	8.6	872	99¾	86⅜	99	+ 14
Sunbe 5½92	7.6	642	82¾	72	72	+ ½
Sunra 4¼87	4.3	83	98¾	94⅞	98¾	+ 5¼
Sunsh 8½95	10.9	4783	94	52½	78	− 14
SunsS 8½95	11.3	5224	94	49½	75½	− 16⅝
Sunsh 8s95	11.8	5524	92	47	68	− 16

NEW YORK BONDS

		Sales $1,000	High	Low	Last	Net Chg.
Sunsh 9¾04	10.5	3258	103	58½	93	− 3
Sunsh 9s94	15.0	733	70	55	60	...
Sunsh 9½94	14.8	820	90	58	64	...
Sunsh 9½95	15.4	563	82	61	61¾	...
Sunsh 10¾95	13.0	192	95	81	83	...
SupOil 9⅝99	9.6	278	103	94¼	100⅛	+ 6⅛
SupOil 14⅜91	12.9	724	115	110¼	111⅝	+ 1⅛
—T—						
TRE 9¾02	cv	56	427	283	423	+ 209
TRW 5½92	6.1	309	91	78⅞	89¾	+ 10¾
TRW 8⅛04	8.6	200	94½	77⅛	94½	+ 13
TRW 9⅞s	9.7	178	102	95⅜	102	+ 9
Tallyl 8⅛97	9.1	155	88⅞	75⅛	88⅞	+ 19⅞
Tandy 10s94	9.8	1319	105½	99⅛	102	+ 2⅞
Telcm 13⅜99f	...	68	117	100	103	...
Teledy 6½92	7.0	268	93½	79⅛	93	+ 13⅝
Teledy 7⅞94	8.4	733	98	84¼	94	+ 9¼
Teledy 7s99	8.2	3226	86⅞	70⅛	85	+ 14½
Teledy 10s04A	9.9	13349	102½	90	100¾	+ 7¾
Teledy 10s04C	9.9	16417	102⅞	90¼	100⅝	+ 8½
Telex 9s96	9.0	2305	100½	81	100½	+ 19½
Telex 11¾96	11.8	479	105	99	100	+ ½
Tenco 7s93	7.4	3810	96⅞	84⅛	94¾	+ 10⅝
Tenco 7s88	7.0	1087	100	91¾	99⅜	+ 2⅛
Tenco 8¼91	8.2	1600	102½	93¾	100¼	+ 6¼
Tenco 8⅜02	9.1	808	95	82	92⅛	+ 9⅛
Tenco 8⅞03	9.2	1001	99	86	96	+ 9
Tenco 9½04	9.4	2424	101½	91¼	101½	+ 11⅞
Tenco 12⅛05	11.2	1876	109½	101	108	+ 2
Tenco 13⅜91	12.6	1733	109¼	105⅛	106	...
Tenco 14½06	13.0	4328	117½	109½	111¼	− 3
Tenco 15s06	13.3	6412	118	111	112½	− 6½
Tenco 14½91	13.3	2210	112½	108½	108⅝	− 2¼
Tenc dc6s11	9.0	43498	69	57¼	66½	+ 6¼
Tenco 13.70s92	11.2	2009	123	115	122⅜	+ 4⅜
Tenco 13⅝07	12.2	1284	113¼	108⅞	111¼	− ¾
Tenco 11⅛13	10.3	1755	108	100	107¾	+ 6
Tenco 12⅝88	11.5	562	110	107	109½	+ ½
Tenco 6¾87	6.8	270	100½	98½	100	...
Tenco 9¼96	9.1	2140	102⅞	97¼	102	...
Tenco 10¼16	9.9	1550	104	97¾	104	...
Tenco 9s97	8.9	1333	101¾	97	101¼	...
TVA 7s97	7.5	3467	95½	80⅛	93	+ 12¾
TVA 7s97r	7.5	1437	96	78⅞	93⅜	...
TV 7.35s97B	7.7	3916	97	81⅛	95	+ 12½
TV 7.3597Br	7.7	1429	97	80½	95⅛	...
TV 7.35s97C	7.7	3705	97⅛	82⅜	95⅞	+ 12⅛
TV 7.3597Cr	7.7	1502	96¼	82⅛	96	...
TVA 7.4s97	7.8	2847	97¾	82	94⅝	+ 13
TVA 7.4s97r	7.7	1759	97⅜	81¼	96⅝	...
TV 7.35s98A	7.9	1774	96⅞	80⅜	93⅝	+ 11⅝
TV 7.3598Ar	7.7	838	104¼	81⅝	95⅜	...
TV 7.35s98B	7.8	4301	96¾	81	94½	+ 12½
TV 7.3598Br	7.8	1147	96¼	20	94⅝	...
TV 7¾s98C	7.8	3549	99⅞	84⅛	99	+ 14⅛
TV 7¾98Cr	8.0	2121	100	83¼	97⅜	...
TVA 7.7s98	7.9	3120	99⅝	83⅝	97	+ 12¾
TVA 7.7s98r	7.9	935	98¾	84	97⅞	...
TerR 4s19	8.0	285	50	40	50	+ 5½
TerR 4s19r	8.4	51	47½	40	47½	...
Tesoro 5¼89	cv	509	91¾	79	87¼	− ¼
Tesor dc12¾01	13.6	8299	96¾	83	94	+ 6¾
TexcC 13¼99	13.1	6362	103¾	98¼	101	− 1½
TexC 13⅝94	12.3	10986	113½	100⅞	111⅛	+ 5¼
TexC 13s91	12.2	28747	108¼	99¾	106½	+ 4
TexC 10¾00t	10.6	5169	102	96½	101⅝	+ 3⅛
TexC 11¼00	10.8	2576	104	96	103¾	+ 6⅝
TexC 11s89	10.6	10085	105⅝	102⅜	103⅜	...
Texco 5¾97	7.8	4917	75½	62½	74	+ 8
Texco 7¾01	9.3	10400	86¼	70	83½	+ 8⅞
Texco 8⅞05	9.7	12605	93⅞	75⅝	90	+ 8¼
Texco 8½06	9.8	14611	91	72½	87⅛	+ 8¼
TxNO 3⅜90	4.0	43	86	81½	85⅛	+ 10½
TxNO 3⅜90r	3.9	15	86	75⅜	86	...
TxPac 5s00	7.4	123	69¼	59½	68	+ 9
TxABnc 15½92	14.3	1871	115½	104	108½	− 2
TxAOil 12s99f	...	10903	83	25	27⅜	− 54¼
TexEst 12s09	cv	10096	118½	108	110¾	− 1¼
TxInd 7¾92	8.2	140	97	88⅛	95	+ 7
TxInd 9s08	cv	6857	108	94	99½	− 2
TxIns 4.8s90	5.2	132	91⅝	81⅞	91⅝	+ 13⅝
TxInt 11½old	26.1	3495	151	35	44	− 28
TxInt d13⅛93	26.3	818	86	48	50	− 34
TxOG 7½92	8.1	53	93	89	93	+ 5
TxOG 7⅜92	8.5	82	99⅛	77½	87¼	+ 9½
TxOG 8¼94	9.0	260	97	86	91½	+ 2½
TxOG 10¼95	10.1	798	104	98¼	101½	+ 4½
TxOG 8¼97	9.1	189	95	85½	91	+ 5½
TxOG 9s98	9.6	279	94⅝	90	94	+ 8½
TxOG 16⅝91	14.6	743	119	110	113¾	− 3¼
TxOG 11½02	11.2	48	103½	99½	103	+ 5
Texfi 4¾96	cv	277	55	44	53½	+ 9½
Texfi 11¼91	cv	461	92⅛	78⅞	91½	+ 12½
Textrn 7½97	8.5	139	91⅝	84⅜	88	+ 11½
Textrn 12¾10	11.4	30	112	111½	112	...
Textrn 11s95	10.1	115	110	105	109	+ 7⅛
Textrn 9¼16	9.8	10	94	94	94	...
Thckry 9s90f	cv	71	95¾	91½	95¾	+ 2¾
Thermo 8½05	cv	2366	131½	116½	122½	+ 3½
Tidwtr 7¾05	cv	1198	68½	42	46¼	− 20¼
Tidwtr 7s10	cv	14331	68	38¼	44¼	− 23¾
Tiger 11½95	13.1	3852	93	69½	88	+ 8
Tiger 8⅝05	cv	1118	83⅞	62	72	...
Time 9⅞09	10.1	32	99	89⅛	97¾	+ 10¾
Timplx 7¾08	cv	4528	118	95	115	+ 2
ToddSh 14s96	13.3	2822	106	97	105	...
TolEd 9s00	9.3	2454	98⅞	9	97	+ 14½
TolEd 7½02	9.1	1142	84	69⅞	82⅜	+ 11⅜
TolEd 8s03	9.2	1039	89¼	73½	87⅜	+ 15¾
TolEd 9.65s06	9.7	1725	100¾	82⅛	99⅜	+ 14⅜
TolEd 9⅝08	9.8	609	99¼	83½	98⅛	+ 16¾
TolEd 11s09	10.5	1593	106	94⅛	104⅝	+ 10⅜
Trchmk 7¾10	cv	11979	137	102½	110¾	+ 8¾
vjTowle 9½00f	cv	5218	71	41	61	− 4
Tracr 9s07	cv	8447	120	101½	107	+ 1
TrailF 8½96	8.7	115	98⅜	96	97⅞	+ 23⅞
TrailF 8.2s87	8.2	648	100¼	96	99 25/32	+ 1 17/32
TWA 4s92	6.5	6845	66½	56	61½	− 3⅛
TWA 5s94	7.9	3851	65½	53⅜	63	− 1
Trans 10⅝04	10.0	920	106⅝	94¼	106⅜	+ 10½
TranF 7⅞91	7.9	889	101	94⅛	100	+ 5⅞
TranF 8½01	8.3	67	102	99	102	+ 3⅛
TranF 9⅞99	9.4	405	105	95	105	+ 10
TrGPL 6¼87	6.3	314	99¾	96	99½	+ 3⅛
TrGPL 8⅜89	8.4	814	101¾	95⅝	99⅞	+ 4¼
TrGPL 8⅞90	8.8	1257	101⅜	94⅜	101⅛	+ 4¾
TrGPL 9½90	9.4	825	103	97½	101	+ 2
TrGPL 8⅞91	8.9	210	100⅛	94⅞	100⅛	+ 4⅛
TrGPL 16¼89	14.5	75	113½	111	112⅛	− ⅞
TrGPl 15⅝92	13.8	30	115¼	112	113	+ 8⅝
Trnwl dc11¼07	11.3	4341	101½	90¼	99¾	+ 7¾
Trvlr 8.7s95	8.6	2534	103	93⅞	101½	+ 6⅝
Tring dc11½03	11.9	522	99	87	97	+ 14½
Trinty zr01	...	9889	29⅜	24½	28	...
Trinit 10s06	cv	5071	107	91	100	+ 7¾
TritEn 13½94	12.9	2515	106	98½	104⅜	+ 2⅜
TucEP 8⅛01	8.5	1147	95⅝	82⅛	95⅝	+ 13⅝
TucEP 7.55s02	8.2	947	92½	76⅞	92½	+ 16½
TucEP 7.65s03	7.7	717	90⅞	76⅝	90⅝	+ 14
TucEP 10½05	9.8	1132	108	98½	106⅝	+ 8⅝
TCFox 10¼98	11.5	3412	94	79¾	89	+ 5⅜
TCFox 13¼00	13.2	6392	106⅞	94	100⅝	+ 2⅝
TycoL 6¾06	cv	4063	128	108	123½	...
Tyler 10½98	10.5	159	100	86½	100	+ 14⅜
Tyler 12⅞94	12.7	60	103¼	101	101	...
—U—						
UCCEL 7¼95	cv	1737	82	72¾	82	+ 9¼
UGI 11s90	10.5	101	105	100½	105	+ 4⅝
UNC 7½06	cv	691	101½	85	87	...
UNC 11½96	11.9	1083	102	96½	96½	...
USX 4⅝96	6.2	14701	76½	65¼	74⅜	+ 6⅞
USX 7¾01	8.9	3565	90½	74⅛	87⅛	+ 13⅛
USX 5¾01	cv	29074	75½	60¾	63½	− 5⅜
UT Crd 8¼02	8.9	80	92½	89	92½	+ 17½
UT Crd 8.85s03	9.2	85	98⅛	88⅜	96½	+ 14½
UT Crd 11¼93	10.2	25	110⅛	107	110⅛	+ 9⅞
UBk 7.35s01	8.6	1076	89⅞	71½	85	+ 14
UnCa 7½96	7.9	110	95	91	95	+ 12
UnCa 10⅞10	10.2	114	107	100	107	+ 24½
UnCa 11s13	10.2	61	107⅞	103¼	107¾	+ 11¾
UCarb 5.3s97	7.4	3081	73¼	59½	72	+ 11⅜
UCarb 8½05	9.7	19749	89	67⅜	87¾	+ 16½
UCarb 7½06	9.8	505	82	63	76¼	+ 12⅛
UCarb 14½91	13.3	20832	111	103	109⅛	+ 3⅝
UCarb 9.35s09	10.0	16438	96½	71	93¾	+ 17¾
UCarb 10s06	cv	20215	122½	102½	115	+ 11
UCarb 13¼93	12.0	2456	115	97¼	110⅛	...
UCarb 14¼96	12.5	79461	121⅜	100⅜	114	...
UCarb 15s06	12.2	68549	132¾	103⅝	122½	...
UnCp dc14½01	14.1	180	104	101⅞	103	+ 3
UnEl 10½05	9.8	1846	107¼	97¾	107¼	+ 7¾
UnEl 8⅞06	8.9	1087	99⅞	84⅞	99½	+ 14⅝

NEW YORK BONDS

		Sales $1,000	High	Low	Last	Net Chg.
UnEl 8⅝07	8.9	1272	98¼	82½	97	+ 13½
UnEl 15⅜91	14.2	1188	113	107½	108	− 2
UnEl 15s92	13.8	1050	115	109	109	− 2
UnEl 13s13	11.6	314	118	110⅜	111¾	+ ¾
UnEl 9⅜16	9.3	105	101	98	101	...
UnEl 8⅞96	8.6	2	103	103	103	...
UOilC 6⅝98	7.9	1103	84	68⅛	83¾	+ 15¼
UOilC 8⅝06	9.4	2030	94¾	82¼	91⅝	+ 7½
UPac 4¾99	cv	171	453	336½	448½	+ 78½
UPac 8.4s01	8.6	694	99	86	97¾	+ 8¼
UPac 11⅞10	11.0	331	115	105	108⅛	− ⅛
UTexP 13s95	13.0	2	100	100	100	...
Unisys 13½91	12.7	424	109	106	106	+ 1
Unisys 11½10	10.6	941	113	100¼	108	+ 8
Unisys 9¼95	9.3	30	101	99⅛	99⅛	+ 1⅛
Unisys 7¼10	...	25283	124	98	117¼	+ 15¼
Unisys 8.2s96	8.5	472	98½	87	96⅛	+ 11⅞
Unisys 13⅞92	11.3	579	125	115	122¼	+ 9
Unisys 12½15	11.3	187	112	105⅝	111	+ 3⅛
Unisys 10¾95	10.4	100	105¾	102	103½	+ 1½
Unisys 7⅝11	cv	16109	135	101¼	135	...
UnAL 5s91	5.8	1284	86¼	74	86¼	+ 11¼
UnAL 4¼92	5.2	1714	83	70¼	81⅝	+ 11⅝
UBkNY 7¾87	7.8	375	100	97⅛	100	+ 2
UBrnd 7¼88	7.4	511	99	91⅛	97½	+ 4
UBrnd 5½94	cv	6836	85	71¼	82½	+ 9¼
UBrnd 9⅛98	9.7	2125	94	75	94	+ 17
UBrnd 10¼05	10.9	2331	95	77	94⅛	+ 16⅛
UtdCbl 7⅞05	cv	588	129	117	119	...
UEnRs 13⅜94	12.6	95	106¼	105⅞	105⅞	+ 3⅞
UEnRs 13s93	11.8	58	110	101⅞	110	+ 8⅛
UGsP 8⅜89	8.4	815	101⅝	94⅝	100⅛	+ 5⅜
UGsP 10⅛90	10.0	220	103⅞	96½	101	+ 3
UGsP 9¾90	9.7	99	101	99⅞	100⅛	+ 3
UGsP 10½89	10.3	336	103	100½	101½	+ 2¾
UGsP 15½91	14.5	247	109½	106½	107	− 2
UJer 7¾97	8.5	445	94½	79¾	91	+ 12
UnMM 13¾00	13.5	711	109	98½	102	...
UsairG 8¾09	cv	7299	122	106	115	− 1
USGy 4⅞91	5.4	215	94	80⅛	90	+ 12
USGy 7⅞04	9.5	355	94	82½	92⅜	+ 11⅞
USHo 5½96	cv	1200	88	55⅜	59	− 11½
USHo 10s87	10.0	2558	101	94½	99⅝	+ ⅝
USHo 12¾89	12.6	1397	103¼	99	101	+ 3
USHo 13¼94	13.3	5501	105½	96¾	99⅜	...
USLsg 15¾87	15.5	51	106	101½	101½	− ¾
USBO 7¾02	8.9	705	90	76	87	+ 10½
USPIC 8s96	8.4	688	96	84	95¾	+ 9¾
USTNY 8½01	8.7	295	98	81¼	98	+ 18¾
UnTec 5⅜91	6.0	375	92½	77	90⅛	+ 13⅞
UnTec 4½92	5.3	330	85	70¾	84½	+ 8⅛
UnTec 9⅜04	9.2	700	103	91⅞	102⅜	+ 7⅜
UnTec 11¼12	10.6	87	110⅞	101⅝	106½	+ ⅞
UnTel 9.4s99	9.4	461	102	88	100½	+ 5⅝
UnTel 11s00	10.7	162	104	100	102½	+ 2½
UnTel 10¾88	10.6	10	102¾	101¼	101¼	+ 2⅞
UnTel 9¾10	7.5	3698	136	108¼	130½	+ 20¼
UTelO 7.6s02	8.4	130	90	77¼	90	+ 12¼
UTelO 9s08	9.0	145	100	89¾	100	+ 19
UnUtil 5s93	cv	1255	106	84½	96	+ 11
UnVaBk 7¾97	8.3	360	93⅞	81	93⅝	+ 10⅝
Univar 9¾99	9.9	160	98	87⅜	98	+ 3
UtaP 10¼05	9.7	871	106¼	97⅝	105¾	+ 9¼
UtaP 9s06	8.9	1265	101⅜	87½	101	+ 12½
UtaP 8¾06	8.8	675	99⅞	86	99⅞	+ 15¾
UtaP 8⅜06	8.8	1021	96½	81½	95½	+ 11½
UtaP 8½07	8.9	965	96⅜	83	95¼	+ 12⅛
UtaP 8¼07	8.8	1108	94½	80½	93½	+ 12½
UtaP 9⅛08	9.1	2515	101	87⅜	100	+ 10
UtaP 10⅛09	9.4	1718	107¼	95½	107¼	+ 12⅛
UtaP 10¼09	9.7	1177	107½	96⅜	106	+ 9⅞
UtaP 13s12	11.5	428	114	108¼	112⅝	− ⅛
Utilicp 6.65s11	cv	149	102	96½	101	...
—V—						
Valer 7¾91	8.5	1709	91⅜	83	90¾	+ 5½
Valer dc16¼01	18.7	36608	108	80	87	− 20¾
ValerNG 16¾02	15.2	1405	115½	108	110	− 4
ValerNG 13½03	13.1	3940	104¾	96⅛	103	+ ⅝
VerP 9⅝98	9.6	1981	103¼	91½	100¼	+ 5¼
VerP 8½98	9.3	302	100	88⅛	91¼	+ 2
Vestrn 9s11	cv	25104	115	64	68½	...
VaSw 5s2003	7.8	144	64½	62	64	+ 14¾
VaRy 3s95	3.3	79	91	87	91	+ 3½
VaRy 3s95r	3.5	23	88½	86⅝	86⅝	+ 4½
VaRy 6s2008	8.1	544	75	59	74	+ 15¾
VaRwy 6s08r	8.2	116	73½	58¼	73½	...
vjVough 6¾88f	...	653	92½	56¾	68	− 15¼
Vul 10¼2000	10.0	125	103	95⅛	102⅞	+ 9⅞
—W—						
WMAC 8⅜88	8.3	1201	101	96	101	+ 4⅜
WaRR 4¼91	4.9	121	87⅛	76	87⅛	+ 10⅛
WaRR 4¼91r	4.9	80	87	80⅛	87	...
Wachov 8¾09	cv	7009	143½	117	131	+ 12
WaltJ 7⅞97	8.6	110	92	84½	92	+ 16
WaltJ 8s98	9.0	513	94½	78⅝	88⅝	+ 13⅝
WaltJ 9½96	9.5	795	102	92¼	100½	+ 10
WaltJ 13¾03	11.6	12	119	110	119	+ 11⅝
WaltJ 10⅞08	11.0	50	98½	90	98½	+ 11½
WaltJ 13¼05	12.2	55	113¼	108¾	108¾	+ 5¾
WarC 9⅛96	9.4	967	99	78	97	+ 19
WarC 10⅞95	10.7	1711	105	92⅜	102	+ 7
WarC 11½13	11.1	5111	106	86¾	103¾	+ 12⅝
WarL 8⅞00	8.9	577	100½	88⅝	100	+ 12⅜
WasteM 01s	...	23626	51½	31¼	48¼	+ 15¾
Wean 5½93n	cv	1071	53	36½	42	− 8
Wean 5½93	cv	1696	52½	34	38	− 11½
vjWedtc 13s04f	cv	17604	113¾	8	12	− 98¼
vjWedtc 14s96f	...	3088	100	12⅛	20	...
WellF 7⅞97	8.2	1246	97	83½	96⅝	+ 13⅛
WellF 8.6s02	9.0	1054	98	83	95⅝	+ 9⅝
WellF 14½91	12.9	879	113⅜	108⅝	112	+ 1½
WellF 12.3s90	11.3	242	113¾	104¼	109	+ 4¾
WellF 11.4s87	11.4	212	103	100 3/16	100 3/16	− 3 5/16
WellF 9½93	9.0	265	107	99½	105	...
WelFM 12s05	cv	6136	117½	106	115½	+ 9½
Wendys 7¼10	7.3	13266	119½	98	99	− 3
WAirl dc10¾98	10.7	13182	101⅞	85	100¼	+ 14¾
WCNA 10⅞97f	...	7852	58	12½	13⅞	− 41⅛
WCNA 10.7s98f	...	12941	60	10⅝	14¾	− 43½
WCNA 13¼92f	...	3632	62	12	12½	− 49½
WElec 8⅜95	8.3	2672	102	91¾	101	+ 8⅜
WElec 7½96	7.7	650	98⅛	87	98	+ 11¼
WPI 10s01	12.1	2717	101	81	82⅜	− 5⅝
WUC 5¼97	cv	17889	55½	31	32½	− 15¾
WUC 10¾97	21.1	14831	81½	36	51	− 26
WUTI 5¼87	5.4	4296	98	73	98	+ 4
WUTI 5¼87r	5.8	216	95½	74	91	...
WUTI 6½89	10.7	4487	83½	47⅝	61	− 19
WUTI 5s92	9.1	4117	74¾	47	55	− 7¾
WUTI 8.45s96	14.6	4881	76⅞	50⅛	58	− 12
WUTI 7.9s97	13.4	4283	69	51	59	− 6¼
WUTI 8.1s98	14.0	4046	72	51	58	− 7¼
WUTI 9¼97	13.5	1836	78	52⅛	68¾	− 6¼
WUTI 16s91	22.1	57722	105	49½	72⅜	− 32½
WUTI 13¼08	19.1	19670	93¾	45	69½	− 22
WUTI 13⅝94	19.2	576	96½	61	71	− 25⅛
WstC 8½91	8.2	648	103½	92	103½	+ 12⅞
WstC 7.6s97	8.0	596	97½	83	95⅜	+ 10⅛
WstC 10⅞90	10.7	631	103⅞	100⅝	101⅞	− ⅛
WstC 14¾91	13.3	853	114½	108¾	111	− ½
WstC 11⅞96	11.7	150	102⅞	101⅝	101⅝	+ 4¾
WstC 8⅜96	8.3	11	101	101	101	...
WstgE 5⅜92	5.9	869	91	79⅝	90½	+ 10⅞
WstgE 9s09	cv	9286	199	139	186¼	+ 40
WstgE 10¾89	10.0	157	107¾	104¾	107¾	+ 3¾
Wstv 9¾2000	9.4	78	104	91	104	+ 15½
Wstvco 8⅛07	8.9	121	92	80¼	91⅛	+ 11⅛
Wstvco 12⅛12	11.2	5	108	108	108	+ 10
Weyh 5.2s91	5.8	574	92	82	90⅛	+ 8⅛
Weyh 7.65s94	7.7	1223	100	88	98⅞	+ 11⅞
Weyh 8⅝00	8.7	1197	101	88¼	99½	+ 10
Weyh 8.9s04	8.8	555	101	89	101	+ 16¾
Weyh 7.95s06	8.9	518	93⅛	80⅝	89¼	+ 13
Whirl 5¾86	5.8	56	99⅜	98 9/32	99⅜	+ 2 11/32
Whirl 9⅝00	9.4	156	104	95	102	+ 12⅞
Whitkr 4½88	cv	410	94⅝	86	94½	+ 8¾
Whitkr 10s88	10.0	919	103	99	100½	+ 1¼
Whitkr 9⅝93	10.3	59	93	86½	93	+ 8⅞
Whitkr 10s96	10.4	2893	98⅞	85	96⅛	+ 8¾
Wms 9.40s96	9.6	225	98½	87⅛	98	+ 6⅝
WilmEl 12¾96	cv	5618	104½	24⅝	97	+ 6½
WisBl 7¼07	8.3	1292	89⅛	74	87⅝	+ 11⅝
WisBl 8s14	8.4	2684	95	78	95	+ 14⅝
WisBl 8¼16	8.7	1228	98½	81	95	+ 11
WisC 4s2004	7.1	476	58	44¼	56	+ 13⅜
WisC 4s2004r	7.4	40	54	44	54	...
WisC 4½29f	...	70	44	37½	44	+ 2⅜
WisG 10⅝95	10.2	211	106	100	104⅜	+ 4⅜
WisPL 13⅜91	12.9	1678	111½	100⅛	103½	− 4¾
Witco 4½93	cv	34	259⅛	239	256	+ 92¾
Woolw 7⅜96	7.6	885	97½	84⅜	97½	+ 11¼
Woolw 9s99	8.9	5287	101½	88⅛	100⅝	+ 8⅞

NEW YORK BONDS

		Sales $1,000	High	Low	Last	Net Chg.
WdAir 11¼94	11.3	1885	101	88⅛	100	+ 11⅜
WdAir dc14s92	15.9	8421	91	71⅛	88¼	+ 2¼
WylLb 5¼88	cv	760	118	95⅜	99⅝	− 4⅛

−X-Y-Z−

		Sales $1,000	High	Low	Last	Net Chg.
XeroxCr 15¼91	13.9	712	115½	110	110	− 4¼
XeroxCr 16s91	14.1	1302	119	113¼	113⅝	− 2¾
XeroxCr 12⅞88	12.4	539	108	103½	103½	− 3
Xerox 6s95	cv	17324	100½	82	95½	+ 9½
Xerox 8⅝99	8.6	1421	101½	88¾	100	+ 10
Xerox 10½88	10.1	1038	107¾	102¾	103¾	+ ⅛
Xerox 10⅝93	9.8	325	110	101	108	+ 3½
Xerox 8⅛91	8.1	5	100⅛	100⅛	100⅛	...
vjYngS 4½90f	...	1049	70½	48	55	− 12
YngtS 4½90r	6.4	10	70½	70½	70½	...
vjYngS 10½00f	...	9272	83	45	59	− 11
vjYngS 9⅞91f	...	3694	89	48	64	− 19⅞
Zapt 10⅞01f	...	34858	70⅞	23	28	− 41
Zapt 10¼97f	...	28676	68¾	22⅛	26⅝	− 41⅜
ZapOff 8⅝96	8.6	229	102½	91¼	100	+ 12
Zayre 8s96	8.2	259	99	86	97½	+ 15¼
Zayre 7¼10	cv	9689	133	95½	104	− 1¾
Zayre 9½16	9.5	50	99½	99½	99½	...
Zenith 6¼11	cv	4377	112	92	97	...
Zurn 5¾94	cv	514	154	121½	135	− 5

Sales figures are unofficial.

cv-Convertible bond. ct-Certificates. d-Deep discount. f-Dealt in flat. m-Matured bonds, negotiability impaired by maturity. NA-No accrual. r-Registered. rp-Reduced principal amount. st-Stamped. t-Floating rate. wd-When distributed. ww-With warrants. xw-Without warrants. zr-Zero coupon.

pr-Exchangeable into debentures.

vj-In bankruptcy or receivership or being reorganized under the Bankruptcy Act, or securities assumed by such companies.

Annual Market Statistics

NYSE LEADERS

Of the total volume of 35,680,016,341 shares traded during 1986 on the New York Stock Exchange, the 25 most active securities accounted for 5,854,831,000 shares, or 16.4% of the aggregate sales. Individual volume, and closing prices, with the net change for the year of the 25 leaders are shown in the following table.

Issue	Sales(hds)	Last	Chg
AT&T	5286867	25	....
USX	4350553	21½	− 5⅛
IBM	4076029	120	−35½
Mobil	2626518	40⅛	+ 9⅞
Exxon	2413458	70⅛	+15
Eastman Kodak	2404128	68⅝	+18
Phillips Petroleum	2276391	11¾	− ⅜
Goodyear	2254147	41⅞	+10⅝
General Motors	2213572	66	− 4⅜
Navistar	2171853	4¾	− 3¾
Sears Roebuck	2100626	39¾	+ ¾
Texaco	2064733	35⅞	+ 5⅞
American Express	2015020	56⅝	+ 3⅝
Commonwealth Ed.	1980060	33⅞	+ 4½
BankAmerica	1979047	14⅝	− 1
Schlumberger	1965209	31¾	− 4¾
General Electric	1896217	86	+13¼
Union Carbide	1875448	22½	....
Merrill Lynch	1872818	36½	+ 2⅛
Occidental Petro	1869620	27½	− 3½
Ford Motor	1840320	56¼	+17⅝
RJR Nabisco	1776431	49¼	+17⅞
Southern Co.	1753171	25⅜	+ 3⅛
Chrysler	1744272	37	+ 6
Philip Morris	1741802	71⅞	+27¾

AMERICAN LEADERS

Sales, closing price and the net change for the 10 most active American Exchange stocks for the year 1986.

Issue	Sales(hds)	Last	Chg
Wickes	2701511	3½	− 1¼
BAT	1202292	6 13/16	+ 2 5/16
Wang Labs B	1080797	11⅝	− 8
Lorimar Tele	589472	16⅛	...
Texas Air	573136	33¾	+18¾
AM International	476752	6⅜	+ ⅜
Echo Bay Mines	434958	23	+ 9¾
Horn Hardart	411380	12¼	+ 4⅝
First Australia	411315	8⅛	....
Amdahl	397890	23⅜	+ 8¾

AMERICAN EXCHANGE

STOCK VOLUME	
Total 1986	2,978,540,000 shares.
Total 1985	2,100,860,000 shares.
Total 1984	1,545,010,000 shares.
Total 1983	2,081,270,000 shares.
Total 1982	1,337,820,000 shares.
BOND VOLUME	
Total 1986	$810,264,000
Total 1985	$645,182,000
Total 1984	$371,990,000
Total 1983	$395,190,000
Total 1982	$325,240,000

WHAT NYSE STOCKS DID

	1986	1985	1984	1983
Advances	1597	1957	1109	1695
Declines	699	356	1185	621
Unchanged	22	19	57	46
Total issues	2318	2332	2351	2362

NYSE STOCK SALES

Total 1986	35,680,016,341 shares.
Total 1985	27,510,706,353 shares.
Total 1984	23,071,031,447 shares.
Total 1983	21,589,576,997 shares.
Total 1982	16,458,036,768 shares.
Total 1981	11,853,740,659 shares.
Total 1980	11,352,293,531 shares.
Total 1979	8,155,914,314 shares.

NYSE BOND SALES

Total 1986	$10,475,399,000
Total 1985	$9,046,452,000
Total 1984	$6,982,291,000
Total 1983	$7,572,315,000
Total 1982	$7,155,443,000

ISSUES TRADED

	1986	1985	1984	1983
N Y Stocks	2318	2332	2351	2362
N Y Bonds	2697	2980	3089	3101
Amer. Stocks	954	936	924	944
Amer. Bonds	309	290	261	250

AMERICAN STOCK EXCHANGE

The following tabulation gives the 1986 sales, high, low, last price and net change from the previous year in stocks listed on the American Stock Exchange.

—A—

Stock	Div.	P-E Ratio	Sales 100s	High	Low	Last	Net Chg.
ACI Hld		...	87255	14⅝	6¾	14½	+ 7
ACI pf	1.20	...	55072	14⅜	10	14	+ 2¾
AL Lab s	.12	18	19339	17¼	9⅝	11½	+ ⅞
AMC s	.10	125	10954	16⅛	8¾	8¾	– 2¾
AM Intl		213	476752	8⅝	4⅞	6⅜	+ ⅜
AM Int pf	2.00	...	41432	30¼	24½	28½	...
AOI		19	26073	4	2¼	2½	– 1⅜
ATT Fd s	.34i	...	27397	41¼	29⅜	37	+ 5¾
AcmePr	.04e	2	3917	6⅝	2½	5⅜	+ 3
AcmeU	.32	46	5647	12⅛	6⅜	8¼	– 3¼
Action	.12e	12	42183	15⅞	7¾	9⅛	– 4½
Acton		...	28339	3¼	1¼	2⅜	+ 1
Actn wt		...	2081	⅝	1/16	⅛	...
AdmRs		33	7112	2⅞	1¼	1⅝	– 1
AdRusl	.08i	79	53694	23⅝	13	20⅝	+ 6½
AirExp		18	20373	14⅝	6⅝	13½	+ 5¾
Alamco		...	21550	1⅜	¼	5/16	...
AlbaW		...	7321	9¾	6¼	7	+ ½
Alfin s		15	142201	40	7⅞	8½	– 16⅝
AlnTre		...	2205	3	1⅜	1⅝	+ ⅛
Aloha		10	13545	28⅝	10⅝	28½	+ 17½
AlphaIn		...	60497	12⅜	6⅝	6⅝	– 4⅛
AlpinGr		39	30378	11¾	5¼	8⅛	+ 4¼
Altex n		...	19765	½	⅛	¼	– 3/16
Altex wt		...	925	1/16	1/32	1/32	...
Alcoa pf	3.75	...	4247	49½	34¼	45½	+ 10½
Alza s		38	122785	26¼	14¼	18⅝	+ 3¼
AmBrit	.08	...	12797	6⅛	2⅝	4¾	+ 1¾
Amdahl	.20	43	397890	25¾	13½	23⅜	+ 8¾
AmBilt	.15	6	8885	15½	9¾	12	+ 1¼
AmCbl n		...	44758	17	12½	14⅛	...
AmCap		7	15268	8¾	3¾	3⅞	– 2⅞
AExFF wt		...	145286	5½	2⅞	3	...
AFruc A		14	66815	17	6⅝	12¾	+ 6¼
AFruc B		13	18168	16⅞	6¼	12⅝	+ 6¼
AHlthM		6	41611	7⅜	2⅝	2¾	– 2⅛
AIsrael	.30e	6	9706	17½	7½	17⅛	+ 9¼
AList s		21	5616	18½	7½	10⅞	+ 3⅜
AMzeA	.52	67	24305	23½	13¾	19½	+ 5¾
AMzeB	.52	64	3326	22⅛	13⅝	18½	+ 5⅛
AMBld		...	87568	7¼	2	3⅜	– 3½
AmOil		...	22553	5½	2⅜	5	+ 1⅜
APetf		...	3503	53	38⅜	43⅛	– 2⅛
APrec s	.18	60	6444	14¼	8	10¼	+ 1¾
AmRlty	2.50e	11	5608	9¾	6⅛	6¼	– 1⅝
AmRoyl	.71j	...	133496	14⅜	3½	5½	– 6¾
ASciE		88	37517	13⅜	4	4⅜	– ⅜
ASci wt		...	1784	2	¾	⅞	...
ATechC		10	27867	10½	3⅞	4	– 4
A ahp pr		...	1435	67	64½	64½	...
A ahp sc		...	1724	14	10½	13¾	...
A xon un	3.55	...	2676	73¾	49	73¾	+ 19⅝
A xon pr	3.55	...	69512	58	44¼	56⅞	+ 8⅝
A xon sc		...	40823	16⅛	5½	14¾	+ 7¾
Amrcr n		36	31734	13⅛	8¾	12¾	...
Ampal	.06	8	24528	2⅞	1⅝	1¾	– ½
Andal		12	17668	16	6⅝	8¾	+ 1
AndJcb		...	6508	2½	1¼	1⅞	– ⅝
Andrea	.72	20	1851	15⅞	8⅞	10¾	+ 1
Angeles		...	8157	15⅝	7¼	8⅛	...
Angel wt		...	3324	4⅛	13/16	1⅛	+ ⅜
AnglFn	1.86e	...	2435	19⅞	15⅝	17	+ ⅛
AngEn n		...	7757	1⅞	¾	1¼	...
AngEn wt		...	3522	½	3/16	¼	...
ArzCm n		...	490	8¼	7⅜	7¾	...
Arley		12	27255	11⅜	5¾	9⅞	+ 4
Armtrn		...	4404	7⅜	2½	3⅛	– 1⅛
Armel		...	42085	10	4¾	6⅞	+ 2
ArrowA	.20	...	3250	12	8¾	10	+ ⅞
Arundl		6	6557	30¾	19¼	19⅝	– ⅝
Asmr g	.20	125	115250	9⅜	5⅛	7½	– 1⅛
Astrex		...	7060	17⅞	6⅜	6⅜	– 8⅝
Astrotc		...	254845	3⅛	9/16	9/16	– 9/16
Astrot pf	1.35j	...	3290	16⅜	5	5⅛	– 7¾
Atari n		11	36631	15¼	11¼	14⅛	...
AtlsCM		...	100945	1¼	⅜	¾	+ 5/16
Atlas wt		...	2676	5	3⅛	4	+ ⅞
Audiotr		...	2836	3¼	1⅞	2¼	– ¼

—B—

Stock	Div.	P-E Ratio	Sales 100s	High	Low	Last	Net Chg.
BAT	.20e	...	f12022	7	4½	6 13/16	+ 2 5/16
BDM s	.12	22	44043	33	21¼	25⅝	+ ⅝
BRT s	.82i	9	19210	17¼	7⅛	15⅛	+ 7⅝
BSD		26	3298	3⅞	2⅜	2⅜	– ⅜
BSN s		22	34606	18½	11½	15¾	+ 4¼
Badger	.50	13	5930	19⅝	12	14	+ 1⅞
Baker		13	2810	19⅜	13¾	16¼	+ 2
BaldwS	.32a	...	11026	11⅞	8⅝	10⅛	+ 1⅛
BalyM wt		...	10739	4⅞	1¾	1¾	– ½
BanFd	6.67e	...	3013	33⅝	25⅝	25⅞	– 1⅝
Banstr g		...	4987	7⅜	5¼	5½	– 1¾
BnkBld	.40	18	15315	13⅞	7¾	12¼	+ 3¾
Barco		...	3876	6¼	3	3⅞	+ ⅜
Barnwl	.10j	22	1647	6⅝	5	5⅛	– 1⅛
BaryRG		13	28273	9⅜	4⅜	8⅞	+ 3⅜
Baruch		...	3304	10½	5½	5⅝	– 4⅝
Beard		14	19064	12⅞	8	8⅜	– 1¾
BeldBlk	.60j	...	9437	10⅞	4½	5⅝	– 4⅜
Beltran		4	3460	1⅞	⅝	1⅛	+ ½
BergBr	.32	17	128504	37¼	16⅜	20⅝	– 11⅜
BethCp	.42t	...	2610	4⅝	2	2	– 1
BicCp	.48	14	21548	35	23¼	29⅝	+ 4⅜
BigV	.44	14	15583	16	10⅛	14	– 2
BinkMf	1.00	10	5007	32⅛	22¼	22⅝	– 7½
BioR B		21	1907	23⅛	13½	17⅛	+ 1⅞
BioR A		22	15524	23¼	13⅝	17¼	+ 2
Blessg s	.34	13	6196	21⅞	16	18¼	+ ½
BlockE		...	25609	1 1/16	¼	15/16	+ 9/16
BlountA	.45	26	16168	16¾	12¼	12⅜	– 3⅛
BlountB	.40	26	2452	16⅜	12¼	12¼	– 3
BolarPh		21	60170	32⅞	13¼	21⅝	+ 4⅛
Booth		475	20782	9	2⅞	4¾	– ¾
BowVal	.20r	...	16452	11¼	6⅞	10½	+ ⅝
BowlA s	.40	13	1600	13⅜	8¾	12⅛	+ 3⅜
Bowmr		17	22567	6	2⅜	2¾	– 1¾
Bowne	.50	13	66245	28½	19¾	27⅞	+ 7½
Brscn s	.80	...	28276	21¾	12¼	19⅜	+ 6¾
BrnFA	1.24	14	4992	58	41½	52⅞	+ 11⅛
BrnFB	1.24	16	41867	64½	44¾	60⅝	+ 14⅛
BrnF pf	.40	...	3227	6⅜	4⅛	5⅛	+ 1
Buckhn		...	7531	4⅞	2⅞	3¾	– ¼
Buckh pf	.50	...	4228	6½	5	5½	...
Buell s	.32	11	5213	26	14⅞	22	+ 6⅞
BushIn		19	17619	21⅞	7¼	17	+ 8⅞

—C—

Stock	Div.	P-E Ratio	Sales 100s	High	Low	Last	Net Chg.
CDI		14	9092	39⅜	21¾	27⅛	+ 1⅞
CMI Cp		...	91793	9⅜	2⅛	2⅜	– 5⅝
CMX Cp		6	6373	2	⅞	1	– ¼
CSS		27	8066	12½	7¾	9⅞	+ 1⅛
Cablv n		...	95336	21¼	13½	18⅞	...
CaesNJ		11	12675	16⅞	10	10¼	– 1⅛
CagleA		11	9628	17¾	7⅜	13⅞	+ 6⅜
CalJky s	.65i	...	4216	27½	19¼	20¼	– 6¾
Calprop	.90t	10	14640	13⅜	7⅜	8	+ ½
Camco	.44	11	16867	18¾	11½	13¼	– 2⅞
CMarc g	.28	...	15625	19¾	13	13¾	– 1⅝
CdnOc g	.64	...	6539	18⅜	11½	17⅛	– 1⅛
CWneA n		10	5962	37⅜	20	21	...
CWineB		10	7162	51¾	21¾	22¾	– 10½
Cardis		7	42194	10	5⅞	7⅝	– 1⅜
CareE B		17	16597	7⅞	2⅞	3¾	– 2⅞
CareE A	.10	8	22002	7⅜	3⅛	3½	– 2
Carml n		...	2256	8	7⅛	8	...
CaroP pf	5.00	...	z43730	63½	48	61	+ 12⅛
Casblan		12	15665	8⅜	2½	6¼	+ 3⅝
CastlA	.80b	120	4249	19½	13¼	13¼	– 4
CasFd	2.20a	...	7963	31¾	25¼	27	+ ⅛
Centenl		39	5397	10⅞	6¼	9	– ⅜
CFCda n	.10e	...	26308	5 3/16	4 1/16	4 15/16	...
CenM pf	3.50	...	z78810	41⅜	29½	39⅝	+ 10⅛
CentSe	1.70e	...	9689	14	11	11⅞	– ⅝
CenS prD	2.00	...	159	29	25⅝	26¾	+ 1¼
Centrst	1.10r	...	110863	15⅛	6⅞	11	+ 4⅛
CtryBu		10	1002	30¾	14⅝	21⅛	+ 6
Cetec	.20	...	5764	9	4⅝	5	– 2
ChDev n		34	9570	19	8¼	16⅞	...
ChDvA n		34	12455	18½	8¾	16⅞	...

AMERICAN STOCK EXCHANGE COMPOSITE

		P-E Ratio	Sales 100s	High	Low	Last	Net Chg.
ChmpH		...	189129	4 1/8	1 3/8	1 11/16	− 5/16
ChmpP	.72	16	13403	45 1/2	18 3/4	38 5/8	+ 19 3/8
ChtMdA	.24	12	144979	24 3/4	17 3/4	18 3/8	− 3
ChtMdB	.24	12	3190	24 1/4	17 3/8	18	− 3
ChiRv	1.20a	13	2998	27 3/8	18 1/2	20	+ 1/8
ChfDv g		...	11794	9 7/8	5 3/8	6	− 3 1/4
ChfDv wt		...	2250	7 1/2	6 5/8	6 7/8	...
ChftD pf	4.75	...	z9550	34 1/8	28	31 1/4	− 5 1/8
ChftD pf	4.00	...	z5300	34	25	30 1/2	− 1 1/2
Citadel		6	60362	60 3/4	34 1/2	53 3/8	+ 17 3/4
CitFst s	.60b	13	24984	24 1/2	15	23 3/8	+ 8
CitFst pf	2.50	...	442	91 3/8	58 1/2	90 1/2	+ 30 1/2
CtyGas	1.20	12	3864	41 3/8	32 1/2	40 1/2	+ 6 1/8
Clabr pf	3.31	...	20756	20 3/4	18 3/8	20 1/8	...
Clabr wt		...	28350	15/16	9/16	5/8	...
Clarmt	2.14e	...	3036	55 1/4	44	54 3/8	+ 5 1/4
ClarkC	.30e	12	1716	13 7/8	8 1/8	12	+ 1 7/8
Clarost	1.10e	11	2017	55	35 3/4	51	+ 12 1/4
Cognitr		...	6264	5 7/8	2 1/4	2 5/8	− 1 1/2
Cohu	.20	20	10891	12 1/8	5 1/2	6 1/2	− 3 1/4
ColnF wt		...	29275	8	3 1/4	5 3/8	+ 5/8
Comfd s	.50	7	36624	33 1/2	14 7/8	29	+ 12 3/8
Cominc	.17r	...	23840	10 3/8	7 1/2	9 3/8	+ 1 1/8
Comtrn n		11	19802	11 7/8	6 3/4	8 5/8	...
CompD		3	3468	24 1/4	12 1/4	19 7/8	+ 7
CmpCn		...	72431	11 5/8	5 3/4	8 1/4	+ 7/8
CmFct s		25	41102	18 1/4	6 7/8	17 1/2	+ 9 5/8
Cmptr s	.03e	24	24306	16 3/4	7	15 1/8	+ 7 7/8
Cnchm	.40a	10	5667	25	18 5/8	18 7/8	− 1
ConcdF		38	4526	13	7 5/8	9 7/8	+ 2
Connly		15	1864	18 3/8	10 7/8	12 1/8	− 6
ConrCp		...	11737	19 1/8	4 1/2	5	− 11 5/8
Conqst		...	97782	8 3/8	3 1/4	3 5/8	− 3 7/8
Conq wt		...	25786	3 7/8	1/16	3/16	− 2 13/16
Conq wtP		...	4139	5/8	1/4	1/2	...
Conq un		...	8473	4 3/4	3 3/4	4	...
CnsEP n		...	7822	3 3/4	1	1 1/4	...
ConsOG		...	43847	5	5/8	3/4	− 4
Constn n		...	27037	15 3/4	8 1/4	9	...
ContAir		...	45881	16 3/4	13 1/2	16 1/8	+ 2 1/4
ContMtl		9	7135	31 3/4	18 1/4	20 1/4	− 3 3/4
Convst	.55j	...	8413	12 1/2	1 5/8	2 1/4	− 9 1/8
Copley	1.65e	14	11179	20	16 3/8	19 3/4	+ 2 7/8
CosmCr		12	26949	6 1/2	3 1/2	3 5/8	− 1/8
Courtld	.11e	...	15216	4 3/4	2 5/8	4 3/8	+ 1 5/8
CrstFo	.15e	12	3237	16 5/8	10 3/4	14 1/8	+ 2 1/8
Cross	1.60	20	20290	49 1/2	34 3/8	47 3/8	+ 10 3/4
CrowlM	1.00	12	765	41	32 7/8	32 7/8	− 7 3/8
CrnCP		...	11430	26	13	13	− 5
CrCPB		...	6810	22	11 5/8	12 3/4	− 2 5/8
CwCP pf	1.92	...	2184	34 1/4	23 1/4	23 1/2	− 2 1/2
CwC pfD	2.25	...	4480	26 1/8	24 5/8	25 1/4	...
CrownC		9	4163	27	8 1/8	24	+ 15 3/4
CrutcR		1	32937	1 1/8	1/4	5/8	+ 1/4
Cubic	.39	115	40211	24	14 1/4	16 1/8	− 6 1/4
Curtice	.96	13	8110	35 1/8	25 5/8	29 1/4	+ 2
CustEn		...	36194	7/8	5/16	7/8	+ 1/4
CypFd n		...	10892	10 1/8	9 5/8	9 7/8	...
—D—							
DWG	.08t	...	67860	3 1/8	1 1/2	2 5/8	+ 3/4
DamnC		...	1054	6 3/4	4 3/4	6 3/8	+ 3/4
DamEA	.23j	...	34182	8 1/8	3/4	7/8	− 6 1/8
DamEB	.29j	...	34850	8 3/8	3/4	13/16	− 5 15/16
Damson		...	136464	4 1/8	3/16	5/16	− 3 5/16
Dams pf	.63j	...	2916	19 1/2	2	2	− 16 1/2
Dams pf	.75j	...	3985	23 1/4	2 1/4	2 1/4	− 19 5/8
Datarx n		...	1956	7 1/2	5 1/4	6 5/8	...
DataPd	.16	21	174278	18	11 1/8	11 1/2	− 4 7/8
Datarm		4	25695	17 7/8	6 1/2	6 5/8	− 2 1/4
DeLau n		...	41063	19 1/4	9 5/8	12 3/4	...
DeRose		...	4305	8	2 1/2	2 1/2	− 3/8
Decorat		...	1032	5 1/8	3 1/8	3 7/8	+ 1/4
DelLb s	.40	11	2073	34 3/8	27 1/2	28 1/8	− 1/8
DelVal	1.74	11	6103	20 1/8	15 3/4	19 1/4	+ 3
Delmed		...	290082	2 1/4	7/16	5/8	+ 1/8
Dsgntrn	.17t	...	4337	5 1/2	2 1/2	2 3/4	− 1 1/2
Desgnl		8	15585	15 3/8	7 3/8	8	− 2 1/4
DevlCp		22	10014	15 7/8	11 3/4	14 5/8	− 3/4
DevnRs	.60	244	17544	8 3/8	4 1/2	4 7/8	− 3
Diag A		18	16321	12 1/8	6 3/4	7 3/8	− 3/8
Diag B		15	6471	9 3/4	5 3/4	6	− 1 1/8
DckMA g		...	4796	7 3/4	5 1/8	7 1/2	...
DckMB g		...	884	7 3/4	5 1/4	7 1/4	...
Digicon		...	21675	1 3/8	3/8	1/2	− 3/4
Digic wt		...	1451	3/16	1/16	1/16	− 1/16
Dillard	.12	16	194901	45 1/8	32	37 7/8	+ 3/8
Diodes		...	10868	6 3/4	2 7/8	3 3/8	− 3/8
DirActn		29	4190	6 7/8	3	4	− 1 5/8
DiviHtl		...	20126	9 5/8	5 3/4	9	+ 1 1/2
DomeP		...	f10248	2 3/8	9/16	5/8	− 1 1/2
Domtr s	1.00	...	42658	26 3/8	15 5/8	25 1/2	+ 8 7/8
Driller		...	2822	1 5/8	13/16	7/8	− 1/8
DrivHar		...	1669	9	4 1/2	5	− 3 7/8
Ducom	.20	...	21222	35 1/2	14 1/2	16 3/8	− 14
Duplex	.60	12	11862	22 1/2	17 5/8	17 7/8	− 2 3/4
DurTst	.40b	19	19622	21 1/4	13 3/8	14	− 2 1/8
Dyneer	25.50c	...	3120	28	1 5/8	1 3/4	...
—E—							
EAC	.40j	...	12003	12 1/4	6 1/8	6 3/4	− 2 3/8
EECO s	.24	23	19875	14 7/8	9 1/4	13 3/4	+ 3 7/8
ESI	.29t	12	16982	12	5	5 1/4	− 2 1/2
EaglCl		...	18790	4 1/8	1 3/4	1 7/8	− 3/8
EAL wt80		...	2151	3/16	1/64	1/64	...
EAL wt83		...	3785	1/8	1/64	1/16	...
EAL pfwi	2.84	...	5409	22	19 1/8	19 1/4	...
EAL pfwi	2.72	...	487	23 1/2	15 3/4	16 3/4	...
EAL pfwi	3.24	...	1488	26 1/4	17 1/8	18	...
EAL pfwi	3.12	...	1283	22 1/2	17 3/8	18 5/8	...
EstnCo	1.00	10	2281	24 3/8	18 3/4	20	+ 1 1/8
Estgp	2.90e	9	4767	33 1/4	27 1/4	27 3/4	− 4 7/8
EchoB g	.14	...	434958	24	13	23	+ 9 3/4
ElecSd		...	15414	10 7/8	6 1/8	9 1/8	+ 2 3/8
Elsinor		...	37759	4 1/2	2 3/8	2 3/4	− 1/2
Elswth n		...	10882	10 3/4	8 1/2	8 7/8	...
EmMed	.03e	...	6221	18 1/4	11 5/8	12 1/4	− 1
EmpA n	.02e	...	16870	5 5/8	4 1/4	4 1/2	...
EmCar	.04	4	10737	10 7/8	5 5/8	9 1/2	+ 4
Endvco	.69t	6	28478	7 1/2	5 1/4	5 3/8	− 3/4
EgyDv wt		...	3887	1/4	1/64	1/64	− 3/64
EnDvl	1.00	...	14028	16 3/8	4 1/2	4 3/4	− 8 1/4
ESD		...	7769	18 1/4	3 3/4	4	− 10 1/4
Enstr pf	.52e	...	3360	3 3/8	1 3/4	2 3/8	− 5/8
EntMk s		...	174747	15 3/8	2 7/8	7 1/8	+ 4
Eqtyg n		...	2283	10 7/8	8 1/2	8 1/2	...
Erolnd s		13	11456	19	6 5/8	14 5/8	+ 7 5/8
Espey	.40	13	9636	30	15 3/4	16 3/8	− 2
Esprit		...	13168	2 3/4	1 1/8	1 3/8	+ 1/4
EsqRd	.72e	114	1125	41	33 1/2	35 3/8	− 1 3/4
EtzLav		...	7062	16 1/2	8 3/8	9	− 3/8
EvrJ B	.10	18	1370	16 3/4	9 7/8	14 1/8	+ 4 1/4
EvrJ A	.20	15	22819	13 1/4	9 5/8	12	+ 2 1/8
Excel	.40b	9	19472	16 3/8	10	10 3/8	− 1/2
—F—							
FPA		...	6668	12 5/8	7 7/8	10	− 1/2
Fablnd	.60	10	7198	34 1/4	22 1/8	29	+ 5 3/8
FairFn s		12	43745	19 7/8	10 3/4	16	+ 4
FalCbl n		...	11251	20	19 3/4	19 3/4	...
Farly pf	2.93e	...	37869	25	15 3/8	22 1/2	+ 7 1/8
Fidata		2	21343	7 1/8	4 3/8	4 5/8	− 3/8
FtAust	.54e	...	45617	12 3/8	6 7/8	8 3/4	− 3/4
FAusP n	.57e	...	411315	11 3/4	8	8 1/8	...
FtCtrl n		28	6979	6	3 5/8	4 1/2	...
FtConn	1.00a	8	2019	15 5/8	11 1/2	14 1/2	+ 2 7/8
Fstfed n		...	8815	10 1/2	10	10	...
FWymB	.50j	13	11966	14	6 1/4	7 3/8	− 6 3/8
Fstcrp	.30	6	10734	17 1/4	10 1/2	11	− 5 7/8
FischP	.93t	23	14703	22 7/8	12 1/2	14 1/2	− 3/8
FitcGE	.35e	13	7882	20 1/4	12 1/2	20	+ 7 5/8
FitGE pf	4.00	...	1054	36	30 1/4	33 3/4	+ 3 1/4
vjFlanig		...	2014	5 1/2	3 1/2	4 1/8	− 7/8
FlaRk s	.50	10	16059	31 1/8	16 5/8	25	+ 7 5/8
Fluke	1.14t	15	32945	30 7/8	19 7/8	22	− 6 3/4
Foodrm		7	6462	20 3/4	13 3/4	16 1/8	+ 1 3/8
FooteM		...	2462	9 7/8	5	5 3/8	− 2 3/8
Foote pf		...	394	33 3/8	23	23	− 6 7/8
FthillG		...	82823	7 1/2	4 7/8	5 5/8	...
FordCn g	12.00e	...	1102	141 1/2	97 1/2	110 1/4	− 12 3/4
ForstC A	.30	17	4466	33 1/2	22	30 1/8	+ 4 1/8
ForstC B	.24e	17	3354	33 1/4	22 1/4	31 1/8	+ 5 3/8
ForstL s		40	136664	24 3/4	13 3/4	23 3/4	+ 9 1/2
Forum n		...	6573	12 3/4	12 5/8	12 3/4	...
Frnkln		...	2384	15	10 1/2	13 1/4	+ 1/4
FrdHly		86	2435	9 1/8	6 1/2	7 3/4	+ 3/4
FreqE s		18	23396	26 1/8	16 3/4	23 1/8	+ 5 3/8
Friedm	.28b	13	6228	11	7 5/8	8 3/4	− 3/4
FriesE s		8	32902	11	3 7/8	4	− 3 7/8
Frischs	.22b	52	13019	42 1/4	20 3/8	39 3/4	+ 15 3/8
FurVlt	.20	31	70405	15 1/4	9	12	+ 2
—G—							
GRI		108	8083	7 3/8	4 1/4	6 1/2	+ 2 3/8
GTI		...	11148	3 3/8	1 3/4	3 1/4	+ 1

AMERICAN STOCK EXCHANGE COMPOSITE

Stock	Div	P-E Ratio	Sales 100s	High	Low	Last	Net Chg.
GalaxC		33	24722	16½	10⅝	11⅞	+ ¼
GalxyO		...	62425	1¼	3/16	¼	− ⅞
Garan	.60	28	6588	31	22⅝	26⅝	+ 1¼
GatLit		...	32081	8⅞	3⅜	5⅛	− 2¾
GelmS		63	7247	17	11¾	15⅛	+ 2⅞
Gemco		...	11218	2½	15/16	1⅝	− ⅛
GnEmp		...	3867	3½	1½	1⅞	− ¾
GnMicr	.10b	13	5100	19⅛	12½	13⅛	− 3¼
Genisco		39	9712	7⅛	3⅞	4¼	− 1½
GenvDr	.20	27	8934	16⅝	10⅜	11¾	+ ⅝
GeoRes		5	12512	14⅞	11	11⅞	− ⅞
GeoR wt		...	6698	5½	3	3⅜	− ½
GeoRs pf	1.00	...	5773	12⅞	10¼	11¾	+ ⅜
GiantF	.60	15	93131	33⅝	23¾	25	− 1½
GntYl g	.25e	16	38184	18⅞	9⅝	13⅛	− 1⅝
Glatflt s	.50	15	21177	27⅜	20½	24⅜	+ 5⅛
Glnmr	1.00b	47	14130	43⅝	21	32⅝	+ 2⅞
GlobNR		14	32463	5⅝	2¾	4½	+ 1
GldFld		...	49140	13/16	5/16	⅜	− ¼
GorRup	.80	14	3316	24¼	16⅞	17¼	− 6⅝
GuldLP n		28	1338	43¾	25½	40	...
Graham		...	3910	12¾	5¼	5⅝	− 2⅝
GrahMc	.40j	...	46656	6	½	¾	− 4¾
GrndAu	.20j	213	9080	24⅛	15¾	23⅜	+ 4⅝
Grng n g		...	7878	6⅝	4⅜	5 13/16	...
Grant		32	6345	10⅝	5⅛	7	− 2⅞
GrTech		18	12598	17⅞	8⅞	14	+ 2
GrtLkC	.56	22	129062	44½	30	36	− 2¾
Grenm s		...	76039	26⅜	8⅜	8¾	− 12⅝
Greiner		12	14709	18½	11½	13¾	+ 1
Gruen n		...	10590	8¼	5⅛	5⅜	...
GrdCh s		11	11054	11	10⅜	10⅜	+ ⅛
GuldM n	.67e	...	18942	12⅜	9¼	11⅝	...
GlfCda n	.52	...	109416	12⅜	8⅞	11⅜	...
GlfCd pr	.16	...	46139	3⅞	3	3 3/16	...
Gull	.05e	37	17641	16⅞	9½	13¾	− 1⅝
Gundle n		...	5354	8¼	8	8⅛	...
—H—							
HAL		5	15309	21¾	8⅛	21¾	+ 12¾
HMG	.60	10	1036	11¼	9	9⅛	− 2
HUBC s	.40	13	4391	19½	11⅛	14½	+ 3¼
Halifax	.05e	...	2935	6⅜	3¾	4	− 1
Halmi		19	212476	5⅛	2⅜	3	+ ½
Hamptl	1.37t	7	6942	17¾	9⅛	12¼	+ 2½
Harley n		...	32130	13⅞	7¼	10½	...
HarpIn		9	20352	12¼	6¼	6⅝	...
HarisT n	.36e	...	6840	11⅜	10	10¾	...
Harvey		...	10357	3½	1⅜	1⅝	+ ¼
Hasbr s	.09	11	364504	30⅞	16½	19½	+ 2⅛
Hasbr pr	2.00	...	24099	63½	37⅜	44½	+ 5¼
Hasting	.40	9	1417	42⅞	28	28¼	− 4¾
Hll n		12	28129	12⅞	6¾	7	− 1¾
HltMn n		14	16669	9¾	6⅞	7⅞	...
HlthCr s	1.56	11	20658	19⅛	12⅞	16½	+ 1⅞
HlthCh		...	37807	12⅜	8⅛	9⅞	+ 1½
HelthM	.68	13	4098	17⅞	13⅞	15⅝	+ ⅛
Hltvst n	.70e	...	37144	23½	19¾	21	...
Heico	.10	8	19039	38⅜	15¼	29⅞	+ 14
HeinWr	.25e	12	5078	11½	7⅞	10	+ 1⅝
Heldor		...	6524	3⅝	1⅝	2⅛	− ⅛
HelmR		19	28682	¾	5/16	⅜	...
HeritEn		7	118200	12⅞	2⅝	7⅜	+ 4¾
HertE wt		...	431	3⅞	2⅞	3½	...
HershO		...	9356	4¾	3¼	3½	− ½
Hindrl		...	7478	5⅝	2	4¼	+ 2⅜
Hiptron	.20	13	4547	17¾	11⅛	12⅜	− 1½
Hofman		12	3691	4½	2¼	4¼	+ 1¾
HollyCp		5	9391	21¼	9⅞	15⅞	+ 5⅝
HmeGp		17	355246	31½	17	21	− 3½
HmIns pf	2.95	...	81266	25⅝	21¾	23¼	− ⅛
HmeSh s		63	274983	44⅝	12⅝	37⅛	...
HmeSh wi		...	145	22¼	6¼	19	...
Honybe n		...	1703	7⅛	6	7⅛	...
Hormel	.60	17	26182	35⅛	22⅛	34¼	+ 8⅝
HrnHar		...	411380	19¼	6½	12¼	+ 4⅝
HrnH wt		...	73658	6⅞	⅝	2⅛	+ 1 7/16
Htll wtA		...	3216	10¼	6⅞	9	...
Htll wtB		...	6722	6⅝	3¼	5⅛	...
HotIP wt		...	4197	9⅜	5⅞	7⅛	+ ⅝
HouOT	.49e	...	121260	4⅛	1⅝	1⅞	− 1⅝
HovnE s		14	28973	21¾	7	18½	+ 11⅛
HowlIn	.25e	7	2433	25⅞	14¼	17	+ 2½
HubelA	.84	13	5223	34½	25	28	+ 2⅝
HubelB	.84	15	47494	36¼	24⅛	30¼	+ 5⅜
Hubbl pf	2.06	...	327	93¾	64½	79	+ 14½
HudsFd n	.10	13	65636	21¼	10¾	15¼	...

Stock	Div	P-E Ratio	Sales 100s	High	Low	Last	Net Chg.
HudGn	.40	15	2928	28	17¾	18⅛	− 3¾
Husky g	.20	...	285787	8¼	4⅞	8⅛	+ ½
—I—							
ICEE n		...	10908	7¼	3½	5⅝	+ ¾
ICH s		6	205796	32⅝	15⅞	19¾	+ 1⅞
ICH pf		...	36798	25¾	5¼	22½	...
ICO		31	8862	1¼	¼	5/16	− 11/16
IPM		41	4607	5	2¼	4⅞	+ 1⅝
IRE n		6	4230	11⅞	6	8	...
IRT Cp		...	18741	14¼	5¼	6⅛	− 3⅜
ISS	.16	22	6555	11⅝	5	6½	+ 1½
ImpGp	.10e	9	37123	5⅝	3	3⅛	− ⅝
ImpInd		...	6312	⅞	⅛	⅛	− ⅜
ImpOil g	1.60	9	153130	37⅜	25⅛	37⅛	+ ⅝
Instron s	.12	19	18633	16¾	10⅛	14	+ 3¾
InstSy		24	137322	2½	1½	2⅛	+ ⅜
InsSy pfA		...	214	101	100	100¾	...
InsSy pf	.25t	...	2599	3¼	2¼	2½	...
IntlgSy		20	203347	8⅛	4½	7⅛	+ 2⅜
IntCty g	.60	9	20602	12	10	10½	− 1½
Intmk s	.10	...	11341	21⅞	10	10	− 3½
Intmk pf	.02e	...	1397	14⅜	9⅜	9½	...
IntBknt		10	199707	10⅜	3	5	+ 1⅝
IntBk wt		...	76988	4⅛	½	1⅛	+ ½
IntHyd		325	11829	9¼	5¾	6½	− 1⅜
IIP	1.00	...	6270	14⅝	10⅛	13½	+ 2⅝
IntPwr		...	1902	6⅜	3¾	3¾	− ¼
IntProt		21	7169	8⅛	3	7½	+ 4⅜
IntSeaw		4	2853	15⅜	8½	9¾	+ ¾
IntThr		...	194146	13	¾	13/16	− 2 9/16
InThr pf		...	16722	5⅛	11/16	¾	− 2⅜
Intwst		...	1796	11	4	6½	+ ⅛
Ionics		39	17083	23½	13¾	14¾	− 5¾
IroqBrd		100	9515	44¾	19¾	33	− 6⅞
—J—							
Jaclyn	.50b	16	3372	15⅛	11¼	13⅝	+ 2¼
Jacobs		45	10572	10⅝	6¼	9	+ 1
JMads n	.30	...	6779	12	8⅝	9⅛	...
JetAm		9	49648	4¾	2⅛	4⅜	+ 1¼
Jetron	.77t	11	12084	10	6	6⅜	− 1¾
Jwlmst n		13	10568	16½	9	9⅝	...
JohnPd		...	10540	4⅛	1¾	4	+ ¾
JohnAm	.22j	17	48299	9⅛	2¾	3⅛	− 3
JohnInd		7	24624	19⅜	8⅝	13⅞	+ 4⅞
JneInt n		...	9982	16⅝	15¾	16⅜	...
JumpJk		10	10718	7⅞	2⅞	4⅝	+ 1¼
—K—							
KnGs pf	4.50	...	z18410	50¾	39	48¾	+ 10¼
KapokC		...	10678	5⅞	2	2⅜	− 1
Kappa		10	32316	10⅝	5	5⅛	− ½
KayCp s	.24b	8	24471	27⅜	14¾	23⅝	+ 8⅞
KayJw s	.40	12	12529	23	12⅞	19¾	+ 6⅝
KayJw wi		...	273	22½	19½	19⅞	...
KearNt	.40	...	5529	19⅛	12¼	13⅝	+ ⅝
KlyOG n	1.10e	...	9429	12½	8	9½	...
Kenwin	.80	...	884	23	14⅞	14⅞	− 4½
Ketchm	.90t	...	7253	25½	15⅝	22⅜	+ 2⅛
KeyCoB	.25e	12	6296	9½	3¼	4¾	+ 1½
KeyCoA	.25e	9	5372	8¼	3	3⅝	+ ½
KeyCa		...	47275	6½	3⅛	5¾	+ 2⅝
KeyC wtA		...	7745	1⅝	7/16	15/16	+ 9/16
KeyC wtB		...	4894	1 11/16	1	1½	...
Kidde wt		...	37611	5¾	1½	1⅝	− 1½
Kilern		12	3862	8⅝	4¼	5½	+ 1¼
Kinark		...	9780	5	2⅜	2⅞	− ⅝
Kirby		...	61914	3¼	1¾	2⅜	...
Kit Mfg		9	6673	12¼	4⅞	7⅜	+ 1½
KleerV	.03e	42	11374	2½	1⅛	1¼	− 1
Knoll		21	38741	20⅜	9⅛	11½	− 3
KogerC	2.40	423	40728	31⅜	25¼	29⅝	+ 4⅜
—L—							
LSB Ind		...	19684	4	1¾	2½	+ ½
LSB pf	2.20	...	441	20¼	19⅞	19⅞	...
LaBarg		...	6228	2⅞	11/16	⅞	− ¾
LaJoll n		...	2447	6	4¾	5¼	...
LaPnt		...	3322	6¼	3⅜	3⅝	− ⅝
LdmkSv	.15e	...	27284	21¼	8½	9½	− 9½
LndBnc	.64	9	15360	20¾	15⅞	16½	− 1¼
Lndmk	.40	358	10167	25⅜	16¾	17⅞	− 3⅜
Laser		15	44161	18½	9¾	12⅝	+ 2¼
Lauren		39	8207	9	5½	5⅞	− 2¾
LazKap		46	1711	10⅞	4	9⅝	+ 5¾

AMERICAN STOCK EXCHANGE COMPOSITE

Stock	Div.	P-E Ratio	Sales 100s	High	Low	Last	Net Chg.
LearPP	2.25j	...	15241	17¾	1	1⅛	− 15⅝
LeePh s		7	73874	19¼	4	10⅝	+ 6½
Lehigh	.37j	14	6942	44⅞	30¼	44¾	+ 12¾
LeisurT		10	31148	8⅛	4⅜	5¼	− 1⅝
LeisT pf		...	4290	26¾	23¾	25¾	...
Levitt		25	4844	14	5¾	10	+ 4¼
LbtFin	.50	12	23761	54⅞	29	35¾	+ 5¼
LifeRst		...	14055	2 3/16	¾	13/16	− 1 3/16
Lfetime		30	80071	3⅝	⅞	3	+ 2
Lilly un		...	90380	5¾	1⅞	2⅜	...
LinPr n	.17e	...	5281	10⅜	9⅜	10⅛	...
LncNC n	1.48	...	7184	14⅞	12¾	13¾	+ ⅛
LncNC wt		...	11801	1¾	⅞	1	− ⅜
LncNC un		...	1240	15¼	14	14	− 1
Lionel		2	217956	10⅞	5¼	5¾	+ ¼
Lionl wtB		...	16743	3¼	7/16	¾	+ ⅛
Litfld		...	2386	4¼	3	3¼	+ ⅛
Lodge		...	6696	2⅝	¾	⅞	− ¾
LoriCp		14	5782	24⅜	9	11⅝	− 7½
LorTel n		16	589472	33⅜	15¼	16⅛	...
Lumex	.08	18	29106	27⅝	15¼	20⅝	+ 2¾
Luria		17	26887	15⅛	9¾	10⅝	− 1
Lydal		13	5845	18	14	14¼	− ⅞
LynCSy	.20	16	39829	16¾	9⅝	15¼	+ 1¾
LynchC	.20	49	8478	34⅞	11¾	19¼	+ 7¾
—M—							
MCO Hd		...	19596	16¾	8⅞	9⅜	− 4⅜
MCO Rs		...	29191	1⅞	¼	5/16	− 1 9/16
MSA	.95e	15	40017	11¾	8½	10½	+ 1¾
MSA wt		...	10223	3⅜	1⅛	1¾	+ ⅝
MSI Dt		33	13758	14⅜	9¾	11⅛	+ 1
MSR		...	13106	2⅝	1⅜	1⅜	− 1⅛
MacGrg		350	56487	20	8¼	10½	+ ¾
MacSch	.20	24	31441	32½	18⅞	25⅞	+ 4⅞
Magcslk		22	3021	12⅝	7⅜	8	+ ⅝
Mag Bk		...	12925	17⅜	7¼	9⅜	− 3¼
MePS	1.40	10	5609	32	19½	28⅛	+ 8½
Malart g	.20e	15	6107	12¾	6⅝	7⅞	− 3
Mangd		...	4089	12¼	4½	6¼	− 5⅞
ManfHo		...	32324	16½	8⅞	8⅞	− 1⅛
MrthOf		...	14937	5⅝	2⅜	2¾	− 2¼
MrkIV s		13	30125	26⅝	12½	17⅜	+ 3¼
MarsG n		...	2490	9	6	6⅜	...
MartP s	.06i	61	6511	20⅞	14¼	17⅝	− 3¼
Matec		19	6050	6⅝	4½	5¼	...
MatRsh	.09j	...	29069	14⅝	4¾	5½	− 6¾
MatSci		15	32643	24⅜	14½	22⅞	+ 7⅝
Matrix		20	111777	26⅝	14¼	15½	− 8⅛
MattW n		5	9858	12¾	8¾	10	...
MayEng	.10j	...	15210	8½	1¼	1½	− 6¾
McDow		...	4121	5⅞	1⅝	2	− 1⅞
McFad		19	16694	7	1⅜	1½	− 5¼
McRae A	.22e	8	2059	5⅞	3½	4	+ ⅝
McRae B		7	1871	5⅝	3½	3¾	+ ½
Media s	.64	17	17003	49½	36	42½	+ 2¾
Mdcore		...	44615	8⅜	2½	3	− ½
Mdcor wt		...	9476	3	⅜	½	...
Mediq s	.10	18	71480	9⅞	5⅜	6	− 1¾
Mediq pf	.06	...	13313	9¾	5⅜	6	...
Mem	.60	24	1406	20⅞	14¼	14¼	− 3⅛
MetPro	.15	20	8741	17⅜	11⅞	12	− 5¼
Metex		10	4851	16¾	9¾	9¾	− 6⅝
MichStr		20	153135	7⅜	4¼	5⅛	− 1¾
MchGn		...	79175	5¼	1	1⅝	− 2⅛
Micrn n		...	1273	6½	5⅛	5¼	...
MidAm	.10j	34	4453	10¼	7⅜	7½	− 1½
MidInd	.40	11	1644	40⅞	28¾	33½	+ ⅜
MinP pf	5.00	...	z28350	68	47¼	60⅛	+ 10⅛
MinP pf	7.36	...	1261	101	73	96	+ 24
MinP pf	8.90	...	1425	105¾	87	104	+ 14⅜
MissnW	.38t	56	3677	13½	7⅝	11⅛	+ 3¼
MtchlE	.24	28	85890	13⅝	9⅛	11⅜	− 1⅞
MonP pf	4.40	...	z8640	55⅜	40⅛	52	+ 11¾
MonP pf	4.50	...	z20860	59	43¼	56	+ 12
MoogB	.20	13	2715	20⅜	13¼	14⅝	− 4⅜
MoogA	.28	13	43116	20½	12½	14⅝	− 4⅜
MMed		17	22174	28⅛	18⅝	25¾	+ 3⅝
MorgnF		44	32607	2¾	1⅛	1¾	+ ⅝
MtgRt wt		...	19607	4⅜	1¾	3⅜	+ 1⅝
MtgGth	1.60	14	29613	23⅜	17⅛	22	+ 4½
MtgPl n	.85e	10	34353	9⅞	6⅞	7¾	− ⅞
Motts	.05j	...	3237	16	8¼	13½	+ 5
MtMed		23	17579	8⅜	2¾	3	− 3⅜
MovStr		...	615	15½	7⅜	8¼	− 6⅛
MovieL		...	2276	8⅝	3	3¾	− 3⅛
MyerIn	.28b	12	4944	12⅝	8¾	11¼	+ 1½
—N—							
NRM	.50e	...	50442	13⅛	2⅛	2⅞	− 9⅜
NRM pf	2.60	...	14871	19⅜	8½	17⅝	+ ⅛
NVHme n	.32e	17	25454	20¼	9	19¼	...
Nantck	1.40t	11	16358	12⅜	6	6½	− 2¾
NtGsO	.40b	21	2990	11⅛	9	9⅜	− 1½
NHltC	.28	15	38723	23¾	14¾	16⅝	− 1⅝
NtPatnt	.10	...	131565	26½	10¼	11	− 11½
NwLine n		8	9835	8¾	5	6	...
NMxAr		6	4443	24¾	15	18⅜	+ 2½
NProc	1.25e	15	29188	32⅝	23¾	29¼	+ ¾
NWldP		16	69159	22⅜	8⅜	10¾	+ 1¾
NYTme s	.36	22	218926	42	23¼	35½	+ 11
NewbC	.25r	...	9115	7	3½	4½	+ ⅞
Newcor	.32	...	6154	14½	7	7⅞	− 3⅛
NewLs s		13	49656	19	8⅛	11¾	+ 2⅜
NwpEl	1.50	18	3307	25	16¼	21⅞	+ 5⅜
NichIn		66	24079	12	5⅛	5¼	− 3⅛
Nichols		13	20152	12⅝	7	7¾	− 1¾
NoelInd		41	12915	10¾	4⅛	8¼	+ 3⅛
NCdO G		...	6715	10⅜	6⅝	7¾	− 2½
NeMtge	.20	10	12714	11½	7	8	...
NIPS pf	4.25	...	1492	47⅞	33¾	43½	+ 9⅛
NuHrz	.16t	22	10032	5⅛	2⅞	3¼	− ⅛
NuHr wt		...	2514	1½	11/16	¾	...
NuclDt		...	7435	6⅜	2	2½	− 2¾
Numac		...	24921	9¾	5⅛	6⅜	− 3⅛
—O—							
OEA		13	5849	26⅜	18⅞	20⅝	− 2⅜
OBrien s		110	23286	17½	4⅛	9⅞	...
OdetA		40	5862	10¼	5⅝	6	− 1½
OdetB		45	1306	11	6	6¾	− 1
OhArt	.24a	20	1615	49⅝	25½	43¼	+ 7½
Olsten s	.20	22	22728	31⅜	19⅜	23¾	+ 3⅜
OneLibt	1.72	12	13162	18⅛	14⅜	16¼	+ 1½
OOkiep		...	3844	6¼	3	4⅜	− ⅜
Oppenh		...	69854	18	5⅛	6⅜	+ 1
OriolH A	.15	11	4518	11¾	6⅛	6⅞	− ⅛
OriolH B	.20	10	6878	12	6⅛	6½	− ¼
Ormand		...	2387	1⅝	11/16	11/16	− 3/16
OSulvn s	.32	17	7788	25⅞	17½	18¾	− ⅝
OxfrdF	.06e	12	29731	27	15⅛	17¼	− ⅞
—P-Q—							
PLM A	.16	7	8339	8⅜	4⅜	6½	...
PLM B	.08	8	10827	9	4⅜	6⅝	+ 1⅜
PSE n		...	13030	14⅛	6⅝	9⅛	...
PGEpfA	1.50	...	7713	19⅞	14	18⅛	+ 4
PGEpfB	1.37	...	4264	17⅞	12¾	16¾	+ 3¾
PGEpfC	1.25	...	1405	16½	12	15¼	+ 3¼
PGEpfD	1.25	...	11434	16	11⅞	15⅛	+ 3⅛
PGEpfE	1.25	...	17822	16¾	12⅛	15⅞	+ 3⅜
PGEpfG	1.20	...	15987	15⅞	11⅝	15⅜	+ 3⅝
PGEpfF	4.34	...	10106	35¼	30⅜	31⅜	− 3⅝
PGEpfY	3.20	...	13858	31⅝	28⅜	30¾	+ 1¼
PGEpfW	2.57	...	37975	29⅜	24⅝	28¾	+ 3¾
PGEpfV	2.32	...	46425	28⅜	21⅞	27⅝	+ 5
PGEpfT	2.54	...	17443	29	24	28½	+ 3¾
PGEpfS	2.62	...	17964	29⅜	25	28⅝	+ 3⅛
PGEpfH	1.12	...	11358	15¼	10¾	14¼	+ 3
PGEpfR	2.37	...	32544	29	22¾	28⅜	+ 5
PGEpfP	2.05	...	31691	26½	19⅝	26	+ 5¼
PGEpfO	2.00	...	25540	25⅞	18⅞	24¾	+ 5
PGEpfM	1.96	...	31344	25½	18¾	24⅜	+ 5
PGEpfL	2.25	...	2201	26½	20⅞	26	+ 4½
PGEpfK	2.04	...	44532	28	19¾	25¼	+ 5¼
PGEpfJ	2.32	...	1392	26½	20¾	24⅞	+ 3⅛
PGEpfI	1.09	...	10914	16	10⅝	14⅛	+ 3¼
PacLt pf	4.36	...	1960	58½	41	53⅛	+ 12⅜
PacLt pf	4.40	...	1322	60	41¼	54¼	+ 11¾
PacLt pf	4.50	...	2758	59½	43	56¼	+ 14¼
PacLt pf	4.75	...	1619	65	45	59⅛	+ 13⅜
PacLt pf	7.64	...	2624	99¼	73¼	92	+ 18
Pacif pf	5.00	...	z32725	66	47	62½	+ 13¼
PWRlt n	.73e	...	35164	12⅞	8¾	9¼	...
PallCp s		31	130176	33⅝	21½	26⅜	+ 3⅞
Pantast		...	17020	13⅞	7⅜	8⅞	+ ¼
PatntM		90	41334	7⅞	2¼	4½	− 3¼
PatTch		36	29919	9½	3¼	3⅝	− 1⅜
PaulPt		6	10383	17½	8½	10	+ ½
PayFon		12	4997	5⅛	3	4⅛	+ ½
PEC Isr		18	z55050	16	8	8¼	− 4¼
PeerTu	.40b	17	3080	10⅝	6½	6½	− 2⅞
PenEM	.60a	21	1511	34⅛	25	29⅜	+ 2⅜
PenTr s	.68	11	12094	24	12½	20⅜	+ 7
PE Cp		...	26639	1	3/16	¼	− ¼

AMERICAN STOCK EXCHANGE COMPOSITE

		P-E Ratio	Sales 100s	High	Low	Last	Net Chg.
PenRE	2.20	15	14135	35 5/8	24 1/8	31 3/8	+ 5 1/8
PenobS	.40	6	1307	14 5/8	10 5/8	11 7/8	+ 7/8
Penril		...	10495	9 1/8	3 5/8	3 5/8	− 3 1/2
Pentron		13	41081	3 3/8	1 1/4	1 3/4	− 5/8
PeriniC	.80	467	7100	34	25 3/4	28	− 1 5/8
Perinil	.48	...	5723	16 7/8	10 7/8	14 1/4	+ 2 3/4
Perini pf	1.10	...	5189	14 1/4	11 5/8	12 1/8	+ 1/4
PtHeat n		...	3304	14 1/4	13 3/4	14	...
PhilLD	.22e	6	238750	15 3/4	1 3/4	12 3/4	+ 10 7/8
PicoPd		...	9531	3 1/8	1 5/8	2	− 7/8
Pier 1 wt		...	21016	35 5/8	9 1/4	21 1/2	+ 12 1/4
PionrSy		...	17120	4 3/8	1 7/8	2 1/4	− 7/8
PitWVa	.55e	11	3774	6 7/8	5 1/4	6 1/4	+ 7/8
PitDsm		...	3357	21 1/4	15 3/4	19	+ 2 7/8
Pittway	1.80	15	5009	107 1/2	78	97	+ 18 1/8
Pizzaln	.06j	51	40373	12 1/4	6 1/4	10 1/8	+ 3 1/4
PlcrD g	.30	...	74264	23 7/8	15 1/8	22 3/8	+ 5 1/4
PlyGm s	.12	15	72401	15 1/2	10	13 1/8	+ 1/4
PlyR A		...	956	4 1/8	2 3/4	2 7/8	− 1/8
PlyR B		...	1146	4 1/8	2 7/8	3	...
PneuSc	1.00	227	592	25 1/2	21 7/8	25	+ 1 1/2
PopeEv		...	37378	4 1/8	1 3/8	1 3/4	− 1 3/4
PortSys		10	32052	12 7/8	5 3/4	6 3/8	− 4 3/4
PostlPr	.20	13	30748	16 3/4	12 1/4	15 1/4	+ 1/4
PrairO s		...	4017	6 1/2	3 7/8	6 3/8	+ 1 1/8
PrattL	.72	12	10625	32 3/4	21 1/2	28	+ 4 1/4
PrecA n		13	3618	8	6 1/4	6 1/4	...
PremRs			7983	1/2	3/16	3/16	− 1/4
PrpdLg		41	76459	18 1/2	10	11 1/2	− 1/4
PresR A	1.20	8	505	17 1/8	12 3/8	13 1/4	− 4 1/8
PresR B	1.20	8	4947	13 5/8	11 3/8	12 1/8	− 1/2
Presid		31	15457	4 3/4	3	3 3/8	− 1/4
Presid pf		...	6557	7	5 1/8	6	...
PricCm		...	59673	14 3/8	8	10 3/4	+ 3 1/4
Prism		4	24823	13 3/4	3 1/4	4	− 6 1/2
ProfCre		28	29367	9 1/4	2 1/4	2 1/2	− 5 5/8
PropCT	1.68	13	17168	26 7/8	19 1/2	24 1/8	+ 4
ProvEn	1.80	10	2998	34 1/2	24	30 3/8	+ 5 3/4
PSCol pf	4.25	...	z51025	50 1/2	37 1/2	45 1/4	+ 6 1/4
Pgt pfC	2.34	...	6591	28 1/8	21 3/8	27	+ 4 3/8
Pgt pfE	4.37	...	8640	34 5/8	30 1/2	30 7/8	− 3
Pgt pfD	2.34	...	7380	27 1/8	24 1/2	26 7/8	+ 2 3/8
PuntaG		8	7765	6 3/4	1 1/4	2	− 3
Queb g s	.16	...	6852	14 3/8	8 5/8	11 1/2	+ 2 1/4

—R—

		P-E Ratio	Sales 100s	High	Low	Last	Net Chg.
RAI	.51t	11	8542	9 7/8	6 1/8	6 5/8	+ 1/4
RBW		42	16312	10	6	6 3/4	− 1 1/4
RMS El		...	2638	4 3/4	1	1 3/4	− 3 1/8
Ragan	.12	51	16807	23 3/8	16 5/8	21 1/4	− 5/8
Ransbg	.72	51	43236	22 7/8	10 1/2	11 1/8	− 9
Raven	.42	11	4916	14 3/8	10	13 5/8	+ 2 1/2
ReCap s		...	23982	24 3/4	6 1/2	14	+ 7 3/8
RltSou	1.60e	10	5917	20 5/8	16 3/8	17 7/8	+ 1 3/8
RltSo wt		...	6615	3 3/8	1 3/8	1 3/8	− 1/8
Redlaw		...	20780	4 3/8	2 1/8	2 1/2	− 1/2
RegalB	.60	12	11502	19 5/8	15 3/8	17 1/2	+ 1 1/4
ResMtg n	.50	...	11697	10 3/8	8 3/4	9 1/4	...
Resrt A		550	121284	77	41 1/2	44	− 3
Resrt B		...	4332	150	47	124	+ 74 1/2
RstAsB		8	9653	12	6 3/4	8 1/8	+ 5/8
RstAsA	.15e	7	6677	10	6 1/8	7 3/8	+ 1
RstAs pf	.50	...	9396	8 3/4	5 7/8	7 1/2	...
RexNor	.10e	10	5989	6 1/8	3 7/8	4	...
RioAl g	.65	...	3708	19 5/8	13 3/4	14 7/8	− 1 1/8
RobtM un		...	2522	7 3/4	6	7 1/8	...
Rckwy	.32	17	40888	26	12 7/8	13 5/8	− 5 3/4
Rogers	.12	70	11890	24 1/2	17 1/4	18 1/4	− 1 7/8
RoonyP		...	111664	2 1/8	1/2	9/16	− 15/16
RoyPlm	1.00c	5	8484	8	6 1/4	6 3/8	− 1/2
Rudick s	.32a	11	10032	18 5/8	11 3/4	15 1/4	+ 2 1/2
Rudck pr	.56	...	274	36 1/2	24 5/8	29 5/8	+ 4 1/2
Rymer wt		...	11404	9	3 7/8	6 5/8	...

—S—

		P-E Ratio	Sales 100s	High	Low	Last	Net Chg.
SFM		...	2186	4 7/8	3 3/4	4	...
SFN pfA	1.22	...	69425	8 3/8	7 1/2	7 3/4	− 1/2
SJW	1.57	11	2877	39 7/8	30	33 1/8	− 5 7/8
Sage		...	13556	9 1/4	5 1/2	6 1/4	− 1 1/8
StJoeG n	.05e	81	45832	13 7/8	9	9 3/4	...
Salem		...	2393	6 1/8	4 1/4	4 3/8	− 1 1/4
Samsn n	1.60	...	5209	15 5/8	11 3/8	12	...
SCarlo		...	19771	6 1/8	3/4	2 1/4	+ 1 1/4
SDgo pf	.88	...	1532	12 3/8	8 3/8	11 3/8	+ 2 1/2
SDgo pf	.90	...	2018	12 1/2	8 5/8	11 7/8	+ 3 1/8
SDgo pf	1.00	...	1128	13 3/4	9 1/2	12 1/2	+ 2 5/8

		P-E Ratio	Sales 100s	High	Low	Last	Net Chg.
SDgo pr	9.84	...	z30200	106	88	100 3/4	+ 12 1/2
SDgo pr	7.80	...	1509	101 1/2	74 1/2	95 1/2	+ 22
SDgo pr	7.20	...	1327	94 1/2	68 1/2	91	+ 21 1/8
SDgo pr	2.47	...	3481	29 1/2	23 1/2	28 5/8	+ 3 5/8
SDgo pr	2.68	...	2997	30	25 1/8	28 3/8	+ 2 7/8
Sandsk n		...	817	7 3/4	4 5/8	7 1/8	...
Sandy		...	16802	16 1/2	3	3 3/4	− 11 1/8
Sanmk s	.48t	12	16958	8 1/8	3 1/2	4 7/8	+ 1/2
SaxnO n	.08	...	14952	8	1/2	13/16	− 6 15/16
Sbarro s		26	40617	20 1/8	8 3/4	14 1/2	+ 5 1/2
Scand n		...	52428	9 5/8	6 3/4	8 1/8	...
Sceptre		...	6535	3 3/8	1 3/4	1 13/16	− 1 5/16
Scheib s	.30	13	13544	18 7/8	13 7/8	15 1/8	+ 3/8
SchoolP		5	4162	5 1/4	2	4 7/8	+ 2 7/8
Schwab	.48	14	2046	14 3/4	10 7/8	11 5/8	− 1 7/8
SciMgt	.10	...	11673	7	4	4 1/8	− 1 1/4
SciLsg		14	25423	20 1/4	8 1/8	9 5/8	− 5 1/4
Scope	.43	13	2112	36 1/2	31 5/8	31 7/8	− 3 1/4
ScurRn	.50	...	1455	16 5/8	10 1/2	13 3/4	− 2 1/8
SbdCp	.50	7	1597	157	83	146	+ 59 1/2
Seamn n	.20e	...	24199	9	6 7/8	7 3/8	...
Seaport		...	2864	1 7/8	7/8	7/8	− 1/4
Seapt pf		...	z6250	6 1/4	3 3/4	3 7/8	− 1
SecCap	.20	...	29481	12 3/8	4 1/4	4 5/8	− 6 5/8
SeisPro	1.30e	...	5495	3 5/8	7/8	1 1/8	− 1 3/8
Selas		...	5581	6 1/8	2 7/8	3 1/4	− 1 1/4
SeligAs		9	5675	16 1/2	5 3/8	7	+ 1 1/4
Semtch		150	16068	3 7/8	1 1/4	1 1/2	− 1 7/8
Semtch rt		...	5041	1 1/4	7/16	1/2	...
Servo		10	7303	23 1/2	10 1/2	16 7/8	+ 6 3/8
Servotr	1.07t	12	3505	10 7/8	7 5/8	8 1/8	− 2 3/4
Seton	.10	11	6964	15 1/4	8 1/4	10	− 1/4
ShaerS	.70e	13	5235	18 5/8	11 1/4	12 1/8	− 3 1/8
SierHS		...	29646	8 1/4	3 7/8	4 3/8	− 2 1/4
SierSp s		44	59702	13 1/4	3 1/2	4	− 5 1/2
Siercn		...	2731	8 7/8	5 1/4	6	− 3/4
Sifco	.10e	6	4158	8 5/8	4 7/8	7 1/2	+ 2 5/8
SikesA	.26	12	18721	20 1/8	10 3/4	16 3/4	+ 4 1/8
Silvrcst		17	8562	7 1/8	3 5/8	4 1/2	+ 3/4
SmthA	.80	5	15222	32 1/8	20 1/8	21	− 2 5/8
SmthB	.80	5	29243	29 5/8	19 1/8	20 1/2	− 3 1/8
Smth pf	2.12	...	6917	37 7/8	28 5/8	29 1/2	− 1 1/4
Solitron		18	32832	10 3/4	5 7/8	6 1/4	− 2 1/8
SorgInc	.10e	11	12420	18 3/4	10	14 1/2	+ 3 1/2
SoTex		...	112	3/8	1/4	1/4	...
SCEd pf	1.02	...	18457	14 5/8	10 1/2	13 7/8	+ 3 1/4
SCEd pf	1.06	...	21747	15 1/8	11	14 1/8	+ 3 1/8
SCEd pf	1.08	...	8907	14 5/8	10 3/8	13 1/2	+ 2 5/8
SCEd pf	1.19	...	8790	16	11 3/4	14 7/8	+ 2 3/4
SCEd pf	4.56	...	1599	73 1/2	49	63	+ 12
SCEd pf	1.45	...	28353	20 1/4	14 3/4	19 1/4	+ 4 1/4
SCEd pr	1.30	...	342	60	40 1/2	53 1/2	+ 10 1/2
SCEd pf	8.54	...	8619	108 1/2	96 7/8	105 5/8	+ 10
SCEd pf	7.58	...	9713	101 1/2	75	97 1/2	+ 22
SCEd pf	8.70	...	4362	107	85	103 3/4	+ 18 3/4
SCEd pf	8.96	...	3057	107 3/4	89	104 3/4	+ 13 3/4
SwBcp n		7	8020	5 1/2	3 3/8	3 5/8	− 1/8
SwstRlt	.69j	...	5755	7 1/8	2 5/8	3 1/8	...
SpedOP		73	4488	9 5/8	5 7/8	5 7/8	− 1 1/4
Spelng n		7	56242	16 7/8	8 1/4	8 7/8	...
Spendth		...	20561	4 1/8	9/16	13/16	− 2 9/16
Spndt wt		...	3207	1	1/16	1/16	− 5/16
StHavn	.08	...	6279	5 3/4	2 5/8	3	− 1 3/4
StHav wt		...	5152	13/16	1/16	1/16	− 11/16
StdShr	10.50e	12	3893	101 1/2	73 3/4	94 1/2	+ 19 3/4
Stanwd		117	9435	18 1/8	8 1/8	15 1/4	+ 4 5/8
StarrtH		37	13774	24	13 1/4	14 7/8	− 3 3/4
Statex		...	3756	9 1/4	6 7/8	8 1/2	+ 1 1/8
Stepan	.80	12	2651	35 3/8	20 3/4	29 1/4	+ 8 3/8
StrlCap		...	1174	8 1/8	6	6	− 1/8
SterlEl		163	5960	2 3/4	1 3/8	1 5/8	+ 1/8
SterlSft		13	214347	21	10 3/8	11 1/4	− 7/8
StrutW		...	8180	2 1/2	7/8	1 3/4	+ 1/8
SumitE	.10t	...	7116	5 5/8	1 1/8	1 3/4	− 3 1/2
SumtE pf	.22j	...	1363	13 5/8	5 1/4	5 1/2	− 7 7/8
SunCty		3	1391	10 5/8	6 5/8	8 1/4	+ 1 1/2
SunbNu		...	21076	15 1/2	9 3/8	9 7/8	− 1 7/8
SunJr	.48	13	1576	28 3/8	20	23 1/2	− 1 1/4
SuprFd	.32	15	41927	27 3/4	16 3/8	22 1/4	+ 3 3/4
SupInd s	.25b	9	35409	16 3/8	9	12 1/4	+ 1 1/8
SuprSr	.40	13	8965	23 7/8	17 3/4	20 5/8	+ 2 3/4
Susqueh		23	10582	5 3/4	3 3/8	3 5/8	− 5/8
SwftEng		13	14545	5 3/8	1 1/4	4 1/8	+ 2 3/8
Swift pf	.45t	...	45382	6 7/8	4 5/8	6 3/8	...
Synaloy		...	10781	6 5/8	3 1/2	4 5/8	+ 3/8
SystEn	.03j	...	5015	6 3/4	3 5/8	4 3/8	− 2 1/8

AMERICAN STOCK EXCHANGE COMPOSITE

Stock	Div.	P-E Ratio	Sales 100s	High	Low	Last	Net Chg.
—T—							
T Bar		55	20292	8	5	7 3/4	+ 2 5/8
TEC	.16j	...	2476	7 1/4	3	3 3/8	– 3 3/4
TIE		...	321360	7 1/8	2 3/4	3 1/4	– 3 5/8
TII		10	14524	11 3/8	6 1/2	7 5/8	– 1/4
TPA Am		...	3399	3	2	2 7/8	...
TabPr s	.20	17	10619	15 1/4	11 3/8	13 3/8	+ 1 1/2
Taiwan n		...	24267	19 7/8	13	19	...
TandBr		18	10356	12 1/4	8 3/8	8 5/8	– 7/8
Tasty s		16	16129	27 1/4	13	23 3/8	+ 9 1/2
Team		...	3279	3	1 5/8	2 1/4	– 1/2
TchAm		...	31913	3 7/8	2 5/8	3 1/8	+ 3/8
TchSym		11	49319	19	12 1/2	14 1/2	+ 5/8
TchOp s	1.52e	16	10218	34 3/4	20	27	+ 5 3/8
TechTp		11	32520	8 3/4	4 1/2	4 7/8	...
Techtrl	.48	9	6970	18 3/8	13	15 3/4	+ 1 7/8
Technd		8	4950	2 7/8	1 1/8	1 5/8	+ 1/8
TejnR s	.05e	315	17192	64 1/2	27 1/4	47 1/4	+ 19
Telecon		...	13929	4 1/4	1 3/8	3 3/8	+ 1 3/4
Telflex s	.28	16	37091	30	19 7/8	23 1/2	+ 3 3/8
TelDta	.22a	15	41830	21 5/8	12 5/8	18 3/8	+ 5
Telsci		...	21387	11 1/2	4 1/4	4 3/4	– 4
Telesph		...	48689	4 7/8	2 1/2	2 5/8	– 1 1/4
Tempo	.16	26	29261	21 1/4	6 1/2	10 3/8	+ 3 7/8
Tenney		23	5692	5 1/2	3	3 3/8	– 1 3/4
TexCd g	1.20	10	9904	24 1/4	17	23 3/4	+ 2 1/4
TexAir		69	573136	40 7/8	14 1/8	33 3/4	+ 18 3/4
TexAE	.24t	...	22543	4 7/8	1	1 1/4	– 3 1/2
TxAE pf	2.57	...	8765	19 5/8	10	12	– 5 5/8
ThorEn		...	2397	1 3/4	5/8	5/8	– 1/2
ThrD B	.06	16	938	4 3/8	3 1/2	4	+ 3/8
ThrD A	.10	15	2149	4 1/2	3 3/8	3 5/8	...
Tofutti		...	35629	9 1/8	3	3 3/4	– 4 3/4
TolEd pf	4.25	...	z50850	46 1/2	33	44	+ 11 1/2
TolEd pf	8.32	...	z60280	84 1/2	64 1/2	80 1/2	+ 16
TolEd pf	7.76	...	1684	80	60	78 3/4	+ 16 3/4
TolEd pf	10.00	...	z64250	99 1/2	78 1/4	95 3/4	+ 13 3/4
Tortel		...	5418	4	1 3/4	2	– 1
TotlPt g	.36	14	177401	22 3/8	13 3/4	19 1/2	+ 3 7/8
TotPt pf	2.88	...	5951	34 3/4	26 1/2	34	+ 6 1/2
TrnsLx	.08r	6	17630	16 7/8	10 3/4	11 3/4	– 2
TrnsTec	.64	12	27906	25	14 3/8	20 1/4	+ 2 1/4
Tranzon	.44	10	2393	19 3/8	15 1/4	16 1/2	+ 3/4
TriSM		7	7630	20 3/4	9	15 1/8	+ 5
TriaCp	1.24t	15	10421	18 5/8	11	14 3/4	+ 2 3/8
TriHme		...	2642	6 7/8	2 7/8	2 7/8	– 1 1/4
Tridex		94	12387	11 1/2	6 1/2	8 1/2	+ 2 1/8
TubMex		...	21659	2 3/8	1 1/4	1 1/4	– 7/8
TurnBd		...	33601	29 1/4	11 1/2	13 7/8	– 1/4
TrnBd pf		...	216514	8 7/8	6 3/8	8 1/8	...
TurnrC	1.30	10	7289	30 5/8	19 5/8	20 5/8	– 5 1/8
TrnEq	.80e	81	21963	9 5/8	7 1/4	7 1/4	– 1 1/8
—U—							
USR Ind		...	2659	3 3/8	1 5/8	1 3/4	– 1/2
Ultmte		14	119424	34 3/4	13 1/8	21 5/8	– 2 5/8
Ultra	.08e	75	141263	12 5/8	8 1/8	9 3/4	+ 1 5/8
Unicorp	.60	9	35075	15 1/2	10 1/4	12 1/8	+ 7/8
Unimar	1.76e	...	36034	11	6	6 5/8	– 3 7/8
UnVly n		8	5736	9 3/8	6 3/8	6 3/8	...
UnCosF	.50	6	14398	25 1/8	18	18 1/2	– 5 1/2
UFoodA	.10a	1	22671	4	1 5/8	2	+ 3/8
UFoodB	.20e	2	10756	4	1 1/2	2 1/2	+ 7/8
UtMed	1.23t	64	20771	15 1/8	7 1/2	7 5/8	– 4 7/8
USAG wt		...	5579	24	14	19 3/4	+ 1/4
USAG pf	3.00	...	15	115 1/2	96	110	+ 20 3/4
UnitelV		111	14752	12	5 1/4	7 3/4	+ 2 1/4
Unitil	1.80	9	1334	36 7/8	23 7/8	28 3/4	+ 4 3/4
UnvCm		15	7209	14 7/8	10 1/4	10 1/2	– 1 7/8
UnivRs		...	26792	7 7/8	2	2 3/4	– 4 1/4
UnvPat	2.25t	...	23665	21 1/8	11 1/2	13 1/4	+ 1 5/8
USACaf	.36	14	64475	8 3/8	4 5/8	7 3/4	+ 3
—V—							
VHT n	.69e	16	18064	9 1/2	6 1/2	7 3/8	...
VHT wt		...	8735	1 1/4	3/8	9/16	...
VST	1.13e	8	22943	10 3/8	7 3/4	8 1/2	– 1 1/2
VTX n		10	2976	8	6 3/8	6 5/8	...
VallyRs	1.52	11	1041	28 7/8	20 1/8	27	+ 6 1/2
Valspar	.64	17	13648	48 1/8	29 3/8	42 1/2	+ 12
VangTc		19	18251	14 3/4	8 7/8	11	...
Verit		8	9525	20	8 3/8	10	+ 1 3/4
VtAmC	.40b	22	13911	21 1/2	13 7/8	18 1/4	+ 1
VtRsh		...	7330	6 1/2	3 5/8	5 3/4	+ 1 1/4
Vernit	.20	10	48192	13 3/8	7 3/4	8 1/4	– 2 1/4
Versar n		...	4167	9 7/8	7 1/2	8 1/8	...
Vertple		15	7457	5 7/8	2 3/8	3 1/2	– 5/8
Viatech		9	3301	12 1/2	5 3/4	10 3/4	+ 5 1/8
Vicon		36	9814	7 1/2	4 1/8	5 3/4	+ 1/4
Vintge		...	3940	5 1/2	2 1/8	2 1/2	– 1/4
Virco	.04r	9	2682	23 7/8	15	16 1/4	– 1 7/8
VisualG	.30b	12	3139	11 1/4	7 7/8	9 3/8	+ 1/8
Voplex	.40	9	6449	13 1/2	6 7/8	7 3/8	– 1 1/2
VulcCp	.80a	24	2078	28 7/8	20	25 3/4	+ 3 3/8
Vyqust		13	16892	13 1/2	4 7/8	5 1/2	– 3/4
—W—							
WTC		...	13160	6 1/4	2 1/2	4 5/8	– 1 1/8
WlkEn n	.64j	...	27209	6 1/4	1 1/8	1 3/8	– 5
WangB	.16	116	f10807	21 3/4	10 1/2	11 5/8	– 8
WangC	.11	115	2755	21 3/4	10 3/4	11 1/2	– 9
WrnCpt		21	50619	7 5/8	3 7/8	5 1/8	+ 1 1/4
WshH s		5	41200	25 1/2	8 5/8	12	+ 2 3/8
WshPst	1.12	21	21135	184 1/2	115	156	+ 37 1/4
WRIT s	1.28	17	18203	26 5/8	18 5/8	22 3/8	+ 3 3/4
Watsc A	.20	11	1768	10 3/4	6	7 5/8	+ 1 1/8
Watsc B	.16	13	1610	11 7/8	7 1/2	9 3/8	+ 1 1/8
Wthfrd		...	35421	3 1/8	5/8	3/4	– 1 7/8
Wthfd pf		...	3463	10 1/8	1 7/8	2 1/8	– 6 1/8
WebInv n	.84e	...	13564	9 1/8	6 5/8	7 5/8	– 1/8
WebIn wt		...	10566	1 1/4	3/8	3/8	– 3/16
Webcor		...	48952	3 1/2	9/16	5/8	– 3/4
Wedco		...	2265	4	2 5/8	2 3/4	– 1/8
Wedgtn	1.56	10	16843	17 1/8	9 1/4	15 5/8	+ 6 1/8
Weiman	.16	9	4532	10 1/4	4 3/8	5	– 1/2
WeldTb		...	2948	12 1/2	7 7/8	11 1/4	+ 2 3/8
Weldtrn		13	9543	10 5/8	6 3/4	7 5/8	– 2 5/8
Wellco s	.38i	4	6563	18 1/2	7 3/4	13 3/4	+ 6
WellAm		...	11343	2 5/8	5/8	1 1/4	+ 1/2
WelGrd		...	8863	4 7/8	2 5/8	4 1/4	+ 1
Wesco	.66	5	4157	51 3/4	35 7/8	37 7/8	+ 2
Wespcp		...	8342	2 1/8	9/16	11/16	– 3/16
WTex pf	4.40	...	z13650	53	40 3/4	52 1/8	+ 11 5/8
WstBrC		...	14989	10 3/4	3 3/8	3 3/4	– 5 7/8
Wstbr g	.20	10	27376	14 1/4	9 3/4	13 3/8	+ 1 1/8
WDigitl		14	222751	20	9 7/8	18 1/2	+ 8
WstHlth		22	16908	8 3/4	4 1/8	4 1/8	– 3 1/4
WIRET	1.66	17	19816	26 1/8	19	25 3/4	+ 6 5/8
WhrEn s		19	86285	23 7/8	11 1/2	14 1/8	+ 3/4
Wichita		...	7884	2 5/8	3/4	3/4	– 1 1/2
Wickes		17	f27015	7	3 1/4	3 1/2	– 1 1/4
Wickes wt		...	66617	4 1/4	1 15/16	2 1/4	+ 1/8
Wick pfA	2.50	...	91291	39	29	30 1/4	+ 5/8
Wiener	.40	14	4568	12 3/4	8 3/8	9 1/4	...
WintIn	1.40a	6	7918	18 1/2	15 1/8	16	– 7/8
WisP pf	4.50	...	z19690	61 1/2	46 3/4	57 1/2	+ 8 1/2
WolfHB		...	2106	5 3/4	3	3 1/2	+ 3/8
Wdstrm	.40	15	11771	26 3/4	8 7/8	23 7/8	+ 14 7/8
Worthn		...	31053	15 3/8	9 5/8	11	– 1 7/8
Wrathr	.02	...	27989	23 5/8	15 3/4	17 3/8	– 2
—X-Y-Z—							
YankCo		...	23822	10 5/8	4	4 5/8	– 2
YnkCo pf	1.15	...	3653	9 1/2	7 1/4	7 3/4	...
Zimer		...	20140	8 7/8	2 7/8	4	– 1

Sales figures are unofficial.

g-Dividend or earnings in Canadian money. Stock trades in U.S. dollars. No yield or PE shown unless stated in U.S. money. n-New issue in the past year. The range begins with the start of trading in the new issue and does not cover the entire year. s-Split or stock dividend of 25 per cent or more in the past year. The high-low range is adjusted from the old stock. Dividend begins with the date of split or stock dividend. The net change is from an adjusted previous year's closing price. v-Trading halted on primary market.

Unless otherwise noted, rates of dividends in the foregoing table are annual disbursements based on the last quarterly or semi-annual declaration. Special or extra dividends or payments not designated as regular are identified in the following footnotes.

a-Also extra or extras. b-Annual rate plus stock dividend. c-Liquidating dividend. e-Declared or paid in preceding 12 months. i-Declared or paid after stock dividend or split-up. j-Paid this year, dividend omitted, deferred or no action taken at last dividend meeting. k-Declared or paid this year, an accumulative issue with dividends in arrears. r-Declared or paid in preceding 12 months plus stock dividend. t-Paid in stock in preceding 12 months, estimated cash value on ex-dividend or ex-distribution date. z-Sales in full.

pf-Preferred. rt-Rights. un-Units. wd-When distributed. wi-When issued. ww-With warrants. wt-Warrants. xw-Without warrants.

vj-In bankruptcy or receivership or being reorganized under the Bankruptcy Act, or securities assumed by such companies.

AMERICAN BONDS

The following tabulation gives the 1986 sales, high, low, last price and net change from the previous year in bonds listed on the American Stock Exchange.

		Sales $1,000	High	Low	Last	Net Chg.
AMC 13.6s00	13.1	5	103½	103½	103½	...
AMC 11⅞01	...	2	100	100	100	...
AP Ind 12⅜01	13.0	60	97½	95	95	...
APL 10s92	12.3	145	82	77	81	+ 3
Action 11¼92	11.0	377	103	88	102	+ 10½
Alpine 13½96	13.5	32	100¼	100	100	...
ACent 7s90	cv	164	72½	65	69½	− 1¾
AmFruc 9.4s00	10.8	913	87¾	72½	87	...
Alsrli 11¾97	cv	1593	108½	88¼	107	+ 17
AMaiz 11¾00	cv	7503	128	105	111½	+ 4
Andal 5½97	cv	127	73	51	68	+ 16
Angles 12½95	14.6	2762	95	83	85½	+ 1¾
Anth 11¼00	cv	3294	120	98	103	− 5
Arrow 12s98	14.2	650	100	79	84⅜	− 1¾
Arrow 14s00	13.9	114	103½	99	101	+ 2
Arrow 9s03	cv	2327	91	58	69	− 13
Arrow 13¾04	15.1	2387	104½	86	91	− 9
BSN 7¾01	cv	4320	121½	100¼	109½	...
BayCol 6¾91	cv	3	120	120	120	+ 1
BergBr 7⅝10	cv	20298	122	85	94	− 14
BergBr 6⅞11	7.6	582	99½	88	90	...
BioRd 15s00	14.4	65	108½	104⅛	104⅛	− 1⅞
Bless 10s92	10.2	69	98	90	98	+ 10
Bowmr 13½95	cv	2574	112	99	100¾	− 3¼
Candg 7s11	cv	1601	107	83	83	...
CareE 9s05	cv	3636	104½	63	65½	− 32
ChambD 8s96	cv	3896	141½	101	134	...
ChtMd 11s93	12.5	16	88⅛	86	88⅛	+ 1½
ChtMd 12⅝97	13.1	13	99	95	96⅛	+ 4⅞
ChtMd 12⅞05	17.7	2	72⅞	72⅞	72⅞	...
ChckFul 8s06	7.1	2740	116	102½	112¼	...
Clabr 14½04	14.4	637	104	95	101	+ 6
CmpC 7¾98	cv	14716	79⅞	59½	75⅞	+ 12⅛
Conair zr93	...	20	39	39	39	+ 7
Condec 10s97	18.7	776	67	50	53½	− 6½
Condec 14⅞00	17.4	217	91⅞	85	85¼	− 3¾
ConOG 9s88f	...	165	90¼	46	46	− 44
ConOG 9¼92f	...	66	64⅛	48⅞	48⅞	− 15⅛
ConOG 12s95f	...	1924	73	25¼	41¼	− 31¾
ConOG 11½93f	...	2307	69⅞	26	41	− 29
ConOG 9s94f	cv	346	75	55	55	− 26
ContAir 11s96	12.2	52	92	89⅞	89⅞	...
ContHlt 14⅛96	...	105	102	101	102	...
CustE 15s97f	cv	1099	85⅜	36½	85⅜	+ 23⅝
DWG 5½87	5.4	1	102	102	102	...
DamsO 13.2s00f	...	10114	76½	15	57½	− 12½
DamsO zr87	...	4790	82	20	78	+ 3
DamsO 12s03f	...	8417	62½	20½	48	− 10
DamsO 15s97	cv	26	52	51	51	...
DamsO 12s97	cv	125	58	50	58	...
DamsO 14s93	cv	60	48	35	37½	...
DamsO 12⅞93	cv	1621	47	40½	41¾	...
DamsO 14⅝93	cv	6	38½	38½	38½	...
DeLaur 12½01	13.2	543	98	94½	95	...
Delmed 10½02f	cv	5716	98½	17½	66	+ 43½
Delmed 10½97f	...	1379	95	20½	66	+ 45
Derwod 8s91	cv	29	75½	74½	75	− ½
DevCp 12s94	14.6	8	82¼	82¼	82¼	+ ⅛
DiagR 8½98	cv	2986	96½	83½	87½	+ 4
Digicn 10½01	...	4097	42½	9	11	− 25
Digicn 12⅞93	23.4	17	55⅛	55	55	+ 1
DorchG 8½05f	cv	1663	66	50	63½	− ⅝
Ducom 7¾11	11.1	1788	103	67¾	70	...
DuroT 5¾92	cv	48	114	101½	108¼	+ 6¼
EasAir 5s92	cv	8970	76	48	58	− 1¾
EasAir 4¾93	cv	3611	62	45	53⅛	− ⅞
EasAir 11½99	cv	59238	89	68	77	− 5⅞
EasAir 11¾05	cv	16237	93	72½	79	− 10⅜
EasAir 17½97	15.6	11823	115	98¼	112	+ 1⅜
EasAir 17½98	15.7	11726	114⅞	98½	111½	+ ¾
EasAir 16⅛02	15.5	28735	108⅞	98¼	104	− 1½
Eckerd 11⅛01	11.8	4608	97½	90½	94	...
Elgin 6¾s88	cv	24	104	98	98	− ½
Elsinr 14s97f	...	1243	73	64	72½	+ 1½
Elsinr 15½99f	...	2466	96	82	82	− 9¼
EntM 8½06	cv	4794	112	92	98	...
Eskey 10¾03	cv	2675	80	65½	73	+ 6
FarWst zr89	...	14	68½	66⅛	68½	+ 4½
FarWst zr95	...	9	30	26	30	+ 6
Farley 7s11	12.1	1390	65	50	58	+ 8
Farley 7½94	9.4	1116	100½	63⅛	80	+ 16½
Farley 12⅜03	12.4	742	102	83⅛	100	+ 16
FtCty 6¾91	cv	63	80	71½	75	+ 3¾
Fthill 12½98	14.7	2	85	85	85	...
Fthill 9½03	cv	2353	104	90	93¼	+ 6¼
FrstCty 7¼11	cv	1178	105¾	100	104½	...
FoxTv pr13s	13.0	9114	104	100	100⅛	...
Galaxy 9s94f	cv	192	66	35	35	− 31
GDef 14½03	13.9	4	104	104	104	+ 4¼
GDef 13s95	12.7	60	102	99	102	...
GTFla 7½02	8.5	200	91½	76¾	88	+ 11
GTFla 8⅛03	...	109	93	79⅛	93	+ 12⅛
GTFla 9⅜05	9.1	411	103	91½	103	+ 14
GTSwt 7½02	8.6	276	88	75¾	87½	+ 14½
GTSwt 7¾03	8.6	298	90	76½	90	+ 13¾
GeoRs 13s91	12.7	1777	107	98½	102½	+ 2½
GeoRs 13¾96	13.0	1334	106	100¾	106	...
GreyhC 6s86	cv	214	98¾	96½	98¾	+ 1¼
HanP 11½90	11.5	98	101⅛	91¼	100	+ 9⅞
HarteH 04f	...	11299	72¾	58¾	70⅞	+ 10⅞
HarteH 13⅞95	...	70	101⅝	101½	101½	...
HlthCr 14⅜95	14.0	15	103	102½	103	...
HlthCh 10⅜99	cv	7263	99½	86	97	+ 10½
Heldr 9s91t	cv	199	92	69	84	+ 12½
HomShp 11¾96	12.2	212	98¼	96	96¼	...
HudFd 8s06	cv	2286	102	97½	100	...
HudGn 7s11	cv	1407	100½	88	88¾	...
InstSy 7s91	cv	43	87	69	87	+ 21
InstSy 11s94	cv	2068	112	100	107½	+ 7½
Intmk 11⅞99	12.7	270	97	87	93¼	+ 5¾
Intmk 13.20s98	13.2	21	102	92	100	...
Intmk 13.2s98	13.5	35	100	95⅛	98	...
IntBkn 10s98	11.2	5888	96	71¼	89	+ 16½
IntCtr 14½06	...	31787	58½	41	53¾	...
IntCtr 12¾01	12.9	58	99½	98½	98½	...
IntHyd 10s10	...	7405	105½	91½	99	...
IroBr 12s99	12.4	541	99½	92	97	+ 11
JetAm 14s87	cv	5593	111	85	109	+ 5½
JohnAm 9¾95	cv	8514	97	73½	80	− 3½
Kane 12¾01	12.4	23	103	100¼	103	...
KayCp 13½98	13.4	2096	103	94¼	100⅞	+ 6⅜
Knoll 8⅛03	cv	4256	116½	72	74	− 24½
Koor 12s96	12.0	391	104	98	100	...
LSB 13¾95	14.5	1284	98	79⅛	95⅛	+ 15⅛
LaBrg 14½93f	...	1048	90	18	39¾	− 49¼
LeisT 6¾s96	cv	172	70	55	68	+ 12¾
LifeRst 13s97	cv	3463	83	51	55	− 18½
LundE 6½88	cv	20	92	88½	92	+ 2
Lynch 06	cv	2190	106	94½	94½	...
MCO 5s97	cv	174	70	65	69	+ 4
MCO 12½99	13.4	1034	99	87	90¾	+ ½
MaplLf 11s98	10.7	1374	104½	97	103	+ 6
MarkIV 7s11	8.2	875	100	82	85	...
MarkIV ⅛¼¾01	12.5	15	101¾	101¾	101¾	...
Matrx 8¼10	cv	3462	128	94	103½	− 19
Matrx 7½11	cv	3857	114	90	96	...
Mayfl 7⅞06	cv	4652	102½	89	95	...
Mediq 7¼06	cv	2953	108	84	85	...
MetrB 15⅝99t	14.9	84	106½	103	105	− 1
MetrB 13⅛02t	13.5	141	99⅜	96½	97½	− 1¼
MetrB zr88	...	12	67½	67⅛	67½	+ ⅜
MetrB zr89	...	11	64⅛	64	64	− ⅛
MetrB zr90	...	3	52	52	52	+ ⅞
MetrB zr91	...	143	50⅛	47	47	− 1
MetrB zr93	...	20	36½	36½	36½	+ 4½
Metrmd 98f	...	15831	80½	63	79½	+ 15½
Mite 10s97	9.9	894	101½	88	100⅝	+ 11⅝
Moog 9⅞06	cv	7144	112	101½	104	− 4¾
MtgRty 6¾91	cv	114	123	95½	123	+ 25
Multm 16s05A f	...	756	69⅜	54	67½	+ 13
Multm 16s05B f	...	12666	70½	55	69¼	+ 13½
NCNB 7¾02	10.5	3	74	69	74	+ 5½
NRM 12¼89	12.1	20	101	101	101	...
NRM 89t f	...	3	83	83	83	...
NwbEn 12s95	cv	2728	113	83¼	104	+ 17½
Nich 15s00	14.2	540	108¼	102½	106	+ 1
Nich 14⅞99	13.9	264	112	103	107⅛	+ 4⅛
Noeast 6½86	cv	85	99⅝	98¼	99⅝	+ 1¾
Oakwd 7½01	cv	8438	104½	87¾	92½	...
Openh 18s01	15.7	796	118	103	114½	− 1½
Openh 12¾03	12.4	2245	105½	92½	102½	+ 9⅝
Openh 12¾02	12.4	3587	105	92½	102½	+ 9½

AMERICAN BONDS

		Sales $1,000	High	Low	Last	Net Chg.
OriolH 12⅝97	14.0	15	90½	88	90½	+ 10½
OriolH 12⅞00	14.4	15	100	89⅝	100	+ 10
Ozark 8¾10	cv	1284	144½	113	144½	+ 36½
PenEng 5s93	cv	425	43½	29	30	− 6
PaRIE 9¾03	cv	15	200	141	200	+ 53½
Penril 10⅞93	13.0	40	83½	82	83½	+ 1⅛
PopeEv 13½02	15.9	96	95	82⅞	85	− 5
PrceC 13s96	13.1	60	99	99	99	...
PSvEG 6s98	7.8	319	79	64¼	77	+ 11½
Pulte 8½08	cv	8396	113	89	93	+ 5⅜
PuntGl 6s92f	cv	908	63	45½	47⅞	− 7⅛
RyanMtg 12½14	12.1	5	103	103	103	...
RMS 9¾95	cv	138	75	60	65	− 6
ResrtInt 16⅝04	15.0	7359	117	110	110½	− 1½
ResrtInt 10s99	11.4	9982	99¾	77¾	87⅝	+ 10⅛
ResrtInt 10s98	11.4	9905	98	78½	87⅞	+ 9½
ResrtInt 11⅜13	12.2	15536	99⅝	82	92⅞	+ 9⅞
RestAs 9s93	cv	1447	104	89	96½	+ 14½
Rudick 8s11	cv	3603	108½	99¾	107	...
RyanH 6s91	cv	315	156	95¼	156	+ 62
RyanM 16s12A	15.0	2693	109	100½	106½	− 1½
RyanM 14s12B	13.4	350	107	102½	104½	...
RyanM 13¾12C	13.3	465	107	103¼	103¼	− ⅜
RyanM 12s12D	11.8	631	105	101	102	− 1
RyanM 12¾12E	12.4	1122	105¾	102	103	− ½
RyanMtg 12½12	12.1	682	105	102⅛	103	+ ½
RyanM 12s13G	11.7	639	105½	101	102⅝	+ ⅝
RyanM 12s13H	11.6	293	106¾	101¼	103¾	+ 2¾
RyanM 11¾13I	11.5	692	104½	100	102½	+ 1½
RyanM 11½13J	11.1	562	103¾	100	103¼	+ 2¾
RyanM 11⅜13K	11.1	606	103¾	100	102½	+ 1½
RyanMtg 12s13I	11.6	689	105	101½	103¾	+ 2¾
RyanM 12⅜13M	12.0	771	105½	102	103	+ ¼
RyanM 12⅞14	12.5	1030	107	102	103⅛	...
RyanM 12¾14o	12.4	736	106	102½	103	...
RyanM 12½14P	12.2	1084	105⅝	100¾	102¾	− ¾
RyanM 12s14	11.7	355	105⅝	101⅛	102⅝	+ ⅝
RyanM 11⅞14	11.5	215	104⅛	101	103	+ 2
RyanMt 11.4s15	11.3	64	105¼	100	100½	...
RyanM 11¼15	11.0	106	103	101	102	...
RyanM 11s13AA	10.8	70	107	98	102	+ 5
RyanM 12⅛13BB	12.0	137	107⅛	100½	101	+ ½
RyanM 12¾13CC	12.4	58	104	101⅝	103	...
RyanM 12½15	12.1	18	103	101⅜	103	...
SCIHld 15s97	13.1	327	118	114	114⅝	...
SCIHld 1zr90	...	4	62¼	62¼	62¼	...
SCIHld 4zr93	...	25	37½	37½	37½	...
SCIHld 5zr94	...	343	40	37½	37½	...
SCIHld 6zr95	...	43	34	34	34	...
Sage 8½05	cv	3681	82½	72	78½	+ 5½
Sanmk 12⅞01	...	18	103	101	101	...
SatAir 4s87	cv	15	116⅛	112⅛	116⅛	+ 16⅝
SciLsg 8¼03	cv	4185	87	65	71¾	+ 6½
SvceCp 10s00	10.0	596	99⅞	83	99⅝	+ 15⅝
SvcMer 11¾96	12.2	1243	99½	95¼	96	...
ShlrG 13¾01	27.4	9332	79	40¼	50¼	...
ShlrG 13s00	16.1	904	82¼	72	80½	...
SCE 4¼87O	4.3	339	99½	92	99⅛	+ 4¾
SCE 4¼87P	4.3	438	103⅝	91¼	98¾	+ 6¼
SCE 4⅜s88Q	4.6	339	99	88½	96	+ 7⅝
SCE 4⅜89R	4.6	219	96	85	95½	+ 9
SCE 4½s90S	4.8	227	93	82	93	+ 9
SCE8⅛94 Y	8.0	2529	102¼	88¼	102	+ 12
SCE7⅞s95 Z	7.9	1440	100	85¾	99⅝	+ 13⅛
SCE8s96 AA	8.1	1821	101	84¼	99⅛	+ 10⅛
SC7⅜s97 BB	7.8	858	102	80	94⅜	+ 12⅞
SC8¼s99 CC	8.5	1332	99	84⅜	97½	+ 12
SCE 8⅞00	8.9	2664	101¼	89	100¼	+ 10¾
SCE 8⅞01	8.9	1146	102	88¼	100¼	+ 9⅜
SCE 8¼02	8.7	1775	99⅜	82⅜	95	+ 12⅝
SCE 9⅝03	9.3	2622	107	92	103¼	+ 9⅛
SCE 16s12	13.9	654	120	114⅛	115	− 3
SCE 12s12	10.8	279	114	107	111½	+ 6½
SCE 12⅜14	...	297	114⅛	108	114⅛	+ 4⅛
SCE 13s15	11.5	194	115½	110½	113⅛	+ 2⅝
SCE 10s90	...	107	104	100	103	...
SwBell 8¾07	9.0	8449	100	84	97½	+ 11¼
SwBell 6⅞11	8.3	3580	83	67½	83	+ 12¾
SwBell 7¾09	8.7	2035	92⅞	75½	89½	+ 11½
SwBell 7⅜12	8.4	5044	88⅛	72	88	+ 13¾
SwBell 7⅝13	8.7	3165	90¼	73⅛	87¼	+ 12⅞
SwBell 8¼14	8.7	4112	95	79	94½	+ 13½
SwBell 9¼15	9.0	4070	103¼	87⅛	102½	+ 12
SwBell 8½16	8.9	3226	97⅞	80	95¾	+ 13½
SwBell 8¼17	8.8	2700	99½	79	93¾	+ 12⅝
SwBell 8¾18	8.9	2256	100	83⅝	98	+ 11¼
SwBell 9⅝19	9.2	13702	105	90¾	104½	+ 11⅜
SpellA 12¼93	12.0	146	104¾	100⅛	102	...
Spndt 12½94f	...	2019	80	20½	20¾	− 65¼
Stwd 7½89	cv	933	96	87	95⅜	+ 3⅜
StrlSft 8s01	cv	3894	103	84	86	...
Storer 10s03	11.9	11544	97	77½	84	...
Susq 5½s88	cv	231	92⅛	81	90½	+ 9½
T Bar 96	...	530	125	100½	125	...
TPA 10s06	7.9	418	105	100½	101½	...
TeamI 13s04	cv	1986	83	55	79	− 2½
TechT 10s96	11.4	433	90½	77⅛	88	+ 12
TxAir 15¾92	14.2	1553	112	104½	111	+ 4½
TxAir 10s05	8.7	44	133	115	115	− 6
TxAr 15¾92b	14.4	4377	112	103¾	109	+ 2¾
TxAr 14⅜90	13.7	171	108	102	105	+ 1
TxAr 14.9s95	...	2	114	114	114	...
TxAr 14¼93	13.3	72	107	99	107	...
vjTexIA 10⅞98f	...	2603	124⅝	,96	124	+ 28
TrnLux 5s87	cv	488	123	97	101	+ 1
TrnLux 9s05	cv	1792	118	100	100	− 9
TrnsTc 9s03	cv	5714	115	94	107	+ 7¼
Tridx 6s88	cv	1134	90	73½	84	+ 7
Tridx 9s96	cv	88	96	90	93¼	...
TCastl 13¾97	13.1	2215	107½	100½	105	+ 4¼
TCastl 7s99	10.8	209	68	65	65	+ 7¼
TurnBd 89	...	93	73	69⅝	71	...
TurnBd 90	...	8	61	61	61	...
TurnBd 92	...	271	53	45	50	...
TurnBd 91E	...	245	102	99¾	100	...
TurnBd 93F	...	1178	108	100	104	...
TurnBd 10¼93	12.1	1718	91½	79¾	85	...
Ultrs 7¾06	cv	7068	112	98	101½	...
Unimx 7½92	cv	232	73	60	70	+ 10
Unimx 10¾97	cv	106	73	62¾	73	+ 10
UnValy 14¼01	14.1	349	105	100	101¼	...
USAir 5½87	5.5	1173	99½	94⅛	99⅛	+ 6⅛
USAir 6s93	cv	79	90	84	88⅛	+ 7⅝
USAir 5¾93	cv	38	152	133	136	− 10
UnivRsc 15¾96	15.5	3662	104	71	101½	+ 2¾
ViacomIn 5¼88	cv	5	300	300	300	+ 49½
Vyqst 13¾01	...	1	100	100	100	...
Wainoc 10¾98	13.8	7513	78	60	78	+ 5⅞
Wang 7¾08	cv	13223	93½	80	82	+ 2
Wang 9s09	cv	15925	108	93½	98½	− 3¾
WarC 7⅝s94	8.9	359	87	69	86	+ 16½
Watsc 10s96	cv	243	103½	101	101	...
WldTb 10s95	12.2	33	81¾	74⅛	81¾	+ 7⅝
Wesco 10⅛91	10.0	400	103¼	97	101	+ 4⅞
Westbr 11.7s96	13.1	725	100½	89	89	...
WstDig 6¾11	cv	2900	125	96	121½	...
WPac 9⅛02	10.7	26	85	77	85	+ 16½
Wherhse 6¼06	cv	2486	101½	80	82	...
Wickes 1287	12.0	145	101	94¼	99⅞	...
Wickes 12s94	12.0	6288	110⅛	90¾	100	+ 5⅞
Wickes 7½-10s05	10.5	12164	78	59¾	71⅜	+ 11⅞
Wickes 15s95	13.5	413	116	104	110¾	+ 3½
Wickes 11⅜97	11.9	2686	101	89	95½	+ 7½
Wickes 13⅞92	13.0	1	106½	106½	106½	...
Wickes 11⅞00	12.2	4794	101	95½	97	...
Wilshir 6s95	cv	10	82	82	82	− 21
WilsSp 6½88	6.6	64	98⅝	90⅛	98⅝	+ 8⅝

Sales figures are unofficial.

cv-Convertible bond. ct-Certificates. d-Deep discount. f-Dealt in flat. m-Matured bonds, negotiability impaired by maturity. r-Registered. st-Stamped. wd-When distributed. ww-With warrants. xw-Without warrants. zr-Zero coupon.

vj-In bankruptcy or receivership or being reorganized under the Bankruptcy Act, or securities assumed by such companies.

GOVERNMENT NOTES AND BONDS

Over the counter U.S. Government Treasury bonds and notes 1986 price range.

			High	Low	Last	Net Chg.
9.75 Jan	1987	p	102.18	100.7	100.7	− 1.22
9.00 Feb	1987	n	102.3	100.9	100.9	− .30
10.00Feb	1987	n	103.14	100.16	100.16−	1.24
10.88Feb	1987	n	103.17	100.6	100.15−	2.21
12.75Feb	1987	n	105.5	100.22	100.22−	4.13
10.25Mar	1987	n	103.18	101	101	− 1.24
10.75Mar	1987	p	104	101.3	101.3	− 2.8
9.75 Apr	1987	p	103.11	101.4	101.4	− 1.5
9.13 May	1987	p	102.30	101	101.7	− .12
12.00May	1987	n	105.26	102.4	102.4	− 3.9
12.50May	1987	n	106.10	102.8	102.8	− 3.25
14.00May	1987	n	108.2	103	103	− 5
8.50 Jun	1987	p	110.1	100.9	101.5	+ .11
10.50Jun	1987	n	104.23	102.5	102.5	− 1.14
8.88 Jul	1987	p	103.4	100.24	101.18+	.6
8.88 Aug	1987	p	103.6	100.23	101.23+	.12
12.38Aug	1987	p	107.20	103.23	103.23−	2.26
13.75Aug	1987	n	109.11	104.24	104.24−	3.28
9.00 Sep	1987	n	103.16	100.30	102	+ .12
11.13Sep	1987	n	106.12	102.5	103.18−	1.13
8.88 Oct	1987	p	103.14	100.24	102.3	+ .23
7.63 Nov	1987	n	102.5	98.29	101.11+	1.30
8.50 Nov	1987	p	103.8	100.5	102.1	+ 1.5
11.00Nov	1987	n	106.20	104	104	− 1
12.63Nov	1987	n	109	105.3	105.11−	2.13
11.25Dec	1987	n	107.18	104.25	104.25−	1.1
7.88 Dec	1987	p	102.21	99.4	101.20+	1.26
8.13 Jan	1988	n	103.2	99.31	101.31	......
12.38Jan	1988	n	109.18	104.4	106.7	− 1.26
10.13Feb	1988	n	106.5	103.3	104.2	+ .3
10.38Feb	1988	p	106.18	103.17	104.11−	.1
8.00 Feb	1988	p	102.31	100.4	101.29	......
12.00Mar	1988	n	109.30	106.20	106.21−	1.5
7.13 Mar	1988	n	101.26	99.6	100.31	......
6.63 Apr	1988	p	100.30	98.10	100.11	......
13.25Apr	1988	n	112.11	108.22	108.22−	1.25
8.25 May	1988	n	103.22	99.20	102.15+	2.1
7.13 May	1988	p	101.28	99.3	101.1	......
9.88 May	1988	n	106.11	102.22	104.17+	.28
10.00May	1988	p	106.18	102.29	104.22+	.26
7.00 Jun	1988	p	101.21	100.1	100.31	......
13.63Jun	1988	n	114.2	110.6	110.6	− 1.29
6.63 Jul	1988	p	101.3	99.24	100.12	......
14.00Jul	1988	n	115.2	111.8	111.8	− 1.28
6.13 Aug	1988	p	100	99.10	99.20	......
9.50 Aug	1988	p	106.11	101.28	104.23+	1.24
10.50Aug	1988	n	108.7	104.3	106.6	+ .31
6.38 Sep	1988	p	100.16	99.27	99.31	......
15.38Oct	1988	n	119.20	114.26	114.26−	2.15
11.38Sep	1988	p	111.12	106.9	107.31+	.16
6.38 Oct	1988	p	100.12	99.30	99.31	......
6.25 Nov	1988	p	100.6	99.22	99.25	......
8.75 Nov	1988	n	106.3	100.6	104	+ 2.21
8.63 Nov	1988	p	105.6	99.29	103.24+	2.22
11.75Nov	1988	n	111.26	107.14	109.4	+ .14
10.63Dec	1988	p	109.16	104.24	107.21+	1.20
6.25 Dec	1988	p	99.29	99.22	99.26	......
14.63Jan	1989	n	119.13	115.2	115.13−	1.2
8.00 Feb	1989	p	104.4	99.4	103	......
11.38Feb	1989	n	111.25	106.23	109.16+	1.14
11.25Mar	1989	p	111.27	106.17	109.24+	1.26
14.38Apr	1989	n	120.3	115.6	116.14−	.4
6.88 May	1989	p	101.21	97.16	100.26	......
9.25 May	1989	n	108.4	101.15	105.26+	2.31
11.75May	1989	n	113.18	108.2	111.7	+ 1.22
9.63 Jun	1989	p	108.17	102.4	106.31+	3.13
14.50Jul	1989	n	121.24	115.7	118.8	+ .17
6.63 Aug	1989	p	101.11	99.19	100.8	......
13.88Aug	1989	n	120.19	114.19	117.5	+ 1.2
9.38 Sep	1989	p	108.12	101.12	106.26+	3.27
11.88Oct	1989	p	115.15	108.29	113.2	+ 2.15
6.38 Nov	1989	p	100.7	99.13	99.19	......
10.75Nov	1989	n	112.11	105.18	110.19+	3.11
12.75Nov	1989	p	118.12	111.21	115.21+	2.13
8.38 Dec	1989	p	105.31	98.14	104.23+	4.22
10.50Jan	1990	n	112	104.25	110.10+	3.26
3.50 Feb	1990		96.1	88.11	95.9	+ 4.3
11.00Feb	1990	p	113.29	106.11	111.29+	3.27
7.25 Mar	1990	p	102.25	97.8	101.24	......
10.50Apr	1990	n	112.21	104.28	110.25+	4.7
8.25 May	1990		106.26	100.10	104.28+	3.1
11.38May	1990	p	115.19	107.25	113.23+	4.2

			High	Low	Last	Net Chg.
7.25 Jun	1990	p	103.2	100.6	101.24	......
10.75Jul	1990	n	114.3	105.26	112.10+	4.18
9.88 Aug	1990	p	111.10	102.23	109.22+	4.31
10.75Aug	1990	n	114.12	105.29	112.16+	4.20
6.75 Sep	1990	p	100.29	99.8	100.2	......
11.50Oct	1990	n	117.14	108.26	115.11+	4.20
9.63 Nov	1990	n	110.29	101.30	109.13+	5.13
13.00Nov	1990	n	123.6	114.20	120.21+	4.1
6.63 Dec	1990	p	100.1	99.17	99.20	......
11.75Jan	1991	n	119.4	110.1	116.31+	4.30
9.13 Feb	1991	k	109.15	100.13	108.2	+ 5.19
12.38Apr	1991	n	122.10	112.24	120.4	+ 5.9
8.13 May	1991	p	106.3	99.12	104.26	......
14.50May	1991	n	131.13	121.24	128.17+	4.16
13.75Jul	1991	n	129.2	118.24	126.7	+ 5.8
7.50 Aug	1991	p	104.1	97.3	102.15	......
14.88Aug	1991	n	134.10	123.23	131.9	+ 5.8
12.25Oct	1991	p	129.8	112.20	121.9	+ 6.7
6.50 Nov	1991	p	100.10	97.12	98.18	......
14.25Nov	1991	n	132.16	121.22	129.30+	5.31
11.63Jan	1992	n	121.9	110.9	119.9	+ 6.20
6.63 Feb	1992	p	100.9	99.3	99.5	......
14.63Feb	1992	n	135.12	129.20	132.24+	6.14
11.75Apr	1992	k	122.15	110.31	120.19+	7.7
13.75May	1992	n	132.9	120.13	129.19+	6.24
10.38Jul	1992	p	116.19	104.26	115.2	+ 7.28
4.25 Aug	1987-92		96.5	88.10	95.9	+ 4.2
7.25 Aug	1992		103.1	91	101.25+	8.11
9.75 Oct	1992	p	114.6	101.29	112.17+	8.3
10.50Nov	1992	n	118.14	105.25	116.9	+ 7.30
8.75 Jan	1993	p	109.20	97.2	107.31	......
4.00 Feb	1988-93		96.13	88.2	95.14+	4.2
6.75 Feb	1993		100.30	87.19	99.12+	9.20
7.88 Feb	1993		105.10	93.2	103.25+	8.3
10.88Feb	1993	n	120.19	107.16	118.12+	8.10
7.38 Apr	1993	p	103.7	95.9	101.11	......
10.13May	1993	n	116.31	103.29	115.2	+ 8.16
7.25 Jul	1993	p	102.26	98.27	100.24	......
7.50 Aug	1988-93		103.7	90.26	100.31+	7.15
8.63 Aug	1993		109.14	96.15	107.24+	8.1
11.88Aug	1993	n	126.31	112.24	124.13+	8.25
7.13 Oct	1993	p	101.19	99.14	100.1	......
8.63 Nov	1993		109.22	96.14	107.25+	8.5
11.75Nov	1993	n	126.31	112.8	124.4	+ 8.30
9.00 Feb	1994		111.21	98.10	109.21+	8.6
4.13 May	1989-94		96.3	88.12	95.10+	4.1
13.13May	1994	p	136.5	120.3	133	+ 9.25
8.75 Aug	1994		131.24	96.20	109.3	+ 9.7
12.63Aug	1994	n	134.2	117.21	130.28+	10.5
10.13Nov	1994		119.1	104.8	117.3	+ 9.9
11.63Nov	1994	p	128.12	112.6	125.25+	10.15
3.00 Feb	1995		96.3	88.12	95.9	+ 4
10.50Feb	1995		121.25	105.24	119.17+	10.24
11.25Feb	1995	p	126.24	110.5	123.30+	10.25
10.38May	1995		121.11	105.15	119	+ 10.13
11.25May	1995	p	127.4	110.5	124.12+	11.5
12.63May	1995		135.27	118.26	132.27+	11.5
10.50Aug	1995	p	122.25	105.23	120.6	+ 11.6
9.50 Nov	1995	p	116.26	100.3	114.6	+ 10.30
11.50Nov	1995		129.20	112.21	127.7	+ 11.22
8.88 Feb	1996	p	113.12	98.15	110.9	......
7.38 May	1996	p	103.1	93.8	100.19	......
7.25 Nov	1996	p	101.23	98.31	100.5	......
7.00 May	1993-98		101	82.16	99.6	+ 14.8
3.50 Nov	1998		96.4	87.26	95.7	+ 3.29
8.50 May	1994-99		108.24	91.27	105.29+	11.10
7.88 Feb	1995-00		104.16	85.28	102.8	+ 13.6
8.38 Aug	1995-00		108.16	89.21	105.10+	12.14
11.75Feb	2001		139.21	114.23	134.1	+ 16.2
13.13May	2001		152	124.24	145.15+	16.31
8.00 Aug	1996-01		106.2	86.21	103.10+	13.24
13.38Aug	2001		154.6	127.3	147.24+	17.10
15.75Nov	2001		175.30	146.27	168.28+	18.28
14.25Feb	2002		162.27	134.27	155.27+	17.4
11.63Nov	2002		139.19	113.12	133.15+	16.14
10.75Feb	2003		131.22	106.24	126	+ 15.19
10.75May	2003		131.26	106.24	126.3	+ 15.22
11.13Aug	2003		135.15	109.16	129.11+	16.16
11.88Nov	2003		142.30	115.17	136.9	+ 16.30
12.38Aug	2004		148.17	120	141.17+	17.23
13.75Aug	2004		162.15	132.2	155.9	+ 19.14
11.63Nov	2004	k	141.16	114.31	135.13+	16.23

Government Notes and Bonds

			Net High	Low	Last	Chg.
8.25 May	2000-05		108.25	86.31	104.19	+14.8
12.00May	2005 k		146.5	117.27	139.7	+17.1
10.75Aug	2005 k		133.18	107.8	127.5	+16.5
9.38 Feb	2006 k		122.5	95.25	115.20	.....
7.63 Feb	2002-07		103.26	81.14	99.2	+14.8
7.88 Nov	2002-07		106.13	83.24	101.17	+14.6
8.38 Aug	2003-08		110.19	88.4	105.11	+13.21
8.75 Nov	2003-08		113.30	91.9	108.15	+13.15
9.13 May	2004-09		117.20	94.8	111.22	+13.22
10.38Nov	2004-09		129.31	103.18	123.8	+15.10
11.75Feb	2005-10		143.12	114.11	135.19	+16.21
10.00May	2005-10		126.5	100.11	120.5	+15.16
12.75Nov	2005-10		154.4	122.20	145.2	+17.10
13.88May	2006-11		166.4	133.10	156.4	+18.11
14.00Nov	2006-11		168.8	134.5	157.28	+18.30
10.38Nov	2007-12		131.15	103.14	124.12	+16.17

			Net High	Low	Last	Chg.
12.00Aug	2008-13		148.19	117.12	140.14	+18.15
13.25May	2009-14		163.3	128.3	153.8	+19.19
12.50Aug	2009-14k		155.2	122.6	146.1	+18.31
11.75Nov	2009-14k					
			147.4	115.23	139.26	+19.14
11.25Feb	2015k		144.26	113.7	137.28	+19.31
10.63Aug	2015k		138.6	107.31	131	+18.25
9.88 Nov	2015k		130.14	102.6	123.2	+17
9.25 Feb	2016k		125.28	100.29	117.6	......
7.25 May	2016k		101.18	92.8	95.15	......
7.50 Nov	2016k		102.18	98.30	100.4	......

k—Non U. S. citizen exempt from withholding taxes. n—Treasury note. p—Treasury note and non U.S. citizen exempt from withholding taxes.

MUTUAL FUNDS

The following table shows the closing net asset value for 1985, the dividends paid in 1986, and the closing NAV for the year.

	NAV 12-31-85	Divs 1986	Cap Dist	NAV 12-31-86
AARP Invest Program:				
Cap Grw				21.19
Gen Bnd				15.96
Ginnie M				16.19
Gro Inc				21.28
TxFr Bd				16.89
TxF Shrt				15.64
ABT Midwest Funds:				
Emrg Gr	15.50			8.77
Growth I	12.34	.46	g2.70	11.34
Int Govt	10.48	.86		10.76
LG Govt	10.90	1.07	.10	10.77
LG Gwth	12.21		g1.09	12.83
Sec Inc	10.94	.05 g	.20	11.10
Util Inc	16.42	.87 g	.33	14.98
AcornFd r	37.82	.50	g6.07	37.27
Adtek Fd				11.50
Advest Advantage:				
Govt r	†10.00	.07 g	.26	9.94
Growth r	†10.00	.03 g	.33	10.54
Income r	†10.00	.40 g	.28	10.39
Specl r	10.00			8.92
Afuture Fd	13.38	.11		12.49
AIM Funds:				
Charter	7.55	.17	2.38	6.22
Constel	21.79		6.75	21.16
Conv Yld	12.27	.66 g	.49	11.73
Grnway	10.18	.06 g	.98	10.11
HiYld Sc	10.00	1.20		9.73
Summit	6.49	.05 g	.66	6.68
Weingr	18.19	.17	4.78	17.63
Alliance Capital:				
Alli Conv	9.45	.55		9.48
Alli Gov	9.40	1.03		9.26
Alli HiY	10.07	1.32	.09	9.71
Alli Intl	16.74	.03	2.75	21.07
Alli Mtge	9.97	.98	.21	9.74
Alli Tech	20.52	.01		23.11
Chem Fd	11.15	.10	5.16	6.87
Cntrpt	12.24	.37	.32	14.11
Surveyr	13.97	.04	4.48	11.51
Alpha Fd				6.97
AMA Funds:				
Am Med	40.20			49.16
Growth	11.24	.16	g1.79	10.56
Income	9.00	.70		9.41
Med Tec	11.76		.19	13.38
American Capital Group:				
Comstk	14.78	.38	1.79	14.60
Corp Bd	7.31	.81		7.29
Enterpr	14.14	.27	2.65	12.78
Exch Fd	52.12	1.40	1.05	57.21
Fed Mtg	13.99	.53	.15	14.20
Fd Amer	11.38	.32	1.33	10.49
Govt Sec	12.04	.90	.64	11.69
Growth	27.41	.10	5.78	22.86
Harbor	13.99	.84	1.56	13.43
High Yld	10.46	1.33	.01	9.79
Muni Bd	19.66	1.56		21.23
O T C	10.16	.02	.91	8.30
Pace Fd	21.67	.65	.84	22.56
Prov Inc	4.75	.30	.44	4.59
TxE HY	11.91	1.03		12.07
TxE Ins	11.91	.83		12.26
Venture	14.42	.23	.30	14.55
American Funds Group:				
Am Bal	11.65	.64	g2.02	10.83
Amcap F	9.60	.19	1.25	9.63
Am Mutl	17.74	.74	2.08	17.99
Bnd FdA	14.01	1.44	.40	14.21
Eupac	18.63	.17	g1.25	24.58
Fund Inv	14.36	.40	g2.75	14.21
Govt	14.76	1.43	.06	14.96
Gth FdA	14.51	.28	.79	15.76
Inc FdA	11.78	.88 g	.59	12.03
I C A	13.51	.44	2.45	13.19
Nw Econ	19.54	.38	2.25	19.41
Nw Prsp	9.10	.21	1.25	9.99
TxEx Bd	10.50	.80	.12	11.48
TxE MD	†14.29	.17		14.44
TxE VA	†14.29	.21		14.80
Wash Mt	11.04	.51	.66	12.30
Am Grwth	8.32	.29	1.09	7.57
Am Heritg	2.37		.36	1.42
Am Invest	7.17		.60	6.45
AmInv Inc	9.32	1.11		8.85
AmNat Gw	4.56	.06	.44	4.59
AmNtl Inc	20.06	.76	2.03	19.11
API Tr r	11.59	.62	.72	11.81
AMEV Funds:				
Capital	12.31	.13	g1.06	13.73
Growth	14.37	.15	.59	16.37
Special	21.88	.14	1.23	24.80
US Govt	10.16	1.00		10.36
Amway Mt				7.82
Analytic	148.45	3.36	7.69	13.70
Aquila: Aquila:				
Haw TF	10.37	.79	.01	11.09
TF Ariz	9.60	.60		10.07
TF Ore	9.60	.34		10.07
Armstrng	7.76	.16	.51	7.99
Axe-Houghton:				
Fund B	11.97	.66	2.78	11.10
Income	5.29	.50		5.60
Stock Fd	8.98	.04	1.80	8.11
Babson Group:				
Bond Tr	1.63	.16		1.69
Entrprs	12.78	.05	1.73	12.12
Grwth	12.88	.35	1.97	12.95
TxFr L	9.02			9.30
UMB Bd	10.94	.83	.03	11.37
UMB Stk	12.74	.51	1.01	12.78
Value	13.04	.87	.18	14.64
Baird Cp				14.62
Bartlett Funds:				
Basic V	12.37	.78	1.08	12.20
Cp Cash	1.05	.08		1.06
Fixed In	†10.00	.62		10.16
Beacon Hll	23.26			24.65
Benham Capital Mngt:				
CalTFI f	10.10	.67		10.67
CalTFL f	10.43	.80	.09	11.50
NtTFL f	10.90	.88		12.00
Ca TNT f	11.20	1.08	.78	11.04
GNMA f	10.34	1.01		10.45
Tgt1990 f	68.16	2.18	4.44	79.01
Tgt1995 f	42.99	1.27	.70	54.57
Tgt2000 f	26.77	.97	2.64	35.51
Tgt2010 f	11.43	.32	1.01	17.68
Berger 100	17.36		1.16	19.71
Berger 101	16.16	.59	3.00	14.98
Blan StGr	†8.00			8.62
Boston Company:				
Cap Apr	32.11	.62	g5.78	32.42
GNMA	†12.50			12.63
Mng Inc	11.80	.43	.14	11.91
Spcl Grw	20.95	.31	g4.96	17.21
Bos I Ser	11.20	.12		13.24
Bowser GF				
Brndywin	10.00	.03		11.61
Bruce	85.34	1.29		109.39
Bull & Bear Group:				
Cap Grw	15.81	.20	5.91	10.37
Eq Incm	11.41	.38	2.01	11.03
Golcnd	9.55	.03		12.86
High Yld	14.55	1.84	.02	13.57
Tax Free	16.88	1.31	.06	18.17
US Govt	15.00	1.10		15.07
Cal Trust	10.41	.73		11.90
CalMun T	10.67	.76	g1.66	9.23
Calvert Funds:				
Equity				19.89
Income				16.98
Mng Gr				23.48
Resrve				16.36
Rsrv Ltd				10.67
Wash A r				18.45
Calvin Bullock Funds:				
Agg Gr	7.57			9.41
Bal Shs	13.47	.67	.53	14.81
Growth	9.18	.10	g2.84	7.74
Canadn	8.30	.17	1.20	7.14
Div Shs	3.35	.13	.40	3.53
US Govt	12.48	1.20		12.49
Hi Incm	10.83	1.39		9.93
Mo Incm	12.16	1.17		12.62

109

MUTUAL FUNDS

	NAV 12-31-85	Divs 1986	Cap Dist	NAV 12-31-86
Tax Free	10.41	.86		11.19
Cardinl Fd	13.48	.35	1.08	14.64
Cardinl Gv	†9.53	.90		9.35
Carnegie Funds:				
Capp Gr	13.35	.35	g1.34	14.01
Capp Tr	9.65	.31	g .35	10.77
HY Govt	10.43	.73	g .57	10.22
Century Sh	18.22	.27	1.11	18.30
Chepsd Dol				12.45
ChestSt Ex	58.37	1.41	.20	65.34
CIGNA Funds:				
Agg Gr	12.61	.08	.49	12.10
Growth	14.95	.35	3.52	12.91
High Yld	10.21	1.24		10.54
Income	7.53	.64		8.20
Muni Bd	7.69	.60	.26	8.41
Valu Fd	12.90	.43	1.32	12.26
Clarmnt C	11.06	.05	g .26	12.09
Clipper	36.26		1.41	41.55
Colonial Funds:				
Adv Gold	14.38	.58	g .43	17.99
Cal TE	†7.14	.28		7.46
CashTr 1	49.45	4.93	g .60	49.16
CshTr II	48.81	3.79	g .31	47.71
Eq Inc	16.61	3.70	g3.21	15.81
Fund	16.39	2.12	1.32	17.80
Gov Mtg	14.66	1.54	g .49	14.36
Govt Sec	12.40	1.53	g .56	12.72
Growth	11.61	.63	.54	13.20
High Yld	7.55	.93		7.69
Income	7.18	.81		7.23
Optn Inc	8.29	1.10	g .93	7.58
OptInc II	11.22	1.52	g1.24	10.47
SS Indx	†12.14	.01		11.38
Tx E HY	12.85	1.10	.03	13.73
Tx Insd	7.28	.64	g .10	7.94
Columbia Funds:				
Fixd Inc	13.04	1.21		13.37
Growth	27.91	.40	6.48	22.88
MunBd r	10.82	.84		11.75
Specl r	23.92		.74	26.97
Commonwealth Trust:				
A & B				1.49
C				2.08
Composite Group:				
Bond Stk	9.93	.60	g .71	10.01
Fund	10.93	.45	g1.67	10.95
Income	9.57			9.43
Tax Ex	7.10		g .12	7.56
US Gov	1.07			1.07
ConnMtlInv Accts:				
Govt	10.73	.91	.11	10.90
Growth	10.94	.24	.07	11.97
Totl Ret	10.91	.30	.04	11.87
Copley Fd	9.36			11.02
Corp Pfd				46.61
Coutry Cap	17.90	.38	3.10	15.92
Cowen IGr	†10.00			10.04
Criterion Funds:				
Cm IncS	10.13	.30	g .88	9.96
Gov Inst	10.00	.76	g .40	9.78
Inv Qual	10.41	1.18	g .70	10.14
Lowry M	9.78	.35		8.52
Pilot Fd	9.47		1.00	9.47
Qlty TF	10.45	.74		11.40
Sunblt G	16.31	.16		18.43
US Govt	10.08	.75	g .47	9.67
CmbrInd G	30.65	.60		33.63
Dean Witter:				
Cal TxFr	11.41	.77	g .40	12.25
Convrt r	10.51	.82	.09	11.03
DevlGr r	8.80	.01		8.88
DivGro r	16.35	.52	.48	18.48
High Yld	13.71	1.80		14.08
Ind Val r	12.67	.32	1.75	12.64
NatRes r	7.37	.22		7.96
NY TxFr	10.57	.72	.09	11.57
OptionI r	10.12	1.25		9.59
Sears Tx	11.41	.77	.86	11.85
Tax Adv	10.40	.78		10.29
Tax Ex	10.79	.87	g .48	11.49
USGovt r	10.53	1.02		10.33
WWIT r	13.35	.10	1.98	15.44
Delaware Group:				
Dectr I	16.16	.80	g2.00	16.86
Dectr II	†9.53			10.18
Delchs F	7.83	1.02		8.05

	NAV 12-31-85	Divs 1986	Cap Dist	NAV 12-31-86
DTR Inv	10.04	.84		9.97
GNMA	9.34	.99	.05	9.27
US Govt	9.33	.98	.08	9.22
TxFr Pa	7.34	.60		8.05
TFr USA	10.71	1.18	.26	11.78
TF USAI	9.87	.76		10.90
Delw Fd	20.78	.55	g4.31	18.34
Delta Td	6.82			7.18
Destiny I	12.92	.32	g2.54	12.43
Destiny II	10.13		g .30	15.93
D.I.T.				
Cap Gr	13.65	.13	g2.03	13.13
Cur In	10.13	1.14	g .22	10.15
Gov Sec	†10.00	.81	g	10.26
OTC Gr	22.03		2.29	23.71
DFA FxIn	101.60	7.63	.79	101.90
DFA Small	8.83	.10	.65	8.70
D G DvSrs	25.79	1.50	1.68	24.79
DodgC Bal	31.93	1.62	3.55	32.62
DodgC Stk	30.95	.94	3.90	31.66
Double Ex	11.12	.87	.09	11.85
Drexel Burnham:				
DB Fund				21.28
DSTGv r				10.70
DSTOp r				10.12
DST Cv r				9.66
DSTBd r				11.70
DST Gr r				11.80
DST E r				12.63
FenInt r				12.26
TxFr Ltd				
Dreyfus Group:				
A Bonds	14.61	1.34	.25	14.99
CalT Ex	14.13	1.10		15.47
Cap Val	16.75	.06	g .65	18.66
Cnv Sec	8.30	.55	g .85	8.87
Dreyf Fd	13.86	.59	g2.70	12.55
Dreyf Lv	18.07	.52	g4.73	16.23
GNMA	15.73	1.47		15.70
Growth	11.59	.21	g2.60	10.50
Insr TE	16.86	1.27		18.40
Intrmd	13.16	1.01		14.12
Mass Tx	15.25	1.17		16.75
New Ldr	18.11	.01	g .01	20.34
NYT Ex	14.59	1.12		15.89
Str Inc	†13.50	.12		13.65
Str Inv	†12.50	.06		12.83
Tax ExB	11.97	.97		13.01
Third Cn	7.50	.31	g .96	6.51
Eagle Gth				6.83
Eaton Vance Funds:				
Cal Mn r	10.00			10.68
EH Stk	14.68	.58	2.64	13.49
Gov Obli	12.26	1.20	g .25	12.36
Growth	7.08	.14	g .80	6.84
Hi Inc r	†10.00	.41		10.04
Hi Mun r	10.00	.87		10.41
High Yld	5.22	.60		5.32
Inc Bost	9.85	.78		10.23
Invests	8.88	.47	1.51	7.64
Muni Bd	8.42	.68		9.25
Naut Fd	13.32			12.15
Spc Eqty	19.58	.05	3.12	16.15
Tot Ret	18.57	.66	1.17	10.67
VS Specl	12.38	.08	1.04	10.63
Empir Bld	16.59	1.16	g .19	17.72
Equitec Siebel:				
AggrGr r	10.00			
HiYld r	10.00	.09		9.68
TotlRet r	11.97	.20	.02	
USGvt r	10.00	.09		9.93
Eq Strat	12.89			16.95
Evergrn	12.67	.14	1.66	12.47
Evrgrn TR	17.87	1.09	1.11	19.18
Fairmnt	53.64	.58	11.56	49.50
Farm B Gr	14.89	.40	1.73	14.19
Federated Group:				
Fed Flt	†10.00	.43		10.04
Fed StkB	15.24	.86	g1.06	15.34
Cash Tr	11.02	.06		10.66
Exch Fd	43.27	1.22	g .77	48.39
FIMT	10.00	.63		10.51
FT Intl	15.47	.08	g2.17	21.60
GNMA	11.39	1.12	.03	11.43
Grow Tr	13.24	.26	g .78	15.38
Hi Yld	10.63	1.31	g .03	10.91

	NAV 12-31-85	Divs 1986	Cap Dist	NAV 12-31-86
Incm Tr	10.87	1.05	.07	10.74
Intrmd	10.03	.88	.06	10.24
SIGT	10.37	.88	g	10.44
SIMT	10.18	.55		10.38
Stock Tr	20.20	.64	g1.44	21.60
US Govt	10.01	.86		10.00
Fidelity Investments:				
Aggr TF	10.66	.93		11.56
Cal HYld	10.81	.80	g .05	11.80
Congr St	68.20	2.10		83.60
Contra	12.16	.25	g2.15	11.29
CT ARP	10.51	.75	.02	10.40
Eq Incm	27.51	1.70	g3.08	27.29
Europe	†10.00			10.81
Exch Fd	55.80	1.60	2.53	62.94
Fidel Fd	18.08	.66	g4.08	16.05
Flex B	7.12	.70		7.36
Freedm	15.63	.35	g .98	16.31
GNMA	10.46	.94	.01	10.81
Govt Sec	9.79	.90		10.28
Gro Co	16.83	.07	4.65	14.11
Gro Inc	10.00	.16		13.33
Hi Incm	9.51	1.10	g .31	9.72
High Yld	12.44	.99	.44	13.29
Ins Muni	10.23	.73		11.33
Ltd Muni	8.88	.62		9.58
Mageln	45.21	.46	g6.84	48.69
Mass TF	10.72	.82		11.66
Mich TF	10.28	.79		11.38
Minn TF	10.09	.77		10.99
Mtge Sec	10.48	.99	.03	10.58
Muncpl	7.42	.55		8.28
NY Ins	10.26	.71	g .01	11.28
NY HiY	11.41	.89	g .17	12.26
Ohio TF	10.12	.77		10.97
OTC Prt	15.93	.02	g1.27	16.47
Ovrsea	18.25		2.14	28.68
Pac Bas	†10.00			10.94
Puritan	12.52	.92	g .76	13.34
Qual Div	15.11	1.10	1.94	14.97
Sel Air	9.50			10.72
SelAGI r	10.02			11.83
Sel Bio r	10.00			10.35
SelBrk r	11.09	.02	.02	12.12
Sel Brd	†10.00			9.78
SelChm r	12.39		.06	15.66
SelCmp r	11.36		.04	12.21
SelDef r	14.31	.03	.20	14.79
Sel El r	11.11			8.46
Sel EIU r	†10.00			10.08
SelErg r	10.93			11.53
Sel Fd r	11.51			14.10
Sel Fin r	27.86	.21	.33	31.56
SelHth r	27.15		.36	32.78
SelLsr r	17.76	.01	.04	20.51
SelMetl r	8.49	.10		11.15
Sel Papr	†10.00			12.02
SelPrC r	10.19			10.97
SelRetl r	9.80			11.19
SelSL r	10.10			12.88
SelSoft r	11.11			12.65
SelTch r	21.99		.08	20.27
SelTele r	11.00			13.18
SelUt r	22.30	.22	.14	27.31
Shrt T	†10.00	.21		9.96
Specl Sit	13.49	.09	g .97	16.21
Tex TF	†9.97	.13		10.38
Thrift Tr	11.03	.66	.22	11.55
Trend	45.02	.61	g10.64	39.83
Value	21.76		1.99	23.06
Fidu CapG	21.42	.10	3.68	17.90
Financial Programs:				
Dynam	8.56	.06	2.09	7.06
Hi Yield	8.37	1.01	g .17	8.38
Industl	4.66	.10	g1.02	3.96
Income	9.37	.42	g2.41	8.00
Select	6.84	.68	.32	7.10
Tax Free	15.00	1.18	g1.38	15.59
Wld Tch	8.31			9.68
FBS Gov	†7.50	.61	g .03	7.90
FSP Egy	8.32	.14	.17	8.60
FSP Eur	†8.00	.01		8.77
FSP Fin	†8.00	.03		7.41
FSP Gld	4.06	.08	.05	5.49
FSP HS	10.69		g1.37	12.50
FSP Ls	11.18		2.76	10.69
FSP PaB	8.52	.04	g1.73	12.69

	NAV 12-31-85	Divs 1986	Cap Dist	NAV 12-31-86
FSP Tc	8.85		g1.07	9.67
FSPUt	†8.00	.06	g .01	8.65
First Investors Fund:				
Bond Ap	12.94	1.32	g .24	12.94
Discovr	11.42	.12	g .80	9.03
Govt Fd	12.14	1.11	g .27	12.19
Growth	6.37		g .41	5.70
High Yld	†14.84	.30		14.90
Income	5.96	.76		5.94
Intl Sec	12.66	.01	g1.44	16.53
NY TxFr	13.03	.95		14.25
Nat Resr	4.49	.21		3.63
90-10	12.43	.67		12.50
Optn Fd	4.99	.11	g .51	4.68
Tx Exmt	9.48	.76	.01	10.14
FstTr US				
Flagl CpCs	†10.00	.28		9.84
Flagship:				
Cp Cash	47.44	3.58		45.91
Mich	9.68	.73	g .08	10.77
No Caro	†9.58	.48		9.75
Ohio	9.76	.75	g .07	10.60
Virgn	†9.58	.47		9.85
Flex Bond	20.84	1.88	.17	21.31
Flex Fund	11.45	.42	1.27	10.91
Fortress Investment:				
GISI	†9.97	.79		9.76
Hi Incm	12.35	1.51		12.32
Hi Qual	10.01	.34	g .05	11.18
44 Wall St				3.09
44 WS Eqt				5.75
Founders Group Funds:				
Growth	8.14	.39	1.06	8.30
Income	14.75	.66	.88	15.30
Mutual	9.75	.29	3.22	7.87
Special	26.68	.29	3.47	27.98
FPA Funds:				
Capital	11.41	.37	1.47	11.08
New Inc	9.37	.84	.03	9.50
Paramt	13.18	.53	.93	12.44
Perennl	18.84	.51	1.70	18.47
Franklin Group:				
AGE Fd	3.70	.49		3.67
Cal Ins	10.52	.84		11.79
Cal TxFr	6.74	.59		7.22
Corp Csh	9.27	.59		8.82
D N T C	10.81	.25		9.95
Equity	5.83	.11	g .60	6.25
Fed TxF	11.08	1.01	.02	12.06
Gold Fnd	7.16	.34		8.99
Growth	14.40	.26	g .24	15.95
Income	2.09	.22	.02	2.24
Ins TxFr	10.79	.85	g .08	11.87
Mass TF	10.56	.82		11.25
MN Ins	10.87	.85		11.87
N Y Tax	10.92	.96	.18	11.64
OHIn TF	10.60	.85		11.53
Optn Fd	6.59	.13	g1.01	5.93
Mich TF	10.59	.83		11.54
US GvSc	7.52	.84	.01	7.42
Utilities	7.09	.56	.01	8.18
Freedom Funds:				
Global	†9.60			10.16
Gold Gov	15.41	1.11	g .61	16.03
Gov Plus	10.00	.44	.02	10.38
Reg Bnk	10.53	.29	g1.48	10.92
FundTrust:				
Aggr f	12.32	.15	g .37	13.27
Grow f	12.03	.31	g .24	13.08
Gro Inc f	11.86	.33	g .36	12.88
Incom f	10.69	.91	g .05	10.62
GabelliA	†10.00			11.29
Gatewy Gr	†10.00			10.04
Gatewy Op	14.69	.34	g1.46	14.63
Geico ARP	25.74	1.75	.28	24.88
GenAgg G	17.03	.04	g .21	19.34
Genl Elec Invest:				
Elf TxE	10.95	.91	.74	11.45
Elfn Inc	11.78	.95	.65	11.99
Elfn Tr	28.83	.99	4.19	27.48
S&S LT	11.77	1.09	.32	12.42
S&S Pro	40.84	1.57	10.11	35.48
GenlSec r	12.89	2.51	g2.13	11.57
Genl TxEx	13.69	1.07		14.89
Gintel Group:				
Cap App	†10.00		.91	11.00
Erisa	39.48	1.20	1.35	45.23

MUTUAL FUNDS

	NAV 12-31-85	Divs 1986	Cap Dist	NAV 12-31-86
GIntl Fd	83.71	1.68	32.06	66.62
Grad EstG	13.73	.25	1.18	15.21
Grad Opp	10.99	.04	.80	11.64
GIT Investment:				
Eq Spec				16.03
Income				9.48
TxFr HY				11.45
Grth IndSh	11.82	.22	3.52	9.10
GrF Wash	10.20	.09	.44	11.12
GT Global:				
Europe	13.68			19.22
Intl	12.50		g .61	18.39
Japan	12.40	.02	g .16	19.68
Pacific	17.64	.01		29.98
Guardian Funds:				
Bond	11.57	.79	.03	12.41
Park Av	21.20	.33	3.81	20.74
Stock	15.40	.22	.59	17.15
Hamilton Group: Hamilton Group:				
Hamltn Fd	6.81	.42	1.24	6.76
Harbor G	10.00			10.24
Hartwll Gt	11.40		1.95	12.01
Hartwll Lv	13.54			16.15
HeartInd	13.46	.09	.83	14.01
Hrtg Cap	9.74	.06	g .04	10.83
HorcM Gr				21.29
Hutton EF Group:				
Bond r	12.00	.96	g .39	12.91
Growth r	15.50	.24	g1.67	15.86
Optnln r	9.08	.10	g .99	8.19
GovSec r	10.20	1.02	g .11	10.41
BasVal r	11.43	.30	g .52	12.15
Cal Muni	10.36	.83	g .19	11.08
Nat Mun	11.07	.91	g .56	11.97
NY Muni	10.67	.84	.28	11.32
PrecMt r	9.22	.03	.22	12.93
SplEq r	13.15	.05	1.00	13.02
IDEX	10.85	.29	.48	12.07
IDEX II	10.00	.02		10.14
IndsFd Am	5.92		2.06	3.07
Industrial Group:				
Ind Am				8.75
Ind Govt				9.33
Ind Opt				8.83
Integrated Resources:				
CapAp r	11.81	.29	g .35	13.17
HmInv r	10.72	.92	g .10	10.67
Tax Free	12.14	.95		12.52
Int CapG	†6.32			6.40
Investment Portfolios				
InvPG r	8.46	.87		8.53
InPHY r	9.20	.96	.05	9.83
InvPOp r	8.44	1.08	.02	7.48
InPEq r	10.49	.04	.21	10.75
ITB Group:				
InvT Bos	11.91	.34	g1.05	11.98
InvT Hip	14.56	1.56	g .43	14.11
InT MTF	15.62	1.17	g .05	16.83
IDS Mutual Fund Grp:				
IDS Bnd	5.02	.49	g .18	5.30
IDS Disc	7.56	.09	g .50	7.45
IDS Eqty	9.28	.24	1.30	9.43
IDS Extl	5.06	.56	.15	5.16
IDS Fed	5.11	.44	g .44	5.24
IDS Gth	19.33	.14	2.69	20.35
IDS HYd	4.30	.36	g .10	4.59
IDS Intl	7.14	.04	g1.51	9.26
IDS Mgt	5.90	.16	g .27	6.87
IDS MN	†5.00	.12	g .01	5.18
IDS Mutl	11.97	.86	g1.14	12.45
IDS ND	9.23	1.76	g2.19	8.52
IDS Prec	4.14	.08		5.94
IDS Prog	7.15	.25	g .93	6.68
IDS Selct	8.42	1.81		9.08
IDS Stck	18.47	.61	2.29	19.16
IDS Tax	3.78	.30		4.25
IDS Ag r	7.94		.11	9.67
IDS Eq r	6.84	.22	g .10	7.43
IDS Inc r	5.83	.50	g .09	6.22
IFG Funds:				
Divrsf f	11.36		g1.22	12.11
Intmn f	10.14			10.44
Intl Fd f	12.23		g2.15	16.07
Intl Eqty	10.11	.02	g .67	14.37
Inv Resrch	5.03	.03	1.27	5.15
IRI Stock	9.59	.30	.88	9.91

	NAV 12-31-85	Divs 1986	Cap Dist	NAV 12-31-86
I S I Group:				
Growth				6.48
Income				3.38
Trst Sh				10.22
Istel Fund	13.89	.64	1.08	13.29
Ivy Funds:				
Growth	15.90	.46	g4.48	13.44
Inst Inv	146.31	6.15	g40.67	125.53
Intl	†11.10			12.40
JP Growth				13.62
JP Income				9.96
Janus Funds:				
Jan Fnd	13.19		2.20	12.47
Janus VI	12.16	.80	.82	12.07
Jans Vn	24.88	1.48	1.04	27.45
John Hancock Funds:				
Bond Fd	15.85	1.53	.50	15.89
Globl Tr	11.69	.02	.10	14.76
Growth	14.50	.17	g2.20	14.03
Spcl Eqt	6.05		.05	5.71
Tax Ex	10.35	.75	.50	11.10
Gtd Mtg	10.75	1.03	.16	10.72
US Govt	9.24	.83		9.71
Kauf Fund	1.11			1.13
Kemper Funds:				
Cal Tax	13.30	1.07		14.59
Income	8.79	.94		9.08
Growth	12.21	.10	g3.57	10.06
High Yld	10.83	1.26		11.45
Int'l Fd	18.18	.28	g6.32	19.30
Muni Bd	8.89	.72		9.81
Optn Inc	10.83	1.31	.12	9.70
Summit	5.38		g1.02	5.11
Technol	12.22	.17	2.72	11.12
Total R	15.10	.56	g1.96	15.25
US GvSc	9.47	1.04		9.90
KY Tax Fr	6.43	52.92		6.96
Keystone Mass Group:				
Cust B1 r	17.07	1.62	.07	17.65
Cust B2 r	19.68	2.00	g .14	19.89
Cust B4 r	8.04	.96	.07	7.77
CustK1 r	9.26	.56	g1.49	8.67
CustK2 r	7.65	.13	g1.51	7.64
Cust S1 r	21.26	.42	g4.52	19.77
Cust S3 r	8.67	.14	g1.93	7.93
Cust S4 r	6.39	.01	.88	5.98
Intl Fd r	5.68	.06	g1.11	7.16
PrecM r	10.82	.37	g .08	14.59
TaxEx r	10.34	.78		11.34
Tax Fr r	8.32	.68	g .26	8.84
Kidder Group:				
KPEQI r	15.42	.45		17.49
GovtIn r	15.42	1.17		15.11
SpclGr r	13.46	.04		13.92
TFI Ntl	14.44	1.16		15.89
TFI NY	14.49	1.10		15.64
Ldmk NY	†10.00	.16		10.17
Ldmk US	†10.00	.19		9.72
Legg Mason Funds:				
Sp Invst	10.00	.02	g .22	10.51
Totl Ret	10.09	.16	g .04	10.04
Val Tr	26.70	.42	g2.78	26.10
Lehman Group:				
Captl	19.75	.25	g4.04	17.87
Invst	19.86	.54	g4.55	17.37
Opprt	24.29		g2.79	22.60
Leverage	8.85		g1.53	7.26
Lexington Group:				
CpLdr fr				13.90
Gold Fd				4.49
Gnma				8.22
Growth				11.80
Resrch				19.16
Liberty Family Fds:				
Am Lead	12.43	.50	g1.23	12.49
Tax Free	9.58	.76		10.72
US Gvt S	8.77	.86		8.62
Lib MutG				10.04
Ltd Term	12.41	.87	g .01	12.90
LndnrDv r	24.42	5.43	3.26	23.74
LindnrFd r	19.16		5.58	16.12
LMH Fund	25.85	1.10	4.42	24.01
Loomis Sayles Funds:				
Cap Dev	25.02	.16	g7.46	23.12
Mutual	21.53	.94	2.75	22.86

MUTUAL FUNDS

	NAV 12-31-85	Divs 1986	Cap Dist	NAV 12-31-86
Lord Abbett:				
Affilatd	9.91	.55	1.14	10.50
Bnd Deb	10.56	1.19	.14	10.29
Devl Gro	8.20		.39	7.88
Fd Valu	9.63			9.75
Govt S	3.20			3.27
TxFr Cal	9.73		.03	10.69
TxF Natl	10.18		.07	11.23
TxFr NY	10.44		.11	11.29
Value Ap	11.88	.23	.86	12.73
Lutheran Brotherhood:				
Broth Fd	16.79	.65	.40	16.96
Bro Inc	8.99	.90		8.97
Bro MBd	7.44	.60		8.34
MacKay Shields:				
CapAp r	†10.00	.02		9.63
Conv r	†10.00	.24		9.86
CorpB r	†10.00	.69		9.80
GovtP r	†10.00	.58		9.99
TF Bd r	†10.00	.40		10.12
Value r	†10.00	.02		9.03
Mass Financial Services:				
MIT	12.12	.40	1.75	12.09
Finl Dev	11.99	.77	g2.45	10.89
Grth Stk	11.14	.14	g2.98	9.44
Cap Dev	12.48	.18	1.94	11.21
TxFr CA	†4.66	.34	.02	5.26
Special	8.19	.01	1.05	8.59
Sectors	†8.41	.01		9.57
Emg Gr	16.34		1.64	16.82
Gv Guar	10.40	.98	g .11	10.32
Intl Bd	10.69	.78	g .65	11.46
Gov HiY	†9.53	.71	.24	9.76
TxF MD	10.13	.74		11.01
Finl Bd	14.31	1.47	.40	14.66
Hilnc Bd	7.22	.94	g .10	6.92
Muni Bd	10.03	.78	g .39	10.63
Muni HY	10.21	1.02	g .08	10.31
TxFr NC	10.69	.77	g .16	11.53
TxFr VA	10.34	.76	g	11.12
TxF MA	†10.08	.77	.01	11.02
Totl Ret	9.78	.59	g .88	10.19
Mathers				16.96
Meeschr C				25.87
Merrill Lynch:				
Basc Val	15.79	.58	.86	17.06
CalTxE r	10.60	.76	.05	11.63
Captl Fd	22.57	.44	2.10	24.40
Corp Dv	10.51	.84		10.90
EqBd 1 r	13.11	.61	.74	13.24
Fed Sec	9.96	.86	.44	9.87
Fd FT r	13.37	.10	.08	15.18
Hi Incm	8.29	.98		8.34
Hi QualP	11.45	1.07		
Inst Int		.12		9.98
Intl Hldg	12.28	.30	1.27	14.28
Inter TP	11.32	1.03		11.87
Muni Ins	7.53	.60	.01	8.18
Mun HY	9.86	.83	.18	10.67
NY Mn r	10.34	.73	.07	11.24
Ltd Mat	9.75	.56		9.90
Munil r		.03		9.94
NatRes r	9.99	.04	.28	12.75
Pacific	19.59	.11	.19	34.20
Phoenx	12.00	.29	1.01	12.39
Retire r	10.19	.34	.19	11.03
RetInc r		.59		9.98
RetGIB r		.19		10.16
Sci Tech	10.65	.10	.53	11.94
Sp'l Valu	14.29	.05	.62	13.97
MetL Eqlc	†9.31			9.58
MetL HI	†7.40	.27		7.44
Mid Amer				5.98
MidA HGr				4.34
Midas Gld	†7.00			7.89
Monitrd	18.25	.38	.78	18.73
MSB Fund				20.60
Mutl Beac	17.24	.31	g .94	18.64
Mutl BnFd	12.87	.32	g1.66	13.66
Mutual of Omaha Funds:				
Amer	10.44	.92		10.65
Growth	6.56	.10	.42	7.09
Incom	9.17	.80	.27	8.94
Tax Free	10.81	.86	.64	11.69
MutlQl Fd	19.22	.85	g1.56	20.04
Mutl Shars	57.54	2.34	g4.52	60.39
NtlAvia Tc	10.63	.18	.99	11.02

	NAV 12-31-85	Divs 1986	Cap Dist	NAV 12-31-86
Natl Ind	12.67	.13	1.32	11.64
National Securities Funds:				
Balanc	15.13	.88	2.61	13.85
Bond	3.44	.46		3.16
Cal TEx	12.09	.99		13.20
Fed Sec	11.65	1.20	.29	11.22
Preferd	8.16	.76	.33	8.50
Income	7.10	.46	.36	7.84
Real Est	8.96	.28	.43	9.82
Stock	9.92	.44	2.03	8.99
Tax ExB	9.20	.76		10.26
Totl Ret	6.62	.38	.08	7.42
Grwth	9.70	.20		11.01
Fairfld	10.72	.09	2.68	8.28
Natl Telcm	13.57	.16		13.80
Nationwide Funds:				
Fund	12.48	.39	.81	13.47
Growth	8.52	.30	1.21	8.56
Bond	9.93	.91	.04	10.21
New England Funds:				
Equity	21.94	.73	5.02	20.60
Grwth	26.32	.22	3.97	26.65
Income	11.01	.93		11.65
Gvt Sec	13.03	1.04	g .03	13.48
Ret Eqty	24.17	.42	g2.73	26.18
Tax Ex	7.53	.68	g .60	7.75
Neuberger Berman Mngt:				
Energy	19.14	.88	1.66	18.47
Guardn	39.30	1.51	g4.50	38.13
Liberty	4.33	.36		4.73
Ltd Mat	†10.00	.43		10.16
Manhtn	8.86	.08	g1.24	8.95
Partner	17.16	.44	g2.25	17.37
Newton Gr	31.29	1.06	11.73	20.74
Newtn Inc	8.46	.73		8.47
NY Muni	1.19	.08	g .06	1.25
Nicholas Group:				
Nichls r	32.18	.88	.19	34.87
Nichll r	15.54	.42	.51	16.22
Nich Inc	3.96	.38		4.01
NodCal Inc	10.60	.54	.53	11.23
NomuraP f	12.38	.30	g .06	21.13
Noeast Gr	15.24	.13	.52	18.36
Noeast Tr	12.68	1.46		13.70
North Star Funds:				
Apollo	10.45	.18	g .34	10.18
Bond	10.37	.90	g .28	10.39
Region	20.53	.42	g6.45	18.42
Reserv	†10.01	.33		10.19
Stock	14.54	.37	g1.80	14.25
Nova Fund	15.53	.04	2.28	14.38
Nuveen BF	8.24	.60	.21	8.96
OldDom In	24.05	1.27	g1.61	24.98
Omega Fd	14.12	.28	2.12	13.44
Oppenheimer Funds:				
Aim Fnd	21.25	.11	3.88	26.99
Directr	20.98			21.92
Eq Incm	8.30	.47	.61	8.46
Opp Fnd	10.79	.12	1.05	9.88
GNMA	14.29	.35		14.31
Gold Spc	6.31	.14		8.45
High Yld	17.37	2.24		16.73
NY TxE	11.77	.84	.23	12.68
Prm Inc	20.81	.29	2.38	18.26
Regncy	14.82	.21	.13	15.63
Sel Stk	11.59	.24	.66	12.22
Special	21.07	.77	g4.20	18.90
Target	19.30	.38		20.49
Tax FrB	8.80	.67		9.81
Time Fd	15.38	.23	2.08	16.21
USGov T	10.17	.98	.19	10.18
Ret Gov	11.09	1.00	g .52	10.42
OTC SecFd	18.68	.06	g2.54	16.99
Pacific Horizon:				
PcH Agr	21.26	.05		25.48
PcH Cal	13.07	.97		14.45
PcH HY	15.93	1.83		16.41
Paine Webber:				
Asst All				9.76
MstrGr r				9.52
Mstrln r				10.03
PW Atls	13.90	.09	g3.04	15.94
PW Am	14.97	.76	1.06	15.04
PW Cal	10.09	.78		11.18

MUTUAL FUNDS

	NAV 12-31-85	Divs 1986	Cap Dist	NAV 12-31-86
PW GN	10.32	1.13		10.21
PW HiY	10.38	1.40		10.36
Pw Inv	10.52	1.19		10.75
PW Oly	10.55	.20	.31	10.86
PW TxE	10.45	.82		11.39
Park Ave	17.77	1.18		19.05
PaxWld Fd	13.34	.50 g	.71	13.19
Penn Mutl	7.43	.13 g1.11		6.98
Penn Squ	9.70	.39	1.25	9.21
Permt Prtf	11.60			13.18
Phila Fund				6.70
Phoenix Series Fund:				
Bal Ser				12.75
Conv Ser				17.44
Gwth Ser				16.40
High Yld				9.64
Stk Ser				12.67
Tot Ret				12.38
Pilgrim Group:				
Par Fnd	22.79	1.69		22.01
Pil Ginn	15.95	1.60		15.33
Pil HiYd	8.05	.96		8.00
Pil Mag	8.91	.25	.34	9.81
Pil Pfd	†25.00	2.13		25.04
Pioneer Funds:				
Bond Fd	9.53	.92		9.60
Pionr Fd	23.13	.67 g5.25		19.72
Pionr II	17.54	.52 g1.03		18.14
Pionr III	15.06	.36 g1.17		15.18
Price Rowe:				
Cal TxF	†10.00	.19		10.30
Cap Apr	†10.00			10.84
Eqty In	11.01	.52 g	.26	12.96
GNMA	10.09	.92		10.23
Growth	17.95	.38 g4.18		16.96
Grw Inc	14.18	.71 g1.57		12.98
High Yld	10.75	1.30 g	.13	10.87
Income	8.73	.77		9.13
Intl Bd	†10.00	.28		10.01
Intl Stk	18.08	.22 g2.75		25.78
New Am	11.85	.10	.30	13.14
New Era	18.67	.50	3.25	17.76
Nw Horz	15.12	.09 g2.64		12.38
S-T Bond	5.16	.42		5.19
TxFr Inc	9.03	.70		10.07
TxFr HY	10.68	.88		11.92
TxFr SI	5.09	.30		5.27
Primry T	10.00			10.04
Principal Preserv:				
S&P 100	9.42	.36	.04	10.43
TX EX	9.02	.63		8.81
GOVT PI	9.37	.83	.13	9.71
Princor Funds:				
Cap Ac	17.42	.52	2.15	17.16
GSIF	11.19	1.14	.28	10.97
Growth	18.31	.32	2.24	18.47
Prudential Bache:				
Adjust R	24.06	1.84		23.07
CalMn r	10.97	.79	.45	11.54
Equity r	9.04	.06 g1.22		9.04
Global r	7.48	.01 g1.10		9.64
GNMA	15.94	1.21 g	.40	15.94
GovtPl r	10.49	.72 g	.34	10.58
GvPl II	†	.05		10.00
Govt Sec	10.66	.98	.23	10.84
Grwth r	12.88		g2.87	11.40
HiYld r	10.33	1.06	.09	10.66
HY Mn r	15.37	1.18 g	.78	16.18
InVer r	10.13	.58	.14	10.94
Muni Md	10.24	.73		10.95
MnNY r	11.15	.79 g	.47	11.74
MuniAz r	10.82	.76 g	.38	11.45
MunMa r	9.99	.75	.22	11.39
MunMi r	10.91	.80	.65	11.46
MunOh r	10.88	.80 g	.15	11.59
OptnGr r	9.01	.16 g1.31		8.72
Resrch r	10.37	.18	.50	12.24
Util Fd r	12.88	.64 g1.47		14.78
Putnam Funds:				
CCT Arp	47.67	3.85		46.04
CCT Dsp	48.17	5.33		48.89
Cal TxE	14.58	1.19		15.96
Captl Fd	8.03	.05	1.03	7.80
Convert	15.30	.96	.44	16.24
Enrgy R	11.82	.30		11.25
George	13.13	.80	.11	14.66
Gnma Pl	†11.39	.47 g	.21	11.38

	NAV 12-31-85	Divs 1986	Cap Dist	NAV 12-31-86
Gro Inc	12.82	.65 g1.13		13.69
Hlth Sci	17.64	.20	2.74	17.44
Hi Incom	12.40	1.12	.49	12.47
High Yld	15.73	2.12		15.62
H Yld II	†12.00	.88		11.62
Income	7.33	.79		7.42
Info Sci	12.75	.03		14.08
Intl Equi	23.54	1.53	.13	30.39
Investr	11.90	.20	1.77	11.62
NY TEx	15.96	1.44		17.37
Option	11.08	.20 g1.11		10.56
Option II	11.63	.40 g1.40		10.82
OTC Em	22.03		2.29	23.71
Tax Ex	23.72	1.94	.14	26.27
TF HY r	13.13	1.06	.18	14.32
TF In r	13.25	1.07	.04	14.55
US GGtd	14.70	1.51	.01	14.71
Vista Bs	17.69	.59	2.84	17.52
Voyage	18.89	.15	2.73	19.59
Quaser As	59.12		9.22	56.85
Quest for	24.68	.20	2.59	25.49
Rainbw Fd				5.41
ReaGra Fd	15.86	.47	1.83	15.14
Rch &Tang	13.44	.28 g .63		14.50
RightTm f				29.89
Rochester Funds:				
Conv Gr	†10.00			9.96
Conv Inc	†10.00	.20		8.47
Growth	9.36			9.11
Tax Mg	10.39			10.61
RoyceF r	8.70	.04 g	.88	8.33
Safeco Group:				
Cal TxFr	10.87		.11	12.02
Equity	10.50	.29	2.03	9.54
Growth	15.56	.31	1.59	14.00
Income	14.03	.78	.73	15.28
Muni	12.76		.21	13.97
Salem Gro	10.97	.16 g	.09	12.53
SBSF Fd	13.75	.49 g1.60		12.72
Scudder Funds:				
Cal TxFr	10.35		.15	11.01
Cptl Gro	15.64	.23 g2.46		15.59
Devl Fd	20.43		g3.99	20.71
Gen 90	10.38		.27	10.53
Global				12.43
Gvt Mtg	15.34		g .08	15.50
Gro Inc	15.35	.17 g	.78	15.02
Income				13.41
Intl Fnd	31.03	.49 g5.93		39.79
Muni Bd	8.40		.24	8.93
NY TxFr	10.73		.30	11.30
TxFr 90	10.03		g .10	10.34
TxFr 87	9.99		g .08	10.03
TxFr 93	10.59		g .24	11.04
Security Funds:				
Action	9.00	.25	.27	9.69
Bond Fd	8.39	.95		8.32
Equity	4.93	.18	.32	5.23
Invest	8.87	.56	.42	8.92
Omni	5.00	.24	1.32	2.91
Ultra Fd	8.44	.62	1.61	6.71
Selected Funds:				
Selct Am	13.35	.48	2.29	12.65
Selct Spl	20.55	.64	3.45	17.83
Seligman Group:				
Captl Fd	12.70		2.43	12.72
Colo Tx	7.14	.29	.03	7.17
Com Stk	13.94	.50	3.37	13.03
Com Info	10.00		.35	11.39
Growth	6.06	.10	1.70	5.25
Income	13.18	1.09	.85	13.44
La TxEx	7.45	.58	.08	7.98
MD Tx	7.33	.53		7.76
Mass Tx	7.62	.58	.18	8.03
Mi TxEx	7.89	.60	.29	8.37
Minn Tx	7.52	.57	.21	7.90
Mo Tx	7.14	.22		7.42
Ntl TxEx	7.72	.63	.33	8.34
NY TxE	7.76	.59	.25	8.24
Ohio Tax	7.62	.60	.12	8.15
Pa TxQ	7.14	.22	.01	7.69
Cal THY	6.20	.50	.26	6.57
Cal TxQ	6.27	.48	.13	6.78
Govt Gtd	8.10	.66	.53	8.15
Secu Mtg	7.76	.65	.34	7.33
High Yld	7.60	.91		7.83

MUTUAL FUNDS

	NAV 12-31-85	Divs 1986	Cap Dist	NAV 12-31-86
Sentinel Group Funds:				
Bal Fund				12.35
Bond Fd				6.58
Com Stk				23.61
Growth				13.96
Sentry Fd	12.36	.32	1.21	12.70
Sequoia	44.01	1.61	8.54	39.29
SFT EQTY	10.80	.45		11.25
Shearson Funds:				
Aggr Gr	12.63		.84	15.00
ATTGr r	88.50	2.27	g23.70	77.36
ATTInc r	86.19	5.40	2.51	99.20
Apprec	23.26		g1.65	26.16
Fund Val	7.02	.32	g .74	6.31
Glob Opp	27.98	.15	6.18	30.07
High Yld	19.02	2.22		18.89
Cal Muni	15.04		.33	16.18
Mng Gvt	13.40		g .30	13.34
Mg Muni	14.57		g .43	15.58
NY Muni	15.48		.29	16.71
Spl Conv	13.00	.15		13.04
Spl GlBd	†15.00			15.52
SplGro r	14.00			14.12
Spl Hln	14.00	.22		14.17
Spl Intl r	†18.00			19.89
Spl Mtgs	†12.00			11.97
Spl TE r	15.74			17.20
Spl Ing r	11.46		g .15	11.76
SplLtg r	9.20		g .29	9.23
Spl Opt r	13.88	.36	1.50	14.09
SplPlus r	16.00			14.59
Shrm Dean	5.49			5.23
Sierra Gro	11.63		.52	11.05
Sigma Funds:				
Capitl Sh	8.35	.16	.48	8.66
Incm Shr	8.77	.89		9.05
Invest Sh	9.17	.32	1.15	9.89
Special	8.73	.13	.80	9.21
Trust Sh	13.23	.77	1.11	13.63
Venture	11.47	.05	.97	11.06
Wrld Fd	11.41		.61	15.75
Sit NB Gr	26.39	.05	3.82	25.37
Smith Barney:				
Equity	16.25	.42	4.18	13.98
Inc Gro	10.10	.67	.13	11.40
Inc Ret	9.51	.87	.01	9.43
US Govt	13.95	1.44	.04	13.89
Soeast G r	11.33		.51	12.59
So GenFnd	16.52	.60	g2.22	17.71
Sovern Inv	22.62	1.10	1.73	24.73
State Bond Group:				
CmSt Fd	6.30	.10	.71	6.35
Diversf	7.15	.25	.85	7.42
Progrss	9.40	.14	.36	10.10
Tax Ex	9.93	.77	.05	10.68
State Farms Funds:				
StF Bal	16.31	.74	1.08	17.29
StF Gr	11.72	.34	1.15	11.95
StF Mun	7.24	.58		7.99
State St Research:				
Exch	104.19	2.70		118.32
Grow	64.63	1.82		70.51
Invest	76.08	2.25	11.50	75.42
Steadman Funds:				
Am Ind	2.89			2.32
Assoc Fd	.93		g .07	.89
Inves Fd	1.45			1.60
Oceang	5.05			4.48
Stein Roe Funds:				
Man Bnd	9.36	.83	.74	9.26
Capit Op	23.81	.20	.85	26.75
Discvr	11.22	.04	.03	10.56
HY Bnds	10.00	.55		9.96
HY Muni	11.10	.92	.15	12.06
Int Mun	10.14	.57		10.77
Mgd Mn	8.93	.78	.92	9.22
Specl Fd	18.41	.34	3.80	16.95
Stock Fd	17.43	.25	3.22	16.97
Total R	25.04	1.35	2.70	25.07
Univrse	18.58	.21	3.62	17.48
Strategic Family Fds:				
Cap Gain	8.32			6.54
Invest	3.91	.30		4.65
Silver	4.38			3.95
Strattn Div	26.62	2.28	.50	29.21
Strattn Gth	20.09	.28	2.07	20.02
Strong Funds:				
Income	10.30	.70		12.65
Invest	19.41	.95	.42	22.18
Optnty	10.00			15.99
Total R	19.56	.70	1.04	21.61
Tel Inc Sh	16.03	1.08	3.09	15.67
Templeton Group:				
Foreign	13.15	.36	1.07	15.41
Gro Inc	11.36	.40	.48	
Income	10.00	.10	.02	10.20
World	13.94	.44	1.28	14.74
Global I	37.19	1.09	2.20	40.81
Global II	12.22	.32	.43	12.72
Tenneco Group:				
Fund SW	11.33	.05	1.85	9.33
Income	5.06	.48		5.36
PBHG	10.08	.07		12.32
Trend	13.42	.33	3.76	10.72
Thomson McKinnon:				
Global r	10.00			9.92
Grwth r	12.65	.35	g1.92	13.28
Income r	10.27	1.10		10.21
OppFd r	13.14	.03	1.27	12.41
TxExm r	10.45	.70	g .44	11.46
USGovt r	10.41	.90	g .22	10.53
Transatl	17.96		g5.32	22.92
TrFd Bd f	10.00	.42		10.26
TrFd Eqt	11.16	.45	.17	12.46
Trust Portfolios:				
EqP Gr	11.62	.02	g1.33	11.92
EqP Inc	12.31	.78	g1.09	12.52
Fixed In	10.76	1.02	g .16	11.07
Twentieth Century:				
Giftrst r	6.40		1.43	6.75
Growth	16.21	.18	5.08	14.06
Select	29.56	.52	3.46	31.61
Ultra r	8.10	.01		8.92
US Govt	100.40	8.43	g .56	100.93
Vista r	5.22		.65	5.95
Unified Mgmt:				
Growth	21.28	.35	1.60	22.20
Income	12.33	.89		12.65
Mun Gen	8.40	.61	.02	9.27
Mun Ind	8.31	.53		9.33
Mutual	16.01	.59	.17	17.07
United Funds:				
Accuml	8.73	.25	2.18	7.78
Bond Fd	6.09	.56		6.42
Cont Inc	18.16	.75	1.52	19.31
Gold G	5.07	.22	.08	6.83
Govt Sec	5.73	.48	g .51	5.65
High Inc	13.82	1.73	.08	13.95
HiInc 2	5.00	.27		4.95
Income	16.20	.49	2.28	17.03
Intl Gth	6.93	.13	1.62	7.13
Muni Bd	6.95	.54	.69	7.18
Muni Hi	5.00	.41	.02	5.30
Nw Conc	5.59	.07	.26	6.14
Retire S	6.41	.27	.94	6.05
Sci Enrg	9.98	.24	1.52	10.00
Vangrd	6.27	.17	.97	6.26
United Service Funds:				
GBT Fd	15.32	.38		16.68
Growth	7.97	.07		8.82
Income	11.05	.86	.37	10.43
LoCap r	7.33			6.83
NewPr r	.96		.02	1.31
Prspct r	.55			.72
USv Gld	3.60	.29		4.63
USAA Mutl Fd Grp:				
Cornr Fd	10.97	.30	.21	
Gold Fd	6.00	.10		
Growth	15.03	.19	1.59	
Income	11.89	1.28	.06	11.98
Sunblt E	16.57	.07	.35	
TxE HY	12.81	1.07	.09	13.79
TxE IT	11.75	.91		12.35
TxE ST	10.47	.65		10.71
ValleyF r	11.16	1.05		10.67
Value Line Funds:				
Val Line	14.27	.23	1.75	14.68
Aggr Inc	†10.13	1.07		9.69
Convrt	10.97	.51	g .71	11.53
Income	7.09	.48	.91	6.81
Lev Grth	20.90	.34	2.60	22.79
Muni Bd	10.70	.91	g .36	10.81

MUTUAL FUNDS

	NAV 12-31-85	Divs 1986	Cap Dist	NAV 12-31-86
Spl Situa	14.37	.04		15.07
US Govt	13.15	1.32 g	.38	12.77
Van Kampen Merritt:				
High Yld	†14.27	.65 g	.04	14.21
Ins TxFr	16.19	1.24	.11	17.95
TxFr HI	15.00	1.36		16.77
US Govt	16.25	1.49 g	.35	16.57
Vance Exch Funds:				
Capt Ex	75.50	1.61	.32	84.71
Dep Bos	48.67	1.04		54.34
Dvrs Fd	83.47	1.57	.14	89.37
Ex Fd	121.99	2.05		129.74
Ex Bost	108.58	2.14	.26	123.64
Fid Exch	64.73	1.22	.62	72.98
2nd Fid	70.43	1.56	.54	76.28
Van Eck:				
Gold Res	9.25			11.69
Int Inv	9.48	.40	.20	12.04
Wld Trd	9.70	.15	.05	13.41
Vanguard Group:				
Convrt	10.00	.17		9.68
Explor	33.78	.02	3.27	27.66
Explr II	21.02	.04	.47	18.99
Morgan	13.82	.43	2.88	11.50
Naess T	40.67		5.67	35.10
Prmcp	35.57	.56	.73	42.57
QualDv 1	17.94	1.36	3.29	17.07
QualDv 2	8.36	.85		9.52
QualDv 3	23.18	1.64		22.47
Star Fnd	11.45	.86	.71	11.34
TCF Int	30.92	1.03	6.55	38.65
TCF usa	31.17	1.16	6.15	28.68
GNMA	9.94	.99		10.05
HiY Bnd	8.86	1.09		9.20
IG Bond	8.47	.88		8.73
ST Portf	10.55	.89		10.82
US Treas	10.00	.46		10.25
Index Tr	23.00	.89	1.72	24.27
Mun HiY	10.00	.84		10.67
Mun Insr	10.94	.89	.17	11.86
Mun Intr	11.39	.87	.02	12.29
Mun Lng	10.23	.84	.19	11.12
Mun Shrt	15.22	.87	.01	15.44
Cal Ins	10.00	.50		10.51
NY Ins	10.00	.46		9.99
Penn Ins	10.00	.50		10.23
VSPE r	10.46	.44	.05	11.18
VSPGI r	6.34	.21		9.22
VSP HI r	15.31	.13	.80	17.64
VSP Sv r	16.35	.16	.70	17.59
VSP Tc r	11.64	.08	.30	11.93
Welsley	15.31	1.33	.47	16.27
Wellgtn	14.51	.94	.34	15.85
Windsr	14.51	.85	2.59	13.95
Wndsr II	11.00	.43	.52	12.39
WF US	11.69	.28	1.94	10.32
WF Intl	7.79	.07	.80	11.26
Venture Advisers Group:				
Incm PI	11.31	1.55		9.87
MuniPI r	9.94	.89 g	.04	10.20
NY Vent	9.04	.10	g1.68	9.20
RPFBd r	7.98	.75 g	.09	7.96
RPFEq r	19.11	.10	g2.20	19.23
Vik Eqind	11.82	.20		13.37
Wall Street	9.04	.06	3.06	6.96
Wealth M	10.00			8.32
Weiss Peck Greer:				
Tudor r	22.75	.07	g5.48	20.08
WPG Fd	24.42	.68	g6.02	20.64
WPG Gv	†10.00	.67 g	.17	10.33
WPG Gr	†100.00			99.21
W Hum Gr	12.25	.24	.35	13.33
Westrgrd	10.74	.09	.26	9.57
Wood Struthers Winthrop:				
DeVg M				12.80
Neuwth				13.27
Pine StF				12.50
Yes Fund	7.96	.83		7.76

f-previous day quotation. r-redemption charge may apply. g-short term gains included. †-NAV since fund inception. z-quote not available.

OVER-THE-COUNTER

Over-the-counter quotations from the National Association of Securities Dealers through NASDAQ, its automated communications system. The quotes for the National Market Issues are for actual trades. The quotes for the remaining issues are the best bid and best offers. Prices don't include retail markup, markdown or commission. Volume represents shares that changed hands. These figures include only transactions effected by NASDAQ market makers but may include some duplications where NASDAQ market makers traded with each other.

	Sales 100s	High	Low	Last	Net Chg.
—A—					
AA Importing	1717	5	4	4¼	– ⅛
Abingtn SvBk	10134	12¼	8¼	10¾	+ 1⅜
AcaJoe Intrcn	25527	4⅞	1½	2¼	– 2⅜
ACS Indust	1155	4½	3¼	3½	...
AdelphiaCm A	17748	16	14	15¼	+ ¾
Adobe Systm	25276	27¾	11½	25½	+12
Advance Ross	10252	6⅝	5⅛	5¾	+ ⅜
AdvInMn Sof	9285	5¾	1¾	3⅞	– ⅛
AeroSvc Intl	8298	1	½	9-16	+1-16
Aiguebelle R	3730	2¾	1¼	1 5-16	–1 1-16
AJRossLog ut	16031	4¾	2½	2⅝	– 1⅞
AldenElect A	5538	8 3-16	4¾	5⅝	– ⅞
Alex Energy	14684	1 13-16	⅜	¾	– ⅞
All Amer Tel	18980	15½	3½	4⅛	– 5⅝
AllegBev deb	1256	146	67	68½	–61
All Seasons	28038	3⅛	½	2	– ⅛
Allwaste Inc	12455	6	5	6	+ ¾
Aloette Cosm	11945	12	8¾	9½	– 1⅛
AloScher Hlth	1009	20½	10	20	+ 9¾
Ameribanc	2890	22	14	14½	– 1
Amercn Advent	57245	3¼	⅛	⅜	– 2¼
AmAggrg .60a	5120	20	9½	16½	+ 6¾
AmBancrp 10i	3676	31	18⅝	26	+ 7⅜
AmCont'l pf	5458	26¾	23½	25	+ 1½
AmCmty Dev	5132	4¾	¾	1 3-16	–3 3-16
AFncl pfF 1.80	870	17⅞	12⅛	15⅝	+ 3⅜
Am Fncl pf E	157	10¼	8¼	9½	+ 1¼
Am Fncl pf D	2025	10½	8⅜	9⅞	+ 1¼
AmGuarn Fnc	16957	1⅛	9-16	11-16	+ ⅛
AmH Patient	14686	8½	4½	7⅝	+ 1⅝
AmLandCr ut	2582	10½	4¼	8	+ 3¾
Am Learning	7746	10	8	9	– 1
qAm Monitr	2914	7¾	⅜	1 1-32	+7-16
Am Natl Pet	12692	1 7-16	15-32	½	–13-32
Am Pacific Cp	1560	2¼	1⅜	1 15-16	...
AmPassage M	21257	9	1¼	1¾	– 6¾
ARecreatn .12	10861	7½	6⅝	7½	+ ¼
Am W Air deb	1179	103	84½	91	– 8½
Amity Bk .15d	4459	12	7¾	7¾	– 3¾
Ampal pf.20a	756	7¾	4½	5	– 1½
AmVstrFcl pf	3402	25	23⅞	23⅞	– ⅞
Anchor Fncl	76	22½	22	22	...
AppldCirc Tc	34000	1⅝	¼	½	–11-16
Arden ItlKitch	11099	3¾	1⅛	1 11-16	–1 15-16
Artistic Grtg	8771	3¾	2¼	2⅜	– ⅞
Aryt Optronic	15615	13⅜	5¾	6	– 5¾
ASDAR Corp	104944	1 1-16	1-32	3-16	+ ⅛
Asea AB .84d	32135	54⅞	28 11-16	49⅝	+18 15-16
AspenRibb ut	4457	7	3¾	5	+ 1⅙
AssocMtg Inv	7283	3⅜	1⅛	2	+13-16
Astradyne Cm	8029	2¾	1 3-16	1¼	– ¾
AtlantcFn deb	600	104	81½	81½	–22
Automotve Fr	2285	3¾	1	2	– 1
Aztech Intl	13546	3½	⅝	⅝	– ½
—B—					
Badger .72a	403	30	21½	24	...
BcOk pfA1.87h	771	24	3¾	4½	–19½
Banc1 pfA5.50	946	100	76½	84½	+ 7½
BncTex pf1.46	5842	8¼	1¼	1¼	– 6¼
Bank Leumi	291	22	20	21½	+ 1
Bnk of NH .72	3233	32½	22	28	+ 4½
Bk ofSanFran	5340	10½	7¾	8¾	– 1½
BkMidA pf2.50	973	19	7	8¾	– 9¾
Barry Blau	13565	5¾	2¼	2⅞	– 2¾
Base Ten B	1031	12½	6¾	7¼	– 1¾
BaukolNoon 1	657	13	9½	13	+ 3½
Beaman .03	10871	9¾	4¾	4¾	– 1¼
Bear AutoSvc	57346	15½	7⅝	7⅝	– 5⅞
Beverly Svgs	35773	8⅞	6½	7½	+ ⅞
Bioassay Sys	17111	7	⅛	⅛	– 6¼
Bio Logicals	26448	2¼	1	1½	+3-16
Bio-Medic ut	1881	13⅝	5⅜	12¾	+ 6⅝
Biothrpdic ut	18151	25	14	18¾	– 1
BirdInc pf1.85	4915	16½	13	15¼	+ 1½
BKLA Bancrp	785	9½	7	7⅝	– ⅛
Blinder Intl	91212	4	1½	2 23-32	+19-32
Bluefield Supp	3408	21	15¼	21	+ 5¾
Bobbie Brooks	32134	2⅜	⅞	1 5-16	+ ¼
Bonray Corp	850	10	7	8½	+ ¼
Bowater .17d	29095	5⅛	3¾	5	+ ¾
Brajdes Corp	3527	5½	2⅝	5	...
Branford SvB	11169	16¾	10¼	14½	+ 3¼
Braniff Inc	43973	6⅛	3⅞	5¾	...
Bralorne Res	5866	2½	¾	¾	– 1⅝
Brenner .10d	236	8½	7½	8½	+ 1
Brenton Bank	2725	11¼	7½	7½	– ½
Broadvw Fin	14203	5½	1⅞	2⅜	– ¼
BroknHill .42d	111246	12¾	8⅝	11⅝	+ 1⅝
Brougher Ins	10371	16⅝	8¼	9	– 6¾
Buckeye F 10i	18139	16	6¾	13½	+ 6¾
—C—					
Cabot Medcl	40633	2 11-16	¾	1 3-16	–13-16
CabotMed ut	22826	8¾	2⅜	3 9-16	–3 7-16
CabotMed wt	12947	13-16	1-16	5-32	–19-32
qCacheInc ut	5725	14¼	1	8½	+ 1¼
Cade Industrs	103074	1 23-32	¾	27-32	– ⅞
Calif MicDev	8293	6¼	5½	6	...
Calmar .40	33287	31¼	20¾	21¾	+ ¾
CanonInc deb	162	403	282½	339	+34½
Carolina Fst	2449	12¾	11	11¾	– ¼
Cavalier Hms	9639	6½	2½	3¼	– 3⅛
CB Fncl 1.85	961	45½	38½	39	– 4½
CB&T Fncl Cp	41	18	17	18	+ ½
CedarIncF I	85	8	8	8	...
CEM Corp	5559	11¼	8½	8¾	– 1½
CnBkgSys .40g	x10407	24⅜	13⅜	21¾	+ 8⅜
CentBk Svgs	29773	13⅛	11	12¼	– ½
CentJersSL 5i	4598	26	16¾	19	+ 2¼
Central PcMin	37962	27-32	17-32	21-32	+ ⅛
CenTr pf3.50	2993	25	23¾	23¾	– 1¼
Cerner Corp	10575	17¾	14¾	15½	– 1½
Chandler Insr	22475	12¾	4½	4⅞	– 5⅛
ChapEn pf1.20	8405	10⅝	½	½	– 9⅜
Chefs Intl Inc	63956	½	3-32	¼	...
ChemClear	23915	8⅞	5¼	6	...
Circle Fine	10957	3⅞	1⅞	2⅞	– ⅝
CircleIn 1.37d	7359	15¾	12¾	14½	+ ½
CtznSB FSB	1810	8⅛	8	8	...
Citzn SecGrp	3349	5	4¼	4¼	– ½
City Resourcs	23176	3 15-16	1 3-16	3⅝	+2 7-16
Clabir cl.B	1392	6½	5¾	6	– ¼
Clevite Ind ut	22615	12	5¾	6	– 5⅝
CodnellTec ut	90	22	10½	10½	– 4½
ColnlCmcia pf	30998	2 1-16	11-16	1 7-16	+11-16
ColumbnE LP	303	2¼	1¾	2	...
Comet Entrpr	35860	⅝	1-16	7-16	+ ⅜
Commrc Bank	551	9	8	8	- 1
CmcrlProg A	5587	5⅜	1	1½	– 2⅛
CwlthRlTr wt	993	13½	11	13½	+ 2½
Commu Group	7212	4⅞	2½	3⅜	+ ⅞
CmtyNBk ut	520	14	8¾	13¼	+ 4½
Compact VSys	87742	8½	3⅝	4⅜	– 2¾
CmptrHrzn ut	64	15¼	10½	(z)	...
Computr Pwr	834	5	2⅜	2⅜	– 2⅝
CmptrPwr ut	2963	12½	4¾	5¾	– 6¾
CmptrSvc .04d	931	65¾	26½	48¼	+19½
Conn Bancorp	4041	10	9	9½	– ¼
ConsrvSB .25d	2676	13½	10	12	+ 2
Cons Equities	325	5½	5¼	(z)	...
Consol Hydro	50997	15¼	10½	14	...
CnslRestr deb	83	64½	36	54	– 1½
Consumr Plst	5199	8½	8	8½	+ ¼
ContlHealth ut	7	27½	(z)	(z)	...
Convex Cmpt	29868	10½	7½	9⅝	+ 1⅝
CoreSt pfA3.07	4526	29¾	26	26¾	– ⅝
CornerstF .60	3536	30½	22¼	25	+ 2½

OVER-THE-COUNTER

	Sales 100s	High	Low	Last	Net Chg.
Correct Corp	10873	9½	7¼	7½	-1⅝
Costco W deb	481	119¼	83½	97	-4½
County Svgs	19559	9	5¾	6	-3
Cousins Home	87092	7¾	1⅞	3⅛	-2⅝
CR PL Inc	3914	8¼	8	8	-¼
CraftHouse 10i	6030	7½	2	6	+4
Cronus Ind wt	6474	14	3½	3½	-1
CrownAm .40	7146	14½	9¼	10¾	+½
C-TEC B .80	1699	22½	18¼	20	...
Cutco Ind .14	5305	4⅝	2¼	4	+¼
CVD Equip ut	8617	6⅜	1¼	1½	-4⅞
—D—					
Dai ei Inc .14	1093	21⅝	6⅞	15⅝	+8¾
Daily Journal	892	9¼	7	8¾	-½
Data Measur	45	8½	8	8½	+½
DataSwit wt	21118	5⅛	1⅜	1¾	-¼
DensePac Mic	41181	8⅛	1¼	1½	-⅞
Dense-Pac ut	18715	22	2¾	3¼	-2⅛
Depositrs SB	2434	4¼	2¼	2¾	-⅛
DetCdaTun .50	786	13½	13¼	13½	+¼
Develcon Elec	7644	3⅝	2	2⅛	-1 7-16
DNA Plant ut	16079	28½	13	13¾	...
DomngzW 1.10	1709	20	17¼	19½	+2¼
Dominion Mtg	150	5½	4¼	5⅜	+¼
Donegal Grp	6077	9	6	6⅜	-2¼
Doskocil Co	183907	2 5-16	13-16	1	-5-16
DoverReg Bsh	2114	10	8¼	8½	-1
Dresdnr 7.53d	5001	226½	157	210	+26½
DrugSyst .45d	3691	8¼	3½	5	+⅜
DryClean USA	6395	14	12½	14	+1¼
DSP Tech ut	10475	7½	4	4¾	-¼
Duramed Ph	16189	8¾	6	8¾	+2½
Dynapac Inc	96470	3 3-16	1-32	(z)	...
—E—					
EA Engineer	13734	10½	7⅝	7⅝	-2⅜
Eastover Bnk	8012	4¼	2¼	2¼	-⅝
EAViner wt90	51	2⅝	2½	(z)	...
EA Viner Hld	6045	4⅝	3 7-16	3⅝	-¼
EAViner wt89	60	2¾	2½	(z)	...
EDAC Corp	8560	5 25-32	1⅜	2	-3 7-16
EDAC Corp ut	8319	6 1-16	1 7-16	2 1-16	-3 13-16
Elcotel	13276	7⅛	6	6⅜	-⅛
ElecGsTch ut	13252	5¾	2	2	-3¼
ElPollo Asado	41969	8⅝	4⅝	6½	+1⅝
EmplCasl s.60	12866	44½	27¾	32¾	+5
Energy Vent	1176	9	7¼	7½	+¼
Eqtbl of Ia	1268	23⅜	17	22½	+5½
EssxCoGs 2.32	1833	35½	24½	35½	+9½
EvergrnB s.96	4562	31	22⅞	25¾	+2⅞
—F—					
Falconbrg Ltd	56474	18⅝	11⅝	12⅛	-2½
Falstaff Brew	14841	8¾	5⅛	6¾	+½
Family Mutl	25936	10¼	8¾	9⅝	+¾
Farmers Cap	22	125	112	125	+13
FedNatRes Cp	9031	2⅛	1⅛	1⅛	-1
Fidelcr pfBwi	50	33	33	33	...
Financial Ind	781	5¼	3⅝	5¼	+1⅝
FineArtAcq ut	3447	11½	4⅞	5¾	+⅞
FABk&T B.40	1480	15	9	10½	+1
FstBshTex .30	1211	6½	4¾	4¾	-1¾
FstCarInvs .50	1397	32½	25	29½	+4½
FstColo Fncl	3367	10⅜	6	6	-1
FstCmBcs .24	1302	13¾	7½	11¾	+4¼
F Data Mgmt	30796	15¾	4¾	7½	-8½
FstFSvBk Ga	1545	12½	10	11	+1
FFSB Decntr	239	10½	10	10½	...
FFdSL Tex 2k	15931	17½	5½	5½	-9½
FFSL LaGrn	881	12	11½	11¾	...
FstFidel pf 4	3071	80	58	64½	+4½
Fst Fincorp	2069	5½	4¾	4¾	...
F Granite .80a	318	29¼	23½	27	+3½
F Jer pfB2.88	3448	57¾	39¼	43¾	+3
Fst Natl Penn	520	37	29½	30	-6
FPeopB pf1.99	3603	32¼	20½	25¼	+4¼
FstSvBk FSB	714	11	9½	11	...
FstSecFin .36	1683	35⅜	28	32½	-2⅞
Firstsouth FA	3871	41¾	(z)	1	-26
FisonPLC .37d	76141	39	23	31⅜	+6⅛
Fla RockTank	7645	12¾	8	9	-1½
FMI Fincl wt	89922	3⅜	2⅛	2 7-16	-½
FNB Corp .24	2338	19	14	15	-3½
FNB Rochstr	1370	9	8¼	8¼	-¾
FNW Bcp .60	1992	40¾	25½	34	+8½
ForBetrLv .10	372	11½	5	11	+5⅞
Fox Tech Inc	3906	3½	⅞	1	-⅝
Fox Tech ut	1844	4	⅞	1	-¾
Framingham	39033	13⅜	8¾	12½	+3½
Frontier Svg	5962	4¼	2	3¼	+¾
—G—					
GAC Liq 1.75d	5060	5½	3½	4	+½
Gainsco Inc	11228	6¾	5½	5½	-1¼
Gamb AB .03d	21791	17¾	10	13¾	+4¼
Gateway Bncp	5033	11	9	9	-1¾
Gen Sciences	16048	7	4¾	6½	+½
GenTelCal pf5	7690	13⅝	9	13	+3⅝
GnTelCal pf56	8982	12	8½	11¾	+3
GeneseB 1.20a	2558	53½	44½	44½	-2½
Genetic Engnr	12954	1⅜	⅜	½	-½
Glamis Gl	28376	6⅝	3⅞	5¾	+1½
Glaxo Hld .06d	769106	17¾	10⅞	15⅜	+4¼
GoldCoAm ut	20205	17¾	10½	15¾	+3½
Great Am Mtg	10133	17½	15	16	+½
Griffith Con	2195	7⅝	5⅞	7¼	+1¼
Grossman wi	7611	8	6½	7¾	+1
GroveHall SB	14430	11⅛	7¾	10¼	+½
GrubbREIT ut	2087	18¾	15	18	+2¼
GuarntBsh .06	14106	12⅛	8¼	8¼	-1¼
Gulf & Miss	5591	8	7	7	-¾
—H—					
Hadson Cp wt	219	9-16	¼	9-16	+3-16
HalseyDrug ut	11893	14¼	6	7½	-2
HamlOl pf1.95	7400	18¾	15	18	+1
Hammer Tech	349747	9⅞	1-16	7-32	-2 5-32
HarlyvNtl .84	503	38½	32	36	+2
HwthnFncl .80	5311	22	12⅜	18¼	+5⅜
Hlth Images	17962	4¼	3¼	3⅞	+⅝
Hrtg NIS Bk	51655	11¼	9	10⅜	+¾
HinesLmb 14t	983	22½	3½	3¾	-18¾
HiPort Indust	1991	12	5	6¾	+1¾
HllywdPk 1.60	11314	28½	20	26¾	+6¾
Home Natl Cp	498	38	32½	37½	+4
HmOwners pf	3826	50¾	50⅜	50¾	+⅜
HrznAir pf1.20	25290	12¼	7⅜	12¼	+3⅜
Horzn FclSvc	4610	7¼	6½	6⅞	-⅜
HosposblPr ut	2322	17½	6½	10¾	+3¼
Hunter EnvSv	7957	5¾	5¼	5⅜	...
Hygeia Sci	42176	13¼	6	10	-¼
—I—					
ICN Biomed	10039	18½	6	14⅞	+3⅞
IDB Bankhold	130	50	46	49	+3
Imark .25d	962	5	3¼	4	+⅜
ImatronInc ut	6668	11¼	3	5	+⅜
ImatronInc ut	15007	3½	3	3¼	...
IndpBC Mass	2721	28¼	19	23	-5
IndBC Mi .40a	3504	11½	8⅜	8½	-1¾
IndInsGrp 1.40	16793	41½	33¼	35	-⅛
IndSqInc 1.62a	5089	19	15	17¼	+1
IndustTrn Sys	940	5	3¾	3¾	-1¼
IndTrnSys ut	3593	5⅝	4¼	4⅜	-1¼
IndTrnSys wt	93	⅝	⅜	⅝	+⅛
Informix Cp	24807	11⅛	7	9¾	+2⅛
Inmac Corp	18933	14¼	10⅜	13¼	+2¾
InstfmGulf So	3527	8⅜	8¼	8⅜	+⅛
Instrmarium	22977	15½	8½	12⅞	+4⅜
Integrt Barter	1714	7⅜	1⅛	1⅛	-¾
Integ Cmp ut	4301	6⅛	5	6⅛	+1⅛
Interactv Tec	7758	7¼	4⅛	5¼	-1⅝
InteractT ut	7027	8⅝	4½	5⅝	-2¾
Intercare ut	27110	4	2¾	2¾	-⅝
IntrcontlLf .18	8500	18⅛	9	10¼	-⅞
Intl Consumer	6750	3⅜	2	2¼	+¼
Intl Dairy Qn	458	87	40½	81	+3
IntlGene Eng	42600	5	2¾	3¼	-1¾
Intl Lease pf	14994	39¼	27⅛	36¼	+9
Itl ThorBrd ut	9433	5½	¾	¾	-3
InvestSB pf.95	11918	16	11⅞	14¼	+2⅛
Invest SvCp	1349	10¾	10	10⅛	-½
Invstrs Title	165	23	20	20	-2
Irwin Un 1.12	705	53	40	41	-2
Israel In 2.35b	620	24½	19½	24¼	+4¼
—J—K—L—					
Javelin Intl	9069	3 11-16	2 5-16	2⅞	+9-16
JeffersonBc 6i	2745	16¼	11¾	14¾	+3
JeffrsnBk .30d	3473	20¼	13¾	20¼	+6½
JoslynCp 1.44	15364	34¼	28	30¾	-¾

OVER-THE-COUNTER

	Sales 100s	High	Low	Last	Net Chg.
JPM Industries	x90190	5⅜	1¾	5¼	+ 3½
Justice Invest	4332	6⅛	1¼	1⅜	− 3
KC LifeIns .96	9385	36¾	25½	25¾	− 1¼
KyInvestor .28	551	13¾	11¼	12¼	+ 1
KingCity FSB	6	6	5¼	6	+ ½
KingIntl Cp	532	10	7¼	9⅛	+ 1⅞
Kinnardl .10d	1480	6¼	3¼	3½	− ⅛
Kleinert's Inc	3386	11¾	6¾	11	+ 4
Knutson Mtge	8350	10⅝	9	9	− 1
Kurzweil Mus	28577	6⅞	1⅞	1 15-16	− 3 9-16
LafayetteBc 1	569	41	27½	35	+ 3
Lakeland Ind	18980	9⅜	6⅛	7⅞	+ 1⅛
Lakeland SvL	1429	14½	13	14½	+ ½
LamarLife .90	828	92	54½	75	+ 20½
Landsing .60d	4611	9¾	3½	3½	− 6¼
Lndsgl VI .45d	3910	10	5	5	− 5
LaneFncl Inc	8107	13¼	13	13¼	...
Lexington SB	13663	11½	9⅞	11½	+ 1½
Lincoln Svgs	3924	5	1	1⅛	− 1
LouisvG pf7.45	1977	25¼	18¼	24⅞	+ 6⅝
LouisvGs pf5	1158	16¾	11½	15½	+ 3
LBS B SC .42d	2795	20½	16	17½	+ 1

—M—

	Sales 100s	High	Low	Last	Net Chg.
Magellan Pet	14031	4¼	1¾	2 7-16	+ 7-16
Manatron Inc	3441	5⅜	4¼	5⅛	...
MarPetro .63d	2018	13¾	9½	10¼	− 3½
MauryFed SB	645	14	11½	14	+ 2
Maxicare deb	1522	126½	88	92½	− 9
Mayfair Indus	3477	8½	(z)	8⅜	− ⅛
MCI Com deb	1876	92	77½	77½	− 8¼
MCI Com wt	261062	¾	1-16	1-16	− ⅝
McM Corp .24	2071	11½	8	11	+ 2½
McCormk Cap	1118	5¼	5	5¼	+ ¼
MedinetInc wt	1185	1¼	(z)	1-16	− 3-16
Merrill Corp	43340	22	11	14¾	− 3¼
Meyers Parkg	1672	28	19	21	+ 1½
Michael Anth	12684	9½	8¾	9	− ⅜
MichaelJ .36a	1382	11½	8½	8¾	− 1
Microbio Sci	25379	8	2½	5⅛	+ 1⅝
MicroHlth ut	3614	5⅞	4⅝	5	...
Midcon Bank	20942	16¾	9	14	+ 4½
MidABSy .30d	927	14¾	(z)	14¼	...
MidFed SvBk	73	10¼	10	10	− ¼
MidSoInsr .20	15565	23	12¾	13	− 7½
Midway pf1.85	22749	32¾	19	30	+ 10⅜
MineSafAp .52	6895	44	32½	34	− 6
Minl Resr .22d	320773	9 13-16	6 23-32	8¼	+ ⅛
MOSCOM Cp	9980	5	1¼	1½	− 3½
MotoPh pf1.20	3601	13¼	9¼	12	+ 2¾
MSI Electron	1345	3½	2⅛	2¼	...

—N—O—

	Sales 100s	High	Low	Last	Net Chg.
Natl FSI Inc	22907	14⅞	3⅛	3½	− 8⅜
Natl Paragon	10922	3	1⅛	1¼	− 1⅝
Navigator	17734	26¾	17½	17½	− 2
NtwkSec 87wt	2908	3	½	¾	− 1
Newman Com	26706	4⅝	⅞	15-16	− 3 3-16
NeworldBk ut	12065	26⅞	(z)	(z)	...
NooneyRIT 1d	1371	20	15	15¼	− 4¾
NoAm Biologc	65732	3	15-16	1⅜	+ ⅜
NoAm Svgs	5606	12½	5¾	6¼	− ⅜
NorthnTr Bpf	5271	51¾	50¾	51¼	+ ¼
Northland SL	359	15	11	13	+ 2
Nowest Eng	1564	9	3¾	5¼	+ 1
NthwestIll .90	275	22	19	20	+ 1
NwstNatGs pf	615	40½	30½	35¼	+ 4½
Novo Corp ut	1746	3¾	1⅝	1⅞	− ⅞
NowscoWl .28	6466	12⅜	6¾	7⅝	− 4¾
Occupatn Med	12157	3¾	2	2½	+ ¼
OCE-NY	15485	48⅜	29½	43⅛	+ 13⅝
Office Land	29030	7⅛	3⅜	5⅜	+ 2
Offshr Log pf	2652	4¼	1⅛	3¼	+ ¼
OffshLog pfA	4340	2¼	⅝	1½	− ⅛
OKC Limited	738	12⅞	3½	5	− 6⅝
OldKent pf1.82	7936	42½	33¾	34¼	− 1½
OldRep pfE 1	3620	52¾	34	34	− 10¼
OldRep pfF 4	8020	57½	49	49	− 3¼
OlympicItl BT	8328	10¼	8⅜	8½	− 1½
Oncogene Sci	70411	11⅜	3½	3⅝	− 4¾
OrangJ ut	193	8¾	3¼	3¼	− 4¼
Overmyer .40	3211	6¾	2¾	4¾	+ 2
Overseas Inns	613	4½	2¾	3	+ ¼
Ovanic ut wi	542	5	4	5	+ ¼
Oxford Enrgy	10806	9¼	5⅜	8	+ 2¼

—P-Q—

	Sales 100s	High	Low	Last	Net Chg.
Pacif Gold Cp	38180	31-32	⅜	7-16	− 3-16
PacInland Bc	1241	6½	4¾	5½	− 1
PacoPhar wi	4160	8¾	3¼	7¼	+ 1½
P&F Indus ut	2004	10	9½	9¾	...
PaperCp B2.50	5008	32¼	27¼	30½	+ 3¼
PCA Intl	24619	7⅜	1⅛	1 9-16	− 3 13-16
PegasusGl wt	48605	13-16	5-32	25-32	+ 19-32
PeoplesSv NB	14640	13⅛	9⅞	11⅞	+ 1⅝
PeopSv Brktn	13969	8	6¾	7½	+ ½
PetHlcoptr .08	4089	8⅞	6½	7½	− ⅛
PetHelcNv .08	12659	8⅜	6¼	7½	− ¼
PharmknL ut	1297	11¾	4⅜	6	− ½
PhoenixFin ut	15548	3 7-16	13-16	13-16	− 13-16
PHP Health	3278	7	6	6	...
Piezo Elec Pr	295066	13-32	1-16	1-16	− 1-16
Pioneer Amer	1	33	30	33	+ 3
PionFd pf1.88	1511	26¼	22½	22¾	− 2¼
Plains Resour	21343	1¼	½	9-16	− 5-16
Plains pf1.30	5111	8½	3	3⅛	− 3⅞
PNCFpfA 1.80	53	200	137	(z)	...
PNCF pfC1.60	1020	41½	27	34	+ 7
PNCF pfD1.80	2407	41½	27¾	35	+ 7¼
PoeAssoc .32	6400	14½	9	12	+ 2⅞
Precision Res	4015	5¼	1¼	5¼	+ 3½
PremierFn .68	1203	13¾	9½	9¾	− 2¾
Pres Airways	34251	6	2⅜	2⅜	− 2¼
ProMed .32d	6935	5⅝	3⅛	5⅜	+ 2⅛
Provdnt Bcrp	257	27	15¼	22¼	+ 6¼
Psicor Inc	14076	7⅜	4½	5½	− 1¾
Pulawski Svgs	4861	18½	16	18½	+ 2¼
PutnmTr 1.16	1072	70	44	64	+ 20
Pyramid Oil	2823	3	2	2¼	− ¾
Quantech Elec	9941	5¼	1⅞	3½	+ 1½
QuebecStr Rv	3761	4½	2⅜	3¼	+ ⅝

—R—S—T—

	Sales 100s	High	Low	Last	Net Chg.
Rada Electrnc	9259	10⅜	2½	2½	− 6¼
RadaElec bd	21181	4⅛	1⅛	1⅛	− 2¼
Radiant Tech	5139	2⅞	¾	⅞	− 1⅞
Radva Corp	12546	5¼	2½	2¾	− 2½
Railroad SL	2185	12	9¾	10	− ¾
RainierRl .75d	35270	9⅜	7¼	9	+ ⅝
Rauch Indus	3570	6½	3⅛	4¾	+ 1¾
RelLifeIn 1.06	453	25¾	21	22	− ¾
Resdel Indust	539	4½	4¼	4¼	...
Retiremt 1.01d	5779	25¼	22½	23	− 2
RHNB Cp .36a	2774	29½	18	28	+ 9½
Right Mgmt	3874	6⅛	5¼	5½	− ½
Ripley Co Inc	745	9¾	7	9	+ ¾
RobBruce .45	7185	6⅞	3½	3¾	− 3
Rockwood Ntl	8639	4⅛	3	3	− 1⅛
RockMChoc 1	17246	5⅞	2	2¼	− ⅞
Rodime PLC	46118	13¾	4¾	4¾	− 6½
Ross Industrs	2383	4¾	3	3	− 1¾
Rubicon Corp	3594	5	3	3¼	− 1½
Rubicon wt	1577	1⅝	½	½	− ¾
SageAllen .24	934	18	14	15½	+ 1½
SMoncaBk .60	1884	37½	24⅝	37½	+ 12⅞
SantosLtd .09d	49244	3⅞	1 29-32	2⅝	− 15-16
Saxton Industr	5471	2¼	7-16	9-16	− 1½
Saztec Intl	12282	6½	4⅞	6	+ ⅜
Science Accss	1737	2½	2¼	2⅜	− ⅛
SciAccess ut	1981	6⅛	5½	6	+ ¼
SciAccess wt	323	1¼	¾	1⅛	...
Seaboard Svg	3203	11⅛	8¼	8¼	− 2⅞
SeahawkOil 5i	16828	1⅜	½	⅝	− ¾
SeattleTr .60f	4927	63	41	62½	+ 17½
SeismicEnt ut	3558	12⅛	1¾	1¾	− 8⅛
Seneca Foods	3143	18½	12½	14	...
ShanleyOil Gs	38270	27-32	⅛	7-32	− 13-32
Shaw's Super	15673	23½	19	20⅞	+ ⅝
ShoreIn SvBk	9824	10	3½	3¾	− 3¾
Silicon Graph	27390	14½	12	13	+ ½
SilverKing Mn	54049	3¼	1 9-16	2 3-16	+ 1-16
SmmnFN .48a	382	19½	14¾	14¾	− 4¼
SircoIntl Cp	2283	6½	4½	5	+ ½
SJNB Fnc .15f	693	8	5¾	6	− 2
Skyline Chili	2301	5	4½	4⅝	− ⅛
Somerset Grp	1431	17	10½	16¼	+ 4¾
Sonora Gold	13612	6 3-16	3½	5⅛	+ 1⅝
Sound Advice	13501	8¼	4	4⅛	− 3¾
SoAtlantc Fin	12104	11	4¾	7¾	+ 2⅛
Southn Elec	9397	6¾	2	3	− 3

OVER-THE-COUNTER

	Sales 100s	High	Low	Last	Net Chg.
SoFedSL TC	558	9⅝	8½	8¾	– ¼
Sthrn Mineral	5699	7	3	3½	– 3½
SthrnPac Petr	84766	9-32	3-16	7-32	...
Starpointe Sv	12287	14⅛	11¼	12¾	+ 1⅛
StarTech Inc	49501	3½	2¼	2¾	+ ⅛
Stater Bros	26273	22¾	10¾	18¾	+ 6⅝
Status Gm ut	513	8¼	2¾	4¼	+ ⅛
StorageEq wt	5122	3⅝	1½	1½	– 1⅛
Strober Orgn	6725	12⅜	11	11	– 1⅛
StuLnMkt wt	34883	10	3¾	8⅞	+ 4⅝
SuburbBcsh A	4016	8¾	6¼	6⅜	– 2⅛
Sun Equities	952	4½	2	2⅜	– 1⅛
Sun Resorts	14384	8¼	2¾	4⅝	+ 1⅝
SunResrts ut	15318	22¾	7	13¾	+ 6¼
SunRsrts wt	5701	6¾	½	4	+ 3½
Sunrise Fedl	122	14¼	12	14	+ ¼
Syntech pf2.75	4002	28¾	17	22¼	+ 5¼
Systonetics	1961	3⅞	1	1	– 1⅛
TalmnHF wi	19131	8⅜	8⅜	8⅜	...
TaroVit Inds	22382	4½	2¼	2¼	– ⅞
TaylorDev 5i	2816	2⅜	1⅛	1⅛	– ⅞
TCellSci ut	13161	24½	10½	13½	– 9¼
Techdyne Inc	6691	5¼	1⅜	1½	– 3¾
Techn Develp	7534	5¼	1¾	2½	– 2¾
TeecoProp wt	3442	1 5-16	13-16	13-16	–7-16
TelOffsh 1.14d	32269	8¼	4	5	– 1⅞
Telecalc Inc	7345	12¼	3½	5	– 5
TennisLady ut	4819	6⅞	1⅝	1⅝	– 4⅛
Termiflex ut	358	6	5	5	– ½
Terra Mines	33850	2½	1⅛	1⅜	–7-16
TevaPhar .09d	5966	7¼	3⅜	6⅝	+ 3⅛
Texstyrene	25280	17¼	4¼	4¼	– 5⅞
Thermal Indus	9503	10	4¼	5	+ ¾
Therm Procss	10812	6⅛	4⅞	5¼	– ¾
Thunander .12	15768	8⅜	4¾	5¾	+ 1
TideldRlt .19d	1455	5¼	3¾	3¾	– 1½
Tinsley Labs	2135	11½	7¾	8½	– 2¾
Tolland Bank	1929	13	11	12¼	+ ½
Total Ericksn	14801	2 15-16	1⅝	1⅝	– ⅞
TotalHlth Sys	16833	8	4¾	6¼	+ 1
TothAlum Cp	279366	4 5-16	⅞	1⅝	+ ⅝
TrnsFncl Bc	791	23	18	21	+ 1
Tribune Swab	7466	1¾	1⅜	1⅜	– ⅜
TricoProdct 1	2173	50	38	43	– 7
TrioTech Intl	18016	9½	2⅛	2⅜	– 6⅝
TriStarPic ut	8042	10¼	9⅜	9¾	– ½
TriStarPic ut	6773	25	12½	12¾	– 2½
TriStar 93wt	3184	1¼	½	1 1-16	–1-16
Turf Paradise	4146	8½	7	7⅞	+ ⅜
202 Data Sys	10727	4⅝	2¾	3⅛	– ¼

	Sales 100s	High	Low	Last	Net Chg.
–U–V–					
Unifi Inc wt	18362	24	6	17½	+11½
UtdCntsBcp 2	3554	74	48½	54½	+ 4½
UtdFnclBkg 6i	1842	18	13¼	13½	– ¾
Utd HearneR	40872	1 11-16	9-16	¾	– ¾
UnNBCen Jer	1552	44⅜	31	33	+ 1⅝
Utd Savgs A	2855	11¾	9¼	9¼	– ¾
UtdSvgBk Ore	16181	10¼·	6½	10¼	+ 2½
UtdSvgs Mont	3552	9¼	8¼	8¾	...
UtdSvcAdv pf	12963	4	2	2⅝	...
UtdVa pfA2.75	198	65	44½	56	+11½
USMedical En	9764	2¾	½	⅝	– 2⅛
US Rlty Prt	5090	24¾	22¼	22½	– 2
US Sugar	449	59½	52	57	+ 5
UnivMedB ut	127563	3 27-32	2⅛	2 7-16	– ⅜
UnivrslMed ut	2850	25⅛	(z)	11½	– 6¼
UnSec ut	1426	19¼	7½	11	+ 3½
UnivrVolt ut	413	12½	7¼	7½	– ¾
Univrsty Bnk	5365	9½	6	6⅞	– 2⅛
Vacu Dry	8529	10¾	6¾	6¾	– 2½
Valley WstB	41	3	3	3	...
Velcro Ind .92	11055	33	20¾	24¾	– 8¼
Vertex Comm	10571	7⅛	2¼	2⅜	– 4¼
VHC Limited	3934	4¾	2½	4	+ 1⅛
Victoria Creat	19257	11¼	8½	9	– 2
VistaResr .20d	1257	32½	29	32¼	+ 3¼
VoluntBsh .52	911	16	12	13	...
–W-X-Z–					
WacoalCp .36d	418	44	17½	37¾	+20⅛
Waldbm A .05f	17769	49¾	23½	48	+21¾
WalkerTel wt	8472	2⅝	¼	⅜	– 1⅞
Warren Five	16191	11⅛	8¼	10	– 1
Wessex Corp	28339	8½	2⅞	3½	– 2½
Wstn Allenbee	95306	6⅝	⅞	2¼	+1 5-16
WstnNwtn SB	21226	11	7½	10¼	+ 2½
WestTelCm B	796	22½	12¾	12¾	...
WestonRoy A	12751	24	12½	23	+10⅜
Westwood .20b	726	12	7¼	12	+ 3¾
WestwOne deb	256	99¾	95¼	95¾	– 3½
WholeslClb pf	2511	25¼	20½	20½	– 4½
WileyJ B .98	2725	43	30½	33	–10
Wisc RlEstTr	2695	5¼	3¾	4½	+ ¾
WolfFncl Grp	4107	4¼	2	4⅛	+ 1⅛
Worlco DataS	8769	3⅝	⅞	2¾	+ 1⅝
Worldwd Cmp	14231	3⅞	2	3¼	– ⅛
WTD Indust	30893	14⅛	9	12⅛	+ 2⅞
X-RiteInc .06d	22279	12¾	7⅛	12¼	+ 4
ZZZZ Best Co	2029	4¼	3	3⅛	– ⅞
ZZZZ Best wt	11105	13¼	11¼	11¼	– 1⅝

National Market Issues

	Sales 100s	High	Low	Last	Net Chg.
—A—					
Aaron Br Art	4778	6¼	5½	6	...
Aaron Rents	38967	20	14	15¼	− 2
Abrams .24	1881	8¼	5⅛	7½	+ 1¾
ABS Ind .80	8219	22¾	12¾	18	+ 5
Acadmy Ins	205575	10	1 15-16	2⅛	−1-16
AcaJoe	195499	8¼	1⅝	2½	− 5
Acceleratn 5i	61505	16¼	7⅜	7¾	− 5
Acceptnc Ins	14502	10¼	8½	9¼	...
AccurayCp .28	138870	45½	15½	45½	+21
Aceto Cp .14f	9909	21¼	16¾	16¾	− 1⅛
ACMAT Corp	8771	26	10¼	12½	− 7
AcmeSteel Cp	25918	10¾	7⅝	9⅞	...
AC Teleconn	13006	8⅜	3½	3½	− 3⅝
Activision Inc	195980	1¾	15-16	1⅜	− ⅛
ActMedia Inc	60301	32½	23¼	27½	+ 3½
Acuson Corp	45159	13¼	7½	12¾	...
Adac Labs	100332	4⅜	½	1½	+ ¼
Adage Inc	65947	8	1⅞	2⅜	− 4
AdRsl El	41702	21½	14	15¼	...
Adaptec Inc	35870	13¼	9½	11⅛	...
ADC Telecm	x50585	21¾	13	20½	+ 6½
AddWes B .90	7754	42	32½	36¾	+ 3
ADIA Sv s.10	x24774	16¾	10¼	15¼	+ 5
Admac Inc	50998	15¼	2	2⅞	− 8⅝
Advnc Circuit	78519	12¼	2	2⅞	− 6⅛
AdvCptr Tech	9522	6¾	3	4	+ ⅛
AdvGenetc Sci	61388	6½	3⅝	3⅞	− ¾
Adv Magnetc	17855	10¼	6	6¼	...
AdvSemi Mat	36664	14¼	2¼	3	− 6
Adv Telecom	83660	11¼	6¼	9⅞	+ 3½
ADVO Systm	86177	7¾	4⅞	7	...
AEC Inc .32	3891	14¼	9¼	10½	− 2
AegonNV .47f	31332	47¾	37¼	40⅛	− 3¼
AEL Indust A	44797	15¼	10	10¾	− 4
Aequitron Md	91877	8⅜	3½	6⅛	+ 1
AEP Industr	35649	18¼	6½	8	...
Aero Services	43833	4¼	2⅜	3⅛	...
AeroSv pfA.96	1976	15⅜	13	13	...
Aero Syst Inc	40493	2⅝	1⅜	1 9-16	...
AffilBkCp .25h	4694	96¼	6	7	− 9½
AffilBksh .50h	80261	17½	9½	11¼	− 5½
AgencyRAC s	x86666	22⅜	11¾	22¾	+10¾
Agnico E .20	97061	25¼	14⅛	19	+ 3½
AID Corp .32	15638	15¼	10⅞	11½	− 1¼
AIFS Inc	29347	13	7¼	8	...
AIM '84	24830	21	18¼	20	+ 1
AIM '85	7941	20¼	17	18	...
AIM Telephon	18991	4⅝	2⅜	4¼	+1 11-16
AirCargoEq s	x25828	9¼	3½	3⅞	...
AirMdwst .10b	74082	11½	2⅜	2¾	− 7⅜
AirWisc Srvc	120527	15⅜	8½	11¼	− ½
AlabFed SvLn	30651	22½	14¼	18	+ 3¼
AlaskaBc .18d	7510	9	3¼	3⅜	− ⅞
AlaskaMut Bc	47939	15⅝	2⅜	2⅜	−12½
AlaskaNBk 5k	6820	14	2¼	2½	−11
AlaTennR 2.20	6572	40½	27¼	28	−10¼
ALC Commun	52551	10¼	1 5-16	2⅜	− 7⅝
AlcoHealth Sv	135667	25½	15⅜	17⅞	+ 2⅜
AlexBald s1.36	x143261	49	27¾	45	+16½
AlexBrwn .10f	82096	38¼	21½	26½	...
Algorex Corp	14177	8¾	3	3⅞	− 3⅝
Alico Inc .85	3565	98	72	77	− 5
AllAmGour s	x81825	16¼	8⅝	12¾	...
Allegh Bev .40	257077	30½	8¼	8¾	−17
AllghWstE .24	84425	29½	12¾	24⅛	+ ⅜
AllenOrB .24a	6168	41½	25½	31½	− 8½
AllianceF s.88	4370	33	22	23½	...
Alliant Cmptr	25556	20½	15¾	20	...
AlliedBcsh .40	392373	22	11½	11¾	− 9⅛
Alld Cap .72a	x7001	24¾	14¼	23¼	+ 8⅞
Allied Resrch	36695	6⅞	4¾	5⅜	+ ½
Allison's Pl	20147	14⅛	4	4½	...
Alloy Cmpt	10933	10	4½	5½	...
Alpha Micrsys	28949	7¾	4	4⅝	− 1⅝
Alternacare	26317	5⅜	1½	2	− 2¾
Altos Computr	232052	19¼	9¼	11¼	− 1½
Altron Inc	8862	12	5¾	6¼	− 5¼
Ambassdr Fn	15124	7¼	2⅞	3⅜	...
AmCapcity Gr	38628	17¼	9½	10¼	...
Amcast .44	57520	15¾	9¼	12¼	− 1½
Amcore s.27d	x8174	18½	14	14¾	...
Ameribanc In	12851	14	5	8¼	− ⅝
AmBCon s.60a	x2243	23	13½	17	+ 3
ABkrs Ins .50	130637	17¼	11½	14	− ⅛
Amer Barrick	168270	16¾	6⅜	15⅛	+8 7-16
AmBus Phone	6473	8	3¾	4¼	− 3⅜
Amer Carrier	91028	16½	9½	12½	− 1½
AmCitBus Jrn	13836	40¼	17¾	26¼	+ 8½
Amcole Enrg	12703	8⅝	2⅝	3¼	− 2⅞
Am Consum P	4509	9⅞	8¼	9	...
AmContl .10d	41805	15¼	6⅜	11½	+ 1
AmCruise 10i	8038	9¼	2¾	3⅛	...
Amer Ecology	29195	50¼	13¼	14	−13¼
Am Exploratn	15692	4¼	1⅝	2½	− 1⅛
AmFed SL .60	40585	23⅜	6¼	7½	− 8½
AmFiltrn s.72	x5787	22½	15	20⅜	...
Amer First 5k	18000	7¾	2¼	3	− 4
AmFstFed ut	21182	20¼	10¾	12	...
AmFst TaxEx	23281	22¾	19½	21½	...
AmFletcher 1	121026	56	31¼	48¼	+16¾
AmGreetg .66	450253	42	24	26¼	− 6⅜
AmHealth Cos	56434	18¾	13	14¾	...
AmHm Shield	64311	8⅜	3½	5⅞	+ 2⅜
AmIncLife .40	121050	15⅛	9⅝	14½	+ 3⅞
AmIndem 1.12	12746	24⅛	16⅜	18	− 1½
Am Integrity	168551	29⅜	4¾	6½	−16
AmLandCr 5i	14157	8¾	4	7	+ 3
AmLandCr wt	3019	2½	⅜	1⅜	+ 1
AmLocker .28	3599	13¼	10¾	12½	+ 1⅝
Am Magnetics	23535	7¾	3⅞	5¼	− ½
AmerMngmt s	x37555	22½	10⅝	19¼	+ 6¾
Amer Midland	186814	25-32	11-32	½	+1-16
Amer Nursery	9416	7¾	6⅛	6½	...
AmNtlIns 1.20	108342	50¾	30	41	+ 6¼
Am Nuclear	12388	2½	1⅝	2¼	+ ½
APIO	7410	10¼	7	7½	− 1¾
Am Physician	49648	5⅞	2⅜	2 13-16	−3-16
AmReliance G	19021	14	8½	10¾	...
Am Restaurnt	3455	4⅛	1½	1¾	− 1
AmSv NY	189466	25⅛	15	15¾	+ ¾
AmSv NY pfA	43461	25¾	21	21¼	...
AmSBWsh 15i	32820	19	12¼	13¼	...
Am Secur 1.02	35567	40	16¾	31¾	+ 2¾
AmShare Hsp	8567	4½	1⅜	2	− 2½
AmSoftwr .08d	88434	16¾	8½	16⅜	+ 3⅞
Amer Surgery	116036	1¼	7-32	5-16	− ⅛
Am Televsn A	230444	20	14½	16⅜	...
Amertek Inc	38984	5⅝	1 15-16	2⅛	− ⅜
Am Traveller	25388	10	5	5½	...
AmVestor s.20	22767	8⅞	4⅝	6⅜	+ 1⅝
Amwest Airln	331229	13½	7⅜	9¾	− 1
AmwstIns .12	12830	13¾	8½	10	+ 1
AmerWestn 5i	44847	15	6	6½	+ 1⅜
Am Woodmrk	27226	15¾	10	12¾	...
AmeriFirst	98676	10¼	8	9⅛	...
Ameritrst 1.76	128321	49½	35¼	37⅝	+ 2⅛
Ameriwest Fn	13649	23½	15¾	19¾	− 3
Amgen	338131	29⅜	12⅜	22⅛	+ 8⅝
Amistar Corp	16149	10	3½	4¾	− 3¾
AmoskBk s.56	x77810	27½	16⅜	21½	+ 4⅛
AmskgC 1.20a	2992	91	37½	66	+28½
Ampad Cp .40	60940	24¼	11½	22	+ 3½
Analogic Corp	154713	15⅝	9½	10¾	− 4¼
AnalysisT .10d	20609	11½	8¾	11	...
Analysts Intl	40762	9⅝	3¾	9	+ 1¼
Anaren Micrw	57929	14⅛	6⅝	6¾	− 7¼
Anchor Glass	75879	28¼	20⅞	25⅜	...
Andersen Grp	8448	11¾	7½	7½	− 1½
Andover Cntrl	32141	13	6¾	10¼	+ 3
AndvrSB .15d	52779	17½	12⅞	15⅛	...
Andover Togs	21562	17¼	6¼	6⅜	...
Andrew Corp	125881	35¾	13½	16¼	− 2¾
Andros Anlyz	26383	13	6¾	9¼	+ 2⅜
Animed Inc	90965	12½	3⅛	3⅝	− 4⅛
Anitec I s.30	x115098	20¾	12	18¾	+ 5⅝
ApogeeEn s.12	x94226	20¼	7⅝	8½	− 1
Apollo Comptr	890403	20¾	9¼	16⅛	+ 2⅛
Apple Bank	110408	33⅛	16⅜	25¾	+ 8⅝
Apple Comptr	2381573	43⅞	21¾	40½	+18½
Appld Biosyst	209926	55	28	32¼	+ 2¼
Applied Data	8874	6½	2½	3½	− ¾
Applied Matl s	x128174	16⅝	8	9½	...
Applied Solar	4489	14¼	8¼	10¾	+ 2½
Arabian Shld	8707	5½	1¾	3	− 1½
Arbor Drugs	60435	24½	14¾	17¼	...
Archive Corp	91156	12⅝	3¾	5	− 3½
ARC Intl Corp	43344	6 5-16	3	3¼	−3-16
Arden Group	14201	28¾	19¼	26⅝	+ 3⅝

OVER-THE-COUNTER

	Sales 100s	High	Low	Last	Net Chg.
Argonaut Grp	33997	22	17½	21	...
ArgoSyst Inc	75980	24½	15½	18½	−4¼
Aritech Corp	22920	16	10¼	13	...
Ark Restrnt	22198	13¾	3	4¼	−6½
ArmorAll Prd	51728	12½	10¼	10¾	...
ArnoldInd s.40	x6754	45	21¼	40½	+16⅝
ArrowBk s.96	x1523	41	26	34¼	+7¾
Artel Commn	36865	7½	1⅞	2⅛	−4½
Asbestec Ind	13833	19½	8¾	14	...
Ashton Tate	607037	46½	18⅛	44½	+26⅛
AskCmptr Sys	291369	17	9	10½	−2⅝
Aspen Ribbon	31897	3⅜	1¾	2 9-16	+⅝
Assoc BCp .48	9186	24	16	18½	+1¾
AssocComA s	x20440	31	14⅞	26	+10½
AssocComB s	x20996	31	14½	24½	+9¼
Associated Co	2928	9¼	5½	5½	−¾
Assoc Host .12	37736	13½	7⅜	8	−3½
AIRCOA .23d	33424	18¾	7¾	8	...
Astec Industr	18513	13½	10⅜	10½	...
AST Research	310976	31½	10⅝	12⅞	−17⅞
Astrocom Cp	14328	4⅞	1⅞	2	−1⅜
Astro-Med	15489	13¾	6	7¾	−2⅜
Astronics s.20	x4455	10¼	7	8¼	+⅞
Astrosystms	63839	10½	5⅝	9½	+2⅜
A T & E Corp	139965	21	8¼	11½	−2¼
Atcor Inc .48	74779	29¾	11¼	13½	−11¼
AtheyProd s	x12236	13½	9½	10½	+½
AticoFncl .20	8660	19¼	14¼	18	+2¾
ATI Medical	29193	9½	4½	7⅛	...
Atkinson .84	25389	19¾	14	14¾	−4¼
Atlantic FSB	2459	16	9½	10¼	...
AtlntaGs s3.20	x80951	24¼	18⅜	23¾	+5
Atl Amer .24	x33107	15¾	9⅝	9⅞	−1⅝
Atlant Bncp	863	16	12½	16	...
AtlantcFed SL	34958	18¼	9¼	16⅛	+5¼
AtlantFin .15d	131603	19⅛	9¾	10	−½
AtlFin pfA1.05	75669	16¾	11	11⅜	−¼
Atlantc Perm	8109	11¾	6¼	7¾	...
Atl Research	118184	32¼	21	28¼	+4
AtlSoeast Air	207720	15¼	9⅝	10⅜	−⅜
Atwood Ocncs	23554	16	12⅛	12¼	−2½
Austron Inc	7680	3¾	2	2⅛	−1⅝
Autoclave .16	5094	9	4¾	5¾	−1
Autodesk Inc	110556	40¼	21¼	38½	+13¾
Autodie Corp	22179	29	17¾	21	+3¼
Automatd Sys	15567	10½	5	5¾	−4½
Automatix Inc	107086	6 13-16	29-32		−2 27-32
Autotrol Cp 5i	8200	10¼	5¼	5¾	−2
AutoTrol Tec	31012	8½	3¼	4	−¾
Auxton Cmptr	67471	14¼	6⅜	11¼	+3½
Avant Garde	36249	12	2¾	4	−1¾
Avantek Inc	349754	22¾	13⅞	15¼	−3⅞
Avatar Holdg	26546	25½	15⅝	18¾	...
AW Cmptr A	44510	5⅛	2⅜	2⅝	−⅜
Aztec Mfg .08	21779	4⅝	2¾	3⅞	+⅜
—B—					
Baird Corp	25177	10¾	6⅜	8¾	+⅞
BakerFent 1a	14027	50½	42½	43¼	−¾
BalchmB .02d	18702	18½	3⅞	7¾	...
BaldLynA s.20	x1729	32	13⅛	22	...
BaldLyonb .20	48606	28¼	17	21½	...
Baldwin Piano	10092	12¼	10½	12¼	...
Baltek Cp .05	18358	17½	7¼	13	+4¾
BaltmrBc s.30	x100195	24½	14¾	17½	...
BanPonce 1.20	32364	36⅜	24	33¼	+8¾
BancoPop 1.32	15253	39½	23¼	32	+8
BcHawaii 1.60	65335	55¾	26¼	50	+14½
BcMiss s	x4204	25	14¼	21	...
BancOkla .10h	36327	17¼	1½	2¾	−14¼
BancTec Inc	55935	12⅝	5¾	9¼	+1⅞
BancSrv s.16d	x2764	16¼	9½	13	...
BangorHyd 1	39992	15⅝	6⅝	14⅜	+4¼
BankDela 1.32	9328	46	32½	40¼	+6¼
BankEast s.48	x42126	19⅞	8¾	17⅝	+8¼
BkGrant s.52	x2755	34½	23½	30½	...
Bk NEng s1.12	x340125	39½	26⅛	29¾	+3
Bk Stamford	5584	15¼	12¼	14	...
Bankers First	48008	19½	13¾	14	−½
Bankrsnote s	x38703	17	5⅝	10¾	+5⅛
Banking Cntr	89880	12⅞	11¾	12	...
Bks of Ia s.79h	4847	64½	48½	50	−6½
BkMidAm .25f	37981	11⅜	3½	3½	−5⅝
Bknorth 1.28g	3900	41½	28¾	34¾	+5½
BnkSouth s.48	x25113	29	18⅛	22¾	+4¼
BkVermnt .15f	51818	38	10	32	+12⅞
BantaGeor .40	133653	24¾	16¾	18	−2¾

	Sales 100s	High	Low	Last	Net Chg.
Barden Corp 1	2078	31¼	23½	25	−½
Baron DataSy	25529	12¾	7	9¼	−2¼
Barris Industr	266610	28¾	13⅛	15¼	−5⅞
Barristr Info s	x35805	24¼	6¼	7½	−2½
Barry's Jwlry	29069	14¾	9¼	9¼	...
Barton Valve	10969	2½	⅝	⅞	−11-16
Base Ten A	14698	13	6	7¾	−2½
BasicAmM 10i	24190	12	7⅛	9	−1⅜
BasicRes Intl	238239	1 11-16	13-32	⅞	−⅝
BassFurn .80a	48025	50¼	33¼	37¾	−1¼
BattlmntA .10	663702	22¼	10⅞	18½	+6⅛
BaymnFSL s	x15860	44	6¾	15¾	...
BayBks s1.32	x88800	52	31⅛	37½	+6
BaylyCorp .12	28663	18⅛	6	13½	+7½
Bayou Resour	896	5¼	2½	3	−1
BayPacif Hlth	32812	7¼	5⅜	7¼	+1⅝
BayView FSL	119880	16	11⅝	12⅜	...
BeautiCntrl	56844	28	9¾	10¾	...
BeeBa's Crtn	80926	27½	10	14¾	+¾
Begley Co .72	1111	24	16¼	17	+¾
BEI Holding	103778	12½	5⅞	9⅝	+1⅛
Bel Fuse Inc	16435	10½	5¼	8⅛	+2⅛
Bell W Co .07h	12789	8½	3⅞	4¼	−2⅜
Ben & Jerry's	17437	27	12¾	13½	−4½
Bench Craft	36529	20	6¾	15½	+5⅛
Benihana Natl	39333	15¼	5⅛	6	−7¼
Ben Franklin	14175	8	7	7⅝	...
Bercor Inc	27285	14¾	6	6½	−8
Berkley s.24	x191002	40¼	20¾	26¼	+3¼
BerklineCp .50	11803	18¼	12¼	15¾	+2¾
BerkGas s1.14	x2535	22	11¼	18½	+7¼
Berkshir Hath	33210	3250	2220	2820	+390
Best Buy Co s	x112237	32¾	13⅛	23¾	+9¼
Betz Labs 1.40	141543	44¾	32½	40¼	+4¼
BGS Syst Inc	15799	13¾	7	7½	−5
BHA Group	7624	7¾	6	7½	...
Big B Inc	52771	19	10⅞	11⅝	−3⅞
Big Bear 10i	78713	25	9½	20½	+2
Bindley Wstrn	76221	13¼	9⅜	12⅜	+2⅞
Binghmtn SB	40858	21½	12	14	+⅝
BingoKing Co	51482	16½	5	5⅜	−3¼
Bio-Logic Sys	29133	14¾	6¾	8⅜	+⅝
Bio Medicus	38951	10¼	4¼	9⅞	+5¼
Bio-Medic wt	2330	3⅞	2	3 13-16	...
Biogen NV	467624	20⅝	5½	7⅛	−7½
Biomet Inc s	x90603	20¼	10¼	19	+8⅛
Bio Response	169786	10¾	2⅞	3	−4
Biotech Capitl	63156	13¼	3½	9	+5 7-16
Bio-Tech Gen	132548	23½	6¼	9¾	+3
BioTch Rsrch	16376	9¼	5½	5¾	−2¾
BioTech Intl	17924	11⅞	4⅛	4¾	−4¾
Bird Inc	38896	12	6⅞	9⅛	−⅜
Birminghm St	71806	20¼	12⅜	18	+5⅝
Birtcher Corp	8347	6⅛	1⅞	2¼	−2⅜
Bishop Gr 10k	10311	7	1⅝	1⅞	−1⅝
BIW Cbls .07h	11185	11¼	3¼	4	−4⅝
BlackInds .30d	9827	30	12	12¾	−1
Blasius Ind	2777	6⅛	3¼	3½	−¼
Blockbuster	40068	17	5½	11¾	+6⅛
BlockDrg .54g	35368	29¼	20¾	27¼	+6½
BlRidgeBB ut	588	16½	12	12½	−2½
BMJ Fncl s.40	x3868	23	13⅛	17½	...
BNH Bncshr s	3670	36	15½	17	+1½
BoatBcsh 1.84	110209	47½	27½	35⅛	−1½
BobEvans s.28	x89097	23⅛	16⅜	18¼	+1½
Bogert Oil s	x18740	11	5⅜	8⅝	...
Bohemia 3i	40964	18⅞	12½	16¾	+1¾
Bolt Tech .08b	24871	8	1	1¼	−4⅜
Bombay PalR	18445	5½	4	4⅞	...
Bonnvlle Pac	39111	11	5	9	...
Boole Babbge	17452	6⅞	4	5¾	+1⅝
BoontonEl 10k	3821	5⅝	3¾	4⅛	+⅛
Boothe Fcl .30	16421	24¼	17⅛	22¼	+3¼
Boston Accst	7036	8	6¼	6½	...
BostonBncp 1	49191	38¼	29⅛	34½	+2
Boston Digital	12127	8½	2⅞	4⅜	+⅜
BostonFiv s.48	x99624	38¼	20	33½	+12½
Boulevrd .40	14308	18¼	15⅝	16⅜	...
BPI Systms	44024	4⅞	1¼	1⅝	−1½
BR Commun	34938	9½	6¾	7	−⅞
BradleyRET 1	5689	17½	13	16¾	+3¼
Brady A s.20	x16287	25	18½	24¼	+5½
Brae Corportn	29587	12¼	6	6½	−5
BraintreeSv s	x11536	19½	12	12¾	...
BranchCp 1.28	23597	44	34	37	+2¾
Brnd Insultn	108829	14¾	2⅞	12¼	+9⅜

OVER-THE-COUNTER

	Sales 100s	High	Low	Last	Net Chg.
Breakwtr Res	96048	5⅝	3⅜	4 5-16	−1-16
BrencoInc .12	40852	6½	3⅝	5¼	+1⅜
Brendle's Inc	46332	19¼	11	12½	...
Brentwood In	14459	8	4	4⅞	−2⅛
Bridge Comm	113541	18⅛	10⅝	15⅛	−1⅞
Bridgefrd Fd	1270	7¾	4¼	5⅞	+1½
BR Intec	67622	21¼	11	12	−3
Britton Lee	78984	10	3½	4¼	−5⅛
BrdwyFin s.36	x4891	24¼	13⅝	17¼	+2¼
Brookfld Fedl	1870	37⅝	20½	33	...
Brown & Co	17674	13⅜	7⅞	8	−2⅜
Brown Trnsp	18803	15⅞	15⅛	15⅝	...
Bruno'sInc .18	235518	23¾	14¾	15⅛	−2⅜
BT Financl s	x2099	22½	16	16¼	−½
BTR Rlty s.06	x4851	10	4¾	6½	+1⅝
Buehler I .06d	24000	13½	6⅞	6⅞	−5⅛
Buffets Inc s	x15698	22	10¼	15¼	...
Buffton Corp	26036	6¾	1½	4⅜	−15-16
Builders Trns	116953	33½	15¾	16½	−9¾
Bull&Bear Gp	14982	16	8¾	9½	−4¾
Burnhm Sv .24	59196	17¾	13¾	16¾	+1⅞
Burnup Sims	72821	8½	3⅜	3¾	−3⅛
Burr Brown s	x43682	18	10½	11¼	...
Burriitt Int s	x34319	25½	11½	22	+8½
Businessland	523689	12½	3⅝	11¼	+3⅝
BMA Co 1.10	62873	32	23¼	25⅞	−5⅛
ButlerJO s.12	x6930	19	8¼	10½	−4½
ButlerMfg 1.32	18665	33	28¾	29½	−3
ButlerNatl Cp	16323	2⅞	1	1⅛	−15-16
—C—					
C Cor Electrn	14106	8¼	5	7⅞	+1½
Cable TV Ind	6318	3¾	1⅝	2⅛	−⅞
qCache Inc	109125	3¼	⅛	1⅜	+¼
CACI cl.A s	x52310	3 1-16	1⅞	2¼	−⅝
Cadbury 1.07d	259828	29½	18⅝	27¾	+4¾
Cadmus C .32	x9494	33	17⅝	28¾	+11⅛
Cadnetix Cp	175182	12⅜	4⅝	7½	−1⅜
Cal Amplifier	17379	3⅞	½	⅝	−1
Cal Biotech	217734	29¾	11½	12¼	−½
CalFstBk 1.08	2326	40¼	29	32½	...
Calgene Inc	46528	16¼	8	9	...
CalGold Mines	22697	4⅞	1⅞	2 1-16	−1 7-16
Cal Mcrowave	101419	12¾	8¼	9	−2⅞
CalWtrSv 2.80	5039	60½	43¾	53¼	+8
Calny Inc .16	111442	16¼	6⅝	7¼	−7
Calumet .28	16660	10¾	6½	9¼	+1¾
Calumet wt	3017	¾	1-16	1-16	...
Cmbrdg BioSc	89774	14¾	4⅝	5⅜	−1⅝
CanalRand 3t	1485	7¾	4⅛	5⅝	−⅜
Canon Inc .31d	52795	37⅝	26⅛	31⅜	+3¼
Canonie Envir	32679	24¾	13	21¾	...
Canrad Inc	5170	16¾	8⅜	12¼	+4
CCB&T s.80	x3481	50	28	39	...
Cap Fed Sac	37883	16⅛	7¾	9	+¼
CaptolBc .84a	x13773	36⅝	22⅝	27½	+2⅜
CaptlFSL .25d	32945	10¾	5¾	6	−1¾
CaptlWire .10d	31293	15½	9	11	...
CaptlSwst .21d	8571	29¾	17½	28¾	+10
CapTrns s.15d	x1452	12¼	5	10⅛	+4½
CaptainCrab s	93901	1½	½	¾	...
CardnlDis .08g	24545	25¼	13¼	17¼	−2⅛
CareerCom	125075	10 5-16	3¾	7⅛	+3 1-16
Caremark Inc	267007	24⅞	7⅛	22⅝	+8
Carl Karcher	83037	20⅞	13⅝	16⅞	+⅜
Carmike Cine	19055	9¼	7⅝	8	...
Carriage .10d	105200	13¾	6¾	7½	−¼
Carrington L	101527	33	9¼	20½	+7½
Carver Corp	69686	17¾	7¾	10⅜	−⅝
Cascade s.40	x4676	27	15	20	+4¾
Casey'sGnSt s	x84239	17½	8½	14⅝	+5½
CatalystEn s	188219	27⅛	9¾	24⅜	+12¼
CayugSB .07d	8501	14¾	11¼	12½	...
CB&TBsh s.36	x9269	26	17¼	22	+7½
CCA Industrs	89172	4¼	1⅝	2¼	+¼
CCA Ind A	5684	1	7-16	½	...
CCB Fncl 1.12	6441	45	32¾	36½	+3
CCNB Cp .40a	x3521	23⅛	13½	16¾	+2⅞
CCX Netwrk s	x15069	21	11⅛	14¾	+3⅛
CDC Life Sci	25691	13¾	12¼	13⅛	...
CEL Comm	53534	8⅝	1⅞	2⅛	−1 5-16
Cellular Com	69211	22½	13¾	21¼	...
CenCor Inc s	x34576	15¼	10⅛	12	+⅞
Centrbnc .40d	7755	34	23	33½	+9½
CenterrBc 1.80	64406	51¾	27¾	35¾	+1¾
Centocor	206728	45½	9	28½	+6¾
Centrafrm Gr	38840	20¾	13⅛	15⅞	−4⅞
CentBc s1.50g	x20377	63	38¾	51¼	...
CnBshSo s.88	x39612	22	15⅛	18¼	+6⅜
CentCo-op Bk	22434	12¾	7½	11¼	...
CentFidBk .96	56728	36½	24¾	28½	+2⅞
Cent Holding	3788	12	3¾	7¼	+3½
CenJerBc 1.40	11058	45½	32¼	33¾	−1½
Central Pac	21598	9¾	6⅛	6⅜	−¾
CenPenn .10d	9946	22	13	13	−4¼
CenResLf .20	26415	14⅛	7⅝	7¾	−3⅜
CentlSprinkl s	x43477	21	8½	10⅛	−2¾
CnWiscB s.44g	x7585	19	13⅛	15	...
Centuri Inc	66693	2 7-16	1	1 1-16	−⅜
CentComm A	80967	16½	12⅜	15	...
CentPapr .09f	4446	11	8¼	9	−1½
Ceradyne Inc	66535	21¼	10¼	13	−2¼
Cerbrnic A .06	18594	19¼	5⅝	9	+⅝
Cermetek Mic	20965	4¼	¾	1 3-32	−1 21-32
CertfdColl s	x96976	15⅛	8	9⅛	−4⅜
Cetus Corptn	875491	42½	8⅝	18⅝	−7⅞
CF&I Steel	34156	9	3	3½	−3½
CFS Fncl Cp	44673	22¾	13¾	14¾	+⅜
C H Heist Cp	1255	7¼	4	6	+½
Challengr .10d	6467	9	4¾	5½	−3½
Champ Part s	x44287	11	3½	7⅝	+3⅞
Chancellor Cp	32569	15¼	7½	9¼	+¾
Chapmn Enrg	117605	6	⅛	9-32	−2 23-32
Chapparl Res	59412	15-16	7-32	19-32	−7-32
Chargit Inc	47047	12	3-16	13-32	−7 19-32
Charlotte Chs	5038	10	6½	8¼	−1¼
CharShop s.10	x346312	24⅜	10¼	19⅞	+2⅜
Charter Crell	13160	16	10¼	11	...
ChartFSL s5i	x44804	14¾	4⅛	7	+2⅞
Chartwell Grp	31783	29¾	14½	27¾	...
ChathamM .80	9959	31	22	26½	+3½
Chattem .56	9716	28¼	20	22¾	+2¼
Check Techn	13065	10¼	4½	8¼	...
CheckpntSys s	x147078	14¾	8	9½	+1
Chemex Phrm	74322	11	5	6⅝	−⅜
ChemFab	11344	5¼	1½	3¼	−1½
ChemLawn .40	170651	31⅛	14⅜	15¼	−5
Chem Leaman	1779	25½	14½	22⅞	+6⅜
CherokeeGr s	x111324	34½	9¼	23	+13½
Cherry Cp .12	14584	14½	10	12¼	+2¼
ChespkInd 10i	8973	6⅞	2⅜	2⅜	...
ChspkUtl s1.15	x2332	25⅞	14½	24½	+9½
Chicago Dock	5508	23½	21½	21¾	...
Chi Chi's Inc	851605	12⅜	6⅜	6½	−2¾
Chi Pacifc Cp	113018	35¼	21¾	33¼	+10¼
Chief Auto s	x91788	19⅝	8¼	15⅞	+2¼
Child World	52938	20¼	10¼	13¼	+1
ChildDisCtr A	16548	5⅞	1¾	2	−2
Chili's Inc	148043	26	17⅜	23½	+3⅜
Chips	49941	11¾	5	11⅜	...
Chiron Corp	200751	31¾	12⅛	20⅞	+8⅛
Chittendn 1.08	17139	52	27¼	43½	+15¼
Chronar Corp	62367	16	7	11⅝	+1
Church D .21	x74893	15⅜	10¾	12⅞	+½
CIMCO	19997	11¾	9¼	10¼	...
CinciFncl 1.32	39591	79⅞	59¼	62¼	+2½
CinciMicr .15d	131536	14¼	6¾	7½	−4½
Cintas .15d	20849	59¾	42½	48½	+6
Cipher DataP	261619	22¼	9¾	11⅛	−6¼
CipricoInc 10i	19312	9	5⅞	6¼	...
Circadian Inc	70881	14½	5	7	−3⅝
Circle Expr s	x53463	12¼	6¾	10	...
Circon Corp	57529	14¼	5¼	6¼	+¾
CitznBnkg s.96	x13210	51	19	19½	−4⅛
CitizenFid s.80	x82432	37	23⅝	30⅞	+6⅜
CitzFclCp .03d	2717	5	4	4	...
CitFncGr 1.08	102704	46	32⅜	39⅛	+6⅜
CitizensGr .48	649	16	13½	14¼	−¾
CitInCoAm A	512	4½	3⅞	4¼	...
CitizenSv Fncl	3880	33	15	22½	+7
Citizen&So 1	442992	30½	19⅜	24½	+3⅞
CitznUtilA s5i	x53315	31	19¼	24¼	+4¼
CitznUtB s1.08	x14105	30½	19⅛	23¾	+3⅝
CityFedFn .40	428943	18⅛	9¾	11¾	−⅜
CityFed pf2.20	13226	37¾	27¼	33½	+4¾
CityF pfB2.10	25694	32	23¼	25	+¾
CityFd pfC.40	44578	3⅝	2 13-16	3 3-16	+3-16
CityILT ut .25t	353213	6⅞	3 15-16	4⅝	+11-16
CityNatl s.52	x55541	23¼	15½	20½	+4⅝
CitySB Merdn	11676	11	8½	10⅝	...
CitytrBnc 1.12	14504	60	42	51	+8½
CJI Indus	693	26	14¾	16½	...
Clairson Intl	21410	11½	9¾	10⅞	...
Clark Mfg .96	51926	31⅞	22¾	26¼	+½

OVER-THE-COUNTER

	Sales 100s	High	Low	Last	Net Chg.
Classic Corp	10482	4¼	2 5-16	3	− ⅝
Clear Channel	10945	19¾	11⅜	12½	− 4⅜
CleveTrRl 1.40	9958	19¼	11¾	12½	− 4½
Clevite Indus	2883	8¼	5½	6⅛	...
Clevite wt	1662	¾	7-32	¼	...
Clothestime s	x257901	23¾	9½	17	+ 5
CML Group	79498	22¼	8½	16½	+ 5
CNB Bsh s.84	x2199	71	23	25	...
CNL Fncl .22	668	4¼	3	4	+ ⅞
Coast Fedl SL	77416	20⅞	12½	12⅝	− 4⅜
CoastRV Inc	39202	11	5¼	5¾	− 2⅛
Coastal Bncp	27681	35¾	25¾	35⅛	+ 3⅝
Coast SvgLn	417956	19½	11¼	14	...
Coated Sales	296533	10¼	4⅛	8¼	+ 3¾
Cobanco .20h	11069	15	8	11½	+ 2½
Cobb Resourc	10940	3⅜	1 7-16	1⅞	− ⅝
Cobe Lab s	x88917	25¾	14	18¼	+ 2⅛
CocaBtCn .88a	47541	58	26½	32½	− 15¼
CochraneF .12	972	15½	10¾	15½	+ 4½
Codenoll Tech	19070	18	9¼	9¾	− 2¼
CodenollTc wt	6798	5⅜	1½	1⅞	− 1⅝
Coeur d'Aln 2i	55318	22⅞	11⅛	17¼	+ 4
Cogenic Enrg	99802	3¾	3-16	⅞	− 1 11-16
Coherent Inc	130035	18¾	9⅝	11¾	− 5
Collabrt Rsch	80007	10¾	4¼	4¾	...
Collagen Cp s	x90254	19	8¾	10	+ ¾
CollectvFSB s	x106545	16⅜	8½	11¼	+ 2⅜
Collins Indust	22024	6 13-16	2⅝	3	− ⅜
ColnlABk .60g	7509	38½	16½	25½	+ 9
ColBkgrpA .60	28978	28¼	19	23¼	+ 4
ColonGas 1.60	21622	26¾	17⅜	21½	+ 4⅛
ColonialGr A	99638	31	15¼	19¼	...
ColLifAcc 1.12	10595	50¼	28¾	41⅛	+ 5
ColorSyst Tec	102554	29½	9	13½	+ 4⅛
Color Tile Inc	171777	33	16¼	29½	+ 8½
ColoNtBk .37h	131829	22¼	12¾	13	− 9¼
ColmbFedl .20	14815	19	10	14¾	+ 4¼
ColumbFst Fd	33026	22¼	12¾	14½	+ 1¾
ColmbsM s.60	x5710	49	16¾	41⅝	+ 18⅞
Comair Inc	128406	11⅛	6⅝	7⅞	− ⅞
Comarco s	x26782	15¼	6⅛	8¼	− 2
COMB Co s	x513041	38	7⅛	22¼	+ 14⅜
Comcast s	x219286	20⅛	14⅜	17⅛	...
Comcoa Inc	15835	7¼	4 1-16	7	+ 2½
Comerica 2.20	78107	60⅝	34	47½	+ 2⅜
Comdial Corp	71812	3⅛	⅞	2 1-16	− 5-16
Command Air	5063	5⅞	3⅜	5⅛	+ 1¾
ComrcBc .36g	2335	20	14½	18½	...
CmrcBcp A pf	882	26½	19½	24	+ 3½
CmrcBsh s1.08	x16228	42¼	30⅞	34½	+ 3⅛
ComrcUn s.60	x98756	33¼	21¾	27¾	+ 5⅜
CmclBCol .36g	5308	16½	12	12½	− ½
ComrClH s1.20	x29291	65½	47½	61	+ 11¾
CommrclFdl s	x111756	19⅜	11⅛	16¾	+ 5⅛
Comrcl Natl 1	8634	29	12½	13½	− 11½
CmclSecB s.84	704	38¾	32½	37½	...
CmclShrg .56g	49969	15½	10½	13⅛	+ 1⅞
CmwthBc 1.12	4932	39½	26½	33¼	+ 6¼
Cmwlth Mtge	12351	10	8¼	8½	...
Cwth S&L Fla	34600	19¼	9¼	15½	+ 6½
Cmw Hou	124702	20	6⅞	9⅜	− 1¾
CmtyBkS s.70	x6741	21½	14	16¾	...
Comunty Bcsh	13466	17⅞	15	17½	...
Communty SB	45431	18	10¼	11⅜	...
CmtyShrs s.40	x13179	16½	9¼	9¾	− 1¾
ComSyst s.20	x74157	10	4⅝	6	...
COMNET	16937	9⅛	4⅝	8	+ 2½
CompU Card s	x194613	23¾	11¼	14	− ½
CompU Check	2671	7¾	4½	5¾	− ¼
CompuChem	19248	11¾	6¼	6¼	− ¼
Compnt Tech	15844	13	4¼	5⅛	− 2⅝
ComprhCr .36	383548	23¼	10⅛	11¾	− 9⅜
Compresn Lab	108468	15¾	4⅜	5¼	− 4¼
Comptek .16	7879	9¾	5¾	7¼	− 2
Compuscn Inc	40555	3½	1 1-16	1 1-16	− 2 1-16
Computr Auto	31049	4¾	1⅝	3½	+ ⅝
C C T Corp	187083	12¾	2¾	3½	− 3⅜
CmptrData .10	22718	10¼	6⅝	6⅞	− 1⅞
CmptrEnt Sys	34033	10⅛	4	7¾	...
Comptr Horzn	33829	14¼	7⅛	10½	− ⅝
Computr Ident	23418	7½	1¾	2	− 4¾
CmptrLng .12	30183	9½	4¾	5¼	− 2⅝
Computr Mem	175801	3½	1 11-16	2 7-16	+ 1-16
ComputrPrd s	203946	8⅞	3⅝	5	− 2⅞
Cmptr Resrc	5868	3⅛	⅝	¾	− 1
CmptTsk s.05	x89968	18⅝	11¼	11⅞	− ½
Comshare Inc	19397	15½	6⅝	12½	+ 2
Comstock Grp	24083	14⅛	5½	7	− 4½
Comtrex Sys	17571	9¼	2	2⅛	− 3⅛
Concept Devel	58509	8⅝	2	5	+ 1⅜
Concept Inc	97360	15⅝	7⅝	13	+ 5⅛
Concord Cmpt	2236	9	4	7	+ 3
Concurrent C	65374	24¾	11	16¼	...
CongressSt Pr	1756	15	9½	10	− 4½
Congrs Video	22172	8⅛	2	2¼	− 4⅝
CongrsVid wt	2470	2⅞	¼	¼	...
ConiferGr 1.20	86833	58¼	20¾	54½	+ 19½
ConnWtrS 1.52	16552	26	17½	22½	+ 3½
ConsCapIn 3a	84960	26	11	12⅜	− 2½
CnCapIOp Tr	782	18	9	10¾	...
CnCpIOpT wt	67	¼	¼	¼	...
CnCapRl 1.68a	27857	17⅜	2¾	3½	− 8¾
ConsCapST 3a	72452	26	7¾	8¼	− 4¼
Consol Fibres	6587	9	5⅛	5⅜	− 1¾
ConsPapr 1.60	63273	59½	35¼	51½	− 2
ConslProd .08	8707	5⅜	2⅜	3⅛	− ⅜
ConsTmL .15d	x2007	35	23¼	28½	+ 3½
CnstlBc s.92	x14509	33	19⅜	22¼	+ 1¾
Consul Restrt	39750	5¾	1⅝	1¾	− ¾
ConsmrFin .07	5264	6⅛	3¾	4⅝	− ⅛
ConsumW s.88	x13999	22½	15⅞	16¾	− ⅜
ContlBcrp 2.04	49231	69	31½	56¼	+ 11¼
ContlFedSL 5k	3024	16	4¼	4½	− 8
CntlGnIns s.10	x5160	8⅞	5¼	5¾	+ ½
ContlHlth Affil	37995	13⅜	7¾	8	− 2⅜
Cont'l MdSys	22466	8¼	6⅞	7½	...
Continum .04h	34962	15	4¾	9	− 4½
Control Laser	45356	13½	4½	5	− 2⅛
ContrlResIn s	x68798	21½	5	18¾	...
ConvFdM 10i	x18749	21¼	7¼	14	+ 7⅝
Convergnt Tec	1217128	14	4⅛	6	− 5⅞
Conversion In	117315	7 11-16	2 9-16	3⅝	...
Cooper Devlp	356808	3⅝	1	1 7-16	− ⅛
Cooper Laser	215179	6⅛	2 1-16	2⅜	− 2 5-16
Co-opBk s.20d	x63346	19¼	11¼	16½	+ 4½
CoorsCo B .50	372840	31⅝	16	24	+ 2⅜
Copytele Inc	144225	20	5½	11½	− 3½
Corcom Inc	9710	8½	4⅜	4¾	− 1¾
Cordis Corprn	424010	19¼	8¼	16⅜	+ 5⅛
CoreStFin 1.36	228099	44⅛	31⅜	35¾	+ 3⅞
Corvus Systm	587486	4 1-16	½	15-16	− 13-16
Cosmetic Frg	23260	9¼	5½	6	...
Cosmo Comm	35464	5⅝	2¾	3⅞	− ⅛
Costar Corp	2891	10⅞	5½	9¼	+ 3¾
Costco Whol	330302	19½	8½	13⅜	+ 1⅝
CottonSLf .24	4853	8¾	5½	5¾	− 1¼
Courier s.40	x9379	20¾	16⅝	20	+ 16⅝
Courier Dspch	13310	5½	3⅞	5½	+ ½
CousinsPr s.32	x33081	21⅝	13⅛	19½	+ 6¼
Covingtn Tech	78172	2⅛	⅝	11-16	+ 1-16
CPI Corp .28	102596	38	14¾	34⅜	+ 8⅞
CPL RE .79d	9228	10¾	8½	9	− ⅜
C P T Corp	169064	7	2¾	3¼	− 2⅞
CrackerBrl .14	32236	22½	13¼	18¼	+ 4
Craftmtc Cntr	56657	13¾	5⅞	5⅞	...
Cramer Inc	3843	7	3¼	4¼	− 1⅝
Crawford .52	21902	26¼	18	25¼	− 3¾
Crazy Eddie s	x642815	21⅝	8¾	11½	+ 2¼
CriterionG A	9263	18½	16¼	16¼	...
Cronus Indust	136971	31⅛	12⅝	18¼	+ ⅝
CrossLnd .40	416577	24¾	12⅜	15⅞	+ 2
CrssL pfA 1.81	96126	28⅜	21½	22	...
CrossTrk .60h	271570	28	12⅞	16⅝	− 6⅛
Crown Ander	18709	11	6⅝	8⅛	+ ⅞
Crown Auto	5135	4¼	3	3¼	− ¼
Crown Books	53444	19¾	9⅛	14½	+ ½
C S P Incorp	51158	14⅝	5	5¾	− 6
C-TEC s.92	x4111	24	18	19	...
Cullen Frst .20	47656	24⅝	12⅛	13	− 8⅛
Cullum .50	92680	26½	17⅜	23¾	+ 3¾
Culp Inc .08	23364	12	8	11½	+ 3½
CVBFnc s10i	x673	21¼	9½	20	...
Cybertek Cmp	48679	12½	4¾	9¾	+ 5
Cycare Syst s	x37578	17⅜	7⅛	7⅜	− 3½
Cyprus Minrl	236773	24⅞	14⅜	16¼	− ⅜
Cyprs Semicn	224757	10½	6½	7⅛	...
Cyprss Savgs	7577	10½	4	4¼	− 3⅜
Cyprss Svg wt	2791	3	½	½	− 1¾
Cytogen Corp	66535	12⅞	6	6¾	...

OVER-THE-COUNTER

—D—

	Sales 100s	High	Low	Last	Net Chg.
D&N SvgBk	65159	19¼	11⅝	11⅝	− ⅝
Dahlberg Inc	35641	14¾	6½	9½	− 4¾
DairyMartA s	x18817	15	9	11	− 2⅞
DairyMartB s	x11966	15⅜	9½	10½	− 3⅜
Daisy Systms	742486	29½	7⅝	8⅜	−21⅛
Damon Biotch	154188	10½	2⅞	4¾	− 3⅜
Danners Inc	4772	21	8	8	− 8
DArtGrp A .13	14108	178	86	149	+32
Data Archtect	30516	12½	7	8¼	− 1¼
Data Card .24	108411	27½	10⅜	11	− 9
Datacopy Corp	76485	10⅛	4½	5⅞	− 1⅜
Data I-0	93647	13⅝	8⅛	8⅝	− 2
Datametrics	1313	3⅜	2⅜	2½	...
DataSwtch Cp	104352	8⅝	4⅞	5⅜	− ⅞
Datamarn Intl	2785	10¼	6	9½	+ 3¼
Datascope s	x31383	25	17	21½	+ 3½
Datasth Cmpt	14031	3⅞	1⅞	2¾	−5-16
Data Translat	16633	19	9¾	17⅝	+ 6⅝
Datavision	73661	3⅞	1	2¾	+ 1⅜
Datron Systm	19848	8⅜	4¾	7	+ ¾
Datum Inc	36022	7¼	4¼	4¼	− 1¼
Dauphin 1.20	33230	39¼	28¼	29¼	+ 1
DavisW s.19f	x12465	18½	7½	15¼	+7 23-256
Dawsn Geoph	10873	6	3⅞	4⅝	+ ¼
Daxor Corp	54342	7⅜	4½	5½	− ¼
DaysInn Corp	x185078	14½	6⅜	10⅛	+ 3¼
D B A Sys Inc	57474	17½	10¾	17	+ 2
DDI Pharm	29828	4½	2⅜	2⅞	+ ⅜
Deb Shops .30	73376	36¼	20	29	+ 6¼
Decom Systm	13399	4	1¾	3 1-16	+1 5-16
DecomSyst wt	3459	1	1-16	⅛	+1-16
DecorCorp 5i	7386	14	7¾	8¼	− 3¼
Defiance Prec	48300	12¼	6	6¼	− 4⅛
Dekalb B .36h	137637	27¼	14¾	17½	− 7
DelawarO .01d	735	15¼	14	14¾	...
Delchamps .28	84582	27¾	12⅝	21¾	+ 4⅜
DeltaData sys	10838	1¼	⅜	⅜	− ¼
DeltaUS	14287	1¾	⅜	⅝	−3-16
DeltaNGs 1.04	8439	14⅝	10¼	13¼	+ 2⅞
Deltak Corptn	3377	5⅝	4¼	5¼	+ ⅜
DentoMed Ind	93426	9¼	1⅝	3	− 5¾
D E P Corp s	x33670	15	7¾	10⅛	+ 2
DepositG 1.32	22511	42¼	30¼	35	+ 4½
Derby SvBk	33395	24	17½	19¾	+ ¾
Designhouse	6242	6¼	2	2¼	− 2¾
Dest Corp	87819	6⅝	2½	2⅝	− 1¼
Detector Elect	11649	8⅜	3¾	4	− 1⅛
DeTomaso Ind	15544	23½	10¼	11½	− 2¾
Detrex Cp 1.20	4506	45¾	34½	38½	+ 4
Devon Group	29647	18¼	13	16½	...
DeVry Inc	17199	10¾	8¼	9½	+ 1¼
Dewey Electr	4758	5	2	3¾	+ ¾
DH Technolgy	38606	6½	2¾	4⅝	+ 1⅝
Diagnostic	49584	16½	5¼	6⅛	+ ½
Diagnstc Prod	43240	27¼	14¾	26¾	+11½
Dial REIT	6849	19¾	18	19¼	...
DiamCryst .80	15140	37½	30	34½	+ 3¼
Diasonics Inc	633178	5 1-16	2⅝	3 1-16	− 1¼
Dibrell Br .88	23221	29	23	25	− ¼
Diceon Elect	44051	27¼	12	24¼	+ 4¾
DickeyJn .12	3878	18	11	13½	− ½
Dicomed Corp	39899	10¾	1¾	2¼	− 2⅜
Digilog	13759	8	3⅝	7⅛	+ 3⅛
DigitlComm s	x267375	32¼	15½	27	+ ¾
Digitech Inc	248952	8¾	21-32	5¾	+5 3-32
DimeSB ofNY	241718	18½	13¾	18⅛	...
DimeSBk .10d	45990	13½	12½	13¼	...
DinnerBell .40	6807	17¼	11¾	16½	+ 4¼
Dionex Corp	x41529	29¼	12⅜	26¼	+ 5
Dionics Inc	4881	5	2½	2⅝	− 2
Distrib Logic	25366	8½	4¼	4⅝	− 2
DivrsHum Rs	8663	8⅜	4¼	4¼	− 3¼
DixieYarn Inc	12227	19	17½	18	...
Dixon Ticondr	10170	15¼	10¼	13½	− 1
DNA Plant Tc	140422	21¼	10⅝	11¼	+ ⅛
DOC Optics	10948	11	7⅜	9	+ 1½
Dollar Gen .20	160662	24⅛	12⅛	13⅛	− 7⅛
DomBksh s.72	x92965	25⅜	17⅜	19⅛	+ 1½
DomnFedSL s	x2260	23	15½	16¼	...
Donovan	16	33½	32	32	− ⅜
DorchHug .32	17526	28¼	12¼	22½	+ 7¾
Dotronix Inc	27417	7⅝	1 15-16	5¾	+3 7-16
Dougl Lom .50	14350	26¾	16¼	19¼	+ 2⅝
DowB Hickam	31549	19½	10¼	14	+ 2¾

	Sales 100s	High	Low	Last	Net Chg.
DranetzTc .24	8793	15½	8½	9	− 1½
Dresher s.13	x35674	14¾	6½	11⅛	+ 1⅛
DressBarn s	x133022	28	12¾	22⅜	+ 9⅛
Drew Ind	95611	15-16	13-32	7-16	−5-16
DrexlerTech s	x102604	26¼	8½	14	+ 3½
Dreyers Grnd	148516	32¼	13½	15½	− 6
DSC Commun	1061193	12¾	5⅜	5¾	− 3¼
DST Systm .20	13721	26¼	10¾	26	+14¾
Dual Lite .08d	21166	14⅜	6⅞	13⅜	+ 6¼
Dumagmi Min	13471	9	2¾	7¾	+4 13-16
DunkDonut .28	92250	38	22⅜	30¼	+ 7¼
Duquesn Sys s	x43086	35½	14⅜	31¾	+17⅜
DurakonInd s	x71075	18	9⅞	11⅝	− 1⅝
Durham 1.36	15270	50½	40¼	41½	+ 1
Duriron Co .56	37950	14¾	9⅜	11⅞	− 1⅛
DurrFillm .16	65433	17⅛	10¾	11⅛	− 1¼
Dyatron Corp	17398	8⅜	3	5⅛	+ ⅝
Dycom Ind s	x17381	18	4⅞	11¼	+ 4¾
DynamicRs s	x10526	10¼	6½	9½	+ 3⅛
Dynascan Cp	53385	14⅜	3½	13¼	+ 6¼
Dynatech Cp	156837	36¾	18¼	30¾	− 3¾

—E—

	Sales 100s	High	Low	Last	Net Chg.
E&B Marine	27749	16¾	6¾	7	− 5
Eagle Bancsh	7860	19	14½	16	...
Eagle Telphnc	112495	3 1-16	1 5-16	1 13-16	+7-16
EagleTelph wt	92	9¼	¾	1	+ ¼
Eastern Bcp	53321	26⅞	21	23½	+ 7
East Weymth	x3502	19	7	9⅞	...
Eastover 2	2495	19½	16	18⅜	− 2½
Eaton Fncl s	x42393	21⅛	12½	13¼	− 1⅜
EatonVn s.28	x16548	29¾	16	21½	+ ⅞
ECI Telecom	26483	13½	1⅜	2¼	− 6¼
Edgecomb Cp	16753	6⅛	5	5⅛	...
Edison Contrl	2173	10	8	9	...
EdisnSlt 1.40g	948	26½	15¾	22	+ 5½
Ehrlich Bober	11755	9¾	9¼	9⅜	...
EIL Instmnts	11166	12	6½	8½	+ 1¾
EIP Micro .12	4570	9¼	5¾	6½	− 1¾
El Chico Corp	39500	8¼	3⅜	3⅝	− 4¼
Elan	74863	18⅜	7½	14¼	+ 1¾
ElbitCm .75d	21680	10⅜	6¼	7½	− 1⅛
Elco Indus .84	17155	26½	16½	16¾	− 3⅝
Eldec Corp	30202	15	9¼	10⅛	...
EldrBeer .22g	2919	26	19½	20	− 2
Eldorado Bcp	5333	9⅜	7	8⅛	+ 1¼
Eldorado Mtr	22855	12½	3⅜	5½	...
Electro Biolgy	93665	10⅜	5½	5¾	− 2⅞
Electro Cathet	106946	25	3	4½	−13⅝
Electro Nucln	98673	19⅞	9¼	11¼	− 7⅜
ElctmgtcSci s	x39416	18⅝	11⅞	15	+ 1⅜
ElMissiles Cm	18367	5½	1⅝	1⅞	− ¾
ElTelcmA .08	8798	15¾	7¾	9½	+ 1
Electro Rent	70361	19⅝	10⅜	14	− 3⅞
Electro Scienc	55174	18¾	8½	10¼	− 5⅜
ElectrSen .10d	4400	10¼	4⅝	5½	+ ½
E Town 2.80	3477	51½	41¼	47	+ 3
ElPasoEl 1.52	295958	19¾	12¾	18¾	+ 3¼
Elron Electrn	32463	9	4⅝	5⅛	− 2⅞
EMC Corp	89584	20¾	11	17	...
EMC Insr .48	58163	15⅛	9	10	− ½
Empi Incorp	7235	9⅞	4	4½	− 3¾
EMS System	26704	3⅝	1⅞	2 11-16	+1-16
Emulex Corp	271420	12⅜	5⅜	8¼	− 3¼
Encore Cmptr	179131	3	1 1-16	1⅝	− 1
Endata Inc	72273	8⅛	4	6¾	+ 2½
Endotronics s	x46269	35½	12¼	20¾	...
Energas 1	28674	17¾	13¼	14⅞	− 1⅛
Energy Convr	74462	30	9	12½	−13¾
Energy Factr	50861	23	8⅜	13	− 7⅞
EnrgyNo 1.24g	7563	23¾	17	19	+ 1¼
Enginr Measr	23852	12¾	7¾	8½	+ ⅜
EnginrSuppt s	x24265	15¾	8⅝	15	+ 5⅞
Engraph s.17	x9825	14	9½	10	− ⅜
Enseco Inc	54728	21¾	12¼	15	+ 2½
EntrtnPub .10	37624	18¾	12¼	15½	− 1½
Entre Comput	81882	9¾	2⅛	2 9-16	−4 5-16
Envirn Treat	125504	32¾	18½	27¾	− ⅜
EnvironTect s	7734	7⅞	3¾	4⅞	+ ⅛
Envirodyn Ind	108713	25¼	8⅛	22⅛	+14
EnzoBiochm s	x101336	15⅝	8⅜	8¾	− 1⅛
Epsco Inc	10847	12¼	8¼	9⅝	+ ¾
Epsilon Data	54996	14	4⅛	8⅞	− 2⅛
Equatorl Com	186888	17⅝	2⅜	3½	− 4⅞
Equion Corp	21969	8⅞	4⅝	5¾	− 1⅞
EqtblBcp s.68	x29369	23⅝	16	23	+ 2¾

	Sales 100s	High	Low	Last	Net Chg.
EqtIowaB 1.28	x34561	23¾	16	23	...
Equity Oil 5i	35826	7	4¼	4⅝	− 2⅛
Ericsson 1.05d	166429	42¼	27⅝	31⅛	+ 1½
Erie lackawn	3331	109	90	108½	+18½
ERLY Ind 10i	28191	17½	5¾	11¼	+ 1
Escalade Inc	7076	10½	3⅞	8¾	+ 4¼
Essex Corptn	4424	5	3¼	4	+ ⅝
Evans Inc .04	50510	18¼	9¾	13	− 3
Evans Suthrld	71810	28¾	13⅛	25¼	+ 7
Evergood Prd	9650	4	2¼	2¾	− ½
Exar Corp	16417	18½	8¼	10	− 3½
ExchgIntl s	x23362	14⅜	6½	9¾	+ 1⅜
Excel Bncp	58103	15⅛	10⅝	12⅞	...
Exovir Inc	68960	22	10⅜	12⅜	− 1¾
ExpeditrIntl s	x55933	14⅛	7¾	13	+ 4⅝
Expsaic s.18d	x26207	18½	12	13½	+ ½
E-Z-EM Inc s	x27395	18⅞	9½	10½	− 2½
—F—					
F&MNatl .58f	4305	34½	23½	27½	+ 3¼
FabrcWhol .12	39056	13¼	6	7⅞	− ¼
Fairfield Noble	17647	19½	10½	13	+ 2¼
Fairhaven SB	18179	10⅛	7⅝	9¼	...
FairLanes .16	35519	9½	5⅜	8⅜	+ 2¾
FamilyStkH s	x29369	13¾	4⅝	11	...
Famous Rest	62961	2⅞	1⅜	2⅛	+ ½
F&M FnclSv s	x678	21⅝	16⅝	17¾	...
Faraday Labs	2587	4⅛	2¼	4	+ 1
Faradyne El s	20419	8	2¾	3	−11
Farm Hm .50d	158857	26	19	22	− 1¾
Farm Fresh	94327	19¼	11⅜	14¼	+ 2⅞
FarmHsFd 5k	53227	5⅝	4⅜	4⅝	− ¾
FarmerBros 1	1958	54¼	42	51	+ 3½
FarmersGr s1	x361646	46¼	32⅝	38¾	+ 4⅝
Farragut Mtg	7136	6⅞	5¾	6½	...
FarrCo s.24	x8859	13¼	10	9½	− 1⅝
F D P Corp	21501	8	3½	3¾	− 3¾
FedScrWk .40	3930	15½	9⅜	9⅜	− 1⅜
FedGuarnt .48	4902	19	13	17¾	+ 4¾
Federatd Grp	186155	20	6¼	6⅝	−12⅜
Ferrofluidics	123104	5⅛	2½	3	− 1
FHP Corp	43184	11¾	7¾	9⅝	...
FFB Corp	132145	17⅜	13⅜	14	...
Fibronics Intl	56056	17	4¾	6⅜	−10⅛
Fidelcor 1.40	140601	47½	31⅞	35¾	+ 3⅞
Fidel A pf3.25	3092	75	51¾	57	+ 5⅜
FidelB pf2.15	26166	37¼	29½	30¾	...
FidFed SL s	x29137	17	9⅝	11⅝	+ 1⅛
FidFSL Tenn	13117	19¼	15½	16⅝	...
5th3rdbc s1.44	21872	65	42½	45½	+ 2⅝
FiggieIntA .88	62116	54½	37¼	54	...
FiggieIntB .76	25929	58¾	22½	54½	+14¼
Filtertek s.44	x27091	20½	8½	16¼	+ 6½
FinalcoGr .20	8635	4⅝	2½	3	− 1
FnclNews Net	512087	22⅛	7 1-16	9⅞	+ 2½
FnclSec SvLn	10825	5⅞	¾	1¼	− 4⅝
FnclTrCp 1.60	1500	48	37¼	44½	+ 5½
Fingermatrx	126417	10½	5½	6⅜	− 2⅝
Finnigan Corp	99610	21½	8½	10¼	− 7⅞
FstAlabB s.64	x181566	26½	16¼	21⅝	+ 5⅜
Fst Albany	21396	13¾	6¾	7⅞	+ ⅜
Fst Amarillo	4413	11¼	7	8¾	− 1
Fst of Am 1.60	62565	52¾	41	42	− 1
FstofAm pf.99	749	30⅝	24¼	24⅜	− ⅞
F of A pfD7.20	805	94½	75	87	+10
FABkT A .40g	93089	16	9⅜	10⅛	+ ⅝
1stAmBk Svg	112738	11⅜	9⅞	9⅞	...
FstAmFdSL s	x9592	22½	10¾	14¼	+ 2⅝
FstAmFncl 1	17917	56	25½	48½	+13
FstAmSv .05d	64568	26	15¾	16½	...
FstAmTenn 1	124420	33¾	23¼	25¾	+ 2⅝
FstBcpOhio s	x14166	38½	16½	28¼	...
FstBcSec s.60	x2234	38½	19	22½	...
Fstbk III s.64	x3548	25½	14	16½	...
FstCapitl s.80	x5077	32¼	23	26½	+ 2¾
FstCitBsh A	1499	38½	26½	29½	...
FstCitBsh B	308	50	35	45	...
FsColBsA s.40	x26897	22⅜	11⅝	19⅝	+ 7
FstColum Fcl	8209	30	13	16½	− 4¼
FstComrc Bcp	5162	6¾	4½	5⅛	+ ⅛
FstComrc 1.20	42913	25½	13⅞	14¾	− 7¼
FstComrcl .72	7389	30½	18½	21½	+ 2¾
FsCmtyB s.80	1958	50	25½	27	...
FstCntRE .41h	25603	8½	2¼	2 15-16	−3 1-16
Fst Eastn 1.50	8128	66¼	43¼	51	+ 4½
FstEmpir 1.40	10486	99	69¼	77	+ 8
FstExecutiv s	x966886	23⅛	14½	15	− ⅜
FstE pfE2.33d	27068	26⅝	22⅛	23	− 1⅛
FstE pfF2.87	27570	28⅝	25½	26¼	+ ⅜
FstE pfG1.56	151538	28⅜	19⅞	20⅜	...
Fst Exec wt	31565	8½	4½	5⅜	+ ⅞
Fst Family	42189	21	3	4	...
First Farwest	2080	17¼	13½	14¾	+ 1¼
FstF Alabama	409	11¼	10¼	11⅛	...
FstFBkNH .40	8717	49½	17½	41½	+23¾
FstFdCaro .32	362	14	9	11	...
FF Caro pfA	9136	16½	11¾	13	+ 1¼
FFSB Mont s	x3355	10⅜	6⅝	9½	− 1½
FstFdSv Ark	76643	10¾	4½	4⅝	...
FFSL Chatt	2790	16¾	15¼	16¾	...
FFSL Co .36g	3377	12¾	9¼	10	...
FFSL Ch .32	x28493	19	11⅝	17⅛	+ 5
FFSL FM s.40	x44108	34¾	16⅞	28¾	+11⅛
FFSL Ka .18d	31613	27	15⅝	18¼	+ ¾
FFdSv Mad s	x22768	19¾	8⅜	14½	+ 5⅞
FFdSLSC .10f	60648	16⅝	8⅝	9½	− ⅛
Fst Fed Mich	267654	30	16⅛	22⅞	+ 6¾
FstFSvBCal s	x45739	24	15½	20¾	+ 4¼
FFSL Brk .16	10477	22¾	12¾	21	+ 7¾
FFSL Panma	4954	8⅝	8⅛	8⅝	...
FstFncB s1.60	x1282	49	31⅞	47½	+14¾
FstFinclCp .40	30496	22	15¼	17¼	− ¼
FstFncl Mngt	47545	27¾	17¼	23¾	+ 2½
FstFlaBks .44	52528	37⅜	22	29⅞	− 2⅛
FHawaii s.90	x29897	27½	16⅜	20¾	+ 3⅝
FstHmFd .05d	10644	13¼	10⅞	12⅞	...
FstIllinois s.44	x80219	17¾	9¼	16½	+ 2⅛
FstIndiana Cp	x15659	25¾	15½	16¾	− ⅜
FstICAlsk 10k	6568	12¾	2½	3¾	− 9
F Intst Iowa	61234	3¾	2¼	2¾	+ ⅜
FstIntWis s.54	x15649	21¾	14¼	15	− 1
FstJersNt 1.80	58510	57⅜	29¾	43¾	+ 3⅞
FstKyNtl s.84	x32562	31	20⅝	24½	+ 3⅛
Fst Liberty F	11730	24½	16½	18¾	+ ¼
1stMdBc s.88	36985	38½	24¾	27⅞	+ ¾
FMichBk .60g	19454	23⅜	16¾	17⅜	− 2¼
FMdwstB 1.20	7210	35½	26¼	29¾	+ 3¼
FstMtlSv s10i	x17724	15⅞	11	13¾	− 2¼
FstMutl SvB	19543	8⅝	5⅛	6⅜	+ ¾
FstBcpGa s.35	x2636	31	15½	27½	...
FstNtlCin 1.48	24576	50	34	35	− 2⅛
FstNatlCp Cal	3477	11	7	10¾	+ 3⅝
FstNHBk s.60	x21308	33	17⅜	28½	+10
FstNoS&L .44	5141	21¼	14	14	− ¾
FstOhioB 1.04	6923	34	25	26¼	− 3
FstOakBrk .60	4660	30½	21	22¾	...
FstPeople Bk	24213	29¾	13	18¾	+ 4¾
FstSBFla .80a	40087	37¼	19¾	36	+ 6¼
FstSec Ut 1.10	89630	35	19½	22¾	+ ¾
FstSecKy s.40	x11010	26½	14⅜	17¼	− 5⅛
FstSvcBk Svg	53790	9¾	7½	8½	...
FstSource .44	4088	22¾	16¾	17	− 2
FSouthnFd SL	78536	22⅛	12½	14	− ⅝
Fst Tenn 1.12	122394	36⅝	24½	30¾	+ 5¾
Fst Union s.68	x502045	29⅞	22½	24⅛	+ 2⅝
FstUtdBcsh 1	1893	33½	28	29	− 2½
FstUnFSv s.40	x9573	16½	9⅝	12⅛	+ 2⅛
FstValley s.84	x32418	34¾	21⅜	26½	+ 4¼
FstWstFin .28	145140	11⅞	7	9	+ 1⅞
FirsTier 1.10	x8974	30½	23	24¾	− ½
FIserv Inc	10708	15	12⅜	13⅞	...
FlaglerA .26g	2256	13	10½	12	− ½
Flexsteel .48	27442	20¼	11¾	18½	+ 4
Flight Intl	11523	6¼	3¼	6 1-16	+2 15-16
Florafax Intl	34853	6	2¼	2 15-16	−1 13-16
FlaComB .56g	972	40	30	32	+ ½
FlaEmpl .10d	7748	10	4⅜	7½	+ 3⅛
Fla Express	96554	14⅜	5¾	7⅛	+ ⅜
FlaFedl SvLn	149296	22⅝	12½	12⅝	− 4⅞
FlaNtlBk s.44	x116538	29¼	17	18	− 2⅞
FlaPubUt 1.24	815	28½	16½	27	+10¾
Flow System	115846	13¼	5¾	6⅛	− 4¼
Fluorocrbn .28	37818	18¼	10⅜	12	− 4¼
FMI Fncl .10d	137509	13⅜	5¼	11⅞	+ ¾
Fonar Corptn	230266	11¾	4½	6½	− ⅞
Fd Lion A s.04	x238250	14⅝	6½	11⅛	...
Fd Lion B s.03	x148665	18½	6⅝	12¼	...
FrmostAm .96	97681	43¼	28¾	38¼	+ 6¼
ForestOil .52f	52986	19	6¼	8⅞	− 5⅛
Forschner Gr	4123	15¾	9¾	14½	+ 3¼
FortuneF .05d	99761	34½	14¾	24¼	+ 3¾
Fortune Syst	188021	2¾	1	1¼	− ⅝
Ft Wayne s.50	x12959	25¾	16¼	20	+ 2½
ForumGr s.06	x410105	11¾	7⅞	8⅜	...

	Sales 100s	High	Low	Last	Net Chg.
FosterLB .02h	83123	6¼	2⅛	2¼	− 2½
FourFnc s.88	x21363	28¼	20¾	20⅝	− ¼
Frankfrd s.92	x1912	28⅝	15	22⅛	...
Frnkln Cmptr	4022	5	1½	2⅛	...
FranklinEl .56	15710	20¼	15½	18½	+ 2
Franklin S&L	1442	18½	10¾	11¼	...
Freedom FSB	44726	18¾	11¼	12½	+ ½
Frem Genl .48	164329	34	15¼	16⅛	− 8¼
Fretter Inc	100743	21¼	9½	9⅝	...
Frontier Insur	5159	8½	7¼	7⅜	...
Frost Sull .12	15310	4⅞	3¼	3⅞	+ ½
FrozenFd .07d	2704	13¼	10	10⅜	− 1⅝
Fuddruckers	113939	6½	1⅜	1⅝	− 4¼
Fuller HB .36	85953	31	14½	25⅛	+ 7¼
FultonFin s.72	x5193	37	20¼	22¼	+ ¾
Funds Net Inc	32217	5 15-16	3¾	5⅞	+ 1
Funtime	2764	6¾	3¾	3¾	− 2¼
—G—					
Galactic Res	199453	12⅛	4⅝	5½	− 1⅝
Galileo ElOpt	38743	38¾	13	25	+ 11¼
Gallagher s.20	x61107	33¼	22½	26¼	+ 2⅛
GaloobL Toy s	x211775	18¾	6¾	10⅝	...
Gaming& Tch	20191	6⅝	1 7-16	6	+ 3½
GammaB .02h	62702	9¼	3⅝	7⅛	+ ¾
Gandalf Tech	47389	7¾	5¼	7⅛	− ¼
Gander Mtn	24375	14	8¼	9½	...
Gantos Inc	66254	26½	13½	13¾	...
Garden Amer	39055	20	10	15	...
Gartner Grp	33480	12⅝	9½	10⅛	...
GatewayBks s	x74163	25⅜	15	20⅝	...
Gateway Med	89724	6¾	1¼	3¾	...
GatewyCom s	x1745238	17	5½	5⅝	...
Gemcraft Inc	84327	15½	5¾	7	− 2⅛
Genentech s	x759140	98¾	32¼	85	+ 50⅛
Gen Automatn	11798	4½	3¼	4	...
Genl Bindg .40	10051	18½	12½	17¾	+ 3
GenCeram .09	9505	21¾	11½	20¾	+ 8¾
Genl Computr	16919	17¾	7½	7½	...
Genl Kinetics	3604	6⅝	4½	5¼	...
GnMagnplt .10	4876	12¼	6	7	− 3¼
Gen Paramtrc	20586	13	9	10	...
GenPhysc .20d	6409	24¼	13¾	19¼	+ 4½
Genetic Labs	8508	4¼	1½	2½	...
Genetic Systm	81262	10¾	5¼	10⅜	+ ¼
Genetics Inst	101361	32½	17¼	18¼	...
GeneveCap .10	1089	104½	54	72	+ 16½
Genex Corp	117544	5⅝	1½	1¾	...
Genicom Corp	44403	13¼	6⅛	10¼	...
Genmar Indus	90230	12¾	8⅛	10¼	...
Genova .10	7269	5¾	4⅜	4¾	− ½
Gentex Corp	45476	5¼	2 13-16	3 7-16	− 1-16
Genzyme Cp	95640	14⅜	6⅝	8	...
Geodynamcs	18121	17¼	9¼	10	− 2½
Geonex Corp	15822	12¼	7¾	11	...
GaBndFd 10k	4638	10	4½	5¾	+ 1¼
GeoWash .09h	7981	4 11-16	2⅛	2⅝	− ½
Georgia Gulf	18825	20	19½	19½	...
GerMedC .08g	34203	9¾	5⅞	6¼	+ ⅛
Germania s	x13007	18	8¼	9⅝	− ½
GibsonCR .20	x3449	11½	7¼	10½	+ 2½
GibsonGrt .25	337214	29⅜	14¼	16	− 3⅜
Giga Tronics	20612	18½	12	13	− 1¼
Gilbert As 1.70	14781	37½	31¼	35	+ 3¼
G+KServ .20	x8760	15	10	14½	...
GNI Inc	6136	2	15-16	1⅛	− ⅜
Godfrey s .32	32392	20	9⅜	17⅞	+ 8½
Goldn Poultr	13213	12¼	8¾	10	...
GoldnRlt 1.25	7475	12¾	10	11½	− ¼
GoldenEnt .24	32272	16	10¼	14	− 1⅝
GoldnVall Mic	34927	25½	19¼	24	...
GoodGuys Inc	80525	18½	3⅛	4⅝	...
Goodmark Fd	57405	15¾	9⅝	11⅝	− ⅝
GoodyProd .32	x21370	19	10½	14⅞	...
GotaasL .10d	200710	31¾	13¾	26¼	+ 7⅛
Goulds Pu .76	105869	19½	14¼	16⅛	− ⅜
Gradco Systm	56112	17¾	6½	6½	− 5¼
GranitCo .20d	1877	14½	11½	12	...
GranitSB .02d	7125	18⅛	14	18	...
Grantree Corp	45974	9⅛	5⅛	5⅝	− 3⅛
Graphic Inds	15849	20½	13	17	+ ⅝
GraphcMd 10i	16621	9⅛	3¾	4¾	+ ¾
Graphic Scan	780587	11	5⅛	9½	+ 2
GrtAmCp .35h	944	18	6½	7	− 11
GrtAmPt .60d	40364	4⅛	2½	2 15-16	− 1 1-16
GrA Recreatn	12998	7-32	⅛	⅛	...
GrtCountry B	61185	23¾	18¼	19¼	...

	Sales 100s	High	Low	Last	Net Chg.
GrtFalls .42	3682	7	5⅝	7	...
GrtLkFSL .40	75876	27¾	17	19⅝	+ 2½
GrtSoFed SBk	18076	10⅝	5¼	5⅞	− 1⅞
GrtWstnB .48g	35808	32	9¼	10	− 15¾
GrtWalv 1.30d	9408	8⅞	5½	6	− 1¾
Grnery Reh s	x47483	19	9	12½	...
GrenadaSun s	x5508	22¾	14¼	14¾	...
GreyAdvrtsg 2	x2553	125	82	92	...
Griffin Tech	9871	6¾	1¾	3⅜	− 3⅛
GristMill Co	55731	10½	2⅞	3⅜	− 6¾
Groundwtr Tc	29173	29	23	23½	...
GrowthFd Fla	22410	6⅛	4¾	5⅛	− ¼
Grubb RE .88	20144	9⅜	7⅛	8⅞	+ 1⅛
GTECH Corp	209532	30¼	11¾	21	+ 2½
GTS Corp	17776	10¼	1⅛	1⅜	− 1⅝
GuarnFncl .40	42583	18	9¾	15	+ 2¼
Guarant Natl	126354	9¾	6¼	8	+ 1⅝
GuardnPk .33	3807	21½	13½	21	+ 7½
Guest Supply	64075	30	9	9½	− 11
Guilford .25d	38676	19½	13⅛	17⅛	+ ⅛
GulfAppTc .20	12348	8¼	5¾	6½	− ¾
GWC Cp 1.32	37343	23¼	19	19¾	− ¼
—H—					
H&H OilTool	4153	3¾	2¼	2¾	− ⅝
Haber s	74607	16¾	2½	3⅜	− 13⅜
Haber Inc pf2	808	28	4½	7¼	...
HaberInc wt	1895	7¼	½	½	...
Hach Co s.16	x1235	15½	14½	15½	...
Hadco Corp	16659	6½	2⅞	2⅞	− 3¼
Hadson Corp	152949	7⅜	2 5-16	5⅝	+ 3 3-16
HalRoach St	55866	17¾	6½	7½	+ 13-16
HamltnOl .07h	113364	16¼	9½	14¼	− ¾
HambrgHml s	x4170	8⅛	3½	4½	...
Hammond Co	5774	7½	3⅜	5	+ 1
Hana Biologic	28839	10½	6¾	7	...
Hanover .50d	4126	12	6	6¾	− 4¼
Hanovr Ins .56	34856	70	51½	63½	+ 12
Harken Oil Gs	44108	2½	13-16	2½	+ 1 11-16
HarlysGrp .32	35088	20	14¼	14¼	...
HarlynProd s	x5625	6¼	3	3⅛	− 2¾
Harman Intl	9074	15¼	12	12½	...
HarmonIn .13	22704	11¾	6⅝	7½	− 2⅛
Harper Gr .34	38103	35½	19½	24¾	+ 4¾
Harper Intl	19004	12⅛	6¼	7⅝	...
HartfdNt s1.20	x198301	31¾	23	24¾	...
HartfdSt s1.60	x32219	51	304	47⅛	...
Harvard Ind	64685	15¾	8½	11⅜	+ 1⅝
Harvrd Secur	5514	8	4¾	6¼	...
Hathaway .10f	12076	8⅞	4⅛	4⅜	− 4⅛
Hausermn .50	7229	25½	17¾	19	− ¼
HavertyF s.34	x24295	17⅜	10¼	12	...
Havrty A s.30	5152	15½	11½	12½	...
Hawkeye Bcp	47802	8⅜	1	1 3-16	− 1 15-16
HawknCh .08f	1818	5¾	3¾	4½	− ¾
HBO&Co .10h	1123916	18¼	8½	9¼	− 9⅛
HCC Indus .06	3751	9¼	4¼	4⅜	− 4⅛
HDR PowrSys	4452	9¼	7	7¼	...
HlthcareSv Gr	48318	18	10½	13	− 3⅜
HlthcrSv Am	56794	12¼	5⅜	6⅜	− 4½
Healthco Ind	123754	27	14¾	20¾	+ 5⅞
HlthSo Rehab	17832	10⅛	6	8⅜	...
Hlthdyne Inc	169456	5⅛	2⅝	4¼	+ ⅜
HealthWays	18605	6⅜	2⅞	3¼	− 3
HeartFSL .05d	23232	22¼	13	17¾	+ 4¾
Heartland Ex	18696	10½	9	9¾	...
HechngrA s.16	x142687	23¾	14¾	16½	...
HechngrB s.06	x25935	24	15⅛	16¾	...
Heekin Can	54643	26¾	17	19	+ 1¼
HEI Corp Tex	19382	5⅞	2	2¼	− 2⅜
HEIIncorp Mn	7898	4¾	1⅛	1⅜	− 3⅛
Helen of Troy	40600	8 9-16	3⅜	8	+ 4½
Helix Technlg	12467	27¼	18¼	22¼	+ ¼
Hemotec Inc	19998	4⅝	2⅜	2 15-16	− 13-16
Henley Group	1206811	24¼	17¼	22⅝	...
HenleyGrp wi	93255	25¼	20¾	21⅛	...
Her Fin Ser	8176	15¼	12¼	13	...
Herley Mcrwv	33469	13⅝	4¼	10¼	+ 1¼
Hetra Comptr	3468	4⅜	1⅜	1½	− 2⅛
HiberniaCp s1	x97593	25¼	14	21¼	+ 2¾
Hibernia SBk	1186	12¾	9½	11¾	...
Highland Supr	209419	39¼	15¾	17½	− 9⅜
HighPlains Oil	2267	6½	4½	6	− ¼
HMO Am Inc	77306	10⅛	4⅝	5½	− 1⅝
Hodgsn House	860	7	3¾	4¾	...
HoganSys Inc	243754	12⅛	6½	10⅝	+ 3⅝
Holmes DH 1g	27002	30¼	18	18	− 8

OVER-THE-COUNTER

Stock	Sales 100s	High	Low	Last	Net Chg.
Homac Inc	4421	4½	2⅞	3⅜	...
Home&Cty SB	66258	24½	15	16⅞	...
HomeBenefc 1	23368	46½	31⅜	35½	+ 2½
HmFBFla .40	78896	33¼	17½	29¾	+12
HmFedSv s.20	x1194	20	11½	14	...
HFSB NO s.24	1771	9¼	7	7½	...
HomeFSLGa s	x8977	12¼	7¼	10	...
HomeFSL Rk	6148	19¼	13¼	14	– ¾
HmFedSL SF	10483	19½	13¾	17	...
HmFSL Tenn	15047	12¾	11½	12¼	...
Home Intensv	11157	7⅛	2½	3⅛	...
HmInters pf1	1381	11	7¾	8	...
HmIntnsCr wt	15	1¾	1¼	1¼	...
HomeOwner s	x59364	31¼	10⅛	21	...
Home S&L NC	3278	15½	11½	12¼	...
Home SvgBk	80161	10¾	9⅞	10	...
Home Unity	8295	8⅝	6⅞	7⅞	...
HON Indus .64	55281	39¾	17¼	37	+ 6½
Hooper H s.32	x5705	16⅛	7¾	10¾	+ 1½
Horizon Air	44834	9⅝	4⅝	9⅜	+ 4½
Horizon Bank	7428	17	12½	16¼	...
Horizon Indus	30111	7	4	6½	+ 2½
HorznRes .01d	2836	4¼	2⅞	3¼	+ ⅜
Hosposable Pr	9408	12¾	5⅜	8¾	+ 2⅜
Hosposbl wt	11029	5⅝	1	2⅛	...
HwrdBc 1.20g	3622	43¼	26¾	38½	+11¼
HowardBk NJ	141555	48½	17½	37⅝	+ 2⅞
HPSC Inc	55130	16½	11½	12¾	+ 1¼
HPSC Inc wt	33444	7	3	5½	+ 2½
Huffman Koos	12857	10	8¼	9½	...
HuntgBsh .84g	85825	37¾	22¼	24	– 2¼
Huntgdn Intl	42051	24	8¼	23½	+10⅝
Hurco Cos Inc	14008	5¼	2½	3¼	– ¼
Hutchinson T	34264	13	6½	9¾	+ 2
Hyde Athletic	45082	11	4⅞	9½	+ 3⅛
Hyponex Corp	58700	19	5	12¼	– 2⅞
Hytek Micrsys	12103	8¾	2¼	2⅞	– 5⅜

—I—

Stock	Sales 100s	High	Low	Last	Net Chg.
IBI SecurSv A	11456	3⅝	1⅝	1¾	– 1½
ICOT Corprtn	177214	12⅝	3⅞	8¼	+ ¼
ICP .28d	23291	10⅛	5¼	9½	+ ¼
IDB Commun	15625	8	5⅞	7⅝	...
IDC Services	26332	11⅞	7	9¼	+ 1⅞
IdealSchl Sup	8266	10¼	9	9¼	...
IEC Electronc	26865	11½	4⅛	5¼	– ⅞
IFR Systems	27435	16	8¼	9¾	...
IIS Intel .11d	11881	6⅛	2⅞	3⅜	– 2⅝
ILC Technolg	11562	10¼	3¼	4¾	– 4½
III Marine .68	6732	35½	25½	30½	+ 4½
Imatron Inc	338579	4 13-16	1 13-16	2⅛	...
ImatronInc wt	30227	1⅞	7-16	15-16	+7-16
Immucor Inc	34868	13⅜	6¼	10¾	+ 3⅝
Immunex Cp	188489	20¼	6⅜	11½	– 2⅜
immunogntc	44191	3 3-16	1½	2⅛	+ ⅛
ImperialBc 5i	23673	17¼	12⅞	12⅞	+ 1⅜
Imreg Inc A s	x213930	13⅜	5⅝	6⅛	...
IMS Intl s.16	x317438	27⅞	15⅝	24	+ 8⅜
Inacomp Cmp	37553	7¾	3	3¾	– 1⅜
Inca Resource	12282	2⅜	15-16	1⅛	–9-16
Incstar Corp	38778	6¾	2¾	4⅜	+ ⅝
IndBcPa s1.08	x23508	36¼	23⅝	24¾	+ ⅝
Indep Bksh 7i	8231	5½	2	2¼	– 2
IndpFed SvBk	232	10½	7	9	...
IndpHldg .05d	8167	26½	13¼	17	+ 3¾
IndnHBk s.84g	x8102	38¾	29	34	...
IndianaFn Inv	2453	8¾	4⅜	6	+ 1⅝
IndnaN s1.10g	x50637	47½	30⅛	33¾	– ⅞
Ind Accus .25d	3741	7⅝	4¼	5¾	+ 1
Ind Electrcs	17515	3⅛	1⅝	2	+ ⅛
Indust Resour	37280	3⅞	1 9-16	1 15-16	–9-16
IndustTrn Cp	422	9¾	7	7¼	...
InertiaDy s	x18611	11	3	10½	...
InfintyBrd A	46896	13½	10¾	11¾	...
InfoResour s	x115817	28½	16½	19½	+ ¼
Info Solutions	4831	4¼	1¾	1⅞	– 1⅛
Inform Intl .22	17547	17¾	12½	13¼	– ¼
Inform Scienc	15072	3¾	½	¾	– 1⅛
Infotron Syst	57679	19	7	7¾	–10½
Initio Inc 8i	4859	3⅝	2¼	2⅞	+ ⅝
Inlnd Vacuum	34833	9	4⅛	5⅞	+ 1⅛
Inmed Corp	5191	11¼	5	5	– 6⅛
Innovatn Sftw	32199	20¼	7	13⅞	+ 6⅞
Innovex Inc s	x78517	20	6	11½	...
Instinet Cp s	x125711	14¼	4⅜	8 1-16	...
InsitfrmE 10i	88430	28¾	9⅞	13¾	+ 3⅛
InsitGr wt s	x21808	15¼	2⅜	7¾	...
InsitfmGL s5i	x69796	17⅞	6¼	10¼	...
Insituform NA	141567	25½	9¾	13⅞	+ 3½
Insitufm SE	24487	11½	7½	8⅜	...
Inspeech Inc	28975	26¼	18¼	24¼	...
Intech Inc 5i	5758	4⅝	2⅛	2¼	– ⅞
Integrt Circt	10018	8¾	4⅝	6⅝	+ 1⅝
Integrt Device	239967	23	6½	9¼	– 7¾
Integrat Fin	4178	6	¼	¼	– 5⅛
Integrt Gene	181038	18¾	3¼	9⅛	+ 3⅞
ISSCO	42700	17½	7⅝	11½	– 4¾
Intel Corportn	1922618	32¼	16⅜	21	– 8¼
Intel Corp wt	134885	8½	4¼	6⅛	– 1
IntelliCorp	134437	16¾	4⅛	5	–11
InterTelInc A	18527	2	1	1¾	– ⅛
Interactv Rad	4081	7¼	3¾	4⅝	– ⅞
Interand Corp	27903	17	6	7¼	– 3
IntrchFn .50	1524	32½	14½	27¼	+11¼
InterfaceSys s	x27178	12⅛	6	7⅛	– ¾
IntrfaceFS .20	54235	19¾	9	17¼	+ 1¾
Intergraph	1214047	40½	15¼	17	–19¾
Intergroup	3577	12	9¾	12	+ 1¼
Interleaf Inc	67913	12¾	7½	10¾	...
Intrmagn Gen	129423	10⅛	3¼	3½	– 4¼
Intermec Corp	64954	17¾	12¾	14¾	– ¾
Intermet s.18	x83644	13¼	5¼	12⅛	...
Intermetrics	11139	8½	3½	3⅞	– 3⅜
IntlAm Home	54324	6¾	3½	4	– ¾
Intl ContnrS s	x20278	15⅞	4⅝	6	...
IntlCap Eqpt	32528	8¼	2⅞	3¼	– ⅞
IntlClinic Lab	141019	17⅝	10¼	10⅞	– 1¾
IntlDairyQ A	43114	35½	18½	23¼	...
IntlDairyQ B	2902	35¼	20	24	...
IntlGame Tch	59676	14⅞	7⅞	11⅛	+ 2¼
IntlHoldng 10k	10133	19½	8	11¼	– 6¼
Intl HRS Ind	72371	5 15-16	2½	3	+7-16
IntlKings Tbl	60662	30	15¾	16¼	– 3½
Intl Lease Fin	123398	28	15⅜	25½	+ 8⅞
ItlMobile Mch	241073	20⅝	6⅜	13½	+ 5½
ItlMob pf.90d	1485	26¾	12½	18½	...
IntlMobM wt	14765	11¾	3	6½	...
IRIS Incorp	155850	2⅝	1 1-16	2 1-16	+ ⅜
IntlResDev .36	16218	9¼	5½	5½	– 1⅞
Intl Robomatn	8274	14¼	8	8¼	...
IntlShiphold s	x12576	17	9½	9¾	– 1⅞
IntTotlzrSys s	x57955	4⅞	3¼	3⅞	...
Interphase	13391	12¼	4⅜	8¼	+ 3⅞
Intrprov Pipe	1797	32¾	26½	28⅜	– 2⅝
Intertrans Cp	54460	20¾	12⅜	15¼	+ 2¼
IntrWstF .37h	31397	19	13½	14	– 1½
Invacare Corp	20859	8⅞	4	8⅛	+ 3⅜
Investr SB .16	78196	12¼	7¾	11	+ 2¾
INVG M .50d	5227	28½	10	11½	–17½
Iomega Corp	369842	23	5⅜	5¾	– 6¼
IowaSthn s1.92	x19547	36¾	22¾	32	+ 8
IPLSystems A	18151	3½	1⅛	2⅛	+ 1
Irwin Magnet	33386	8½	7⅛	7⅞	...
Isco Inc .16	14623	17	8¼	10	– 3
I S C Syst Cp	356443	18⅝	8¾	9¼	– 5⅜
Isomedix Inc	32974	17¾	6¾	7½	– 5½
Itel Corp	335650	16⅛	5¼	13⅜	+ 3⅝
ItelCl.B pfA	1484	60	57½	58	...
Itel pfB 8.64a	9953	59¾	52½	58⅛	...
ItoYokad .39d	15428	117½	57⅞	101½	+41¼
Iverson Tech	22505	18	9¾	14	+ ⅝
IWC Res s1.36	x7005	25½	16½	20	+ 2

—J—

Stock	Sales 100s	High	Low	Last	Net Chg.
Jack Henry	19748	7½	3	3⅛	– 3
Jackpot Ent	58957	8¼	5⅜	6⅛	...
JacobsnSt s.50	x19426	45¼	21¼	37¾	+16¼
Jacor Commn	110244	8⅝	4⅝	6⅛	+ 1¼
Jaguar .16d	2540195	9¼	4 7-16	7 15-16	+3
J&J SnackF s	x16319	22	7¼	9¾	...
J Baker Inc	91083	20	13¾	15½	...
JB Hunt s.12	x79111	30	13⅝	25¾	...
JB's Rest .04h	74249	10¾	5	5½	– 4⅞
JBildner Sn	15101	14½	10½	11¼	...
Jefferies Grp	83201	17¾	9½	10¼	– 5
JeffBshr s1.12	x6325	39½	27½	29½	– 2⅛
JeffrsnNB s5i	x7987	12¾	10	11¾	...
Jffrs Sm s.24a	x40027	39	12⅜	38½	...
Jeffrey Martn	57343	7¼	4	6⅞	+ 2⅜
Jerrico s.12	x401053	26⅜	15¾	18⅞	...
JG Indus Inc	16866	10½	3¾	7	+ 3¼
Jiffy Lube	61403	23¼	16½	18¼	...
J L G Indus	14999	8¼	3¾	4¼	– ¾
JMB Rlty 1.64	5300	18½	15¾	16¾	+ ½

OVER-THE-COUNTER

	Sales 100s	High	Low	Last	Net Chg.
JohnAdams Lf	20482	18⅛	5¼	6	− 6¼
John Hanson	69042	10	5¼	5¼	...
Johnson Elect	10353	6¾	2⅝	2¾	− 3
Johnstown SB	2269	9⅝	8¾	9⅛	...
Jones Medicl	9108	6⅜	4⅝	5	...
JonesVn s.14f	x8106	3⅝	(z)	3⅝	...
JonesIntcbl 5k	55489	16¾	3⅞	11⅜	+ 3⅝
JonesIncbA 5k	144044	17	3⅝	11	+ 3⅛
Joseph Intl	52165	12⅛	7	11	+ 2⅞
Joule Inc	10328	8¾	4⅞	7⅞	...
Judy'sInc s.06	x4190	6	2⅜	4¼	+ 1½
Juno Lighting	44508	37⅛	22½	29¾	+ 5¼
JustinInd .40	35795	20⅞	12⅞	13¾	− 4⅝

—K—

	Sales 100s	High	Low	Last	Net Chg.
KahlerCorp s	x4295	23	11½	19	...
Kaman A .52	76587	28	21¼	22½	− ½
Kenan Trnspt	754	16½	13¼	14¾	...
Kasler Corp	68394	14½	5¾	6¼	− 4¼
Kaydon .05d	35680	15¾	7	14⅝	+ 3⅛
Kaypro Corp	86045	4	1¼	1⅜	−3-16
Keane Inc s	x1428	10⅝	5	5¼	...
KeithleyIn .13	2736	13½	11	13	+ 1¼
KellySrv A .70	39057	61½	45	49	+ 2½
KellySrv B .60	2869	62½	44	51	+ 8½
Kemper s.60	x336262	35½	14⅝	25	+ ⅝
Kencope Enrg	11684	3½	1 5-16	1 15-16	−1 9-16
Kenilwrth Sys	231687	1¾	13-32	19-32	−11-32
Kenington Ltd	9387	8⅜	5½	8⅜	+ 1⅛
Kent Elec Cp	6857	6¾	4	4	...
KyCentLif 1.10	14437	63¾	34¼	54¾	+ 1¾
Kevex Corptn	15913	8¾	3⅞	3⅞	− 2½
Kevlin Micrw	9861	5¾	2⅜	2⅜	− 2⅞
Kewaunee .44	4498	13¾	10¼	10⅜	− 3⅛
KeyCentr 1g	10608	42½	25	36¼	...
KeyTronic Cp	91177	17¼	6¼	6⅞	− 3⅞
KeystnFn s.76	x12276	31¼	19½	20¾	− 1
KeystnHtg .80	2311	35½	23	23½	− 4
Kimball B .60	18185	32	24½	30	− 1¾
Kimbark OilG	6861	5⅞	⅞	1 1-16	−1 1-16
Kincaid Furn	45554	16½	6¾	10¾	+ 2½
Kindrcar s.06	x526782	17¾	11⅝	13⅞	+ ⅝
KingRoad Ent	46593	8½	2¾	3	− 5
KLA Instrum	223176	26¼	11	13⅝	− 9⅜
KLLM Trnspt	28919	18	12¾	17¼	...
Kloss Video	4704	4⅛	1⅞	2¼	− 1⅛
KMW Systm s	x10266	10⅛	7⅛	8	+ ¾
KnapeVo 1.40a	x2317	19⅝	12¾	17	+ 3⅜
Koss Corp	7658	5⅛	3⅛	4½	...
Kreisler M	1401	9¾	7¾	9¼	+ 1¼
KruegerW .36	128376	18⅞	12⅜	13½	− ¾
Krug Intl s.03	x25690	16¾	7¾	9	+ ⅞
K Tron Intl	18251	7⅜	3¼	6¼	+ 2⅜
Kulicke Soffa	104768	16⅜	7	7¼	− 5⅞
Kustom El 5k	7322	8½	4⅛	4⅝	− 1⅝
KV Pharm s	x35969	16½	5½	12	+ 6¼

—L—

	Sales 100s	High	Low	Last	Net Chg.
Lacana Minng	10228	8¼	5¼	6⅝	− ¼
LacledeSt .25d	9515	22½	16	16½	− ⅛
LaddFurn s.12	x86103	16¾	8⅝	15⅝	+ 3⅞
LA Gear Inc	111437	24½	7¾	8¼	...
Laidlaw In .20	55015	22½	11¾	20½	+ 3¾
Laidlaw A s.14	x3407	16⅜	6⅜	16⅜	...
LaidlwB s.14	x137947	13⅞	6⅜	13⅝	+ 6
LkSunape .06d	7251	23	12½	19	...
Lam Reserch	89506	13¾	3¾	4½	− 5⅝
Lancastr s.64	x59570	20¾	14	19	+ 4⅞
Lancer Corp	20633	19	10¼	10⅞	− 5¼
Lance Inc 1.08	56192	40½	30	39½	+ 7¾
Landmrk Bk	7651	16¼	11¼	15	...
Landmrk Fncl	650	12¼	11⅝	11⅝	...
Land Linc .48	18987	16½	12	14	− ⅝
LandsEnd Inc	24319	30¼	23¼	24¼	...
Lane Co .80a	x103256	63	41	52¼	+ 11¼
LanglyCp .45d	12046	9⅛	6⅛	7⅝	+ ⅞
LaPetiteAcd s	x85701	25¾	12	16	...
Laser Corp	24602	12	3⅞	4⅛	− 4⅛
Laser Precision	29542	9½	3⅝	8	+ 4⅜
Lawrence SB	34310	15	10⅝	11¾	...
LawsnPr s.24	x44412	26¼	18¼	21¼	+ 1½
LaZBoy 1.60	21445	72½	52¼	63	+ 9½
L C S Industr	20924	21½	5¼	7¼	− 5
LD Brinkman	83431	10¼	4¾	5	− ⅞
LeaderDevl 5i	6488	9¾	4⅝	4½	− 2¼
Lee Data Corp	210121	8¾	4¾	6⅝	+ ⅝
Leiner Nutritn	17950	22¼	9⅜	17½	+ 7½
LeisurCncpt s	x68173	17¾	3½	4	...
LescoInc s.01d	x18251	16½	7¼	12½	+ 5⅛
LewisPlm .28	30950	10	7	7½	...
Lexicon Cp s	x83139	6⅞	2⅝	2⅞	− 2⅛
LbrtyH A .24	12195	14¾	8¾	10¾	− 1¼
LbrtyH B .20	4401	14½	9	10¾	− 1½
LibNtlBc s.76	x12481	41	27¾	29	− 3¼
Liebermn En	61151	26⅜	13⅝	16⅝	− 5½
Liebert Cp .12	74654	31½	20¾	26⅜	+ ⅜
LifeInvestr .24	3412	50	41¾	49½	+ 1¼
Lifeline Systm	26635	9⅝	3½	4	− 3¼
Lifetech Inc	18144	10	8⅜	9½	...
LillyIndA .42	32164	18	12½	14	− 1
Lin Broadcast	314238	57¼	23⅞	55⅜	+ 18¼
LincFncl s.73	x4430	32⅝	20½	21	...
Lincoln Food	32768	17½	8¼	9½	...
Lincoln Logs	35461	5¼	4	4	+3 9-16
Lincoln SvBk	14467	29¾	17¾	22¼	...
LincTel 2.20	10621	55	29¼	48½	+ 8½
Linda Cedar	5079	7½	2¾	4	+ 1¼
LindbgCp .16a	10946	8⅝	4¾	6¼	+ 1⅝
Linear Corptn	19186	8¾	3½	8¾	+ 5
LinearFilms s	x98453	28¾	13¼	16¾	+ 1½
Linear Tech	83800	10	6	8½	...
Liposome Co	28414	8	6¼	6⅝	...
LiquidAir 1.60	5515	36½	25¾	30½	+ 3¾
LiquiBox s.60	x6349	70	31	44	+ 12½
LittleArthr .70	2116	35	25	34	+ 9
LivngWell Inc	4401	9	3	3⅞	− 4⅛
LizClaibn s.25	x566382	48½	23⅛	42¾	+ 18½
LoanAm Fncl	1878	18	9¾	9¾	− 2¾
LocalFedS .30	38603	21¾	8⅜	9¾	− 6¾
Lodgistix	21162	6½	2 7-16	2 11-16	−1 13-16
London House	3283	9½	6	6⅝	− ⅜
LoneStar Tech	187066	10¾	6⅛	6¼	− 2¼
LongLake En	44630	9¼	6⅜	7¾	...
LngvwF 1.60	35643	38¼	21¼	37¼	+ 9¾
Lotus Develop	705454	58	20⅛	51¾	+ 26¾
LaBancshr .72	105066	16	7¼	7⅜	− 8
LouisVtn 2.07d	4629	49	30⅛	39¾	+ 8
Lowell InstSv	47487	11½	8⅞	9	...
Lowrance El	4152	8½	7⅞	7⅞	...
Loyola Cap	10198	15	13	13⅝	...
LPL Invest A	6256	12⅛	11¼	11¼	...
LSB B NC .68	4328	26	19	20	+ ¼
LSI LightSyst	53760	25¾	13	14⅜	− 1⅜
LSI Logic s	x738118	20½	8	10¾	+ ⅞
L T X Corp	87273	19¼	6½	7¾	− 5¼
Luskin Inc	14945	14½	3¾	4½	− 8¼
Lynden Inc	2265	25	14	14½	− 8
Lyphomed s	x312296	25⅞	10¾	18⅜	+ 6⅜

—M—

	Sales 100s	High	Low	Last	Net Chg.
MacDermd .52	6031	27½	17	24¼	...
Machine Tech	37229	10¼	2⅞	3½	− 3¾
Machine Vsn	132093	6	7-16	½	− 4½
Mack Trucks	179227	14⅞	9⅝	10⅞	+ ¼
MacMillan Bl	8853	31½	23⅜	29½	...
Mad GsEl 2.36	35057	41½	22⅜	34¾	+ 7⅛
Magma Engy	14910	9⅜	5⅛	5½	− 3
Magma Powr	63354	22¼	12⅜	14⅜	− ⅞
MagnaGr .68g	20354	24¾	17¼	17¾	...
MAgnaIntl .48	372226	26⅜	14	16¾	+ 1⅝
MailBoxes	14237	18¾	15	18½	...
Major Realty	67925	13¼	8	9½	+ 1¼
MakitaEl .22d	15780	47¾	23⅞	44⅜	+ 19⅞
Malrite Comm	19781	17⅜	8¾	9¼	− 2¾
MalriteCom A	24956	16¾	7¾	8¼	− 3½
MgmtAsst .75t	34086	2¾	1¾	2	...
MngtSci Amer	207684	16¼	10⅞	12¾	+ 1¾
Manitowoc .80	105131	22¾	15¾	18¾	− 3¼
Manf Natl 1.44	81237	53½	38	39	− 1¼
Marble Fncl	21461	24	20½	22	...
M A R C Inc	50084	25¾	8	10¼	− 10
Marcus .33	19811	30	14	21¾	+ 2½
Margaux Cntr	118522	5⅝	2 1-16	2 1-16	−1 15-16
Marietta Cp	19240	16½	8	9¼	...
MarineCp s.22	14610	17⅛	10¾	12	+ 5¾
Marine W 1.48	16864	51	34½	38½	+ 1¼
Marine Trnprt	12011	9	6¾	6⅞	− ⅜
MarkT Bsh .88	4205	35	25	31¾	+ 6¼
MarketFct .32	5696	14¾	7¾	7¾	− 2½
Marquest Md	43236	11¼	7	8⅛	− ⅛

OVER-THE-COUNTER

	Sales 100s	High	Low	Last	Net Chg.
Mars Stores	42214	17	4⅝	5	− 9
Marsh IIsl s.80	x51351	38¾	25½	27½	+ 1¾
MarshSup s.40	x17711	18⅛	10	14¼	+ 3¼
Marten Trnsp	27307	20	12¾	17½	...
MaryIndN 1.30	185193	50⅞	34¾	40	+ 4⅛
Masco Indus s	x129179	27¾	8⅞	22¾	+12
MascoIndus pf	35961	30	28	29¼	...
MassBnk .08d	35933	17¼	15½	15½	...
Masscomp	90475	9½	5⅛	6	+ ⅞
Masstor Syst	273293	4⅛	1⅛	3⅛	+ 1⅜
Matrix Sci .10	24380	38	27½	35⅛	+ ⅝
Maverck Rest	9841	2⅝	15-16	1	− ¼
Maxco Inc	25084	3⅝	2⅜	2⅜	− ⅜
Maxicare Hlth	882016	28½	12½	15⅝	− 5⅜
Maxtor Corp s	x412164	20½	7	17⅜	+10⅛
Maxwell Labs	24597	18¼	8¾	12¾	− 2¼
May Petrolm	96965	4¼	1⅜	2⅛	− ⅝
MayfSpA s.04	x13614	26½	11	20½	+ 8¾
Maynard Oil	16334	4¾	3¾	4 1-16	−7-16
Mays JW Inc	3145	18½	11½	18	+ 6
MBI Bus Cntr	160211	16¾	4⅞	5¼	− 2¾
MCI Communi	4470453	13¼	6	6¼	− 5
McCmkCo 1	124481	45⅝	31⅞	39⅜	+ 5⅛
McFarInd En	24155	13	8½	10	− 1⅛
McGillMfg 1	4279	35	29¼	31¾	− 2½
McGrath Rent	29519	16¼	9	12¼	− ⅛
Mechancl Tch	8124	9¼	5⅝	8½	+ 2⅝
Mechtron Intl	22477	16	6¾	8¾	− 7¼
MedalistIn .40	43882	19¼	11	16½	+ 5¼
Medar Inc	69941	13	6¼	6¾	− 1¼
Med Care Intl	106095	7⅛	3⅝	3⅝	− 1¾
MedChemPr s	x25646	14¼	7	10½	− ⅛
MedcoCont Sv	82944	42¼	26¼	32½	+ 6
Medex Inc .06	14844	9¾	6	7⅝	− 1⅜
Medford SvBk	70837	21½	12⅞	14⅞	...
Medicl Graph	8004	12½	6¼	11½	+ 4⅝
Med Steril	14463	13¾	5	5½	− 2¼
Medicare Glas	13470	5	3¼	3½	− 1
Medcn Shoppe	22092	33½	21½	29⅝	+ 5⅝
Meditrst 2.40a	78073	29¾	19¼	27½	+ 8
Megadata Cp	9912	5¾	2⅛	2⅞	− ¾
MellonPt .76d	59858	11⅝	8¾	11⅛	+ 2⅜
MelridgeInc s	x75911	19½	8¼	11	+ 2⅝
Mentor Corpn	124322	19½	11	16¾	+ 1
Mentor Graph	334695	19⅝	11⅛	15¼	− 4¼
MercBc s1.40	x72591	37⅛	27⅛	28	+ ¾
MercBsh s1.08	x47454	47¼	34½	39¼	...
MrchBsh s.80g	x1071	35½	18	30½	+11
MerchBNY 1g	752	158	106	158	+49
MerchBcp 1.12	16259	47¾	31¼	41	+ 9
MerchBc Nor	2712	15½	13¾	14½	...
MrchBkA .30d	1051	26¼	18½	21½	...
MrchBk B	43547	29½	12½	20¼	+ 5¼
Merchants Gr	6344	10¾	7	7⅜	...
MerchNtl s.60	x63342	40¾	22½	25¾	+ 2⅛
MercuryG .24	136618	25½	15¼	17⅜	− 2⅜
Meret Inc	9484	5¾	2½	4⅜	+ 1¼
MeridnBcp s1	x100856	27½	19	21⅛	+ ⅝
MeridBc pf2½	3885	56	29	46¾	+ 5¾
Meridian Diag	15721	10¼	3½	4½	...
MeritorSB .20	695000	13⅛	7¾	8¾	− 1⅜
Merrimac Ind	8549	16½	8½	8½	− 7¼
MerryGo Rnd	73128	21⅜	11¾	16	+ 1½
MerryLnd s5i	x23071	14¾	8⅛	11¾	+ 3
Mesaba Aviat	35398	6⅜	2⅝	3	+ ⅛
MetCoilS .09d	27974	12½	5¼	5¾	− 6½
Methode A .07	61623	9⅜	5	5⅝	− 3¼
Methode B .06	2223	9¼	5½	5½	− 3¼
Metro Airlines	68400	13¼	8	11½	+ 1⅛
Metrobnc s.80	x7825	21¼	13	18¾	+ 5⅜
Metrobnk LA	885	10½	9½	9½	...
MetroFdSL s	x43548	24⅝	12⅛	18⅛	+ 6
Metromail Cp	113654	29¼	20⅞	23¼	− ¼
Metro Mobile	63240	21½	12¾	21½	...
MetroSL Tex	17939	19	10¼	10¾	− 8
Metro Tel .03g	6326	4½	2⅝	3½	+ 1
Meyer Fred	82195	14⅝	12⅝	13⅛	...
MichNatl 1.20	76522	44	30⅜	33¼	+ 1
Micom Systm	227711	29¼	9¾	13½	− 8¾
MicroBilt	15552	10½	6⅝	7½	...
Micro D Inc	50583	6	2½	4⅜	+ ½
Micro Mask	16344	10¼	1⅞	3⅛	− 3⅜
Microdyne .06	37854	6⅝	3⅜	4	− 1⅜
Micropro Intl	172034	3¾	1¾	2 9-16	+1-16
Micron Techn	628029	17⅛	3⅜	4½	− 4
Micropolis Cp	323179	19⅝	4⅞	18¾	+10
Microsemicp	125517	9¼	6¼	7⅛	− ⅞

	Sales 100s	High	Low	Last	Net Chg.
Microsoft	254419	51¼	25½	48¼	...
Micros Systm	17513	3	2	2¼	+ ⅛
MicrowvFlt 5k	5289	4½	1¾	2	− 1⅝
Microwv Lab	5088	6¾	6	6¼	...
MidAmBcp .56	6895	34½	21	21¾	− 5½
MidANtlB 1.60	1962	36½	25	34	+ 7
MidPacifc Air	40425	5⅞	2¼	2½	+ ¼
MidlsxWt 1.66	4172	32¼	23½	26¼	+ 3
MidlnticB 1.36	160406	52⅛	29⅛	40⅜	− 3⅜
MidMaine SB	3273	15	12½	14	...
MidStFSL .40	22669	28¾	18	21¾	+ 3
MdHudson SB	4847	24½	14¼	15¼	...
Midway Airln	268811	14⅞	3⅞	13⅛	+ 6¼
Midwest Fncl	17249	24¾	14	17¼	+ 2
MillerHrm .44	242455	31	19½	20¼	− 3⅛
Millicom Inc	57448	14⅝	3½	10¾	+ 6½
Milipore s.28	x302460	35	21	31½	+ 8¾
Miltope Grp	22975	23¾	15¼	16	− 2
Milw InsGrp	10476	12	10¼	11	...
Miniscribe Cp	560869	9⅝	2⅞	8¾	+5 5-16
Minntech Cp	17392	9½	5	7⅞	+ 2½
Minntonka Cp	349101	21	10⅜	18⅝	+ 7⅞
Minstar Inc	224716	35½	18¾	22¼	− ¼
Mischer Corp	3280	15⅜	8½	8½	− 6⅛
M-I Schotten	11274	7	5¼	5⅞	...
Mitsui Co .52f	1731	103½	42	66¼	+25¾
MLX Corp	28064	7¾	3¼	5½	...
M Kamenstein	6751	3⅞	1¾	2¾	+ ¾
MMI Medical	9605	9	3⅜	4½	− 2¾
MNX Incorp	25054	21¾	13½	19¾	...
Mobile Com A	116231	19⅜	7⅝	18	+ 6¼
Mobile Com B	125423	19⅜	7¾	18⅛	+ 6½
MobileGs 1.04	2344	22½	13	21½	+ 8¼
MOCON .10	25631	11¾	5¼	5⅝	− 1⅝
Modine M .76	40953	28½	22⅜	26	+ 2¾
Modulaire 10i	16926	15¾	5½	5¾	− 6
Modular Tech	18180	8¾	3½	3¾	...
Moleculr Bios	118543	6⅞	3¼	5½	+1 7-16
Moleculr Gnet	95521	15½	6	6⅜	− 4⅛
Molex Inc .03	105608	56	28¾	46½	+10
MonrchA s.14	x12087	13½	2½	3⅛	− 3⅞
MonfortC .45b	18902	63	18¼	48	+19½
Moniterm Cp	21559	7	3½	4½	...
Monitor Tech	13836	5¾	1⅝	2	− 2
Monlithc Mem	500205	22½	10	12¼	− 3⅞
Monoclnl Antb	90437	29	5½	5⅞	−12⅝
MooreFin 1.20	24992	34⅛	21½	22½	− 3⅝
Moore Handly	27274	19½	5¾	8	...
MooreProd .88	5173	36	26¾	31	+ 2¾
MorFloInd .01	6713	19¼	12	14	− 4⅝
Morgan Olmst	16674	7⅞	4⅛	4⅝	...
Morgan Prdct	68148	27¾	14	18	+ 2¾
Morino Assoc	13129	21	15½	18¾	...
Morlan Intl	51228	9	4⅝	5⅝	+ ⅝
Morrison .48g	149863	27	16⅝	21⅜	− ⅝
Moseley Hldg	225109	9¾	3¼	3¼	− ⅛
MosineeP s.26	x26718	19¼	11½	13	+ ¾
MotrClAm .30	19072	22	12¾	19½	+ 3⅛
MtBakerBnk s	x9628	17¼	8	17	...
MtnrBsh s.17d	x1022	30½	20	25	...
MPSI System	37489	8⅝	4¼	6	+ 1⅝
Mr Gasket	58921	15	4⅜	5¼	− 3¼
MS Carriers	23967	34	25	31	...
MTech Corp	25990	17¼	15½	16	...
MTS Syst .28	22030	32½	12¼	29¼	+ 4½
Mueller P 1.70	3555	27½	20	20¼	− 5
Multibk s.52	x68902	32½	20¼	23¼	+ 1⅝
Multimedia	72318	47¼	26⅞	41	+10⅞
Municipl Dev	7524	11¾	8	9	...
Musto Explor	114508	4 3-16	1⅝	1 13-16	−1 5-16
Mutual FSL	1203	9½	7½	8¼	...

—N—

	Sales 100s	High	Low	Last	Net Chg.
NAC RE Corp	56090	42	25¼	26¼	−10¾
Nanometrics	7238	7½	3¾	4¾	− 1½
NapaValley s	x4805	15⅜	9	13¼	...
Napco Intl	6232	21½	15¾	16½	− 1
Napco Sec Sys	39622	13½	8½	9¼	− 1
NashFin 1.04a	14233	38¼	29½	35½	+ 4¼
NashCBTr .52	4903	26¾	18½	20¼	− 1
NathansF .07	20164	8¼	3⅜	7¾	+ 4¼
NBAlaska s.50	5406	35¾	27½	28	− 6¼
NatlBanc Cm	578	17¾	16½	17½	...
NtlBshTex .78	61795	24	11⅞	12¼	−11½
NatlBusSys s	x38514	16⅛	9⅛	12⅛	...
NatlCap RE	10115	3¾	1½	2¼	− 1

OVER-THE-COUNTER

	Sales 100s	High	Low	Last	Net Chg.
NatlCityBc 10i	14120	21½	11⅞	15¼	+3⅛
NatlCity s1.50	x194296	49⅜	36⅝	45⅞	+20¾
NCmBkNJ 3a	6376	128	89	114	+17
NtComrB s.52	x13360	22½	14	17¾	+1¾
NtlCmptr s.20	x229230	23⅝	13	13½	−3⅜
NtlContrl .05d	7759	7	3¾	6⅞	+2⅛
Natl Data .44	186845	25⅝	13⅝	21¼	+3
Natl Guardian	57686	13¾	7	7¾	−4¼
NtlHardgd 10i	5028	10¾	6¼	7½	+¾
Ntl Hlthcare	129854	17¼	2⅞	3½	−8½
Natl HMO Cp	13197	7½	3½	4	−½
Natl Lumber	17904	7	4	4 1-16	−15-16
Nat Microntcs	138861	4¾	15-16	1 15-16	−1 9-16
NtlPennB s.80	x772	38½	16	27½	+9½
Natl Pizza s	x35518	18¼	11¾	16¾	+4¾
NatlProp .10d	435	10½	9	9	...
NatlSanit .04d	18217	13	9¼	11¾	...
NSB Albany	14344	25¼	17	17¼	−1¼
NatlSecIns .54	1814	22	13½	20	+6½
NatlTech Syst	16555	4½	1⅝	1¾	−¾
NatlVideo Inc	2102	4⅛	3¼	3½	...
Nat Western L	22243	23	16¼	18⅜	+1¾
Nationwd Pwr	25823	3	¾	15-16	−1 9-16
Natures Bnty	28204	5⅞	2 5-16	2¾	+7-16
Nature Sunsh	4486	5½	2½	4½	+1¼
NBSC Corp .80	1946	35	22	28	+6
NCA Corportn	14575	8	3¼	4½	+⅝
NEC Cp .54d	114427	79	30¼	63⅞	+31
NEECO Inc	20284	7⅜	6½	6¾	...
Nelson Resrch	80471	8½	2⅞	5 9-16	+5-16
NEOAX Inc	9110	16½	2¾	6¼	...
Nestor Inc	x15316	8½	3⅛	3⅛	...
Network Syst	899815	20⅜	10⅛	13⅞	−6⅜
Netwrk Secur	80995	8⅛	4½	5	−⅝
Networks Elct	11428	5⅝	3½	4⅞	+⅜
Neutrogena s	x16756	43½	26¼	38⅛	+11⅛
NevNatl Bncp	6307	11½	5¼	6	...
NewBruns Sci	49674	13⅝	8	11¾	+3½
NewCen Br	21129	24	16¼	21⅞	+5⅛
NewCent Entr	59142	5½	1¾	2	−¾
NewCentE pf	11224	5½	1¾	1⅞	−¾
NewCenP pfB	1532	5	2½	2⅝	...
NEngBsSv s	x44358	30¼	15	22	+6
NwEngCrit Cr	17181	16	10	14⅝	...
NewEng SvBk	53213	15⅝	13⅜	15⅛	...
NH SvBk s.48	x45824	29½	15⅝	25⅞	+9¼
NMilfSB .30d	63514	28	19½	22⅞	...
Newnan FdSL	60	18¾	16	17¼	...
NewportCp .06	162087	23½	10¾	12	−11¼
Newport Elect	11781	8	3	5⅜	+2⅜
Newport News	9725	12¼	8½	8¾	...
Newport Phar	283298	15⅛	4⅛	4¼	−8⅞
NeworldBk .30	115448	28	18	23¼	...
NYCity Shoes	14925	6⅛	3½	3⅞	...
NYMarine Gn	13875	49½	34	42	+8
NFS Fncl Cp	20458	19	13¾	17	...
NiagaraEx .20	25903	16	9½	10¼	...
NI CalDev Ltd	117745	3 5-16	¼	⅝	−⅜
Nichls Hmshl	23509	12½	8¼	9¼	...
Nike Inc B .40	815017	20½	10⅜	11¾	−2⅜
NMS Pharm	48738	6⅛	2½	3½	−⅜
NobelIns .29f	53160	18¼	11¾	17	+5⅛
Noble Drill	78606	3¾	1½	2⅝	−¼
Nodaway 10i	6240	9⅝	5⅝	5⅞	−½
NolandCo s.40	x9021	27¼	16½	21¼	+4¾
NordsonCp .72	17590	31	17	29½	+11
Nordstrm s.26	x353734	51¼	23¾	41¾	+17⅞
NorskDtB s	x133967	33¼	24½	26⅛	+¼
Norstan Incp	27069	8	5	7¾	+1¾
NoAmCom Cp	28779	11¼	8⅜	8¾	...
NoAm Hldg s	x18916	7¾	2½	7¼	+4¾
NoAmHldg A	5867	7⅝	6	7⅝	...
NoAmNtl .01f	10728	16½	9¼	9¼	−2¾
NoAtlantc Ind	23873	8⅝	6	6⅜	−1⅝
NoCarFSL s	x8223	12½	5½	6	...
NCaroNG 1.92	5516	32½	23	29½	+6½
NorthForkB s	x27149	24½	12⅜	21¾	+8¼
NoHills Elec	7856	3½	1½	1⅝	−⅝
Noest Bc 1.40	21003	61¾	38	53¾	+15¼
Northeast Svg	185820	26½	7¾	16½	−1⅛
N'east pfA2.25	18431	36½	27¼	29¾	+½
NorthnAir Frt	12648	6½	3¾	5	+¾
NthrnTrst s.92	x66421	47	28	39⅛	+10⅞
NorthSide SB	78904	19⅜	14⅞	16¼	...
Northview Cp	3360	18½	10¼	11⅛	−3⅞
NowstNtG 1.56	74656	25⅛	16⅜	21⅝	+2⅞
NwstTel s	x4523	5¾	2½	4¾	+1¾
NwstNtlLf .86	176343	33⅞	23⅞	31	+6⅞
NWPS 2.40	24956	38⅝	20½	33½	+8⅝
NWTelcm 1.20	1421	25½	17½	25	+5
Norwesco .16	6448	6¾	4½	5¼	+¾
Norwich Savg	28550	12	10½	11¾	...
NovaPhrm Cp	350659	24¼	6¾	10⅛	+3 3-16
NovaPhrm wt	78491	39½	6 13-16	13	+6⅛
NovaPhar wt B	75955	19⅝	2⅝	6	+3¼
Novamtrx Md	49211	10⅝	4½	7½	+2⅛
NovarElec .02	16354	17	6¼	7½	−7
Novell Inc	183988	26½	14	25¾	+6⅝
Novo Corptn	49639	3¾	1¾	2 1-16	−15-16
Noxell B s.64	x113403	47	29	42	+12½
Nuclear Metal	15903	19¼	13½	17½	+4¼
NuclrSup Svc	28107	30¾	13¾	17¾	+3¼
NuMed	98667	9¼	6	6	−1⅝
Numerex	20207	6⅝	3	3⅜	−2⅛
Numerica .56	85101	24⅜	15½	21¼	+5¼
Nutmeg Indus	14655	15	5½	14½	...
Nu Vision Inc	47248	21	9¼	11¾	+1

—O—

	Sales 100s	High	Low	Last	Net Chg.
OakHill Sprtw	48563	10¾	3⅜	6⅜	+2½
Occidentl Neb	15537	8⅛	1¾	1¾	−4⅞
Oceanrg Intl	39736	3¾	⅞	1 3-32	−27-32
Ocilla Indust	75048	14½	5	5½	−6¼
OCG Technolg	84265	4¼	⅝	1¼	−⅞
OgilvyGp s.80	x150171	42	24½	29¾	+⅞
OglebayN 1.40	18841	29½	18¼	20¾	−4½
OhioBcp s1.40	x2980	50½	30½	38½	...
OhCaslCp 3	86381	91	46¼	77¾	+8
OilDriCp s.20	x11799	31	18½	28¾	+7¾
Oilgear 1.20	1073	25½	22	24	−¼
Old Dom Syst	31078	7	3⅞	4	...
OldFash Food	5998	5¾	4⅜	4⅞	+⅜
OldKentF s.80	x66261	26⅝	20⅞	21¾	...
OldNtlBc s.84	x6492	39½	16⅝	30½	+4¾
OldNB Wa .20f	30319	42½	31	42	+24⅞
Old Repub .78	125984	42¼	27	27⅜	−8¼
OldSpagh Wr	18364	8	3¼	3½	−4½
OldStone s1.56	x37844	34¼	23¼	28¼	+2⅝
OldStn pfB2.40	3755	28½	23	25¾	...
OldStn pfC2.60	9448	22¾	19⅞	20½	−2
Oliver's Strs	101187	12⅛	3⅜	4¼	...
Olson Ind	3464	37½	10	29½	+17¾
Omnicom .98	166279	28½	16⅞	20⅛	−⅜
OMI Corp	223796	7 7-16	3 3-16	3¾	+7-16
OMI Corp pf	6449	22⅜	16½	16¾	...
OneBncp s.30	x72418	24	14½	16⅞	+1¾
OnLine Softwr	23570	16¼	4¼	14¼	+3¼
OneValley s1	x1409	41⅜	35¾	35¾	...
Opticl Coating	57628	21⅝	13⅝	16⅛	+2⅜
Opticl Radiatn	144652	32¼	14	17½	−11¾
Optical Specl	24966	6	1	1 9-16	−1 7-16
Optrotech Ltd	15970	12¾	2⅝	3¾	−8
Opto Mechank	21459	7¼	4½	5⅜	−½
Oracle Systm	136781	28⅞	13	20¾	...
Orange Juls	6336	9¼	3¼	3⅜	−3⅞
Orbanco Fincl	13006	15½	12⅛	13⅞	−½
Orbit Instrum	162712	13¼	5⅝	10⅞	+3⅞
OreMetl 2.50b	20720	8⅝	4	4⅞	−2
Orfa Corp Am	203239	6⅞	1¼	1⅞	−3⅞
Orion Resrch	19940	7½	4	4½	−1¾
OshKosh A .26	63955	70¼	33¼	55¼	+19¾
OshKosh B .26	2347	63	34	49	+14¼
Osh Trk B.20d	103467	33	19¼	24	+4½
OshmanSG .20	36523	23¼	13¼	13¾	−1¾
Osmonics Inc	13827	16¾	7	7¼	−7⅜
OTF Equits	52248	7⅞	2⅜	4⅝	+1⅜
Otter Tail 2.84	34025	49¼	27¾	47⅛	+12⅛
Overland Exp	43415	10¾	2¾	2¾	−7⅞
OwensMnr .30	50473	20⅜	13¼	18	...

—P-Q—

	Sales 100s	High	Low	Last	Net Chg.
Paccar 1.40a	83926	58¼	41	46¾	+¼
Pace Membr	257824	21	7½	8⅛	−6½
Pacer Corptn	12209	6⅞	4⅜	5⅛	...
PacifiCare	22939	17¼	10¼	10¼	−7
PacFstFnc SB	224615	21	8¼	16	+4¾
PacNucl Sys	50539	14¾	4⅝	6¾	−4¼
PacSowst Air	59248	16½	6½	16	...
PacTelecm .88	36844	17¼	13	16	+1
PacWestrn .12	42366	6½	4¾	5½	+¾
PackageSys s	x3655	7¼	3⅝	5¾	+1¼
Paco PharmS	56198	23¾	13½	21	+2¾

OVER-THE-COUNTER

	Sales 100s	High	Low	Last	Net Chg.
PageAmer Gr	81120	1⅞	½	9-16	-¼
PalmSpr SvB	727	13	8¼	11	...
PAM Transpt	18036	15¼	13½	15	...
PanAm Mtge	15430	9⅝	5⅛	8½	+3⅜
Palmetto Fedl	28929	23	12¼	16¾	+4½
Panatech Res	36431	5⅞	1½	2⅛	-2⅜
Pancho's .13g	28732	14½	7¾	10⅞	+1⅜
P&C Foods	13415	11⅛	8¼	10⅛	...
ParTechnl Cp	17453	23¼	11½	12½	-5¼
ParisBus Frm	15618	9⅜	4½	4⅞	...
Parisian Inc	40090	29¾	9⅞	23½	+8
Park Comm	8996	34½	22	28¼	+5
ParkOhio .50h	61720	14¼	5	6½	-4¾
Parkway .20d	6284	25½	19	20⅜	+⅝
Parlex Corp	8787	19½	14¼	17¼	+3¼
Par Pharmct	119760	19½	13	15¼	-1¼
Pasql FdA s	x74746	20	12¼	18	+1⅜
pasql FdB s	x2512	20	10½	18	+7
Pasta & Chees	61277	16⅞	7¾	16¼	+7
Patlex Corp	60348	20¼	7¼	14½	+3
PatrickInd 10i	27342	14½	7⅜	8	-1⅞
Paul Harris	64764	25⅛	11⅝	13⅞	+1⅞
PaxtonFrk .54	7455	21½	15½	18½	-¾
Paychex Inc s	x63472	25¾	11¾	23¼	+10⅝
Payco Amer	28520	24½	15¼	16½	+½
Pay'n Save	41102	16⅛	5⅛	5¾	...
PCS Inc	22857	14¾	13	13¾	...
PDA Engineer	35674	19½	7	10¼	-7¼
PeerlessMf .72	1242	14¼	10	10	-3½
Pegasus Gold	131671	11¼	5⅜	11¼	+4½
Pennbncp 1.20	22566	57¼	37	37½	-10¾
PennEntr 2.20	6132	41	26	36¾	+3½
Penn SvgsBk	17685	17	13¼	13½	...
Penn Va 1.60a	11746	50½	39½	46½	-⅝
Pentair .66	66629	33½	21¾	25⅝	-5⅜
Penwest Lmtd	20710	19½	11¼	19	+7½
PeopleBc s.48	x6635	18	12⅜	14	+⅞
PeopleBcWa 1	19806	56½	46¼	48½	-1½
PeopleBk .12d	972	18½	14	14½	-1½
People Htge	70122	18¼	16¾	17⅞	...
Peoples SvBk	16951	15⅛	12½	15⅛	...
Peoples West	53002	21½	16⅜	18⅛	...
Perceptn Tec	33296	25	15	18	...
Perceptnc Inc	48809	10⅞	6¼	6⅝	-3
Perle System	6010	10	4	4½	-4
PerpetualSB s	x95927	20	11⅝	13¾	+⅞
PerpSB pf.85d	49821	14¾	11¾	12¼	+¼
Petrol Indus	7009	2 9-16	1	1⅜	-⅜
PETCO Co	36744	2⅜	½	25-32	-1 7-32
Petrolite 1.12	33278	29	22¾	27	-1½
Petrmnrl .05d	8119	2⅞	1	1⅜	-1½
P&F Ind A s	x60211	5⅝	2¼	4	...
P&F Indus wt	7262	½	1-32	1-32	...
Pharmcia .10d	506012	27⅛	16½	22⅛	+3⅝
Pharmacntrl	187198	19⅝	5¾	7½	-¾
Pharmkntc Lab	112393	3 5-16	1 5-16	1¾	-3-16
PhilipCrs s.35	x56889	19⅝	6	9	...
PhilipG ADR	535873	25⅞	15⅝	19⅞	-2½
Phoenix Amer	11818	5¾	3	3⅜	+⅜
Phoenix Med	7140	5¾	2½	2¾	-1½
PhoneA Gram	11782	4⅝	1⅝	3¾	+1¼
Photo Contrl	3925	6	3⅞	4¼	-1¾
Photronics Cp	17184	7¼	4	6⅛	+2⅛
Physcnl Oh s	x15287	11¾	5	7¼	+1¼
Pic N Save s	x451000	30⅜	17⅝	21⅛	+⅝
Piccadilly s.48	x33507	26¼	16½	20	-1⅝
PiedmtBk s.44	x1873	24	14¾	18¼	+3½
PiedmtFed 5i	13759	18¼	10¼	15¾	+5½
PiedmntM .36	22030	27½	13⅜	16¾	-1¾
PionFed s.18d	x31841	11¼	5⅛	6¾	+¼
PioneerFn Sv	10130	13¾	11¼	13	...
Pioneer Gr .40	37674	35½	19¾	24¼	-2
PioneerHi 1.04	260173	43¾	29½	30	-8
Pioneer SvBk	44132	11⅜	6	7½	+⅛
Pionr SB Inc	6089	15¾	11	11	...
PionrStEl .12	28435	10½	5	6¾	-3⅜
PiperJaf .20	1093	26½	19½	20	...
PlantersCp .70	9576	26¾	18½	22	+2½
Plasti-Line	12333	20¾	12½	13	...
PlazaCB .10g	6925	9	5¼	8	+2½
PlenumP 1.04	15069	77	45	48¼	-3¼
Plexus Corp	22303	13¼	5¼	5⅜	...
Plymth Five	33217	14¾	11¾	12¾	...
P N C F 1.52	268583	51	34⅞	41¼	+6¼
Po Folks Inc	33901	11⅜	3¾	4	-5⅝
Policy MgtSys	327116	28	15	23	...
Polk AudioInc	22014	18	11½	14½	...
Polycast Tech	4387	11½	6½	8½	+1¼
PolycastTc wt	754	3½	2¼	3½	+1
Polymeric Resr	5607	5⅛	2¾	4⅜	+1⅝
Polymer Intl	8466	10⅛	6⅝	7⅝	...
PolyTech Inc	41250	16½	5	5⅝	...
PonceFd s.36a	x86470	15½	9⅛	11⅛	+1⅜
Popular Bcshr	18920	5¾	2⅞	5⅜	+1⅞
Ports of Call	73221	10⅞	6¾	7⅜	...
PorexTech Cp	81013	35⅛	23¾	27¼	+1⅝
PossisCorp s	x37443	37½	15½	23½	+4⅝
Poughkps SvB	59752	27	14⅞	15¼	-2⅝
Powell Indust	20682	2½	1⅛	1¼	-⅝
PrattHotel Cp	123348	5⅝	1½	3	+1⅜
Prec Cast s.12	x67569	33½	13⅛	32¾	+9⅝
PfdHlthCare s	x11568	18⅝	7¼	12½	+4
PrfdRiskLf .88	3211	41½	31	35½	+3½
Preferred SB	11879	7¾	5	5½	-1¼
Present Co	24530	11⅜	5⅝	6	-1
PresLf s.36	x41823	33½	11½	28	+15⅝
Preston Cp .50	95461	24	15¾	23½	+6½
Preway Inc	95994	3⅜	½	11-16	-1 3-16
Priam Corp	441027	7½	2⅛	2⅜	-3¾
PriceComm s	x7913	10¾	5¾	9⅛	+1⅝
Price Co s	x470075	55¾	28¼	32¾	-2¼
PSS Pub	39262	22¾	9	13½	+1
Prime Bank	7643	15	10¾	11⅝	-½
Prime Capital	17219	12½	8⅞	9⅜	...
PrimeMd Sv	40729	8	3½	3½	...
Princevl .16	173283	11¾	6½	8	+1⅜
Printronix Inc	38628	14⅞	9¾	10	-3
Prod Oprtr .16	38989	4¾	3¾	4	-⅜
Profess Invest	20652	11⅛	5¾	6½	-¼
Prof Sys .30h	13513	18⅛	8¾	8¾	-6¼
Program Syst	8692	10½	7½	8¼	+¼
ProgrsFSB 10i	5139	22¾	13½	14½	+1
ProgrsOh s.06	x158870	38½	20¼	31	+10½
ProgrsBk .28	x16177	24¾	12⅜	17½	+4
Progroup Inc	34086	10⅝	7	8	+⅞
PropTrA 1.20	39003	14¼	9	9⅜	-1¾
Prospect Grp	212312	10⅝	8	8⅞	...
ProtectvLf .70	87629	25½	17⅝	18	-4
Provident Am	11396	5	1½	2⅛	+⅛
ProvLfAcc .84	140879	33	22⅞	24⅝	-1¾
Prud Fncl Svc	5144	12	8¾	10	+¼
PrudentBc 10i	9388	20¾	14¼	14¾	+¼
Pubco Corp	113586	1 3-16	17-32	⅝	-½
Publishrs Eq	30308	9	4⅞	5½	+⅛
PbSvcNC 1.80	14697	28⅛	20⅛	26⅛	+5⅝
PugetSBc s.72	x59585	26¾	20	21	+⅝
PulaskiFn s.36	x16647	20⅞	12¾	16½	+2¾
Pulitzer Pub	20108	31	28¼	30½	...
PuritnBen s.20	x49609	31¾	14	29½	+13⅞
Pyramid Tech	44019	17⅜	3¾	5	-12
QED Explor	10094	3⅛	1⅞	3⅛	...
QMS Incorp	176479	16⅜	8⅞	14⅛	+5
QTNT Co	97368	1¼	3-32	3-32	-21-32
Quadrex Corp	126901	16½	4	9½	+1
QuakerCh .50	38989	20½	12	16¾	+3¼
Quality Systm	13877	4¼	1¾	2⅛	...
Quantronix	13934	11¾	5¾	6	-1½
Quantum Corp	251223	27	16	20¾	-6
Quarex Ind	6584	5¼	2½	2¾	-⅝
QuesTech Inc	2334	7½	4¾	5¼	-1¼
Quest Medical	91479	6⅝	3⅛	3¾	-½
Quiksilver	9791	8½	6⅝	7⅛	...
Quincy Cp 10i	32172	21	15⅞	15⅞	-1¾
Quintel Corp	6273	5¾	3	4	-1¼
Quipp Inc	2155	20	12½	20	...
Quixote Cp s	x94399	15½	8¾	11¾	+2¾
QVC Network	117561	26	15½	16¾	...

—R—

	Sales 100s	High	Low	Last	Net Chg.
Radiatn Syst	84766	15⅞	8⅜	8⅞	-5⅜
Radiatn Tech	76817	11¼	2¼	2¾	-8¼
Radionics Inc	11511	12	6¾	8⅞	+1⅞
Ragen Corp	53013	6½	1⅝	2⅜	-1¼
RainierBc 1.08	152860	43¾	30½	33	-1⅜
Ramapo Fn s	x4032	24⅝	15⅛	17	+1¾
Ramtek Corp	63033	6¾	2¾	5⅜	+2
Rangaire .18f	17194	10⅜	7¾	8⅞	+½
RaxRestr .01b	41137	10¾	4⅞	5	-1¼
RaymndC s.47	x26298	23	13¾	17¼	+2⅞
ReadiCare	77410	5¼	1 3-16	1½	-¼
Reading Co	28141	28	19⅜	23½	+1⅜
REIT Cal 1.28	25345	18¼	13½	17⅛	+2⅞
Recoton Corp	29281	14½	6¾	7	-3⅞

OVER-THE-COUNTER

	Sales 100s	High	Low	Last	Net Chg.
Redkn Lb .20g	26401	35½	14¾	25	-8
Reed Jewelers	4654	10¼	8½	8½	...
Reeves Comm	204275	16⅛	5⅜	8	-4⅛
Refac Techn s	x35842	15½	5¾	9¾	-5⅝
Reflectone	16747	20¾	13	14¾	-4
RegencyEl .20	163559	8⅜	4⅝	6⅛	...
Regency Eqt	237072	1⅜	⅜	9-16	+3-16
Regina Co	33442	21¾	11⅝	20	+8
Regis Corp .18	22493	18¾	10½	14¾	-2½
Reid Ashman	14738	6	1	1⅛	-4⅛
Reliability Inc	13148	10	3⅛	3⅞	-1
RentACenter s	x50909	26	17⅛	24½	+7
Repco Incorp	5142	5¾	2⅞	4¼	...
Repligen Corp	50269	11⅝	5¾	8¾	...
RepubAm .10d	146236	18	14¼	15¼	...
RepAuto .04h	22151	10	6⅝	8¾	-¾
RepublicPic A	38575	14¾	7¾	8	-⅜
RepblSvgs Fin	7026	6⅝	3¼	4½	-1¼
Republic Svg	5616	19	15½	19	...
ResrchInc .40	6141	11¼	7¾	11	+¼
Research Ind	39870	9¾	3¾	4½	-1¾
ReservOil Mn	12553	4½	2¾	2¾	-¼
Resourc Explr	19130	2⅝	1 7-16	1 9-16	-11-16
Respns1 .81d	13716	13	10½	12¼	+½
Respns2 .72d	19521	12½	9	10¼	-1¼
Respns3 .60d	16133	10¾	7¾	9¼	-½
RestMgm s.07	x27399	13½	7½	7½	-2⅜
Reuter Inc	25498	19	8⅞	12½	+3⅜
Rtrs ADR .41d	467361	51	20	49⅞	+17½
Rever AE 1.56	7152	16½	12¾	15½	+2¾
Rexon Incorp	32739	9⅜	3⅞	6½	+1
ReynldsA s.76	x146126	41½	25⅛	33	+4⅜
Rheometrics	5574	9¼	5	6½	-2⅜
Ribi Imunchm	153897	11½	5	5¾	-1
RichardsnEl s	x27449	24½	13¾	17¾	+3⅝
RichmHill SB	73217	16⅛	11⅝	13¼	...
Richton Intl	30595	7⅞	3⅝	4⅛	-3¼
Ridgewd Prop	5775	27	21	25	+1½
Riedel Envirn	31487	21	10½	14¼	...
RiggsNtl s1.10	x43682	41½	28	29¼	-1¾
Ritzy's GD	19059	3	15-16	1⅛	-⅛
RivForBc s.16	x7381	16	11½	15	...
Riverside G	7175	13¾	4¼	11⅛	+6⅛
RLI Corp s.28	x30034	20⅛	11½	13¾	+1⅛
Roadrunner E	15588	7⅞	5½	7	...
RoadwSrv 1.10	318692	45¾	29½	34½	-¼
RoanokEl s.56	x14070	20¾	12¼	14¼	+⅝
Robbins Myer	7334	13¾	7	9	-3½
RobesonIn 10k	17420	7¼	2¾	4¼	-1
RoboticVs Sys	35621	11½	3⅝	4	-4½
Robsn Nu .06	31870	13¾	9⅞	12½	-1⅛
RochstrC SB	210336	15⅞	10⅜	11¼	...
Rockwd Hold	12256	12	4½	6¾	+¾
RckyMt Undr	39116	9⅜	2½	4⅛	-3⅝
RogersCbl Am	94053	16⅝	9⅞	11⅛	-2⅛
Ronson Corp	15794	2⅜	⅞	15-16	...
Ropak Corp	33291	19½	7½	8¾	-3½
RoseStore s.16	x10706	23	10⅛	16¼	...
RoseStrB s.16	x66249	23¼	10⅞	16	+4⅝
RosptchCp .60	25555	24½	16¼	21	+4
Ross Stores	314277	18¼	4¼	4¾	-13¼
RoTech Med	7680	5⅝	3⅜	3¾	...
Roto Rootr .20	19872	23¼	14¼	16½	-2
Rouse Co .60	127500	34½	25¾	31⅜	+5⅛
RoweFrn .16a	26995	19¼	9⅞	14	+4
Rowley Scher	15837	12¾	3¼	4	-5¼
Royale Airline	13965	7¾	2⅜	2¾	-4½
Royal Palm S	63373	9¾	3¾	4⅝	-4⅞
Royal Resour	26992	7⅝	1⅝	2⅞	-⅛
RPM Inc .72	104755	23¾	13¾	19¾	+2¼
Rudy's Restr	21904	8	3½	3¾	...
RSI Corp s	x27873	12¼	2½	10⅞	...
Rule Industr	17060	9¼	6½	7¼	+¾
Rusty Pelican	55991	15⅜	5	8⅜	-3½
Ryan Beck Co	32815	16	8¼	8¾	...
Ryan'sFam s	x220403	26	10⅛	21⅜	+11¾
—S—					
Saatchi 2.68d	199154	44½	24½	32⅜	-3⅜
SafeCard s.24	x366585	33⅛	15	30⅛	+20½
Safeco Cp 1.70	219869	64	32⅝	53½	+7⅛
Safeguard Hth	86291	13¼	5	5½	-6¼
SAGE Softwr	22338	14½	12½	13¼	...
Sahara Resort	12947	7¼	3⅛	6⅞	+3¾
StJoeBc .72g	4974	43½	27½	40	+8¾
StJude Med s	x112657	17¾	9¼	15	+4½
StPaulCo s1.50	x448765	54	35¾	40¼	+⅜
Salem Carpet	74835	11	3¼	8¾	+3⅜
Salick Health	80567	19⅞	10¾	11⅝	+¼
San Bar	7129	9½	5	5	-2½
S&K Famous	6338	11⅝	6	8⅝	+2⅝
Sands Regent	21531	13¾	7½	8½	-1½
Sandwch Chef	8852	9⅞	5½	5½	-3¼
Sndwich Coop	21289	16	12	14¼	...
Sanford Cp	35048	31¼	20¾	27	+5¾
SanFran FSL	47426	12⅝	10⅜	11⅝	...
Saratoga Std	29775	4⅜	2⅜	3 3-16	+1-16
Satell Music	99358	13⅞	3¾	4⅜	-2
Savana F .88a	18900	37½	22	24	-7½
Saxon Oil	60907	⅝	7-32	9-32	-9-32
SAY Industrs	43474	12½	5	7½	-1⅝
SaversInc .40h	8094	13	½	⅞	-10⅞
Savoy Indust	78942	1½	½	½	-11-16
Scan Optics	105590	15¼	6¾	8⅝	-2½
Scan Tron s	x53772	19⅛	10⅛	13⅝	+1½
SchererRP .32	103013	20¾	9¾	13⅝	-1¾
Scholastic Inc	19872	38½	18½	36½	+17
Schulman .44g	43651	44¾	16½	41⅛	+12⅞
SCI SystemsIn	197383	21⅜	13½	17⅝	+2½
SciCom Data	5213	5⅞	3¾	4 7-16	-1 1-16
Science Dynm	14840	6⅛	3⅜	4⅛	-⅛
Sci Commun	41518	13½	8	12¾	+2½
SciMedLf Syst	x19397	14	3⅞	13½	+4⅛
Sci Micro Syst	47625	7¼	4	4⅝	-¼
Scientific Sys	27442	5	1⅞	2	-1½
Scientfc Softw	29793	11½	3⅜	3¾	-4
Scitex Corpn	93140	16¼	2⅜	3¾	-4¼
ScoaIndB 9i	29816	21½	14	21	+5⅞
SCOR US Cp	62340	14½	10½	12	...
Scott Cable	24460	15	9¼	11	+¼
Scott String	1565	15½	13½	13½	...
Scripps H .80	13322	89¾	47½	79	+30½
SCS Compute	9961	8¾	4⅞	6¼	...
SeacstBkA .44	8181	19⅞	15¼	17	+⅞
SeaGalley Str	41412	7⅜	1⅞	1⅞	-2⅜
Seagate Tech	1767626	21	4¾	19⅛	+11⅞
Seagull pf A	229	31½	31	31	...
Seal Incorp	11548	6¾	3	5⅛	+1⅞
Sealright .03d	36373	25½	18½	19⅝	...
Seamans Furn	54257	46½	25	42	+16¾
Seaway FT .68	3743	23½	16¾	22	+3½
SecNtlBL s.24	x32121	10½	5¾	6⅞	+1⅛
SecAmF s.06	x4392	12	6¾	9⅝	+½
Secur Bcp s1	x11012	21¾	20	21¾	...
SecurFed SBk	1515	8⅝	8⅛	8⅛	...
SecurTag Sys	48858	11⅝	1¼	1 13-16	-1-16
SEEQ Technol	205418	3¼	7-16	⅞	-2⅛
SEI Corp	64769	27¾	14	18½	-5
Seibels Br .80	50958	22¾	14½	14¾	-6
SelectInsur .92	35537	24¾	16¼	21¾	...
Selecterm Inc	5675	11½	4¾	5¼	-1½
Semicon Inc	10293	8⅛	5⅛	5⅞	-1½
Sensrm El .10	490545	11¾	7⅛	9¾	+⅜
Svc Fracturng	13171	5⅝	2	2½	-1⅜
SrvcMerch .08	853630	15⅛	7⅜	7¾	-4⅝
ServicoInc 10k	12701	27	15¼	18½	-3
SevenOak s.16	x65409	21⅛	13¼	13⅛	-1
SFE Tech .10e	41576	10	2⅝	3 5-16	-4 1-16
ShrMedSys .72	438216	42½	26⅞	40½	+5¼
Shawmut 2.04	97928	55½	30⅛	45⅜	+3¾
Shelby FedSB	469	11¾	9¼	11	...
ShelbyWil s.16	x84482	28¼	14¼	17	-⅛
Sheldhl Inc	29095	12	6	11½	+2½
Shelton SvLn	1784	13	11½	12¾	...
SHLSystmhs s	x128039	12	(z)	11⅞	...
Shoe City	12658	11½	7¼	8½	...
Shoneys s.16	x261654	31	19⅛	24⅞	+1⅜
Shoneys South	59821	18¾	11¾	13	+½
Shopsmith Inc	7227	6¾	2¾	3½	+½
Shorewood Pk	23762	11½	8¾	10½	...
SierraCap IV	5795	9⅝	7½	8¾	...
SierR83 .65d	3877	11	9	10½	+¼
Sier84 .62d	4609	10	8	9	-¼
SigmaAld s.28	x102826	40¼	26½	37¾	+20⅝
Sigma Design	31330	18¼	13⅛	17¾	...
Sigma Resrch	6379	4⅝	¼	1 1-16	-2 11-16
Sigmaform Cp	15343	10	4¾	5¼	-4¾
Silicon Generl	99223	7¾	2⅞	4¼	-½
SiliconSys Inc	101200	19	10	11⅛	-2¼
SiliconVal Grp	40509	20¼	9¼	12½	-3¾
Siliconix s	x97875	19¼	9¾	10¼	-1⅛
Silvar Lisco	122672	8¾	3⅞	4¼	-1⅜
Silver StMing	360933	2 1-32	11-16	1 11-32	+17-32

OVER-THE-COUNTER

	Sales 100s	High	Low	Last	Net Chg.
Simmons Air	101589	14¾	5¾	7¼	– 3¼
SmpsnInd s.56	x55016	21⅛	10⅝	13½	– 3
Sippican Inc	30462	14½	10½	12¼	+ 1⅜
SIS Corporatn	3403	7	4	5¼	– 1¼
Sizzler Rest s	x114335	19	10¼	15½	– ¾
Skaneateles 5i	7938	14¼	9½	9½	...
SKF AB 1.19d	13848	52⅞	39	49¾	+10½
S-K-I Ltd .05d	17434	11½	8¾	10	+ 1¼
Skipper's .08	24465	11¼	7½	7½	– 2¾
Sky Express	6876	2¾	⅞	1	– ¾
SkyWest Inc	14288	10¼	8¾	9½	...
SmithLab Inc	150824	3⅞	2⅜	2¾	...
Smithfld Fd s	x61671	23	8⅞	17¾	+ 8¼
Snelling .40d	2610	8¾	6	7½	+ ¾
SocietyCp 1.92	60115	71½	35½	56½	+ 2½
SocietyS .07f	x174881	28¼	12½	22¾	+ 9⅝
SofTech Inc	37949	12½	7	7	– 3¼
Software AG	86351	21¾	10	11¾	– 5⅜
Software Publ	92293	8½	4¾	7	– 1¼
SomrsetB .80a	3465	37½	25	29½	+ 3¾
Somerset Svg	28961	12⅛	10⅜	10⅝	...
SonestaA s.20	x2188	15	10⅝	11¼	– ⅜
SonocoPr .80	54470	41	29¼	38	+ 7¼
SoonerDef Fla	31142	9½	5⅛	6	+ ⅞
SoonrFSL .15h	29467	17½	8	13½	– 2¾
Sound Warhs	55860	31⅛	13½	13⅞	– 8⅝
Southbrk ADR	23668	14¾	4½	5	– 5
SoCaro FSB	17323	19¾	14	15	...
Se Mich s1.04g	x7383	20	12	17¾	+ 4⅞
SoeastnSL .12	12274	17½	11½	12	– 1
SCaroNatl s.50	x61633	27¾	19⅞	22¼	+ 1⅝
Southrn Bksh	145	42	39	40	...
SoCalWtr 1.90	15568	35	23¼	26¾	+ 3⅜
SthnHome SB	5601	22½	14	21½	+ 7½
Sthn Hospitlty	38058	5⅝	2¾	3	– 1½
SthnNtlNC .76	14895	26½	20¾	22¼	+ ¼
Southingtn SB	x8228	20	12	16½	...
SthlandFcl .52	150674	31¾	13⅛	13½	– 7½
Sthlife Hldg	26961	11	7½	7¾	...
SouthTrust .68	70053	25¾	19	23½	+ 4⅜
SthwstNtl s.70	x1739	36½	17½	22½	+ 4¼
SthwstWt s.80	x1739	21½	14½	19½	+ 3
SowstnEIS 2	913	39¾	29¾	38	+ 7¾
Sovereign .10	158976	10	6⅝	7¼	+ ⅜
Sovran F 1.36	242549	44½	32¼	33¾	+ 1½
SpanAmMd s	x38557	13	12¼	6⅛	– 5¼
Spartan Motor	38555	3⅞	1⅛	3	+ 1¾
SpartnMtr wt	623	¾	⅜	½	...
Spartech Corp	85584	2⅜	1	1 9-16	+1-16
Spearhead 10k	34815	9¼	2⅞	7⅜	+ 4
SpecContrl .06	70752	13¾	5½	9⅞	+ 1¼
Speclty Cmpst	2006	7¼	4½	5¾	+ ¾
SpecltyRet 10i	6249	9	5¾	5¾	– ¾
SpecsMusic s	x12363	8½	5⅞	7½	...
Spectradyn s	x121875	21¼	10¾	17	+ 3½
Spectran Corp	102312	21½	1¼	2⅛	–19⅜
SPI Pharm .06	80007	43½	10¾	28	+16¼
Spire Corp	19004	16⅝	7	8½	– 7¾
SPI Suspensn	33747	7⅞	1¾	2¾	– 3¾
Sporting Life	19947	9¼	4½	5½	...
Springboard S	10914	8¼	7	7¾	...
SprouseR .60d	3155	45	25	27	...
Square Indus	3181	12½	8	8½	– ¾
SRI Corp .80	36239	24¾	16¼	22¾	+ 5⅞
Staar Surgical	69015	15⅞	7	7½	– 2⅝
Staff Build .20	62014	12⅜	5⅞	9⅞	+ 1¼
StanWest Mng	91559	4⅞	1⅞	3⅛	–9-16
Stanadyn 1.20	23251	43¾	21½	35½	+ 5½
StdCmTb s.44	x17931	33	20½	21¾	+ 5
Std Microsyst	201359	21¾	9⅛	10½	– 3⅞
StdRegistr .80	50390	50¼	31½	36⅛	+ ⅝
StanfordTel s	x25999	33	10⅛	12⅛	– 2¼
Stanley Inter	14212	12½	9⅞	10½	...
Stanline .28g	20737	13¼	7⅞	8¾	+ ⅛
Stansbury Mn	161271	4¼	9-16	1 9-16	+9-16
Stars To Go	17986	14½	8	8¾	...
StateOMaine s	x1657	9½	7	9½	+ 2½
StateSBos s.36	x189973	28⅞	19¼	23⅜	+ 2¾
StatsmnG .05g	62779	8⅜	4½	4¾	– ⅜
StatewdB .72	22928	25½	17	19	–10¼
Status Game	30199	6½	3	4	– ⅛
SteelTech .03d	14262	24	13⅛	23½	+10⅜
Stendig Ind B	65	14	8	11½	...
Stendig cl.B	8407	14	8	11¼	+ 1¾
Stepsaver Dat	35827	5⅝	3⅛	5	...
Sterner LghtS	35720	18⅜	4⅜	12⅛	+ 1⅜

	Sales 100s	High	Low	Last	Net Chg.
Stereo Village	69735	13¼	7-16	1 1-16	–7 13-16
Sterling Inc	27130	16⅛	10	14	...
StewrtInfo .76	60373	29	18½	19¾	– 3¼
Stewrt Sndw	5878	2⅝	1	2⅛	– ⅜
StewrtStev .20	50961	16¾	10	12¼	– 3¼
Stockhldr Sys	18402	10½	6¼	6½	– 2¾
StockrYal s.10	x6641	16	8¾	10	+ ⅞
StockSL s.17	x15716	17½	8½	12	+ 3½
StokelyUS .12	57357	15⅛	7⅜	7½	– 6
StrategicP B	15901	12⅝	11½	12¼	...
Stratus Cmptr	381845	24¾	15¼	21⅛	– 2⅝
Strawbrig .93g	47091	63½	37	40½	– ⅞
Stryker Corp	49524	44	23¼	32	+ 8
StuartDept Str	70317	18¾	6¼	7½	– 6
StuartHal .05g	33261	9½	3⅜	5⅝	+ ¼
StudntLVt .36	27969	55½	41	54	...
SturmR 1.50d	2432	44	32½	36	– 1
STV Engineer	8588	20¾	10	13½	+ 2½
Subaru s.38	x355364	39	18½	19¼	+ ¼
SubrbBcA .22	17073	21½	14⅞	16⅜	...
Sudbury Hldg	32166	9⅞	7⅝	9⅛	+ ⅛
SuffldSvgs .12	45278	24⅝	13½	17⅜	+ 2½
SuffolkB s.25d	1561	34	27½	30	...
Sumitomo 1.16	2397	30½	20	25	+ 5¼
Summa Medl	98787	5¾	2⅛	2⅜	– ⅛
Summcp s.36	x10580	23¼	13	15	– 3
SummitB s.68	80514	29½	20⅞	25	...
SummtHth .12	119313	11½	5⅛	6⅛	– 3⅜
SummitHld 1f	374	41	33	34	...
SummitSavg s	4042	9¼	3¾	4⅞	+ 1⅞
Suncoast Plas	224646	5⅛	1	2⅞	+ 1¾
SunairElec .24	19925	9⅝	5⅜	6¼	– 1¾
SuncoastSL A	5138	10	7	9¾	+ 2⅝
SunGard Data	103943	16	9¾	13½	...
Sunlite Inc	8551	4⅛	2⅜	2¾	– 1⅜
Sun Microsys	436850	24⅜	11¼	24	...
SunWorld Intl	31220	7⅞	2¾	3	– 4⅜
Sunrise Med	48355	15½	9¾	11½	+ 1¼
Sunstar Foods	3046	5¼	3⅝	4⅜	– ½
Sunstate Corp	2410	12¾	10	11⅞	+ ⅞
Sunstate pf	1513	25½	21	22½	– ½
SunState S&L	13847	10	7	8	...
SunwstFn s1	x18830	35¾	15¼	32½	+ 4⅞
SuperiorE 10k	15220	12⅛	7	9½	– 1¾
Super Rite .20	30887	27¼	12⅛	12⅜	– 8⅝
SuperSkyIntl s	x15733	13⅛	24½	10	...
Supertex Inc	19649	4½	1¼	1¾	– 1⅞
Supreme Eqpt	8443	10⅜	4¼	6¼	– 1⅛
SusqhnBs s.72	x9010	29½	18¾	20⅜	+ 1⅛
SurgCare Affil	7368	10	5½	6¾	+ ¼
Survival Tech	10131	28½	8½	13¼	+ 4¼
Sutron Corp	5536	4⅜	1¾	2	– 2¼
Svenska .48d	2986	43	21⅜	42⅜	+19⅞
Sybra Inc	9210	13¼	10	10½	...
SylvanLearn s	x28782	14¼	5¾	6¾	...
Symbion Inc	48087	4	2⅜	2⅝	...
Symbol Techn	70575	19¼	9¼	18⅞	+ 6⅝
Symbolics Inc	580904	15⅜	3⅞	4⅜	– 9⅞
SymTek Systs	4561	21	12½	16½	+ 2¾
Synbiotics s	x15971	15½	(z)	7¾	...
Syncor Intl	141236	10⅛	5⅛	6⅝	+ ½
Synergen Inc	53282	18⅜	7⅝	8½	...
Synercom Tch	72518	18¾	4⅝	5⅞	...
Syntech Intl	59838	14⅝	7	8⅝	+ 1¾
Syntrex Inc	51328	5⅞	2⅞	3⅜	– 1⅛
Syntro Corp	20188	8⅛	3⅛	4¼	...
Syrac Supp .28	1860	14¾	10½	14⅜	+ 3⅞
Syscon Cp .20	49354	20	11¾	19⅞	+ 6⅜
System Indus	31336	9½	5⅞	5⅞	– 1⅝
System Integr	101026	17	6	8⅞	– 2⅛
Systems Assc	53013	16	5¾	12¼	+ 1½
SysCmptr Tec	99825	7	3⅜	4⅛	– 1
Systematic .12	72507	30¼	13⅞	17⅝	– 7⅝

—T—

	Sales 100s	High	Low	Last	Net Chg.
TacoVilla Inc	4460	5¼	2½	3½	– ¼
Taco Viva Inc	15224	3⅝	1¾	1⅞	– 1⅛
Tandem Cmpt	1041238	39½	18⅞	34¼	+12
Tandon Corp	1131160	7⅞	1⅞	2 5-16	–2 9-16
Taunton SvBk	28139	12¾	11	11	...
TBC Corprtn	21462	14	8¾	12½	+ 1¼
TCA Cabl s.24	x31978	16¾	(z)	16¾	...
TCBYEnt s.24	x290070	39¾	8¾	17⅝	+ 7½
T Cell Sci	30539	5⅛	2¼	3⅜	...
TCF Banking	73605	15¾	11¼	12⅛	...
TCTC s	x637	31	22	24½	- 3½

OVER-THE-COUNTER

	Sales 100s	High	Low	Last	Net Chg.
Tech Data	22184	12¼	7¼	10	...
TechCom Intl	9187	19	6	14½	...
Technalys .17	6028	14½	5⅜	8	− 3½
Technicl Com	4589	9½	2⅜	3¼	− 5¾
Teknowledge	104008	16	8	9⅜	...
TecmPd 3.20a	8434	130	105½	120½	+ 7
Tekelec	19271	12¼	5¼	5⅝	...
Telco System	144963	18¼	2¾	3	−11¼
Tel Plus Intl	343453	9⅞	6	7¼	− 1
Telecrafter Cp	15040	13¾	2½	2¾	− 9⅞
TelecmNtwk s	x33487	15¼	5½	5½	...
Telecredit .36	104493	54¾	20¾	54	+24¼
TelecommA s	x696425	29⅛	17½	22⅞	+ 4⅝
Tele Comm B	10545	56¼	21½	22¾	−13
TeleComm wt	84416	39¼	18⅛	26½	+ 7¾
Telemation s	x8446	4¾	1¼	(z)	...
TeleQuest	20788	13¾	3	3	...
Telesis Syst	17000	7¾	3⅜	4¼	...
Televideo Sys	148747	4 1-16	1¾	2	− 1
Tellabs Incorp	117441	15¼	9⅜	11½	− ⅜
Tel Man Inc	34464	16	12¼	12½	...
Telos Corp	18970	10⅜	5⅜	5¾	− 3¾
Telxon s.01d	x145954	27½	9⅛	20½	+ 5¼
Temco Home	39687	8⅝	3⅛	3⅛	− 3½
Templeton En	126934	2 15-16	1½	1 9-16	...
Temtex Indus	8667	7½	3⅞	4¾	− 2¼
TendrLv Care	42102	13¼	3⅝	6⅜	+ 2¼
TennantCo .96	48188	26½	20½	24¼	+ ¾
TeneraLP wi	9377	5½	2¾	3	− ⅞
TermData 10k	28887	10¾	1 5-16	2	− 1⅜
Termiflex Cp	3580	6¾	5	5¼	− ¾
Therml Profls	37881	13⅝	1⅜	1⅝	− 4¾
Thermedics s	x127767	19¾	7½	13¼	+ 5
Thermo Anlyt	35794	13	5¾	6	− 2⅝
Thermo Inst	24770	10½	7⅜	9¾	...
Thetford .20	7672	17¾	7½	12¾	+ 1½
ThNelson .16g	54531	11¾	5¾	7¾	+ ⅞
Thomson CSF	1128	52½	42	48⅝	...
ThornApple V	4016	5¾	3¾	5¼	+ ⅝
Thousand Trl	162445	15⅛	1¾	3⅛	− 5⅛
3Com Corp	252328	16⅝	7	16⅛	+ 4⅝
Tierco Group	1903	10¼	6½	6½	− 2
Timberland	5928	8¼	4¾	6	+ ¼
Tipton Center	21934	15¾	11¾	13¼	...
TMK United	41843	14¾	9¼	12½	...
Tom Brown In	235100	1⅞	3-16	½	−7-16
TonyLam .40h	10310	15	8	9½	− 5½
Tops Market	54617	25¾	18	19	...
Toreadr Roylt	13699	7¼	2½	3	− 3
TotalSystSvc s	x14603	29½	13¼	23½	+ 9¼
TowerFed SB	10793	15¾	8½	9	...
Town& Cntry	12107	17¼	9¾	13½	+ 1⅛
Toys Plus Inc	25453	9½	4	4⅛	− 4¼
Tradition Ind	23377	16½	11¼	12½	...
TrakAuto Cp	26994	18¾	11	13½	− ½
Transducer	3201	8	4¾	5¾	− 1⅜
TransInd s	x4307	15	8	8½	− 1¼
Trans Leasing	27935	9½	3	4	...
Transntl Ind	9117	8½	5	6	...
Transnet Corp	58000	3⅜	1 15-16	2 1-16	−3-16
Transtech Ind	7887	9	4¾	6½	+ 2
Trnstectr Sys	21263	4¾	1⅞	2¼	− ½
TrnsW Air pf	32958	36¼	31	31	...
TrnsWorld Bc	3198	10½	7¼	7¾	− 1
TrnsW Music	38713	24	14	21¼	...
TraveRE .78d	14834	11¾	9	9⅛	− ¾
TravInc 1.20d	11882	17¾	14⅜	14⅝	− 1⅛
TRC Cos Inc	24537	21½	9½	14¾	+ 1½
Trenwick Grp	67714	25½	14⅞	16½	...
Triad Systems	83881	13⅛	8½	9⅝	− ¼
Triangl Micro	38565	6⅜	3⅝	4¼	− 1⅝
Trilogy Ltd	411687	2	7-32	5-16	−1 3-16
Trimedyn Inc	97948	16⅛	5½	11½	+ 5¼
Trion Inc .11	10474	9¾	6	7¼	+ ½
TriStar Pictrs	262696	16⅛	8½	8¾	− 2⅛
TriStarPic wt	79730	9½	3⅞	4	− ⅜
Triton Group	490730	2¼	⅞	1	−5-16
TritonGrp pfC	22175	15⅞	9	9½	− ¼
TRowe Price	76085	45	25⅝	30½	...
TrusJoist .48	26338	36¾	24	28	+ 3¼
TrustAmer Sv	2601	9½	8½	8¾	...
TrstCoNY s.88	x2159	30¼	18¾	21	...
Trust Cp 1.50	x37416	42⅜	28¾	28¾	...
Trust Cp pf	3874	53	40	43	+ 3
Trust NJ 1.20	3466	76½	39¼	71	+31

	Sales 100s	High	Low	Last	Net Chg.
TRV Minerals	10586	2⅛	11-16	¾	− ⅝
TS Indus	45885	25½	13½	25½	+11½
T S I Inc .08	13352	15¼	8½	10	+ ¼
TSO Financial	111647	18½	10¼	12¼	+ 1⅛
TSR Inc	23199	9⅜	3¾	5¼	− 2¼
Tucker Drillg	11164	7⅛	4⅞	5¼	− ¼
Tuesday Morn	40330	28	13	13¾	...
TVX Broadcst	31783	12¼	7¾	9¾	− 1½
20CentInd s.25	x111202	25¼	15	17¼	...
Twistee Treat	176140	5 1-16	2	2⅛	− 1½
II Morrow Inc	11662	11¼	6¼	9⅜	+ ⅜
Tyco Toys Inc	102239	9	6¼	7⅝	...
Tylan Corp	15089	12½	2¼	2 7-16	−8 13-16
TysonFdA s.04	x305714	38¼	12⅝	27¼	+13½
—U—					
UltraBncp .88	13588	36½	21	28	+ 5½
Ungrmn Bass	390032	16¼	7⅜	9¼	− 6⅞
Unicare Fncl	5101	10⅜	8	8⅜	...
Unibncp .20	16442	26½	15½	23	+ 6
Unibc pfA 1.53	10935	26	17	22⅝	+ 4⅞
Unifast Indust	21046	7⅞	2⅞	7⅜	+ 4½
Unifi Inc s	x229139	17⅞	9¼	15⅛	+ 5¾
UniforceTm s	x18069	15½	7¼	13¾	+ 5⅝
Uni-Marts A	20310	9	7⅞	8¼	...
Unimed Incrp	35970	18¼	8	10¼	+ ¾
UnFSLCa .05d	102189	22¾	14½	17⅞	+ 3¼
UnionNtl 1.14g	20815	47¼	31	32⅛	− 2⅞
Union Planter	91833	40	18	37	+ 8
Un Special .30	19010	22¼	14¾	19½	+ 4¾
Union Warren	75181	38¼	17½	33	+13⅛
UtdArtA s.04	x311773	21¾	12⅜	17⅝	+ 4¼
UtdBcpAl 10i	15371	10⅛	1¾	1¾	− 7¼
UtdBAriz .72	116668	32⅞	29	32¾	+ 3⅜
UtdBk SvBk	28809	33½	16⅝	31¼	+14¼
UtdB Colo 1.08	102876	35½	21¼	21⅝	− 7¾
UtdBnkr .20h	34748	9	4¾	5⅛	− 3⅞
UtdCaroB 1.04	27520	33¾	26¾	28	+ ¼
Utd Cities 1.60	21993	33	23	23¾	+ ½
UtdDoRT .96	19147	17½	12½	16⅞	+ 3½
UtdEd Softwr	24148	6 3-16	3½	5¼	+ 1¼
UtdFcl Group	45154	10	1⅝	1¾	− 4¾
UtdFireC s.80	x19643	33	19⅛	33	...
Utd Guard 10k	23171	12⅞	4½	5⅛	− 3⅝
Utd Healthcar	202177	15⅞	7½	8⅜	− 1⅞
UtdHome Life	1193	9½	7¼	7½	− ½
UtdInsur Cos	28811	27	17½	19½	...
UtdMoBcsh 1g	6537	47½	38	39	− ½
UtdNMxF .25d	14007	14¾	9	12	+ 1½
Utd Presdentl	34096	18⅞	9⅝	18¾	+ 8½
UtdSvrsB .72	47051	36	24¼	26¼	+ ¾
Utd SavingBk	8567	19	13¼	13½	...
UtdSvgLn s.24	11584	16¼	10	10	− 5
UtdStation .24	170393	25¾	13½	16⅞	− 8⅛
UtdTelcntrl El	14932	8¼	5	6½	+ ⅛
Utd Television	22675	36¾	16	28½	+ 4¼
United Tote	6084	8½	5	6	+ 1
UtdVtBncp .84	2819	30	19¼	28½	+ 8¾
UtdVaBks s.92	x80140	35⅞	22⅜	28⅝	+ 5¾
US Antimony	37088	4⅝	1⅛	1 3-16	−3 1-16
US Bncp pfA	3026	34	24	24½	− 5
USBcOre s.80	x162486	27⅜	19¼	23⅝	...
US Capital Cp	20380	5⅛	⅞	1	− 2⅜
US Design Cp	59519	5⅜	1	2⅜	− ½
US Energy Cp	11150	3⅜	1¼	1⅜	− 1⅜
US Facilities	28057	9¾	8	8½	...
US Hlthcr .12	1135520	22⅞	11⅛	11⅝	− 8¾
USHealthInc s	x31751	3½	1½	1⅞	− ⅜
US Intec	22469	20¾	9¼	12	− 3¾
US Play Card	3926	15	7	8½	− 6¼
USPlayCrd wt	342	6	4	4½	− ½
US Prec Metl	45608	3⅞	1⅝	1 13-16	− ¾
USP RlEsInv	3440	11¼	8⅛	8½	− 2½
US Shelter .12	18997	4⅝	1½	2	− 2⅛
US Surgicl .40	194926	27	15¼	22⅛	+ 3½
USTrckL 1.20a	71180	15⅜	7⅜	7¾	− 5¼
US Trust s1	x62600	44¾	27½	33¼	+ 3⅜
Univrsl Furn	59718	38¼	14¼	31¼	+ 7¾
UnivHlthB 10k	496474	17⅛	6⅝	7	− 7½
Unvrsl Holdg	18385	6⅛	3⅜	3¾	− 1¼
UnivSec Instr	53013	8⅛	3½	5	+ 1¼
Unvrsl Voltrn	29624	5½	3⅛	3⅜	− ¼
UnivFedSv .30	57778	18¼	8½	11¾	− ½
UnivNtBk .40	739	25⅜	21¾	22½	+ ½
UpRight Inc	43793	11¾	5½	7¾	+ 2⅛
UpperPen 2.10	8263	27¾	22	25¾	+ 3½

OVER-THE-COUNTER

	Sales 100s	High	Low	Last	Net Chg.
USA Cafes .36	62745	8⅜	3⅜	8⅛	+3⅜
USBC Pa s.88	x5608	30	17	18	−4¾
USLICO .80	60912	31⅜	22⅝	23⅞	−2⅜
UST Corp s.74	x18980	42	25	38½	+12⅞
U T L Corpn	113866	26	14½	15⅞	−⅛
—V—					
--V V--					
VBand Sys s	x66781	24¾	11½	21¼	+9⅜
ValidLogic Sy	188664	12⅛	3½	4⅞	−4⅜
Vallen Corptn	2719	19½	16¾	16¾	−½
ValleyBcp s.80	x9695	30⅝	21¼	22¼	−⅞
ValleyFed SL	53595	33	8½	23½	+3⅜
ValleyForg .14	2083	7½	5	6¼	+1⅛
ValleyN s1.60a	x6820	59	39	44	−2
VallNtlCp 1.44	179850	50¼	28¾	38⅝	−2⅞
ValleyUtah .72	21479	31½	21¾	30	+8
ValmntInd .60	9116	19¾	14½	15	−1¼
ValtekInc .16	15876	11⅜	7⅛	11¼	+2
ValueLine .40	22968	28¾	18¼	23¼	−5
Vanguard SB	27253	19¼	13	14½	−½
Vanzetti Syst	15810	9½	2½	3	−2
VariCare s.03	x10402	8¼	4⅞	5½	−1¼
Varlen Cp .60	17705	15	10½	15	+3½
Velo Bind Inc	56246	15½	9¼	12¼	+½
Ventrx Labs	176984	7½	2½	2¾	−1⅜
VtFnclSv s.80	x4176	30	18¼	26½	...
Veronex Resr	59427	6½	2 11-16	5 5-16	+5-16
VersaTch s.20	x21628	21¼	12¾	13¼	−½
Vestar Inc	7532	9¾	8	9¾	...
ViconFiber Op	10947	3⅞	1¾	1¾	−1
VicorpRst .06h	246804	23½	10½	11	−7⅝
VictorBcs .30h	8347	22	11	12⅛	−8⅝
VictoryMkt s	x21346	24⅞	10¼	23⅞	...
Video Display	9016	8¾	5¾	8¾	+1¾
Video Library	7208	5⅝	3½	4⅛	...
VieDeFrn .22d	62327	12⅛	4⅝	5⅜	−1¼
ViewMaster s	x91123	28¼	7¾	18	...
Viking Freight	49225	22¼	10⅝	20¼	+5
Vipont Lab	100487	19	9¾	11⅜	−6
ViratekInc s	x190091	98½	10⅛	63	+52⅜
Va Beach s.16	x27904	8⅝	4¼	6⅞	+1⅛
VaFstSvg .05d	x6857	14¼	6⅝	6¾	−⅛
VistaOr LtdPt	119822	7½	1⅞	2⅞	...
Visual Elect	13877	5	1⅞	2⅛	−1⅛
Vitramon 5i	7134	13¼	7	12¼	+5¼
VLI Corp	156602	6⅝	3	3½	−2⅜
VLSI Tech	279866	18	8¼	10⅝	−4⅛
VM Software	x53103	21	11¾	20	...
VMS ut 1.06d	15211	10¼	9	9¾	+⅜
VMS MtgII ut	4452	9½	7¼	8	...
V M X Inc	95233	9¼	2¾	2⅞	−2¼
Vodavi Tech	118249	11⅛	3¾	4¾	−4⅛
VoltInfo Scien	65401	33½	16½	27¼	+7¼
VolvoAB 1.17d	99527	61½	23½	50⅛	+9⅛
Vortec Cp .08g	24520	10⅛	2¾	3⅛	−6¼
VSE Corp .20	5194	17¼	7⅝	14	+2⅝
Vulcan Pack	21059	4⅞	1¾	2⅝	+¾
VWR Corp .60	17936	17¾	10	16	...
—W—					
Walbro Cp .40	51435	36	16	19¾	+2¼
Walker Telcm	72804	9¾	3½	4	−5⅜
Wall to Wall	24957	9¼	4¼	5¼	−3¾
Waltham SvB	35841	12½	10⅜	12	...
Warehouse Cl	51803	11¼	3⅜	3⅝	−7⅝
Warwick Ins	43820	12½	5¾	8½	+¾
Wa Enrgy 1.84	59809	30⅛	19⅜	28⅞	+4¾
WaFedSL .80	78509	40¾	29⅛	35¾	+9¼
WaMutSB s.40	x232506	26¼	10⅝	23	+11⅝
WashScien .15	19025	11¾	6¾	10¾	+¾
Waterford Gls	96355	22⅝	15⅜	17	...
WatersInst s	x7244	11⅛	3⅛	5¾	+2¼
WattsIn A .02d	93602	16¾	13	16	...
WausauP .48g	46380	34½	21½	29	+7¼
WaverlyP s.32	x8047	16¾	11½	12¼	−1⅛
Wavetek Corp	57384	11	6⅜	7	−⅜
Waxman .08	28004	17¾	12⅛	15¾	+3½
WD 40Co 1.32a	51730	33½	20¼	33½	+10
Wearever Prc	12891	12¼	10¼	10½	...
Webb Co .30h	72540	16¾	10¾	16	+3⅞
Webstr Cloth	22422	12¾	9	9½	...
Webster Fncl	14185	11¾	11¼	11½	...
WeighTron .40	15626	14¼	8¾	13¼	+3¾

	Sales 100s	High	Low	Last	Net Chg.
Weisfields .50	2886	18¾	13½	17¼	...
Welbilt Corp	33906	27	14¾	23½	+8½
Wendt Bristl	99	5¾	5⅛	5½	...
WendtBris wt	2	⅞	(z)	⅞	...
Werner Entrp	52068	21⅞	15	18¾	...
WesamBcp .70	12935	52¾	21¼	49	+27
Wespac I .19d	18417	7½	2½	2⅝	−3⅞
Wespac II .13d	6354	4	1	1⅛	−2⅛
Westcorp	74664	13⅝	8¼	8⅞	...
Westerbeke	6777	8¾	4	4¼	...
Western Bank	5185	7⅛	4	5¾	...
WstnCap Inv	161887	21½	13¼	13⅝	−1¾
Wstn Comercl	5534	4¼	1¾	2½	+¼
WFSBPR .50g	20183	21	13¼	15	−1¾
WstnFed SL	92857	25⅝	6⅜	16½	+1⅝
Western Fncl	10914	10¼	6½	7	−¾
WstnMicro Tc	24365	10½	5⅞	6¾	−1¼
W Microwave	13083	11½	5¾	6	−4
WstPublish Gr	260610	21⅛	11⅞	12¾	...
WstSteer s.20	x9818	17¾	10½	11⅜	+⅛
WstnTelCm A	44594	27½	11⅜	13⅝	...
Wstrn Waste	31805	16¼	10¾	13¾	+3
WestMass Bsh	5855	8¾	7¾	8¼	...
WstmrInd .60	59696	24½	16¼	20½	−¼
WestportBc 1g	1905	50	26	38	+12
WestwOne s	x93974	37¼	21⅜	26¼	...
Wstworld Hlth	146036	15⅜	½	⅞	−11
Wetterau 1.04	127142	43¼	25	38¾	−⅜
Weynbrg 1.44	823	97	74	79	+4½
Wholesale Cl	66546	9½	5	5⅜	−1¼
Wicat Sys Inc	275204	7⅜	2⅜	2⅝	−1⅝
Wiland Servcs	8662	5½	3⅜	3½	−1¼
WileyJ A 1.10	22250	39½	30½	33½	−6
Willamet s1.03	x115278	46	29⅜	40¾	+9⅞
WilliamsA Cp	241534	30⅛	8⅝	17½	+2
Williams Inds	7856	15¼	8⅝	11¼	+1¼
William Son s	x26206	22¾	12¼	18¼	+5⅝
WilliamW .60g	2967	23½	11¾	14	+1½
Wilm SvgFd	23992	10⅞	10⅛	10¼	...
Wilmgtn s.72	x44302	25½	18¼	23	+4
Wilson Foods	156413	11⅜	5¼	9	+3¼
Wilton Entprs	14555	2¾	1 3-16	1 9-16	−7-16
Wndmere .03b	121841	7¼	4⅞	6¾	+1¾
Wings W Air	34707	9¼	4¼	5½	...
WiscSoG 1.04g	1555	29	18	18¾	−1¼
WiserOilCo .40	35545	19¾	13	13¾	−1½
WNS Inc	30921	22	12½	18¾	+4¼
Woburn S .10d	31263	11⅛	9⅞	9⅞	...
Wolohan L .20	54907	10⅞	5¾	8	+1⅜
Wolverine s.16	x43194	14¾	5¾	9⅛	+2½
WoodhdDn .60	16244	15	10¼	11¾	−2¼
Worcester Co	76552	13⅛	11⅞	12⅞	...
WOW Inc	374533	29¼	16½	19⅞	...
Worthing s.36	x172904	20⅜	12⅝	16½	+1⅞
WrightWm .38	5819	13⅞	11⅛	13⅜	+1½
WriterCp .15d	13077	11⅜	6¼	6¼	−2¼
Wyman G .80	84450	25	16	16½	−4¾
WyseTech Inc	261341	18½	10⅞	17¼	+3⅝
—X-Z—					
Xebec	110560	4¼	1⅜	1 9-16	−15-16
Xicor Incorp	222866	12	4¼	6½	−2¼
Xidex Corprtn	783251	22¼	11½	12¼	−2⅞
Xidex Corp wt	40381	8	2⅝	3	...
XL Datacom	33447	25¼	15	16	−6¾
Xoma Corp	56665	17½	8	11⅞	...
Xplor Cp s.45d	x773	6¾	2¼	2¼	...
Xyvision Inc	54401	15¾	10¾	13½	...
YellwFr s.62	361909	41½	27½	36⅞	+7⅞
YorkFncl .60g	13065	26¼	13½	17⅛	+1⅝
Zehntel Inc	52488	4¾	2⅞	3⅜	...
Zenith Lab	81107	24¾	18	23	−1¾
ZenNatlIns .80	163656	33½	20¾	25¾	...
Zentec Corp	42764	4¾	1⅛	3⅞	+2½
Zeus Compont	8135	10	3⅝	5¼	−3½
ZieglerCo .48a	14344	20	13¾	17	+3¼
ZionsUtah 1.44	18254	63½	31¼	39¼	−5½
Zitel Corp	18787	5¼	1¼	1⅝	−1½
Ziyad Incorp	72162	7⅛	3	3⅜	−2⅛
Zondervan	158818	29⅜	8¾	27⅝	+14½
Zycad Corp	113057	11⅛	3⅜	4	−6¾
Zygo Corp	2603	13¼	6¼	6½	−3½
ZyMOS Corp	80798	2 15-16	1	1	−1 9-16

Foreign Securities

Unless noted, all issues are American Depositary Receipts, or ADRs, representing ownership of securities physically deposited abroad. Quotes are in U.S. dollars. n-Not ADR.

	Sales 100s	High	Low	Last	Net Chg.
GREAT BRITAIN					
Beecham G .05d					
	844715	6 15-16	4½	6 19-32	+1 15-32
Burmah Oil .33d					
	48830	6 7-16	3 25-32	5⅝	+1 13-16
Rank Organ	55841	9 3-32	5⅞	7⅝	+1⅜
JAPAN					
Fuji Photo .10d	317184	47½	19	45¾	+25½
Japan Airlines	2636	167	90⅝	165½	+74
NissanMotr .12d	54635	8⅝	5½	6¾	+1 3-16
TokioMarine F					
	6736	622¼	209¼	559	+334½
ToyotaMotr .07d					
	287651	29⅛	12	26⅝	+14½
MEXICO					
TeleDeMex .01e	455658	5-32	1-16	3-32	−1-16
SOUTH AFRICA					
AngloAGld .55d					
	132972	8 9-16	4 7-16	7 5-32	+1 17-32
AngAm SAf .58d	81880	16¾	9¼	14¼	+3⅜

	Sales 100s	High	Low	Last	Net Chg.
BlyvoorGld .65d					
	75392	6⅛	3 15-32	4 15-16	+9-16
BuffelstnG 3.41d	69864	30⅛	14⅝	16½	−6⅝
DeBeersMn .22d					
	753679	8 1-16	4 13-16	7½	+2 25-32
Driefontn 1.14d	115444	20¼	10⅜	15⅛	+1⅜
FrStConG 1.09d					
	157771	13⅞	6 9-16	11	+½
Gold Fields .58d	32963	14¾	7¾	13	+2¾
Highveld Steel					
	47136	2⅛	15-16	1 3-16	−13-32
KloofGold .42d	166458	9⅛	4½	7 5-16	+1⅛
Lydenbrg Plat	30410	10⅜	6⅛	8⅛	+1 15-16
OrangeFS 2.92d	41306	35¾	16⅛	28¾	+3⅝
StHelenGd 1.54d					
	35700	15⅛	8 7-16	11⅜	+¼
Sasol Limitd					
	14312	2 29-32	1¼	1 31-32	−7-16
VaalReefs .74d					
	316281	9	4 11-16	8 7-32	+2 5-32
WelkmGld .74d	31547	9¼	4 5-16	7 9-16	+2⅛
WstDeepL 2.63d	46950	45	22⅜	38⅜	+8½

z-Sales in full.
a-Annual rate, also extra or extras. b-Paid in 1985, no regular rate. c-Payment of accumulated dividends. d-Paid so far in 1984, no regular rate. e-Cash plus stock paid in 1985. f-Cash plus stock paid in 1984. g-Annual rate plus stock dividend. h-Paid in 1985, latest dividend omitted or no action taken at last meeting. i-Percent in stock paid in 1984. j-Percent in stock paid in 1985, latest dividend omitted. k-Percent in stock paid in 1985. p-Granted temporary exception from Nasdaq qualifications. q-In bankruptcy proceedings. t-Liquidating dividend. ut-Units. wt-Warrants.

OVER-THE-COUNTER
ANNUAL NASDAQ INDICES

1986

	High	Low	Last	% Chg.
Composite	411.16	323.01	348.83	+7.36
Industrials	414.45	326.56	349.33	+5.80
Financial	553.42	424.52	460.64	+8.77
Insurance	467.05	381.59	404.14	+5.78
Utilities	362.86	295.97	316.09	+4.81
Banks	457.59	346.35	412.53	+18.08
Transportation	365.81	288.13	348.84	+19.63

1985

	High	Low	Last	% Chg.
Composite	325.16	345.91	324.93	+31.4
Industrials	330.17	258.85	330.17	+26.6
Financial	423.52	298.20	423.49	+35.0
Insurance	385.45	276.33	382.07	+41.8
Utilities	303.84	234.87	301.57	+26.4
Banks	350.08	230.23	350.08	+52.0
Transportation	296.91	236.20	291.59	+21.9

1984

	High	Low	Last	% Chg.
Composite	287.90	231.93	247.35	−11.2
Industrials	336.16	250.18	260.73	−19.4
Financial	298.62	252.34	298.62	+ 7.6
Insurance	283.91	226.87	283.11	+ 9.9
Utilities	280.54	194.33	238.66	−11.4
Banks	229.77	192.99	229.77	+12.8
Transportation	290.70	194.33	239.29	−14.8

1983

	High	Low	Last	% Chg.
Composite	328.91	230.59	278.60	+19.9
Industrials	408.42	270.55	323.68	+18.3
Financial	284.39	206.86	277.53	+33.7
Insurance	287.34	217.33	257.63	+13.8
Utilities	391.37	257.12	269.39	− 5.9
Banks	203.75	155.68	203.75	+30.3
Transportation	293.76	194.27	280.80	+43.6

1982

	High	Low	Last	% Chg.
Composite	240.70	159.14	232.41	+18.7
Industrials	281.64	177.70	273.58	+19.3
Financial	216.40	154.45	207.50	+15.8
Insurance	236.76	163.78	226.40	+16.5
Utilities	316.17	168.02	286.23	+57.6
Banks	160.73	127.84	156.37	+ 9.2
Transportation	205.81	145.26	195.48	+16.5

1981

	High	Low	Last	% Chg.
Composite	223.47	175.03	195.84	− 3.2
Industrials	283.03	204.62	229.29	−12.3
Financial	182.10	154.61	176.20	+14.4
Insurance	204.77	166.10	194.31	+16.5
Utilities	190.59	148.69	181.67	+ 9.6
Banks	144.06	118.59	143.13	+20.9
Transportation	201.71	155.99	167.88	+ 2.2

Foreign Markets
Closing Prices of Selected Issues

TOKYO
(in yen)

	1986 Close	1985 Close
Ajinomoto	1,990	1,150
Asahi Chem	798	781
Bk of Tokyo	935	760
BridgestnTire	725	522
C. Itoh	749	433
Daiwa House	1,800	900
Daiwa Secur	1,720	785
Eisai	2,280	1,320
Fuji Bank	1,860	1,560
Fujitsu	1,060	1,080
Isuzu Mot Ltd	315	350
Kajima Corp	1,460	471
Kansai Elec	3,900	2,160
Komatsu Ltd	486	518
MaruiDeptStr	2,850	1,550
Marubeni	468	338
Mazda	372	390
MitsubishiEst	2,490	1,200
MitsubishiInd	418	385
Mitsui & Co	530	432
MitsuiRealE	1,890	1,090
Nikko Secur	1,490	725
Nintendo	12,400	....
NipponKogaku	870	1,060
NipponGakki	1,560	1,600
NipponSteel	169	155
NomuraSecur	2,960	1,060
Ricoh	1,000	1,050
Sekisui House	1,720	850
Sharp El	1,100	....
SumitomoBk	2,420	1,710
SumitomoCh	389	248
Taisei Const	910	321
Takeda Chem	2,640	1,040
Teijin	693	490
Tokyo Elec	7,900	2,880
Toshiba	755	370
YamaichiSec	1,530	734
Yasuda F&M	914	540

LONDON
(in pence)

	1986	1985
Allied Lyons	321	268
Babcock	183	179
Barclays Bk	515	477
Bass Ltd	738	658
BOC Group	372	289
British GE	184	164
Britoil	171.5	....
BTR PLC	271	378
Cable&Wi	330	595
Cadbury Sch	187	158
Charter Con	273	196
Coats Viyella	463	158
Consol Gold	672	439
Dalgety	279	238
Glaxo	1,048	1,540
Grand Metro	457	398
Guest Keen	273	263
Guinness	289	....
HansonTrust	189.5	198
Johnson Mat	215	133
Legal Gen	257	732
Lonrho	248.5	202
Lucas Indust	477	485
MIM Hold	104	126
Nat'l WestBk	548	692
Nrthrn Food	249	286
Racal Elect	191	160
Redland	403	342
Reed Int'l	304	687
Rio Tinto	705	519
STC	174	100
Tate&Lyle	562	545
TaylrWoodrw	307	485
Thorn EMI	470	401
Trust House	178	346
T I Group	490	369
Ultramar	160	201
Utd Biscuit	232.5	240
Vickers	407	301
Wellcome	233.5	....

SOUTH AFRICAN MINES
(in U.S. currency)

	1986 Close	1985 Close
Bracken	1.70	1.45
DeelKraal	2.70	1.85
Doornfontein	10.13	9.63
DurbanDeep	10.62	6.50
East Rand Gold	4.12	....
East Rand	5.38	4.50
Elandsrand	8.50	5.25
Elsburg	2.30	1.65
General Mng	c8.13	c6.06
Grootvlei	3.25	3.63
Harmony	10.00	8.50
Hartebeest	4.75	3.10
Impala	10.87	....
Johannesb C	c9.25	c51.00
Kinross	12.62	12.00
Leslie	1.20	1.50
Libanon	16.62	12.75
Loraine	5.38	3.60
Randfontein	8.80	6.70
Rustnbg Plat	9.75	6.75
Southvaal	41.00	28.75
Stilfontein	5.63	5.88
Unisel	6.87	4.88
West Areas	3.50	2.60
Winkelhaak	17.75	16.50

c-In British pounds.

FRANKFURT
(in marks)

AEG-Tele	328.20	240.80
Allianz Vers	2,291	2,073
BASF	274.70	270.50
Bayer AG	316.60	275.50
BMW	583.50	569.50
Cont'l Gummi	342.50	165.50
Commerzbnk	308	365
Daimler-Benz	1,233.5	1,246
Degussa	468	427.50
Deutsche Bk	822	925
Dresdner Bk	407	451.50
Hoechst AG	269.40	293.50
Lufthansa	180	225
Nixdorf	747	....
Porsche	1,050	....
RWE	240.5	....
Schering AG	677	633
Siemens	747.5	755
Thyssen-Hut	124	170.40
Veba	299	295.50
Volkswagen	427	498.30

BRUSSELS
(in Belgian francs)

ARBED	1,945	2,615
Gevaert	6,400	5,100
GB-Inno-Bm	9,140	5,200
GrpBrLambrt	3,600	2,545
Metal Hobokn	8,000	5,950
Petrofina	9,980	6,750
SocGenerale	3,380	2,380
Solvay	8,350	6,100

MILAN
(in Lire)

Buitoni	7,350	3,880
Ciga	3,801	12,010
Fiat	14,490	5,950
Generali	133,000	77,050
La Rinas	999	960
Mont Ed	2,885	2,729
Olivetti	13,590	8,780
Pirelli	5,000	3,495
Snia Visc	4,780	5,399

Foreign Markets
Closing Prices of Selected Issues

PARIS
(in French francs)

	1986 Close	1985 Close
AirLiq	701	650
Aquitaine	315.90	201.40
BSNGrD	4,360	2,750
Club Med	684	470
Imetal	86.10	77
L'Oreal	3,845	2,855
Hachette	2,880	1,490
Lafar Coppee	1,370	800
MachBull	41	48.35
Michelin	2,560	1,649
MoetHen	2,380	2,355
PeugtCtn	1,185	507
Source Perrier	780	470
Total CFP	409	289

SWITZERLAND
(in Swiss francs)
Zurich

	1986	1985
Brown Bov	1,835	1,840
Ciba-Geigy	3,570	4,000
Credit Suisse	3,800	3,700
Nestle	9,775	8,925
Sandoz	11,000	10,950
Sulzer	560	490
Swissair	1,190	1,790
Swiss Alum	475	685
Swiss Bancp	562	575
Union Bank	6,000	5,240

Basel

vHoffmn-LaR	12,275	11,900
Pirelli Intl	438	380
v-1/10 share.		

STOCKHOLM
(in Swedish Krona)

AGA b	170	179
Alfa Laval b	222	179
Electrolux b	311	194
Kone oy	245	....
Swenska Cel b	289	175

AMSTERDAM
(in guilders)

	1986 Close	1985 Close
AKZO	157.10	145.50
Ahold	115	88.50
Algemene Bk	524	600
Amst-Rot Bk	89.70	115.80
Elsevier-NDU	251	195.50
Fokker	57.30	75.70
Heineken's	177.50	233.50
Holec	31.80	284
Hoogovens	42.90	80.60
Nation Neder	80.20	91
Nedlloyd	176.70	209.70
Robeco	95	86.20
Rolinco	83.50	74.50
Rorento	50.10	46.60
Wessanen	84.80	246.50

HONG KONG
(in Hong Kong dollars)

Bk of East Asia	22.20	24.60
Cheung Kong	40.25	21.30
Hang Seng Bk	41.50	46
Hong Kong El	13	8.50
Hong Kong Lnd	6.75	6.85
HongkongShBk	9.25	7.70
Hutchsn Whmp	46.25	27.50
Jardine Mathsn	22.50	13.70
SunHungKaiP	18.60	12.80
Swire Pacific	20.20	31.25
World Intl	3.80	2.60

SYDNEY
(in Australian dollars)

ANZ Bk	5.60	4.40
Central Norse	14.80	6.06
Coles GJ	6	4.25
CRA	7.36	5.48
CSR	3.58	3.56
Leighton Hld	0.80	0.90
Natl Aust Bk	5.60	4.44
News Corp	18.20	9.06
Pacific Dunlop	4	....
RensGldFlds	9.50	5
Santos	4.15	5.36
SouthrnPacPet	0.21	0.17
Westrn Mining	5.46	3.20
Westpac	4.85	4.52
Woodside Pete	1.50	1.15
Woolworth	3.95	3.34

Doron Ben-Ami

Foreign Bonds

		Sales $1,000	High	Low	Last	Net Chg.
—A—						
Asian 7¾96	8.6	41	93	86	90	+ 4⅛
AsiaDv 11⅛98	9.3	22	119⅞	119⅞	119⅞	...
Asian zr92s	...	454	66	51¼	66	+ 15⅜
Austla 9⅛96	9.1	391	103	94¾	100	+ 5¼
Austla 9s96	9.0	303	102	94	99½	+ 8⅜
Austla 8⅞97	9.0	214	101⅛	96	98⅝	+ 7⅝
Austla 9⅛93	9.1	684	104	97	100⅛	+ 5½
Austla 12¾92	10.4	142	122¾	112	122¾	+ 14⅞
Austla 13⅜07	11.1	111	121½	111	121	+ 6¼
Austla 11⅜93	9.7	230	117¼	104⅛	117¼	+ 13⅛
Austla 12⅛08	10.4	201	117½	108⅝	116½	+ 7½
Austria 8⅝92	8.7	13	99½	86½	99½	+ 12⅝
—B—						
Brazil 8¼87	8.5	49	97	94	97	+ 8⅞
—C—						
CaisAut 9⅛97	9.2	338	100⅞	94	98⅞	+ 4⅞
Caisse 9.3s96	9.2	174	101	92¼	101	+ 8¾
Caisse 11⅛90	11.0	40	103½	101	101	− 2
Cuba 4½77mf	...	218	12	10	10	− ½
Czec 6s60mf	...	7	95	62	62	− 3
—D—						
Denm 14s88	13.7	1418	107½	102⅛	102½	− 4½
Denm 14⅝88	13.8	615	112	105	106	+ ⅜
—E—						
EurCS 9s96	9.1	184	103⅛	93¾	99	+ 4
EurCS 8⅞96	8.9	521	100¼	93	100	+ 9⅜
EurCS 9⅛97	9.1	477	103¾	93⅜	100	+ 6
EurCS 9¾99	9.7	50	101	92¼	101	+ 8
EEC 11.6s99	11.0	52	106½	99½	105	+ 6
EurIn 8⅞96	8.7	754	103	90⅝	102	+ 12
EurIn 9s97	8.8	383	102⅜	93	102⅜	+ 11⅜
EurIn 8⅜92	8.3	183	101⅞	94¼	101	+ 10¾
EurIn 9¼98	9.3	298	100⅛	94⅛	100	+ 12
EurIn 9⅛98	9.0	204	102¼	92¾	101	+ 9¾
EurIn 9⅞99	9.9	135	101½	100	100	+ 5
EurIn 9⅞87	9.7	629	102	99¾	102	+ 2
EurIn 10s99	9.5	61	105¾	94¼	105¾	+ 8¼
EurIn 10.15s99	9.5	300	106½	100⅜	106½	+ 9½
EurIn 11⅞00	11.2	229	111	105	105⅞	+ 7⅛
EurIn 12¾88	12.2	317	107	104	104⅜	− ⅝
EurIn 13½00	11.8	66	118	113	114	+ 1
EurIn 14⅝91	11.5	54	127	112½	127	+ 12½
EurIn 13⅜92	...	80	125¾	112	125¾	+ 14¾
—F—						
Finlnd 8¾92	8.6	253	102	94¼	102	+ 7⅞
Finlnd 14¾86	14.7	364	104¾	100 17/32	100 17/32	− 4 15/32
Finlnd 13⅝87	13.1	494	108	104⅜	104⅜	− 2⅝
Finlnd 11¾93	10.7	15	117½	110	110	+ 14¼
—H—						
HydroQ 10s08	9.3	436	112	97	107¼	+ 14⅝
—J—						
Japan 11⅞91	10.2	1	116	116	116	...
—M—						
Mexco 8½87	8.6	130	98½	90	98½	+ 6
Mexco 8⅛97	11.6	562	74	64⅛	70¼	+ 6
Mexco 10s90	10.4	234	97	88	96	+ 6
Mexco 15s88	14.4	1939	105	96	104⅛	+ 2⅛
—N—						
NipTT 8⅛87	8.1	126	100 1/16	99½	100 1/16	+ 5/16
NorgKb 9⅛98	9.2	191	102	94	98¾	+ 4¾
NorgKb 9⅞99	9.9	16	100	95	100	+ 12¾
—O—						
Oslo 8¾97	8.8	218	100	88⅛	99⅛	+ 11
OsterBk 1988	...	142	90	78¼	88¼	+ 12¾
OsterBk 11¼90	10.5	10	107¼	107¼	107¼	...
—S—						
SocNC 9s92	9.0	61	99⅝	97½	99⅝	+ 9⅝
Stkhlm 8⅞92	8.7	135	102	95¼	102	+ 6¾
Stkhlm 9¾94	9.7	40	100½	90	100½	+ 11½
Swed 9s97	8.9	449	103	92½	101¼	+ 8¾
Swed 9¼98	9.3	305	100	97½	100	+ 6½
Swed 11⅝99	11.0	127	105½	101⅜	105½	+ 1½
Swed 10⅝90	10.4	80	105	102	102	...
Swed 11⅜00	10.6	171	107	100	107	+ 6
Swed 14⅝88	13.3	754	114	108½	110⅛	+ ⅜
Swed 12¼89	10.8	133	113½	106	113	+ 8
Swed 12¾97	10.5	34	131½	117	122	+ 22½
Swed 12s10	...	1	128¼	128¼	128¼	...
SwedEx 15½90	13.4	20	115½	115½	115½	+ 2
—U—						
UK 8⅞93	8.9	85	99½	97⅝	99½	+ 3
—V—						
Venez 8¾92	8.8	200	100	85	100	+ 15

Sales figures are unofficial.

cv-Convertible. ct-Certificates. d-Deep discount. f-Dealt in flat. m-Matured bonds, negotiability impaired by maturity. na-No accrual. r-Registered. rp-Reduced principal amount. st-Stamped. t-Floating rate. wd-When distributed. ww-With warrants. x-Ex interest. xw-Without warrants. zr-Zero coupon.

pr-Exchangeable into debentures.

vj-In bankruptcy or receivership or being reorganized under the Bankruptcy Act, or securities assumed by such companies.

Foreign Indices

FT Ordinary Index
(UK)

1986

High	Low
1425.9	1094.3

1985

High	Low
1146.9	911.0

1984

High	Low
952.3	755.3

1983

776.2	598.4

1982

637.4	518.1

Banca Commerciale Italia
Index (Italy)

1986

High	Low
908.2	454.67

1985

High	Low
460.04	228.56

1984

High	Low
230.31	192.06

1983

214.93	160.45

1982

212.66	147.23

Swiss Bancorp Index
(Switzerland)

1986

High	Low
625.5	497.2

1985

High	Low
587.9	388.7

1984

High	Low
388.5	354.5

1983

386.6	294.4

1982

288.3	237.0

ANP-CBS Industrial Index
(Holland)

1986

High	Low
301.0	240.4

1985

High	Low
255.6	185.6

1984

High	Low
147.2	118.7

1983

154.2	100.1

1982

85.8	63.2

Foreign Indices

Rand Daily Mail Gold Index (S. Africa)

1986
High	Low
1950.0	1011.4

1985
High	Low
1154.5	846.6

1984
High	Low
1099.0	738.1

1983
1099.5	661.5

1982
988.3	335.5

CAC General Index (France)

1986
High	Low
414.3	267.8

1985
High	Low
265.8	180.9

1984
High	Low
183.0	155.6

1983
156.7	96.1

1982
111.6	93.9

Commerzbank Index (Germany)

1986
High	Low
2278.8	1762.4

1985
High	Low
1951.5	1111.8

1984
High	Low
1107.9	917.7

1983
1044.0	727.9

1982
763.4	650.2

Belgian Stock Exchange Index (Belgium)

1986
High	Low
4131.69	2766.91

1985
High	Low
2986.36	2090.7

1984
High	Low
165.08	135.28

1983
136.77	100.5

1982
103.89	86.42

Asia-Pacific Stock Market Indices
Hang Seng Index (Hong Kong)

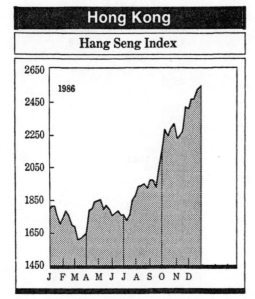

Hong Kong

Hang Seng Index

1986

1986

January	8	High	1826.84
	31	Low	1695.78
	31	Close	1695.78
February	17	High	1783.08
	28	Low	1695.30
	28	Close	1695.30
March	4	High	1695.77
	18	Low	1561.72
	27	Close	1625.94
April	28	High	1848.65
	2	Low	1603.27
	30	Close	1836.99
May	8	High	1865.65
	19	Low	1765.02
	30	Close	1787.90
June	18	High	1789.78
	6	Low	1747.37
	28	Close	1754.19
July	31	High	1855.46
	10	Low	1718.30
	31	Close	1855.46
August	18	High	1950.12
	1	Low	1874.11
	29	Close	1913.00

September	30	High	2068.44
	2	Low	1903.02
	30	Close	2068.44
October	28	High	2355.93
	6	Low	2084.93
	31	Close	2315.63
November	28	High	2418.75
	5	Low	2203.71
	28	Close	2418.75
December	31	High	2568.30
	5	Low	2400.72
	31	Close	2568.30

1985

January	17	High	1388.42
	2	Low	1220.74
	31	Close	1365.02
February	19	High	1435.17
	7	Low	1312.43
	28	Close	1372.25
March	1	High	1401.15
	19	Low	1300.97
	29	Close	1382.04
April	16	High	1521.30
	1	Low	1389.13
	30	Close	1520.56
May	17	High	1647.88
	2	Low	1516.21
	31	Close	1613.87
June	4	High	1643.35
	18	Low	1427.08
	28	Close	1570.61
July	25	High	1692.06
	9	Low	1565.04
	31	Close	1680.62
August	19	High	1711.51
	21	Low	1650.78
	30	Close	1656.10
September	2	High	1616.17
	27	Low	1511.80
	27	Close	1511.80
October	30	High	1694.68
	1	Low	1520.99
	31	Close	1665.39

HONG KONG

November	13	High	1747.18		December	24	High	1206.83
	1	Low	1680.65			10	Low	1115.01
	29	Close	1716.95			31	Close	1200.38
December	30	High	1752.62					
	3	Low	1664.06		**1983**			
	31	Close	1752.45		January	20	High	908.56
						4	Low	761.61
1984						31	Close	887.04
January	31	High	1102.38		February	25	High	1066.30
	3	Low	871.06			3	Low	888.08
	31	Close	1102.38			28	Close	1021.55
February	6	High	1134.12		March	1	High	1033.59
	27	Low	1022.85			21	Low	955.11
	29	Close	1059.29			31	Close	996.01
March	19	High	1170.35		April	14	High	1067.36
	30	Low	1014.38			6	Low	998.48
	30	Close	1014.38			29	Close	1019.43
April	19	High	1115.85		May	3	High	1033.15
	2	Low	1023.96			24	Low	877.68
	30	Close	1037.06			31	Close	918.59
May	1	High	1034.73		June	20	High	967.79
	21	Low	893.01			9	Low	863.10
	31	Close	915.30			30	Close	964.35
June	11	High	966.12		July	21	High	1102.64
	29	Low	901.07			1	Low	983.72
	29	Close	901.07			29	Close	1072.02
July	2	High	868.63		August	3	High	1059.11
	13	Low	746.02			31	Low	965.94
	31	Close	800.15			31	Close	965.94
August	31	High	926.78		September	1	High	955.24
	1	Low	826.74			30	Low	758.33
	31	Close	926.78			30	Close	758.33
September	27	High	1014.98		October	31	High	865.22
	13	Low	911.78			4	Low	690.06
	28	Close	1002.50			31	Close	865.22
October	26	High	1056.84		November	7	High	896.53
	8	Low	963.50			24	Low	823.75
	31	Close	1015.13			30	Close	852.90
November	29	High	1136.11		December	6	High	881.58
	5	Low	1027.48			1	Low	848.78
	30	Close	1128.10			30	Close	874.94

Nikkei Average (Japan)

1986

January	8	High	13,056.42
	21	Low	12,881.50
	31	Close	13,024.30
February	27	High	13,642.14
	1	Low	13,043.61
	28	Close	13,640.83
March	31	High	15,859.75
	1	Low	13,727.86
	31	Close	15,859.75
April	21	High	15,827.28
	8	Low	15,014.06
	30	Close	15,825.50
May	30	High	16,670.77
	17	Low	15,674.03
	31	Close	16,629.09
June	30	High	17,654.19
	3	Low	16,669.54
	30	Close	17,654.19
July	25	High	18,050.59
	10	Low	17,469.82
	31	Close	17,509.71
August	20	High	18,936.24
	4	Low	17,263.10
	20	Close	18,787.40

September	1	High	18,820.75
	17	Low	17,336.62
	30	Close	17,852.86
October	9	High	17,650.23
	22	Low	15,819.55
	31	Close	16,910.63
November	28	High	18,325.50
	5	Low	16,713.71
	28	Close	18,325.50
December	16	High	18,933.07
	2	Low	18,190.97
	27	Close	18,701.30

1985

January	31	High	11,992.31
	4	Low	11,558.06
	31	Close	11,992.31
February	28	High	12,321.92
	5	Low	11,823.43
	28	Close	12,321.92
March	28	High	12,604.02
	11	Low	12,263.85
	29	Close	12,580.76
April	1	High	12,677.15
	18	Low	12,052.82
	30	Close	12,426.29
May	30	High	12,790.27
	16	Low	12,369.30
	31	Close	12,758.48
June	26	High	12,910.29
	3	Low	12,473.41
	28	Close	12,882.09
July	5	High	13,040.10
	31	Low	12,232.27
	31	Close	12,232.27
August	22	High	12,734.05
	13	Low	12,326.71
	31	Close	12,716.52
September	24	High	12,755.60
	6	Low	12,453.85
	30	Close	12,700.11
October	15	High	13,055.52
	1	Low	12,685.36
	31	Close	12,936.47
November	6	High	12,892.40
	14	Low	12,589.51
	30	Close	12,779.53

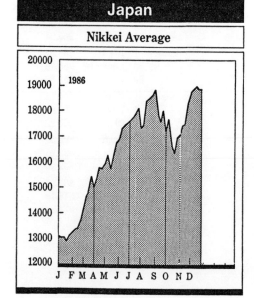

Japan

Nikkei Average

JAPAN

December	17	High	13,128.94	**1983**			
	3	Low	12,774.55	January	8	High	8210.02
	27	Close	13,083.18		25	Low	7803.18
1984					31	Close	8103.47
January	30	High	10,235.73	February	16	High	8145.41
	4	Low	9927.11		22	Low	7918.16
	31	Close	10,196.10		28	Close	8085.57
February	1	High	10,200.81	March	31	High	8478.80
	18	Low	9921.81		1	Low	7988.85
	29	Close	10,030.70		31	Close	8478.80
March	31	High	10,968.41	April	28	High	8636.56
	1	Low	9920.27		5	Low	8420.34
	31	Close	10,968.41		28	Close	8636.56
April	2	High	11,050.19	May	9	High	8719.88
	24	Low	10,761.82		23	Low	8528.64
	28	Close	11,016.28		31	Close	8617.57
May	4	High	11,190.17	June	27	High	8900.04
	31	Low	9940.14		8	Low	8445.45
	31	Close	9940.14		30	Close	8870.95
June	30	High	10,428.43	July	28	High	9112.07
	1	Low	9913.17		19	Low	8866.66
	30	Close	10,428.43		29	Close	9078.75
July	6	High	10,461.91	August	22	High	9203.75
	23	Low	9703.35		9	Low	8874.22
	31	Close	9998.50		31	Close	9189.43
August	30	High	10,586.27	September	28	High	9445.32
	1	Low	9948.40		19	Low	9141.25
	31	Close	10,584.20		30	Close	9402.59
September	28	High	10,649.25	October	12	High	9563.25
	6	Low	10,458.49		25	Low	9232.77
	28	Close	10,649.25		31	Close	9356.79
October	31	High	11,252.98	November	17	High	9416.95
	2	Low	10,540.05		10	Low	9244.24
	31	Close	11,252.98		30	Close	9320.24
November	30	High	11,438.64	December	28	High	9893.82
	26	Low	11,162.96		1	Low	9336.60
	30	Close	11,438.64		28	Close	9893.82
December	4	High	11,577.44				
	11	Low	11,250.83				
	28	Close	11,542.60				

Commercial & Industrial Index
(Philippines)

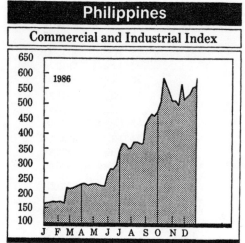

Philippines

Commercial and Industrial Index

1986

1986			
January	23	High	169.67
	2	Low	160.85
	31	Close	168.39
Feburary	28	High	219.22
	10	Low	164.87
	28	Close	219.22
March	31	High	230.26
	12	Low	209.16
	31	Close	230.26
April	14	High	236.93
	18	Low	227.72
	30	Close	232.23
May	2	High	231.69
	29	Low	225.05
	30	Close	226.71
June	30	High	312.79
	2	Low	226.71
	30	Close	312.79
July	14	High	391.33
	7	Low	324.63
	31	Close	351.46
August	14	High	377.78
	1	Low	353.08
	29	Close	368.42
September	29	High	482.42
	1	Low	386.26
	30	Close	476.83

October	17	High	587.03
	1	Low	465.91
	30	Close	533.80
November	28	High	567.48
	20	Low	486.55
	28	Close	567.48
December	2	High	567.99
	9	Low	489.90
	30	Close	548.03
1985			
January	2	High	106.31
	15	Low	100.66
	31	Close	104.18
February	7	High	117.60
	1	Low	103.85
	4	Low	103.85
	5	Low	103.85
	28	Close	114.71
March	28	High	135.55
	1	Low	114.71
	4	Low	114.71
	29	Close	132.48
April	9	High	132.55
	18	Low	130.47
	19	Low	130.47
	22	Low	130.47
	30	Close	131.98
May	8	High	132.73
	9	High	132.73
	17	Low	128.58
	31	Close	130.06
June	3	High	130.06
	21	Low	126.83
	27	Close	127.25
July	25	High	131.46
	17	Low	126.37
	31	Close	131.46
August	30	High	143.00
	21	Low	132.94
	30	Close	143.00
September	13	High	165.17
	2	Low	141.48
	30	Close	163.27
October	25	High	181.60
	1	Low	163.42
	31	Close	178.11

THE PHILIPPINES

November	4	High	176.04
	29	Low	169.00
	29	Close	169.00
December	2	High	168.62
	11	Low	155.64
	27	Close	160.86
1984			
January	25	High	149.02
	3	Low	144.57
	31	Close	146.12
February	1	High	146.52
	20	Low	138.43
	21	Low	138.43
	29	Close	139.30
March	12	High	138.40
	28	Low	128.85
	30	Close	130.34
April	26	High	132.80
	3	Low	127.77
	30	Close	131.99
May	30	High	134.73
	11	Low	131.37
	31	Close	134.46
June	6	High	134.76
	29	Low	128.67
	29	Close	128.67
July	4	High	129.93
	5	High	129.93
	31	Low	121.10
	31	Close	121.10
August	3	High	119.50
	21	Low	107.58
	31	Close	112.35
September	3	High	112.35
	27	Low	104.89
	28	Close	105.03
October	26	High	119.72
	15	Low	102.16
	31	Close	118.24
November	5	High	118.68
	29	Low	107.91
	29	Close	107.91

December	6	High	110.88
	26	Low	105.21
	28	Close	106.31
1983			
January	31	High	100.66
	4	Low	90.39
	5	Low	90.39
	31	Close	100.66
February	28	High	115.57
	1	Low	101.70
	28	Close	115.57
March	1	High	115.71
	22	Low	107.78
	30	Close	110.09
April	7	High	110.79
	15	Low	106.94
	29	Close	109.05
May	27	High	111.28
	23	Low	109.07
	31	Close	110.69
June	29	High	111.74
	9	Low	107.73
	30	Close	110.18
July	13	High	116.11
	22	Low	109.95
	29	Close	113.43
August	3	High	113.13
	30	Low	110.46
	31	Close	110.81
September	12	High	127.72
	6	Low	111.19
	30	Close	126.18
October	28	High	142.26
	3	Low	125.97
	28	Close	142.26
November	2	High	145.65
	10	Low	141.93
	29	Close	142.18
December	29	High	145.63
	9	Low	140.39
	29	Close	145.63

Straits Times Index (Singapore)

1986

January	8	High	644.89
	23	Low	588.41
	31	Close	607.32
February	20	High	640.29
	7	Low	611.33
	28	Close	623.27
March	4	High	626.23
	18	Low	570.29
	31	Close	593.02
April	2	High	597.41
	28	Low	563.34
	30	Close	570.20
May	30	High	656.00
	2	Low	573.38
	30	Close	656.00

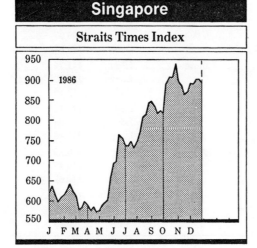

Singapore

Straits Times Index

June	23	High	776.89
	2	Low	683.30
	30	Close	741.22
July	2	High	749.75
	10	Low	721.98
	31	Close	741.94
August	29	High	838.48
	1	Low	741.31
	29	Close	838.48
September	1	High	853.18
	30	Low	804.26
	30	Close	804.26

October	31	High	937.37
	2	Low	812.34
	31	Close	937.37
November	3	High	940.64
	21	Low	863.67
	28	Close	866.89
December	19	High	901.61
	1	Low	871.83
	31	Close	891.30

1985

January	31	High	833.51
	16	Low	764.38
	31	Close	833.51
February	28	High	839.04
	14	Low	802.92
	28	Close	839.04
March	7	High	853.24
	27	Low	817.06
	29	Close	820.49
April	4	High	820.64
	22	Low	787.99
	30	Close	791.81
May	20	High	828.96
	7	Low	789.31
	31	Close	812.41
June	3	High	812.41
	17	Low	778.05
	28	Close	782.69
July	23	High	778.70
	15	Low	717.95
	31	Close	771.95
August	2	High	771.21
	28	Low	745.67
	30	Close	752.65
September	26	High	788.88
	4	Low	750.12
	30	Close	776.06
October	25	High	785.02
	15	Low	746.46
	31	Close	766.61
November	7	High	781.26
	29	Low	691.81
	29	Close	691.81
December	13	High	655.13
	23	Low	596.18
	30	Close	620.04

SINGAPORE

1984			
January	31	High	1071.01
	3	Low	1013.59
	31	Close	1071.01
February	8	High	1071.91
	23	Low	1013.72
	29	Close	1017.85
March	7	High	1023.17
	28	Low	980.46
	30	Close	994.44
April	13	High	1007.36
	2	Low	981.45
	30	Close	993.19
May	2	High	994.68
	23	Low	928.57
	31	Close	950.67
June	7	High	951.08
	27	Low	879.71
	29	Close	885.90
July	31	High	945.80
	12	Low	867.18
	31	Close	945.80
August	6	High	994.87
	28	Low	920.42
	31	Close	929.26
September	3	High	922.29
	20	Low	890.13
	28	Close	902.68
October	1	High	893.43
	31	Low	839.73
	31	Close	893.73
November	7	High	838.17
	21	Low	785.24
	30	Close	817.56
December	10	High	821.63
	18	Low	792.28
	28	Close	812.59

1983			
January	31	High	777.59
	5	Low	712.29
	31	Close	777.59
February	28	High	827.44
	7	Low	774.06
	28	Close	827.44
March	31	High	867.65
	3	Low	822.93
	31	Close	867.65
April	27	High	956.67
	5	Low	858.08
	29	Close	954.87
May	5	High	968.46
	24	Low	913.39
	31	Close	937.84
June	17	High	984.44
	1	Low	939.70
	30	Close	967.54
July	6	High	984.31
	27	Low	925.07
	29	Close	935.08
August	25	High	992.62
	29	High	992.62
	8	Low	910.67
	31	Close	989.30
September	26	High	990.56
	19	Low	963.41
	30	Close	989.35
October	3	High	962.84
	6	Low	924.12
	31	Close	943.80
November	21	High	955.88
	8	Low	921.08
	30	Close	941.10
December	30	High	1002.03
	5	Low	926.98
	30	Close	1002.03

All Ordinaries Index (Australia)

Australia			
All Ordinaries Index			

1986			
January	31	High	1075.1
	2	Low	1010.8
	31	Close	1075.1
February	4	High	1075.6
	13	Low	1039.7
	28	Close	1050.1
March	25	High	1168.8
	3	Low	1053.3
	27	Close	1136.5
April	18	High	1218.7
	1	Low	1129.7
	30	Close	1210.6
May	7	High	1247.0
	21	Low	1172.3
	30	Close	1241.0
June	6	High	1230.2
	30	Low	1179.8
	30	Close	1179.8
July	1	High	1175.5
	28	Low	1094.7
	31	Close	1123.5
August	29	High	1192.3
	4	Low	1120.2
	29	Close	1192.3
September	26	High	1259.0
	18	Low	1199.2
	30	Close	1246.9

October	31	High	1377.2
	1	Low	1253.6
	31	Close	1377.2
November	7	High	1401.8
	18	Low	1314.7
	28	Close	1379.6
December	31	High	1473.10
	2	Low	1376.80
	31	Close	1473.10

1985			
January	31	High	773.3
	7	Low	715.3
	31	Close	773.3
February	20	High	798.9
	11	Low	765.3
	28	Close	792.2
March	29	High	829.7
	11	Low	783.9
	29	Close	829.7
April	30	High	875.2
	1	Low	828.6
	30	Close	875.2
May	20	High	904.6
	2	Low	863.3
	31	Close	873.4
June	3	High	872.3
	18	Low	840.2
	28	Close	860.8
July	25	High	940.7
	1	Low	860.2
	31	Close	936.0
August	15	High	956.9
	7	Low	931.8
	30	Close	937.8
September	30	High	987.0
	2	Low	937.0
	30	Close	987.0
October	25	High	1052.2
	1	Low	994.3
	31	Close	1027.0
November	4	High	1015.1
	29	Low	990.6
	29	Close	990.6
December	30	High	1001.6
	16	Low	974.8
	30	Close	1001.6

AUSTRALIA

1984			
January	9	High	787.9
	17	Low	765.0
	31	Close	765.9
February	6	High	778.3
	29	Low	737.6
	29	Close	737.6
March	30	High	750.5
	8	Low	718.3
	30	Close	750.5
April	16	High	764.5
	3	Low	744.9
	30	Close	756.0
May	3	High	767.5
	31	Low	654.8
	31	Close	654.8
June	4	High	681.5
	18	Low	646.3
	29	Close	658.9
July	27	High	683.6
	3	Low	656.2
	31	Close	681.5
August	22	High	751.9
	1	Low	687.3
	31	Close	733.2
September	28	High	739.2
	10	Low	712.5
	28	Close	739.2
October	16	High	754.5
	2	Low	738.9
	31	Close	753.7
November	16	High	782.5
	29	Low	745.3
	30	Close	749.0
December	3	High	740.0
	18	Low	714.3
	28	Close	726.1

1983			
January	21	High	540.6
	4	Low	487.8
	28	Close	536.6
February	2	High	545.1
	23	Low	495.4
	28	Close	498.8
March	8	High	527.1
	1	Low	490.8
	31	Close	512.7
April	26	High	603.0
	5	Low	515.7
	29	Close	592.2
May	26	High	619.9
	6	Low	588.5
	31	Close	618.6
June	6	High	614.9
	8	Low	593.3
	20	Low	593.3
	30	Close	605.0
July	27	High	678.5
	6	Low	603.5
	29	Close	672.1
August	24	High	708.4
	12	Low	661.7
	31	Close	701.3
September	12	High	736.7
	22	Low	706.5
	30	Close	718.0
October	7	High	709.5
	25	Low	677.0
	31	Close	687.4
November	29	High	745.4
	2	Low	685.4
	30	Close	744.7
December	30	High	775.3
	7	Low	735.0
	30	Close	775.3

Composite Index
(South Korea)

1986			
January	31	High	160.42
	24	Low	153.85
	31	Close	160.42
February	24	High	177.78
	5	Low	161.73
	28	Close	175.91
March	31	High	199.76
	3	Low	179.33
	31	Close	199.76
April	17	High	217.00
	25	Low	193.39
	30	Close	202.71
May	30	High	229.47
	9	Low	198.14
	30	Close	229.47
June	26	High	250.68
	4	Low	228.57
	30	Close	243.36
July	30	High	274.15
	1	Low	249.32
	31	Close	273.75
August	20	High	273.97
	6	Low	262.51
	29	Close	264.78
September	11	High	268.18
	29	Low	252.39
	30	Close	253.45

October	7	High	258.43
	24	Low	225.92
	31	Close	240.79
November	22	High	269.18
	11	Low	247.54
	28	Close	266.50
December	2	High	279.47
	23	Low	266.43
	26	Close	272.61

1985			
January	7	High	145.51
	29	Low	137.81
	31	Close	138.90
February	1	High	138.84
	22	Low	133.37
	28	Close	134.72
March	5	High	135.72
	20	Low	133.92
	29	Close	135.08
April	22	High	139.48
	30	Low	134.15
	30	Close	134.15
May	31	High	134.09
	20	Low	131.40
	31	Close	134.09
June	17	High	140.77
	4	Low	133.58
	28	Close	137.20
July	31	High	137.38
	8	Low	134.33
	31	Close	137.38
August	22	High	139.59
	16	Low	134.84
	29	Close	136.44
September	30	High	138.91
	6	Low	134.87
	30	Close	138.91
October	24	High	142.42
	15	Low	138.39
	31	Close	140.89
November	29	High	148.84
	5	Low	140.65
	29	Close	148.84
December	26	High	163.37
	3	Low	149.74
	26	Close	163.37

South Korea
Composite Index

Weighted Price Index (Taiwan)

1986

January	27	High	889.41
	3	Low	839.73
	31	Close	882.95
February	28	High	943.95
	3	Low	885.14
	28	Close	943.95
March	18	High	986.20
	31	Low	926.13
	31	Close	926.13
April	1	High	932.96
	15	Low	890.18
	30	Close	902.87
May	30	High	946.19
	2	Low	885.86
	30	Close	946.19
June	16	High	990.92
	2	Low	954.24
	30	Close	955.21
July	11	High	995.99
	31	Low	935.83
	31	Close	935.83
August	4	High	914.39
	26	Low	877.92
	29	Close	906.22
September	30	High	947.11
	16	Low	906.81
	30	Close	947.11
October	22	High	1017.16
	1	Low	946.17
	30	Close	994.44
November	10	High	1026.78
	3	Low	978.96
	29	Close	996.24
December	29	High	1039.11
	10	Low	995.46
	29	Close	1039.11

1985

January	17	High	840.57
	30	Low	787.22
	31	Close	787.75
February	8	High	793.71
	13	Low	775.17
	28	Close	781.37

Taiwan

Weighted Price Index

March	8	High	824.49
	28	Low	773.15
	28	Close	773.15
April	4	High	773.65
	29	Low	739.39
	30	Close	739.63
May	20	High	745.90
	13	Low	723.18
	31	Close	730.53
June	24	High	725.09
	13	Low	687.10
	28	Close	703.09
July	1	High	706.46
	30	Low	636.02
	31	Close	637.04
August	30	High	666.11
	1	Low	643.83
	30	Close	666.11
September	19	High	713.12
	2	Low	674.88
	27	Close	710.02
October	30	High	781.66
	11	Low	709.67
	30	Close	781.66
November	6	High	794.60
	20	Low	738.14
	29	Close	776.50
December	27	High	830.31
	2	Low	779.70
	27	Close	830.31

TAIWAN

1984							
January	30	High	829.43	July	4	High	901.94
	5	Low	764.50		12	Low	872.62
	30	Close	829.43		31	Close	894.48
February	24	High	892.34	August	10	High	924.05
	6	Low	838.05		1	Low	891.04
	29	Close	868.40		31	Close	909.84
March	19	High	910.41	September	4	High	895.61
	5	Low	848.19		24	Low	859.67
	30	Close	869.28		27	Close	879.92
April	30	High	938.30	October	3	High	891.35
	5	Low	859.24		29	Low	825.22
	30	Close	938.30		30	Close	830.36
May	15	High	969.25	November	1	High	838.12
	28	Low	853.67		13	Low	792.24
	31	Close	869.77		30	Close	835.04
June	21	High	919.91	December	14	High	865.36
	1	Low	871.09		28	Low	830.76
	29	Close	887.09		31	Close	838.07